C000184747

ISBN 978-0-331-84739-0
PIBN 11209179

No. 9281 Vol 2172

United States
Circuit Court of Appeals
For the Ninth Circuit.

UNITED STATES OF AMERICA,
Appellant,

vs.

WILSON A. HOLLAND,
Appellee.

Transcript of Record

Upon Appeal from the District Court of the United States for the Southern District of California, Central Division.

No. 9281

United States
Circuit Court of Appeals
For the Ninth Circuit.

UNITED STATES OF AMERICA,
Appellant,

vs.

WILSON A. HOLLAND,
Appellee.

Transcript of Record

Upon Appeal from the District Court of the United States for the Southern District of California, Central Division.

INDEX

[Clerk's Note: When deemed likely to be of an important nature. errors or doubtful matters appearing in the original certified record are printed literally in italic; and, likewise, cancelled matter appearing in the original certified record is printed and cancelled herein accordingly. When possible, an omission from the text is indicated by printing in italic the two words between which the omission seems to occur.]

Page

Amended Judgment 20

Answer 9

Affidavit of Service of........ 11

Appeal:

Designation of Contents on (Circuit Court of Appeals)........ 389

Designation of Contents on (District Court) 31

Notice of 28

Order Extending Time to Docket........ 29

Statement of Points on........ 384

Stipulation and Order re Transmittal of Original Exhibits 30

Attorneys of Record, Names and Addresses of... 1

Clerk's Certificate 35

Complaint 1

Affidavit of Service of........ 7

Notice of Filing of........ 6

Index Page

Judgment 14

Amended 20

Second Amended 24

Motion of Defendant for Judgment 19

Motion for Directed Verdict 337

Order Denying Same 364

Names and Addresses of Attorneys of Record 1

Notice of Appeal 28

Notice of Defendant of Motion for Judgment 18

Notice of Filing of Complaint 7

Order Denying Defendant's Motion for Judgment 24

Order Denying Motion for Directed Verdict 364

Order Directing Filing of Jury Verdict 13

Order Extending Time to Docket Appeal 29

Order re Transmittal of Original Exhibtis 31

Reporter's Transcript of Proceedings (for Detailed Index see "Testimony") 36

Statement of Points on Appeal 384

Stipulation and Order that Certain Voluminous Exhibits Need Not Be Printed 388

Stipulation Designating Contents of Record on Appeal 31

Stipulation Designating the Record Necessary for the Consideration of the Appeal Herein 387

Index Page

Stipulation re Transmittal of Original Exhibits 30

Testimony 36

Exhibits for Defendant:

A—Application to Los Angeles County Civil Service Commission........ 208

B—Application No. 33178 to Los Angeles County Civil Service Commission 230

C—Application No. 12640 to Los Angeles County Civil Service Commission 182

D—Application No. 14096 to Los Angeles County Civil Service Commission 191

E—Application No. 20387 to Los Angeles County Civil Service Commission 199

F—Report of Physical Examination........ 215

G—Schedule of F. E. R. A. Salary Payments Made to Wilson A. Holland from June 7, 1934 to July 25, 1935... 249

K—Report of Department of Roentgenology, U. S. Veterans' Bureau dated 8-24-36 308

Index Page

Exhibits for Plaintiff:

20—Excerpt from "Diagnostic Standards Tuberculosis of the Lungs and Related Lymph Nodes" 332

21—Letter dated March 12, 1937 to Veterans Administration from Wilson Alvin Holland 173

22—Statement of Claim for Insurance —Total Permanent Disability 176

23—Letter dated November 9, 1937 to H. L. McCoy from Wilson A. Holland 344

24—Letter dated April 1, 1937 to Wilson A. Holland from H. L. McCoy... 346

25—Letter dated May 9, 1938 to Wilson A. Holland from H. L. McCoy..... 347

26—Letter dated April 19, 1937 to Wilson A. Holland from Ben F. Ryerson, Jr. 349

27—Letter dated October 28, 1937 to Wilson A. Holland from H. L. McCoy 350

28—Letter dated January 8, 1938 to W. S. Rawlings from Wilson A. Holland 354

Instructions to the Jury..... 364

Motion of Defendant for Verdict..... 337

Requested Instructions of the Defendant..... 377

Index Page

Witnesses for Defendant:

Close, Otho H. (deposition)
—direct 267
—cross 272

Howe, Homer S. (deposition)
—direct 240
—cross 243
—redirect 245
—recross 246

Merritt, Donald M.
—direct 278
—cross 289

Shulman, Dr. Leon
—direct 309
—cross 318
—redirect 325
—recross 327

Witnesses for Plaintiff:

Burton, Roy W.
—direct 115
—redirect 120

Carleton, Harold A. R.
—direct 105
—cross 113

Cohn, Dr. Harry
—direct 121
—cross 140
—redirect 149

Index Page

Witnesses for Plaintiff (Cont.):

Holland, Wilson A.
—direct 37
—cross 48
—redirect 57
—recross 58
—redirect 58
—recalled, direct 328
—recalled, direct 342

Holland, Mrs. Wilson A.
—direct 101

Mentzer, Dr. Mary Jones
—direct 150
—cross 167
—redirect 170

Smith, Clarence (deposition)
—direct 251
—cross 262

Wyres, Robert E.
—direct 59
—voir dire 64
—direct 65
—cross 90
—redirect 98

Verdict 14

NAMES AND ADDRESSES OF ATTORNEYS:

For Appellant:

BEN HARRISON, Esq.,
United States Attorney,
Federal Building,
Los Angeles, California.

ERNEST D. FOOKS, Esq.,
Attorney, Department of Justice,
Federal Building,
Los Angeles, California.

For Appellee:

ALVIN GERLACK, Esq.,
845 Mills Building,
San Francisco, California. [1*]

In the Central Division of the United States District Court for the Southern District of California.

No. 8415-RJ

WILSON A. HOLLAND,

Plaintiff,

vs.

UNITED STATES OF AMERICA,

Defendant.

COMPLAINT—GOVERNMENT INSURANCE

Plaintiff complains of the Defendant and alleges:

*Page numbering appearing at foot of page of original certified Transcript of Record.

I.

That Plaintiff is a citizen of the United States, and a resident of the Southern District and State of California and of the County of Los Angeles therein.

II.

That this action is brought under the War Risk Insurance Act of October 6, 1917, and the World War Veterans Act of June 7, 1924, and amendatory acts, and is based upon policies or certificates of insurance issued under said acts to the plaintiff by the defendant. [2]

III.

That Plaintiff served in the armed forces of the Defendant on active duty in its Army between the 6th day of May, 1917, and the 3rd day of August, 1920.

IV.

That while serving the Defendant as aforesaid, Plaintiff applied for, and was issued a policy of yearly renewable term insurance in the amount of $10,000.00, which said policy was reinstated and converted on April 1, 1927, to one of the Defendant's United States Government converted insurance policies, No. K-613,076 in the principal sum of $10,000.00. That plaintiff ever since the issuance of said policy, up to and including the 30th day of November, 1933, has paid all premiums that were due on said policy, and that said policy was in full force and effect up to and including the said 30th day of November, 1933.

V.

That while the above named policy was in full force and effect the Plaintiff contracted certain injuries, diseases and disabilities resulting in, and known as, pulmonary tuberculosis and chest trouble, and other disabilities, as shown by the records and files of defendant's Veterans Administration and United States Army Hospitals.

VI.

That said diseases, injuries and disabilities have continuously, since August 30, 1933, rendered, and still do render, plaintiff wholly unable to follow any substantially gainful occupation, and such diseases, injuries and disabilities are of such a nature, and founded upon such conditions that it is reasonably certain they will continue throughout Plaintiff's lifetime in approximately the same degree. That Plaintiff has been, ever since August 30, 1933, and still now is, totally and permanently disabled by [3] reason of, and as a direct and proximate result of, such disabilities above set forth.

VII.

That Plaintiff made and submitted to the Defendant's Veterans Administration, due proof of his permanent and total disability.

VIII.

That on or about February 12, 1937, the Plaintiff made application to the Defendant through its Veterans Administration and the Administrator of Veterans Affairs thereof, after submitting due proof on or about August 30, 1933, of his permanent and total disability, for the payment of insurance installments under his said policy No. K-613,076 on account of permanent and total disability, and that said Veterans Administration and the Administrator of Veterans Affairs thereof, have refused to pay Plaintiff said insurance, and on the 14th day of May, 1938, disputed Plaintiff's claim to said insurance benefits, and disagreed with him concerning his rights to the same.

IX.

That under the provisions of Plaintiff's said policy he is entitled to the payment of $57.50 for each and every month transpiring since August 30th, 1933, together with a refund of all premiums paid since said date, in the total amount of $33.90 per month since said date.

X.

That Plaintiff has employed the services of Alvin Gerlack, an attorney and counsellor at law, duly licensed and admitted to practice before this Court and all Courts of the State of California. That a reasonable attorney's fee to be allowed to Plaintiff's attorney for his services in this action, is ten per centum [4] (10%) of the amount of insurance recovered in this action, including premium refunds, payable at the rate and in the manner provided by Section 500 of the World War Veterans Act of 1924 as amended.

Wherefore, Plaintiff prays judgment as follows:

First: That Plaintiff since August 30, 1933, has been and still is, permanently and totally disabled.

Second: That Plaintiff have judgment against the Defendant for all of the monthly installments of $57.50 per month due under his said Policy No. K-613,076 since August 30, 1933, together with a refund of all premiums paid since said date.

Third: Determining and allowing to Plaintiff's attorney a reasonable attorney's fee in the amount of ten per centum (10%) of the amount of insurance recovered in this action, including premium refunds, payable at the rate and in the manner provided by Section 500 of the World War Veterans Act of 1924, as amended, and for such other and further relief as may be just and equitable in the premises.

ALVIN GERLACK,
Attorney for Plaintiff. [5]

United States of America,
Southern District and State of California,
County of Los Angeles—ss.

Wilson A. Holland, being first duly sworn, deposes and says:

That he is the Plaintiff in the above entitled action; that he has heard read the foregoing Complaint and knows the contents thereof.

That the same is true of his own knowledge and belief except as to those matters stated upon information and belief and that as to those matters he believes them to be true.

WILSON A. HOLLAND.

Subscribed and sworn to before me this 15th day of June, 1938.

[Seal] RAY STURGE,

Notary Public in and for the County of Los Angeles, State of California.

[Endorsed]: Filed June 27, 1938. [6]

[Title of District Court and Cause.]

NOTICE OF FILING COMPLAINT AGAINST UNITED STATES UNDER TUCKER ACT OF MARCH 3, 1887, AND WORLD WAR VETERANS ACT, AS AMENDED.

To the Honorable, The Attorney General of the United States, and to Honorable Benj. Harrison, United States Attorney for the Southern District of California:

Sirs:

Please Take Notice that Plaintiff's Complaint in the above entitled cause was duly filed with the Clerk of the United States District Court for the Southern District of California on the 27th day of June, 1938, which Court has jurisdiction of the cause set forth in said Complaint, and in which District Plaintiff resides.

Dated: June 27th, 1938.

ALVIN GERLACK,

Attorney for Plaintiff,

Mills Bldg., San Francisco, Calif. [7]

Receipt by copy of the within Notice of Filing Complaint against the United States under the Tucker Act, together with copy of said Complaint is hereby admitted this 27th day of June, 1938.

BENJ. HARRISON,
United States Attorney,
By A. DI GIROLAMO,
Attorneys for Defendant,
United States of America.

[Endorsed]: Filed June 27th, 1938. [8]

In the United States District Court, Southern District of California, Central Division

No. 8415-RJ

WILSON A. HOLLAND,
Plaintiff,

vs.

UNITED STATES OF AMERICA,
Defendant.

AFFIDAVIT OF SERVICE ON UNITED STATES ATTORNEY AND MAILING NOTICE TO ATTORNEY GENERAL UNDER TUCKER ACT AND WORLD WAR VETERANS ACT AS AMENDED.

United States of America,
State of California,
County of Los Angeles—ss.

U. E. Malott, being first duly sworn, deposes and says:

That he is the Clerk for the attorney for plaintiff in the above entitled action. That on the 27th day of June, 1938, he served a copy of the complaint on file herein, together with a copy of the Notice of Filing Complaint against the United States under the Tucker Act of March 3, 1887, and the World War Veterans Act as amended, on the United States Attorney for the Southern District of California, by giving to and leaving with said U. S. Attorney, true and correct copies of each of said papers.

That on the 27th day of June, 1938, he mailed to the Attorney General of the United States, full and complete copies of each of said foregoing papers, by registered mail, postage thereon fully prepaid, and deposited the same in the U. S. Postoffice at ...., addressed as follows: "The Honorable, the Attorney General of the United States, Washington, D. C."

Registered, Return receipt requested".

U. E. MALOTT.

Subscribed and sworn to before me this 27th day of June, 1938.

[Seal] W. A. PERILMUTER,

Notary Public in and for the County of

State of

[Endorsed]: Filed June 27, 1938. [9]

[Title of District Court and Cause.]

ANSWER

Comes Now the defendant, the United States of America, by Ben Harrison, United States Attorney for the Southern District of California, Ernest D. Fooks, Attorney, Department of Justice, and Attilio di Girolamo, Attorney, Department of Justice, and for answer to plaintiff's complaint, denies, and alleges:

I.

For answer to Paragraph I in plaintiff's complaint, defendant, for want of information, denies the allegations contained therein.

II.

For answer to Paragraph II in plaintiff's complaint, defendant, admits the allegations contained therein.

III.

For answer to Paragraph III in plaintiff's complaint, defendant, admits each and every allegation contained therein.

IV.

For answer to Paragraph IV in plaintiff's complaint, defendant admits that while in the service plaintiff applied for and was granted a $10,000.00 war risk term insurance policy and alleges that premiums on said policy were paid to include the month of August, 1920; defendant further alleges that effective April 1, 1927, plaintiff reinstated and converted said insurance in the amount of $10,-

000.00 and that premiums were paid thereon to include the month of November, 1933. [10]

V.

For answer to Paragraph V in plaintiff's complaint, defendant denies each and every allegation contained therein.

VI.

For answer to Paragraph VI in plaintiff's complaint, defendant denies each and every allegation contained therein.

VII.

For answer to Paragraph VII in plaintiff's complaint, defendant denies each and every allegation contained therein.

VIII.

For answer to Paragraph VIII in plaintiff's complaint, defendant denies each and every allegation contained therein and alleges that on, to-wit, the 16th day of March, 1937, the plaintiff filed a claim with Veterans Administration for permanent and total disability benefits; that said claim was denied by the Insurance Claims Council on the 9th day of May, 1938; that on the said 9th day of May, 1938, the Director of Insurance did notify by registered mail the plaintiff of said denial.

IX.

For answer to Paragraph IX in plaintiff's complaint, defendant denies each and every allegation contained therein.

X.

For answer to Paragraph X in plaintiff's complaint, defendant being without knowledge, information, or belief concerning the employment of counsel by the plaintiff, denies allegations concerning same. Defendant avers that attorneys' fees are governed by Section 500 of the World War Veterans Act as amended.

Wherefore defendant prays judgment as follows:

I.

That plaintiff take nothing by the action filed herein; that said action be dismissed, and that judgment be for defendant, with its costs. [11]

II.

That the Court grant the defendant such other and further relief as it deems just and proper in the premises.

BEN HARRISON,
United States Attorney.
ERNEST D. FOOKS,
Attorney,
Department of Justice.
ATTILIO DI GIROLAMO,
Attorney,
Department of Justice.

[Endorsed]: Filed Aug. 19, 1938. [12]

[Title of District Court and Cause.]

AFFIDAVIT OF SERVICE BY MAIL

United States of America,
Southern District of California—ss.

Bertha W. Ink, being first duly sworn, deposes and says:

That she is a citizen of the United States and a resident of Los Angeles County, California; that her business address is 360 Pacific Electric Building, Los Angeles, California; that she is over the age of eighteen years, and not a party to the above-entitled action;

That on August 19, 1938, she deposited in the United States Mails in Los Angeles, California, in the above-entitled action, in an envelope bearing the requisite postage, a copy of Answer addressed to Alvin Gerlack, Attorney-at-Law, Mills Building, San Francisco, California, Attorney for Plaintiff, at which place there is a delivery service by United States Mail.

BERTHA W. INK.

Subscribed and sworn to before me, this 19th day of August, 1938.

R. S. ZIMMERMAN,

Clerk, U. S. District Court, Southern District of California.

[Seal] By L. B. FIGG,

Deputy.

[Endorsed]: Filed Aug. 19, 1938. [13]

At a stated term, to wit: The February Term, A. D. 1939, of the District Court of the United States of America, within and for the Central Division of the Southern District of California, held at the Court Room thereof, in the City of Los Angeles, California, on Wednesday, the 1st day of March, in the year of our Lord one thousand nine hundred and thirty-nine.

Present:

The Honorable: Jeremiah Neterer, District Judge.

(Calendar of Hon. Geo. Cosgrave)

[Title of Cause.]

This cause coming on for further jury trial; Alvin Gerlack, Esq., appearing for the plaintiff; A. di Girolamo, and Gerald J. Meindl, Attorneys, Department of Justice, appearing for the Government; Byron Oyler being present as court reporter and reporting the proceedings; and the jury and counsel all being present as heretofore, the Court orders it so noted.

* * * * * *

At 4:29 o'clock p. m. Court reconvenes and counsel and the jury being present as before, the Court orders it so noted.

Verdict in favor of the plaintiff is presented and read by the Clerk and ordered filed and entered herein, as follows: [14]

[Title of District Court and Cause.]

VERDICT

We, the Jury in the above-entitled cause, find for the plaintiff and fix the date of his total and permanent disability, as that term is defined in his policy, beginning August 30, 1933.

Dated: Los Angeles, California, March 1, 1939.

C. M. NEUNER,

Foreman of the Jury.

[Endorsed]: Filed Mar. 1, 1939. [15]

In the Central Division of the United States District Court, for the Southern District of California.

No. 8415-C Law

WILSON A. HOLLAND,

Plaintiff,

vs.

UNITED STATES OF AMERICA,

Defendant.

JUDGMENT

This cause came on regularly to be tried on the 28th day of February, 1939, and was thereafter regularly continued to the 1st day of March, 1939; Alvin Gerlack, Esq., appearing as counsel for the plaintiff and Hon. Ben Harrison, United States Attorney for the Southern District of California and Attilio De Girolamo, Esq., attorney, Department of Justice, appearing as counsel for the defendant.

A jury of twelve persons was impaneled and sworn to try said cause. Witnesses on the part of plaintiff and defendant were sworn and examined and documentary evidence on behalf of the parties hereto, was introduced. After hearing the evidence, arguments of counsel and the instructions of the court, the jury retired to consider of their verdict and subsequently returned into court their verdict in words and figures as follows, to-wit:

[Title of District Court and Cause.]

VERDICT

"We the Jury in the above-entitled cause, find for the plaintiff and fix the date of his total and permanent disability, as that term is defined in his policy, beginning August 30, 1933.

Dated: Los Angeles, California,
March 1, 1939.

C. M. NEUNER
Foreman of the Jury [16]

And the Court having fixed plaintiff's attorney's fees in the amount of ten per centum (10%) of the amount of insurance recovered in this action; said ten percentum (10%) to cover plaintiff's attorney's services for all courts in connection with his services in the above entitled cause, and

The court having found that due proof of the plaintiff's total and permanent disability was furnished to the defendants, Veterans Administration on March 12, 1937.

It is ordered, adjudged and decreed that the plaintiff, Wilson A. Holland, do have and recover of and from the United States of America, the defendant, the sum of Seventeen Hundred and Twenty Five Dollars ($1,725.00), being thirty (30) accrued monthly installments of insurance at the rate of Fifty Seven Dollars and Fifty Cents ($57.50) per month, beginning September 12th, 1936, same being six months prior to the receipt of said proof up to and including the monthly installment due February 12th, 1939, less plaintiff's attorneys' fees as herein provided, less a policy lien of $608.30.

It is further ordered, adjudged and decreed that the defendant, the United States of America, deduct ten per centum (10%) of the amount of insurance recovered in this action and pay the same to Alvin Gerlack, of San Francisco, California, plaintiff's attorney for his services rendered before this court, which amount is to include legal services performed, not only before this court but such other courts to which said case might be appealed, said ten per cent (10%) to be payable at the rate of ten per centum

(10%) of all back payments and ten per centum (10%) of all future payments which may hereafter become due on account of such insurance maturing as a result of this judgment, said amounts to be paid by the defendant's Veterans Administration or its successor if any, to said Alvin Gerlack or his heirs, out of any payments to be made to said Wilson A. Holland, or his beneficiary or estate in the event of his death before two hundred and forty (240) of said monthly installments have been paid.

Dated: March 2nd, 1939.

JEREMIAH NETERER

U. S. District Judge

Approved as to form as per rule #8.

GERALD J. MEINDL

Attorney

Department of Justice. [17]

Judgment entered Mar. 2, 1939.

Docketed Mar. 2, 1939.

Book C. O. 1, Page 514.

R. S. ZIMMERMAN,

Clerk

By R. B. CLIFTON,

Deputy

[Endorsed]: Filed Mar. 2, 1939. [18]

[Title of District Court and Cause.]

NOTICE OF MOTION

To the above named Plaintiff and to his Attorney, Alvin C. Gerlack:

You and each of you are hereby notified that at the calling of the Law and Motion Calendar in the Court of the Honorable Jeremiah Neterer, one of the Judges of the above entitled Court, at his Court Room in the Federal Building, City of Los Angeles, State of California, on the 20th day of March, 1939, at 10:00 o'clock A. M., or as soon thereafter as counsel may be heard, the defendant by its counsel will move the Court to vacate the jury verdict heretofore rendered in the above entitled cause on March 1, 1939, and judgment entered thereupon on the 2nd day of March, 1939, and for a judgment in favor of the defendant notwithstanding the verdict.

Said motion will be based on the following two grounds:

I.

That plaintiff has failed to produce due proof of his permanent total disability as required in the terms of the policy sued upon herein and that due proof is a jurisdictional prerequisite.

II.

That the verdict of the jury is contrary to the evidence and that defendant's motion for directed verdict based on the evidence should have been granted.

BEN HARRISON,
United States Attorney.
ATTILIO DI GIROLAMO
Attorney,
Department of Justice.
Attorneys for Defendant.

[Endorsed]: Filed Mar. 11, 1939. [19]

[Title of District Court and Cause.]

MOTION

Comes now the defendant by Ben Harrison, United States Attorney for the Southern District of California, and Attilio di Girolamo, Attorney, Department of Justice, and moves the Court that the jury verdict rendered herein on the 1st day of March, 1939, and judgment entered thereon on the 2nd day of March, 1939, be vacated and a judgment be entered for the defendant notwithstanding the verdict, and in accordance with defendant's motion for directed verdict.

The defendant bases its motion on the following grounds:

I.

That the plaintiff has failed to adduce due proof of his permanent total disability while the insurance remained in force and that such proof is a jurisdictional prerequisite.

II.

That plaintiff has failed to prove by substantial credible evidence that he became permanently and totally disabled while his war risk insurance policy remained in force and that the jury's verdict was contrary to the evidence.

BEN HARRISON
United States Attorney.
ATTILIO DI GIROLAMO
Attorney,
Department of Justice.
Attorneys for Defendant.

[Endorsed]: Filed Mar. 11, 1939. [20]

[Title of District Court and Cause.]

AMENDED JUDGMENT

This cause came on regularly to be tried on the 28th day of February, 1939, and was thereafter regularly continued to the 1st day of March, 1939; Alvin Gerlack, Esq., appearing as counsel for the plaintiff, and Hon. Ben Harrison, United States Attorney for the Southern District of California, and Attilio di Girolamo, Esq., attorney, Department of Justice, appearing as counsel for the defendant.

A jury of twelve persons was impaneled and sworn to try said cause. Witnesses on the part of plaintiff and defendant were sworn and examined and documentary evidence on behalf of the parties hereto was introduced. After hearing the evidence, arguments of counsel and the instructions of the court, the jury retired to consider of their verdict and subsequently returned into court their verdict in words and figures as follows, to-wit:

(Title of Court and Cause)

VERDICT

"We the Jury in the above-entitled cause, find for the plaintiff and fix the date of his total and permanent disability, as that term is defined in his policy, beginning August 30, 1933. [21]

Dated: Los Angeles, California,
March 1, 1939.

C. M. NEUNER
Foreman of the Jury"

And the Court having fixed plaintiff's attorney's fees in the amount of ten per centum (10%) of the amount of insurance recovered in this action; said ten percentum (10%) to cover plaintiff's attorney's services for all courts in connection with his services in the above-entitled cause; and

The Court having found that due proof of the plaintiff's total and permanent disability was furnished to the defendant's Veterans Administration on March 12, 1937,

It is ordered, adjudged and decreed that the plaintiff, Wilson A. Holland, do have and recover of and from the United States of America, the defendant, monthly installments from and after September 12, 1936, same being six (6) months prior to the receipt of said due proof in accordance with the terms of the insurance in force on August 30, 1933, to-wit: insurance in the amount of $10,000.00 payable in monthly installments commencing on September 12, 1936, in the sum of Fifty-seven and 50/100ths Dollars ($57.50) each; and the further sum equal to all premiums paid by plaintiff to the defendant on or subsequent to August 30, 1933, without interest, after deducting any sums due to the United States for any outstanding lien and interest thereon created by plaintiff upon his insurance policy.

It is further ordered, adjudged and decreed that the defendant, the United States of America, deduct ten percentum (10%) of the amount of insurance recovered in this action and pay the same to Alvin Gerlack, of San Francisco, California, plaintiff's attorney, for his services rendered before this Court, which amount is to include legal services performed, not only before this Court but such other courts, if any, to which said case might be appealed, [22] said ten percentum (10%) to be payable at the rate of ten percentum (10%) of all back payments and ten per centum (10%) of all future payments which may hereafter become due on account of such insurance maturing as a result of this judgment, said amounts to be paid by the defendant's Veterans

Administration, or its successors, if any, to said Alvin Gerlack, or his heirs, out of any payments to be made to said Wilson A. Holland, or his beneficiary or estate in the event of his death before two hundred and forty (240) of said monthly installments have been paid.

Dated: March 13, 1939.

JEREMIAH NETERER

Judge of the United States District Court.

Approved as to form as per Rule #8.

A. DI GIROLAMO

Attorney,

Department of Justice.

Judgment entered Mar. 13, 1939.

Docketed Mar. 13, 1939.

Book C. O. 1, Page 550.

R. S. ZIMMERMAN,

Clerk,

By R. B. CLIFTON,

Deputy.

[Endorsed]: Filed Mar. 13, 1939. [23]

At a stated term, to wit: The February Term, A. D. 1939, of the District Court of the United States of America, within and for the Central Division of the Southern District of California, held at the Court Room thereof, in the City of Los Angeles, California, on Monday, the 20th day of March, in the year of our Lord one thousand nnie hundred and thirty-nine.

Present: The Honorable Jeremiah Neterer, District Judge. (Calling Calendar of Judge Cosgrave, District Judge.)

[Title of Cause.]

This cause coming on for hearing on motion of defendant to vacated judgment entered March 2nd, 1939, and for judgment notwithstanding the verdict, filed March 11th, 1939, pursuant to notice filed same date;

*   *   *   *   *   *   *

. . . it is by the Court ordered that the motion of defendant be, and the same is hereby denied, with exception to defendant. [24]

[Title of District Court and Cause.]

SECOND AMENDED JUDGMENT.

This cause came on regularly to be tried on the 28th day of February, 1939, and was thereafter regularly continued to the 1st day of March, 1939;

Alvin Gerlack, Esq., appearing as counsel for the plaintiff, and Hon. Ben Harrison, United States Attorney for the Southern District of California, and Attilio di Girolamo, Esq., attorney, Department of Justice, appearing as counsel for the defendant.

A jury of twelve persons was impaneled and sworn to try said cause. Witnesses on the part of plaintiff and defendant were sworn and examined and documentary evidence on behalf of the parties hereto was introduced. After hearing the evidence, arguments of counsel and the instructions of the court, the jury retired to consider of their verdict and subsequently returned into court their verdict in words and figures as follows, to-wit:

(Title of Court and Cause)

VERDICT

"We the Jury in the above-entitled cause, find for the plaintiff and fix the date of his total and permanent disability, as that term is defined in his policy, beginning August 30, 1933. [25]

Dated: Los Angeles, California, March 1, 1939.

C. M. NEUNER
Foreman of the Jury"

And the Court having fixed plaintiff's attorney's fees in the amount of ten per centum (10%) of the amount of insurance recovered in this action; said ten percentum (10%) to cover plaintiff's attorney's services for all courts in connection with his services in the above-entitled cause; and

The Court having found that due proof of the plaintiff's total and permanent disability was furnished to the defendant's Veterans Administration on March 12, 1937,

It Is Ordered, Adjudged and Decreed that the plaintiff, Wilson A. Holland, do have and recover of and from the United States of America, the defendant, monthly installments from and after September 12, 1936, same being six (6) months prior to the receipt of said due proof in accordance with the terms of the insurance in force on August 30, 1933, to-wit: insurance in the amount of $10,000.00 payable in monthly installments commencing on September 12, 1936, in the sum of Fifty-seven and 50/100ths Dollars ($57.50) each; and the further sum equal to all premiums paid by plaintiff to the defendant on or subsequent to September 12, 1936, without interest, after deducting any sums due to the United States for any outstanding lien and interest thereon created by plaintiff upon his insurance policy.

It Is Further Ordered, Adjudged and Decreed that the defendant, the United States of America, deduct ten percentum (10%) of the amount of insurance recovered in this action and pay the same to Alvin Gerlack, of San Francisco, California, plaintiff's attorney, for his services rendered before this Court, which amount is to include legal services performed, not only before this Court but such other courts, if any, to which said case might be appealed, [26] said ten percentum (10%) to be payable at the rate of ten percentum (10%) of all back payments, and ten percentum (10%) of all future payments which may hereafter become due on account of such insurance maturing as a result of this judgment, said amounts to be paid by the defendant's Veterans Administration, or its successors, if any, to said Alvin Gerlack, or his heirs, out of any payments to be made to said Wilson A. Holland, or his beneficiary or estate in the event of his death before two hundred and forty (240) of said monthly installments have been paid.

Dated: March 28, 1939.

JEREMIAH NETERER
Judge of the United States District Court.

Approved as to form as per Rule #8.

A. DI GIROLAMO
Attorney, Department of Justice.

Judgment entered Mar. 28, 1939. Docketed Mar. 28, 1939. Book C. O. 1, Page 616.

R. S. ZIMMERMAN,
Clerk.
By R. B. CLIFTON,
Deputy.

[Endorsed]: Filed Mar. 28, 1939. [27]

[Title of District Court and Cause.]

NOTICE OF APPEAL.

Notice is hereby given that the United States of America, defendant above named, by its counsel, Ben Harrison, United States Attorney for the Southern District of California, and Ernest D. Fooks, Attorney, Department of Justice, hereby appeals to the Circuit Court of Appeals for the Ninth Circuit from the final judgment in favor of the plaintiff entered in the above-entitled cause on March 2, 1939.

BEN HARRISON,
United States Attorney.
ERNEST D. FOOKS,
Attorney, Department of Justice,
Attorneys for Appellant.

[Endorsed]: Filed June 1, 1939. [28]

In the United States Circuit Court of Appeals for the Ninth Circuit

No.

UNITED STATES OF AMERICA,

Appellant,

vs.

WILSON A. HOLLAND,

Appellee.

ORDER EXTENDING TIME TO FILE THE RECORD ON APPEAL AND TO DOCKET THE CAUSE.

Good cause appearing therefor,

It Is Hereby Ordered that the time within which to file the record on appeal and docket the above-entitled cause in the United States Circuit Court of Appeals for the Ninth Circuit be, and the same hereby is, extended to and including the 30th day of August, 1939.

Dated this 10 day of July, 1939.

DAVE W. LING,

United States District Judge.

[Endorsed]: Filed Jul. 10, 1939. [29]

[Title of District Court and Cause.]

STIPULATION AND ORDER FOR THE TRANSMITTING OF ALL EXHIBITS INTRODUCED AT THE TRIAL TO THE CIRCUIT COURT OF APPEALS.

(Rule 75 (i))

It Is Hereby Stipulated by and between the parties hereto through their respective counsel that all of the exhibits introduced on the trial of the above entitled cause may be sent to the Circuit Court of Appeals for the Ninth Circuit pursuant to rule 75 (i), Rules of Civil Procedure for the District Courts of the United States, and that the court may make such order for the safekeeping, transportation and return thereof as it deems proper.

Dated this 25th day of August, 1939.

BEN HARRISON,
United States Attorney for the Southern District of California.

ERNEST D. FOOKS,
Attorney, Department of Justice.
Attorneys for the Defendant and Appellant.

ALVIN GERLACK,
Attorney for the Plaintiff and Appellee.

It Is So Ordered this 26th day of August, 1939.

PAUL J. McCORMICK,

United States District Judge.

[Endorsed]: Filed Aug. 26, 1939. [30]

[Title of District Court and Cause.]

STIPULATION AS TO THE RECORD ON APPEAL.

It is hereby stipulated by and between the parties hereto through their respective counsel that the following hereinafter enumerated parts of the record, proceedings and evidence be included in and shall constitute the record on appeal herein pursuant to Rule 75 (f) of the Rules of Civil Procedure for the District Courts of the United States.

1. Complaint,
2. Notice of filing complaint,
3. Affidavit of service of complaint,
4. Answer,
5. Affidavit of service of Answer,
6. Minute Order directing filing of jury verdict and the verdict,
7. Judgment,
8. Amended Judgment,
9. Second Amended Judgment,
10. Defendant's Notice of Motion for Judgment Notwithstanding the Verdict,
11. Defendant's Motion for Judgment Notwithstanding the Verdict,

12. Minute Order Denying Defendant's Motion for Judgment Notwithstanding the Verdict, [31]

13. Certified Reporter's complete transcript of all proceedings and all Exhibits introduced in evidence at the trial including the hereinafter designated exhibits as follows:

Government's Exhibit "A" (2 photostats)

Government's Exhibit "B" (3 photostats)

Government's Exhibit "C" (3 photostats)

Government's Exhibit "D" (3 photostats)

Government's Exhibit "E" (3 photostats)

Government's Exhibit "F" Report of physical examination dated April 19, 1937, VAF—San Fernando, California (6 pages)

Defendant's Exhibit "G" Schedule SERA salary payments, (2 pages)

Defendant's Exhibit "H" Deposition of Donald M. Merritt (27 pages) and Exhibits attached thereto,

Defendant's Exhibit "I" Deposition of Dr. Mary Jones Mentzer (20 pages)

Defendant's Exhibit "J" Depositions of Clarence H. Smith and Otho H. Close (21 pages)

Defendant's Exhibit "J-1" Filing card,

Defendant's Exhibit "J-2" Form 617, State of California, dated 5-11-34,

Defendant's Exhibit "J-3" Form 626, State of California, dated 6-1-34,

Defendant's Exhibit "J-4" Form 620, State of California, dated 6-2-34,

Defendant's Exhibit "J-5" Letter dated June 3, 1934, bearing signature of Wilson A. Holland,

Defendant's Exhibit "J-6" (8 photostats)

Defendant's Exhibit "J-7" (5 photostats)

Defendant's Exhibit "J-8" (6 photostats)

Defendant's Exhibit "J-9" (8 photostats)

Defendant's Exhibit "J-10" (9 photostats)

Defendant's Exhibit "J-11" (3 photostats)

Defendant's Exhibit "J-12" (3 photostats)

Defendant's Exhibit "J-13" (65 photostats)

Defendant's Exhibit "J-14" (33 photostats) [32]

Defendant's Exhibit "J-15" (40 photostats)

Defendant's Exhibit "J-16" (10 photostats)

Defendant's Exhibit "J-17" (11 photostats)

Defendant's Exhibit "K" U. S. Veterans' Administration Form 21-M, dated August 24, 1926.

Plaintiff's Exhibit 1. Government Life Insurance Policy, No. K-613,076, amount $10,000.00, payable to Wilson Alvin Holland,

Plaintiff's Exhibit 2. X-Ray negative marked, "Pacific Colony, 170-R, Spadra, California," and card signed H. L. Roberts, X-Ray Technician, dated August 30, 1933,

Plaintiff's Exhibit 18. X-Ray negative, Los Angeles City Health Department, 7-8-37, R-642,

Plaintiff's Exhibit 19. X-Ray negative, Los Angeles City Health Department, 2-27-39, R-642,

Plaintiff's Exhibit 20. Diagnostic standards of National Tuberculosis Association, 1938.

Plaintiff's Exhibit 21. Letter dated 2-12-37 (Claim for insurance benefits) bearing signature of Wilson Alvin Holland,

Plaintiff's Exhibit 22. U. S. Veterans' Administration Form 579, dated April 19, 1936 (3 pages)

Plaintiff's Exhibit 23. Carbon copy of letter dated November 9, 1937, addressed by Wilson A. Holland to H. L. McCoy,

Plaintiff's Exhibit 24. Letter dated 4-1-37, addressed by H. L. McCoy to Wilson A. Holland,

Plaintiff's Exhibit 25. Letter dated 5-9-38, addressed by H. L. McCoy to Wilson A. Holland,

Plaintiff's Exhibit 26. Letter dated 4-19-37, addressed by Ben F. Rynearson, Jr., to Wilson A. Holland,

Plaintiff's Exhibit 27. Letter dated October 28, 1937, addressed by H. L. McCoy, to Wilson A. Holland,

Plaintiff's Exhibit 28. Carbon copy of letter dated 1-8-38, addressed by Wilson A. Holland, to W. S. Rawlings (4 pages),

Plaintiff's Exhibit 29. Report of physical examination of Wilson A. Holland, VAF—San Fernando, California, dated 4-19-37,

14. Notice of Appeal,

15. Order extending time to August 30, 1939, to file the record on appeal and to docket the cause,

16. Stipulation and Order for transmitting all Exhibits [33] introduced at the trial to the 9th Circuit Court of Appeals.

17. This stipulation designating the contents of the record on appeal.

18. Certificate of Clerk authenticating the record.

BEN HARRISON,
United States Attorney for the Southern District of California.

ERNEST D. FOOKS,
Attorney,
Department of Justice.
Attorneys for Defendant and Appellant.

ALVIN GERLACK,
Attorney for plaintiff and appellee.

Dated this 25th day of August, 1939.

[Endorsed]: Filed Aug. 26, 1939. [34]

[Title of District Court and Cause.]

CLERK'S CERTIFICATE.

I, R. S. Zimmerman, Clerk of the District Court of the United States for the Southern District of California, do hereby certify the foregoing 34 pages, numbered from 1 to 34, inclusive, contain full, true and correct copies of the Complaint; Notice of Filing Complaint; Affidavit of Service of Complaint; Answer; Affidavit of Service of Answer; Minute Order Directing Filing of Jury Verdict; Verdict; Judgment; Defendant's Notice of

Motion for Judgment; Defendant's Motion for Judgment; Amended Judgment; Minute Order Denying Defendant's Motion for Judgment; Second Amended Judgment; Notice of Appeal; Order Extending Time to Docket Appeal; Stipulation re Transmittal of Original Exhibits, and Stipulation Designating the Contents of Record on Appeal, which together with Reporter's Transcript of Testimony and original Exhibits transmitted herewith, constitute the record on appeal to the United States Circuit Court of Appeals for the Ninth Circuit.

Witness my hand and the Seal of the District Court of the United States for the Southern District of California, this .... day of August, A. D. 1939.

R. S. ZIMMERMAN,
Clerk.

By

Deputy Clerk. [35]

[Title of District Court and Cause.]

TESTIMONY.

Mr. Gerlack: I shall call Mr. Holland, the Plaintiff in this action.

Now, I think we have stipulated to most of the facts regarding his service.

The Court: I think I shall say to the jury that it is admitted by the pleadings in the case that the Plaintiff was in the World War and while he was in the War a policy was issued to him, that his policy was kept in full force and effect until mid night of November 30, 1933.

Mr. Di Girolamo: If the Court please, I have here more definite data.

(The documents referred to were passed to the Court.)

The Court: I think that is a general outline.

Mr. Di Girolamo: With the grace period, the insurance was in force until December 31, 1933.

The Court: Oh, yes, December 31, 1933.

Mr. Di Girolamo: Yes, a 31-day period.

The Court: December 31, 1933. While the claim that [47] he became totally and permanently disabled in August, that is not so material, having become totally disabled on December 31, some months later.

Where admissions are made *on* proof is necessary. That is a conceded fact.

Mr. Gerlack: Shall I proceed, your Honor?

The Court: Yes, proceed.

WILSON A. HOLLAND

a witness called in behalf of himself, being previously duly sworn, testified as follows:

The Clerk: Will you state your name to the Court and jury, please?

The Witness: Wilson A. Holland.

Direct Examination

By Mr. Gerlack:

Q. Mr. Holland, you are the Plaintiff in this action? A. Yes, sir.

(Testimony of Wilson A. Holland.)

Q. Where are you residing at the present time?

A. My residence address is 2727 Cunard Street, Los Angeles.

The Court: Mr. Witness, speak to that last man over in the jury box. If he hears then they all will be able to hear.

By Mr. Gerlack:

Q. Where are you spending your time?

A. I am a patient at the United States Veterans' Hospit- [48] al at San Fernando, California.

Q. How long have you been a patient there?

A. This time I have been a patient there since last October, since October 1st. Previous to that I have spent a little over a year there during 1936 and 1937.

Q. What were you treated for there?

A. Active tuberculosis.

Q. How much time have you spent in bed since you went into the hospital last October?

A. Well, practically all the time.

Q. How did you get your meals in the hospital?

A. On a tray.

Q. Do you get up daily?

A. I am allowed to go to the bathroom.

Q. That is the only time you get out in 24 hours? A. That is right.

Q. Except when you got up for this trial?

A. That is right.

Q. Now, will you tell us how you felt, so far

(Testimony of Wilson A. Holland.)

as your bodily manifestations were concerned, on August 30, 1933?

A. Well, at that time I felt very tired all the time. It just seemed as though I could never get rested. I would go to bed at night and put in a full night's sleep, from eight to ten hours, and when I would wake up the next morning it just seemed as though I had never been to bed, like [49] I had been working all night instead of sleeping. I was rather nervous, in fact, little things seemed to upset me, like noise. I occasionally had some night sweats at that time. I coughed some and raised some sputum; but the main feeling I had was one of fatigue. I was just always tired.

Q. How long have you experienced that feeling?

A. Well, more or less, ever since I first was told I had tuberculosis.

Q. When was that, Mr. Holland?

A. That was in 1924.

Q. Did you take treatments for tuberculosis in 1924? A. Yes, sir.

Q. Where?

A. I first was a patient in a private hospital in St. Joseph, Missouri; and then, I think early in January of the year 1925, I went to the United States Veterans' Hospital at Fort Lyon, Colorado.

Q. You were hospitalized by the Government there? A. That is right, sir.

Q. How long were you there?

A. I stayed there until the Spring of 1925 and then I returned home.

(Testimony of Wilson A. Holland.)

Q. Were you there again at a later date?

A. No, I didn't go back to the hospital then.

Q. Were there any operations performed on you at Fort Lyon? [50]

A. No operations at Fort Lyon other than an attempt to remove some pus from my lungs once.

Q. What was done to you in that respect?

A. They simply stuck a needle between my ribs and took some pus out.

Q. Is that what is known as a rib recection?

A. I don't believe so. A rib recection I had earlier in the private hospital in St. Joseph, Missouri.

Q. Did you get better or worse after that hospitalization?

A. Well, after the hospital—I will put it this way—I came to feel better at the time I left the hospital and then later on I didn't feel quite so well again, and later, again, I felt better. It is a sort of thing you don't feel exactly the same all the time.

Q. Did you follow an occupation after you got out of the hospital in 1925?

A. Well, not immediately, not for some two years.

Q. You did after that?

A. More than two years later, I did.

Q. Who advised you that you were able to go to work?

(Testimony of Wilson A. Holland.)

A. The Veterans' Bureau of Doctors told me I was able to go to work.

Q. It was on their advice that you went back to work? A. Yes, sir.

Q. How long had you been working at Spadra prior to [51] August 30, 1933?

A. About six months it was.

Q. Was that a Civil Service status you had there? A. Yes.

Q. What was your grade in Civil Service there?

A. I was called an institution bookkeeper, Grade 2.

Q. What was your salary there?

A. The basic salary was $120.00 a month plus maintenance.

Q. How much was that?

A. Well, the State estimates everything over maintenance at $35.00 a month.

Q. How much did you actually receive?

A. In addition to $120.00 a month I was allowed an additional $11.00 a month for my quarters outside. Being a married man there was no accommodations for me on the hospital grounds.

Q. Now, why did you quit that employment?

A. Why, I was just so worn out, so tired out that I just had to rest, and upon the advice of a physician that I should rest I did so; but even without his advice I felt that I could not carry on for the time being any further.

(Testimony of Wilson A. Holland.)

Q. What did you do after that?

A. Well, I rested for a few months until I didn't have any more money with which to eat.

Q. By the way, is this the policy that was issued to [52] you? A. Yes.

Mr. Gerlack: Are you familiar with this, Mr. Di Girolamo?

Mr. Di Girolamo: We admit the policy.

Mr. Gerlack: We offer this as Plaintiff's Exhibit.

The Clerk: Plaintiff's Exhibit 1.

(The document referred to was received in evidence and marked "Plaintiff's Exhibit No. 1".)

Mr. Gerlack: May I read it to the jury, your Honor, the part dealing with permanent disability?

The Court: The Court will instruct them as to that.

Mr. Gerlack: Very well.

Q. Mr. Holland, after you ceased your employment there what did you do next?

Mr. Di Girolamo: What date is that, please?

By Mr. Gerlack:

Q. When did you quit, August 30 or 31?

A. I think it was the last day of August.

Q. The 31st? A. I believe so.

Mr. Di Girolamo: What year?

Mr. Gerlack: 1933.

Q. Did you do anything after that, Mr. Holland?

(Testimony of Wilson A. Holland.)

A. Well, for the first few months I rested. I stayed home and rested. [53]

Q. In what manner did you rest?

A. Well, I stayed in bed nearly all the time.

Q. 24 hours a day?

A. No, not 24 hours a day. I got up for my meals, but I daresay I spent 20 hours a day in bed.

Q. How did you feel during that time?

A. Well, I was resting. I felt a great deal better, but I was still tired. My nervousness improved quite a little bit.

A Juror: What improved, please?

The Witness: My nervousness, my feeling of nervousness had improved, but I couldn't overcome this feeling of fatigue so quickly or easily as that.

By Mr. Gerlack:

Q. Did you attempt to work again after that?

Mr. Di Girolamo: Now, just a minute. Mr. Gerlack knows the correct form of question to ask. I object to his using the phrase "Did you attempt to work."

The Court: Proceed, gentlemen.

By Mr. Gerlack:

Q. Just answer the question.

A. Yes, I attempted to work after that.

The Court: Just what was said there, Mr. Holland?

The Witness: I went back to work with the State Relief Administration. They wanted me to

(Testimony of Wilson A. Holland.)

take a job and come to work there because I was familiar with the California [54] State System of Accounting procedure. It seems that my name had been gotten out of the Civil Service list as one who was experienced in that line of work. Since it was necessary for me to go back to work I accepted this position. I remained on that job up until the Summer of 1935, and then I got this job with the United States Treasury Department in San Francisco where I remained until I finally had a hemorrhage from the lungs and had to enter the hospital at San Fernando, California in the Summer of 1936.

By Mr. Gerlack:

Q. You have not done anything since then, Mr. Holland? A. No, sir.

Q. Now, how much wages did you receive on this S. R. A. job?

A. The initial salary was set up at $125.00 a month, and then when the office was transferred to San Francisco they made some adjustments in all of the salaries, and I believe they raised that to $170.00 a month. There had been an intermediate adjustment for all accountants and they were raised to $150.00. They seemed to feel that $125.00 was hardly the sort of salary for men to receive who were doing that type of work. $170.00, I believe, was the final salary we received.

(Testimony of Wilson A. Holland.)

Q. Just tell us how you felt, so far as your health was concerned, while you worked on that job, Mr. Holland?

A. Well, it didn't differ from what I just told you [55] about the way I felt when I was working at Spadra, at the State Hospital, except if anything is worse because I got to coughing more at that time and I got so tired. Sometimes I didn't think I could pull the day through and very frequently I didn't. I just simply had to go home in the afternoon or at other times I just begged for a day off or sometimes a couple of days, and I would just stay in bed 24 hours a day and rest. Then, feeling a little refreshed, I came back. Other times I would feel extremely fatigued. One time, three months after I went to work on this job, I just got so all in I had to take a week off and I went down on the desert with a friend of mine, somewhere on a ranch down there, and I just spent my time out there living in the sunshine and eating good food. I stayed in bed whenever I felt like it which was just about all the time. Then I would come back to work again. That is the way I carried on all the way through this employment.

Q. What were your duties, were they arduous or light?

A. It wasn't what you would call a difficult job. My fellow workers who had more or less similar jobs didn't regard them as difficult.

(Testimony of Wilson A. Holland.)

Q. I know, but was your work supervisory or what?

A. Well, it was a little of each. I had some supervisory work and then a little later on I had less supervisory work. I actually worked on the accounts themselves trying to set them up in the general ledger. [56]

Q. Now, how long did you work for the Treasury Department, the Treasury Accounts Division?

A. I was there approximately ten months. I believe my appointment dated from some time in August, 1935, and it was early in June, 1936, that I had to leave and enter the hospital after this hemorrhage from my lungs.

Q. How did you get on, how did you feel on that job compared to the way you felt previously?

A. Well, there was no change. You might express it as no change.

Q. When you were not at work, for instance, on evenings, and Saturdays and Sundays, did you enjoy dancing and social activities?

A. Oh, no.

Q. What did you do?

A. That has been out for a good many years. Why, I went to bed. I was always so tired when I got home at night that I didn't feel like eating and went to bed.

Q. You spoke of going home early in the afternoon. How much of the time did you do that?

(Testimony of Wilson A. Holland.)

A. Well, it is a little hard to estimate that, but it happened rather frequently.

Q. Rather frequently?

A. Naturally I tried not to go home any oftener than necessary.

Q. Who was your superior on that State job? [57]

A. H. A. R. Carleton, the State Director.

Q. He was your immediate superior?

A. He was in charge of the whole office.

Q. Now, how did you feel today when you came here? How do you feel now as compared to the way you felt when you quit your work at Spadra?

A. Well, there is very little difference, very little difference. Of course, the fact that I am resting all the time now, spending all of my time at home in bed, helps somewhat, but I can't overcome this feeling of fatigue. I just want to rest. I can't get away from that, so I shouldn't say there is a great deal of difference in feeling between the way I feel now and the way I felt in 1933.

Q. How do you feel now as compared to the time you worked on the S. R. A. job?

A. I can't say I feel much different.

Q. What would you say comparing the way you feel now, as compared to the way you felt when you worked for the Treasury Department?

A. Just about the same.

Mr. Gerlack: Well, you may cross examine. [58]

(Testimony of Wilson A. Holland.)

Cross Examination

By Mr. Di Girolamo:

Q. Mr. Holland, you obtained an insurance policy while in service in February, 1918, is that right? A. That is right, sir.

Q. And you paid premiums on that insurance until 1920? A. That is right?

Q. Then it lapsed? A. Yes.

Q. Then in 1924 that was the first time you went to a Veterans' Bureau for a medical examination?

A. That is right.

Q. And they found that you had tuberculosis?

A. That is right.

Q. You testified that they prescribed some sort of treatment? A. Yes.

Q. You followed that treatment, did you?

A. I went to the hospital.

Q. Did they tell you what you were supposed to do?

A. Well, they advised hospitalization, that is what they advised.

Q. They advised hospitalization?

A. Yes.

Q. Did they tell you you should rest or exercise? [59]

A. Well, I went to the hospital.

Q. You were suffering from tuberculosis, were you not?

Mr. Gerlack: What time are you speaking about?

(Testimony of Wilson A. Holland.)

By Mr. Di Girolamo:

Q. In 1924?

A. Understand, I didn't enter the Veterans' Hospital in 1924.

Q. I know that, Mr. Holland, but you were examined by the doctors of the Veterans' Bureau, were you not? A. That is right.

Q. Did they advise that you work or that you rest?

A. They did not advise me to do anything other than to go to the hospital.

Q. Just go to the hospital? A. Yes.

Q. Now, the next time you went to the Veterans' Bureau to be examined was in 1925, was it not?

A. 1925? You mean after I left the Veterans' Hospital?

Q. Yes. A. That is right.

Q. And then in 1926 you went again?

A. Yes, I went for an examination again in 1926.

Q. Did you or did you not feel better in 1926?

A. Late in .1926 I *begain* to feel better.

Q. And then you went again in 1927, didn't you? [60] A. Yes.

Q. And you felt better then, didn't you?

A. Yes, sir.

Q. Then you went again in 1931, did you not?

A. Yes, sir.

Q. And you felt better then, didn't you?

(Testimony of Wilson A. Holland.)

A. 1931? Let's see. If I remember, in 1930, I wasn't feeling well.

Q. You didn't go to the Veterans' Bureau in 1930, you went there in 1931, did you not?

A. In 1931?

Q. On March 16, 1931? A. Yes.

Q. Right here in Los Angeles, at Sawtelle?

A. Yes, 1931.

Q. 1931, wasn't it?

A. You say that was in March?

Q. March 16. A. Yes.

Q. And then you went there again about a year later, on February 13, 1932? A. Yes.

Q. Then you did not go back there until June 13, 1936, is that right? That is when you went to San Fernando, is that right?

A. That is right, June 13. [61]

Q. You stayed there from June 13 to June 27, is that right?

A. No, I stayed there over a year at that time.

Q. The first time?

A. I went in there in June, 1936 and left in June, 1937.

Q. Now, in March, 1922 you were working in the United States Post Office in Iowa?

A. That is right.

Q. And you worked there for the duration of the term, five years, until 1927?

A. I didn't work the full duration of my term there. You see, I became so ill in September of

(Testimony of Wilson A. Holland.)

1924 that I didn't work from then on until 1927.

Q. You were not employed at all between 1924 and 1927 at the Post Office in Iowa?

A. I was not on the job. I was on a leave of absence. I still held the position officially.

Q. I see.

In 1927 you left that job to accept a job with the Pickwick Corporation in California, did you not?

A. You mean I left the job in Iowa?

Q. Yes. A. No, sir.

Q. To come here to California to accept a job with the Pickwick Corporation? [62] A. No.

Mr. Gerlack: What date is that?

Mr. Di Girolamo: December, 1927. No, just a minute, this was in June, 1927.

Q. You left there in June, 1927 and came here to accept a job in Glendale, California?

A. Yes.

Q. You accepted a job in a Post Office?

A. Yes.

Q. You stayed there until December, 1927?

A. Yes.

Q. In December, 1927 you quit there to accept in the same month a job with the Pickwick Corporation? A. Yes.

Q. At $175.00 a month, is that right?

A. No.

Q. How much was it? A. $25.00 a week.

Q. Then you worked for that corporation until January, 1931, is that right? A. Yes, sir.

(Testimony of Wilson A. Holland.)

Q. And the reason you left that job is because the corporation went into the hands of a receiver, is that right?

A. They hadn't gone into the hands of a receiver until some months after that.

Q. Well, did you ever state at any time, in writing, [63] that you left because the corporation went into the hands of a receiver?

A. I probably did in filling out applications for employment.

Q. I see.

A. I didn't want to tell them that it was on account of my health.

Mr. Gerlack: Your Honor, I don't see the materiality of this. It is prior to the date we claim as to permanent disability. Unless counsel can show it has a direct bearing on his present physical condition, I will object to it.

Mr. Di Girolamo: I think I can show it. It is material as to the Plaintiff's testimony, what he did in 1922, 1923 and 1924.

The Court: I think it is going into more detail than is really necessary.

Mr. Di Girolamo: All right, your Honor.

Q. Now, when you left the Pickwick Corporation you enrolled in the Southwestern University.

A. As a part-time student, yes.

Q. You remained there until March, 1932?

A. Yes, in the day school.

(Testimony of Wilson A. Holland.)

Q. And you left there to accept the job as Deputy Assessor at $140.00 a month?

A. It was a temporary job for a couple of months or so. [64]

Q. You stayed there until the month of May, is that correct?

A. Something like that, it lasted about two months, I believe.

Q. In May, 1932, you went back to the university? A. Yes, sir.

Q. In March, 1933, you went with the State Narcotic Hospital at Spadra? A. That is right.

Q. You had a salary of $125.00 a month there, did you? A. Yes, sir.

Q. And maintenance?

A. Maintenance, yes, sir.

Q. You worked there until September, 1933?

A. Yes.

Q. That is the time the position was abolished, is that right?

A. At the end of August. The position was abolished as of June 30, the end of the fiscal year, 1933. I remained on until August, through July and August, at which time I left.

Q. In the month of November, 1933, the same year, that is the last month you paid a premium on your insurance, is that right? A. Yes.

Q. The next month, the month of December, you went [65] to work for the State Relief Administration at $125.00 a month? A. Yes.

(Testimony of Wilson A. Holland.)

Q. A $5.00 increase from that which you were getting when you dropped your insurance?

A. Less actual cash.

Q. Yes.

A. I was getting $131.00 actual cash with the State.

Q. And you remained on that job until August, 1935, Mr. Holland?

A. That is about the right date.

Q. And the month of August, 1935, the very same day you left that job which you left in order to accept a new position, you went with the Treasury Accounts Division, did you not? A. Yes.

Q. On that job you were paid $225.00 a month?

A. Yes.

Q. Which is about $100.00 more than you received on the other job?

A. The other job had been increased to $170.00 at the time I left.

Q. Then you went with the Treasury Accounts Division at $225.00 a month and you remained there until June, 1936 although you were kept on the active list, that is, on the eligible list, until August, and you actually quit in August, [66] 1936?

A. I entered the hosiptal at that time.

Q. All right.

All this time that you were feeling so bad, every time you left the job and you went to some other job, why didn't you go back to the Veterans' Hospital where you had been going in 1924 one time,

(Testimony of Wilson A. Holland.)

1925 two times, 1926 once, 1927 three times, 1931 once, 1932 once, and then you didn't go back there at all until 1936. All this time you were feeling so bad, as you testified, why didn't you go back there?

Mr. Gerlack: Just a moment, we object to that as argumentative.

The Court: Oh, he may answer.

The Witness: Why didn't I go back for examination?

By Mr. Di Girolamo:

Q. Yes.

A. Because I had had examinations before. They seldom ever tell you anything at the Veterans' Administration when they give you an examination.

Q. They told you you had T. B. in 1924, didn't they?

A. Oh, naturally. They either tell you to go to the hospital and that is about all.

Q. And that is where you are now, isn't it?

A. Yes.

Mr. Di Girolamo: What about these papers, Mr. Gerlack? [67]

Mr. Gerlack: He signed them all.

Mr. Di Girolamo: You will stipulate these papers bear Mr. Holland's signatures?

Mr. Gerlack: Well, you had better ask him about the signatures. I don't know his signature.

By Mr. Di Girolamo:

Q. Mr. Holland, does this document bear your signature?

(Testimony of Wilson A. Holland.)

A. (Examining document) Yes.

(The document referred to was handed to the Clerk.)

The Clerk: That is Government's Exhibit B.

By Mr. Di Girolamo:

Q. Is that writing your handwriting?

A. (Examining document) Yes.

The Court: You had better have these marked. Mark them all so they can be identified for the record.

Mr. Di Girolamo: All right, your Honor.

Mark these.

(The documents referred to were handed to the Clerk.)

The Clerk: Government's Exhibits C, D, and E.

Mr. Di Girolamo: May this be marked Exhibit A?

The Clerk: Government's Exhibit A.

Mr. Di Girolamo: Your Honor, these documents have been marked Government's A to E for identification.

The Court: Very well. [68]

(The documents referred to were marked as "Government's Exhibits A to E for identification," inclusive, respectively.)

By Mr. Di Girolamo:

Q. Is this your signature? A. Yes, sir.

(Handing document to the Clerk.)

(Testimony of Wilson A. Holland.)

The Clerk: Government's Exhibit F.

(The document referred to was marked "Government's Exhibit F for identification.")

Mr. Di Girolamo: Will you produce the deposition taken by the Defendant?

Mr. Gerlack: Very well.

Mr. Di Girolamo: That is all.

The Court: Any redirect?

Redirect Examination

By Mr. Gerlack:

Q. Mr. Holland, this employment as a bookkeeper for the Pickwick Stages, and also during the time you were a part-time student at the Southwestern University, was that night work, night classes?

A. Part of it was evening classes, up until about 9:00 o'clock.

Q. And this Deputy Assessor's job, did that all take place before you claimed permanent disability on August 1, 1933? [69]

A. Oh, yes, long before that.

Q. Now Mr. Di Girolamo asked you if the Veterans' Bureau told you in 1934 that you had active T. B.? A. That is right.

Q. In 1927 when they examined you and told you your tuberculosis was arrested, did they tell you it was safe for you to go out and follow a job?

A. Yes, sir.

(Testimony of Wilson A. Holland.)

Mr. Gerlack: That is all.

The Court: Any recross examination?

Recross Examination

By Mr. Di Girolamo:

Q. In 1927, on April 1, that is the time you applied for reinstatement of your insurance which had lapsed in 1920, and you were examined again in connection with that application, were you not?

A. Yes.

Q. Were you granted your insurance?

A. Yes.

Mr. Di Girolamo: That is all.

The Court: Reinstatement, you mean.

Mr. Di Girolamo: Reinstatement of the insurance that had lapsed.

The Court: Yes. [70]

Redirect Examination

By Mr. Gerlack:

Q. Were you examined by a Government doctor at that time for that reinstatement, Mr. Holland.

A. Yes.

Mr. Gerlack: That is all.

Mr. Di Girolamo: That is all.

The Court: Anything further with this witness?

Mr. Di Girolamo: That is all.

(Witness excused.)

The Court: Your next witness.

Mr. Gerlack: Dr. Wyres.

ROBERT E. WYRES

a witness called in behalf of the Plaintiff, being first duly sworn, testified as follows:

The Clerk: Will you state your name to the Court and jury, please?

The Witness: Robert E. Wyres.

The Court: Are his qualifications admitted?

Mr. Gerlack: I wonder if counsel has any objection to excusing the Plaintiff. He wants to go to bed.

Mr. Di Girolamo: No objection, if the Court please.

The Court: Very well. **[71]**

Direct Examination

By Mr. Gerlack:

Q. Dr. Wyres, what is your occupation?

A. Physician and Surgeon.

Q. Where is your office at the present time?

A. At Pacific Colony.

The Court: You had better speak up louder, Doctor.

The Witness: Pacific Colony, at one of the state institutions.

By Mr. Gerlack:

Q. Are you employed by the State of California? A. Yes, sir.

Q. What is your occupation at Spadra?

(Testimony of Robert E. Wyres.)

A. I am Assistant Superintendent there.

Q. How long have you been connected with the institution at Spadra?

A. From April, 1929, since April, 1929.

Q. Doctor, you are a licensed and practicing physician and surgeon, licensed to practice in this State? A. Yes, sir.

Q. What medical school did you graduate from?

A. The University of Arkansas.

The Court: Do you admit the Doctor's qualifications?

Mr. Di Girolamo: I do, your Honor.

By Mr. Gerlack:

Q. What is your specialty, Doctor? [72]

A. Neuropsychiatry.

Q. Do you do any work outside of that?

A. Yes, I do a good deal of general in an institution like that.

Q. You don't claim to be a tuberculosis specialist? A. No, I don't.

Q. Have you treated and have you had experience with tuberculosis?

A. Oh, yes, we have always had some tuberculosis. Ever since graduation I have had to deal with tuberculosis, but I don't claim to be a specialist in that line.

Q. What particular experience have you had outside of the usual practice of medicine, in tuberculosis?

(Testimony of Robert E. Wyres.)

A. Well, at another state institution where I was associated I was in the tubercular service, in this insane institution, for a few months. Other than that, I have had none except the general cases that would come in along with my general work.

The Court: About how many would that be?

The Witness: In all cases?

The Court: Yes, tuberculosis cases.

The Witness: Well, I couldnt' tell you the number at all. I can tell you, however, that we do have some cases all the time. At the present time in our institution we have seven or eight cases of active tuberculosis and it is that way all the time, your Honor. [73]

By Mr. Gerlack:

Q. Well, Doctor, do you know the Plaintiff here, Wilson Holland? A. Yes.

Q. When did you first meet him?

A. I believe it was in March, 1933.

Q. How did you become acquainted with him on that occasion?

A. Well, he was sent to us as an accountant.

Q. He came to work at Spadra as an accountant?

A. That is right.

Q. How long did he work there?

A. Five or six months, I would say, approximately.

Q. He quit on the 31st of August, 1933?

A. I believe that is the date.

(Testimony of Robert E. Wyres.)

Q. What kind of a bookkeeper was he so far as qualifications were concerned?

A. The very best, I would say.

Q. He really knew his work as a bookkeeper?

A. That is right.

Q. How was his health at that time?

A. Poor, I would say.

Q. Tell the Court and jury what he looked like at that time.

A. He was lean, lank, and cadaverac looking very much as he is now, undernourished. You would see that he didn't [74] have much energy or that he was not very active, but he was a good bookkeeper and seemed to manage to get by with his work very well.

Q. Were his duties as a bookkeeper arduous at that time?

A. No, it is an occupation where there is no physical exertion. It was light work, and especially so at an institution like we are working in.

Q. Doctor, did you ever make an examination of him during the time he was at Spadra?

A. Yes, sir.

Q. Did you take any x-rays? A. Yes, sir.

Q. Was that a chest examination?

A. Yes.

Q. Tell the jury what examination you made and what your findings were and what your diagnosis was.

(Testimony of Robert E. Wyres.)

A. As a general rule we do not take care of employees, that is, we don't do that now at all, but at that time we didn't make a special effort to treat employees because they were with us for the purpose of working rather than hospitalization. In his case he was complaining to me about some trouble in his shoulder, some pain, and as I recall a stitch in his side.

Well, I thought that we would give him an examination, so I went over his chest and I took some of his history in [75] the meantime. He had told me that he was or had been having trouble with tuberculosis. After a chest examination I decided we would take an x-ray plate, which I did, and from my examination I would say he had tuberculosis without question. The x-ray plate showed it as well as my examination did.

Q. Was his tuberculosis active at that time?

A. I felt so, yes.

Q. What was the degree of advancement?

A. It would be on the borderline between moderately advanced and far advanced.

Q. Have you that x-ray with you, Doctor?

A. I have.

Q. Is that part of the official records of the California State Hospital at Spadra?

A. That is right.

Q. It was taken at that time by the hospital?

A. That is right.

(Testimony of Robert E. Wyres.)

Q. You are able to say that from your experience, that this is an x-ray taken of him at that time? A. Oh, yes.

Q. Does it definitely show, can you point out, Doctor, where that definitely shows tuberculosis?

A. Well, in the shadow-box, I could——

Mr. Di Girolamo (Interrupting): Now, just a minute, before this doctor testifies any further I would like to [76] question him on voir dire as to the admissibility of that x-ray.

The Court: Proceed.

Voir Dire Examination

By Mr. Di Girolamo:

Q. Doctor, did you see that x-ray taken?

A. I did.

Q. Who took it?

A. Our laboratory technician, x-ray technician.

Q. What is his name?

A. H. R. Roberts.

Q. What is his occupation now?

A. He is still our technician.

Q. What?

A. He is our technician still.

Q. You didn't take the x-ray yourself?

A. No.

The Court: Where is that?

The Witness: Pacific Colony at Spadra, the state institution at Spadra.

The Court: These jurors may know where that is, but I don't.

(Testimony of Robert E. Wyres.)

The Witness: It is near Pomona. I say Spadra because that is our post box, but Pomona is our town.

Mr. Gerlack: It is about 25 miles north.

The Court: I know where Pomona is. [77]

By Mr. Di Girolamo:

Q. You didn't take that x-ray, did you, Doctor?

A. No.

Q. You didn't develop this? A. No.

The Court: Were you present when it was taken?

The Witness: No, sir.

Mr. Di Girolamo: If the Court please, I object to the introduction of this x-ray.

The Court: What have you to say about it, counsel?

Mr. Gerlack: I would like to ask a few questions about it.

Direct Examination (Continued)

By Mr. Gerlack:

Q. In connection with your x-ray records at the hospital, have you a record that goes with it?

A. Oh, yes. I believe it is in the folder here. The number in the corner was taken at the time. There is a metal put on the screen and also put on there and that is copied with the patient's name and this is filed as a permanent record.

(Testimony of Robert E. Wyres.)

Q. Is that record part of the permanent record of Spadra Hospital?

A. That is right.

Q. Is that kept in the regular course of bookkeeping at the hospital? [78]

A. Yes.

Q. Kept in the regular course of business in the hospital?

A. Yes, so that he can identify it quickly.

Q. Aside from that, are you able to identify it, from a physical examination, as a doctor, are you able to say from your physical examination of the man and what you found in his chest, are you able to say, basing your answer on your experience as a doctor, that this is an x-ray of Mr. Holland?

A. Well, yes, but I believe I could suggest a better way of identifying it, if he has other pictures recently, by comparing the pictures.

Q. Have you examined him at any time besides August 30, 1933?

A. Not until this morning.

Q. What examination did you make of him this morning?

A. A chest examination under the fluoroscope.

Q. Are you able to say positively that this x-ray is his x-ray?

A. Yes, I am; I satisfied myself.

Q. You can say that, Doctor, from a medical standpoint? A. Yes.

(Testimony of Robert E. Wyres.)

Mr. Gerlack: We submit, your Honor, the foundation is laid in two ways: The doctor identifies his x-ray of the man, [79] and secondly, as something connected with the regular course of business there.

The Court: You think there is no question in your mind, Doctor?

The Witness: No question in my mind.

Mr. Di Girolamo: He testified, your Honor, that they did not examine employees, that they are at the institution to work and not for hospitalization. This is not, therefore, an official x-ray of Mr. Holland. Secondly, regardless of how well satisfied this Doctor is that this is his x-ray, the technician who took the x-ray, the *roetenologist,* is the proper person to testify about the x-ray.

The Court: I don't think that it is very material, even if admitted.

Mr. Gerlack: We did not bring Mr. Roberts in here on account of the expense. We would have to pay for his expenses if he came down to Los Angeles.

The Court: That would not modify any rule of law, but I don't think it is very material on the testimony here. I don't think the objection is very well taken. The mere fact that they did not take x-rays of employees, that they made an exception at this time, and having treated him, of course, he would be under the regular rules of the hospital.

(Testimony of Robert E. Wyres.)

Mr. Gerlack: Is your Honor overruling the objection?

The Court: Yes, if you insist on having it admitted. [80]

Mr. Gerlack: Yes. May we offer this as Plaintiff's next in order with the understanding that after the trial this will go back to the State Hospital? The doctor tells me that all records have to go back.

The Court: This may have to go up to the Court of Appeals.

Mr. Gerlack: When the case is ultimately finished, is that the understanding, it may go back?

Mr. Di Girolamo: When the case is all through.

Mr. Gerlack: Yes.

Mr. Di Girolamo: Note an exception.

The Witness: I would like to keep some other sheets in there.

The Court: Everything goes with it.

Mr. Gerlack: Here is the x-ray by itself.

The Witness: What about this card?

The Court: That goes with it.

Mr. Gerlack: Yes, that goes with the exhibit. What exhibit is this?

The Clerk: Plaintiff's Exhibit 2.

(The document referred to was received in evidence and marked "Plaintiff's Exhibit No. 2.")

The Court: Proceed.

(Testimony of Robert E. Wyres.)

By Mr. Gerlack:

Q. Now, Doctor Wyres, at the time of your examination of Mr. Holland here, on August 30, 1933, in your opinion was [81] his tuberculosis then of a temporary or of a permanent nature?

A. It was a permanent or chronic case, I would say, of course.

Q. Chronic? A. Yes.

Mr. Gerlack: Have you the medical report?

Mr. Di Girolamo: Yes.

Mr. Gerlack: At this time I will offer in evidence the Government's medical reports from the Government Bureau.

The Court: Please identify them.

Mr. Gerlack: I think your Honor also knows that under the decision these reports are not admissible in evidence. The practice has been to mark them for identification.

The Court: I am just waiting to see what you will do.

Mr. Gerlack: We will offer them for identification.

The Court: Very well, let them be marked for identification.

Mr. Gerlack: The first one we will offer as Plaintiff's exhibit next in order.

The Clerk: Plaintiff's Exhibit 3.

(The document referred to was received in evidence and marked "Plaintiff's Exhibit No. 3.")

(Testimony of Robert E. Wyres.)

Mr. Gerlack: This is a Report of Physical Examination at Des Moines, Iowa, December 30, 1924: Temperature 97, Pulse 116, Weight 113, Normal Weight, 135, Lowest Weight within one year 80. [82]

"This is a tall, slender, under-nourished black-haired man. Pupils: Equal, regular, react to light and accommodation; Sclera and conjunctive are negative."

Q. That is the eyes, Doctor? A. Yes.

Q. "Chest is long and slender. Excursion is very markedly limited left side."

What does that mean, Doctor, "Excursion is very markedly limited left side"?

A. That is the normal movement of the chest.

Q. Is that a common occurrence?

A. Yes, you will find it in these cases.

Q. "Fremitus is markedly increased both uppers, and absent the entire base of left side. Resonance is a marked dullness thruout left chest, becoming entirely flat below the left 4th rib."

What significance has that?

A. It might have some significance there.

Q. What is meant by "Resonance is a marked Dullness"?

A. Well, resonance here means resonance as anywhere else. There is a normal resonance, and then there is an impairment of resonance. It varies

(Testimony of Robert E. Wyres.)

in different cases. Did he say it was any particular kind of resonance?

Q. No;

> "Resonance is a marked dullness thruout left chest, becoming entirely flat below the left 4th rib."

A. It might have some significance there, yes. [83]

The Court: Just tell us what that word "resonance" means so that we farmers and jurors in the courtroom will know what it is.

The Witness: Well, in using the word resonance, we speak of certain resonance that is produced in the lungs.

The Court: You mean the force of breathing produces a sound?

The Witness: Yes.

The Court: Just so we understand it.

The Witness: It may be diminished or increased. It becomes greater or less in diseased states.

By Mr. Gerlack:

Q. Is that a symptom of tuberculosis?

A. Well, it might be. Tuberculosis renders it abnormal.

Q. Now, Doctor, "There is a scar in the left 7th interspace axillary region which is draining a seropurulent fluid."

What does that mean?

(Testimony of Robert E. Wyres.)

A. It is a combination of two words serous and purulent. Serous and purulent is a description of a type of fluid. A serous fluid is clear with less viscous, or I might say, is less heavy than others. Purulent means containing pus. Combining the two words serous, a light fluid, mixed with this heavy pussy material.

Q. Examination shows further that "Breath sounds are harsh, right 3rd rib to 4th Dorsal Spine. Markedly diminished [84] over entire left chest, *resulint* in atrophy of the left base."

What does that word "atrophy" mean?

A. Atrophy means diminishing or decreasing.

Q. Shrinking?

A. Shrinking is a better word.

Q. Further, "There are a number of fine rales thruout chest more marked below 4th rib front and below 4th Dorsal Spine in the back."

What are rales? And what is their significance in tuberculosis, Doctor?

A. These rales are abnormal sounds produced in the lungs. Air going through various parts of the respiratory system produce abnormal sounds. For instance, air going in produces these abnormal sounds which are not found in normal tissue. In tuberculosis they are found because the tissues are abnormal there.

Q. Anyway, it is one of the symptoms of tuberculosis?

(Testimony of Robert E. Wyres.)

A. Yes, but the rales are not considered so important in the diagnosis.

Q. Now, the special lung examination shows:

> "Right lung—Harsh breathing to 3rd rib and 3rd Dorsal Spine. No rales.
>
> "Left lung—Diminished breathing thruout front. A few fine rales. Following cough to 4th rib, numerous fine rales to lower border. A few fine rales above [85] 3rd Dorsal Spine and front."

What does that mean as far as tuberculosis is concerned?

A. Well, it means that you are getting these abnormal findings. All those conditions mentioned are abnormal. They could become pronounced in tuberculosis, or they could be less pronounced, all of those.

Q. Then it says,

> "Summary: Disseminated fibrosis infiltration left upper lobe. Thickened pleura with purulent accumulation. Left pleura drainage 3 months ago. Not healed."

What does that mean?

A. This fibrosis is a process which undertakes to repair all injuries to any of our tissues, such as a scar on your hand, for instance. The little scar which you speak of when you cut your hand, is a little attempt on the part of nature to heal and

(Testimony of Robert E. Wyres.)
the same process takes place in all parts of the body.

Q. The general diagnosis is Pulmonary Tuberculosis, Chronic, minimal active; Pleuritis chronic purulent.

A Juror: (Interrupting) Would you ask the witness whether fibrosis and scar tissue are the same?

The Court: Will you answer that question?

The Witness: In the repair of tissue they would be the same. In repairing an injury to the body it is the same thing. [86]

By Mr. Gerlack:

Q. In other words, there is fibrosis or scar tissue, and there can be scar tissue and active tuberculosis going on at the same time?

A. Oh, yes, there would be certain lesions which might have been repaired, while there might be active lesions elsewhere in the lungs.

Q. Now, the next examination made of Mr. Holland was at the U. S. Veterans' Hospital at Fort Lyon, Colorado, February 4, 1924.

Physical Examination, general appearance fairly well developed and nourished.

X-ray Report by Dr. Frank R. Ruff, Special Roentgenologist: "Moderate tuberculosis of the right apex and upper Far advanced tuberculosis of the left chest with an empyema which is filled with pus."

(Testimony of Robert E. Wyres.)

What is empyema, Doctor?

A. It really means that there is pus in the plural cavity.

Q. Further,

> "This occupies about half of the lung extending from the 2nd rib to the 7th rib, and there is an adhesion to the left diaphragm."

That was Doctor Ruff's report.

This particular examination goes on to state,

> "Small amount of pus in left side. Rib has been resected and drainage established. Tap this day failed to secure pus, [87] possibly because of thickness of same."
>
> "Heart: No exercise for heart reaction.
>
> "Auscultation, Right Lung: BS increased and harsh slightly prolonged expiration 2nd rib and 3rd Dorsal Spine up. Whispered voice, vocal resonance increased with BVB 2nd rib and 2nd Dorsal Spine up.
>
> "Left Lung: Whispered voice, vocal resonance, and BS diminished base up to 5th Dorsal Spine, also axillary line and *na*teriorly below 4th rib, BS weak with BVB 2nd rib and 3rd Dorsal Spine up.
>
> "Infiltration and consolidation most left upper and lower. Empyema left Chest."

Tell the jury what that means in the language of the layman, Doctor, so that all of us can understand it.

(Testimony of Robert E. Wyres.)

A. Well, the abnormal findings, as I said before —this seems to be pretty much of a repetition of the findings which you just gave, these abnormal signs which are mentioned here. We have the normal condition and the departure from that is what he calls attention to.

Q. Does that mean the man has tuberculosis?

A. It sounds much like it.

Q. Tuberculosis?

A. Yes, it sounds like it.

Q. It says here, "Pulmonary Diagnosis positive; condition active; stage far advanced."

The General Diagnosis is "Tuberculosis, Pulmonary, [88] Chronic, Active, Far Advanced, Empyema left chest."

A. What is the date of that?

Mr. Gerlack: The date is February 24, 1925.

(Handing document to Clerk.)

The Clerk: Plaintiff's Exhibit 4 for identification.

(The document referred to was marked "Plaintiff's Exhibit No. 4 for identification.")

Mr. Gerlack: The next examination taken at the U. S. Veterans' Hospital, No. 80, Fort Lyon, Colorado, May 5, 1925. Apparently it is about the same.

"Slight fibrosis right upper. Old infiltration and fibrosis upper left, thick pleura over most of left, walled off Empyema pocket left base, sinus.

(Testimony of Robert E. Wyres.)

"Pulmonary diagnosis Positive; Condition improved; State Moderately advanced, active."

"General Diagnosis: Tuberculosis, Pulmonary Chronic Active Far Advanced, Tuberculosis Empyema, drainage, left chest."

Unless you want me to read further I will pass that.

Mr. Di Girolamo: Oh, pass it.

The Clerk: Plaintiff's Exhibit 5 for identification.

(The document referred to was marked "Plaintiff's Exhibit No. 5 for identification.")

Mr. Gerlack: In a diagnosis or examination made October 1, 1925,

"Right lung: Shows a marked disseminated fibrosis with a large group of calcified glands in the [89] hilus with a definite infective process extending from the hilus to the periphery involving the upper lobe. There is definite mottling of the lung structures throughout this area.

"Left lung: Shows the same general changes, and in addition there is a definite infective process involving the periphery of the upper lobe, with an infiltration of the lung structures along the course of the bronchi of the lower lobe.

"The changes in both uppers are definite of pulmonary tuberculosis. There is no accumu-

(Testimony of Robert E. Wyres.)

lation within the pleural cavity on the left side at this time."

That is signed by Dr. Thomas A. Burcham.

I offer that as Plaintiff's next in order.

The Clerk: Plaintiff's Exhibit 6 for identification.

(The document referred to was marked "Plaintiff's Exhibit No. 6 for identification.")

Mr. Gerlack: Here is a Wassermann Test which was negative.

The Court: Are you offering that?

Mr. Gerlack: Yes.

(Hands document to Clerk.)

The Clerk: Plaintiff's Exhibit 7 for identification.

(The document referred to was marked "Plaintiff's Exhibit No. 7 for identification.") [90]

By Mr. Gerlack:

Q. Wassermann Tests are made in most hospitals—— A. Yes.

Q. They take them in practically all cases?

A. Yes.

Q. Just as a matter of routine? A. Yes.

Mr. Gerlack: Here is an Eye, Ear and Throat which I won't offer.

(Testimony of Robert E. Wyres.)

Now, the next examination was taken at Des Moines, Iowa, U. S. Veterans' Regional Office, apparently Des Moines, Iowa, October 1, 1925.

Examination shows pulmonary tuberculosis.

> "Auscultation: Right lung: Breath sounds harsh to 3rd rib front Dorsal Spine, numerous fine rales above 2nd rib; Left lung: B.V. breathing to 4th rib harsh breathing to 3rd Dorsal Spine, few fine rales below lower angle of scapula.
>
> "Pulmonary diagnosis: Pulmonary Tuberculosis, chronic, active. Empyema left healed, Pleurisy fibrosis chronic left, Deviated nasal septum."

(Hands document to Clerk.)

The Clerk: Plaintiff's Exhibit 8 for identification.

> (The document referred to was marked "Plaintiff's Exhibit No. 8 for identification.")

Mr. Gerlack: Here is a clinical record. It does not [91] show where it was taken. This is on a form of the United States Veterans' Bureau No. 26141, October 6, 1925, "Tubercle Bacilli found."

Q. Does that mean tuberculosis germs were found in the sputum, Doctor?

A. Yes, that means it was found through a laboratory examination.

Mr. Gerlack: I offer that as Plaintiff's next in order.

(Testimony of Robert E. Wyres.)

The Clerk: Plaintiff's Exhibit 9 for identification.

(The document referred to was marked "Plaintiff's Exhibit No. 9 for identification.")

Mr. Gerlack: The next examination was taken in Los Angeles, California, August 19, 1926. I will just read the preliminary findings.

Right lung—I can't quite make these words out (indicating.)

Mr. Di Girolamo: It says, "Bronchular tuberculosis—B. T. B."

The Doctor can tell you.

The Witness: T. B. means tuberculosis.

By Mr. Gerlack:

Q. No, it is T. V. C.

A. Right lung.

Q. Look at this (indicating.)

A. Well some of those abbreviations I wouldn't be sure of myself. [92]

Q. Does every doctor have his own abbreviations?

A. Sometimes, unfortunately, they abbreviate in their own style, a lot of times.

Q. Fibrosis both upper lobes. Thickened adherent pleural left chest following empyema.

Pulmonary diagnosis: Tuberculosis pulmonary chronic. Pleurisy fibrous chronic.

(Testimony of Robert E. Wyres.)

I can't quite make that out. Oh, yes, "following Empyema left chest."

Mr. Di Girolamo: That is right.

Mr. Gerlack: "Condition improved, quiescent, moderately advanced."

(Hands document to Clerk.)

The Clerk: Plaintiff's Exhibit 10 for identification.

(The document referred to was marked "Plaintiff's Exhibit No. 10 for identification.")

Mr. Gerlack: Next examination taken at Los Angeles, California, March 2, 1927. The examination, according to this, shows it was made of the lungs and that the "shape of the chest was thin and flat, mobility poor, deep apices, permanent"—can you make that out?

Mr. Di Girolamo, is that "permanent clouded" or something like that?

Mr. Di Girolamo: No, it is not clouded.

Mr. Gerlack: I will skip it.

Right lung—I can't make that out either. [93]

The diagnosis was pulmonary tuberculosis, chronic, pleurisy, chronic—another word I cannot make out—healed left base. Condition apparently arrested. Stage moderately advanced.

General diagnosis: Tuberculosis Pulmonary Chronic, moderately advanced, apparently arrested. Pleurisy supperative. Healed left chest.

(Testimony of Robert E. Wyres.)

I offer that in evidence.

The Clerk: Plaintiff's Exhibit 11 for identification.

(The document referred to was marked "Plaintiff's Exhibit No. 11 for identification.")

Mr. Gerlack: The next examination was made at the Regional Office of the United States Veterans Bureau, Los Angeles, California, September 30, 1927.

"Auscultation: Right lung—B. V. B. and I. V. C. over dull area," it looks like here. "No persistent moist rales heard."

"Left lung—I. V. C. apex. No moist rales heard.

"Post anterior *a*mphysema scar and axilla. Fibrosis both uppers. Thickened pleura left base.

"Pulmonary diagnosis: Tuberculosis, chronic, pulmonary. Moderately advanced, arrested. Post anterior emphysema healed left. Chronic fibrosis pleurisy left base."

I offer that as Plaintiff's next in order.

The Clerk: Plaintiff's Exhibit 12 for identification. [94]

(The document referred to was marked "Plaintiff's Exhibit No. 12 for identification.")

(Testimony of Robert E. Wyres.)

Mr. Gerlack: Here is a document dated October 15, 1927 which states, among other things, "After a careful review of all the medical evidence in file, the undersigned members of the T. B. Board conclude that claimant did manifest pulmonary tuberculosis from date of separation from service.

"Definitely arrested."

That document is signed by Dr. O. S. Evenson, Dr. David A. Bahn, and Dr. John F. Marlin.

I offer that in evidence as Plaintiff's next in order.

The Clerk: Plaintiff's Exhibit 13 for identification.

(The document referred to was marked "Plaintiff's Exhibit No. 13 for identification.")

Mr. Gerlack: The next examination was made at the Regional Office of the Los Angeles Veterans' Bureau at Los Angeles, California, on March 16, 1931.

"Examination of Lungs:

"Shape of chest: Long, narrow, thin and frail, mobility limited expansion left chest.

"Palpation: Fremitus negative.

"Percussion—Right lung: Diminished resonance 2nd rib and 4th dorsal spine. Left lung: Diminished resonance 2nd rib and 4th dorsal spine with dullness from the 4th rib down in the axillary and posterior area.

(Testimony of Robert E. Wyres.)

"Auscultation: Right lung: B.V.B. and I.V.C. over [95] impaired area with a few inconstant rales heard both below and above the clevicle.

"Left lung: V.V.B. and I.V.C. over imparied area. Many rales heard following expiratory cough. Breath sounds at the base below the 4th rib is diminished with pleural crepitations over the area of the emphysema scar.

"Fibrosis both upper lobes with thickened adherent pleura following emphysema operation.

"Pulmonary diagnosis, Tuberculosis, pulmonary, chronic, arrested, moderately advanced with chronic fibrous pleurisy left base, post operative emphysema."

I offer this in evidence as Plaintiff's next in order.

The Clerk: Plaintiff's Exhibit 14 for identification.

(The document referred to was marked "Plaintiff's Exhibit No. 14 for identification.")

Mr. Gerlack: The next examination is made at the Veterans' Bureau, Los Angeles, California, February 13, 1932, Special Chest Report.

"Inspection: Chest is long and thin with apical retraction bilateral. There is a 3″ scar

(Testimony of Robert E. Wyres.)

8th and 9th interspace in the posterior axillary line, result of an operation for empyema. Scar is well healed but adherent to the underlying structure. Mobility is limited on the left side. Fremitus is increased over both upper lobes and at the left base.

"Auscultation: Right Lung: Harsh vesicular breathing [96] thruout with increased voice conduction over the impaired area. A few mucus and sonorous rales are heard thruout. Left Lung: Harsh breath sounds of sonorous type. Prolonged expiration thruout with increased voice conduction over the imparied area. There are diminished breath sounds at the base below the angle of the scapula, in the mid-axillary region, with many pleural crepitations over the same area.

"Summary: Fibrosis over both upper lobes with thickened pleura left lower lobe.

"Diagnoses: (a) Tuberculosis, pulmonary, chronic, arrested, moderately advanced. (b) Pleurisy, fibrous, chronic, left, following empyema.

"No Reports:

(Signed) "O. S. ESSENSON, M. D.,

"O. S. ESSENSON, M. D.,

"Attending Specialist, (Tb)"

I offer that in evidence as Plaintiff's next in order.

(Testimony of Robert E. Wyres.)

The Clerk: Plaintiff's Exhibit 16 for identification.

(The document referred to was marked "Plaintiff's Exhibit No. 16 for identification.")

Mr. Gerlack: Next examination was made at the United States Veterans' Hospital at San Fernando, California, or the Veterans' Administration Facility, I believe they call it now, V. A. F. San Fernando, California, 6/13/36—6/27/36.

"Respiratory System: Chest is moderately long, moderately broad and flat, more on the left. Mobility: Poor, [97] restricted both uppers.

"Palpation—Right—Increased over right upper and lower right back. Left—Increased left upper.

"Percussion: Right—Dl above 2nd rib and 7th D. S. Left—Dl above 3rd rib and thruout back.

"Auscultation: Right—I.W. above 3rd rib and 6th D. S. BVB same area. Scattered TPMI rales heard above 2nd rib and 5th D. S. on inspiration after expiratory cough. Breathing sounds over left base are distant with pleural crepitations. Impression: Active infiltration and fibrosis both uppers and upper parts both lower lobes."

(Testimony of Robert E. Wyres.)

The diagnosis on that hospitalization was: "Tuberculosis chronic pulmonary far advanced active; Pleurisy, chronic, fibrous, left base; Cicatrix, old healed, P. O. rib resection; Hypotension arterial;—"

Q. What is Hypotension, Doctor?

A. "Hypo" is below normal; "hyper" is the opposite.

Mr. Gerlack:

> "Hemorrhoids, external, mild, non sumpathetic; Pes Planus, bilateral, 3rd degree; Vericocele, left moderate; Rhinitis, chronic hypertrophic; Deviation nasal septum, left."

The Witness: What is the date of that, please?

Mr. Gerlack: That is June 13 to June 27, 1936.

The Witness: All right.

Mr. Gerlack: I offer that as Plaintiff's exhibit next in order. [98]

The Clerk: Plaintiff's Exhibit 16 for identification.

(The document referred to was marked "Pláintiff's Exhibit No. 16 for identification.")

Mr. Gerlack: The next examination was made at the U. S. Veterans' Hospital at San Fernando on September 18, 1936. It shows about the same findings and diagnoses, that is, tuberculosis, pulmonary, chronic, far advanced, active. The rest of the examination is the same as the last.

(Testimony of Robert E. Wyres.)

I offer this in evidence as Plaintiff's next in order.

The Clerk: Plaintiff's Exhibit 17 for identification.

(The document referred to was marked "Plaintiff's Exhibit No. 17 for identification.")

By Mr. Gerlack:

Q. Now, Doctor Wyres, bearing in mind these different examinations, assuming the evidence that Mr. Holland gave on the witness stand, assuming those facts to be true, and assuming these Government reports to be true, and taking that in connection with your own examination, in your opinion, what were the probabilities on August 30, 1933 that Mr. Holland's tuberculosis would become arrested even if he had taken the best of medical treatment at that time?

Mr. Di Girolamo: Just a moment. I object to that in that this witness is called upon to base an opinion upon the opinions given by other doctors.

Mr. Gerlack: I will clear that up.

Q. Disregard the diagnoses of doctors. Base this [99] absolutely on the evidence, but don't take into consideration their findings.

Mr. Di Girolamo: I will renew my objection. Those examinations when read by counsel were read as prognoses and were opinions made by other doctors. He has read practically every prognosis

(Testimony of Robert E. Wyres.)

and diagnosis and opinion of these different doctors. The witness cannot possibly form an opinion without basing it on the opinions given by other doctors.

Let me cite to your Honor the case of Corrigan versus the United States, 82 Federal 2nd, Page 106.

The Court: Can you differentiate the diagnoses from the doctors and from the opinions given?

The Witness: Yes.

The Court: And the conclusions?

The Witness: Yes.

The Court: Purely upon the diagnoses?

The Witness: Yes, because those histories seem to be pretty well written. There is plenty of information given from the physical examinations.

The Court: Objection overruled.

Mr. Gerlack: May I reframe my question for the purpose of the record?

The Court: Yes, go ahead.

By Mr. Gerlack:

Q. Now, Doctor, I will ask you to base your opinion [100] not upon the findings—you know the difference between findings and diagnoses—disregard the diagnoses—base your opinion merely upon the findings and upon your own examination and findings as shown by your testimony here, and assuming the facts or the evidence as given by Mr. Holland under oath on the witness stand to be true, basing your opinion on those facts, will you tell us

(Testimony of Robert E. Wyres.)

in your opinion what were the probabilities of Mr. Holland becoming an arrested case of tuberculosis on August 30, 1933 even had he taken the best of medical care including going to a sanitarium?

A. Well, I would say a small chance, perhaps one in ten.

Q. You mean that the strong probabilities were that he would not have gotten well even had he taken the best of medical care?

A. That is right.

Mr. Gerlack: You may cross examine. [101]

Cross Examination

By Mr. Di Girolamo:

Q. Doctor, when did you examine him? Do you know the exact date you examined him and had this x-ray taken? A. Yes.

Q. When was it?

A. It was August 30, 1933.

Q. Until when did he remain in that institution?

A. Until when?

Q. Yes. A. I think he left the next day.

Q. The next day?

A. I think his services were terminated the next day.

Q. Doctor, you are not a tuberculosis specialist, are you? A. No, sir.

Q. Did you yourself ever treat a case of tuberculosis? A. Yes, sir.

(Testimony of Robert E. Wyres.)

Q. Is it not a fact, Doctor, that Mr. Holland left in September, 1933 at that hospital? A. No.

Q. Left his employment?

A. I will not be positive about that.

Q. You are not positive?

A. These dates I gave you are approximate.

Q. Doctor, you stated that fibrosis is a healing [102] process, is that right? A. Yes.

Q. By the way, Doctor, you have with you the diagnostic standard? A. Yes, sir.

Q. Mr. Gerlack gave you that book?

A. Yes.

Q. Have you read it? A. I looked it over.

Q. Now, can you tell us what the Diagnostic Standards of that association are for the purpose of ascertaining when a disease is arrested?

A. Well, a disease is arrested if constitutional symptoms are absent. That is, the temperature is normal, no coughing, and the sputum is free and has been for, let us say, six months, and the last two months of which the patient has been taking hourly exercises such as walking, exercises for two times a day, let us say. Also the x-ray findings would show improvement, that is, the lesions would be healed and show an improvement from the x-ray standpoint. In other words, it would show retrogression rather than progression.

Q. That exercise twice a day is equivalent to how many working hours?

A. Give me that question again, please.

(Testimony of Robert E. Wyres.)

Q. You stated that one of the tests was an exercise [103] twice a day.

A. Yes, walking exercise is usually what is used.

Q. Equal to how many hours of work?

A. I would say about an hour twice a day.

Q. Two hours a day? A. Yes.

Q. Now, when a patient whom you have diagnosed as having tuberculosis comes to your attention and subsequently you find the diagnosis, or rather, you make a diagnosis of quiescence, what does that mean?

A. Well, quiescence may even have a tubercle bacilli in the sputum, but there is no progression.

Q. No progression?

A. In the x-ray findings you can tell by your lesion's whether or not there is an increase over a couple of months' period, let us say.

Q. All right. Now, if the next diagnosis shows "apparently arrested," what does that mean?

A. Apparently arrested is just a little less than what you are willing to call an arrested case, if in some four months' period or three months' period they have been quiet as far as their active lesions are concerned.

Q. Now, supposing you have a patient whose diagnosis was first active and then quiescent and then apparently arrested, what do you do next to test whether or not he is arrested? [104]

(Testimony of Robert E. Wyres.)

A. You mean, if you want to be able to call him arrested, is that right?

Q. Yes.

A. Just as I have explained to you under the case of arrested tuberculosis.

Q. Then your next diagnosis shows definitely arrested. What does that mean?

A. Definitely arrested would mean that you had observed him for a longer period, that would be all; you had watched the case longer and it still had not shown any activity.

Q. Now, is it your opinion, Doctor, that a man——

A. May I say this, first of all: Be slow in making a definitely arrested diagnosis.

Q. How slow, Doctor?

A. I would wait for a period of a year, at least.

Q. About a year? A. Yes.

Q. All right, now, suppose you tell us this, Doctor. Take a man whose tubercular condition has been found to be arrested and who worked, let us say, for a period of one year, if that work does not show a reactivation of the tubercular condition, would that suggest to you that his condition was definitely arrested?

A. Just how strong do you mean to use the word "arrested"? Do you mean cured? [105]

Q. No, just arrested.

A. I see. Well, I would feel that he was probably arrested, probably an arrested case if I could

(Testimony of Robert E. Wyres.)

not make any clinical findings or get any clinical findings.

Q. Do you know the difference between primary infection and reinfection in tuberculosis? That is in the book also.

A. I am afraid none of us can draw a definite line between that, but primary means the first infection, of course.

Q. I see.

A. It is common in childhood.

Q. What is reinfection?

A. Reinfection, under the old classification might result from a new infection or from the activity of a primary infection.

Q. Now, Doctor, if you had examined a man in 1924 and found active tuberculosis, and then in 1925 also active tuberculosis, and in 1926 you found quiescence, in 1927 apparently arrested, again in the same year arrested, again in the same year definitely arrested, and then the man keeps on working —such work as has been testified by Mr. Holland here—and then you examined him again four years later, in 1931, and you also found him arrested, with fibrosis, which is a healing process, isn't it?

A. Yes. [106]

Q. And scar tissue is a healing process, isn't it?

A. Yes.

Q. And then you examined him again in 1932 and you also found a tubercular condition, arrested,

(Testimony of Robert E. Wyres.)

wouldn't you say, Doctor, that was a sufficient test to determine that his condition when it became arrested in 1927 was arrested?

A. You have made rather a long and involved question there. May I have the question read?

Mr. Di Girolamo: Read the question:

(The record referred to was read by the reporter, as follows:

> "Q. Now, Doctor, if you had examined a man in 1924 and found active tuberculosis, and then in 1925 also active tuberculosis, and in 1926 you found quiescence, in 1927 apparently arrested, again in the same year arrested, again in the same year definitely arrested, and then the man keeps on working—such work as has been testified by Mr. Holland here—and then you examined him again four years later, in 1931, and you also found him arrested, with fibrosis, which is a healing process, isn't it?
>
> "A. Yes.
>
> "Q. And scar tissue is a healing process, isn't it? A. Yes.
>
> "Q. And then you examined him in 1932 again and you also found a tubercular condition, arrested, wouldn't you [107] say, Doctor, that was a sufficient test to determine that his condition when it became arrested in 1927 was arrested?")

(Testimony of Robert E. Wyres.)

The Witness: Well, under our diagnosis and classification, I would say that he would be, if a satisfactory examination had been made to determine that he was actually arrested, why, I would say that he was; but sometimes just saying that a case is arrested because he has not died from tuberculosis in the meantime, during four years, or whatever period it might be, does not mean really that he is an arrested case.

By Mr. Di Girolamo:

Q. Doctor, didn't you say just a moment ago that in order to determine whether a case is arrested or not after quiescence you try for six months with exercises?

A. Exercises? Exercises would not answer questions. If a satisfactory set of examinations were made for arrested tuberculosis, I would say yes.

Q. Now, the evidence as read to you in these examinations—take for instance No. 1, where they take his temperature, his pulse, examine his right lung and his left lung, using the stethoscope, examining the pleura, where they took x-rays in 1927, are those examinations sufficient examinations?

A. I don't believe it is sufficient to do that.

Q. It is not? [108] A. No.

Q. You are basing your opinion upon these examinations, are you not?

A. Well, here is the thing. They should have had something more than just that. Now, when it

(Testimony of Robert E. Wyres.)

comes to your x-ray findings, and so on, those are the most valuable; but under our classification it tells about your x-rays and you see what effect the x-rays have over that period. Isn't that true?

Q. Well, Doctor, from May 27, 1936—you heard the Plaintiff on the stand? A. Yes.

Q. You were in court when the Plaintiff testified, weren't you? A. Yes.

Q. I presume you heard him state he worked when the medical examinations were made in 1926 as quiescent, three in 1927 apparently arrested, one definitely arrested, one in 1931 arrested, one in 1932 arrested, and he continued to work up until 1936. Isn't that a sufficient test, Doctor?

A. Perhaps.

Q. Perhaps? A. Yes.

Q. Still you are of the opinion that in 1933, when you examined him, his chances were one to ten? A. In 1933? [109]

Q. They were one to ten?

A. That is my statement, yes.

Q. That is your statement? A. Yes.

Q. Did you advise Mr. Holland when you found him to be in that condition, with chances for arrest one to ten, did you advise him what to do?

A. I don't think I told him what his chances were. I did tell him that he had to take care of himself, that he needed rest then.

Q. You told him that? A. Yes.

(Testimony of Robert E. Wyres.)

Mr. Gerlack: Just a moment. I think counsel's question is a little unfair. The doctor assumes something not in evidence at that time. He now asks him what he told Mr. Holland in 1933. In answering that question he based it on what he heard in the courtroom today. I don't think it is fair.

The Court: Oh, there is nothing prejudicial in it. He answered the question.

By Mr. Di Girolamo:

Q. Now, Doctor, you advised him to take a rest?

A. Yes.

Q. Would your opinion change as to his chances had he at the time you advised him to take a rest, taken a rest instead of working as he did until June, 1936? [110]

A. Well, of course, the working changed the outlook somewhat.

Mr. Di Girolamo: That is all, Doctor.

Redirect Examination

By Mr. Gerlack:

Q. What effect did work have on his condition, Doctor?

A. Well, in a tubercular condition, of course, naturally, rest is one of the most therapeutic measures we have.

Q. What is therapeutic?

A. Well, it includes direct therapeutics, light therapeutics, and treatment.

Q. In other words, work would aggravate his condition and make it worse? A. Yes.

(Testimony of Robert E. Wyres.)

Juror Whittingham: May I ask the witness a question?

The Court: What do you want to know?

Juror Whittingham: The witness states that fibrosis or scar tissue shows evidence of healing. I would like to know after it is called healing is it active or inert tissue?

The Court: You may answer that.

The Witness: I don't believe that was made clear.

Now, in a case of tuberculosis, an old chronic case like you have here, there is, of course, some active tissue. Nature is trying to heal the wounds. There might be a lot of [111] fibrosis or scar tissue, or an attempt to heal, and still the case would be very active and the patient would be going down hill with tuberculosis.

Juror Whittingham: I don't think the witness is getting the idea of the question, or perhaps I did not ask it properly. I don't want to know about the activity of tuberculosis, but whether the fibrosis tissue, healed over the spots on the lung, is then active tissue, which the patient makes use of in his lungs, or does it become inert tissue which reduces the capacity of the lungs.

The Witness: It is no good as lung tissue.

Juror Whittingham: Thank you.

The Witness: It is no good to him.

The Court: Anything further?

(Testimony of Robert E. Wyres.)

Mr. Di Girolamo: That is all.

Mr. Gerlack: That is all.

The Court: Well, I think that is all we will be able to hear this morning.

The jurors will not discuss the facts in this case.

You should not permit any person to talk to you in your presence, either here or elsewhere, during the recess of this court. If anyone attempts to talk to you take their names and report the matter to the Court.

The court will take a recess until 2:00 o'clock this afternoon.

(Witness excused.) [112]

(Thereupon, at 12:00 o'clock noon, a recess was taken until 2:00 o'clock of the same date.) [113]

Los Angeles, California
Tuesday, February 28, 1939
2:00 o'Clock P. M.

The Court: Let the record show the jurors are present.

Mr. Gerlack: It is stipulated the jury is present.

Mr. Di Girolamo: It is so stipulated.

The Court: Proceed.

Mr. Gerlack: I will call Mrs. Holland to the stand.

MRS. WILSON A. HOLLAND,

a witness called in behalf of the Plaintiff, having been first duly sworn, testified as follows:

Direct Examination

By Mr. Gerlack:

Q. Mrs. Holland, you are the wife of Wilson A. Holland, the Plaintiff here? A. Yes.

Q. When and where were you married to him?

A. On October 12, 1919, in Siberia.

Q. You have lived with him continuously since that time, have you? A. Yes.

Q. Do you recall when he had a job at Spadra in August, 1933? A. Yes, I do.

Q. You were living with him out at Spadra, or you were living in town there? [114]

A. I was living in town.

Q. When did you see him?

A. He used to come home for week ends, every week end.

The Court: Speak up so that the last man can hear you.

By Mr. Gerlack:

Q. Tell the jury how he appeared to you on week ends when he came home from Spadra.

A. He would come home awfully tired and usually went right to bed and stayed there on Sunday and started back on Monday morning.

Q. Did you go to shows on Saturday night or anything? A. No.

(Testimony of Mrs. Wilson A. Holland.)

Q. He spent all of his time in bed on Saturday afternoons and Sundays? A. Always.

Q. Do you recall when he got out of the San Fernando Hospital the first time? I believe that was in 1937, before he went back the last time, last October? A. Yes.

Q. Tell the jury how he appeared at home during that time as compared when he came home from Spadra?

A. Well, he was more rested. He was able to be about more. He was more active in his mind, too. He was not quite as irritable. His appetite was better, but it didn't take him very long until he started to go downgrade a little [115] more. Then he stayed in bed more.

Q. What did you notice that was unusual about the time he took that job at Spadra?

A. Well, just constantly being tired, always tired and always on the verge of a cold, and loss of appetite.

Q. I didn't hear that last part, Mrs. Holland.

A. Always on the verge of having a cold or getting a cold.

Q. What about his appetite? A. Terrible.

Q. Tell us in what respect?

A. Well, I think I am a pretty good cook. I had to cook for him. I cooked some very good tasting things, but he absolutely could not eat them.

Q. How long did you notice that his appetite was poor?

(Testimony of Mrs. Wilson A. Holland.)

A. You mean during our married life?

Q. Yes.

A. Well, it started from 1923 on.

Q. From 1923 on?

A. During the time he was in bed or in the hospital his appetite seemed to improve some.

Q. What else did you notice about his health that was unusual that you did not notice on a normal person? A. Constantly being tired.

Q. Anything else? [116] A. Irritable.

Q. Did you notice any night sweats?

A. Oh, yes, night sweats.

Mr. Di Girolamo: Just a moment. Don't lead the witness. We object to leading questions.

Mr. Gerlack: All right.

Q. Just tell us the unusual things you noticed that you would not notice about a normal person.

A. Well, when he would rest he would get better and then when he would work some more, in about ten days or two weeks, all of a sudden he would begin to get tired.

Q. Was he tired or was he lazy?

A. He was never lazy.

Q. He never seemed lazy?

A. Not that I know of, but he was always tired.

Q. What else did you notice about his condition, aside from what you have told us here?

A. Night sweats.

Q. Tell the jury about that, how it acted upon him.

(Testimony of Mrs. Wilson A. Holland.)

A. Well, I noticed it especially during the period of time he came from Spadra, he was always tired, and had to go to bed. In fact, I gave him his meals in bed so that he could rest. During the night I noticed a quivering of the body and night sweats, cold, clammy sweats, not from overheating, but it looked very exhausting.

Q. How does he appear to act now as compared to the [117] time immediately after he quit Spadra in the Fall of 1933?

A. Well, his condition is about the same or probably a little worse.

Q. His condition appears to be better now than then? A. No.

Q. What about his weight?

A. About the same. He has been around 115 or 118.

Q. How old is Mr. Holland? A. He is 38.

Q. He is 38 now?

A. He will be 38 in January.

Mr. Gerlack: I think that is all.

You may cross examine.

Mr. Di Girolamo: No questions.

(Witness excused.)

Mr. Gerlack: I will call Mr. Carleton to the stand.

(Testimony of Harold A. R. Carleton.)

I want to state to your Honor that Mr. Carleton is now residing in Portland. We took his deposition on the way from Portland to San Francisco. He happened to be in town for a couple of days and I thought as long as he was here on a business trip we could have him testify personally. [118]

HAROLD A. R. CARLETON

a witness called in behalf of the Plaintiff, being first duly sworn, testified as follows:

The Clerk: State your full name, please.

The Witness: H. A. R. Carleton.

Direct Examination

By Mr. Gerlack:

Q. Mr. Carleton, what is your business or occupation?

A. State Commander for the Volunteers of America in the State of Oregon.

Q. Have you any special training in your own lines?

A. I have been in professional social work for about 20 years.

Q. Where did you formerly reside before you resided in Portland?

A. From 1914 until 1935, in Los Angeles.

Q. You know the Plaintiff here, Wilson A. Holland, do you? A. I do.

Q. When and where and under what circumstances did you first become acquainted with him?

(Testimony of Harold A. R. Carleton.)

A. In the Federal Transient Service. I was the State Director in California. That service was inaugurated in September, 1933, and I believe my first meeting with Mr. Holland was two months subsequent to that, about in November, 1933. [119]

Q. You were the California State head of this organization? A. That is right.

Q. Is that the S. R. A.?

A. Well, it was the Federal Transient Service supported 100 per cent by Federal funds, but the funds came into the State upon application of the respective State Governors and from that point were disbursed by the State Relief Administrator, so that our work was correlated closely with the State Relief program.

Q. How long was Mr. Holland with that organization?

A. I don't recall from memory. Mr. Holland was with us from that time, November, 1933, until along about December, 1935.

Q. Is that November or December, 1933?

A. It may have been December.

Q. Just tell the jury in your own words how he appeared in so far as his health was concerned in the work which he did under your supervision?

A. I might say that Mr. Holland did not come very much under my own personal influence. In order to set up our accounts to begin with we employed a certified public accountant from Los An-

(Testimony of Harold A. R. Carleton.)

geles to set up our accounts. Under the rules and regulations of the department——

Q. (Interrupting) Pardon me, but what was his name? A. Mr. R. Burton. [120]

Q. All right.

A. He came to me and said it would be necessary to have someone familiar with the nature of accounting to set up our system. A few days later he introduced me to Mr. Holland whom he said was familiar with that type of work. Therefore he came directly under Mr. Burton's supervision, more so than he did under mine.

All I recall specifically was that Mr. D. M. Merritt, Mr. Burton's assistant, came to me one day with the complaint——

Mr. Di Girolamo: Just a minute. I move to strike out about the complaint.

The Court: Sustained. What complaint was made?

By Mr. Gerlack:

Q. Was that complaint about his work?

A. No, it was simply that he had received a complaint from some of his co-workers, some of the girls in the office——

Mr. Di Girolamo: (Interrupting) I still object, your Honor.

The Court: Yes, the objection is sustained.

(Testimony of Harold A. R. Carleton.)

By Mr. Gerlack:

Q. By the way, is that Mr. D. M. Merritt, *he* Mr. Merritt who is now with the——

The Court (Interrupting): No, just let him tell what work he did. [121]

By Mr. Gerlack:

Q. What work did he do?

A. Mr. Merritt is now an accountant with the Treasury Accounts Office for the State of California.

Q. Tell the jury what work Mr. Holland did, and how he appeared to you as far as his health was concerned?

The Court: Tell us what work he did and how he did it.

The Witness: Mr. Holland's capacity was pretty largely that of a consulting capacity and advisory capacity in setting up books of account rather than doing any actual work or expecting that of him; and as I recall him, he was quite faithful in his work, except he seeemd to tire quite easily and was out at frequent intervals.

The Court: Out from work?

The Witness: Yes, he was absent from work quite frequently.

The Court: Quite frequently, you say. How frequently do you mean?

The Witness: Well, I would say on the average of a day a week, probably.

The Court: Proceed.

(Testimony of Harold A. R. Carleton.)

By Mr. Gerlack:

Q. How did he appear during that time, compared to the way he appears now?

A. Well, he impressed us as being not a well man at the time, and there was some discussion as to whether or not [122] he should be kept on.

Q. Was that condition obvious as you observed him? A. Yes.

Q. Why didn't you keep him on?

Mr. Di Girolamo: Just a minute, I object, if the Court please.

The Court: I didn't get that question. I didn't understand it.

Mr. Gerlack: The question is, why didn't they keep him on. He said he didn't appear strong.

Mr. Di Girolamo: Just a minute.

The Court: That would be proper on cross examination. He may answer it.

The Witness: Well, your Honor, the Transient Program, as I stated a moment ago, was closely correlated to the State Relief Program, and while we never had instructions in writing, in a written bulletin, it was pretty well understood a man on a nominal salary, and able to give some service to his work, was better off than a man on the relief rolls. The salary Mr. Holland was receiving was quite nominal and it would cost a portion of that amount if he were dismissed and taken over on the relief rolls.

(Testimony of Harold A. R. Carleton.)

By Mr. Gerlack:

Q. How much time was he off from his job on account of his health?

A. Well, I couldn't say definitely as to that. It [123] would be only an impression. As I already testified, it seemed to me it would be an average of a day a week, anyway. I think Mr. Merritt, or perhaps Mr. Burton, who were his accounting superiors, could give a better answer to that than I can.

Q. Now, would you say the character of his services from a professional standpoint were satisfactory or unsatisfactory?

A. I would say they were very satisfactory. He had a very fine technical knowledge of the *word* he was doing.

Q. He really knew his work as a bookkeeper and accountant, didn't he?

A. He really did.

Q. Would you say the amount of work which he did, the work which he turned out, would you make a statement as to how that contrasted with the other men doing the same kind of work?

A. It is difficult to say. He was doing a special job, more or less a consulting job, setting up jobs according to State regulations, taking off reports required by the State regulations, rather than actually doing the work himself. Most of the others in the office, outside of Mr. Burton and Mr. Merritt, were actually doing the work itself, so there was no

(Testimony of Harold A. R. Carleton.)

one to compare him with in that respect.

Q. Would you say that his services, that his duties were arduous or light? [124]

A. Well, I would say that they were technical. As such, he had to have a technical knowledge of the State accounting system, in order to be of value to us, and he had that knowledge. I would not say his duties were particularly arduous

The Court: Would that position require a physical effort, physical exertion?

The Witness: No physical exertion. It might require some mental exertion.

By Mr. Gerlack:

Q. Or was it a light job or a heavy job?

A. No, in ordinary terms it was a light job. Of course, it was an emergency program. We had a great deal of night work that we had to do, and in order to keep up with our various accounts, and various stations, we found it necessary to take care of the emergency situation at that time.

Q. Did he do any night work?

A. We would have liked to have him do night work, but we felt he was not strong enough for overtime work.

Q. You mean he did not do night work?

A. That is right.

Q. Although the others did?

A. Many of the other men did night work.

(Testimony of Harold A. R. Carleton.)

Q. Your impression is that he was off one day a week, Mr. Carleton. How did he appear during the time he was on [125] the job?

A. Well, I say, I never noticed the people in the office. I wasn't close enough to him to keep in touch with him on that. All I can say is I received no complaints as to his services from either of his superiors except the one that I started to mention just a moment ago.

Q. Did you ever notice anything about his mannerism that was unusual so far as you would expect from a normal person? I mean, outside of being tired, did you notice any other unusual things about him? A. No, I can't say that I did.

Q. Did you ever notice him cough or spit?

Mr. Di Girolamo: Now, just a moment, Mr. Gerlack. Your Honor, Mr. Gerlack has tried many of these cases. He knows when he is asking leading questions.

The Court: I think you had better reframe your question.

Mr. Gerlack: Very well.

Q. Did you see anything unusual at all about the fact as to Mr. Holland's condition, other than the fact he appeared tired and went home in the afternoons occasionally?

A. Yes, sometimes we would get a call that he would be unable to report for work in the morning. That was little inconvenient at times when we were dependent upon him.

(Testimony of Harold A. R. Carleton.)

Q. How often would that happen? [126]

A. Well, there were times when he was off two or three days at a time.

Q. Was he docked for that work? A. No.

Q. He was paid just the same? A. Yes.

Q And the State payroll would not show he was off? A. That is right.

Mr. Gerlack: I think that is all. You may cross examine.

Cross Examination

By Mr. Di Girolamo:

Q. Mr. Carleton, you say Mr. Holland was never under your immediate supervision?

A. Not under the immediate supervision of myself, no. I was the State Director and Mr. Burton was the Chief Accountant that installed the system, and Mr. Merritt was his assistant.

Q. As a matter of fact, he never worked under your supervision? A. Not in the same office.

Q. But he did not work under your supervision?

A. That is right.

Q. Now, if Mr. Holland himself testified that he not only supervised, but he actually did the work, then you would say you were wrong in assuming that he only supervised. [127] is that correct?

The Court: Oh, you have his statement in the record, counsel.

Mr. Di Girolamo: I want to test this man's memory.

(Testimony of Harold A. R. Carleton.)

The Court: He has already testified.

Mr. Di Girolamo: All right.

Q. Did you ever keep the records of the actual sick leave in that department?

A. No, we kept a record of vacation time and we had a policy at that time that a person was allowed in six months' period a week of sick leave.

Q. And if the records of your department show during the entire time that Mr. Holland was employed there he was between annual leave and sick leave 22 days, would that be correct, or would the records be false?

A. Well, as I recall it, a person that was giving satisfactory service, and who was out for a day, that was not computed against his record; but if he was out for an entire week at a time, it was.

Q. And in the report that you had of Mr. Holland's efficiency at his job and his assiduity at the job, that was from information you got from others, not from your own observation of him, is that right?

A. Pretty largely. I saw Mr. Holland at work. Occasionally I would have an opportunity to confer with him about various reports. [128]

Q. Now, you testified that there were calls made at times when he would not be able to report for work. To whom were those calls made, to you?

A. No, they would usually come to Mr. Burton or to Mr. Merritt.

(Testimony of Harold A. R. Carleton.)

Q. Then, you would not know about that, other than what someone told you about it?

A. Except that I might call for him and find that he called up in the morning and said he would not be able to come in that day.

Q. Just a moment. I am referring to telephone calls that were made at the office.

A. That is right.

Q. They were not made to you?

A. Not personally.

Q. Not personally? A. That is right.

Q. So that you would not know anything about that other than what someone might have told you?

A. Yes, sir.

Q. Is that right?

Mr. Di Girolamo: That is all.

The Court: Anything further?

Mr. Gerlack: That is all.

The Court: Call your next witness.

(Witness excused.) [129]

ROY W. BURTON

a witness called in behalf of the Plaintiff, being first duly sworn, testified as follows:

The Clerk: What is your name, please?

The Witness: Roy W. Burton.

Direct Examination

By Mr. Gerlack:

Q. Mr. Burton, what is your occupation?

A. Certified Public Accountant.

Q. Where? A. In Los Angeles?

Q. You know the Plaintiff here, Wilson A. Holland, do you not? A. Yes, sir.

Q. When and where and under what circumstances did you first meet him?

A. I believe it was in December, 1933.

Q. Where was that?

A. In the Cotton Exchange Building at Third and Main Streets.

Q. What work were you doing and what work was he doing at that time?

A. I was employed by Mr. Carleton, the State Director of the Transient Relief Program.

Q. Mr. Carleton was the last witness here?

A. Yes. [130]

Q. What were you doing?

A. I was engaged in installing a system of accounts for the State Relief Board.

Q. How did you come to meet Mr. Holland on that occasion?

A. There were numerous people who came in for jobs and Mr. Holland was one of those who had come in for this work. I found that he had this experience with the State, that is, experience in State accounting which, of course, was something that we

(Testimony of Roy W. Burton.)
could use very well in that program and especially in helping set up this system of accounts.

Q. How long did he work with you there?

A. I stayed until May of 1934; Mr. Holland was there when I left.

Q. Just tell the jury how he appeared, so far as his health was concerned, while working under your charge there?

A. When Mr. Holland came to work for the S. R. A. he was quite thin, apparently as thin as he is now, and I felt at the time—of course, I am no physician,—but I felt at the time——

Mr. Di Girolamo: Now, just a minute, I object to what he felt.

The Court: Yes, objection sustained.

By Mr. Gerlack:

Q. Just tell us how he appeared, what his experience was like. [131]

A. He was as thin as he is now. During the course of his employment there he came to me one day and said he was very tired and that he would like to go home, get off for a few days and then go out to a ranch of some friend of his, I believe. I think it was somewhere near Ontario, some chicken ranch, and rest there. He wanted to know if he could get off for a period of approximately ten days. I said yes. He did get off then and went to the ranch, presumably.

Mr. Di Girolamo: I move to strike out what he presumes.

(Testimony of Roy W. Burton.)

The Court: We will disregard where the witness presumed the Plaintiff went.

By Mr. Gerlack:

Q. At least, Mr. Holland was gone from the job?

A. He was gone for the period of time that he requested to be off.

Q. Did the record show he was off on a sick leave at that time?

A. I don't believe so because we did not make records of people who got off due to sickness. There was a rule that was promulgated later, that people off due to sickness had to be reported, but at that time, when it first started, it was not required.

Q. By the way, do you know about his getting off at any other times during the period you worked there?

A. I have no definite recollection of any other times he was off. I do know we did considerable night work there, [132] but he never helped during the time we were doing the night work. We would anywhere from 10:00 to 1:00 or 2:00 o'clock seven nights a week and Mr. Holland did not help us.

Q. Did he work all day, every day when he was there? A. As far as I know.

Q. Do you remember him getting off and going home in the afternoon?

A. I don't recall that.

Q. Did you notice anything else about him except that he appeared to be tired?

(Testimony of Roy W. Burton.)

A. Well, he did not seem to have the energy and he was subject to colds.

Q. How often? Tell us about that. What did you notice in that respect?

A. Well, he was contributing his difficulty to colds.

Mr. Di Girolamo: Just a moment. I move to strike out what he contributed it to.

The Witness: Well, that was his statement to me.

Mr. Di Girolamo: I move to strike out the witness's answer.

By Mr. Gerlack:

Q. Well, did he appear to you to have a cold, as you observed him?

The Court: What did he do that made you think he had a cold?

The Witness: He would cough. He had a cough that he [133] couldn't seem to get rid of.

By Mr. Gerlack:

Q. Did he have that during most of the time he was there? A. No.

Q. How much of the time?

A. Oh, on a percentage basis, probably 20 percent.

Q. Did you notice anything else? What else did you notice about him that gave you the impression that he had a cold?

A. I don't know that there was anything else that I observed.

(Testimony of Roy W. Burton.)

Q. By the way, just for the purpose of the record, you were subpoenaed up here to the court as a Government witness, were you? A. Yes.

Mr. Gerlack: That is all.

The Court: Any cross examination?

Cross Examination

By Mr. Di Girolamo:

Q. Mr. Burton, as a matter of fact, Mr. Holland worked there eight hours a day, did he not?

A. I have forgotten just what our hours were, but I believe that was the amount of time that was normal.

Q. Would you say that he was a hard worker?

A. Yes. [134]

Mr. Di Girolamo: That is all.

The Witness: He worked beyond his capacity.

Mr. Di Girolamo: That is all.

Redirect Examination

By Mr. Gerlack:

Q. That was considered an easy job or a hard job from a physical standpoint?

A. Oh, I wouldn't say it was a hard job. It was one which required technical knowledge in the classification of accounts.

Q. Did he do the work himself or did he advise in the setting up of a system? A. He did both.

Mr. Gerlack: That is all.

Mr. Di Girolamo: No further cross examination.

(Witness excused.)

The Court: Call your next witness. [135]

DR. HARRY COHN

a witness called in behalf of the Plaintiff, being first duly sworn, testified as follows:

The Clerk: State your full name, please.

The Witness: Dr. Harry Cohn.

Direct Examination

By Mr. Gerlack:

Q. Dr. Cohn, you are a licensed physician and surgeon? A. Yes, sir.

Q. Licensed to practice as such in this State?

A. Yes, sir.

Q. What medical school are you a graduate of?

The Court: Are his qualifications admitted?

Mr. Di Girolamo: We will stipulate the doctor is well qualified.

Mr. Gerlack: In view of the Doctor's exceptional qualifications, I think we should know what they are.

The Court: Very well.

By Mr. Gerlack:

Q. Doctor, your specialty is T. B. and contusions of the chest? A. Yes.

Q. State very briefly to what extent you have specialized in that field, Doctor?

A. It covers about 27 years. First, I was Superin- [136] tendent of the Chicago Winfield Sanitorium, then as Tuberculosis Physician for the Cook County Tuberculosis Hospital.

Q. Cook County, is that in Chicago? A. Yes.

Q. Go ahead.

(Testimony of Dr. Harry Cohn.)

A. Then as Medical Director for the Milwaukee County Tuberculosis Hospital. Then as officer for the Federal Board for Vocational Education. That was under the United States Public Health Service.

The Court: You say that was for the United States Public Health Service?

The Witness: Yes.

The Court: For how long?

The Witness: From 1919 until 1923 I was at Washington, D. C., and Fort Baird, New Mexico, and at Camp Kearney, Nebraska.

By Mr. Gerlack:

Q. At Fort Baird, what kind of a hospital was that? A. Veterans' hospital.

Q. A Government Hospital there?

A. At that time it was the largest tubercular hospital in the United States. It has decreased a lot in size since that time.

Q. What was your connection with the Government at Camp Kearney?

A. I was either Acting Medical Officer in Charge or Chief of the Medical Service. [137]

Q. Is that a U. S. Veterans' Hospital?

A. It was first with the Public Health Service and then transferred to the Government.

Q. You mean transferred to the Veterans, is that correct? A. Yes.

Q. How long were you in charge of the hospital?

A. A year and a half or two years.

Q. What has been your experience in tuberculosis since then?

(Testimony of Dr. Harry Cohn.)

A. Well, I have worked for the Los Angeles County as Senior Tuberculosis Physician, and for the past 12 years I have been in charge of the tuberculosis work for the City of Los Angeles.

Q. You are head of the Los Angeles Board of Health for work in tuberculosis? A. Yes.

Q. Did you have occasion to examine Mr. Holland, Doctor? A. Yes, sir.

Q. When did you first examine him?

A. January, 1937.

Q. Where was that examination conducted?

A. In the Health Department.

Q. At 116 Temple Avenue, right across here?

A. Yes. [138]

Q. What examination did you make of him and what conclusions did you reach as a result of that examination?

A. Well, he first gave me a detailed history regarding his experience and pointed out the symptoms which he had. Then there was a physical examination. Then he was examined through the x-ray screen. After that an x-ray picture was taken of his chest. Then certain laboratory tests were made.

Q. Have you those x-rays, Doctor?

A. They are right over there (indicating).

Q. Were those taken by you?

A. They were taken at my direction.

Q. Were they taken in your presence, Doctor?

A. Yes.

Q. You saw them actually taken? A. Yes.

(Testimony of Dr. Harry Cohn.)

Q. Are you able to say by looking at those x-rays and after your examination of Mr. Holland that those are x-rays of that particular individual?

A. Yes, sir.

Q. How many x-rays have you examined in your lifetime, Doctor, or are you able to approximate that?

A. Well, we take about 10 to 12 x-rays a day at the Health Department. In addition to that many are brought in from the outside. So that I look at anywhere from 12 to 20 x-rays a day. [139]

Q. How many years have you been doing that, Doctor?

A. Well, it has been about 12 years that I have been at that particular job.

Q. You have seen x-rays before that?

A. Yes.

Q. Doctor, tell us what those various x-rays show, what the x-rays show as to his condition.

A. I am sorry. Have you a view-box?

Mr. Gerlack: I don't know is there a view-box in the courtroom?

The Court: Doctor, you had better stand over there and explain it to the jurors.

The Witness: (Leaving the witness stand). This is taken in 1937, this picture.

The Court: Stand down in the middle of the jury box so that all of the jurors can see it.

The Witness: This picture was taken in 1937. This is the way the normal lung appears (indicat-

(Testimony of Dr. Harry Cohn.)

ing). The normal lung does not show anything, that is, any shadow. It just looks dark.

This shadow in the central portion here is largely made up of heart shadow, and this shade here is the diaphragm with the intestines and the stomach beneath.

Over here you can see the spine coming down, and the white shadow covers the spine.

The Court: I don't think the juror on the end can see [140] that picture.

The Witness: There are the collarbones, these are the shoulder blades, and these you see here are the ribs which make up the cage in which the lungs lie.

If you will look over here a little you will see a white shadow, and from the top you see the first rib; and this is the second rib, and these ribs are the ribs in the back and the same over here (indicating).

You see a white shadow coming down to the second rib. It becomes softer here (indicating). This is the older tuberculosis, and this represents a more recent tuberculosis, so that there is, as we say, true tuberculosis in the upper portion of both lungs above the second rib.

By Mr. Gerlack:

Q. That was January, 1937? A. Yes.

Q. All right, go ahead.

A. In this corner here—here is that lesion in the diaphragm, it is dark down there, and you have that little adhesion (indicating).

(Testimony of Dr. Harry Cohn.)

That was a picture taken in 1937.

Q. Was the tuberculosis active as shown by that picture? A. Yes.

Q. You examined him with a stethoscope and made other examinations as well, did you Doctor? [141]

A. Yes.

Q. Now, this picture was taken the 27th of February, 1939. Several things happened since that time. I think it is evident the spot extended down that far on the right side—this is the left side over here—and it extended down a little on this side (indicating).

In addition to this, you see here, air beneath the diaphragm on both sides. In other words, he had an operation performed paralyzing this diaphragm and they put air in the peritoneum in an effort to push these diaphragms up, to press the diseased lungs.

Mr. Gerlack: Your Honor, for the purpose of keeing the record straight, may we introduce the first x-ray which the Doctor is showing——

The Witness (Interrupting): No, this is the last one.

Mr. Gerlack: Just a minute. We have an x-ray dated January, 1937. May we have that marked Plaintiff's Exhibit next in order?

The Clerk: Plaintiff's Exhibit 18.

By Mr. Gerlack:

Q. What is the date of the second one?

(Testimony of Dr. Harry Cohn.)

A. June 27, 1939.

Mr. Gerlack: Mark that as Plaintiff's next in order.

The Clerk: Plaintiff's Exhibit 19.

The Witness: A juror wants to ask me a question.

The Court: Proceed. [142]

Juror White: In developing these negatives, does that process have anything to do with the density of the picture?

The Witness: Yes, it gives quite a difference in the appearance of the picture, in the softness or hardness. While the standard technique is used, no two groups of films are identical in makeup. Some have a softer appearance and some produce a harder picture.

Juror White: Are they the same?

The Witness: It is approximately the same. This is a little softer film than this is (indicating). This brings out the detail a little better than this film does, but the amount of tuberculosis is a more extensive in this film, while the other only has it up here (indicating).

By Mr. Gerlack:

Q. Now, Doctor, I will show you a film that has been introduced here, Plaintiff's Exhibit 2, which has been testified was an x-ray taken of Mr. Holland at the Spadra Colony, under date of August 30, 1933, and ask you to examine that and tell us whether that shows any tuberculosis, active tuberculosis?

(Testimony of Dr. Harry Cohn.)

A. Any time there is an inflammation in the lungs there is a change in the density of the film.

Juror White: You are holding that up against a light background.

By Mr. Gerlack: [143]

Q. Hold it here, against the light, Doctor.

A. All right.

Now, you see what we call either a cotton density or a snowflake deposit in the lung, from here above, from here above (indicating), while here the lung field is clear (indicating). These shadows here are made up of the arteries and veins. We call that a Hilon shadow present in most cases. There is an absolute condition here (indicating), but from here up you have something that is——

Juror White (Interrupting): The ribs on this side do not appear in their entirety. What causes that?

The Witness: That is caused by the density of the white shadow. The white shadow comes down here on the left side, being more on the left than on the right, and you will find the picture more indefinite there, while above it is more definite; but the ribs here come over from the spine, as you see (indicating).

By Mr. Gerlack:

Q. That definitely shows he had active tuberculosis? A. Very definitely.

Q. At the time that film was taken, August 30, 1933? A. Yes, sir.

(Testimony of Dr. Harry Cohn.)

Q. Now, Doctor, were you in court this morning when these medical examinations were read?

A. Yes, sir.

Q. You examined those documents personally outside [144] of having heard them?

A. Yes, sir.

Q. You sat at the table and read them, did you not? A. Yes, sir.

Q. Now, Doctor, assuming the facts to be true as shown by those Government records, and basing your opinion not upon the diagnoses, but merely the findings as shown by those medical reports, and basing your opinion upon this x-ray finding, or this x-ray that you have just interpreted which has been introduced in evidence here, and as the testimony shows was taken at Spadra of Mr. Holland on August 30, 1933, and bearing in mind your own examination of him, in your opinion, I will ask you, first, what were the probabilities of his tuberculosis being cured or even arrested, or apparently arrested, even with the best of medical treatment at the time you first examined him in January, 1937? A. They were poor.

Q. You mean by that, that the probabilities were against him?

A. Very strongly against him recovering from the existing tuberculosis.

Q. By the way, what is your present diagnosis of his condition?

(Testimony of Dr. Harry Cohn.)

A. He is classified as far advanced, a far advanced active case of tuberculosis with additional complications. [145]

Q. Now, assuming that, and assuming the findings of these Government reports by Government doctors, in your opinion, what were the probabilities of his tuberculosis becoming arrested even with the best of medical care on August 30, 1933?

A. The odds were very much against his securing an arrest of his tuberculosis in 1933.

Q. At the time the film was taken, do you mean?

A. At the time the film was taken, yes.

Q. Doctor, in your opinion, what is the effect of following an occupation or engaging in any physical or mental labor by persons suffering from active tuberculosis?

A. Generally speaking, it tends to aggravate the existing tuberculosis. There are exceptions, of course, but the rule is what governs.

Q. Doctor, will you give us, for the record, and for the information of the jury here—will you explain this disease of tuberculosis, what it is, how it progresses and what effect the disease has upon its victim?

A. Well, briefly, the disease of tuberculosis, like any other infectious disease, is due to a specific organism, in this case the tubercle bacillus. Fortunately, infection in tuberculosis does not very often mean disease. We know by tuberculosis tests that 30 to 45 or perhaps 50 per cent of the popula-

(Testimony of Dr. Harry Cohn.)

tion have taken into their bodies at some time or other a few tubercle bacilli, but a very small percent- [146] age ever develop the disease of tuberculosis itself.

The disease of tuberculosis develops owing to certain factors peculiar to the individual. In the first place, you have to take within your body the germ. In addition to that, the host has to be in such a condition that he is unable to resist the infection of the germ. In other words, those in good health need not fear the tubercle bacillus; but if the vital forces are depleted from overwork or overstudy or by burning the midnight oil in riotous living, or by infectious diseases from existing illnesses, we may become candidates for tuberculosis should we at that time take within our bodies some tubercle bacilli. They are usually deposited in the lungs by being inhaled. They drop down like pieces of dust.

Q. Is tuberculosis ever hereditary, Doctor?

A. No, it is not hereditary because it has not been proven, except in rare instances of what we call hereditary tuberculosis in a family, but the opportunities for inhaling these bacilli are so great that if the grandfather or the father or mother had tuberculosis they are very likely to hand it on down. They are very likely to hand it down to the offspring due to the reasons that they have intimate contact with one another. Heredity was blamed for direct infection in that way.

(Testimony of Dr. Harry Cohn.)

Now, after the tubercle is inhaled, immediately the body starts throwing up a barrier, trying to wall these [147] germs so that they don't travel any farther. The white blood cells come to the little capillaries and pile on this area. Pretty soon you have a little microscopic mound built up. You cannot see it with the x-ray until it is about six weeks old. You may spread from that one tubercle by working through the barrier, finding its way into the little lymph channel, or many of them may go together and make one large mass of thousands of tubercles, and then you have pneumonia or a quick type of consumption; or it may spread through the blood and you may get tuberculosis meningitis, or bone tuberculosis, or spine tuberculosis. Or, perhaps, it may break down, form a pus, and discharge through the long nasal chamber, and then you have a hole in the lung. However, it is different in every individual and it has to be studied from an individual standpoint. The statements I have made govern generally the things which may happen as a result of tuberculosis.

Q. How does working or following occupation affect the disease? In what manner does it hasten the progress of tuberculosis?

A. That is explained this way. You are already dealing with a wasting disease. Patients with tuberculosis lose weight. They have a fever. They have a rapid pulse. They have a loss of appetite. They get poison into their system or usually have little spots on the lungs. When the patient exercises he just

(Testimony of Dr. Harry Cohn.)

washes more of that poison out of [148] lungs into the blood stream. He gets more poison into it. He loses weight more rapidly. He may cough more. He may have a higher fever and it may break down faster so that with active tuberculosis we say the symptoms are extenuated and the disease is aggravated by work, whereas rest has the opposite result.

Q. Now, Doctor, where a man has active tuberculosis and he is later examined and found the tuberculosis is not active, does that mean the man has an arrested case?

A. Not at all. In any chronic disease, in practically all chronic diseases, you have periods where the disease is quite evident, not only in tuberculosis, but also every chronic disease. Then it quiets down and the unwary patient might assume they are well and do things they shouldn't do and in that way spoil their chances for recovery. That is the delusion and scare particularly in tuberculosis. The patient goes to bed a month or two, possibly, and sometimes it quiets down because he does not absorb so much poison into his system. He gets a false sense of security. He gets up and starts out again and the next thing he knows he has a spread of tuberculosis. He becomes ill again and stays in bed until he gets over his sickness. He may call it a cold or he may call it bronchitis, but it is tuberculosis. Every one of these reactive agents means a spreading of the disease into new territory until you have so much territory infected that a man is sick all the time,

(Testimony of Dr. Harry Cohn.)

[149] and even then he may be sick for a week or two and then it will quiet down.

Q. What symptoms does a man feel in the manifestation of tuberculosis?

A. Unfortunately, he may not feel any symptoms at all. That is the unfortunate thing about tuberculosis. It does not make people sick. They don't have pain with the disease usually. He may have quite extension tuberculosis and not realize that there is anything seriously wrong with him. A man may tire out more easily than he did and cough, but he blames it on something else. Maybe he is working too hard, smoking too much, or not getting enough rest, so that he becomes tired. Outside of that little coughing, a little loss of weight, and tired feeling, the patient does not show any symptoms unless he should expectorate some blood.

Q. Is there any medicine or specific that will take care of the disease?

A. No, no one has ever found, nor is it probable any will ever be found, due to the peculiar formation of the tubercle. The tubercle is in the blood supply. If you can inject chemicals into the body to destroy the tubercle you could not get to the tubercle because there is no blood supply in the tubercle itself. You would destroy the cells around the tubercle, but not the tubercle itself.

Q. In other words, you would kill the man before you [150] killed the germ?

A. That is correct.

(Testimony of Dr. Harry Cohn.)

Q. What is your treatment for this disease, Doctor?

A. The orthodox treatment is a so-called sanitorium treatment, a regime of living, using simple principles like rest, freedom from worry, proper food, and so on. After a while, prescribed exercises are given. While the remedies are simple, it requires a very fine judgment on the part of physicians and nurses in their treatment of cases because you are dealing with human beings while they are sick. They are still human and each individual has to be treated differently.

In the last 10 or 15 years the addition of surgery into the treatment of tuberculosis has materially aided people in recovering from that disease so that the outlook in this day and age is very much better than it was a decade or two ago.

Q. Were you in the courtroom this morning, Doctor, when Mr. Whittingham was asking questions about fibrosis of the witness, one of the jurors?

A. Yes.

Q. Can you answer the juror's question?

A. Fibrosis is simply a scar tissue formation. For instance, if you get your hand cut fibrous tissue forms interlacing it in. The same thing happens in the lungs except it is a different structure, made up of different [151] kinds of cells, and the reaction is different; but the air cells and the diseased part are replaced by scar tissue.

Q. Doctor, what are the principal functions of the lungs?

(Testimony of Dr. Harry Cohn.)

A. The lungs are chiefly an organ for the interchange of gases. In other words, through a rather complicated mechanism you take the red blood cells through the homoglobus portion, which pick up the oxygen which has been breathed in, and deposit the oxygen into the tissues where it is utilized. After it is deposited, they in return pick up carbon dioxide and carry it back to the lungs and deposit it there and out it goes. It is an organ for the interchange of gases.

Q. In other words, the lungs areate blood?

A. Yes, and they carry off gases.

Q. When a man has tuberculosis, which I understood you to say is a consuming disease, where the disease consumes or eats the lungs away and replaces it with scar tissue, has that scar tissue any ability to areate blood?

A. It has no function except to seal up the diseased part. It is not able to do anything.

Q. How much of a person's lung can be lost and still be useful?

A. Well, we have about five times as much lung tissue as is necessary to carry on the vital functions at complete rest. [152]

A Juror: Would you repeat that, please?

The Witness: I said we have about five times as much lung tissue to carry on the function of living at complete rest.

By Mr. Gerlack:

Q. In other words, at complete rest, a man could lose four-fifths of his lungs and keep the one-fifth?

(Testimony of Dr. Harry Cohn.)

A. Yes, but he would have to be very quiet.

Q. Does that explain why a person could live for years with tuberculosis even though they had lost considerable portion of their lungs?

A. That is part of the explanation.

Q. How much of the lung capacity has Mr. Holland left at the present time?

A. Well, I would just have to conjecture that because there are tests that will tell you very definitely how much is left. I would say that he has, at the present time, about two-thirds of his lung capacity.

Mr. Di Girolamo: He still has?

The Witness: He still has, because the air cells at the bottom of the lung have enlarged. He has what we call empyema at the bottom of both lungs. The cells there have to do extra work because of the cells which have been destroyed by the disease of the upper portions.

By Mr. Gerlack:

Q. Are you able to say from reading the x-ray taken [153] at Spadra on August 30, 1933, as to the degree of advancement of his tuberculosis, as to whether or not it was moderately advanced or far advanced?

A. That Spadra film shows tuberculosis which is at least moderately advanced. There are two or three spots in that film—I think it is in the left upper—where they may be a beginning cavity for-

(Testimony of Dr. Harry Cohn.)

mation; if they were proven he would be up in the far advanced stage, but it is not a probability.

Q. Would you say at that time there was no hope of his coming to complete health?

A. No, I will explain that tuberculosis has to start somewhere. This man's tuberculosis is shown by the age of his lesions. It started at the extreme top of the lungs, probably the right lung. It spread to the top of the left lung, and from both of those spots it spread down into both lung fields. In other words, he has had a spread of tuberculosis from one lung to another, and it has traveled downward. Had it remained in one lung his chances of realizing a recovery would have been good, but where you have two lungs diseased, the disease spreads downward, and the chances for securing an arrest is not good.

Q. Is he using both lungs uniformly, Doctor?

A. There has been an effort made in the last x-ray, through the use of starch, to arrest it as much as possible. In other words, they put air into the abdomen by the use of [154] a needle and pushed the diaphragm up and collapsed the lungs a little.

Mr. Gerlack: I think that is all.

Juror Whittingham: May I ask a question?

The Court: What is it?

Juror Whittingham: The doctor this morning said something about calcium salt in the Spadra picture. What has that to do with the Plaintiff's condition?

The Witness: I often refer to calcium salt as lime salt. They are anonymous terms in the healing

(Testimony of Dr. Harry Cohn.)

of these microscopic tubercles. Nature throws that wall of tissue around them, and later lime salt may be carried in impregnating the new tissue. That is the so-called lime or calcium salt deposit which you can see on the top of the Spadra film.

Juror Whittingham: May I ask another question?

The Doctor speaks of passing from one lung to another. Is there any rate or time as to its passing?

The Witness: No, there is no time because the change may take place through the bronchial tubes. He may expectorate through the bronchial tubes and out through the mouth and he might drop something over on the other side and get a seeding and it would start to grow there. On the other hand, some may pass through the blood stream. That is why I say I don't know how long it takes. Here there is not much difference in age, although there may be a year or two [155] difference.

Juror Whittingham: May I ask a question.

The Court: Very well.

Juror Whittingham: This surgical operation performed, driving the air up, is it for the purpose of distributing the mucus gathered in the lungs? Would it be possible for an operation to be performed of that kind, where a pressure would be distributed from one lung to the other, through the bronchial tubes?

The Court: I think, Mr. Juror, that is beyond the scope of our inquiry here. It may be a splendid

(Testimony of Dr. Harry Cohn.)

thing to discuss with a medical student, but I don't think it is an issue here.

Cross Examination

By Mr. Di Girolamo:

Q. Doctor Cohn, when you examine a patient, before you make a diagnosis of tuberculosis, you take his history, don't you?

A. That is one step, yes, sir.

Q. Now, if the objective symptoms are such that may lead to immature conclusions, do you then take x-rays to find out whether or not there is a tubercular condition, bronchitis, or pleurisy?

A. Well, it is a matter of common procedure these days to take x-ray pictures of everybody complaining of chest diseases or chest troubles. We may overlook some [156] serious form of disease unless we do take an x-ray.

Q. Well, the x-ray alone would not tell you without using the stethoscope and making a history, making an examination, of getting the objective findings, and so forth, the x-ray would not tell you it was tuberculosis, would it?

A. Oh, yes, it will. If I have a picture of a man showing moderate tuberculosis in the upper lobe, of a cavity of the size of a large English walnut, I know that man has tuberculosis, although for the purpose of doing a scientific job I would not just say he has tuberculosis and just let it go at that, because the question of treatment requires a study

(Testimony of Dr. Harry Cohn.)

of the patient, how long he has had the disease, and what should be done for him, but the diagnosis could be made from the film alone.

Q. An x-ray plate is black and white, is it not?

A. Yes.

Q. And fibrosis on the plate is white, is it not?

A. Yes.

Q. That is scar tissue?

A. Yes, of course, it is white.

Q. Now, you take an x-ray plate, not made by you, made at a time when you did not examine the man, where you could not tell whether he had moist rales or dry rales, whether or not he had fever, whether his pulse was normal, whether he had night sweats or not, you could not tell whether it was real fibrosis, snow flakes, or what, could [157] you?

A. I could not, did you say?

Q. I say, can you?

A. Yes, of course. I can take a picture 20 years ago, taken 20 years ago, and tell you whether a man had tuberculosis 20 years, if the findings are sufficient to warrant a diagnosis. That is a question of experience, in interpreting x-ray films. When it comes to a case of films like we have here, I have enough experience to tell whether or not he has active tuberculosis from the film.

Q. Just so we understand each other, Doctor. I am not talking about your ability or experience. I wondered whether or not you could do that.

A. Yes, sir, I can.

(Testimony of Dr. Harry Cohn.)

Q. Now, Doctor, you stated before when a tubercular patient goes to bed to rest and thinks he is well and gets up and he breaks down if he does excessive exercising?

A. If he does things detrimental to him he will break down most likely.

Q. The first time you examined this man was in 1937? A. Correct.

Q. He was sent to you by Mr. Gerlack?

A. No, I don't believe he was. I think he came in on his own accord. I know he did come in of his own accord.

Q. He got out of the San Fernando Hospital? [158]

A. He was a patient when he came to see me.

Q. And he came to you in your office when he got out? A. Yes, sir.

Q. Now, Doctor, you gave your opinion that this man, in August, 1933 had a tubercular condition, that according to that x-ray it was on the borderline of moderately advanced and far advanced. What would you say he was in 1935?

A. Well, I have not seen a 1935 x-ray.

Q. In 1937?

A. I would say far advanced.

Q. You would say he was far advanced in 1937?

A. Yes, sir.

Q. Doctor, he was examined the first time in 1924 and they found active tuberculosis. He was

(Testimony of Dr. Harry Cohn.)

examined again three times in 1925. The first examination in 1925 was active, the second apparently active, and the third was active. Then in 1926 he was diagnosed as quiescent. That is a state where it is not necessarily arrested, but it is dormant, isn't it? It is not spreading?

A. It is temporarily inactive. It may become permanently inactive.

Q. In 1927 he was examined three times during that year. The first time apparently arrested; the second time arrested, and the third time evidently arrested, by a Board of Tubercular Examiners.

He went to work in 1927 at the Glendale Post Office at [159] 65 cents per hour and worked there until December, 1927. He left that job in order to accept a job with the Pickwick Corporation, and he worked there until January, 1931. He was examined on March 16, 1931 and his tubercular condition was found to be still arrested in spite of that work record.

When the Pickwick Corporation went into the hands of a receiver he enrolled in the Southwestern University and remained there until March, 1932 at which time he left the University in order to accept a position as Deputy Assessor, where he worked until May, 1932. In May, 1932 he went back to the University and stayed there until March, 1933.

(Testimony of Dr. Harry Cohn.)

Now, Doctor, isn't it significant that this man, through this entire work record, in none of those examinations subsequent to 1926, that there is a reactivation of the tuberculosis? Yet you state that he was on the borderline between moderately advanced and far advanced tuberculosis, although we find that this man went back again to the University in May, 1932, for a whole year, or to be correct, about 11 months when he did not work, and that is the only time he took a whole year's rest.

He had active tuberculosis in 1924; he was active in 1924 and 1925. It is arrested and quiescent to be correct. In 1926 and 1927 it is apparently arrested, evidently arrested. He works along until 1932. In 1932 he goes for a whole year to the University and comes out in March, 1933.

You examine him in 1937 and you say that in August, [160] 1933 he had tuberculosis, that it was on the borderline between moderately advanced and far advanced.

In other words, the only thing that brought the tuberculosis back must have been that year he did not work, while he was at the University? Does that strike you as an inconsistent theory as to the method of arresting tuberculosis and as to the effect of work on tuberculosis?

A. Not at all. It is rather an indictment of the classification, of the method as used in those reports, and the x-ray examinations, simply by plac-

(Testimony of Dr. Harry Cohn.)

ing a stethoscope on a man and saying it is an arrested case of tuberculosis.

Q. Doctor, didn't you state some time in 1938 that you examined this man in 1937 and that you found him suffering from moderately advanced tuberculosis?

A. I certainly did.

Q. So then, according to that, the disease regressed from 1933 to 1937, is that right?

A. No, it did not regress at all. As a matter of fact, it progressed a little bit.

Q. Well, Doctor, in giving your answer to Mr. Gerlacks hypothetical question, you assumed the facts he gave you as being true, did you not?

A. Yes, sir.

Q. So, you assumed that it was true that in 1925 it was quiescent, that in 1927 on three examinations, first apparently arrested, then arrested, and then definitely ar- [161] rested——

Mr. Gerlack (Interrupting) Now, just a minute. That diagnosis of arrested tuberculosis was a doctor's diagnosis. The doctor was not permitted to give his opinion upon the diagnosis of the other doctor, but based upon his own findings.

By Mr. Di Girolamo:

Q. Doctor, do you know of anything in the findings of the examinations, from any of the examinations in the year 1927, which would lead to a conclusion other than arrested tuberculosis?

(Testimony of Dr. Harry Cohn.)

A. Yes, sir.

Q. What are they?

A. May I have the records?

Q. All right, I will give it to you. There are two of them in 1927. (Hands document to witness.)

A. I will take it step by step, with the National Association's classification of what constitutes an arrest of tuberculosis. In the first place, the National Association says there should be an entire absence of constitutional symptoms. This man has a little cough and expectoration. His chest pains. His endurance is not good. He is easily tired. The Tuberculosis Association classification next says the x-ray findings should be those of stationary and healed tuberculosis. There is no x-ray report on this record. That important step was not taken in ascertaining [162] whether or not this man was an arrested case.

Sputum, if any, should be negative for tubercle bacilli. There is no record submitted as to whether or not his sputum was examined, although the man said he expectorated.

The National Association classification says that the man should be taken for at least six minutes in exercise or its equivalent, to one hour walking twice daily. The doctor here makes no statement about this man taking any exercise. He does not say anything about that.

(Testimony of Dr. Harry Cohn.)

So, according to the National Association classification I would not say that that man was apparently an arrested case at the time.

Take each one of the four items, sputum, absence of x-ray, which are necessary under the National Association classification, and we find no sputum examination, no exercises, none of the items were given which is necessary in a diagnosis for arrested or apparently arrested tuberculosis, none of them were included in that examination.

Q. Now Doctor, what does that reference to exercise amount to as compared to work?

A. It is the most important thing in testing whether or not a man has tuberculosis or not. You treat patients to get them to go back to work. How do you know if you don't put them on exercise and try them out? This man wasn't given any exercise as far as the record shows. [163]

Q. I ask you again, Doctor, what is the equivalent of that exercise with respect to work?

A. Well, two hours of walking may be to some people as much as eight hours work. That depends on what your previous occupation was and your condition. A man sitting at a desk will find that two hours walking is hard work while a man accustomed to rigorous exercise would not think much of two hours walking. It is an individual matter.

(Testimony of Dr. Harry Cohn.)

Q. Isn't it the test that there should be so much exercise, the equivalent of one hour's walking in the morning and one hour's walking in the afternoon?

A. No. If you will look at the National Association classification, it says one hour's walking or its equivalent twice daily. You see a man should be able to walk six miles a day or its equivalent.

Q. Now, Doctor, when they examined this man in 1931 or 1932, why would they want to put it on that basis and give him a test of two hours' walking when he had been working for about four or five years, not one hour a day, but eight hours a day?

A. I pointed out to you before a man may be leading a sedentary occupation. The doctor asks a man how much exercise he is taking and he might make his diagnosis on what the man says. The doctor has to find out certain things and examine him in order to determine his condition. He takes an x-ray to determine the man's condition. [164]

Mr. Gerlack: Just a moment, counsel. I think you are assuming something not in evidence. At the time the 1927 examination was made Mr. Holland had not worked for two years prior.

The Court: Proceed.

Mr. Di Girolamo: I am talking about 1931 or 1932.

Mr. Gerlack: I thought you said 1927.

Mr. Di Girolamo: No.

The Court: Anything further?

Mr. Di Girolamo: That is all.

Redirect Examination

By Mr. Gerlack:

Q. You spoke of the National Tuberculosis Association. Did I understand you to say they put out a certain standard by which tuberculosis is judged?

A. They have a diagnostic standard used by practically all of the sanatoria in the United States.

Q. Is that a copy of the Standards of the National Tuberculosis Association, Doctor?

A. This is the 1938 Edition.

Mr. Gerlack: May I have that marked?

(Hands document to Clerk.)

By Mr. Gerlack:

Q. Will you read from that the classification so far as arrested tuberculosis or apparently tuberculosis is concerned? [165]

The Court: Is this redirect examination?

Mr. Gerlack: Yes, your Honor.

The Court: It is not cross of the cross, I presume?

Mr. Gerlack: What is that, your Honor?

The Court: It is not cross examination of the cross examination, is it?

Mr. Gerlack: Counsel brought something out on cross examination which I should like to go into.

The Court: But this Doctor has testified.

(Testimony of Dr. Harry Cohn.)

Mr. Gerlack: Very well.

May we have that marked for identification?

The Clerk: Plaintiff's Exhibit 20.

The Court: Anything further?

Mr. Gerlack: That is all.

Mr. Di Girolamo: That is all.

(Witness Excused.)

The Court: Call your next witness.

Mr. Gerlack: Now, if your Honor please, I have a deposition of Dr. Mary Jones Mentzer, taken at San Francisco. Mr. Spaulding has consented to help me read it. You had better take the original, Mr. Spaulding.

Mr. Spaulding: Will you read the questions?

Mr. Gerlack: Yes. I might state that this deposition of Mr. Mentzer of San Francisco was taken before a Notary Public in San Francisco. [166]

The Court: Proceed with the reading of the questions and answers.

Mr. Di Girolamo: May I have a copy of that?

Mr. Gerlack: Yes.

"Whereupon,

DR. MARY JONES MENTZER,

having been first duly sworn to testify the truth, the whole truth and nothing but the truth, testified as follows, to wit:

(Deposition of Dr. Mary Jones Mentzer.)

"Direct Examination

"By Mr. Gerlack:

"Q. Dr. Mentzer, what is your full name?

"A. Mary Jones-Mentzer.

"Q. You are a licensed physician and surgeon, licensed to practice as such in the State of California? A. I am.

"Q. Of what medical school are you a graduate?

"A. I went to the University of Pennsylvania for my pre-medical and to Women's Medical College of Pennsylvania for my full medical course.

"Q. In what year did you graduate?

"A. 1905.

"Q. And have you practiced continuously since that time?

"A. No—I didn't begin practicing—you mean private practice, don't you?

"Q. No, either institutional or private practice.

"A. Well, I worked as an interne in the Philadelphia [167] Women's Hospital and as resident physician in the Sheltering Arms, and after I came out here I worked in the Poly. Clinic. On the first Monday in March, 1918, I opened a private office and I think in about 1920 I went to Stanford and worked there in the clinic and was instructor in chest diseases. I was also in charge—physician in charge—of the Arequipa Sanitarium for tuberculosis for young women. Then I went to the Southern Pacific Hospital—I am doing general work there

(Deposition of Dr. Mary Jones Mentzer.)
handling the out-patient department in the mornings.

"Q. Doctor, you say you were engaged first, as an interne and then connected with these hospitals —you were practicing during all that time? That is, the work you were doing constituted the practice of medicine? A. Yes, sir.

"Q. You have practiced medicine continuously since your graduation in 1905 until the present time?

"A. I wouldn't say that exactly—you see in about 1905 I married and there was a hiatus there of about five years.

"Q. What practice have you had in the diseases of the chest?

"A. I was instructor at Stanford University—heart and lungs both—that was from approximately 1918 I think to about 1924. No, I gave that up in 1927—when I went to the Southern Pacific and I have been there since 1927. [168] I was at Arequipa for 1917 I think, for about ten years.

"Q. You were confining your medical practices to the diseases of the chest at Arequipa?

"A. Yes.

"Q. Just where is Arequipa, and what kind of an institution is it?

"A. It is an institution for young women in the early stages of tuberculosis—no, I wouldn't say that either—let me say that it is an institution for

(Deposition of Dr. Mary Jones Mentzer.)
young women with apparently 'curable' tuberculosis.

"Q. It is a tuberculosis sanitarium?

"A. Yes.

"Q. Do you still confine part of your practice to tuberculosis and diseases of the chest?

"A. I am particularly interested in that but my work in the Southern Pacific takes in almost any realm.

"Q. You mean the Southern Pacific General Hospital in San Francisco? A. Yes.

"Q. Did you ever have occasion to examine and treat professionally the plaintiff in this case, Wilson A. Holland? A. I did, yes.

"Q. You have your records?

"A. Yes, right here.

"Q. Can you tell when he first came under your professional care? [169]

"A. On September 19, 1935.

"Q. Just tell us, doctor, what examination you made of him at that time and what you found on that examination.

"A. He had a disease of the chest—I took his height, weight, time of the examination, time of taking his temperature, which was 2:10. I examined his eyes, lids, teeth, membranes, tongue, tonsils, glands, thyroid, nails, hands, heart, chest.

"Q. What diagnosis was made as a result of your examination?

(Deposition of Dr. Mary Jones Mentzer.)

"A. Bilateral tuberculosis (both lungs)—pulmonary, more extensive on right. The physical signs were of empyema at the left base. According to the roentgen examination this diagnosis was pleural thickening and adhesions at the left base. He also had acute pleurisy at that time.

"Q. Was his tuberculosis active at that time?

"A. It was active at that time.

"Q. What would you say as to the degree of advancement—whether minimal—moderate degree of advancement—or far advanced?

"A. It was right on the border-line. According to our rules, I would say he had an involvement of about the whole of one lung . . . that can either go on the moderately or far-advanced side according to the National Tuberculosis Association standards followed by us. He told me he had had a cold with a cough and expectoration for about ten [170] days and that he felt well enough along through the days unless something untoward happened—if he had a cold, or became excited—then he wasn't so well. And I think this is very important—he said for about a year and a half he had been troubled with heartburn and occasional constipation, and he was exceedingly nervous—this with heartburn and constipation indicated that he was getting second-stage symptoms—that is why I consider this important. There was nervousness and interrupted sleep, and of course loss of weight. I can give you those figures

(Deposition of Dr. Mary Jones Mentzer.)

if you want them as they were given to me. High weight in 1918, when he entered the army was 140, with a minimum of 90 at the time of the empyema, and 113 in September, 1924. For several years he had carried a dressed weight of 120 to 125. I got him at 120 that day, dressed. He was a man that would call for a weight of about 165. I have a copy here of the x-ray findings.

"Q. Did you order an x-ray taken?

"A. Yes.

"Q. Did you see it yourself? A. Surely.

"Q. Were you able to say from the x-ray and examination—were you able to say that that was his x-ray? A. Yes.

"Q. What were the findings on the x-ray, Doctor?

"A. (Reading from x-ray report): Bony frame work: [171] Right upper chest contracted. Right diaphragm negative. Left diaphragm shows several basilar adhesions over dome and attached to chest wall in axillary region. Heart of the dropped cylindrical type. Aorta negative; trachae distorted to the right; Right lung: Marked old heavy fibrosis scattered about fourth rib and fifth dorsal spine, which contains numerous mottled areas. Pleura thickened over upper chest. Left Lung: Old heavy fibrosis scattered about third rib and fifth dorsal spine, which also contains numerous scattered

(Deposition of Dr. Mary Jones Mentzer.)
coarse mottled areas. Pleura thickened over apex and base. Conclusions: Pulmonary tuberculosis, active. Signed by Dr. G. A. Fogerty, Saint Francis Hospital.

"Q. That was also your interpretation of the x-rays, Doctor?

"A. Also more at the left base than they had.

"Q. Were your findings the same, or not, Doctor?

"A. My findings were practically the same as those except at the left base he says there were pleural thickenings over the right and that the thickenings came up into the axillary. I found it a little more extensive than that and there was quite a flat area and no breath sounds over that at all.

"Q. Was that x-ray compatible with your opinion on your physical examination as to the degree of advancement of his tuberculosis? **[172]**

"A. Yes, moderately between far and moderately advanced.

"Q. You may assume for the purpose of this question, that Mr. Holland was examined at Des Moines, Iowa, by the United States Veterans' Administration on December 30, 1924, at which time the physical examination, among other things, showed breath sounds were harsh over the right 3rd rib to the 4th dorsal spine. Markedly diminished over entire left chest, resulting in atrophy of the

(Deposition of Dr. Mary Jones Mentzer.)
left base. There were a number of fine rales throughout the chest more marked below the fourth rib front and below the 4th dorsal spine in the back. Excursion very markedly limited left side of chest. Fremitus is markedly increased both uppers and absent the entire base of left side. Resonance is a marked dullness throughout left chest, becoming entirely flat below the left fourth rib. There is a scar in the left 7th interspace axillary region which is draining a seropurulent fluid.

"A. Haven't you anything later than 1924?

"Q. Yes, but I want to give you the whole thing.

"A. All right.

"Q. The diagnosis at the time of that examination was pulmonary tuberculosis, chronic, minimal active. Pleuritis, chronic, purulent.

"A. These I found as far advanced in 1935.

"Q. His examination and the x-ray of his chest at that time further showed heart, marked displaced toward the right. [173] Diaphragm on the left side completely obliterated with a dense hemogeneous shadow extending from base up to the second rib anteriorly, with a definite fluid level. The right lung showed a marked disseminated fibrosis with a definite peripheral increase of density and slight mottling of the lung structure. This has the appearance of an old tubercular condition. The left lung, on account of the dense shadow spoken of in the left lung, very little of the lung structure is

(Deposition of Dr. Mary Jones Mentzer.)

noted. There is a definite increase in density and slight mottling in the extreme apex. This condition is the result of an accumulation in the left pleural cavity, with a possibility of an old tubercular infection.

"He was again examined at the U. S. Veterans Hospital, No. 80, at Fort Lyon, Colorado, on February 4, 1925, at which time he had a temperature of 98; pulse 114; time of day 9:30 A. M. His blood pressure was 108/72. Weight 114; normal weight 135; lowest weight within one year, 90 pounds. Sputum negative. The x-ray showed infiltration and consolidation most left upper and lower. Empyema left chest. Pulmonary diagnosis, positive, active, far advanced. The x-ray showed moderate tuberculosis of the right apex and upper far advanced tuberculosis of the left chest with an empyema which is filled with *pu.* This occupies about half of the lung extending from the 2nd rib to the 7th rib and there is an adhesion to the left diaphragm. Small amount of pus in left side. Rib has been resected and drainage established. [174] Tapping this day failed to secure pus, possibly because of thickness of same. Diagnosis: Tuberculosis, pulmonary, chronic, active far advanced B; empyema left chest.

"He was again examined at the same hospital at Fort Lyon, Colorado, on May 5, 1925, at which time the pulmonary diagnosis was positive, improved, moderately advanced. The x-ray showed moderate

(Deposition of Dr. Mary Jones Mentzer.)

tuberculosis of the right apex and upper. Far advanced tuberculosis of the left chest with an empyema which is filled with pus. This occupies about half of the lung, extending from the 2nd rib to the 7th rib and there is an adhesion to the left diaphragm. Diagnosis, tuberculosis, pulmonary, chronic, active, far-advanced; tubercular empyema, drainage left chest.

"He was next examined at Des Moines, Iowa, on October 1, 1925. This examination among other things upon a physical examination, a moderate number of fine rales over base of left lung posteriorly. Pulmonary diagnosis, pulmonary tuberculosis, chronic, active. Empyema left, healed A S D; pleurisy, fibrosis, chronic, left. The x-ray on October 1, 1925, showed the right lung to have a marked disseminated fibrosis with a large group of calcified glands in the hilus with a definite infective process extending from the hilus to the periphery involving the upper lobe. There is definite mottling of the lung structure throughout this area. X-ray of the left lung shows the same general changes and in addition there is a definite infective process in- [175]
volving the periphery of the upper lobe, with an infiltration of the lung structures along the course of the bronchi of the lower lobes. The changes in both uppers are definite of pulmonary tuberculosis. There is no accumulation within the pleural cavity on the left side at this time.

(Deposition of Dr. Mary Jones Mentzer.)

"The next examination made in Los Angeles on August 19, 1926, shows, among other things, a few inconsistent rales below the clavicle. Fibrosis of both upper lobes. Thickened adhesive pleura left chest following empyema. Tuberculosis, pulmonary, chronic, improved, quiescent, moderately advanced.

"A. He told me the last x-ray he had had were in 1926.

"Q. The next examination was made by the United States Veterans Administration at the U. S. *Vetersan* Hospital in Los Angeles, on March 2, 1927, by Drs. Woodward, Middleton and Essenson. Their diagnosis at that time was tuberculosis, pulmonary, chronic, moderately advanced, apparently arrested. Pleurisy chronic, suppurative, healed left chest.

"The next examination was made at the Regional Office of the United States Veterans Bureau on March 16, 1931, and showed among other things, auscultation, right lung, BVB and IVC over impaired area with a few inconstant rales heard both below and above the clavicle. Left lung, BVB and IVC over impaired area. Many rales heard following [176] expiratory cough. Breath sounds at the base below the 4th rib is diminished with pleural crepitations over the area of the empyema scar. The pulmonary diagnosis at that time was tuberculosis, pulmonary, chronic, arrested, moderately advanced with chronic fibrous pleurisy left base, post

(Deposition of Dr. Mary Jones Mentzer.)

operative empyema. This was signed by Drs. Burstien, Essenson and Rene.

"The next examination was at the United States Veterans Hospital at San Fernando, California, on June 13th to June 27th, 1936, at which time the physical examination, among other things showed scattered TPMI rales heard above 2nd rib and 5th dorsal spine on inspiration after cough. Left, I.W. above 3rd rib and 8th dorsal spine. BVB same area. Scattered TPMI rales heard above 2nd rib and 5th dorsal spine on spiration after expiratory cough. Breath sounds over left base are distant with pleural crepitations. Impression, active infiltration and fibrosis both uppers and upper parts both lower lobes. Trachea in mid line, heart small, slightly displaced to left, hilus shadows bilateral are heavy, with a few areas of increased density about the right hilus, there is an interweaving of the trunks above the 4th rib anteriorly, there are no well defined areas of cavitation the descending trunks are somewhat thickened, bases are slightly emphyematous, the C P angles are slightly clouded due to apparent adhesions, the left diaphragm is slightly flattened. The inner portion of diaphragm [177] bilateral shows apparent adhesions. Impression, infiltration and fibrosis upper half of lung field bilateral with empyema both bases and diaphr*am*atic adhesions bilateral. Diagnosis, tuberculosis, chronic, pulmonary, far advanced, active. Pleurisy, chronic,

(Deposition of Dr. Mary Jones Mentzer.)

fibrosis left base. Cacatrix, old healed, post-operative rib resection. Hypotension arterial. Hemorrhoids, external, mild.

"The last examination made was apparently made at the U. S. Veterans Hospital at San Fernando on April 19, 1937. He was admitted on June 13, 1936. This examination showed tuberculosis infiltration and fibrosis both upper lobes, upper part of both lower lobes. Fibrous pleurisy both bases. The x-ray reports as compared with June 16, 1936, shows no reentgenological change. Diagnosis, tuberculosis, pulmonary, chronic, far advanced, active, pleurisy, chronic, fibrous left. This was signed by Drs. Grieger, Beatty and Nalty.

"Q. Now, Doctor, bearing in mind your own examination taken in September, 1935, at that time, what would have been the effect of following an occupation or engaging in any physical or mental labor, what would the effect have been on this man?

"A. Disastrous.

"Q. In what respect?

"A. Well, in the first place, the first principle of treatment in tuberculosis is rest, and we think it would aggravate the condition if any activity were engaged in such [178] as a person would enter into if he or she were to work.

"Q. Do you mean by that, Doctor, that even mental activity would aggravate such a condition and would make it worse, and that if he did not

(Deposition of Dr. Mary Jones Mentzer.)

engage in such activity he would make progress more rapidly than otherwise? A. Yes.

"Q. Bearing in mind your own examination and findings, and assuming the findings which I have just read as far back as in 1925, and also the findings on the last examination in 1936 and 1937, assuming these findings to be true, and bearing in mind your own examination of Mr. Holland in 1935, what were the probabilities at that time in 1935, of him becoming either worse or becoming an arrested case?"

Mr. Di Girolamo: There is an objection there, if the Court please. That objection was made at the time the deposition was taken. The objection is on the ground it is incompetent and irrelevant and is a question based on facts that are not in evidence, "and upon the further ground that it is asking the doctor to state her opinion based upon the conclusions and opinions of other doctors. And on the further ground that it is ambiguous and unintelligible and contains many facts which are hearsay and not properly before this Court."

Mr. Gerlack: And then there is the next question, your Honor:

"Q. I will ask you a further question, in answering [179] this question, eliminating the diagnoses or opinions of these doctors and taking into consideration only the findings given you as read from the reports of their examinations—assuming these find-

(Deposition of Dr. Mary Jones Mentzer.)

ings read to you to be true and basing your opinion upon the findings but not upon the diagnoses, bearing in mind your own examination and your own findings, in your opinion what were the probabilities of Mr. Holland being cured or even attaining an arrestment of his tuberculosis at the time you saw him in September, 1935?"

Mr. Di Girolamo: Your Honor, there is the same objection made as to the former question, on the same grounds, not every fact is in evidence.

Mr. Gerlack: That is true. The fact was not in evidence at that time. Since that time it has been in evidence.

The Court: I don't know that that will help us here.

Mr. Gerlack: What is that?

The Court: I don't know that the answer to that question would help us here.

Mr. Gerlack: I think so. It is incumbent upon the Plaintiff to prove permanency. It is probable that it will last throughout his lifetime. We are no longer permitted to ask the doctor if the man is totally or permanently disabled, so that we are breaking down that definition by showing that the man is suffering from disabilities which would [180] *would* be aggravated by work of any kind.

The Court: No question up to that point, but you say 1935.

Mr. Gerlack: Yes, your Honor.

(Deposition of Dr. Mary Jones Mentzer.)

The Court: We are concerned with total disability in 1933.

Mr. Gerlack: That is true, but the higher court holds you must prove total disability at the time of trial as well as to all the time in between the date alleged.

The Court: If it was total in 1933 it was total in 1935.

Mr. Gerlack: Your Honor must bear in mind at the time of the examination made he was working in the Treasury Accounts Division in the Treasury Department, and at that time he was suffering from active tuberculosis, and at that time it was incurable. This question will elicit the answer to that question.

Mr. Di Girolamo: I don't believe it is material or relevant whether it was curable or incurable in 1935. The issue is 1933.

The Court: If this question were propounded by the Defendant it might be proper. You have to show he was totally and permanently disabled in 1933.

Mr. Gerlack: I think we have shown that. I anticipate, of course, the Government's attempted defense in this case is that he did work and that is the evidence he was not [181] totally or permanently disabled.

The Court: If the Government offers it I will permit it, but it is cumulative for the record and might be followed up almost indefinitely. It is not material to your type of case.

(Deposition of Dr. Mary Jones Mentzer.)

Mr. Gerlack: We submit it is, your Honor. What is the last?

Mr. Spaulding: We were on Line 12 of Page 14.

Mr. Gerlack: Did I understand the Court to sustain an objection to that?

The Court: Yes.

Mr. Gerlack: (Reading)

"Q. In other words, the strong probabilities were in 1935, that he would not get well and would have tuberculosis as long as he lived?"

Mr. Di Girolamo: "I object to that as leading and suggestive."

The Court: Read the answer.

Mr. Di Girolamo: If the Court please, I make the same objèction. The question on Line 25, as read by counsel, says "In other words, the strong probabilities were in 1935 that he would not get well and would have tuberculosis as long as he lived?"

The Court: Oh, you may read the answer.

Mr. Spaulding: (Reading)

"A. Taking into consideration the matter of progress— [182] progress is good, if you get the patient in time—if you begin treatment early—prognosis is good if the treatment is continued a sufficient length of time and the patient is careful. There are three things dependent upon the patient, whether he follows the treatment, gets plenty of rest and plenty of fresh air. This makes it exceedingly hard to say, but from my experience, I would say

(Deposition of Dr. Mary Jones Mentzer.)
that man had very little chance of getting well then or now."

Mr. Gerlack: That is all. And then the cross examination.

The Court: Are you through?

Mr. Gerlack: Yes, your Honor, this is cross examination.

The Court: Proceed.

Mr. Di Girolamo: (Reading)

"Cross Examination

"Mr. Lynch:

"Q. Assuming, as I understand it, that the average treatment for the majority of tuberculosis cases is rest at night, fresh air and sunshine, will extreme cases usually require some types of medicines?

"A. Correct. However, we always consider that good food, peace of mind, plenty of rest and fresh air are the four things which influence the treatment of tuberculosis.

"Q. Assuming that during that—asuming, Doctor, that at that time when you examined him, he embarked upon [183] the program prescribed, and followed out the recommendations that you made to him, do you think that would have brought about an improvement of his condition?

"A. Didn't he do that?

"Q. I don't know, I'm asking you.

"A. Well, I only saw him for a very short time —I don't know those things. But I think he has

(Deposition of Dr. Mary Jones Mentzer.)

been following—I know he has been receiving treatment—he has written me that.

"Q. That is not before the court, that is hearsay.

"A. I know he has been receiving treatment of pneumoclysis and of pneumoperitoneum.

"Q. I am just asking if it is reasonable to assume that if he followed the proper diet and other recommendations made to him that he would show an improvement in his condition?

"A. I don't think we can say—some of these cases will seemingly be going along all right, then they have a hemorrhage, get bronchial pneumonia and are dead in ten days—you can't tell what is going to happen.

"Q. But they do sometimes show improvement?

"A. Some do, yes.

"Q. In other words, there is no such thing as estimating the outcome in tuberculosis unless the tuberculosis has arrived at the last stage?

"A. No. [184]

"Q. Could a man suffering from far advanced active tuberculosis if he followed prescribed treatment, expect eventually to reach such a stage, generally speaking, that his tuberculosis would be arrested?

"A. You mean far advanced with cavity? I would say no, not without surgery—with cavity. Far advanced without cavity—he has a chance of be-

(Deposition of Dr. Mary Jones Mentzer.)

coming quiescent—we say that a good deal—he has a chance of becoming apparently arrested.

"Q. What treatment would you recommend for this man at the present time?

"A. Today? Why, I examind in September, 1935 —I wouldn't be fool enough to recommend anything—I know he is having surgery.

"Q. Assuming that this man was before you today, what type of treatment would you recommend for him?

"A. Well, I can judge his condition as one of cavity. In this case I know that he is to have pneumothorax and bilateral pneumothorax by the treatment he is receiving. In a sanitarium he would get all of his essentials,—he is supposed to be getting all of his essentials now.

"Q. In your opinion, should that bring about some improvement in his present condition?

"A. It would certainly tend to mitigate any aggravation of condition—it ought to, that is—it doesn't always do it. [185]

"Q. It is possible that it would?

"A. Possible—yes.

"Q. You say you examined him in 1935?

"A. Yes.

"Q. You had never seen him before that?

"A. No.

"Q. You haven't examined him since?

"A. I examined him twice at that time.

(Deposition of Dr. Mary Jones Mentzer.)

"Q. What was the occasion for this examination —under what circumstances did you examine him— was he a paid patient?

"A. He was referred to me by an eye doctor—I suppose he had told the doctor something of his history, and he then sent him to me because he knew I was interested in tuberculosis.

"Q. Both occasions for you seeing him were in 1935? A. Yes.

"Q. That is all.

"Redirect Examination

"Mr. Gerlack:

"Q. Now, Doctor, Mr. Lynch asked you if this man would do certain things if his condition would improve—do you mean by that that he would improve to the extent that he would become arrested——?

"A. I wouldn't say that it would become arrested—it might become apparently arrested—that means without [186] physical signs under ordinary conditions of life, for three years. I didn't mean apparently cured.

"Q. Would working at—would he be able to work at an occupation without endangering his health?

"A. No, I wouldn't say that.

"Q. In this man's case, would you say—do you believe—that the probabilities were or were not, at

(Deposition of Dr. Mary Jones Mentzer.)
the time you saw him in 1935, that he would become a completely arrested case? For or against it?

"A. In my opinion they were rather against it.

"Q. Strongly so?

"A. With a history like that—with a history of a man whom everything made nervous—anything brought about a strain, and he was immediately not well—I would say, strongly so.

"Mr. Gerlack: That is all.

"Mr. Lynch: That is all.

(Signed) "MARY JONES MENTZER, M.D."

Mr. Gerlack: That is the Plaintiff's case, your Honor.

The Court: The Plaintiff rests.

Proceed with your evidence on behalf of the Defendant.

Mr. Di Girolamo: I have some depositions to read, also, your Honor.

Mr. Gerlack: Do you want me to read them, read the questions and you can answer them?

Mr. Di Girolamo: I don't care. [187]

Mr. Gerlack: Well, I may answer them from the witness box.

Mr. Di *Girolomo*: All right, Mr. Gerlack, but first I would like to make a short opening statement to the Court and jury.

The Court: Proceed. [188]

Mr. Gerlack: Your Honor, in these converted cases it *in* incumbent upon the Plaintiff, or I might say, one of the conditions of the policy is to prove submission of proof. Due proof means proof that would satify an unprejudiced mind. Usually Mr. Fooks and I, in trying these cases, have stipulated in the event a favorable verdict is rendered we agree on what proof is agreeable.

The Court: No proof has been made.

Mr. Di Girolamo: We do not contend due proof has been made.

Mr. Gerlack: Can we stipulate that in event of a favorable verdict for the Plaintiff that the date of the [190] claim is the date of due proof?

Mr. Di Girolamo: Oh, no.

Mr. Gerlack: Then I will ask your Honor to allow the Plaintiff to open it up.

The Court: Very well.

Mr. Gerlack: Will you produce the statement of insurance?

The Court: Where is it?

Mr. Gerlack: It is a Government document that I am calling for, your Honor. It is a statement. Here it is. We offer it as Plaintiff's next in order.

The Clerk: Plaintiff's Exhibit 21.

(The document referred to was received in evidence and marked "Plaintiff's Exhibit No. 21")

PLAINTIFF'S EXHIBIT NO. 21

845 Mills Building,
San Francisco, California,
March 12, 1937

Veterans Administration, and/or
United States Veterans Bureau,
Washington, D. C.

Attention: Administrator of Veterans Affairs
and.or
Director, United States Veterans Bureau
Re: Holland, Wilson Alvin
C-1 224 075 K-613076

Gentlemen:

I hereby appeal to the above Administrator and/or Director and make claim for the benefits due me under my Government Insurance Certificate or Policy.

I claim that I have been permanently and totally disabled from following continuously any substantially gainful occupation since August 30, 1933.

Claim is also made under Section 408 of the War Risk Insurance Act and Section 305 of the World War Veterans Act of 1924, as amended, and also for the refund of all premiums, if any, paid on account of said insurance since I became permanently and totally disabled.

I have heretofore, to-wit, on August 30, 1933, while I was a beneficiary and a patient of the

United States Veterans Administration, furnished you with due proof of my permanent and total disability.

This claim is being sent you prior to filing suit under Section 19 of the said World War Veterans Act.

Trusting I may have your decision at an early date, either allowing my claim for insurance benefits or denying the same, and thereby creating the necessary "Disagreement" contemplated under Section 19 of said Act, I am

Respectfully,
WILSON ALVIN HOLLAND
U. S. Veterans Facility
San Fernando, California

[Endorsed]: Plaintiff's Exhibit No. 21. Filed Feb. 28, 1939.

Mr. Gerlack: The claim for insurance benefits, dated February 12, 1937, which counsel hands me from the official files of the Veterans' Administration identified by a rubber stamp which reads, "Received March 16, 1937 Mail Sub-Div. Veterans' Administration, Reader No. 55."

Now, is Dr. Cohn's statement there?

Mr. Di Girolamo: I don't have it.

Mr. Gerlack: Did you look in the file? There is a Form No. 579 that accompanied that.

The Court: Would you gentlemen of the jury like a short recess?

We will take a short recess for about 10 minutes. [191]

(At this point a short recess was taken, after which proceedings were resumed, as follows:)

Mr. Gerlack: As long as this document is purely technical I won't read it to the jury, your Honor. I will just introduce it in evidence.

The Court: Very well.

Note all of the jurors present.

Mr. Gerlack: It is so stipulated.

Mr. Di Girolamo: It is so stipulated.

Mr. Gerlack: If your Honor please, I will also offer Plaintiff's next in order, Veterans' Administration insurance Form No. 579 in connection with this claim.

The Court: Any objection?

Mr. Di Girolamo: No objection.

The Court: Very well.

The Clerk: Plaintiff's Exhibit 22.

(The document referred to was received in evidence and marked "Plaintiff's Exhibit No. 22.")

PLAINTIFF'S EXHIBIT NO. 22

Claim Number
C-1 224 075
K- 613 076
Holland, Wilson A.

STATEMENT OF CLAIM FOR INSURANCE—TOTAL PERMANENT DISABILITY

This form is to be executed by the veteran if living and competent, or by the Committee or guardian if veteran is incompetent; if veteran is dead by the personal representative of the estate, or if there is no personal representative, the statement of claim must be executed by the beneficiary under the insurance contract. All information herein requested must be given — if not furnished, reasons for failure to do so must be stated.

Part I

1. Name of veteran—Wilson Alvin Holland

2. File numbers — T—— K 613 076 C 1 224 075

3. Home address — 3023½ Van Buren Place, Los Angeles, California.

4. Mailing address—Veterans Administration Facility, San Fernando, California.

5. Did veteran apply for (a) Disability Compensation x (b) Disability Allowance — (c) Retirement pay — (d) Pension —

6. Make (x) after branch of service in which veteran served — Army x Navy — Marine Corps — Coast Guard —

7. Serial number R-322 237.

8. Date of enlistment May 6, 1917.

9. Date of last discharge August 3, 1920.

10. On what date did the veteran's permanent and total disability cause him to cease work? Aug. 30, 1933 altho I did try to work after that but such work aggravated my condition and made my tuberculosis worse.

11. From what date does the veteran claim to have been permanently and totally disabled? August 30, 1933.

12. What disease or injury causes the veteran to be permanently and totally disabled? Pulmonary tuberculosis and chest trouble.

13. Places and dates *or* residence of veteran since the date on which the alleged permanent and total disability began, and for two years prior thereto—

Street and Number of R. F. D. Post Office State Date

Los Angeles, California, from 2/1/31 to 11/11/34.

San Francisco, Calif., from 11/12/34 to 6/10/36.

Veterans Admin. Hospital, San Fernando, California, from 6/13/36 to date.

14. Name and addresses of hospitals at which the veteran has been treated—

Name Address Date of Admission Date of release

Methodist Hospital, St. Joseph, Mo., 9/19/24, 10/5/24.

Veterans Hospital, Fort Lyon, Colo., 1/25/25, 5/6/25.

Veterans Hospital, San Fernando, Cal., 6/13/36, still hospitalized.

15. Give names and addresses of all doctors who have attended veteran for the disease or injury causing total and permanent disability. Also date of treatment. See my Veterans Administration Folders C-1 224 075.

16. If veteran has been examined or treated by a physician, or physicians, during the last year submit a supplemental statement by such physician, or physicians, preferably on the physician's letterhead, showing length of time under treatment, history of condition, physical and laboratory findings, diagnosis and prognosis, and any other pertinent medical data relating to the veteran's condition.

See Records Veterans Hopsital, San Fernando, California.

17. Does or did veteran have other insurance? If so, please give—

See my Veterans Administration folder.

Name of Company

Amount

Date of issue

Amount and beginning date of disability payments, if any

18. Industrial History

State below occupations since the date on which the veteran was discharged from the service, including names and addresses of all employers, beginning and ending dates of employment, usual number of hours worked each day, number of days worked each week, average weekly wages, amount of time lost on account of illness, reason for termination of employment. If self-employed, give nature of business, period, volume of business, help employed, gross and net income, time lost on account of physical condition. If unemployed, state periods and reasons. Statement should account for the entire period since date of discharge from service. Detailed answers must be made hereto.

See my Veterans Administration Folder.

19. If person executing claim is the legal representative of the veteran or the personal representative of his estate, give date and designation of court of appointment.

This case involves possible litigation and I consider this a very unfair request and not necessary to a proper consideration of my insurance claim on its merits.

Oath of Applicant

21. I, the undersigned, being duly sworn depose and say that each question has been truthfully and completely answered to the best of my knowledge, information and belief, and I hereby make claim for payment of disability benefits under the contract of insurance.

WILSON ALVIN HOLLAND
(Signature of veteran)

22. Subscribed and sworn to before me this 9th day of April, 1937 by Wilson Alvin Holland, to me

personally known, and to whom the statements herein were fully made known and explained.

[Seal] PAUL L. STAYNER
Notary Public in and for the County of Los Angeles, State of California
My Commission Expires May 15, 1940

Part II

Not to be executed unless the veteran has a policy of United States Government life insurance and has paid the additional premium for the Total Disability Provision authorized by Section 311 of the World War Veterans' Act, 1924, as amended.

I hereby make claim for waiver of the payment of premiums and the payment of the monthly income in accordance with the Total Disability Provision attached to and made a part of United States Government life insurance policy, Number K——— in the amount of $————.

―――――――――――――
(Signature of insured)

Section 501 of the W. W. V. Act as amended, provides as follows:

"That whoever in any claim—compensation or insurance, or in any document required by this Act, or by regulations under this Act, makes any sworn statement of a material fact knowing it to be false, shall be guilty of perjury and shall be punished by a fine of not more than $5,000.00, or by imprisonment for not more than two years, or both."

Apr. 19, 1936
Holland, Wilson A.
C No. 1 224 075
T No. ————
K No. 613 076

STATEMENT OF CLAIM FOR INSURANCE—TOTAL PERMANENT DISABILITY

I, Wilson Alvin Holland, believe myself to be entitled to receive any monthly payment of benefits awarded on account of permanent and total disability of the insured under any insurance granted or issued under certificate or policy number K-613076.

My permanent home address is 3023½ Van Buren Place, Los Angeles, California.

I desire checks mailed to above address.

In support of this claim, I make the following statement as true to the best of my knowledge and belief:

1. Under what name, rank and organization did the insured serve? Wilson Alvin Holland, Corporal, Co. D, 53rd Telegraph Battalion, Signal Corps.

WILSON ALVIN HOLLAND

Signature of (Insured) (Guardian, legal or personal representative).

Date: April 9, 1937.

[Endorsed]: Plaintiff's Exhibit No. 22. Filed Feb. 28, 1939.

Mr. Di Girolamo: Now, I offer in evidence Government's Exhibit C for identification. I won't read all of it. I will read only what is pertinent and counsel can read anything he wants to.

The Court: Proceed.

Mr. Di Girolamo: This is an application with the Los Angeles County Civil Service Commission, dated November 28, 1931. (Reading) [192]

I offer that in evidence.

The Clerk: Defendant's Exhibit C.

(The document referred to was received in evidence and marked "Government's Exhibit C.")

GOVERNMENT'S EXHIBIT C

12640

Examination date: Dec. 4, 1931.

Do not file this application if your general qualifications, experience and education do not meet the requirements of the bulletin announcing the examination.

APPLICATION

LOS ANGELES COUNTY CIVIL SERVICE COMMISSION

This application must be filed with the Commission in accordance with the instructions in the bulletin announcing the examination, not later than the last day for filing specified in the bulletin.

This form must be filled out in a complete and legible manner. An application improperly filled out or which shows the applicant to lack the prescribed qualifications, will be rejected.

Use ink.

Elig. No. 6

Gen. Av. 75.49 (10 points: 85.49)

Written 75.83

Gen. Qual. 75

Efficiency ....

Seniority ....

Phys. Tests ....

Prac. Test ....

Exam. No. ....

1. Wilson Alvin Holland.

Notice Sent 2800 Newell St., Los Angeles, Calif.

Telephone Normandy 4628.

"Statements as to age and education will be verified."

2. Examination (give exact title) Junior Field Deputy Accountant (Seasonal Service).

3. Residence (if different from mail address)......

If now working for County, give Department..........

4. How long have you been a resident of Los Angeles County? 4½ yrs. Of California? 4½ yrs

If less than two years in California, give exact date of arrival..............................

5. Where were you born? Redding, Ringgold County, Iowa.

6. I am a citizen of the United States by birth.

If a naturalized citizen, certificate of naturalization must be presented with your application. If a citizen through marriage, give date of marriage. If a citizen through parents' naturalization, give place and date of such naturalization..............................

7. Date of birth: January 9, 1901. What was your age on your last birthday? 30.

8. Height 5 ft. 10. in. Weight 125 lbs.

9. Are you married? Yes.

If a married woman, what was your maiden name?..............................

Are you the sole support of yourself? Yes. Of your family? Yes.

How many persons INCLUDING yourself are dependent on you for support? 2.

If married, is your husband or wife working?? No. Kind of employment?..............................

10. Are you in good health? Yes. Name each serious illness or accident you have had in the last three years: None.

Do you have any defect of sight, hearing, speech or limb? No. If so, what?..............................

11. Honorably discharged soldiers, sailors and marines who served in time of war or armed insurrection are, under Sec. 36½ of the County Charter, entitled to 10% credit.

Do you claim such credit? (Answer "Yes" or "No") Yes.

(If you waive the right to this credit at this time, you will not be permitted later to claim it. If you claim this credit, you must present your "honorable discharge" when filing application.)

12. Do you now or have you ever used intoxicat-ıg liquors? (Answer "Yes" or "No") No.

If so, to what extent? Be specific.........................

13. Have you ever been arrested for the violation f any law or ordinance? No. If so, explain ully........................ ....

Your education and experience are partly deter-ıined by the statements you make below.

14. EDUCATION

Give Name and Location of Schools Attended	Last Grade Completed	Did You Graduate?	Give D Leavi Gradu
(a) Last Common—Public or Private			
lockton Public School, Blockton, Iowa	8	Yes	1
(b) Junior High School			
(c) Last High School—Public or Private			
lockton High School, Blockton, Iowa	12	Yes	1

d) College or University (List all)	Years Attended	Major Subjects	Credits or Degree Obtained	Give Lea Gra
outhwestern University, Los Angeles	1½ yrs.	Accounting	Credits obtained in accounting & Business Law	Att pr t

e) Give in full any other education you have had (Business Coll Correspondence, Coaching Schools, etc.), giving addresses and d

15. If the Commission writes your present em-loyer, will it jeopardize your position? Not em-loyed.

16. Have you ever been dismissed? No. If so, ive circumstances ....

17. What foreign languages do you speak? Russian.

18. Give below full names of five persons as re: erences, not present or former employers, not en ployees of Los Angeles County, and not related t you by either blood or marriage, who are familia with your character.

The references below will be written to only i the discretion of the Commission.

l Name	Home (Mail) Address Number,Street, City and State	Occupation or Business
n Wilcox	707 Decatur St., Los Angeles	Auto Parts busine:
C. DeSilva	2908½ So. Sycamore, Los Angeles	Mechanic
W. Bowman	1345 E. Hill St., Long Beach	Plastering Contrac
. R. A. Holmes	604 W. Wilson, Glendale	Dentist
W. Hadley	4455 Willow, Inglewood	Accountant

19. Application may be rejected if the following is not fully and properly filled in. Account for all time since leaving school (all wo ployment on first line. Be sure addresses are correct. If the firm for which you worked is out of business, indicate to whom we may writ

Employed From Mo.	Yr.	To Mo.	Yr.	Total Time	Position Held Give Title and Duties	Monthly Salary	Cause of Leaving	Employer Firm or Person Kind of Business	
June	1921	Sep.	1921	4 mo.	Drug Clerk—Selling	$50	Accept other position	L. M. Souders—Druggist	....
Sept.	1921	March	1922	6 mo.	Drug Clerk—Selling	$85	Accept other position	J. H. Bremmer—Druggist	Unknown
Mar.	1922	Mar.	1927	5 yrs.	Postmaster—postal activities Supervisor of all	$150	Expiration of term	U. S. Post Office Dept.	....
Apr.	1927	June	1927	2 mo.	Unemployed	———			
June	1927	Dec.	1927	7 mo	Postal Clerk—Distributing mail	65¢ per hr.	Accept other position	U. S. Post Office, Glendale, Calif.	....
Dec.	1927	Jan,	1931	3 yrs.	Assistant Auditor—Supervisor of office detail, cost accounting, stock record, bookkeeping, and preparation of financial statements.	$175	Closing down of manufacturing	Pickwick Corporation & Pickwick Motor Coach Works—Manufacturers of busses	560 So. Los
Jan.	1931	Present		1 yr.	Attending school				

File 2571 No. 6

20. Give date and name of last Los Angeles County examination for which you filed: None.

Give names of all Los Angeles County Civil Service Examinations for which you are now filing (other than this one) or for which you have filed in the last year: None.

Title.................... Passed?.................... Failed?....................

Title.................... Passed?.................... Failed?....................

21. Summarize in your own handwriting your education and experience which you believe will qualify you for the position for which you are applying: The accounting experience gained while in my last position was largely of a type with which an assessor must be familiar, such as stock records, equipment records, etc. Since leaving that position, I have enrolled in the School of Commerce of Southwestern University, majoring in Accounting. I am now in my second year.

It is understood by me that any willful misstatement of facts in this application automatically rejects my application or fails me in the examination and forfeits my right to appeal.

Application sent by mail must be sworn to before a notary public.

22. The following oath must be taken before the Secretary of the Civil Service Commission or one of his assistants or before a Notary Public.

AFFIDAVIT

I solemnly swear that the answers I have made to each and all of the foregoing questions are full and true to the best of my knowledge and belief.

And further, in order that the Los Angeles County Civil Service Commission may be fully informed as to my personal character and qualifications for employment, I refer to each of my former employers and to any other person who may have information concerning me, agreeing, as this information is furnished at my express request and for my benefit, to hold such persons harmless and I do hereby release them from any and all liability for damage of whatsoever nature on account of furnishing such information.

Signature of Applicant

WILSON ALVIN HOLLAND

(The blanks below to be filled in only by Notary Public.)

Subscribed and sworn to before me November 28, 1931.

[Seal] IDA M. MURPHY

Notary Public

My term expries May 8, 1933.

(The blanks below to be filled in only by deputy in the Civil Service Office.)

Subscribed and sworn to before me..............................

L. E. LAMPTON,

County Clerk

[Endorsed]: Government's Exhibit C. Filed Feb. 28, 1939.

Mr. Di Girolamo: Now, I offer in evidence Government's Exhibit D dated January 20, 1922. It reiterates the employment as stated in the other application. Will you stipulate to that, Mr. Gerlack?

Mr. Gerlack: Yes, it has the same information Let it go in.

The Clerk: Defendant's Exhibit D.

(The document referred to was received in evidence and marked "Government's Exhibit D.")

GOVERNMENT'S EXHIBIT D

14096

Did not appear for Examination.

Exam. Date: Jan. 29, 1932.

Do not file this application if your general qualifications, experience and education do not meet the requirements of the bulletin announcing the examination.

APPLICATION
LOS ANGELES COUNTY CIVIL SERVICE COMMISSION

This application must be filed with the Commission in accordance with the instructions in the bulletin announcing the examination, not later than the last day for filing specified in the bulletin.

This form must be filled out in a complete and legible manner. An application improperly filled out or which shows the applicant to lack the prescribed qualifications, will be rejected.

Use ink.

Elig. No...

Gen. Av. ....

Written ....

Gen. Qual. ....

Efficiency ....

Seniority ....

Phys. Tests...................................

Prac. Test ....

Exam. No. ....

1. Wilson Alvin Holland

2800 Newell, Los Angeles, California.

Telephone Normandy 4628.

"Statements as to age and education will be verified."

2. Examination (give exact title): Senior Bookkeeper.

3. Residence (if different from mail address).........

If now working for County, give Department...........

4. How long have you been a resident of Los Angeles County? 5 yrs. Of California? 5 yrs.

If less than two years in California, give exact date of arrival..

5. Where were you born? Redding, Ringgold County, Iowa.

6. I am a citizen of the U. S. by birth.

If a naturalized citizen, certificate of naturalization must be presented with your application.

If a citizen through marriage, give date of marriage...

If a citizen through parents' naturalization, give place and date of such naturalization..

7. Date of birth: January 9, 1901. What was your age on your last birthday? 31.

8. Height 5 ft. 10 in. Weight 126 lbs.

9. Are you married? (Yes)

If a married woman, what was your maiden name?....................................

Are you the sole support of yourself? Yes. Of your family? Yes.

How many persons INCLUDING yourself are dependent on you for support? Two.

If married, is your husband or wife working? No. Kind of employment....................................

10. Are you in good health? Yes. Name each serious illness or accident you have had in the last three years: None.

Do you have any defect of sight, hearing, speech or limb? No. If so, what?....................................

11. Honorably discharged soldiers, sailors and marines who served in time of war or armed insurrection are, under Sec. 36½ of the County Charter, entitled to 10% credit.

Do you claim such credit? (Answer "Yes" or "No") Yes.

(If you waive the right to this credit at this time, you will not be permitted later to claim it. If you claim this credit, you must present your "honorable discharge" when filing application.)

12. Do you now or have you ever used intoxicating liquors? (Answer "Yes" or "No") No.

If so, to what extent? Be specific..............................

13. Have you ever been arrested for the violation of any law or ordinance? No. If so, explain fully..............................

Your education and experience are partly determined by the statements you make below.

.4. **EDUCATION**

Give Name and Location of Schools Attended	Last Grade Completed	Did You Graduate?	Give Date of Leaving or Graduating
Last Common—Public or Private			
ckton Public School, Blockton, Iowa	8	Yes	May, 1914
Junior High School			
Last High School—Public or Private			
ckton High School, Blockton, Iowa	12	Yes	May, 1921

College or University (List all)	Years Attended	Major Subjects	Credits or Degree Obtained	Give Date of Leaving or Graduating
thwestern University, Los Angeles 1121 So. Hill St.	1 yr.	Accounting	None	Still attending evening school

) Give in full any other education you have had (Business College, Correspondence, Coaching Schools, etc.), giving addresses and dates.
None

15. If the Commission writes your present employer, will it jeopardize your position? Not now employed.

16. Have you ever been dismissed? No. If so, give circumstances ....

17. What foreign languages do you speak? Russian.

18. Give below full names of five persons as references, not present or former employers, not employees of Los Angeles County, and not related to you by either blood or marriage, who are familiar with your character.

The references below will be written to only in the discretion of the Commission.

Full Name	Home (Mail) Address Number, Street, City and State	Occupation or Bus
r. R. A. Holmes	604 W. Wilson, Glendale, Calif.	Dentist, retire
. W. Bowman	1345 E. Hill, Long Beach, Calif.	Plastering Con
. W. Hadley	5555 Willow St., Inglewood, Calif.	Cost Accounta
. C. DeSilva	2908½ Sycamore, Los Angeles	Mechanic
. Peters	1001 W. Washington, Los Angeles	Mortician

19. Application may be rejected if the following is not fully and properly filled in. Account for all time since leaving school (all workin ployment on first line. Be sure addresses are correct. If the firm for which you worked is out of business, indicate to whom we may writ

Employed From Mo.	Yr.	To Mo.	Yr.	Total Time	Position Held Give Title and Duties	Monthly Salary	Cause of Leaving	Employer Firm or Person Kind of Business	Presen
May	1921	Sept.	1921	4 mo.	Clerk—Waiting on Customers	$50.00	Take other position	L. M. Souders—Druggist	
Sept.	1921	Mar.	1922	7 mo.	Clerk—Waiting on Customers	$85.00	Take other position	J. H. Bremmer—Druggist	Unknown—Verify by Ass't Postmaster
Mar.	1922	Mar.	1927	5 yrs.	Postmaster—General Supervision of mails, carriers, & clerks	$150.00	Expiration of term	U. S. Postoffice Dep't	First Asst. P. M. Gen
Mar.	1927	May	1927	3 mo.	Unemployed				
May	1927	Dec.	1927	8 mo.	Postoffice clerk—Distributing mail	65c hr.	Take other position	U. S. Postoffice—Glendale, Calif.	
Dec.	1927	Jan.	1931	3 yrs. 1 mo.	Cost Accountant and later Assistant Auditor—Figuring of costs on building of motor busses and later as Ass't Auditor, general factory accounting	$175.00	Production Discontinued	Pickwick Motor Coach Works Bus Manufacturers	P. O. Box 817
Jan.	1931	Present		10½ mo.	Attending Southwestern University				

File 2580 No. 95

20. Give date and name of last Los Angeles County examination for which you filed: Junior Field Deputy Accountant, Dec. 4, 1931.

Give names of all Los Angeles County Civil Service Examinations for which you are now filing (other than this one) or for which you have filed in the last year: Only the one mentioned above.

Title.................... Passed?.................... Failed?....................

Title.................... Passed?.................... Failed?....................

21. Summarize in your own handwriting your education and experience which you believe will qualify you for the position for which you are applying: My accounting experience began when I was appointed a Postmaster in 1922. During the five years I held that office I personally handled all of the accounting records.

My three years in my last position covered are varied an accounting experience as one could find. Being a manufacturing concern with many separate departments, the accounting set-up was necessarily quite extensive. I supervised every detail of it, kept the books, prepared the routine financial and operating statements, etc.

I have completed half of my second year in Advanced Accounting at Southwestern University.

It is understood by me that any willful misstatement of facts in this application automatically rejects my application or fails me in the examination and forfeits my right to appeal.

Application sent by mail must be sworn to before a notary public.

22. The following oath must be taken before the Secretary of the Civil Service Commission or one of his assistants or before a Notary Public.

AFFIDAVIT

I solemnly swear that the answers I have made to each and all of the foregoing questions are full and true to the best of my knowledge and belief.

And further, in order that the Los Angeles County Civil Service Commission may be fully informed as to my personal character and qualifications for employment, I refer to each of my former employers and to any other person who may have information concerning me, agreeing, as this information is furnished at my express request and for my benefit, to hold such persons harmless and I do hereby release them from any and all liability for damage of whatsoever nature on account of furnishing such information.

Signature of Applicant

WILSON ALVIN HOLLAND

(The blanks below to be filled in only by deputy in the Civil Service Office)

Subscribed and sworn to before me Jan. 20, 1932.

L. E. LAMPTON,

County Clerk

By M. H. JETER.

[Endorsed]: Government's Exhibit D. Filed Feb. 28, 1939.

Mr. Di Girolamo: (Reading exhibit)

I offer in evidence an application dated February 19, 1932 which reiterates the same work up to February 1932. (Reading document.)

The Clerk: Defendant's Exhibit E.

(The document referred to was received in evidence and marked "Government's Exhibit E.")

GOVERNMENT'S EXHIBIT E

20387

Exam. Date: Mar. 8, 1932

APPLICATION

LOS ANGELES COUNTY CIVIL SERVICE COMMISSION

Elig. No. 4

Gen. Av. 73.80, plus 10 pts. 83.80

Written 72

Oral ....

Gen Qual. 75

Efficiency ....

Seniority ....

Phys. Tests ....

Prac. Test ....

1. Examination (give exact title): Audit Clerk (Male).

2. Wilson Alvin Holland

Notice Sent: 2800 Newell, Los Angeles, California.

Telephone Normandy 4628

Important — Read Carefully

Instructions:

This form must be filled out in complete and legible manner. An application improperly filled out or which shows applicant to lack the prescribed qualifications will be rejected. Every question must be answered. Use ink.

File your application as early as possible. In case of a tie in final rating, priority in filing determines priority on the eligible list.

Every statement in this application is subject to verification. False statements in applications concerning any matter affecting applicant's eligibility may result in disqualification of applicant, or removal from eligible list.

3. Height 5 ft. 10 in. Weight 125 lbs.

4. Are you married? (Yes)

5. Residence (if different from mail address): Same.

6. If now working for County, give Department..................................

7. How long have you been a resident of Los Angeles County? 4 yrs. 11 mo. Of California? 4 yrs. 11 mo.

If less than two years in California, give exact date of arrival..................................

8. Where were you born? Redding, Ringgold County, Iowa.

9. I am a citizen of the U. S. by birth.

If a naturalized citizen, certificate of naturalization must be presented with your application.

If a citizen through marriage, give date of marriage..............................

If a citizen through parents' naturalization, give place and date of such naturalization..............................

10. Date of birth: January 9, 1901. What was your age on your last birthday? 31.

11. Honorably discharged soldiers, sailors and marines who served in time of war or armed insurrection are, under Sec. 36½ of the County Charter, entitled to 10% credit.

If you claim this credit, you must present your "honorable discharge" when filing application.

Do you claim such credit? (Answer "Yes" or "No") Yes.

12. EDUCATION

Give Name, City and State of Schools Attended (Under a, b, c, d)	Grades Completed	Did You Graduate? (Yes or No)	Give D Leavir Gradu
(a) Last Common—Public or Private			
Blockton Public School, Blockton, Iowa	8	Yes	19
(b) Last Junior High School			
(c) Last High School—Public or Private			
Blockton High School, Blockton, Iowa	12	Yes	19

(d) College or University (List all)	No. of Years Completed (Not Dates)	Course Taken	Credits or Degree Obtained	Give Dat Leaving Graduat
Southwestern University, Los Angeles, Calif.	1½ yrs.	Accountancy	17 credits	Still attendi

(e) Give in full any other education you have had (Evening Sch Business College, Correspondence, Coaching Schools, etc.), gi addresses and dates.

13. If the Commission writes your present employer, will it jeopardize your position? Not employed.

14. Have you ever been dismissed? No. If so, give circumstances ....

15. What foreign languages do you speak? None.

16. Give below full names of five persons as references, not present or former employers, not employees of Los Angeles County, and not related to you by either blood or marriage, who are familiar with your character.

The references below will be written to only in the discretion of the Commission.

Full Name	Home (Mail) Address Number, Street, City and State	Occupation or Business
A. Schoenmann	529-B W. Stoker, Glendale, Calif.	Attorney-at-law
R. A. Holmes	604 W. Wilson, Glendale, Calif.	Dentist, retired
W. Hadley	5555 Willow St., Inglewood, Calif.	Accountant
W. Wilcox	707 Decatur St., Los Angeles, Calif.	Motor Supply Dealer
A. Riegert	1527 E. Seventh St., Los Angeles, Calif.	Fender and Body Worker

19. Application may be rejected if the following is not fully and properly filled in. Account for all time since leaving school (all workin ployment on first line. Be sure addresses are correct. If the firm for which you worked is out of business, indicate to whom we may writ

Employed From Mo.	Yr.	To Mo.	Yr.	Total Time	Position GiveTitle	Monthly Salary	Cause of Leaving	Employer Firm or Person	Kind of Business	Present Address
June	1921	Sept.	1921	4 mo.	Clerk	50.00	To accept other position	L. M. Souders	Druggist	....
Oct.	1921	Mar.	1922	6 mo.	Clerk	85.00	To accept other position	J. H. Bremmer	Druggist	Address unknown—Write Postmaster,
April	1922	Mar.	1927	5 yrs.	Postmaster	150.00	Expiration of term	U. S. Post Office Dept.		First Ass't Postmaster Gen
April	1927	May	1927	2 mo.	Unemployed					
June	1927	Nov.	1927	6 mo.	Postoffice Clerk	65¢ hr.	To accept other position	U. S. Post Office, Glendale, Calif.		Postmaster
Dec.	1927	Jan.	1931	3 yrs. 2 mo.	Assistant Auditor	175.00	Closing down of business	Pickwick Corporation,	Bus Manufacturers	560 So. Los Angeles St.
Feb.	1931	Present		1 yr.	Attending Southwestern University					
Mar. 7 to Pres.					Jr. Field Dep. a/c			Assessor		

File 2601 No. 4

18. Give date and name of last Los Angeles County examination for which you filed: Senior Bookkeeper.

Give names of all Los Angeles County Civil Service Examinations for which you are now filing (other than this one) or for which you have filed in the last year..................................

Title: Senior Bookkeeper

Did you pass? (Yes or No): Did not take exam.

Title: Deputy Junior Field Accountant

Did you pass? (Yes or No): Yes.

19. Do you now or have you ever used intoxicating liquors? (Answer "Yes" or "No") No.

If so, to what extent? Be specific..................................

20. Have you ever been arrested for the violation of any law or ordinance? No. If so, explain fully..................................

21. If a married woman, what was your maiden name?..................................

Are you the sole support of yourself? Yes. Of your family? Yes.

How many persons INCLUDING yourself are dependent on you for support? Two.

If married, is your husband or wife working? No. Kind of employment?..............................

22. Are you in good health? Yes. Name each serious illness or accident you have had in the last three years: None.

Do you have any defect of sight, hearing, speech or limb? No. If so, what?..................................

23. Summarize in your own handwriting the personal qualifications which you believe will qualify you for the position for which you are applying: Have completed nearly two years of Accounting study, and have had more than three years of accounting experience which included the installation of systems, as well as bookkeeping and general supervision of all office detail.

It is understood by me that any willful misstatement of facts in this application disqualifies me in the examination and forfeits my right to appeal.

Application sent by mail must be sworn to before a notary public.

24. The following oath must be taken before the Secretary of the Civil Service Commission or one of his assistants or before a Notary Public.

AFFIDAVIT

I solemnly swear that the answers I have made to each and all of the foregoing questions are full and true to the best of my knowledge and belief.

And further, in order that the Los Angeles County Civil Service Commission may be fully informed as to my personal character and qualifications for employment, I refer to each of my former employers and to any other person who may have information concerning me, agreeing, as this information is furnished at my express request and for my benefit, to hold such persons harmless and I do hereby release them from any and all liability for damage of whatsoever nature on account of furnishing such information.

Signature of Applicant

WILSON ALVIN HOLLAND

(The blanks below to be filled in only by deputy in the Civil Service Office)

Subscribed and sworn to before me Feb. 19, 1932.

L. E. LAMPTON,

County Clerk

By M. H. JETER.

Mr. Di Girolamo: I offer in evidence an application dated November 29, 1933 in which he was asked, "Have you any physical defects?" And the answer is "No."

(Reading document)

(The document referred to was received in evidence and marked "Government's Exhibit A.") [193]

GOVERNMENT'S EXHIBIT A

APPLICATION
CIVIL SERVICE COMMISSION
COUNTY OF LOS ANGELES

1002 Hall of Records

Important—Read carefully

For Office use only

Eligible No. 18

Final Av. 85.94 + 10 pts — 95.94

Written Av. 89.90

Oral Test ....

Gen. Qual. 80

Eff. Rating ....

Sen. Rating ....

Phys. Test ....

Pract. Test ....

Exam. Date Dec. 9, 1933

Exam. Notice ....

Oral Notice ....

Stand. Notice Feb. 1, 1934

This form must be completely filled out. Use ink. Make out a separate application for each position. Every statement is subject to verification. False statements may result in disqualification or removal from the eligible list.

1. Examination Title—Clerk, Grade III (Male) & Senior Clerk (Male)

2. Name in full (Print)—Wilson Alvin Holland

3. Mail Address—2800 Newell St., Los Angeles, Calif. Residence Telephone Normandy 4628

4. State whether single, married, separated, divorced or widowed—Married. How many dependents? One.

5. Birthplace—Redding, Iowa. Date of Birth—Jan. 9, 1901. Age last birthday—32.

6. Length of last continuous residence in L. A. County—6½ yrs.

7. Weight—125 Height—5 ft. 10 in.

8. Have you any physical defect? No. If so, what is it? ....

9. Have you ever been arrested? No. If so, explain fully (Exclude minor traffic violations)..........

10. Are you a citizen of the United States? Yes. Native born? Yes. Naturalized? ....
If Naturalized, certificate of naturalization must be presented at time of filing application.

11. Are you entitled to Veteran's 10% credit allowed by Sec. 36½, Los Angeles County Charter? Yes. If you claim the credit your honorable discharge must be presented at time of filing application.

12. If the Civil Service Commission writes to your present employer, will it jeopardize your position? No.

For Office Use Only

Counter Number or Time Stamp—Received 1933 Nov 29 AM 8:55

28

13. EDUCATION.

Correspondence and/or Other Schools	Course	Lessons Completed or Time Attended

M					Salaries Received
Sep 1933	Present	3 mo.	Unemployed		
Mar 1933	Sep 1933	6 mo.	State Narcotic Hospital, Spadra, Calif.	Bookkeeper	$120.00
May 1932	Mar 1933	9½ mo.	Attended Southwestern University		
Mar 1932	May 1932	2½ mo.	L. A. County Assessor, Los Angeles, Calif.	Deputy Junior Field Accountant Assessing Business Firms	$160.00
Jan 1931	Mar 1932	13½ mo.	Attended Southwestern University		
Dec 1927	Jan 1931	3 yrs. 1 mo.	Pickwick Corporation 560 So. Los Angeles St., Los Angeles	Asst. Auditor—Supervised All clerical work & assisted auditor	$175.00
June 1927	Dec 1927	7 mo.	U. S. Post Office Glendale, Calif.	Postal Clerk	65¢ hr.
Mar 1927	June 1927	3 mo.	Unemployed		
Mar 1922	Mar 1927	5 yrs. 1 mo.	U. S. Post Office Dept., Washington, D. C.	Employed as Postmaster at Blockton, Iowa	$150.00

15. All applicants must subscribe to the following:

I solemnly swear (or affirm) that all the statements contained herein are true to the best of my knowledge and belief.

Signature of Applicant—Wilson Alvin Holland

This space for Civil Service Deputy only

Subscribed and sworn to before me Nov 29 1933

L. E. LAMPTON,
County Clerk,
By O. E. JONES

This application will be acknowledged free of charge if presented in person at the office of the Civil Service Commission.

[Endorsed]: Government's Exhibit A. Filed Feb. 28, 1939.

Mr. Di Girolamo: I offer in evidence report of physical examination made at San Fernando in 1937, "Brief Medical and industrial history:

> "States following service he felt well until April, 1924 when he started hemorrhaging and remained at home until Sept. 1924. States was diagnosed Tbc. in April 1924 by a private physician. Went to Methodist Hospital in St. Joseph, Mo. in Sept. 1924 when he had resection left side, there about three weeks. Then remained home until Jan. 1925 when admitted to VAF Fort Lyons, Colo. and remained there until May, 1925. Discharged not in need of further

hospitalization. States in fall of 1926 was diagnosed quiescent Tbc., and in about six months time went to work and has been able to work steadily ever since. States in Sept. 1935 he had severe cold and from then on has not been able to be free from colds. Had a small hemorrhage, reported to Veterans Administration, San Francisco, Calif., who recommended hospitalization. Returned to Southern California and admitted to San Fernando facility for treatment June 13, 1936."

Approved by F. Nelson, Assistant Chief Outpatient Service.

There is a signed statement by the claimant, "My answers to questions 8 and 9 have been read to me, and I hereby certify that the medical and industrial history are correct and the complaints recorded are all that I am suffering from, to the best of my knowledge and belief." [194]

(Handing document to Clerk.)

The Clerk: Government's Exhibit F.

(The document referred to was received in evidence and marked "Government's Exhibit F.")

GOVERNMENT'S EXHIBIT F.

Read carefully, Instructions, page 8. Use "Additional", page 7, when the space under any caption is not sufficient for notations.

File in S. F.

IL

Exam. by Board of Three at Request of Regional Office (Los Angeles) for Insurance purp.

REPORT OF PHYSICAL EXAMINATION.

C-No. 1 224 075.

(See par. 7, page 8)

Date of admission to hospital June 13, 1937.

Date of discharge from hospital, In hospital, 193

(See par. 9, page 8)

1. Claimant's name, Holland, Wilson A.

Address, Veterans' Admin., San Fernando, Calif.

2. Examined, VAF, San Fernando, Calif. 4/19/37.

3. Age, 36. Color, White. Birthplace, Iowa. Race, W. Color of eyes, blue. Color of hair, brown.

4. Height, 71 inches. Weight (weigh him) 122½ lbs. Highest weight in past year 127½.

5. Permanent marks and scars other than described below:

Healed P.O. scar left lower chest, mid axillary line, result of rib resection for empyema.

6. Rank and organization Corp. Co.D 53rd Tel. Bn. Date of enlistment 5/6/1917; of discharge 8/3/1920.

7. Origin and date of incurrence of disability as alleged by claimant:

States in 1918 in the P.I. he was sick, probably from the flu and had malaria fever in Siberia, also had trouble with diarrhea in Siberia caused from bad water. Had regular straight discharge from service.

8. Brief medical and industrial history:

(In first examinations, this history must cover sufficiently the time elapsing since date of discharge from military service. When previous examinations have been made, the examiner will record only the medical and industrial history covering the period since the most recent previous examination, thereby bringing it up to date of his examination. If, for any reason, such history cannot be obtained, the reason therefor must be stated. The data to be noted are: When, where, by whom, and for what condition has the veteran received medical treatment? When, where, by whom, and at what occupation and wages was he employed, and how continuous was the employment?)

States following service he felt well until April 1924 when he started hemorrhaging and remained at home until Sept. 1924. States was diagnosed Tbc. in April 1924 by a private physician. Went to Methodist Hospital in St. Joseph, Mo. in Sept. 1924 when he had resection left side, there about three weeks. Then remained home until Jan. 1925 when admitted to VAF Fort Lyons, Colo. and remained there until May 1925. Discharged not in need of further hospitalization. States in fall of 1926 was diagnosed quiescent Tbc., and in about six months time went to work and has been able to work steadily ever since. States in Sept. 1935 he had severe cold and from then on has not been able to be free from colds. Had a small hemorrhage, reported to Veterans Administration, San Francisco, Calif., who recommended hospitalization. Returned to Southern California and admitted to San Fernando facility for treatment June 13, 1936.

Approved

[Illegible]

Asst. Chief, Outpatient service.

9. Present complaint (subjective symptoms, not diagnosis:

Cough, expectoration, pleurisy pains both sides. Gas pressure and sharp pain in pit of stomach. Pain in arches of both feet, more on right, causing pain in leg and sacrum. Bothered with hemorrhoids.

Statement by Claimant. My answers to questions 8 and 9 have been read to me, and I hereby certify that the medical and industrial history are correct and the complaints recorded are all that I am suffering from, to the best of my knowledge and belief.

Signature of claimant (or his mark)

WILSON A. HOLLAND.

For the physical examination the claimant must be stripped.

10. Temperature Range 36.4-37; Respiratory rate: Standing..................: immediately after exercise; 3 minutes after exercise................ Pulse rate: Standing: Range 68-84; immediately after exercise................; 3 minutes after exercise................ Any arrhythmia of pulse?................ (If so, describe... (Taken 3 minutes after exercise).................................... Blood pressure: Systolic 96, diastolic 60.

11. General appearance, well developed, poorly nourished but bright and alert; carriage, normal; posture, erect; gait, normal.

Lids and conjunctivae slightly reddened and thickened. Nor corneal scars or ulcers.

12. Eyes: External structures, each eye, Pupils react to light and accommodation. No lid [illegible] ness or muscular imbalance. Fundus Examination: Pupils dilate round and equal.

Internal structures, each eye (if practicable) Media clear. Discs well outlined, normal size, shape and color. Macular regions well defined. Vessels within normal limits.

Impression: No essential fundus pathology.

Vision (Snellen chart): Uncorrected R— 20/20 L— 20/20; corrected R— 20/ L— 20/

13. Ears: Auditory canals: Normal? Yes. Discharge?...................... From external canal or middle ear?...................... Mastoidectomy scar?.................. Appear-

ance of membrana tympani? No perforations or discharge. Bone and air conduction within normal limits. Ordinary conversation heard: Right 20 feet; left 20 feet.

(Test only at prescribed distances—1, 2, 5, 10, 15, 20 feet). Tests for bone conduction (Specify Rinné, Weber, Schwabach): Nasal mucus membranes negative. Turbinates hyperplastic. Septum deviates to right, partial obstruction. No clinical evidence of sinusitis. Pharynx slightly reddened. Tonsils enucleated. Larynx: Epiglottis negative. No tumors, ulcers or paralysis. Cords approximate throughout entire length. Phonation good. Impression: Negative larynx.

14. Nose, throat, sinuses: Normal?..............................
If not, record findings:

L. C. HOBSON,
M. D., EEN&T SP.

INDUSTRIAL HISTORY OF WILSON A. HOLLAND SINCE DISCHARGE FROM MILITARY SERVICE.

From the latter part of 1920 to the autumn of 1921 I was employed as a drug clerk. During the summer of 1921 my weight dropped from 135 to 118 and I had difficulty keeping my position because of physical inability to stand on my feet all day. I left to accept another position as drug clerk which was less strenuous than the first. This position I held until the spring of 1922. I suffered from colds and pleurisy a great deal while in the employment, feeling badly most of the time. In the spring of 1922 I was appointed a Postmaster, in which position I continued until the late summer of 1924 when I became ill with acute pleurisy from which empyema developed. It was at this time that I was diagnosed as tubercular. While holding the position of Postmaster I lost considerable time on account of ill health. As I had no immediate superior at my place of employment I was able to arrange my own hours of work but in spite of this I had difficulty in carrying on the work. From September to December of 1924 to about June of 1927 I was unemployed due to pulmonary tuberculosis and empyema. During a great part of that time I was confined to bed. For the remainder of 1927, when not too ill, I worked part time as a clerk. I suffered greatly from fatigue during this employment and became exhausted after only a short while at work. However, it was necessary for me to work in order to support myself and family. I felt that I should not have been working at all.

During 1928, 1929 and 1930 I was employed in light cost clerk and general clerk positions. The work was routine and did not require the expenditure of much energy but I lost a great deal of time because of ill health and finally gave up the job. For the next two years I felt so badly that steady employment was out of the question. I was weak, tired and exhausted during that period, coughed considerably, raised quite a bit of sputum and believe that I had active pulmonary tuberculosis as I felt just as I did previously when my tuberculosis had been pronounced active.

For a few months in 1933 I held an easy routine bookkeeping position. During this employment my feeling of fatigue and weakness increased to the point where I had to drag myself around. I continued to cough and raise considerable sputum and felt hot and feverish especially in the afternoon. From the symptoms I believe that I undoubtedly was suffering from active pulmonary tuberculosis at that time. For the remainder of the year or nearly so I was unemployed due to my tubercular condition, then tried a light accounting position. On this job I was still manifesting the same symptoms of tuberculosis as previously but due to necessitous circumstances I had to work whether I was able to or not. I certainly did not feel able, knew that I should be resting and as a result was forced to take time off from my work frequently. I resigned to take another office position which I hoped would be better for my health but held it less than a year when I suffered a lung hemorrhage, so resigned to enter this hospital where I have since been under treatment for active pulmonary tuberculosis.

Ever since the War I have felt weak and lacking in stamina. My work has so fatigues me that I have always been exhausted at the end of the day at least, and usually by mid afternoon. A night's rest of eight to ten hours has not refreshed me as it should and I have had to drag myself along chiefly on will power. I have not felt well since leaving the service. I have felt as though I had a cold of which I could never quite rid myself.

WILSON A. HOLLAND,
C-1 224 075

15. Cardio-vascular system: Normal?........................

(If not, record area of heart dullness, murmurs, thrills, dyspnea, cyanosis, oedema. Any aneurism? (If so, describe.) Any arteriosclerosis. (If so, what degree?) Record any electrocardiographic examination made under "Laboratory examinations.")

Heart: PMI in 6th interspace left mid clavicular line, rhythmical, no murmurs heard.

16. Respiratory system: Normal?........................

(If not, give shape and measurements of chest on inspiration, expiration, and at rest. Any difference in mobility on or contour of sides? Record physical signs, in each lung separately, upon palpation, percussion, and auscultation. State quality and location of râles during inspiration following expiratory cough. State areas of infiltration, consolidation, and cavities, by lobes; record area of adhesions or fluid. Any cough, expectoration, or hemorrhage? Record sputum examinations under "Laboratory examinations.")

Thoracic: Long, narrow chest. Expansion diminished more to left. Old empyema operation scar left mid ax. line level 10th rib.

Fremitus: R. Lung, increased upper half front and back. L. Lung, Absent from left lower chest, increased over upper part.

Percussion: R. Lung, D.R. 3rd rib and 6th DS up. L. Lung, DR from base up to 6th DS post.

Auscultation: R. Lung, BVB and WV above 3rd rib and 6th DS. M. rales over 3rd rib and 5th DS. L. Lung, BVB and WV over 3rd rib and 5th DS. Few rales above clavicle and 3rd DS., Apex ant. Many pleural crepitations throughout lower lobes.

Summary: Tuberculous infiltration and fibrosis both upper lobes, upper part of both lower lobes—fibrous pleurisy both bases.

17. Digestive system: Are mouth, teeth, gums, stomach, intestines, liver, gall bladder, and rectum normal? Abdomen: Negative. Rectum: Hemorrhoids, ext., mild.

(If not, describe findings. Record X-ray gastro-intestinal series and examination of stomach contents or feces under "Laboratory examinations.")

Dental Report: Missing teeth 1, 3, 17, 32. No treatment indicated.

CLYDE W. ALLEN,
Acting DDS

18. Spleen; lymphatic glands: Normal?..................... If not, record findings.

Liver, spleen and lymphatic glands not palpable.

19. Nervous system: Are brain, spinal cord, peripheral nerves, and mentality normal?.....................

(If not, record mental and neurological findings: Intelligence, school, and general knowledge, memory for remote and recent events, orientation, retention, mental trends, emotional reactions; state of thinking processes, including attention; insight, cooperation, and deportment; hallucinations, delusions; stations and gait; Romberg's sign, deep and superficial reflexes, muscular atrophies, sensation disorders, tremors, paralyses, contractures, etc. Is the patient competent? Any endocrine disorders? If so, describe symptoms in full. Record seriological tests under "Laboratory examinations.") (Observe provisions of par. 6735, R & P, in determinations of incompetency.)

Apparently negative, patellar reflexes present.

20. Genito-urinary system: Kidneys, bladder, prostate, penis, testicles normal? ....

(Record urine analysis (color, recation, sp. gravity, albumin, sugar, casts, pus, blood, shreds) and permeability tests under "Laboratory examinations.")

Atrophy testicle, bilateral. Complete right, partial left, due to mumps while in service. Opinion of Board: From atrophy of testicle, patient has lost procreative function of testicles.

21. Rheumatism: Articular or muscular? None. What joints affected? ....
Swelling, crepitus, atrophy deformity, limitation of motion, ankylosis? Bones & Joints: Negative. Spine: Apparently normal.

22. Hernia: Inguinal, femoral, ventral, umbilica? None. Side? .... Size? .... If inguinal, complete or incomplete? .... Truss worn? .... Retained by truss? .... Operable? ....

23. Hydrocele? No. Varicocele? No. Side? .... Size? ....

24. Varicose veins? No. Size and location?............ .... Sacculated or ruptured? .... Scars or ulcers?............................ Elastic stocking worn? .... Operable? ....

25. Pes planus (flat or weak foot)? Yes. Side? Bilateral. Degree—first, second, third? Third. (See report attached) Abduction (eversion)? .... Inner border bulged? .... Painful? .... Limp? .... Stand on toes? .... Pes cavus (hollow foot)? No. Side? .... High arch? .... Dorsal flexion at ankle limited on active and passive motion? .... Associated equinovarus? .... Hallux valgus (bunion)? No. Side? .... Painful? .... Describe:

26. Skin (location, type, extent of lesions): Clear.

27. Residuals of gunshot wounds or other injuries:

(Level of injury, location and character of scars, limitation of motion, muscle injury, effect on functions.)

None.

28. Evidence of effects of past or present vicious habits (alcohol, narcotics, venereal infections):

(Report laboratory tests under "Laboratory examinations.")

None.

29. Laboratory examinations:

(X-ray, including gastro-intestinal series; urine analyses; kidney permeability; sputum examinations; blood counts; blood sugar determinations; Wassermann test or modifications for blood and spinal fluid; other spinal fluid examinations; basal metabolism; electrocardiographic examination; examination of stomach contents; of feces, etc., if made.)

X-Ray Report (1/27/37)—Stereo film of the chest as compared with 6/16/36 shows no roentgenological change.

(6/16/36) Stereo of chest shows chest to be long and average width, trachea in mid line, heart small, slightly displaced to the left, hilus shadows bilateral are heavy, with a few areas of increased density about right hilus, there is an interweaving of the trunks above 4th rib anteriorly bilateral, with some discrete mottling above 2nd rib right and 3rd rib left anteriorly, there are no well defined areas of cavitation, the descending trunks are somewhat thickened, bases are slightly emphysematous, the CP angles are slightly clouded, due to apparent adhesions, the left diaphragm is slightly flattened, the inner portion of diaphragm bilateral shows apparent adhesions. Impression: Infiltration and fibrosis upper half of lung field bilateral with emphysema both bases, and diaphragmatic adhesions bilateral.

G. I. Series 11/5/36—X-ray examination after ingestion of barium meal shows the stomach to be very large and low in position with no filling defects. The duodenal cap filled normally under fluoroscope. The 6 hr. film showed a slight gastric retention with the head of the meal at the cecum. The 24 hr. film showed the hepatic and splenic flextures and colon to be low in position with no definite filling defects.

Impression: The above findings show no definite pathology, but the stomach is very large, with the colonic flextures low in position as well as the transverse colon.

C. P. HARROD,
M. D., Roent.

Laboratory Examinations,

Urinalysis (6/13/36) Lemon color; acid; 1.015. Negative except occasional WBC.

Sputum: 4/8/37—Negative T.B. (3/1/37) 1 Negative T.B. 9 (cert.) Negative T.B. Sedimentation time (12/8/36) 120 min. to 12mm.

Gastric Content (9/29/36) Ewald test meal. Ingested 7:30 AM, withdrawn 8:30 AM. Total Acidity 50′. Free HCL 35′. No blood, small amount mucus, digestion fair.

(Continued at #30)

Patient referred from VAF, San Fernando, Calif., for examination and recommendation re flat feet.

Feet:

Examination: Inspection shows feet to be of the long slender type. There is no evidence of marked architectural deformity. There are no scars, areas of gangrene, ulceration, swelling, heat or redness present. Feet are entirely free of callosities. Pulsation of dorsalis pedis and posterior tibial arteries definitely palpable bilaterally. There is no limitation of motion at ankle upon either active or passive movement. No crepitation found. Manipulation showed feet to be neither rigid nor contracted. Patient was able to hop without difficulty. When weight was borne it was noted that a very slight flattening of the longitudinal arches occurred, without pronation of feet or out-flaring of heels.

Diagnosis: Weak feet, slight.

Suggest: Massage, manipulation, exercises, contrast baths, to be self-administered. The proper exercises have been explained fully to patient.

H. W. NEWMAN, M. D.,
Orthopedist.

Holland, Wilson A. C-1 224 075 #3153

30. Additional:

(This space to be used for further details of medical or industrial history or additional description of disabilities if the space in the foregoing pages was not sufficient.)

Laboratory Examinations—continued from #29:

Blood: RBC 5,000,000, WBC 8,700. Poly. 48, Lymph. 39, Monocytes 11, Eosinophiles 2. Hemoglobin Sahli 85. Coagulation time 3½ min.

Wassermann: Negative.

Feces: Negative.

H. C. FORTNER, M. D.,
Path.

31. Diagnoses:

1711 Tuberculosis, pulmonary, chronic, far advanced, active (1)

1335 Pleurisy, chronic, fibrous, left

0285 Cicatrix PO for old empyema left, rib resection

0799 Hypotension, arterial

0705 Hemorrhoids, external, mild,

0587 Pes Planus, bilateral, 3rd degree

0169 Atrophy Testicle, bilateral—right complete, left partial

1300 Pharyngitis, chronic, catarrhal

1501 Rhinitis, chronic, hypertrophic

0417 Deviation nasal septum, right

0312 Conjunctivitis, chronic, OU

0023 Absence acquired, teeth, patrial.

0769 Hyperchlorhydria

32. Is the claimant bedridden? No. Is he able to travel? Yes. Does he need hospitalization? Yes. Will he accept it? In hospital yes. Is an attendant necessary for travel? No. Is the claimant mentally competent or incompetent? Competent. Do you consider a guardian necessary? No. Did you examine him yourself? Board. Date April 19, 1937.

Name of examiner

(See instructions as to signature in composite reports.)

J. J. BEATTY, M. D.,
Chairman.
Title Clinical Director.

W. C. NALTY, M. D.,
Member.

H. GRIEGER, M. D.,
Recorder.

[Endorsed]: Government's Exhibit F. Filed Feb. 28, 1939.

GOVERNMENT'S EXHIBIT B

33178

Exam. Date: Nov. 30, 1932

APPLICATION

LOS ANGELES COUNTY CIVIL SERVICE COMMISSION

Elig. No. 6

Gen. Av. 72.25, plus 10 pts. 82.25

Written 86.89

Oral ....

Gen. Qual. 62.50

Efficiency ....

Seniority ....

Phys. Tests..............................

Prac. Test..............................

1. Examination:

Assistant Property Clerk (Male)

2. Wilson Alvin Holland

Notice sent: 2800 Newell, Los Angeles, Calif.

Telephone Normandie 4628.

Important — Read Carefully

Instructions:

This form must be filled out in a complete and legible manner. Study carefully and answer as directed. An application improperly filled out or which shows applicant to lack the prescribed qualifications is subject to rejection. Every question must be answered. Use ink.

File your application as early as possible. In case of a tie in final rating, priority in filing determines priority on the eligible list.

Every statement in this application is subject to verification. False statements in applications concerning any matter affecting applicant's eligibility may result in disqualification of applicant, or removal from eligible list.

3. Height 5 ft. 10 in. Weight 125 lbs.

4. Are you married? (Yes)

5. Residence (if different from mail address).........

6. If now working for County, give Department..............................

7. How long have you been a resident of Los Angeles County? 5 yrs. 7 mo. Of California? 5 yrs. 7 mo.

If less than two years in California, give exact date of arrival...................................

8. Where were you born? Redding, Ringgold County, Iowa.

9. Are you a citizen of the U. S. by birth?

If a naturalized citizen, certificate of naturalization must be presented with your application.

If a citizen through marriage, give date of marriage....................................

If a citizen through parents' naturalization, give place and date of such naturalization..................................

10. Date of birth: January 9, 1901. What was your age on your last birthday? 31.

11. Honorably discharged soldiers, sailors and marines who served in time of war or armed insurrection are, under Sec. 36½ of the County Charter, entitled to 10% credit.

If you claim this credit, you must present your "honorable discharge" when filing application.

Are you entitled to such credit? (Answer "Yes" or "No") Yes.

2. EDUCATION

Give Name, City and State of Schools Attended (Under a, b, c, d)	Grades Completed	Did You Graduate? (Yes or No)	Give Date of Leaving or Graduating
Last Common or Grammar—Public or Private			
ckton Public School, Blockton, Iowa	8	Yes	1914
Last Junior High School			
Last High School—Public or Private			
ckton High School, Blockton, Iowa	12	Yes	1921

College or University (List all)	No. of Years Completed (Not Dates)	Course Taken	Credits or Degree Obtained	Give Date of Leaving or Graduating
thwestern University, Los Angeles, Calif.	2	Accounting	32	Still attending

Give in full any other education you have had (Evening School, Business College, Correspondence, Coaching Schools, etc.), giving addresses, amount and dates.

13. If the Commission writes your present employer, will it jeopadize your position? Not employed.

14. Have you ever been dismissed? No. If so, give circumstances ....

15. What foreign languages do you speak? None.

16. Give below full names of five persons as ref-
ences, not present or former employers, not em-
oyees of Los Angeles County, and not related to
u by either blood or marriage, who are familiar
th your character.

The references below will be written to only in
discretion of the Commission.

ull Name	Home (Mail) Address Number, Street, City and State	Occupation or Bu
W. Bowman	1345 E. Hill St., Long Beach, Calif.	Contractor
alter Engleke	149 La Verne Ave., Long Beach, Calif.	Ship Master
. R. A. Holmes	604 W. Wilson Ave., Glendale, Calif.	Retired Dent
H. Schoenmann	527-C W. Stocker, Glendale, Calif.	Bookkeeper
C. DeSilva	953 Santee St., Los Angeles, Calif.	Mechanic

19. Application may be rejected if the following is not fully and properly filled in. Account for all time since leaving school (all w with first employment on first line. Be sure addresses are correct. If the firm for which you worked is out of business, indicate to whom

Employed From Mo.	Yr.	To Mo.	Yr.	Total Time	Position Give Title	Monthly Salary	Cause of Leaving	Employer: Firm or Person	Kind of Business	Present Address of Empl	
June	1921	Sep.	1921	3½ mo.	Drug Clerk	$50	Take Other Job	L. M. Souders	Druggist	....	Bl
Sep,	1921	Mar.	1922	6½ mo.	Drug Clerk	$85	Take Other Job	J. H. Bremmer	Druggist	Write Assistant Postmaster	Be
Mar.	1922	Mar.	1927	5 yrs.	Postmaster	$150	Expiration of term	Post Office Department		....	W
May	1927	Dec.	1927	7 mo,	Postal Clerk	65¢ hr.	Take other job	U. S. Post Office		....	Gl
Dec.	1927	Jan.	1931	3 yrs. 1 mo.	Assistant Auditor (Included installation and handling of perpetual inventory. Took physical inventory each 6 months.)	$175	Place Closed Down	Pickwick Corp. & Pickwick Motor Coach Works	Bus Manufacturers	560 So. Los Angeles St.	Lc
Jan.	1931	July	1931	5½ mo.	Student at Southwestern University Los Angeles, Calif.						
July	1931			3 wks.	Stock Clerk (Temporary)	50¢ hr.	Work Completed	General Motors Truck Co.,	Truck Sales	Washington & Alameda Sts.	Lo
Aug.	1931	Mar.	1932	5 mo.	Unemployed—Attended Southwestern University evenings						
Mar.	1932	May	1932	2½ mo.	Deputy Jr. Field Accountant	$160	Work Completed	County Assessors Office		Hall of Justice	Lo
June	1932			2 wks.	Stock Clerk (Temporary)	40¢ hr.	Work Completed	Greyhound Motors & Supply Co.,	Motor Parts	Write Pacific Greyhound Lines, Stores Dept., 711 Decatur Street	Lo
July	1932	Present		4 mo.	Unemployed—Attending Southwestern University evenings						

File 2712 No. 6

18. Give date and name of last Los Angeles County examination for which you filed: Audit Clerk, March 18, 1932.

Give names of all Los Angeles County Civil Service Examinations for which you are now filing (other than this one) or for which you have filed in the last year.

Title: Deputy Junior Field Accountant.

Did you pass? Yes.

Title.. Did you pass?..................

19. Do you now or have you ever used intoxicating liquors? (Answer "Yes" or "No")..............................

If so, to what extent? Be specific......................................

20. Have you ever been arrested for the violation of any law or ordinance? No. If so, explain fully..................................

21. Are you the sole support of yourself? Yes. Of your family? Yes.

How many persons INCLUDING yourself are dependent on you for support? Two

If married, is your husband or wife working? No. Kind of employment?..................................

If a married woman, what was your maiden name?..................................

22. Are you in good health? Yes. Name each serious illness or accident you have had in the last three years: None.

Do you have any defect of sight, hearing, speech or limb? No. If so, what?...................................

23. In your own handwriting state here the personal qualifications which you believe will qualify you for the position for which you are applying: During my service with the Pickwick Corporation and subsidiaries I took inventory many times, and also installed and supervised a perpetual inventory system. I worked on the perpetual inventory personally and assisted in the physical inventory each six months.

It is understood by me that any willful misstatement of facts in this application disqualifies me in the examination and forfeits my right to appeal.

Application sent by mail must be sworn to before a notary public.

24. The following oath must be taken before the Secretary of the Civil Service Commission or one of his assistants or before a Notary Public.

AFFIDAVIT

I solemnly swear that the answers I have made to each and all of the foregoing questions are full and true to the best of my knowledge and belief.

And further, in order that the Los Angeles County Civil Service Commission may be fully informed as to my personal character and qualifications for employment, I refer to each of my former employers and to any other persons who may have information concerning me, agreeing, as this information is furnished at my express request and for my benefit, to hold such persons harmless and I do hereby release them from any and all liability for damage of whatsoever nature on account of furnishing such information.

Signature of Applicant

WILSON A. HOLLAND

(The blanks below to be filled in only by deputy in the Civil Service Office)

Subscribed and sworn to before me Nov. 3, 1932.

L. E. LAMPTON,

County Clerk

By M. H. JETER

[Endorsed]: Government's Exhibit B. Filed Feb. 28, 1934.

Mr. Di Girolamo: Now, Mr. Gerlack, have you got those duplicate depositions?

Mr. Gerlack: I have.

(The documents referred to were handed to Mr. Di Girolamo.)

Mr. Di Girolamo: Defendant's Exhibits A to F are admitted in evidence?

Mr. Gerlack: That is right.

Mr. Di Girolamo: Without objection?

Mr. Gerlack: No, objection to anything that is over his signature. I assume whatever you read was over his signature.

Mr. Di Girolamo: Yes.

Mr. Gerlack: No objection to that.

Mr. Di Girolamo: The deposition of Homer S. Howe is the one I would like to read first.

Mr. Gerlack: I have it right here.

Mr. Di Girolamo: Will you waive all of the preliminaries, Mr. Gerlack?

Mr. Gerlack: Yes. I will take the stand and read the answers, and you can ask the questions.

Mr. Di Girolamo: All right. (Reading deposition. [195]

"HOMER S. HOWE,

produced as a witness on behalf of the defendant, having been duly cautioned and sworn by the Notary Public to tell the truth, the whole truth, and nothing but the truth, testified as follows:

"Direct Examination

"Mr. Lynch:

"Q. Will you state your full name?

"A. Homer S. Howe.

"Q. What is your business or occupation?

"A. Supervisor of Records, State Relief Administration.

"Q. Although your answer is almost self-explanatory, will you give us a detailed resume of your official duties with the State Relief Administration?

"A. Well, it is the filing and storing of all state relief administration records.

"Q. And those records to which you refer, are they the official records of the State of California in connection with the administration of relief?

"A. Yes.

(Deposition of Homer S. Howe.)

"Q. Mr. Howe, you were subpoenaed to bring with you a record of the employment of Wilson Holland during a period of time when he was employed by the State Emergency Relief Administration in connection with the transient service, is that correct? A. Yes. [196]

"Q. And as I understand from previous conversation with you, you have prepared a transcript of the official records of the State of California relating to his employment, is that correct?

"A. A transcript of payroll payments only.

"Q. Now, did you personally make that transcript? A. I did.

"Q. And where did you secure the information that is reflected in that transcript?

"A. From the payrolls themselves.

"Q. And those were the official payrolls?

"A. Yes.

"Q. Those payrolls are required to be kept by law? A. Yes.

"Q. And they are kept in the regular course of business? A. Yes.

"Q. And they are the official records of the State of California? A. Yes.

"Q. And they are under your direct custody, control and direction, are they? A. Yes.

"Q. You have just signed that transcript in the presence of Mr. Gerlack and myself, is that correct?

"A. I did. [197]

(Deposition of Homer S. Howe.)

"Q. May I see it, please? A. Yes.

"(Document handed to Mr. Lynch.)

"Q. And as I understand it, this payroll reflects by weeks the amounts of money and the number of the check by which Mr. Holland was paid for his services rendered to the State Relief Administration? A. Yes.

"Q. And this is a true and correct copy of the official records of the State of California?

"A. It is a certified copy.

"Q. And this reflects his entire period of employment?

"A. No, it does not. The period from December 13th, 1933, to June 6th, we do not have those records. They are in Sacramento.

"Q. And who has charge of those records?

"A. Mr. J. M. Roberts.

"Mr. Lynch: Now, Mr. Gerlack, if you have no objection as to the authenticity of this record—I believe it speaks for itself—I will offer it in evidence at this time.

"Mr. Gerlack: I have no objection.

"Mr. Lynch: I offer in evidence at this time the certified transcript of the schedule of F.E.R.A. salary payments made to Wilson A. Holland from June 7, 1934, to [198] July 25, 1935, as prepared and certified by the witness Homer S. Howe.

"Mr. Gerlack: Now, let me state this: I do not want to stipulate to the accuracy of that, but I will

(Deposition of Homer S. Howe.)
waive any possible objection that it is not the best evidence. And this witness has stated that he is the custodian of the records—is that right?

"A. Yes, sir.

"Mr. Gerlack:

"Q. And you examined and compared the originals of this transcript? A. Yes.

"Mr. Gerlack:

"Q. And this transcript is a correct representation of what those original records show?

"A. Yes.

"Mr. Gerlack: I will offer no objection to the form of it. Of course, I won't stipulate to the accuracy of it.

"Mr. Lynch: Of course, the checks will be offered in evidence at a later time and will speak for themselves. That is all.

"Cross Examination

"Mr. Gerlack:

"Q. You didn't know Mr. Holland personally?

"A. No, I did not. I never met him.

"Q. Did you examine the records to ascertain whether [199] they showed any leaves of absence on account of sickness?

"A. Well, this is off the record.

"(Unreported discussion.)

"Mr. Gerlack: Just put that in the record.

"A. The record reflected no detail on Mr. Holland's sick leave or vacations.

(Deposition of Homer S. Howe.)

"Q. Well, would his personnel records ordinarily show his leaves of absence on account of sikness or annual leave?

"A. It is a part of the regulations that they should, but they don't.

"Q. Was there any reason why they didn't in his case? Do you know why the exception was made in his case? A. No.

"Q. What did the personnel jacket show?

"A. Merely that Mr. Holland was connected with the transient service.

"Q. No explanation was made as to why no personnel records were made in this case?

"A. No.

"Q. Do you know Mr. Carleton?

"A. No, I do not.

"Q. The records show that Mr. Carleton was his immediate superior at this time, is that correct?

"A. Yes, Mr. Carleton was the director in charge.

"Q. The records show that at that time? [200]

"A. Yes.

"Q. Who was responsible for keeping those records?

"A. A personnel officer, and we have had some——and this is off the record.

"(Unreported discussion.)

"Mr. Gerlack: Put that in the record.

"A. We had half a dozen of them, and I don't know which particular one would be responsible for this.

(Deposition of Homer S. Howe.)

"Q. Where are those personnel records now, if you know?

"A. The personnel records in connection with the transient records are on file at 677 Mission Street.

"Q. And is that where you are located?

"A. Yes, sir.

"Q. And you have charge of those records?

"A. Yes, sir.

"Q. This missing personnel record in his case, would that be in Sacramento, if you know?

"A. No, it would not.

"Q. You don't know where it is?

"A. No, and no one else does.

"Q. Personnel records are ordinarily kept of every one, are they?

"A. All administrative employees have personnel jackets set up for them.

"Q. And there is no notation in the record as to where [201] his particular record is?

"A. No.

"Q. By the way, you have made a diligent search to ascertain whether or not the personnel record was there? A. Yes, I did.

"Q. And you couldn't find it? A. No.

"Mr. Gerlack: That is all.

"Redirect Examination

"Mr. Lynch:

"Q. Mr. Holland was an administrative employee? A. Yes.

(Deposition of Homer S. Howe.)

"Q. As opposed to one receiving relief?

"A. Yes.

"Mr. Lynch: That is all.

"Recross Examination

"Mr. Gerlack:

"Q. This was part of the relief program, was it not, the work that he was doing? A. Yes.

"Mr. Gerlack: That is all

"Mr. Lynch: That is all.

(Signed) "HOMER S. HOWE."

Mr. Di Girolamo: Now, I would like to read into the record the payroll, schedule of F. E. R. A. salary payments made to Wilson A. Holland from June 7, 1934 to July 25, [202] 1935.

"June 7, 1934	$19.52
14	34.60
21	34.60
28	34.60
July 5, 1934	34.60
12	34.60
19	34.60
26	34.60
Aug. 2	34.60
9	34.60
16	34.60
23	34.60
30	34.60

Sept. 6, 1934	34.60
13	34.60
20	34.60
27	34.60
Oct. 4, 1934	34.60
11	34.60
18	34.60
25	34.60
Nov. 1, 1934	34.60
8	37.00
15	37.00
22	37.00
29	37.00
Dec. 6, 1934	37.00
13	37.00
20	37.00
27	37.00
Jan. 3, 1935	37.00
10	37.00
17	37.00
24	37.00
31	37.00
Feb. 7, 1935	37.00
14	37.00
21	37.00
28	37.00
Mar. 7, 1935	33.30
14	33.30
21	33.30
28	33.30

Apr. 4, 1935	37.00
11	37.00
18	37.00
25	37.00
May 2, 1935	37.00
9	39.25

[203]

May 16, 1935	$39.25
23	39.25
30	39.25
June 6, 1935	39.25
13	39.25
20	39.25
27	39.25
July 4, 1935	39.25
11	39.25
18	39.25
25	39.25"

Mr. Di Girolamo: I offer this in evidence for the purpose of the record.

The Clerk: Defendant's Exhibit G.

(The document referred to was received in evidence and marked "Government's Exhibit G.")

GOVERNMENT'S EXHIBIT G.

United States of America Exhibit One.

[Seal]

California

State Relief Administration

Schedule of F.E.R.A. Salary Payments Made To Wilson A. Holland From June 7, 1934, To July 25, 1935:

Week Ending	Payroll No.	Amount	Check No.
June 7, 1934	1	$19.52	80756
14	2	34.60	81088
21	3	34.60	81411
28	4	34.60	81750
July 5, 1934	29	34.60	109442
12	36	34.60	127986
19	45	34.60	141194
26	51	34.60	163500
Aug. 2, 1934	57	34.60	203491
9	64	34.60	230779
16	71	34.60	271943
23	79	34.60	312975
30	90	34.60	348963
Sept. 6, 1934	97	34.60	389796
13	107	34.60	429477
20	119	34.60	470644
27	131	34.60	512249
Oct. 4, 1934	138	34.60	553861
11	146	34.60	590317
18	152	34.60	38266
25	158	34.60	81412
Nov. 1, 1934	164	34.60	133009
8	169	37.00	226209
15	176	37.00	62722
22	183	37.00	72114
29	188	37.00	90573

Week Ending	Payroll No.	Amount	Check No.
Dec. 6, 1934	198	37.00	103382
13	204	37.00	127182
20	212	37.00	134365
27	217	37.00	151239
Jan. 3, 1935	222	37.00	155948
10	227	37.00	11187
17	233	37.00	167228
24	238	37.00	186026
31	243	37.00	44490
Feb. 7, 1935	248	37.00	203987
14	254	37.00	227692
21	261	37.00	238117
28	267	37.00	254912
Mar. 7, 1935	272	33.30	249084
14	277	33.30	272737
21	282	33.30	124551
28	287	33.30	295934
Apr. 4, 1935	293	37.00	296805
11	298	37.00	300314
18	303	37.00	302398
25	309	37.00	333861
May 2, 1935	314	37.00	357087
9	319	39.25	349972
16	325	39.25	394323
23	330	39.25	215053
30	335	39.25	387902
June 6, 1935	341	39.25	454934
13	347	39.25	518424
20	352	39.25	583962
27	357	39.25	638353
July 4, 1935	362	39.25	693144
11	367	39.25	766563
18	372	39.25	827172
25	377	39.25	889741
	Total	$2,164.32	

I certify this schedule of salary payments to be drawn from F.E.R.A. payroll records and that it is correct and true.

HOMER S. HOWE,
Supervisor of Records,
State Relief Administration,
San Francisco, California.

[Endorsed]: Government's Exhibit G. Filed Feb. 28, 1939.

Mr. Di Girolamo: Mr. Gerlack, have you a copy of the deposition of Clarence H. Smith and Otho H. Close?

Mr. Gerlack: I have it right here (handing document to Mr. Di Girolamo).

Mr. Di Girolamo: (Reading deposition of Clarence H. Smith.)

"Testimony of

CLARENCE SMITH,

witness produced on behalf of plaintiff, Sworn

"Direct Examination

"By G. B. Hjelm, Esq., counsel on behalf of defendant herein:

"Q. What is your name?

"A. Clarence H. Smith.

"Q. What position do you hold with the State of Cali- [204] fornia at the present time?

(Deposition of Clarence Smith.)

"A. Deputy State Controller.

"Q. And how long have you held that position?

"A. Approximately fifteen or sixteen years.

"Q. Are you then in the warrant department of the State Controller's Office?

"A. I have charge of the disbursing and auditing division.

"Q. And you have been served with a subpoena duces tecum in this case to produce certain warrants and documents? A. I have.

"Q. Will you hand me them in order?

"(Witness hands documents to Mr. Hjelm).

"Q. Now you have handed me certain documents and papers. What are they?

"A. They are claims, as filed with the State Controller, on the part of the Department, and also in conformity with those claims, warrants of the Controller in payment.

"Q. Now, you have been and you are the——these are the official records of the State of California, kept in the usual course of business and required to be kept? A. Yes.

"Q. Now, I will show you—I withdraw that——I will show you a paper here—I will show you what appears [205] to be warrant No. C5145, payable from support of State Narcotic Hospital, and I will ask you to state what that warrant is?

"A. This particular warrant was issued under date of April 7, 1933, in payment of salary due

(Deposition of Clarence Smith.)

Mr. Wilson A. Holland as Institutional Bookkeeper Grade 1, for the period of March 1st to March 31st, 1933, in the sum of $120.00.

"Mr. Gerlack: In view of the stipulation reserving all objections at the time of trial, I won't urge any objection at this time.

"Mr. Hjelm: Do these records disclose the position that Wilson A. Holland held with the State of California for the period from March 1st to March 31st, 1933?

"A. Yes, it is Institutional Bookkeeper, Grade 1.

"Q. And that was in what department?

"A. Narcotic State Hospital.

"Q. In what place?

"A. Spadra, California.

"Q. Does this document—what does this next, second page of this document that you have handed me, what does that purport to show?

"A. This is simply what we term 'Institutional Payroll' setting forth the name of the employees, the capacity in which they are serving, and the rate of compensation per month or per diem, whichever the case may be.

"Q. Does the name of Wilson A. Holland, plaintiff in [206] this action, appear thereon?

"A. Yes.

"Q. And it appears only once on that sheet?

"A. That is correct.

"Q. Now, does his name appear on the sheet following? A. Yes.

(Deposition of Clarence Smith.)

"Q. And what does that sheet purport to show?

"A. This covers maintenance allowance on the part of the Institution for the same period stated before—for the full calendar month of March, 1933, in the sum of $11.00.

"Q. What does—what do you mean, 'maintenance'?

"A. He is allowed this because he could have taken his meals at the Institution—he could have taken maintenance at the Institution, and he wished to do otherwise and they gave him that allowance.

"Q. That was for what period?

"A. March, 1933. Full month of March, 1933.

"Q. And the vouchers annexed to said documents, one appearing to be in the sum of $120.00 and one in the sum of $11.00—that has what significance with respect to this payroll?

"A. Well, the only thing, that is, warrants have been issued in conformity with the Institutional claim filed with us by the officials of the Narcotic State Hospital.

"Q. And the first page seems to be headed 'Claim;' [207] What does that purport to be?

"A. That is the Department of Institutions' claim.

"Q. And does the name of plaintiff, Holland, appear anywhere? A. On the first page.

"Q. Who makes out such claim?

"A. The officials of the Narcotic State Hospital.

"Q. Is that in due course of business?

(Deposition of Clarence Smith.)

"A. That is in conformity with the statute or law.

"Q. And does Mr. Holland's name appear anywhere in the—does Wilson A. Holland's name appear on those payroll documents—does that name correspond with the payee of the vouchers?

"A. That is right——

"Q. One and the same person? A. Yes.

"Q. Do said vouchers have endorsements thereon showing payment of those vouchers?

"A. The warrants bear the first endorsement, Wilson A. Holland.

"Q. And the second one also?

"A. The second warrant—both vouchers, both warrants.

"Q. These documents now, that I pin together here (pinning documents) are the original records and entries in the—in your State department? [208]

"A. Yes.

"Q. I offer them in evidence, as Defendant's Exhibit 1.

"Mr. Hjelm: Will you stipulate, Mr. Gerlack, that before these depositions be forwarded to the Clerk of the Court, that these records may be photostated and the originals returned to the State Department?

"Mr. Gerlack: No, for this reason—I want to be cooperative, but I have tried a good many of

(Deposition of Clarence Smith.)

these cases, and half the time they reduce the photostatic copies down to a third or a fourth the original size, you can't read them, so I have lately taken the position the only way the ends of justice can be served is to send down the originals. I am willing to stipulate that immediately after the trial they can be returned and the photostatic copies sent in place, but I have had some very bad results and experience in photostats.

"Witness: I can assure you they will be as good as the originals—same size in every respect—but we can't let these originals out of our possession——they are State property and we are not allowed to let them out of our possession.

"Mr. Hjelm: Well, can you produce these originals at the trial, then?

"A. Yes, if we are subpoenaed.

"Q. What is the title of your position?

"A. Deputy State Controller. [209]

"Q. As such are you the official custodian of the State of California of warrants covering the State Narcotic Hospital at Spadra from the period April 7, 1933, to July 9, 1934 mentioned in the subpoena—the subpoena states for the period from April 10, 1933, to August 15, 1933 or any other period?

"A. These cover the period from March 1, 1933, to July 9, 1934.

"Q. Have you—on what basis were employees employed at the hospital during those dates, paid?

(Deposition of Clarence Smith.)

"A. Are you speaking of all employees?

"Q. On monthly, daily or weekly basis?

"A. I could not say without checking, but ordinarily I would say on a monthly basis—the great majority of them.

"Q. Take the first month covering that period——what does the payroll show concerning whether or not Wilson A. Holland was an employee of the State Hospital, State Narcotic Hospital at Spadra?

"A. He appears on here as Institutional Bookkeeper, Grade 1, for the period March 1, to March 31st, inclusive, at the rate of $120.00 per month——March, 1933.

"Q. Does the record show—include the vouchers for the payment of $120.00 and $11.00 as per the State records? A. Yes.

"Mr. Hjelm: Then I will offer this as defendant's Ex- [210] hibit 2.

"Q. Have you the same records for the month of April?

"A. Yes. Covering the calendar month of April, 1933, the controller issued warrant A13355 for the amount of $120.00; warrant issued in conformity with payroll claim signed by the officials of the Narcotic State Hospital for Wilson A. Holland.

"Mr. Gerlack: I will stipulate that the witness may read from the records and the records may be returned to the legal custodian or that photostatic copies thereof may be substituted and may be submitted.

(Deposition of Clarence Smith.)

"Mr. Hjelm: You will stipulate we may substitute photostats?

"Mr. Gerlack: Yes, provided they are full size photostats.

"Mr. Hjelm: Is this the original record thereof?

"Witness: Yes.

"Mr. Hjelm: I offer it in evidence as defendant's Exhibit 2.

"Q. You have like records with reference to Wilson A. Holland for the month of May, 1933, as Bookkeeper Grade 1?

"A. Yes. Covering the calendar month of May, 1933, the controller issued Warrant No. F18988, issued June 8, 1933, in favor of Wilson A. Holland, for the sum of $120.00, covering compensation of Wilson A. Holland as Institutional Bookkeeper Grade 1, for the Narcotic State Hospital for the [211] month of May, 1933. Also, Warrant F19020, issued in favor of Wilson Holland, dated June 8, 1933, in the sum of $11.00, the same representing maintenance allowance for the same period of time.

"Mr. Hjelm: I offer that in evidence as defendant's Exhibit 3.

"Q. You have like records with reference to Wilson A. Holland for the month of June, 1933?

"A. Yes, covering the calendar month of June, 1933, for the sum of $120.00, in favor of Wilson A. Holland, covering compensation of Wilson A. Holland as Institutional Bookkeeper, Grade 1, for the

(Deposition of Clarence Smith.)

Narcotic State Hospital for the month of June 1933. Also, Warrant No. E4320, issued July 18, 1933, covering the same period, June, 1933, for the sum of $11.00, the same representing maintenance allowance for the same period of time.

"Mr. Hjelm: I offer it in evidence as defendant's Exhibit 4.

"Q. You have like records with reference to Wilson A. Holland for the month of July, 1933, as Bookkeeper Grade 1, for the Narcotic State Hospital at Spadra?

"A. Yes, covering the calendar month of July, 1933, the controller issued Warrant No. E10,905, issued August 15, 1933, in favor of Wilson A. Holland for the sum of $120.00 covering compensation of Wilson A. Holland as Institutional Bookkeeper Grade 1, for the Narcotic State Hospital for the [212] month of July, 1933. Also, Warrant No. E11,049, issued August 15, 1933, in the sum of $11.00, the same representing maintenance allowance for the same period of time.

"Mr. Hjelm: I offer it in evidence as defendant's Exhibit 5.

"Q. You have like records with reference to Wilson A. Holland for the month of August, 1933?

"A. No, on January 10, 1934, the controller issued Warrant No. A49,866, payable to Wilson A. Holland, in the sum of $84.68, issued in payment of compensation for the month of December, 1933,

(Deposition of Clarence Smith.)

as Bookkeeper for the State Relief Administration."

Mr. Gerlack: Although this record is inaccurate, although it does not say he was paid for August, 1933, I will stipulate he testified this morning he received $120.00 plus $11.00, although, of course, this record does not show it.

Mr. Di Girolamo: Thank you, Mr. Gerlack. Let's get on with the deposition.

Mr. Gerlack: He received it and I want to stipulate to it.

Mr. Di Girolamo: "What is the next document?"

Mr. Gerlack: That is Line 30, Page 9.

Mr. Di Girolamo: (Reading)

"Mr. Hjelm: I offer it in evidence as defendant's Exhibit 6. [213]

"Q. What is the next document?

"A. On February 15, 1934, the controller issued Warrant No. A63,421, in favor of Wilson A. Holland, for the sum of $125.00, issued in payment of compensation for Wilson A. Holland, Bookkeeper, for the month of January, 1934, for the State Relief Administration.

"Mr. Hjelm: I offer it in evidence as defendant's Exhibit 7.

"Q. What is the next document?

"A. Controller's Warrant No. H58,867, issued March 8, 1934, payable to Wilson A. Holland, for

(Deposition of Clarence Smith.)

the sum of $125.00, covering the month of February, 1934, in payment of compensation of Wilson A. Holland as Bookkeeper for the State Relief Administration for the month of February, 1934. In conformity with payrolls.

"Mr. Hjelm: I offer it in evidence as defendant's Exhibit 8.

"Q. What is the next document?

"A. Controller's Warrant No. A81881, dated April 17, 1934, payable to Wilson A. Holland, for the sum of $125.00, covering compensation as Bookkeeper for the State Relief Administration for the month of March, 1934.

"Mr. Hjelm: I offer it in evidence as defendant's Exhibit 9.

"Q. You have like records for April, 1934?

"A. On May 5, 1934, the controller issued Warrant No. [214] F-88505, in favor of Wilson A. Holland for compensation as bookkeeper for the State Relief Administration for the month of April, 1934, in the sum of $135.00.

"Mr. Hjelm: I offer it in evidence as defendant's Exhibit 10.

"Q. What is the next one?

"A. On June 5, 1934, the controller issued warrant No. D66591, for the sum of $19.35 in favor of Wilson Holland, as compensation for Bookkeeper Grade 2, for the period from May 27th, to May 31st (five day period) 1934, at the rate of $120.00 per month, at the Preston School of Industry.

(Deposition of Clarence Smith.)

"Mr. Hjelm: I offer it in evidence as defendant's Exhibit 11.

"Q. What is next?

"A. On July 14th, 1934, the controller issued warrant D-3873, in favor of Wilson A. Holland, for $12.00, covering compensation as Bookkeeper Grade 2, for the period from June 1st to 3rd, inclusive, at the rate of $120.00 per month, for the Preston School of Industry.

"Mr. Hjelm: I offer it in evidence as defendant's Exhibit 12.

"Q. Is that all of the records you produced in pursuance of the subpoena duces tecum?

"A. Yes.

"Q. And all of the records you have now produced and [215] which have been offered in evidence in your presence here are the original records of the State of California, of the State Controller? A. They are.

"Q. And you have had the custody thereof during that period of time? A. Yes.

"Q. And such records—are such records kept in due course of business and pursuant to the rules and regulations and the laws of the State of California? A. They are.

"Mr. Hjelm: I believe that covers everything.

"Cross Examination

"By Mr. Gerlack, counsel for plaintiff herein:

"Q. Mr. Smith, do the records show why his employment was terminated on any of these jobs?

(Deposition of Clarence Smith.)

"A. There is nothing to show in our department or on these records.

"Q. And if his employment were terminated at Spadra on account of his health, that would not show?

"A. No—these are strictly payroll.

"Q. They would not show whether or not his services were satisfactory? A. No.

"Q. In fact they do not show anything of a personal nature? [216] A. That is right.

"Mr. Gerlack: That is all.

"Mr. Hjelm: Do you know anything about whether his services were satisfactory?

"A. No, I haven't any idea whatsoever.

"Mr. Gerlack: You do not know him personally? A. No.

"Mr. Hjelm: Do the records you have produced and which have been introduced in evidence cover the plaintiff's employment at Spadra?

"A. That is right.

"Q. Do they also show with reference to transient services?

"A. Do they mean by that, Relief Administration—there is a division in there called transient service, it might refer to that.

"Q. Does it disclose his services with the S. R. A. and Preston School of Industry?

"A. Yes. State Relief Administration and Preston School of Industry are included here.

(Deposition of Clarence Smith.)

"Mr. Gerlack: When he was at Preston, was he working for the S. R. A.?

"A. No. He apparently worked in three divisions of the government—Narcotic, under the department of Institutions; Preston; and Relief Administration.

"Q. When he was working for S. R. A. was that tran- [217] sient service?

"A. I could not say as to that, although they do have a division called transient service.

"Mr. Hjelm: You don't know of any other services than as reflected by these records?

"A. As far as I know this is all.

"Q. Whether he had any other services during such period of time you do not know?

"A. No, we have checked our files—this is all we find.

"Q. So far as his services for any other people are concerned you know of none? A. No.

"Mr. Gerlack: This shows all the money the State of California has paid him for salary?

"A. That is right.

"Mr. Hjelm: It will be stipulated then that in lieu of the originals that photostats thereof may be made and transmitted with the deposition.

"Mr. Gerlack: Full size photostats.

"Mr. Hjelm. Then that is the stipulation and these original records may be returned to the witness; are they now in order here? A. Yes.

(Deposition of Clarence Smith.)

"Mr. Gerlack: And it is understood that the photostats will be full size photostats of the entire page, of [218] each page?

"Mr. Smith: I will make them up in the same fashion as they are here.

"Mr. Hjelm: That will be all.

"Mr. Gerlack: That will be all.

(Signed) CLARENCE H. SMITH."

Mr. Di Girolamo: I think the Court wants to recess at this time.

The Court: How long will it take you to finish this reading?

Mr. Di Girolamo: I think this will take about an hour, and then I have a doctor to put on the stand.

The Court: Very well, the Court will adjourn at this time.

Bear in mind the admonition I gave you this morning.

The Clerk: The Court will adjourn until 10:00 o'clock tomorrow morning.

(Whereupon, at 5:00 o'clock P. M., an adjournment was taken until 10:00 o'clock A. M., March 1, 1939.) [219]

State of California,
County of Los Angeles—ss.

I, Byron Oyler, hereby certify that on the 28th day of February, 1939, I was the acting court reporter of the United States District Court for the Southern District of California, that as such reporter I took down in Shorthand writing all proceedings in the case of: Wilson Alvin Holland, Plaintiff, vs. United States of America, Defendant, No. 8415-RJ, Law, which was heard before the Hon. Jeremiah Neterer, Judge Presiding, on the date hereinabove mentioned.

I further certify that the attached transcript consisting of pages 1 to 179, both inclusive, are a full, true and correct transcription of my said shorthand notes, and that the same is a full, true and complete transcript of said proceedings.

Dated this 25th day of August, 1939.

BYRON OYLER,
Reporter.

Subscribed and sworn to before me this 25th day of August, 1939.

BYRON OYLER,
Notary Public in and for the County of Los Angeles, State of California. [220]

Los Angeles, California
Wednesday, March 1, 1939
10:00 o'Clock A. M.

The Court: Note all jurors present.

Mr. Gerlack: It is so stipulated.

Mr. Di Girolamo: It is so stipulated.

The Court: Proceed.

(The deposition of Otho H. Close was read by Mr. Gerlack and Mr. Meindl as follows:)

"Testimony of

OTHO H. CLOSE,

witness produced on behalf of defendant, Sworn.

"Direct Examination

"By G. B. Hjelm, counsel for defendant:

"Q. What is your name?

"A. Otho—O-t-h-o H. Close.

"Q. And you are the Superintendent of the Preston School of Industry at Ione, California?

"A. Yes.

"Q. And you have held that position for how many years last past?

"A. Superintendent since August, 1920.

"Q. Do you remember one Wilson Alvin Holland, also known as Wilson A. Holland?

"A. Yes.

"Q. When did you see him? [228]

"A. First on June 11, 1934.

"Q. And then what place did you see him?

(Deposition of Otho H. Close.)

"A. At the Preston School of Industry, Ione.

"Q. Was he employed at that institution?

"A. He was.

"Q. And upon what date did he commence his employment at that institution?

"A. May 27, 1934 he started to work.

"Q. And he continued to work there until when? A. June 3, 1934.

"Q. At what salary?

"A. Salary of $120.00 per month and maintenance.

"Q. Does that mean $120.00 includes maintenance? A. That's right.

"Q. Or $120.00 per month and maintenance besides?

"A. He received $120.00 per month and his room and board valued at $35.00 by the State.

"Q. Now, do you recall the incident of his leaving your institution? A. I do.

"Q. What did he state, if anything, as to why he was leaving?

"A. He stated that he was lonesome; that the distance from Los Angeles to Ione was great and that he believed it was best for him to go back and accept his old position which was still open for him if he wished to return. I recall [229] that conversation clearly.

"Q. Was that job with the transient service?

"A. I do not recall that.

(Deposition of Otho H. Close.)

"Q. Have you with you the records of your institution and the cancelled vouchers for his pay during that period?

"A. The cancelled vouchers were presented by Mr. Smith.

"Q. By Clarence Smith whose testimony has been taken here? A. That is right.

"Q. Do you have any records there with respect to his being at your institution?

"A. Personal records only.

"Q. Let me see that document. (Witness hands card to Mr. Hjelm).

"Mr. Gerlack: These are original records?

"A. They are.

"Mr. Hjelm: Kept under your supervision and custody? A. Yes.

"Mr. Hjelm: I offer the same in evidence as defendant's Exhibit 1-a.

"Q. This appears to be a pink paper here, State of California, Department of Finance, Division of Personnel and Organization, Report of Emergency Appointment. What does that purport to show?

"A. That is form 617. He was appointed on the date mentioned by the Superintendent of Preston School of Industry [230] on what is known as an emergency appointment which is effective for fifteen days.

"Q. This is the original record? A. Yes.

"Mr. Hjelm: I offer the same in evidence as Defendant's Exhibit 2-a.

(Deposition of Otho H. Close.)

"Witness: Also, there is form 626, known as Certification of Eligibles, to the appointing authority, Certificate No. 24,403, which includes the name of Wilson A. Holland as eligible for appointment.

"Mr. Hjelm: This is an original entry, also?

"A. Yes.

"Q. Which has been kept under your supervision and custody? A. Yes.

"Mr. Hjelm: I offer it in evidence as defendant's Exhibit 3-A.

"Witness: This is form 620, report of separation, to the Division of Personnel and Organization, indicating the separation from service of Wilson A. Holland, from the Preston School of Industry, effective June 3, 1934. Reason for separation given, Resignation.

"Q. That applies to Wilson A. Holland?

"A. Wilson A. Holland.

"Q. And this is an original entry and record in your office? [231] A. Yes.

"Mr. Hjelm: I offer the same in evidence as defendant's Exhibit 4-a.

"Witness: This is his resignation, signed in his own hand.

"Mr. Hjelm: You recall that he signed this resignation on June 3, 1934?

"A. I do not—but I assume that it is correct.

"Mr. Hjelm: This is what purports to be the resignation of Wilson A. Holland, directed and addressed to you, Mr. O. H. Close, Superintendent

(Deposition of Otho H. Close.)

Preston School of Industry, Waterman, California, dated June 3, 1934, a part of the record that you have kept with respect to Wilson A. Holland during the period of time he was employed in your institution, in due course and as a part of the original records of that institution? A. That is correct.

"Mr. Hjelm: I offer the same in evidence as defendant's Exhibit 5-a.

"Witness: There are three copies of telegrams, which I think probably are of no interest.

"(Mr. Hjelm looks over telegrams).

"Mr. Hjelm: No, I don't think so.

"Q. Now, you recall the veteran in question—you recall Wilson A. Holland, and I will ask you whether or not there was anything in his behavior, conduct, and/or appear- [232] ance which would—which did indicate to you that he was otherwise unwell?"

Mr. Gerlack: We will waive objection. At this point, your Honor, I objected to the question, but we will waive the objection.

"Mr. Hjelm: What was his appearance?

"A. I recall at least three times I met him—once when he entered the service, and once when he talked to me about retiring, and I believe I met him when he left the school. He did not refer to any ill health to my recollection—he appeared to be a man slightly underweight, but made no complaints about illness—his only reference to himself was the fact that he was lonesome.

"Mr. Hjelm: That's all.

(Deposition of Otho H. Close.)

"Cross Examination

"By Alvin Gerlack: Counsel for plaintiff.

"Q. You recall him personally?

"A. Yes, I do.

"Q. Will you describe him?

"A. As I recall, he was a man at that time about forty years of age, light complected, I would judge about five feet ten in height.

"Q. How much did he weigh?

"A. In my opinion about one hundred and sixty pounds at that time.

"Q. Do you remember the color of his hair? [233]

"A. Well, as I recall it was light.

"Q. Color of his eyes? A. Blue.

"Q. Do you recall, Mr. Close—by the way, did you order a physical examination of him when he entered the institution? A. I did not.

"Q. It was a practice to require that, was it not?

"A. The new employees are examined by the Personnel Board—that is eligible employees, and at that time the State Department of Institutions had not established the practice of examining all of its new employees.

"Q. You are sure of that? A. Yes.

"Q. Do you recall about Mr.—isn't it a fact that while he was at the school for final interview with you he mentioned—you mentioned to him that under a new rule it would be necessary for new employees to pass psyhical examinations?

(Deposition of Otho H. Close.)

"A. There is a telegram here which indicates there was some correspondence or discussion about physical examination and this wire is so long ago I don't remember the incident.

"Mr. Gerlack: May I see that wire? (Witness hands wire to Mr. Gerlack.) He came to work when?

"A. The records show May 27, 1934. [234]

"Q. He came to work May 27, 1934?

"A. That is right.

"Q. And this wire shows you wired him as follows:

> "Quote: Mr. Wilson Holland, 1469 Lemoyne Street, Los Angeles. Have talked with the Department of Institutions regarding physical examination. Not necessary for you to submit to additional physical examination for employment. Will expect you May 26.
>
> Signed O. H. CLOSE.
>
> End quote.

"Q. And that was in answer to his telegram to you dated May 15, 1934, from Los Angeles, addressed to Superintendent Preston School of Industry, as follows:

"Quote: Must notify superiors today of resignation. Advise decision of physical examination. Signed Wm. Holland, 1469 Lemoyne Street. End quote.

"Q. You received that telegram from him and the previously read telegram was your reply?

"A. Yes.

(Deposition of Otho H. Close.)

"Q. I will ask that those telegrams be submitted in evidence.

"Q. And you also sent this telegram to your representative, Norman E. Holden, 908 California Building, Los Angeles, California?—what is his position?"

Mr. Gerlack: At this point there are two typographical errors in the answer. They should read: "A Deputy payroll officer."

(Reading) [235]

"Q. What was the occasion for your telegraphing about a physical examination?

"A. I have no recollection of that whatsoever—I don't know, other than that it is in the records.

"Q. If he were to state that he had an interview with you and that you mentioned that under recent ruling it would be necessary that new employees of the Department of Institutions pass a physical examination, you couldn't say you did not tell him that? A. No.

"Q. And if he were to state after returning to his hotel at Ione he telephoned you that he might not be able to pass such an examination and you agreed to dispense with it, you couldn't say either that you did not tell him that, either?"

Mr. Meindl: There is an objection to that as being incompetent, irrelevant and immaterial.

Mr. Gerlack: I think it is very material, your Honor.

(Deposition of Otho H. Close.)

The Court: It may be answered. Read the answer.

"Mr. Gerlack: If he were to testify under oath that he phoned you from his hotel in Ione to the school, that he might not pass such a physical examination and that you mentioned to him that you would dispense with the requirement or physical examination in view of the fact that he had once worked for the Department, you can't say you would not remember that? [236]

"A. No, I would not remember a detail of that type.

"Mr. Hjelm: Do you have any recollection of making such a statement to him? A. No.

"Mr. Hjelm: Then, so far as you are concerned your statement that you could, in response to his question would be only in so far as it is possible, that you might have forgotten?

"A. That is correct.

"Mr. Hjelm: But you recall this man?

"A. Yes.

"Q. And I will ask you whether or not, if such a statement had been made to you by him, would you recall that?

"A. I might, and I might not, because we employ forty or fifty a year.

"Q. According to your best recollection did you make such a statement?

"A. I don't recall it—it might or might not be true.

(Deposition of Otho H. Close.)

"Q. Do you recall anything now that would have caused you to have made such a statement?

"A. Only that those telegrams in the folder here would indicate that the matter of his physical examination had been a subject of discussion at the time he was employed. [237]

"Q. Had he been disabled, then he would not be accepted in the service? A. No.

"Q. Then the fact that no physical examination was required, what would that indicate with respect to his condition of health?

"A. It indicated that in as much as he had been in the service, we did not request or desire an examination in order for him to work at the institution.

"Q. Would it indicate that so far as you were concerned he was in good health? A. Yes.

"Mr. Gerlack: As a matter of fact, if at that time he had been suffering from active tuberculosis you did not know that?

"A. If it were in a serious state, we might have recognized it. If it were in an incipient state, no.

"Q. If it were shown that in 1933, 1934, he was examined by a doctor——

"Mr. Hjelm: I object to that, no purpose——

"Mr. Gerlack: Withdraw that—for all you know, he might have had tuberculosis and you did not know it?

"Mr. Hjelm: Same objection, unless you limit it to appearance.

(Deposition of Otho H. Close.)

"Mr. Gerlack: What was his appearance?

"A. His appearance did not excite any suspicions in [238] regard to his health or I would have insisted on a physical examination. He might have been suffering with tuberculosis but not suffering to the extent that he gave indications of it to a casual observer.

"Q. If he had active tuberculosis do you know what symptoms——

"Mr. Hjelm: Object, no proper foundation laid—this witness is not a doctor and there is no showing that he is competent to give any testimony as to his being a tubercular patient or not.

"Mr. Gerlack: Do you know if he had tuberculosis or not? A. Not under the circumstances.

"Q. Did you ever see him cough or spit?

"A. No, not to my recollection—I saw him only a week and probably did not talk to him as long as we have been discussing the case here.

"Q. You just saw him on three occasions, very short, first when he came to work and when he discussed his resignation and when he left?

"A. Yes.

"Q. Did you—would you say you spent five minutes with him each time? A. All of that.

"Q. Did you ever see him at work?

"A. No.

"Mr. Gerlack: That is all. [239]

"Mr. Hjelm: So far as you are concerned, then, as a layman, you did not, or did you, observe any-

(Deposition of Otho H. Close.)

thing that would indicate he was otherwise than normal? A. No.

"Mr. Hjelm: That's all.

(Signed) "OTHO H. CLOSE."

Mr. Meindl: We will next take the deposition of Donald M. Merritt. Do you waive preliminaries?

Mr. Gerlack: Yes.

"DONALD M. MERRITT,

produced as a witness on behalf of the defendant, having been duly cautioned and sworn by the Notary Public to tell the truth, the whole truth, and nothing but the truth, testified as follows:

"Direct Examination

"Mr. Lynch:

"Q. Will you state your full name, please?

"A. Donald M. Merritt.

"Q. Where do you reside?

"A. 41 Arguello Boulevard, San Francisco.

"Q. What is your business or occupation?

"A. The accountant in charge of the Treasury Accounts Office of the United States Treasury Department, San Francisco, California.

"Q. And what duties are connected with your position?

"A. The control of funds appropriated under the emer- [240] gency relief acts to agencies in California, and to any agencies whose headquarters are

(Deposition of Donald M. Merritt.)

in San Francisco, but activities extending into the adjacent States.

"Q. Do you have charge of the accounts of the Treasury Department with relation to emergency relief appropriations and payments made thereunder?

"A. Yes, however, the vouchers are examined in the Treasury Accounts Office, and the disbursements are made through the disbursing clerk of the United States Treasury Department.

"Q. You have been subpoenaed to appear here and bring with you records relating to the employment of one Wilson Alvin Holland? A. Yes.

"Q. Have you brought those records with you?

"A. Yes.

"Q. Have you the records here now?

"A. Yes, sir.

"Q. Will you produce them, please?

"A. Yes.

"(Thereupon the witness handed records to Mr. Lynch.)

"Q. Will you state what records you are producing at this time?

"A. A copy of a letter of appointment of Mr. Holland under date of August 7, 1935; copy of a letter of extension of his appointment, dated June 30, 1936. [241]

"Mr. Gerlack: What are those dates?

"A. The first date was August 7, 1935, and the second date was June 30, 1936.

(Deposition of Donald M. Merritt.)

"Mr. Gerlack: Thank you.

"A. A copy of the separation notice dated August 17, 1936; a copy——

"Mr. Lynch: Just a moment.

"Q. You state these are copies. The originals are presumed to be in the possession of Mr. Holland, is that correct? A. Yes.

"Q. They having been sent out to him?

"A. Yes. A copy of a letter of the discontinuance of Mr. Holland's services from the office of the Secretary, under date of October 8, 1936; copy of the Personal History Statement, Standard Form 6 if you want that—signed by Mr. Holland, Application for Position, signed by Mr. Holland. There are two confirmations sent to previous employers. Do you want those?

"Mr. Lynch: No.

"A. The individual record of absence for the year 1935, and the individual record of absence for the year 1936.

"Q. Now, with relation to these records which you have identified, are these the official records of the United States Government? [242]

"A. Yes, they are file copies retained in the San Francisco office.

"Q. These are file copies retained in the San Francisco office? A. Yes.

"Q. And they are under your personal charge and supervision?

(Deposition of Donald M. Merritt.)

"A. To the extent that we have a personnel clerk who maintains the records. Technically they are under my direct supervision.

"Q. And these are records that are required to be kept by law? A. That is right.

"Q. And they are kept in the usual course of business? A. That is correct.

"Q. Mr. Merritt, at this time I show you a letter on the letterhead of the Treasury Department, dated October 8, 1936, addressed to Mr. Wilson A. Holland, and signed 'J. E. Harper, Chief, Division of Appointments,' and ask you if that is a copy of a letter which has been taken from the official file which you have just presented?

"A. Yes, sir.

"Q. And what is that letter?

"Mr. Gerlack: Just a moment. We object to that on the ground the letter is the best evidence." [243]

Mr. Gerlack: We will waive it.

The Court: Very well.

"Mr. Lynch: I will put the letter in evidence if you wish. Go ahead and answer the question.

"A. This letter is the notice to Mr. Holland that by direction of the Secretary his services as an Acting Chief of the Administrative Division at $2700.00 per annum, EO 10, in the Office of the Commissioner of Accounts and Deposits, Field (San Francisco, California), ERR., have been discontinued without prejudice——

(Deposition of Donald M. Merritt.)

"Mr. Lynch: Just a moment. Are we going backwards in this file?

"A. I skipped through a bit.

"Mr. Lynch: That is all right.

"A. (Continuing) —to take effect at the close of business on August 17, 1936.

"Mr. Lynch: At this time I offer the letter described by the witness as the Government's first in order.

"(Document handed to Mr. Gerlack.)

"Mr. Gerlack: No objection.

"(Thereupon the said document was marked 'United States of America Exhibit No. 1.')

"Mr. Lynch:

"Q. At this time I will show you letters clipped together, one dated August 7, 1935, addressed to Mr. Wilson A. Holland, and signed 'J. E. Harper,' and the other letter [244] dated July 25, 1935, addressed to Mr. Wilson Holland, 3908 20th Street, San Francisco, California, and signed by the Accountant in Charge, U. S. Treasury State Accounts Office, and ask you if these two letters were taken from your official file heretofore described by you?

"A. Yes, sir.

"Mr. Lynch: At this time I will offer these two letters in evidence, and ask the witness to state the official character of those letters, if any.

"Mr. Gerlack: May I see them?

"(Documents handed to Mr. Gerlack.)

(Deposition of Donald M. Merritt.)

"Mr. Gerlack: We object to them on the ground they are self-serving declarations."

Mr. Gerlack: We will waive that.

The Court: Very well.

Mr. Meindl: (Reading)

"(Thereupon the said documents were marked 'United States of America Exhibits No. 2 and 3,' respectively.)

"Mr. Lynch:

"Q. At this time, Mr. Merritt, I will show you a document which is entitled 'Personal History Statement, Standard Form No. 6'; it purports to be signed by Wilson A. Holland; and ask you if this is a document that was taken from your official records which you have heretofore described?

"A. Yes, sir. [245]

"Q. What is that document?

"A. All employees are required to prepare this form—the original of which is sent to the Central Treasury Accounts Office in Washington, and the copy retained in the files covering the pertinent information as to name, address, legal residence, record of past service with the Government, if any, military and naval record, and principal employment other than with the United States Government in addition to statement indicating extent of education.

"Q. Is it required that that document be in the handwriting of the applicant?

(Deposition of Donald M. Merritt.)

"A. Yes, this document is to be prepared by the appointee in his own handwriting.

"Q. Do you know whether that is in the handwriting of Wilson A. Holland?

"A. Yes, this is Mr. Holland's handwriting.

"Q. And you recognize it as such?

"A. Yes, sir.

"Q. And this, as you have stated, is an official record of the United States Treasury Department?

"A. Yes, sir.

"Mr. Lynch: At this time I offer the document identified and described by the witness as Government's Exhibit next in order in evidence.

"Mr. Gerlack: To which we object on the ground it states on its face that it is not a true copy. [246]

"(Unreported discussion.)

"Mr. Gerlack: No objection.

"(Thereupon the said document was marked 'United States of America Exhibit No. 4.')

"Mr. Lynch:

"Q. At this time, Mr. Merritt, I will show you a white sheet entitled 'Treasury Department, Accounts and Deposits, Application for Position,' dated July 19, 1935, and purporting to have been signed by Wilson A. Holland on the reverse side, and ask you if that is a document which has been produced by you in response to the subpoena?

"A. Yes, sir.

"Q. Is that an official record of the United States Treasury Department?

(Deposition of Donald M. Merritt.)

"A. The completion of this record was required of all applicants for a position.

"Q. And is it required that that document be in the handwriting of the applicant?

"A. It covers the applicant's history as to education and previous employment, and any special qualifications. It has always been in the applicant's handwriting.

"Q. Do you know whether that particular document is in the handwriting of Mr. Wilson A. Holland?

"A. I recognize Mr. Holland's handwriting.

"Q. You are familiar with his handwriting?

"A. Yes, sir. [247]

"Q. And this as you have heretofore stated is an official document of the Treasury Department which is required to be kept by law, and is kept in the regular course of business?

"A. This document is not forwarded to the Central Office, but it is customary that either this form of application or a similar form be prepared by any applicant preliminary to appointment.

"Q. And you recognize the portions of that document which are in ink as being written in the handwriting of Mr. Wilson A. Holland?

"A. Yes, sir.

"Mr. Lynch: At this time I offer the document identified by the witness as Government's Exhibit next in order in evidence.

"(Document handed to Mr. Gerlack.)

(Deposition of Donald M. Merritt.)

"Mr. Gerlack: No objection.

"(Thereupon the said document was marked 'United States of America Exhibit No. 5.')

"Mr. Lynch: At this time, Mr. Merritt, I will show you a form entitled 'United States Treasury Department, Office of the Commissioner of Accounts and Deposits,' being Form No. D-39, 'Job Analysis Sheet,' to which there is attached a supplemental sheet which purports to be an amplification of the answer to question 8, and I will ask you if that is a document which is taken from the official [248] files of the Treasury Department? A. Yes.

"Q. That was produced here by you in response to the subpoena? A. Yes, sir.

"Q. What is that document?

"A. All employees are required periodically, and if any change of duties takes place, to prepare immediately at that time a statement indicating the nature of the duties with respect to the percentage of time spent on each major activity.

"Q. Is it required that the employees make out these sheets themselves? A. Yes, sir.

"Q. Do you know of your own knowledge whether or not that sheet was made out by Mr. Holland?

"A. The form is signed by Mr. Holland; and question 8, 'Description of duties and responsibilities,' states: 'Described on attached sheet.'

"Q. That document, as I believe you have already testified, is an official record of the Treasury Department? A. That is correct.

(Deposition of Donald M. Merritt.)

"Mr. Lynch: At this time I offer the document identified by the witness as Government's Exhibit next in order in evidence. [249]

"(Thereupon the said document was marked 'United States of America Exhibit No. 6.')"

Mr. Meindl: Any objection, Mr. Gerlack?

Mr. Gerlack: No objection.

The Court: Proceed, gentlemen.

"Q. Mr. Merritt, in addition to the documents produced, have you with you, or have you in your possession any documents relating to the actual term of employment and rate of pay received by Mr. Holland?

"A. The service record card, Standard Form 7, indicates the date of entrance on duty, the position, the salary, together with the office and official station.

"Q. And that is an official record of the United States Treasury Department? A. Yes, sir.

"Q. And kept under your supervision and control? A. Yes, sir.

"Q. Now, will you state when Mr. Holland was first employed by the Treasury Department?

"A. Mr. Holland entered on July 26, 1935, as Acting Chief of the Administrative Division.

"You are also familiar with these facts from your own knowledge, are you not?

"A. That is correct.

"Q. What was his rate of pay?

"A. The salary was $2700.00 per annum. [250]

(Deposition of Donald M. Merritt.)

"Q. When did his services terminate?

"A. Mr. Holland's services terminated officially on August 17, 1936; prior to that time being on a leave without pay status for sixty days.

"Q. During Mr. Holland's employment by the Treasury Department as just stated, was his yearly salary increased or decreased?

"A. Mr. Holland's salary was $2700.00, or was at the rate of $2700.00 per annum during the entire period of employment in the San Francisco Accounts Office.

"Q. The term 'relief' has been used in connection with your testimony. Will you please state whether or not Mr. Holland was what was known as a relief employee?

"A. At the time the office was organized in July, 1935, an attempt was made to secure qualified personnel to fill all the positions. A great deal of the accounting was accomplished through machine accounting facilities in the nature of tabulating equipment. It was necessary to secure as qualified employees as possible to examine the vouchers submitted for payment through the Treasury Accounts Office. In connection with the administrative duties there were certain sections in the nature of stenographic mail file and supply units operating as service units to the two main divisions which required co-ordinating.

"Q. In connection with the previous question, Mr. Merritt, as I understand it, the compensation

(Deposition of Donald M. Merritt.)

received by [251] Mr. Holland was paid to him for his services rendered in connection with his position as opposed to any payments in the nature of relief, is that correct? A. That is correct.

"Q. Was Mr. Holland working under your supervision? A. Yes.

"Q. With relation to his services, were they satisfactory or unsatisfactory?

"A. Mr. Holland's services were satisfactory during the period from his employment up to about the latter part of April or May, 1936, at which time I was detailed to another office, and Mr. Holland left prior to my return.

"Q. During all of the time you were in contact with him, as I understand your answer, his services were satisfactory? A. That is correct.

"Mr. Lynch: That is all. You may cross examine.

"Cross Examination

"Mr. Gerlack:

"Q. Now, on this record, Mr. Merritt, I notice it says here, 'Enter sick leave in red ink,' and the red notations here would indicate that he had sick leave on those days. A. That is correct.

"Q. And what are the blue marks?

"A. The blue is annual leave.

"Q. And what does 'L. W. O. P.' mean? [252]

"A. 'Leave without pay.'

"Q. What would be the occasion for making such an entry?

(Deposition of Donald M. Merritt.)

"A. Well, I think you will find—would you restate your question?

"Mr. Gerlack: Will you read the question?

"(Pending question read.)

"Mr. Gerlack:

"Q. (Continuing) In his case on this record?

"A. If you will hold the record for just a moment——

"Mr. Gerlack: Off the record.

"(Unreported discussion.)

"Mr. Gerlack:

"Q. I notice on this card here which has been marked Government's Exhibit——

"Mr. Lynch: No, I didn't offer it. You can offer it if you wish.

"Mr. Gerlack: We offer in evidence, then, 'Individual Record of Absence for the Year 1935,' for Wilson A. Holland, and attached cards, and ask that it be marked as 'Plaintiff's Exhibit A.')

"(Thereupon the said cards were marked 'Plaintiff's Exhibit.')

"Mr. Gerlack:

"Q. Mr. Merritt, these records are taken from the official records of your office of the Treasury Department, [253] are they?

"A. Administrative procedure requires the maintenance of this form for each employee.

"Q. And these cards were produced here at the taking of this deposition pursuant to the subpoena that was issued? A. Yes, sir.

(Deposition of Donald M. Merritt.)

"Q. And they were kept in the regular course of procedure?

"Mr. Lang: I have no objection to their authenticity.

"Mr. Gerlack: Very well. We will offer them as 'Plaintiff's Exhibit A.'

"And we next offer as 'Plaintiff's Exhibit B,' 'Individual Record of Absence for the Year 1936,' Wilson A. Holland, 'Treasury Department Stock Form 2152,' and other attached papers; and the same is true of that record, also, is it?

"Mr. Lynch: I waive any objection as to the authenticity of the documents.

"Mr. Gerlack: It is stipulated these are official records of the Treasury Department, and kept in the regular course of business? A. Yes, sir.

"Mr. Lynch: We will so stipulate.

"(Thereupon the said cards were marked 'Plaintiff's Exhibit B.')

"Mr. Gerlack:

"Q. The notation on here, Mr. Merritt, '31 Days L. W. [254] O. P.'—that means he was absent from his work 31 days, without pay—that is what that means, does it?

"A. I think that was in just the one column, though.

"Q. I am reading this here. (Indicating to witness on 'Plaintiff's Exhibit.') A. Yes, sir.

"Q. And that was in July, 1936. And it says, '17 Days L. W. O. P.'

(Deposition of Donald M. Merritt.)

"Mr. Lynch: Just a moment. I would ask that the witness be allowed to amplify his answer.

"Mr. Gerlack: Isn't that for redirect examination?

"Mr. Lynch: No. You are testifying yourself. You said that was in July, 1936.

"Mr. Gerlack:

"Q. Is that true—is that the notation for July, 1936? A. Yes, sir.

"Q. And there is a notation under August of '17 Days L. W. O. P.'—that means 17 days leave without pay in August? A. Yes, sir.

"Q. And his service terminated officially on August 17, 1936? A. Yes.

"Q. As a matter of fact, Mr. Merritt, at that time in July and August, 1936, he was a patient in the U. S. Veterans' Hospital in San Fernando, and had been since July 13, 1936, [255] isn't that right?"

Mr. Gerlack: There is an objection there.

Mr. Di Girolamo: We will waive the objection.

Mr. Gerlack: I then asked the question, "Well, you know that of your own knowledge, don't you, Mr. Merritt?"

And then there was an objection to that question, also.

Mr. Di Girolamo: We will waive the objection.

Mr. Gerlack: Then the answer was as follows: (Reading)

(Deposition of Donald M. Merritt.)

"A. I was not in San Francisco at the time Mr. Holland left, but I am quite sure he entered the Veterans' Hospital on or about June 13, 1936.

"Mr. Gerlack:

"Q. And he left the employ of the Government, and the Treasury Department, in that position solely on account of his health?"

Mr. Gerlack: There is an objection there.

Mr. Di Girolamo: We will waive the objection.

The Court: Well, read the answer.

Mr. Gerlack: (Reading)

"A. If you will pardon me just for a moment. The leave without pay which you pick up there—that 31 days in July, and the 17 days in August, and there was also leave without pay in June, from the 19th, which brought it up to the 60 days, which I believe he requested, or at least we carried him on the 60 days leave without pay before he was officially terminated—— [256]

"Mr. Gerlack:

"Q. You know as a matter of fact that his employment in that position was terminated on account of his health, wasn't it?

"A. Yes; as I stated when I was detailed away from here, the acting accountant in charge advised me of Mr. Holland's condition, and that he was leaving.

"Q. He notified you or advised you of that officially as part of your work down there in the Treasury Department?

(Deposition of Donald M. Merritt.)

"A. I don't know that it was an official advice, but he was in contact with me during the time I was away."

Mr. Gerlack: Do you waive the objection there by Mr. Lynch?

Mr. Di Girolamo: We waive the objection.

"Mr. Gerlack:

"Q. Now, you worked with Mr. Holland almost side by side during most of the time he was there, didn't you, Mr. Merritt?

"A. Well, we were very closely associated. I wouldn't say that I worked side by side with him. There were some 135 or 140 employees.

"Q. Well, what I mean by that, you were an executive, and also he was an executive doing work in the same office? A. That is correct.

"Q. And you saw him almost daily, didn't you?

"A. That is right. [257]

"Q. Well, he appeared like a sick man during most of that time, didn't he?

"A. As to Mr. Holland's physical appearance, he was very slight of stature, small-boned, thin-faced, and was not of a robust type that you would come in contact with.

"Q. Did he give you the impression as you looked at him that he appeared to be tubercular?"

Mr. Di Girolamo: There is an objection there, if the Court please.

Mr. Gerlack: I will withdraw it. It was withdrawn, your Honor, anyway.

(Deposition of Donald M. Merritt.)

Mr. Di Girolamo: All right.

"Q. But he did appear thin and emaciated during the time he worked there?

"A. Yes, he was very slight-built, and was not husky in any respect.

"Q. Did he seem to tire quickly or easily?

"A. Well, yes. He was not required to maintain the hours that many of the employees were maintaining in the Voucher and in the Accounts Division. In the beginning months it required a great deal of overtime, and the nature of his duties were more in the initial purchase of supplies and establishing supply records and the development of route tickets for documents which did not require the overtime and long hours that the majority of the employees had to put in. [258]

"Q. In other words, on account of his health he had a little easier time of it than other employees?

"A. No, the nature of the position was such that it did not require working half the night in the machine room over tabulating machines; or, for example, in the voucher examination section the hours of overtime that might be required when a large volume of documents came in that had to be cleared.

"Q. In other words, his duties were more of an executive nature than a clerical nature, is that right? A. That is correct.

"Q. Did you ever know of him going home earlier in the afternoon?

(Deposition of Donald M. Merritt.)

"A. Well, there is no record of that on his absence card, in which all annual leave is charged.

"Q. Well, I am asking you if you would know that yourself, and if he ever did that?

"A. No. According to the administrative procedure any absence, unless through a reassignment of duties and hours, in which he had previously worked overtime, would have to be maintained on the records.

"Q. Was he required during any of that time to go out of the office to perform duties away from the office?

"A. No, his duties were all in the office at 49 4th Street.

"Q. Who kept his personnel records? [259]

"A. The personnel clerk.

"Q. Was he the superior of the Personnel clerk?

"A. The personnel section along with the other administrative sections is under the direction of the Chief of the Administrative Division.

"Q. And who is that?

"A. And Mr. Holland was in the acting capacity.

"Q. Was Mr. Carlton connected with the office?

"A. No, sir.

"Q. Do you know Mr. H. R. Carlton?

"A. Yes, sir.

"Q. And what was his connection, if any, with the office?

"A. Mr. Carlton had no connection with the Treasury Accounts Office.

(Deposition of Donald M. Merritt.)

"Q. Did he come in contact with the office, however?

"A. Mr. Carlton for a period of time, some time after July, 1935, continued his duties with the State Relief Administration, with offices at 49 4th Street, which were across from the Treasury Accounts Office.

"Q. They were in the old Mint Building?

"A. No, it is the Apparel Center Building.

"Q. And you came in contact with him through that source? A. Yes.

"Q. Did you know Mr. Holland when Mr. Holland was connected with Mr. Carlton's office? [260]

"A. Yes, sir.

"Q. Did he appear thin and emaciated during the time he worked for Mr. Carlton?

"A. Yes, Mr. Holland's appearance, as previously indicated, he was of very slight build.

"Q. In other words, he looked about the same during all the time you knew him?

"A. That is correct.

"Q. I understood you to say from a professional standpoint his duties and services were satisfactory? A. That is correct.

"Q. In other words, he knew his profession as an accountant? A. Yes, sir.

"Q. Would you say that so far as the quantity of the work that he was able to handle, that it was unsatisfactory due to his physical condition?

(Deposition of Donald M. Merritt.)

"A. No. There were certain administrative reports that I placed the responsibility on Mr. Holland of preparing each month, and those reports were satisfactory.

"Q. I believe he was exceptionally well qualified, was he not, in knowing the State procedure of accounting of the State of California, and the State and Government procedure from an accounting standpoint?

"A. His knowledge of State accounting was a material aid to him in having an understanding of the appropriation ac- [261] counting with which he came in contact.

"Q. In other words, his employment was not terminated due to any lack of professional qualifications?

"A. No; his *appointment* was due to the necessity of his having to leave on account of his health, and he had sick and annual leave accrued which extended I believe to June 18, 1936, and we requested the Central Office to place him on a sixty day leave without pay status after that date.

"Q. In other words, his leave without pay status began on June 19, 1936, did you say?

"A. I believe it was June 19th; it was in there somewhere.

"Q. It was in there somewhere? A. Yes.

"Q. In other words, he had lost considerable time, and had used up all his sick leave and annual

(Deposition of Donald M. Merritt.)

leave on account of his health in being away from the job prior to that, had he?

"A. Well, during the period of July, 1935, to August 17, 1936, the leave records indicate Mr. Holland had 17 days 1½ hours annual leave, 9 days sick leave, and 63 days leave without pay, of which 60 days was from the period June 19th to August 17th.

"Q. In other words, you would say as an accountant he was above average in ability—I mean professionally?

"A. Mr. Holland had considerable ability and aptitude [262] for placing his knowledge in effect in an operating organization, to differentiate from an accountant who might be working as a single individual.

"Q. Did you ever observe any condition in his appearance in the afternoon as compared to when he came to work in the morning—particularly as to whether or not his face was flushed in the afternoon, whereas it wasn't in the morning?

"A. I don't know that I noticed any particular flushing of his face in the afternoon. It was apparent on a number of occasions when he had a severe cold that it was difficult for him to shake those off.

"Q. Did he appear to have a cold that hung on?

"A. As I stated, it took him longer to get over a cold than the ordinary individual.

(Deposition of Donald M. Merritt.)

"Q. When he walked around the office was he energetic, or did he sort of drag himself around like he was tired?

"A. Well, that is a tough question to answer.

"Q. You have known people who are very energetic, and who talk quick, and make quick movements and are very energetic?

"A. I think he was pretty much of that type—I mean in getting around; he talked rather rapidly. He was in an office adjoining mine, and I didn't have occasion to observe him as if he was sitting at a desk right next to me, and to observe his every move. [263]

"Q. Did you ever notice him coughing?

"A. Yes, on the occasion of these colds I did.

"Q. That was quite a considerable percentage of the time he worked there, was it?

"A. Well, I don't know as to the extent of the time, but I did realize that he was having some difficulty in getting rid of these colds.

"Q. You never saw him spit any blood, did you?

"A. No, sir.

"Q. What would you say as to his lack of endurance? Did he seem to have plenty of endurance, or did he seem to lack in endurance?

"A. I think in the operation of any office over a period of time that you realize those who can work through a double shift if necessary, and those that are possibly not as robust and husky and who wouldn't be able to stand up under that sort of

(Deposition of Donald M. Merritt.)

work, and as I have stated the nature of his duties in coordinating certain major units to the operating units in the office.

"Q. In other words, he had a job which from a physical standpoint you would say was an easy job, would you?

"A. Well, there were probably certain portions of the job that were not exactly easy, and it is possible he kept certain things to himself and carried on anyway in order to accomplish the job and in order to meet the time limits that we have on preparation and submission of certain operating [264] reports.

"Q. In other words, he was really trying to do the best he could?

"A. Yes, I always felt that he was.

"Q. But you couldn't depend upon him for any night work, such as double shift, when it was necessary?

"A. The nature of his work didn't require it.

"Q. Did you ever ask him to, and find that he couldn't?

"A. Not during the period that he was with the Treasury Accounts Office.

"Mr. Gerlack: That is all.

"Mr. Lynch: That is all.

(Signed) "D. M. MERRITT."

The Court: Very well, what is next?

Mr. Di Girolamo: Now, I would like to read in evidence a letter dated October 8, 1936, addressed to Mr. Wilson A. Holland, signed by Mr. J. E. Harper, Chief, Division of Appointments, as follows:

"Mr. Wilson A. Holland,

"Office of the Commissioner of Accounts and Deposits, Field.

"Sir:

"By direction of the Secretary your services as an Acting Chief, Administrative Division at $2700.00 per annum, EO 10, in the Office of the Commissioner of Accounts & Deposits, Field (San Francisco, California), ERR., have been discontinued without prejudice to take effect [265] at the close of business on August 17, 1936.

"Very truly yours,

"(Signed) J. E. HARPER

"Chief, Division of Appointments."

Now, I would like to refer to another document entitled

"PERSONAL HISTORY STATEMENT.

"Department or Establishment Treasury Dept. Accounts Office, San Francisco, Calif.; Date July 19, 1935." Name of Mr. Wilson Alvin Holland.

"Statement of principal employment other than with the United States Government:

Name and Address of Employer	Position and Character of Work	Length of Service
Pickwick Motor Coach Works, 560 So. Los Angeles Street, Los Angeles, Calif.	Ass't Auditor—Accounting Reports & Office Management	3 yrs.— 12/28/27 to 1/15/31
State of California, State Narcotic Hospital, Spadra, California.	Institution Accountant Bookkeeping, Accounting, Reports, Stores & Property Inventory Control.	6 mos. 3/1/33 to 8/1/33
S. E. R. A., Transient Division, 86 Third St. San Francisco, Calif.	Fund Accountant—Bookkeeping, Accounting Reports & Fund Control Accounts	1½ yrs. 12/11/33 to 7/26/35.

(Signed) "WILSON A. HOLLAND"

[266]

"Treasury Department
"Accounts and Deposits
"Application for Position

"Date July 19, 1935

"Character of Position applied for: Accountant.

"Name: Wilson A. Holland, Address: 3809-20th St., San Francisco, California. Phone No. Mission 8371.

"Date of Birth: January 9, 1901. Place of birth: Redding, Iowa. Race: White.

"If veteran of any war, state which: World War.

"Legal residence: State: California. City or Town: Los Angeles. Congressional District: 11-18.

"State Civil Service examination taken: None. Date:.................... Average:....................

"Weight: 125 lbs. Height: 5′10″. Color of eyes: Blue. Color of hair: Black.

"Male or Female: Male. Married: Yes. Dependent Children: None.

"Physical Defects: Limb: None. Sight: None. Hearing: None.

"Present Employment: (Give office, grade, Present salary; also name of supervisor) Fund Accountant, Transient Division of E. R. A., $170.00 Mo.

D. M. MERRITT."

This document is signed by Wilson A. Holland.

Mr. Gerlack: Did you read that card you put in evidence? [267]

Mr. Di Girolamo: Not yet, but I will.

Mr. Gerlack: Pardon me.

Mr. Di Girolamo: (Reading)

"Job Analysis Sheet.

"Name Wilson A. Holland.

"Title of position Acting Chief, Administrative Division.

"Present annual salary $2700.00. Division Administrative.

"Section Unit

"Name and title of employee's immediate superior.

"D. M. Merritt, Accountant in Charge.

"Description of duties and responsibilities: List and describe Each Task Performed. This description should be sufficiently definite and detailed to give a clear word picture of the work. State the per cent of time spent on each task described. (Use additional sheets if necessary.)

"Describe on attached sheet.

"Wilson A. Holland.

"Description of duties and responsibilities.

(a) Direct Personnel Section, Stenographic Section, Mail Section, Files Section and Supply Section 70%

(b) Confer with Division Chiefs and Accountant in Charge on methods and policies, and assist in preparation of memoranda on decisions reached 3%

(c) Make no decisions without higher approval

(d) Have recommendatory authority on classification of employees in Administrative Division, selection of such em- [268] ployees, arrangement of working shifts, selection of types of furniture and equipment, arrangement of office space and general office routine 5%

(e)	Maintain continuous audit of property records	15%
(f)	Make estimates of Administrative expenses	2%
(g)	Supervise maintenance of Administrative expense records, and assist in preparation of such reports	5%
		100%

Then under the question, "Do you supervise others?" there is a list of different people.

Mr. Gerlack: The card you have reference to, the one with the red ink on it, as I recall, there is one for each year, 1935 and 1936, showing the annual leave he took, and the sick leave; the sick leave in red and the annual leave in blue, I believe.

Mr. Di Girolamo: Sick leave, 2 days in September, 1935, in November, 1935, 1 day, total sick leave 3 days in 1935. Annual leave 3 days in September, or rather, 2 days and 3 hours and 20 minutes in September. Total sick leave for the year 1935 3 days. Total annual leave 2 days, 3 hours and 20 minutes.

Mr. Gerlack: Next is the year 1936, I believe. One is 1936 and the other is 1937.

Mr. Di Girolamo: October 1, 1935 is the date of the card, and it shows annual leave none; sick leave none; with- [269] out pay none; military none.

November, 1935, annual leave 2½ days; sick leave 2 days; without pay 3 days.

Mr. Gerlack: That shows the same thing on the other card.

Mr. Di Girolamo: Yes.

Mr. Gerlack: I don't think we should waste any time on it.

Mr. Di Girolamo: Well, that is all on that deposition.

The Court: Very well.

Mr. Di Girolamo: Now, we offer all of these depositions in evidence.

The Court: Call your next witness.

Mr. Di Girolamo: I offer the entire deposition in evidence.

The Clerk: Defendant's Exhibit H.

(The document referred to was received in evidence and marked "Government's Exhibit H.")

Mr. Di Girolamo: And the deposition of Homer S. Howe?

The Clerk: Defendant's Exhibit.

(The document referred to was received in evidence and marked "Government's Exhibit.")

Mr. Di Girolamo: We offer all of the Exhibits in evidence taken in connection therewith.

The Court: Any objection?

Mr. Gerlack: No objection. [270]

The Court: Admitted.

Mr. Di Girolamo: The depositions of Clarence H. Smith and Otho Close.

The Clerk: Defendant's Exhibit J.

(The documents referred to were received in evidence and marked "Government's Exhibit J.") [271]

Mr. Gerlack: I overlooked that.

Mr. Di Girolamo: Very well.

DEFENDANT'S EXHIBIT K

"United States Veterans' Bureau

Los Angeles, Calif. 8-24-26

"Department of Roentgenology

"X-Ray Report of Wilson A. Holland

#122407 File No.

"Examination Chest Ref. by Dr. Essenson

"Diagnosis and Remarks:

"Long narrow chest.

"Left chest slightly contracted lower border. Right chest is broad and thick. Ribs are evenly spaced. Both costo-phrenic angles are obliterated by dense shadows suggestive of pleuritic adhesions. Heart is of the drop heart type. Great vessels apparently normal. Hilum moderately thickened, shadows radiating to the periphery and into the apices. Both upper lobes are moderately hazy.

"Suggestive of fibrosis both upper lobes and pleuritic both lower borders.

"O. S. ESSENSON, M. D.

per hak

"Roentgenologist."

[Endorsed]: Defendant's Exhibit K. Filed Feb. 28, 1939.

I offer that in evidence.

Mr. Gerlack: What date is that?

Mr. Di Girolamo: August 24, 1926.

The Clerk: Defendant's Exhibit K.

(The document referred to was received in evidence and marked "Defendant's Exhibit K.")

The Court: Call your next witness. [272]

Mr. Di Girolamo: We will now call Dr. Shulman.

DR. LEON SHULMAN

a witness called in behalf of the Government, being first duly sworn, testified as follows:

The Clerk: State your full name.

The Witness: Leon Shulman.

Direct Examination

By Mr. Di Girolamo:

Q. State your profession?

A. Physician specializing in diseases of the chest.

Q. You are a duly licensed physician, Doctor?

A. Yes, sir.

Q. In the State of California? A. Yes, sir.

Q. Where did you study, Doctor?

A. I graduated from the University of California in 1911. I interned at the Los Angeles County Hospital from 1911 to 1912. I have been on the attending staff of the County Hospital since that time. I am Consulting Physician to the tubercular sani-

(Testimony of Dr. Leon Shulman.)

torium and the Los Angeles San*i*torium. I am Associate Professor of Chest Diseases at the College of Physicians, member of the National Tuberculosis Association, the American College of Chest Physicians, the American Academy of Chest Physicians and Fellow of the American College of Physicians.

Q. How old are you, Doctor? [273]

A. 53. I have a son graduating this June.

Mr. Gerlack: For the purpose of expediting the trial I will stipulate the doctor read all of these medical reports.

Mr. Di Girolamo: All right.

Mr. Gerlack: You don't have to read them to him again.

The Court: It is stipulated he made all of the reports?

Mr. Gerlack: No. I will stipulate the doctor read them. This doctor never examined the plaintiff, but he read the reports and looked at these X-rays.

The Court: Very well.

By Mr. Di Girolamo:

Q. Doctor Shulman, I hand you Plaintiff's Exhibit 2, an X-ray taken at the Spadra Narcotic Hospital in 1933, and I ask you to examine that X-ray?

(The exhibit referred to was handed to the witness.)

The Witness: You have no viewbox here?

By Mr. Di Girolamo:

Q. It would take too long to bring it here from upstairs.

(Testimony of Dr. Leon Shulman.)

The Court: Is the light sufficient for you to see?

The Witness: Yes. This shows a small white mark in the center——

The Court (Interrupting): You had better stand over there before the jury.

The Witness: All right.

The Court: Explain to them loud enough so that every [274] one can hear you. Go right over there toward the center of the jury box.

The Witness: Pardon me.

The Court: Step down towards the center so they can all see it.

The Witness: I don't know if all of you can see from here. This is the line of the diaphragm. This is the heart here. It is a narrow long heart which is typically found in a person who is tall and narrow. There are adhesions in the right portion here because the diaphragm does not come down convexly. Here is the left side. I will turn it this way so that you will not be confused. This is the left side of his chest over here (indicating).

Extending out from the very center, we see some white marks which go clear up to the top of the left side. That is known as the apex. They also extend to the radiated lines downward on the left-hand side. That is known as the bronchial tree. In other words, it shows here the bronchial tubes, and about those bronchial tubes is scar tissue, calcified glands, and blood vessels.

Up in the left apex here is a rather dense area, sharply and clearly defined. It is not hazy. There is

(Testimony of Dr. Leon Shulman.)

no mottling. The shadows are sharp. It indicates what is known as the fibrosis.

On the right side, on this side, we find a dense hilus permanently established with fibrous shadows in the area. [275] These little areas are calcified glands and calcified areas showing healing.

Now, fibrosis is the ultimate object of any treatment of tuberculosis. That is, in every patient we try to get what is known as fibrosis, in other words, a healing scar. It is like any other part of the body. If you have a wound on the abdomen, it heals up and leaves a scar which we call scar tissue.

Now, that scarred area, as far as functions are concerned, is dead, it is gone, because there is no lung tissue to amount to anything in that area which will have to function; there is not sufficient scar tissue in there to interfere with the ordinary functions of a man's life or of his activities, because we have plenty of lung tissue from here down on both sides, or to be a little more accurate, let us say from the second or third rib down on both sides to give him plenty of aeration.

If there were evidence of activity in this film the shadows would not be sharp and as clear. You could not see them as clearly. They would be hazy, they would be foggy. It is like a picture out of focus in a photograph, you don't see it clearly. That is evidence of activity, evidence of incomplete fibrosis, of incomplete scar, and that is not present in this picture. So, I would say, just from an examination

(Testimony of Dr. Leon Shulman.)

of the film, that we have here negative fibrosis, an arrested condition, with adhesions on both sides, more [276] marked on the left than on the right, pleuritic adhesions.

Q. Now, Doctor, I will show you Plaintiff's Exhibit 18 for identification, and Plaintiff's Exhibit 19 for identification, No. 18 being an X-ray report made on July 8, 1937, and No. 19 made on February 27, 1939. (Handing document to witness.)

I should like to have you point out, if you can, the difference between these two X-rays, if any, and the one you have just viewevd.

A. Here we have the silhouette of the heart again and the diaphragms with adhesions. The first thing we notice is, in this particular picture, the shadows are not as sharp and as clearly defined.

I wonder if you could hold the other film for me, please.

This Exhibit I am holding is No. 18.

Now, if you will notice here, and here, the right upper, and the left upper, the shadows are denser and they are more confluent, they are together more. They are much sharper here. The shadows are not so sharp, except for certain little areas.

Down below there is a mottling on both sides which would show better on the film box, but they show sufficiently here.

In these shadows you still see these calcified glands here, and here, but you see a spread—it is a little larg- [277] er than here—and not so sharply defined; and the same on the left side.

(Testimony of Dr. Leon Shulman.)

This film I am holding in my hand shows an active condition as well as a fibrosis.

Now, the thing about fibrosis, scar tissue, that is permanent. You will see that in every film as long as a man lives, but when activity develops, and healing ceases, and the thing breaks down, the scar softens, and therefore it is not clearly visible on the X-ray film. This is further corroborated by the clinical examination.

Now, this film, what date is this? (Handing film to counsel.)

Mr. Di Girolamo: I believe it is 1939. February 7, 1939, Exhibit No. 19.

The Witness: You see little dark areas in both upper regions, interspersed with the light areas, and you see the mottling practically all the way down, not clearly, to the bases on both sides.

Over here is a lot of mottling, on the right and left sides. The shadows here are dense, but they are interspersed with mottling, more marked on this film than the film just shown you, and extension of the activity. It is progressing, in other words. In this film it is not so good as the other, it is more active, the disease spread from the other parts into the lower lobe. [278]

By Mr. Di Girolamo:

Q. Now, Doctor, you were in court yesterday afternoon, were you not? A. Yes, sir.

Q. And you have examined all these medical reports, have you not? A. Yes, sir.

(Testimony of Dr. Leon Shulman.)

Q. This man's medical history, as portrayed by the medical reports, together with the X-rays shown, and together with his industrial history, taking them all together, have you an opinion, Doctor, whether or not at any time this man, Mr. Holland, the plaintiff in this case, was suffering with tuberculosis? A. Yes, sir.

Q. When, in your opinion, was he suffering with tuberculosis?

A. From the record, as I recall it, it was 1924 and 1925. You mean active tuberculosis?

Q. Yes, active tuberculosis.

A. The examination in 1926 showed evidence of quiescence, that is, the activity was beginning to subside and scar tissue was beginning to become more evident. In other words, the healing process was beginning in 1926.

Q. Now, Doctor, what significance has this X-ray report, made on August 24, 1926, where it says, "Suggestive of fibrosis, both upper lobes and pleuritic adhesions both [279] lower borders."

A. It means the healing is well developed in the chest. The adhesions were due to the empyema, and the pleurisy that existed prior thereto, and the fibrosis shown *indications* that the healing was developing in the upper lobe, where prior to that time there had been what is known as active infiltration.

Q. Doctor, do you adhere to the Diagnostic Standards of the Tuberculosis Association?

A. Yes, sir.

(Testimony of Dr. Leon Shulman.)

Q. What is the accepted test for ascertaining whether or not the peculiar condition has become arrested in accordance with those Standards?

A. Beginning with quiescence, there is beginning fibrosis. The sputum may or may not be positive. There is no fever, or very little fever, about one-half degree, this condition to have existed about two months. If the process goes on to healing, there is no evidence of constitutional symptoms, the sputum is negative, the X-ray shows fibrosis and the clinical examination shows fibrosis, and that condition must have existed for a period of three months, the last months of which the patient is able to do the equivalent of one hour's walking daily, that is the apparently arrested case.

Now, going into arrested, there is no constitutional symptoms, fibrosis is evident, the sputum is negative and the [280] patient is febrifugal, without fever, and the condition must have existed for six months, the last two months of which the patient shall be able to walk one hour a day twice daily, two hours a day, but in divided doses, as it were.

Going on to apparently cured, there are no constitutional symptoms, the sputum is negative, both by animal innoculation and stomach washings, if necessary, the X-ray show no fibrosis, and the patient is able to continue in normal activities for a period not less than two years.

Q. Proceed, please.

A. Well, from the records that I read there was evidence of quiescence in 1926; then there were

(Testimony of Dr. Leon Shulman.)

three examinations in 1927, each of which showed a progressive improvement in condition; that is, the fibrosis was sustained, and toward the end of 1927 it was definitely arrested, in that no constitutional symptoms were determined by the Board, and no physical findings were determined that would indicate any activity.

In 1931 there was an examination which still showed an arrested condition, and also in 1931. In other words, we have, beginning with 1926, when quiescence was entering, but really beginning with 1927 is when the arrestment showed definitely. It continued at least for the period until 1932, according to the examinations, according to the records which I read.

Now, if there was any breakdown it would be evidenced, [281] especially in the presence of the work activity, that is, the physical or mental activity.

As to the matter of physical activity it must be sustained over a certain period of time. In other words, the time element is important. A man may work for a month or so and then not be able to continue any further and he may stop; and it would not show an evidence of breakdown, or it may show evidence of breakdown; but a man may continue over a period of a couple of years with no clinical evidence of breakdown in the chest, and then the conclusion can rightfully be drawn that the man has an arrested condition, because if he didn't have an arrested condition he would break down so that

(Testimony of Dr. Leon Shulman.)
there would not be a very definite indication in the clinical examination of any activity. That was not shown by the examinations I read up to 1932.

Q. Not, in 1932, that is the last medical examination until 1936, so far as the records show. Let me ask you this question, Doctor, have you an opinion as to whether or not Mr. Wilson A. Holland at any time during the year 1933, up to December 31, 1933, was suffering from active tuberculosis or not?

A. Well, I can't say definitely, because I didn't examine him myself, nor have I any record to show, but from the progression of his examinations, the repeated examinations, and the continuity of his work, on those facts, I would say the condition was arrested. [282]

Q. Now, Doctor, let us pick out the month of August, 1933, at which time this X-ray was taken. That is the only other point we have, if it can be termed a point. Are you of the opinion at that time he was suffering from active tuberculosis?

A. Not from what I see in the film.

Q. There is no activity shown there?

A. Just fibrosis.

Mr. Di Girolamo: That Exhibit is Plaintiff's Exhibit 2, for the record.

That is all, Doctor.

Cross Examination

By Mr. Gerlack:

Q. Do I understand you to say, Doctor, you are expert enough in tuberculosis to make a diagnosis of arrested tuberculosis solely on an X-ray film?

(Testimony of Dr. Leon Shulman.)

A. Yes.

Q. That is your statement? A. Yes, sir.

Q. Would you be willing to have that statement and this film shown before the local tuberculosis association of Los Angeles County?

A. I would.

Q. I understood you to say you subscribe to the scheme of classification of the National Tuberculosis Association? [283] A. Yes.

Q. I show you Plaintiff's Exhibit 20 for identification, being the last scheme of classification. (Handing document to witness.)

A. Yes, sir.

Q. That is the yardstick by which all tuberculosis in the United States is judged?

A. Yes, sir.

Q. That is considered authentic on all tuberculosis diagnoses by all tuberculosis specialists?

A. Yes, sir.

Q. Now, Doctor, I want to call your attention to the result of treatment on Page 22:

> "Quiescent: No constitutional symptoms. Sputum, if any, may or may not contain tubercle bacilli. Lesions stationary or retrogressive according to X-ray examination; cavity may or may not be present. These conditions to have existed for at least two months."

That is necessary before an actual and dependable diagnosis of quiescent tuberculosis can be determined after a previous activity, is that correct?

A. Yes, sir.

(Testimony of Dr. Leon Shulman.)

Q. And the examiner cannot make a dependable diagnosis unless he has observed the man two months in order to know these conditions have existed for two months? A. That is correct. [284]

Q. Now, "Apparently Arrested:

"Constitutional symptoms absent. Sputum, if any, must be concentrated and found microscopically negative for tubercle bacilli. Lesions stationary and apparently healed according to X-ray examination; no evidence of pulmonary cavity. These conditions shall have existed for a period of three months, during the last two of which the patient has been taking one hour's walking exercise daily, or its equivalent." A. Yes, sir.

Q. Unless those things are done the diagnosis cannot be called dependable? A. Yes, sir.

Q. Now, "Arrested":

"Constitutional symptoms absent. Sputum, if any, must be concentrated and found microscopically negative for tubercle bacilli. Lesions stationary and apparently healed according to X-ray examination; no evidence of pulmonary cavity. These conditions shall have existed for a period of six months, during the last two of which the patient has been taking one hour's walking exercise twice daily, or its equivalent."

Now, Doctor, those are the standards by which tuberculosis is judged, is it not? A. Yes, sir.

Q. Now, therefore, is it a fact unless an X-ray is [285] taken, and the X-ray evidence shows that

(Testimony of Dr. Leon Shulman.)
any lesions are stationary, or apparently healed, you cannot call that an accurate diagnosis or examination? A. No.

Q. Is it not a fact, Doctor, that these Government examinations do not show an X-ray was taken either in 1926 or 1927?

A. Well, there was one taken in 1926.

Q. But not in 1927? A. None in 1927.

Q. None in 1931? A. None that I saw.

Q. None in 1932? A. Yes, sir.

Q. You cannot say that those diagnoses are really accurate, can you, Doctor?

A. Yes, they are accurate.

Q. You just stated it does not show any X-ray was taken, and it does not show any tolerance test, that the man was observed over a period of six months, giving the tolerance test. A. Yes.

Q. Now, take the disease of tuberculosis, Doctor. A man comes to the sanitorium. Let us say you are the Ward Doctor. He has one diagnosis of moderately advanced active tuberculosis. Let us say the man has been working [286] and quit the day before he came to the hospital. He has been raising one-half cup of sputum mostly in the morning, pulse of 100, temperature of 98 to 100, that is, the afternoon, he has some cough, he feels weak and tired, sort of exhausted, what do you do with him?

A. I put him to bed.

Q. You keep him there 24 hours a day?

A. Yes.

(Testimony of Dr. Leon Shulman.)

Q. At the end of three months the can's condition shows no symptoms. Let us say, he shows practically no constitutional symptoms. Are you justified in saying that the man has attained an arrested condition? A. Not until I examine him.

Q. Suppose you examine him and the X-ray shows he is retrogressive with lesions stationary?

A. No, at the end of three months, I would say he shows the beginning quiescence.

Q. You mean to say he is quiescent until he showed his symptoms fully, from two months, according to this classification? A. Yes.

Q. You cannot say he is apparently arrested until you give him X-rays and a tolerance test?

A. Yes.

Q. Suppose he shows no symptoms of tuberculosis at the end of three months, and he goes back to the job, what would [287] happen to him?

A. If he were not arrested he would break down and there would be a very rapid extension of his condition. He would not be able to continue on the job very long. He would probably show an acute condition with beginning cavity formation.

Q. In other words, work or activity aggravates tuberculosis?

A. If it is active; if it is not active it does not.

Q. There is no question in your mind, Doctor, that active tuberculosis is total disability?

A. Yes.

Q. He shouldn't work? A. Yes.

(Testimony of Dr. Leon Shulman.)

Q. If he continues to work he signs his death warrant?

A. If he has active tuberculosis he should not work.

Q. Doctor, one of the outstanding symptoms of tuberculosis that a layman would observe on a fellow-worker is if a man has frequent colds that hang on? A. Yes.

Q. That is one of the outstanding symptoms?

A. No, not one of the outstanding symptoms, just one of the symptoms?

Q. One of the symptoms?

A. Yes, but not outstanding.

Q. And fatigue is an outstanding symptom, is it not? [288]

A. It is a symptom, yes, certainly.

Q. Now, Doctor, an X-ray is just a link in the chain of diagnosis, is it not? It is not conclusive by any means, is it? A. No, it is not.

Q. An X-ray is not a picture, it is a picture of the shadow, is that right?

A. Yes, it is a photograph.

Q. If you have a cavity and take a front view—they very seldom take side views of lateral views in tuberculosis?

A. Frequently—I would say there are some being taken, more now than before.

Q. Just speaking in general? A. No.

Q. As far as the Government practice is concerned? A. No.

(Testimony of Dr. Leon Shulman.)

Q. If a cavity were within a cavity it might show on the side view and not show on the A. P. and lateral?

A. It would show better on the A. P. than on the lateral.

Q. There is just a chance it would be another thing, a cavity, or tubercular mound which might be hidden behind some of the ribs or bones of the sternum and you might miss it?

A. If it were back of the heart or hilus, then the lateral or oblique view might bring it out. [289]

Q. These are all front views? A. Yes.

Q. To be frank, an X-ray is just a link in the diagnosis? A. Yes.

Q. It is not conclusive in itself?

A. Only in so far as it hooks up and runs it in with the constitutional symptoms and the clinical examinations. Neither one is conclusive, but taken together, then the opinion is conclusive.

Q. As far as you are personally concerned, Doctor, you are unable to detect any tuberculosis in this film taken at Spadra? A. I didn't say that.

Q. What did you say?

A. I didn't find any evidence of active tuberculosis. I found evidence of fibrosis.

Q. As far as you are concerned, you are not able to see any active tuberculosis?

A. No, I didn't see any areas that would indicate activity in this film.

Q. In your opinion? A. No, sir.

(Testimony of Dr. Leon Shulman.)

Q. You do not claim to be infallible?

A. No, sir, I am very fallible.

Q. By the way, did you ever examine this man, or did [290] you ever see him before yesterday when you saw him in this courtroom?

A. Not to my knowledge.

Mr. Gerlack: That is all.

Redirect Examination

By Mr. Di Girolamo:

Q. Doctor, you said something about a front view X-ray. Is that what is known as stereo?

A. No, stereo is a double view, taken in front and in back, so as to give the picture depth. It is like the old stereopticans that had two figures, one on each side. You would put them in the slide and focus it by moving the handle back and forth, and look through the view box, and you got a third dimension of depth.

When you take a stereo of the chest, instead of the areas lying flat as they do in this film, you get a sense of depth, and you can tell from that whether the condition, the lesion, the fibrosis is pointing more to the front or to the back, which is often very important as to what treatment should be given.

Q. Now, Doctor, from a stereo X-ray, where there are any cavities present, you would be able to see those, wouldn't you? A. Yes, sir.

Q. Now, with respect to the question of exercise, whether once or twice a day, as a test in order

(Testimony of Dr. Leon Shulman.)

to corrob- [291] orate whether or not your diagnosis of arrested tuberculosis is definite, when you have such an industrial history as Mr. Holland admitted on the stand yesterday, with that industrial history, would you still deem it necessary to give exercise once or twice a day when you have his own history of this employment?

A. No, it would not be necessary then.

Q. Is that a sufficient substitute for the exercise? A. Yes, sir.

Mr. Di Girolamo: That is all.

Juror Whittingham: May I ask a question, your Honor?

The Court: What is it?

Juror Whittingham: I would like to know the amount of lung depletion shown in the Spadra picture.

The Court: I hardly think that would be fair either on direct or cross.

Juror Whittingham: Thank you.

Mr. Gerlack: We have no objection to the doctor answering that question.

Mr. Di Girolamo: Neither has the Government, your Honor.

The Court: All right, answer the question.

The Witness: The amount of depletion—one, two, three, four, five—about to the sixth rib posteriorially, which would take it to one, two, three ribs anteriorially. These ribs I am pointing to going down are the ribs from [292] the back, and these

(Testimony of Dr. Leon Shulman.)
shadows going this way are the ribs from the front, so I would say up to the third rib on each side.

Juror Whittingham: Is that 20 or 40 percent of capacity?

The Witness: Oh, about 25 per cent.

Juror Whittingham: Thank you.

The Court: Anything further, gentlemen?

Mr. Gerlack: One question.

Recross Examination

By Mr. Gerlack:

Q. Doctor, a stereo, as I understand, has two views. A man lies on an X-ray table with the tube above him. They take one picture and move the tube two or three inches to one side?

A. The chest view is usually taken standing up.

Q. It is moved two or three inches to one side or the other?

A. That is for the stereo effect. It is done for only mechanical reasons.

Mr. Gerlack: That is all.

The Court: Anything further.

Mr. Di Girolamo: The Government rests.

The Court: Any rebuttal?

Mr. Gerlack: I would like to call Mr. Holland to the stand again. [293]

The Court: Make it strictly rebuttal.

WILSON A. HOLLAND

recalled as a witness in his own behalf, in rebuttal, being previously duly sworn, testified as follows:

Direct Examination

By Mr. Gerlack:

Q. Mr. Holland, how did you come to work up at Ione, at the Preston School of Industry?

Mr. Di Girolamo: If the Court please, this is not proper rebuttal.

The Court: I don't think it is. Is it strictly rebuttal?

Mr. Gerlack: We have a right to rebut an inference.

The Court: Place your direct leading question to rebut it.

Mr. Gerlack: Very well.

The Court: Don't open up the field.

By Mr. Gerlack:

Q. What were the real reasons for your resigning at the Preston School of Industry?

A. Well, I was scared of that physical examination. Mr. Close had told me when I went there for my first interview that a physical examination would be required, and then before I left the school —I had gone back to the little hotel there in Ione, and I telephoned him that I wasn't sure I could pass the physical examination. He seemed to [294] like my application and he said the fact I had worked in the State service and in Department of Institutions four months previous, he would see

(Testimony of Wilson A. Holland.)

what he could do about getting the examination waived. Then I came back to Los Angeles and waited here for his answer. He finally wired about the examination, he sent a return wire he would waive examination.

After I got up there, the more I got to think about it—I thought now, here is this job under Civil Service, and if they ask me, "Have you ever had an official physical examination since you started to work in the Department of Institutions?" I would have to reply, "No." They didn't examine me when I first entered the Department of Institutions and I knew if they ever made a physical examination my job would be blown up, I would be taken off the Civil Service list entirely, so I thought I had better go back to this job in Los Angeles. I hadn't been gone a week yet. I knew I could go back.

Q. You merely gave that as an excuse, that you were lonesome?

A. I couldn't tell him I had tuberculosis.

Q. How long were you up at Ione?

A. About a week, or possibly a little less.

Q. You just worked there less than a week?

A. That is about all.

Q. Were you given any examination with the exception [295] of one X-ray examination in 1927 —when an X-ray picture was taken of your chest, when you were examined by Dr.—just a minute, do you remember being examined by Dr. Woodward on April 4, 1927?

(Testimony of Wilson A. Holland.)

A. Yes, I remember Dr. Woodward. He gave me his card. He was leaving.

Q. But he was still in the Government service?

A. Yes, but he was leaving then.

Q. Were you given any X-ray examination on March 16, 1931, in the Regional Office?

A. No, I can't recall any X-ray after 1926.

Q. By the way, how long did those examinations take in the Regional Office?

A. Well, they would usually take between 15 to 30 minutes.

Q. That is the actual examination of yourself?

A. Yes, from the time they thumped you around.

Q. Were you ever given the tolerance test?

A. Never.

Q. The exercise tolerance test of one hour's walking twice a day? A. No, sir.

Q. Never at any time by a Government doctor?

A. No, it never was suggested.

Mr. Gerlack: I think that is all.

The Court: Any cross? [296]

Mr. Di Girolamo: No questions, your Honor.

The Court: Next witness?

(Witness excused.)

Mr. Gerlack: That is all.

The Court: Both sides rest. Step up to the bench, gentlemen.

Mr. Di Girolamo: I would like to make a motion in the absence of the jury, your Honor.

I would like to have permission to argue this motion because I have two important points.

The Court: No, I don't think you have any points. I think we have to submit it to the jury. I will tell you that frankly, argument would not do any good.

Mr. Di Girolamo: It is a question of due proof.

The Court: Yes.

Mr. Gerlack: Well, the question of due proof is this: In the White case where the Government took me to the Circuit Court they held where they deny the claim, issue a denial, that is in effect due proof. It is my contention where a man is a beneficiary, and where the Veterans' Bureau repeatedly examined him, they are in a state of continuous due proof.

The Court: I would have to submit it to the jury.

Mr. Di Girolamo: The last time he was examined by the Bureau was in 1932. He had an arrested condition. He work- [297] ed until 1936 and did not come back until then. How could that be due proof?

The Court: I have thought about that.

Mr. Di Girolamo: If a man is examined and they find him well——

The Court (Interrupting): I will have to submit it to the jury.

Mr. Di Girolamo: May I dictate the motion to the reporter?

The Court: Yes.

Mr. Gerlack: Your Honor, we have three Exhibits, Plaintiff's Exhibits 18, 19 and 20 for identification. We ask those be placed in evidence.

The Court: Very well.

Mr. Gerlack: Any objection?

Mr. Di Girolamo: Those Exhibits are marked for identification.

Mr. Gerlack: I would like to put them in.

PLAINTIFF'S EXHIBIT NO. 20

DIAGNOSTIC STANDARDS
TUBERCULOSIS OF THE LUNGS
AND RELATED LYMPH NODES

Tentative Edition 1938

National Tuberculosis Association
PLAINTIFF'S EXHIBIT NO. 20

*   *   *   *   *

Explanation of Classification and
Descriptive Summary

For statistical purposes, presentation in annual reports of institutions and general convenience, the items in the Classification and Descriptive Summary referring to extent of pulmonary lesions, severity of symptoms and status of the case in subsequent observation (items 7, 12 and 15) may be selected, especially since such use of these has been customary for many years. Accordingly, these items are explained first. In this respect there has been no material change from the previous classification.

Extent of Pulmonary Lesions (Item 7)

Minimal

Slight lesions without demonstrable excavation confined to a small part of one or both lungs. The total extent of the lesions, regardless of distribution, shall not exceed the equivalent of the volume of lung tissue which lies above the second chondrosternal junction and the spine of the fourth or body of the fifth thoracic vertebra on one side.

Moderately Advanced

One or both lungs may be involved, but the total extent of the lesions shall not exceed the following limits:

a. Slight disseminated lesions which may extend through not more than the volume of one lung, or the equivalent of this in both lungs.

b. Dense and confluent lesions which may extend through not more than the equivalent of one-third the volume of one lung.

c. Any gradation within the above limits.

d. Total diameter of cavities, if present, estimated not to exceed 4 cm.

Far Advanced

Lesions more extensive than Moderately Advanced.

a. None.

b. Slight. Constitutional and functional symptoms, such as loss of weight, ease of fatigue, and anorexia are slight and not rapidly progressive. Temperature not more than one-half degree above normal at any time during the twenty-four hours. Slight or moderate tachycardia. Cough, if any, is not hard or continuous; sputum, if any, may amount to one ounce or less in twenty-four hours.

c. Moderate. Symptoms of only moderate severity; fever, if any, does not exceed two degrees. No marked impairment of function, either local or constitutional, such as marked weakness, dyspnea and tachycardia. Sputum usually does not exceed three or four ounces in twenty-four hours.

d. Severe. Marked impairment of function, local or constitutional. Usually there are profound constitutional symptoms, such as weakness and continuous or recurrent fever. Cough often is hard and distressing and the sputum may be copious.

Result of Treatment or Observation (Item 15)

Quiescent

No constitutional symptoms. Sputum, if any, may or may not contain tubercle bacilli. Lesions stationary or retrogressive according to X-ray examination; cavity may or may not be present. These conditions to have existed for at least two months.

Apparently Arrested

Constitutional symptoms absent. Sputum, if any, must be concentrated and found microscopically negative for tubercle bacilli. Lesions stationary and apparently healed according to X-ray examination; no evidence of pulmonary cavity. These conditions shall have existed for a period of three months, during the last two of which the patient has been taking one hour's walking exercise daily or its equivalent.

Arrested

Constitutional symptoms absent. Sputum, if any, must be concentrated and found microscopically negative for tubercle bacilli. Lesions stationary and apparently healed according to X-ray examination; no evidence of pulmonary cavity. These conditions shall have existed for a period of six months, during the last two of which the patient has been taking one hour's walking exercise twice daily, or its equivalent.

Apparently Cured

Constitutional symptoms absent. Sputum, if any, must be found negative for tubercle bacilli, not only by concentration and microscopic examination, but also by culture or animal inoculation. In case there is no sputum, the fasting gastric contents should be obtained and similarly examined. Lesions stationary and apparently healed according to X-ray examination. These conditions shall have existed for a period of two years under ordinary conditions of life.

Unstable (or Active)

Symptoms unchanged, worse or less severe, but not completely abated. Lesions not completely healed or progressive according to X-ray examination. Sputum almost always contains tubercle bacilli.

* *

Died.

* * * * * * *

[Endorsed]: Plaintiff's Exhibit No. 20. Filed Feb. 28, 1939.

The Court: Do you want to come back at 1:30?

Mr. Di Girolamo: I should like to very much.

The Court: The jury may be excused now until 1:30 o'clock. We have some motions to discuss in which the jury is not interested. Bear in mind the admonitions I have heretofore given you.

(Whereupon, the jury retired from the court room.)

Mr. Gerlack: Is there any objection to putting those [298] X-rays of Dr. Cohn's and Spadra in? (No response.)

We ask those two X-rays go in.

The Court: I don't know of anything that has not been disposed of.

Mr. Gerlack: There is just those two X-rays.

The Court: Give me the citation of that White case.

Mr. Meindl: Shall we dictate our motion to the reporter now?

The Court: Yes, proceed, the jury is out.

Mr. Meindl: This is 48 Federal 2nd 584.

The Court: Have you the volume here?

Mr. Meindl: No, your honor.

If your Honor please, the Defendant now moves the Court for an order directing the jury to return a verdict in favor of the Defendant and against the Plaintiff, upon the ground and for the reason that the Plaintiff has failed to prove by any substantial evidence that the insured, Wilson A. Holland, became permanently and totally disabled within the meaning of the insurance policy sued upon in this action at any time while his insurance policy was in force and effect; and upon the further ground that this Court is without jurisdiction in this action, for the reason that Plaintiff has failed to prove by any substantial evidence, or any evidence, that he ever submitted due proof of his permanent and total disability while this insurance policy was in force; and upon the further ground that there is no evidence what- [299] soever of due proof being submitted before this policy lapsed, which is one of the requirements of the insurance policy sued upon, or within any reasonable time after the policy had lapsed.

The Court: Have you any authority upon that?

Mr. Meindl: Yes, your Honor, we have.

The Court: Except the White case?

Mr. Meindl: In the case of U. S. versus Ranes, 48 Federal 2nd 592, Ninth Circuit, has held that due proof is a jurisdictional requirement.

In the case of Boyett versus U. S., 86 Federal 2nd, 66, Fifth Circuit, has held that due proof must be submitted to the Government within a reasonable time after the policy has lapsed.

The authority that we have on what due proof consists of is just general insurance law which has held more or less that way. I can cite no war risk insurance cases because that has not been interpreted in war risk insurance cases. However, there must be some "evidence in some form as is calculated to convince or persuade the mind of the truth of the facts alleged and may be any form of evidence that is worthy enough to enable to the insurer to form an intelligent estimate of its right and while it does not require any particular form of proof which the insurer might arbitrarily demand, it does require such a statement of fact reasonably verified as if established would prima facie require the pay-
[300] ment of the claim."

The Court: What case do you cite?

Mr. Meindl: I am citing O'Reilly versus Guardian Mutual Life Insurance Company, 60 New York 169 at 172.

The Court: 60 New York?

Mr. Meindl: Yes.

The Court: That is, of course, the Court of Appeals?

Mr. Meindl: Yes.

The Court: What page?

Mr. Meindl: At 172.

Citing further 14 Ruling Case Law, Page 1337.

The Court: I haven't any of those volumes here.

Mr. Gerlack: Those cases would not apply to this case because the man was the beneficiary of the Bureau and the very worst view of the evidence would be the man submitted due proof when he submitted himself to the San Fernando Hospital for hospitalization. They had the man themselves. That is better than anything he can submit, and that was to submit himself and let them examine him.

This due proof clause is put in there because a lot of people like myself that have a policy—I have a $10,000.00 policy in force—if I were to buy an automobile and ten years before, they would not have any way to meet that, but this man is the beneficiary of the Bureau.

The Court: What is the technical name of the Bureau?

Mr. Gerlack: The Veterans' Administration. It is an [301] agency of the United States Government which takes care of all affairs relating to veterans. This man is continually submitting due proof. That is our contention. There is nothing technical about it. It is to advise them that the man is making a claim and there is some evidence to back it up. They have a record of every heart beat this man has had since 1917.

Mr. Meindl: May I state one thing in reply to that, your Honor?

The Court: Yes.

Mr. Meindl: We have an examination in 1932. There was arrested tuberculosis, no activity whatsoever. Our records show he was working. That is all the Government had with which to decide whether or not this case should have been paid. That is the only evidence we had at all of the man's condition while the policy was in force. How that can be due proof, I don't know. He never went into the Veterans' Bureau again until 1936. If that is due proof, I would like to know what due proof is.

Mr. Gerlack: Here is my view. It is not a question for the jury to say whether or not due proof has been proved. That is for the Court to decide. The jury should decide whether or not he became totally and permanently disabled while the policy was in force. If they decide that question then this Court should order the type of judgment to fit this case. It may be six months prior to 1936 when he entered the [302] hospital there, which would be the very worst view from the Plaintiff's standpoint; and the Court may decide he submitted himself in 1932.

The evidence of Dr. Cohn, in 1932 there was not an examination upon which they could really make a dependable diagnosis of arrested tuberculosis because they didn't give him the tolerance test, they didn't take an X-ray, they didn't observe him, they didn't make the requisite test anyway; and the evidence of the last witness shows they didn't make the requisite test.

Mr. Meindl: That is immaterial. It is a jurisdictional matter to determine whether due proof has been submitted. Maybe our examinations have been faulty, but that is all we have.

The Court: Have you a copy of what you have said?

Mr. Meindl: I haven't a copy. This is a memorandum sent out from Washington.

The Court: I will look this over. Of course, if the insurer knew nothing about the condition of this man after 1930, when this condition was arrested, why, that is something to think over.

I don't think you need to take any more of this, Mr. Reporter.

(Discussion between the Court and counsel.)

(Thereupon, at 11:55 o'clock A. M., a recess was taken until 1:30 o'clock P. M. of the same date.) [303]

Los Angeles, California
Wednesday, March 1, 1939
1:30 o'clock P. M.

The Court: Note the jury present.

Mr. Gerlack: It is so stipulated.

Mr. Di Girolamo: It is so stipulated.

Mr. Gerlack: May it please the Court, at this time I move the Court to permit the Plaintiff to open up the case on the question of submission of due proof.

The Court: Will you be short?

Mr. Gerlack: Very short, your Honor.

Mr. Di Girolamo: I submit, if the Court please, the Plaintiff has already closed his case.

The Court: Oh, the Court realizes that. Proceed.

Mr. Gerlack: Take the stand, Mr. Holland.

WILSON A. HOLLAND

recalled as a witness in his own behalf, being previously duly sworn, testified as follows:

Direct Examination

By Mr. Gerlack:

Q. Mr. Holland, I will show you a letter dated February 12, 1937, addressed to the Veterans' Administration, and which has already been introduced as Plaintiff's Exhibit 21. That is one of the original claims that you put in for insurance in this case? (Handing document to witness.) [304]

A. Yes, sir.

The Court: That is already in evidence?

Mr. Gerlack: Yes.

Q. At that time or shortly thereafter, you also filed with the Bureau a document entitled Veterans' Form No. 579, in connection with your claim for insurance bearing date "Received by Veterans' Administration April 12, 1937," which has been already introduced in evidence as Plaintiff's Exhibit 22. (Handing document to witness.)

A. Yes, sir.

Mr. Gerlack: Do you want to see it?

(Testimony of Wilson A. Holland.)

Mr. Di Girolamo: No objection to that, but what we do object to that it dates subsequent to his hospitalization in 1936.

By Mr. Gerlack:

Q. Mr. Holland, I will show you a letter dated October 28, 1937 and ask you if you received that from the Veterans' Administration? (Handing document to witness.)

A. Yes, I received that letter.

Q. I will show you another letter dated April 19, 1937 and ask you if you received that from the Veterans' Administration in connection with your insurance claim? (Handing document to witness.)

A. Yes, I received that letter.

Mr. Gerlack: I offer these two in evidence as Plaintiff's next in order. [305]

The Court: Any objection?

Mr. Di Girolamo: There is no objection as to the admissibility of the documents, but it all dates subsequent to his hospitalization in the year 1936, therefore, they can't assist in any way as to the question of due proof.

The Clerk: Plaintiff's Exhibit 23.

The Court: Overruled; it is admitted.

(The documents referred to were received in evidence and marked "Plaintiff's Exhibit No. 23.")

(Testimony of Wilson A. Holland.)

PLAINTIFF'S EXHIBIT NO. 23

917 Dexter Street,
Los Angeles, California,
November 9, 1937.

Mr. H. L. McCoy,
Director of Insurance,
Washington, D. C.

Re: Holland, Wilson A.
C-1 224 075
K-613076

Dear Sir:

This will acknowledge receipt of your letter of October 28th regarding my claim on my above-numbered converted policy.

Please do not misunderstand me. I have never refused any reasonable request for information from Mr. Rollins or any one else. I want to cooperate with the Bureau to the fullest extent. However, Mr. Rollins asked me what I consider some rather impertinent questions and which I cannot possibly see had anything to do with my case.

At the time my insurance lapsed in October, 1933, I was then suffering from active tuberculosis, which I believe was chronic and also far advanced at that time. At the time my insurance lapsed, I was unemployed and unable financially to keep up the premiums on my insurance. Following that, during part of 1934 and 1935 I worked as an accountant. During all of this time I had a feeling of complete

(Testimony of Wilson A. Holland.)

exhaustion which never left me. Most of the time I would get up in the morning feeling as tired as I did when I went to bed. I was coughing, raising a good deal of sputum, and every afternoon I felt hot and feverish. My stomach was also upset during practically all of this time and I was also showing many other symptoms of active tuberculosis at that time. I then quit this job and took another job for the balance of 1935 and 1936, working as an accountant, but manifested all of the same symptoms during that time. Since June 11, 1936, I have done no work whatsoever and have been in Government hospitals most of that time. In fact, I have had active tuberculosis for a number of years.

Trusting this is the information you desire, I am,

Very truly yours,

WILSON A. HOLLAND

[Endorsed]: Plaintiff's Exhibit No. 23. Filed March 1, 1939.

By Mr. Gerlack:

Q. Did you receive that letter from the Veterans' Administration in connection with your insurance claim? A. Yes.

Q. That is the letter of denial. Did you receive this letter from the Veterans' Administration in connection with your insurance claim?

A. Yes, I received that one.

Q. And did you write this letter in answer to one of those letters to the Veterans' Administration,

(Testimony of Wilson A. Holland.)

the original of that? A. Yes.

Mr. Gerlack: We offer those in evidence as Plaintiff's next in order.

The Court: The same objection to all of them, I presume?

Mr. Di Girolamo: Yes, your Honor.

The Court: Same ruling; overruled. [306]

(The document referred to was received in evidence and marked "Plaintiff's Exhibit No. 24.")

PLAINTIFF'S EXHIBIT NO. 24

Veterans Administration
Washington

April 1, 1937

Your File Reference:
In Reply Refer to: FDE
Holland, Wilson A.
C-1,224,075

Mr. Wilson A. Holland
Veterans' Administration Facility
San Fernando, California

Dear Sir:

Your letter of February 12, 1937, has been received.

You will find our Forms 579 and 579a herewith enclosed. You should complete these forms and return them to this Administration at San Francisco, California.

(Testimony of Wilson A. Holland.)

When they are received there, the complete records will be forwarded to this office. Your attention is directed to the fact that you must complete the Form 579 and it is suggested that you also furnish statements from physicians who have treated you from the time you allege to have been permanently and totally disabled.

If you will be kind enough to give this matter your prompt attention it will be appreciated.

Respectfully,

H. L. McCOY

Director of Insurance

[Endorsed]: Plaintiff's Exhibit No. 24. Filed March 1, 1939.

PLAINTIFF'S EXHIBIT NO. 25

Veterans Administration

Washington

May 9, 1938

Your File Reference:

In Reply Refer to: FDF

C-1 224 075

K-

Registered Mail

Mr. Wilson A. Holland

917 Dexter Street

Los Angeles, California

Dear Sir:

In reference to the above entitled claim, you are informed a decision was rendered on May 9, 1938,

(Testimony of Wilson A. Holland.)

by the Insurance Claims Council to the effect that the evidence was not sufficient to establish as a fact that you were permanently and totally disabled at the time alleged or at any time while insurance was in force and, therefore, your claim has been denied.

You may file an application for review on appeal to the Administrator of Veterans' Affairs within one year from the date of this letter which is the mailing date thereof. Any material evidence you are able to submit within a period of one year or prior to the consideration of the appeal, whichever is the earlier, will receive consideration but the submission of such evidence will not extend the period in which you may present an appeal.

An application for review on appeal may be filed with any activity of the Veterans Administration prior to the expiration of one year.

If you do not appeal, then the denial of your claim by the Insurance Claims Council is final.

The case folder is being forwarded to the Veterans Administration at Los Angeles, California, to which office further inquiries may be directed.

Respectfully,

H. L. McCOY

Director of Insurance.

[Endorsed]: Plaintiff's Exhibit No. 25. Filed Mar. 1, 1939.

(Testimony of Wilson A. Holland.)

PLAINTIFF'S EXHIBIT NO. 26

Veterans Administration
Los Angeles, California

April 19, 1937
Your File Reference:
In Reply Refer to: AC.5-bc
C 1 224 075

Mr. Wilson A. Holland,
Veterans Administration,
San Fernando, California

Dear Sir:

This will acknowledge the receipt of forms 579 and 579a. The Chief of the Out-Patient Service of this facility has been requested to secure a report of your physical condition. When this has been received the claim for insurance benefits together with the complete records in your case will be forwarded to the Director of Insurance for consideration.

By direction,
BEN F. RYERSON, JR.
Adjudication Officer

[Endorsed]: Plaintiff's Exhibit No. 26. Filed March 1, 1939.

(Testimony of Wilson A. Holland.)

PLAINTIFF'S EXHIBIT NO. 27

Veterans Administration
Washington

October 28, 1937
Your File Reference:
In Reply Refer to FDF
Holland, Wilson A.
C-1 224 075

Mr. Wilson A. Holland
917 Dexter St.
Los Angeles, California

Dear Sir:

Relative to your communication of September 25, 1937 addressed to Mr. W. S. Rawlings, Field Examiner, Office of Chief Attorney, Veterans' Administration Facility, Los Angeles, California, you are advised that in view of your refusal to furnish the information requested of you, consideration of your claim by the Insurance Claims Council will be withheld and no decision rendered until such time as the information requested of you has been furnished.

Respectfully,
H. L. McCOY,
Director of Insurance

[Endorsed]: Plaintiff's Exhibit No. 27. Filed March 1, 1939.

(Testimony of Wilson A. Holland.)

By Mr. Gerlack:

Q. Mr. Holland, while you were in the hospital in connection with this insurance claim, the Government Hospital in San Fernando, was any demand made upon you by the Government doctors or Government officers for further evidence in connection with your insurance claim? A. Yes.

Q. Was that a statement of your occupational history? A. That is right.

Q. Is that a copy of the history you gave him in connection with the demand?

A. I believe this is a later statement, Mr. Gerlack.

Q. Did you make two statements?

A. Yes, one on demand of the doctors there at the hospital and later, this was on demand of Mr. Rawlings who is Field Examiner.

Q. Who was Mr. Rawlings?

A. He describes himself as the Field Examiner for the Veterans' Administration.

Q. Is he the Mr. Rawlings referred to in some correspondence of the Veterans' Administration?

A. Yes, Mr. W. S. Rawlings.

Q. Have you the original of that statement?

A. No.

Mr. Gerlack: Mr. Di Girolamo, I am looking for the original dated April 19, 1937 in connection with the hospital- [307] ization there.

(Testimony of Wilson A. Holland.)

Mr. Di Girolamo: No, I have not, Mr. Gerlack.

Mr. Gerlack: It should be there somewhere because we have a copy of it here which we took from the medical.

The Witness: Mr. Gerlack, if I may say so, it should be in connection with the examination in April, 1937.

Mr. Gerlack: Yes, that is the date. The examination is there.

Mr. Di Girolamo: The statement is right in the examination.

Mr. Gerlack: It is right on top.

Q. Mr. Holland, do you recall making a statement to the doctor in connection with the medical examination of April 13, 1937?

A. It was about that date.

Q. Is that the statement you made?

A. Yes.

Mr. Gerlack: We offer this in evidence as Plaintiff's next in order.

The Court: Any objection?

Mr. Di Girolamo: There is no objection if it goes in on the question of due proof, but not as evidence to the jury. It is a self-serving declaration. Is it for the purpose of due proof?

Mr. Gerlack: That is its purpose.

The Court: All right. [308]

The Witness: This is a statement of industrial history which I gave them at that time.

(Testimony of Wilson A. Holland.)

By Mr. Gerlack:

Q. Which you gave them at what time?

A. At the same time this examination was made.

Q. After you had put in your claim for insurance? A. Yes.

Q. That is April 19? A. Yes.

Mr. Gerlack: We offer that also.

Mr. Di Girolamo: If the Court please, that doesn't even purport to be a copy of the original statement. Mr. Gerlack says Mrs. Holland made a copy.

Mr. Gerlack: No, Mrs. Davis, who took a copy of the medical reports, copied that and sent it up with the rest of the medical reports.

The Court: Mark this as an Exhibit, Mr. Clerk. (Handing document to Clerk.) It is admitted.

(Testimony of Wilson A. Holland.)

PLAINTIFF'S EXHIBIT NO. 28

917 Dexter Street
Los Angeles, Calif.
January 8, 1938

Mr. W. S. Rawlings, Examiner
Chief Attorney's Office
Veterans Administration Facility
Los Angeles, California

Re: Holland, Wilson A.
K-613 076
C-1 224 075
Industrial History
March 1, 1933 to
Current Date.

Dear Sir:

In conformity with your insistent demand for a complete and detailed statement of my employment record from March 1, 1933 to the current date, and the refusal of the Insurance Claims Council to consider my claim until such information is furnished it, I submit the following:

On March 1, 1933 I was fortunate (in my tubercular condition) to secure a position as bookkeeper at the State Narcotic Hospital, Spadra, California, remaining in this position until August 30, 1933. This was a very easy job of light work—the only reason I was able to hold it. My immediate super-

(Testimony of Wilson A. Holland.)

visor was Dr. Thomas F. Joyce, Superintendent, Pacific Colony-State Narcotic Hospital, Spadra, California. Salary, $120.00 per month plus maintenance. My work consisted of checking invoices and the preparation of same for payment, when I was able to do it; posting to ledger accounts, recording receipts and disbursements of cash, additions and withdrawals from stores, and expense items, etc, preparation of monthly accounting reports etc. I was supposed to be on duty when able eight hours per day, five and one-half days per week, although the average time required to complete the daily work was much less than that except at the end of the month.

On occasions it was necessary to obtain medical treatment for relief from pain after arrival at the office, there being physicians and nurses in the same building as the office. During this employment I suffered unusual fatigue, and felt nervous and irritable. I felt like I continually had a cold. My stomach was troubling me continually. During the afternoons I was hardly able to keep going, and eased up on my work as much as possible. My eyes pained me continually during this time.

My fellow workers commented on my unhealthy appearance and advised me to do something about it. Although unaware of my history of tuberculosis at that time, Dr. Joyce recommended a rest. I am sure that my lung condition was bad. My fellow

(Testimony of Wilson A. Holland.)

workers often helped me with my work and my superiors were lenient, otherwise I could not have hung on. I felt tired, exhausted and "fagged out" continuously.

From September 1, 1933 to December 11, 1933, I rested because I was too sick and weak to work. It had been my intention at the time I was compelled to leave my employment on August 30, 1933, to follow the advice of Dr. Joyce and take an extended rest. However, certain financial plans failed to develop and it immediately became imperative that I obtain work or accept public charity no matter what my physical condition was. Because of my dire need of either a job or relief, and in view of my knowledge of California State accounting procedure, I was fortunate to secure the following employment:

From December 11, 1933 to August 15, 1935, I was with the State Relief Administration, being employed for the purpose of advising and assisting in the installation of an accounting system conforming with State procedure. I was supposed to be at the office seven hours a day, five and a half days per week. I cannot state exactly how much time I lost during this period of employment on account of illness but it was plenty. I should estimate that it totalled several months. About three months after going to work I was so worn out that I went down to the desert for a week to rest. Later in the sum-

(Testimony of Wilson A. Holland.)

mer, too, it again became necessary for me to take a ten day rest. I was often so tired and exhausted in the mornings I could hardly get out of bed. These were not just vacations, but genuine rest cures during which I went to bed, getting up only for meals During the time I worked for the SRA I took no regular vacations because of the time it was necessary for me to be absent on account of my tubercular condition.

I took another rest of several days in the winter of 1935, and between the longer periods mentioned were many absences of one to three days for the purpose of recuperating from fatigue, from colds, etc. All of this I now know to have been caused by my active tubercular condition. In addition to the rests taken during absences I spent most weekends in bed, and undoubtedly I was able to keep going as long as I did before starting to hemorrhage because of the excellent care I took of myself and the light job I had. In spite of the care taken, however, my health continued to decline. As the months went on I suffered more and more frequently from colds. I awoke mornings tired after nine to eleven hours of sleep. After my work became more routine it was difficult and impossible to accomplish what was considered a normal day's work without assistance. Rest periods during the day were necessary to last out the day. I felt tired and feverish in the afternoon and found it almost impossible to concentrate

(Testimony of Wilson A. Holland.)

on my work. My stomach and eyes continued to trouble me. I could not have continued to hold my job except for the fact that I was the only man in the entire office who had had State Accounting experience and the further fact that my salary was being paid from Relief funds. Practically all of our employees were persons who were unable to obtain employment except on relief projects. My tubercular condition must have been taken into consideration by my superiors.

On August 16, 1935, I transferred to another office where I remained until June 10, 1936, at which time I resigned to enter a tubercular hospital. My salary was paid from relief funds. I was selected for this position, as in the previous one, because of my experience in and knowledge of budget accounting and government procedure generally. My work here was of an advisory and supervisory nature and did not require the completion of any specific daily assignment. I occupied myself with personnel matters, mail, and filing problems, purchases of furniture and equipment, accounting procedure and other general office matters. I was supposed to work seven hours per day, five and a half days per week. In this position I was unable to arrange so many absences for the purpose of rest as I did while with the SRA and as a result started hemorrhaging again. In about four or five weeks after starting on the new job I caught a severe cold which became so serious

(Testimony of Wilson A. Holland.)
I had to go to bed for ten days (this, of course was tubercular).

During the winter of 1935-1936 I was frequently absent for one day or part of a day because of feeling so badly. In the spring of 1936 I took another week off to rest, but was unable to recuperate sufficiently to carry on.

In June I began hemorrhaging again, necessitating prompt hospitalization.

It seems hardly necessary to repeat that during my employment with the Treasury Accounts Office I exhibited to an even greater degree the same symptoms of active tuberculosis observed during the other periods of employment stated here. Had I been less ambitious or shown less fortitude I should have given up long before I did. I do not feel that I should be penalized for trying to earn a livelihood and support my family properly and keep them and myself from becoming public charges.

From June 13, 1936 to June 19, 1937, I was a patient at the Veterans Hospital at San Fernando, California, and under treatment for my advanced tuberculosis.

From June 20, 1937 to the current date I have been on home treatment, resting at home. I have not been employed during this period.

I trust that the information given meets the requirements of the Insurance Claims Council and

(Testimony of Wilson A. Holland.)

that my claim will be considered without further delay.

Yours very truly

WILSON A. HOLLAND

[Endorsed]: Plaintiff's Exhibit No. 28. Filed March 1, 1939.

By Mr. Gerlack:

Q. Mr. Holland, how many times were you examined during last October when you entered the Veterans' Hospital? How many times were you examined and by how many doctors?

A. Since last October, do you mean?

Q. Yes.

A. I will have to sort of do a little calculating.

The Court: October of what year? [309]

Mr. Gerlack: 1938.

The Witness: I was examined when I first came in; I have been examined two or three times by my Ward Surgeon; and then the Board had six or seven doctors examine me some three weeks after I came in. I suppose there have been four or five, possibly six examinations by about seven doctors, I should say.

By Mr. Gerlack:

Q. Those examinations you have had in there since 1936, in June, have they been in connection with your insurance claim?

(Testimony of Wilson A. Holland.)

Mr. Di Girolamo: Just a moment. I object to that.

Mr. Gerlack: I will withdraw that.

Q. Since you put in your insurance claim in January, 1937, have you been examined for insurance purposes? A. Just once.

Q. When was that? A. In April, 1937.

Q. That was out at the hospital of the Veterans' Administration?

A. That is right.

Mr. Gerlack: That is all.

The Court: Any cross examination?

Mr. Di Girolamo: No cross examination.

(Witness excused.) [310]

Mr. Gerlack: As I view the situation, your Honor, the question of due proof is addressed solely to the Court.

The Court: What is that?

Mr. Gerlack: I say, your Honor, the question of due proof is addressed to the Court rather than to the jury.

The Court: What do you think about it, counsel?

Mr. Di Girolamo: Well, the question of due proof is purely a jurisdictional question.

The Court: I think it is a matter for the Court to decide.

Mr. Gerlack: I think so.

The Court: You will renew your motion, I presume?

Mr. Meindl: Yes, let the record show our motion was renewed.

Mr. Gerlack: It is so stipulated.

The Court: Let the record show the motion is renewed.

This provision of this policy, "Upon due proof of the total permanent disability of the Insured before the end of the Endowment Period and while this policy is in force, the monthly installments shall, except as hereinafter provided, be payable to the Insured and continued to be so payable during total permanent disability so long as he lives, and payment of all premiums due after receipt of such proof during total permanent disability shall be waived."

This provision must be construed with the further provision which is: The total permanent disability benefits may [311] relate back to a date not exceeding six months prior to receipt of due proof of such total permanent disability, and any premiums becoming due after the date of such disability and within such six months, if paid, shall be refunded without interest.

The Veterans' Bureau prepared and contracted the insurance and it must be construed favorably to the insured. It is so held by all authorities and especially it is true in the Minnesota Mutual Life Insurance case, 29 Federal 2nd 977, which so construes the general provision. Due proof may be made after the policy has elapsed which must be within a reasonable time, and the reasonable time under the circumstances of this case must be the period limited by statute in which an action can be commenced. The grace period of the policy, in my judgment, can have no application since paid premiums may be recovered for six months, and the grace period is only six months.

I think the Circuit Court of Appeals in the Minnesota case was in error when it used the phrase, "Within the grace period."

Due proof is a self-evident proposition, evidence in some form which is calculated to influence or persuade the mind as to the truth of the fact. It is so held in the O'Reilly case, 60 New York 169, to be such proof as the law would judge to be reasonable and satisfactory.

In the case of Foreman against New York Life Insurance Company, 244 Northwest 222, due proof can mean no more than [312] reasonable evidence of disability and the term of the policy shall be submitted. 14 Ruling Case Law, Page 1377 says, "To constitute satisfactory proof it should be such as to make out a prima facie case. Any form of evidence which is substantial and trustworthy evidence to enable the insured to form an intelligent estimate of his plight is sufficient." It means some evidence or notice to the company that the insured has become totally and permanently disabled.

The insured was hospitalized by the Veterans' Administration Bureau in 1936 and continued through into 1937. It was all the evidence that could be produced. It examined the Plaintiff many times by its specialists and the Bureau admitted the Plaintiff himself for examination and had him under their observation for a period of time which testimony shows itself to have been sufficient because it denied total permanent disability when the claim was made.

Upon that phase there can be no doubt in my mind that the Court has jurisdiction and that it is shown that due proof was made.

Upon the other phase of lack of evidence, there is some evidence here that the jury must consider and the Court would be acting arbitrarily, without right, to grant the motion to dismiss, and it is denied.

Mr. Di Girolamo: Note an exception. [313]

(At this point a short recess was taken, after which proceedings were resumed as follows:)

The Court: Note all the jurors present. [345]

Mr. Di Girolamo: It is so stipulated.

Mr. Gerlack: It is so stipulated.

The Court: Gentlemen of the Jury, I think I can say at the outset in view of the inquiry just made by a juror before recess, that in this trial we are not concerned with pensions. That is a gratuity extended by the Government for patriotic service.

This action is predicated solely upon a contract entered into between the Government and the Plaintiff or other holders of policies, and the question of a pension has no bearing in this case whatsoever. It is merely a business contract entered into between the parties.

The issue in this case is made up by the allegations in the complaint and the answer of the Defendant. The pleadings will be sent to the jury room, but they are not evidence in the case, except where admissions are made by the answer, that the fact is consented, and no proof need be made.

The Plaintiff brought this action on a policy of war risk insurance, as stated in the complaint, alleging that said policy was issued while Plaintiff was serving in the Army of the United States, the policy being in the sum of $10,000.00, together with other facts which are not necessary to relate at this time.

The Plaintiff alleges all premiums were paid on the policy prior to his total permanent disability, as claimed, [346] and that is admitted by the Defendant, that is, that the policy was in force until the 31st day of December, 1933. The Plaintiff's claim that he became totally and permanently disabled on August 30, 1933, and that the policy was in full force and effect at that time, that is admitted, as I have stated to you. All claims made by the Plaintiff in his complaint are admitted save under the Plaintiff's total and permanent disability as of August 30, 1933, and that is denied.

Now, in determining the Plaintiff's total and permanent disability, you are instructed that there are two elements involved. It must be total in the first place; and secondly, it must be permanent. These items must be considered together.

Partial disability is not sufficient. There must be a disability and it must be total. It must have been total prior to midnight August 30, 1933. The policy was in force at that time. It must have been total prior to that time, and the Plaintiff alleges that it was August 30, 1933, and if you find that he was totally and permanently disabled on August 30, 1933, you will so note that in your verdict.

Total disability is defined in the policy and by the law as an impairment of mind and/or body which will render it impossible for the Plaintiff to follow continuously in a substantially gainful occupation. It is deemed permanent when it is founded upon conditions found to be present which will render it reasonably certain that it will continue dur- [347] ing the life of the Plaintiff.

Total disability may be stated to be a relative term. It is not confined to the injuries of employment or the strength or facility to pursue continuously his usual occupation. It is not a condition which prevents him from doing anything whatsoever pertaining to the occupation or any occupation, but only to the extent that he cannot do any and every kind of activity pertaining to any gainful pursuit.

The amount of gain is not so material except that the pursuit must be tantamount to a substantially gainful employment.

The term "continuously" is significant. The ability to work, and to apply oneself spasmodically or intermittently does not meet the requirement, the intention being that the insured Plaintiff shall be able to adapt himself to some occupation, some pursuit, or some employment in regular competition with others of average attainment under such conditions of life without serious injury to his health and yet will bring him gainful results, something dependable in earning a livelihood.

Total disability, to be permanent, must be such as is found on conditions today and at the present time that render it reasonably certain that it will continue throughout the lifetime of the Plaintiff, and it is essential that the menal or physical condition of the Plaintiff be so considered, and when so considered, the inquiry is whether the conditions
[348] as disclosed by the evidence are such from which the conclusion may be deduced as to whether it is reasonable to determine that the disability will continue throughout the Plaintiff's lifetime.

Total disability, within the meaning of the law, and the insurance policy, does not mean that the man must be bedridden or bedfast.

Ordinarily when a man works for a period of two or three years at a fair compensation it is evidence of the fact that he is not totally disabled, but if a person is employed at a fair compensation and is carried on the payroll so that he did not in fact perform all services without injury to his health or was permitted to take time off, possibly the length of a week or possibly days, and he did not do the active work in which he was engaged, but merely in a supervisory capacity in which his attainment or experience and practice and intellectual qualities enabled him to superintend or to do such things as others in the same employment could not do, this would not be indicative of any permanent and total disability.

The ascertainment of permanent and total disability involves this question which you must answer as a question of fact, has the Plaintiff at all times since August 30, 1933, or midnight on the 31st day of December, 1933, been totally disabled. If you find that he was disabled prior thereto and suffered an impairment of mind and/or body which has [349] prevented him from continually following in a gainful occupation, and to determine whether it is reasonably certain since that time that his total disability will continue throughout his life. You will take into consideration all of the testimony that will bear upon the development and determination of that fact, what he did, his condition, the condition of living, his condition of health as disclosed by the evidence in this case before you. When you have considered all these facts if you find that the Plaintiff became totally and permanently disabled prior to August 30, 1933 or December 31, 1933, midnight, as complained in the complaint, he will be entitled to recover, otherwise your verdict will be for the Defendant.

Reasonable certainty is certainty that something has been reasonably proven which a careful and experienced man would conclude as a probable result of conditions ascertained and present as a basis for deduction. The burden of proof is upon the Plaintiff to establish these elements which I have named to you by a fair preponderance of the evidence. That is, the scales must evenly balance, must more than evenly balance in his favor. If the scales evenly balance then the burden has not been sustained. It is not a proof beyond a reasonable doubt, but it is the weight of the evidence. Nor does it depend upon the character and number of witnesses testifying to a fact or a certain fact. The testimony of one witness may outweigh the testimony of many witnesses. [350] It is the quality of the testimony, the convincing truth or facts with relation to it that is material.

In determining the issue of fact which is before you and of which you are the sole judges, you will take into consideration all of the evidence which has been presented by the Plaintiff, and also all of the evidence presented by the Defendant and weigh it carefully. You will disregard any opinion you may think I have of any fact which has been established in this case. While I would have the right, under the law, to tell you what I believe to be the fact, it is not my purpose to invade the province of the jury. This question of fact is something for you to decide, and if you feel I have any opinion about the facts in the case disregard it and conclude upon the testimony itself as your independent conclusion upon the evidence as it has been presented.

You are also the sole judges of the credibility of the witnesses who have testified before you, and in determining the weight which you desire to attach to a witness you will take into consideration the demeanor of the witness on the stand, the reasonableness of his story, the interest or lack of interest in the trial, the opportunity of the witness for knowing the things about which he is testifying, and from all these consider what you believe the weight should be. If you feel any witness has shown any bias in the case you will likewise take that into con- [351] sideration in the weighing of the truth with relation to the facts here. Physicians have been called as experts, that is, as persons who by reason of study, experience and practice are admitted by the law to have sufficient knowledge in the structure and functions of the human body and who are able to disclose the effect of certain things on the human body, upon its health and life. This testimony you will consider in the same way, applying the same rules you would as to any other testimony. These are conclusive and binding upon him, but it is for your own information in deciding the case, and should be carried on with the other testimony in the case to determine where you believe the truth in this case lies.

The Plaintiff, of course, is interested in the result of this trial because he is to be a beneficiary if any judgment is returned. You heard his testimony as to his physical ailments. Do you think that he worked when he should not have worked? Do you think he worked when he should have rested? Do you think he did work which was injurious to his health? Take into consideration his testimony and all of the testimony which has been presented.

The wife is likewise an interested party because she will participate as a wife in whatever he receives if he receives anything. Was she fair? Did she show any bias? Or did her testimony indicate she was earnest and sincere? If there is anything to indicate that the witness or any [352] witness on the part of the Plaintiff overstated facts as to his condition bear that in mind.

On the part of the defense you will read all the testimony by the same rules and weigh it carefully, deciding whether it was a fair disclosure of conditions as found to be present, and ask yourself does it bear the stamp of truth?

You will concern each witness with all the circumstances disclosed in this trial, and determine from a fair, deliberate and conscientious study of the issues as to where you believe the truth to be. Each witness has testified, they testified to the truth, and should be given such credit as you believe the testimony is entitled to, whether on the part of the Plaintiff or on the part of the Defendant, and it is for you to determine which you believe did unfold the truth.

Some statements have been introduced in evidence here which were made in relation to certain Civil Service examinations, by the Defendant. You will consider these statements as to his physical or mental condition made for employment or other purposes, they should be considered with all of the evidence and the purpose under which they were made, whether the Plaintiff was over-zealous in seeking employment, or whether he was over-zealous in seeking an enrollment in the Civil Service Board, that he did unconsciously make statements which did not exactly state the conditions [353] of his health at that time.

You should decide, from the evidence in this case, whether you are warranted in considering those statements with all of the evidence in the case with relation to the condition of mind and purposes at that time, and likewise determine the truth with relation to this issue as to total and permanent disability.

You will weigh all of the evidence fairly as twelve fair minded persons with a view to determine justice between the Plaintiff and the Government in this case. This is not a case where the Court and the Jury is authorized to adjudicate a fund and distribute it unless the proof establishes broken condition of the policy. The policy is merely a business transaction between the Plaintiff and the Government and the burden is on the Plaintiff to show the conditions of the policy have been broken, that is, that he became totally and permanently disabled during the time the policy was in force not later than midnight on December 31, 1933. You have nothing to do with the physical or mental conditions other than to find whether he was totally and permanently disabled as of the date claimed and outlined in these instructions.

It will require your entire number to agree upon a verdict, and when you have agreed you will cause it to be signed by your foreman whom you will elect immediately upon retiring to the jury room. [354]

There are two forms of verdict, one form will be for the Defendant and which will read: "We the jury in the above-entitled cause, find for the Defendant"—then date it and have it signed by your foreman. The other form, if you find for the Plaintiff, you will say: "We the jury in the above-entitled cause find for the Plaintiff"—and fix the date of his total permanent disability as that time is defined in his policy—"beginning"—then put in the date. If you find August 30, 1933, put in that date; if you find a date in between August 30, 1933, put in that date and cause it to be signed by your foreman.

The Court will receive the verdict at any time before 4:45 P. M. this afternoon if you should agree; if you do not agree before that time seal it up, sign it, and report to the court at 10:00 o'clock tomorrow morning, all of you, without any exception.

Mr. Gerlack: We are perfectly satisfied, your Honor.

Mr. Meindl: With few exceptions the Government would like to make for the record.

The Court: How is that?

Mr. Meindl: We would like to make a few exceptions.

The Court: You can do that now if you like.

Mr. Meindl: Your Honor, the Defendant excepts to the Court's instructions in defining the term "total disability."

The Court: I think I read the policy.

Mr. Meindl: I understood your Honor to define it accord- [355] ing to the term policy rather than the converted policy, which is at issue in this case.

The Court: In view of the suggestions of the attorney I will read the policy to you.

Mr. Meindl: It is on the second or third page.

Mr. Gerlack: Paragraph 9, I believe, on the second page.

The Court: Total and permanent disability, point it out to me.

Mr. Meindl: Paragraph 9, your Honor.

The Court: Very well.

Total and permanent disability. You will take this definition as the definition of total and permanent disability.

Juror Swan: Are those two terms synonymous, total and permanent? Do they mean the same thing?

The Court: Take the definition which I give you now. I am reading it right from the policy. The policy will be sent into the jury room when you leave the court room.

"Total permanent disability as referred to herein is any impairment of mind or body which continuously renders it impossible for the disabled person to follow any substantially gainful occupation and which is founded upon conditions which render it reasonably certain that it will continue throughout the life of the person suffering from it." [356]

I guess that defines it.

Mr. Meindl: Yes, your Honor, that is satisfactory to the Government.

The Court: Very well.

Mr. Meindl: For the purpose of the record, your Honor, may the Government have an exception to the Court's failure to give Defendant's requested instructions, Nos. 1 to 9, inclusive, as requested?

The Court: You mean all of them?

Mr. Meindl: Yes, for the purpose of the record, your Honor.

The Court: Very well.

Mr. Meindl: We ask that they be incorporated in the record of the report.

The Court: Yes. Have you any exceptions on the part of the Plaintiff?

Mr. Gerlack: We are perfectly satisfied.

(Note: The instructions referred to commence at page 319 of this transcript.)

The Court: You gentlemen will collect all of the Exhibits, give them to the Clerk, and I will send them out to the jury room, if the jury desires them. I will likewise send out the answer and the complaint, also the insurance policy.

Mr. Di Girolamo: If the Court please, with respect to the medical examinations there are parts which are not in [357] evidence.

The Court: Those should not be sent out.

Mr. Di Girolamo: I have no objection.

Mr. Gerlack: I am agreeable either way.

Mr. Girolamo: Yes, so am I. Ordinarily they are not sent out.

The Court: I don't think I will send them out. You may swear the Bailiff.

(Thereupon the Bailiffs were sworn by the Clerk.)

The Court: Now, gentlemen of the jury, you have the complaint, and answer, and the policy. The jury may retire.

Juror Anderson: May we take that chart in, your Honor?

The Court: No.

The Court will adjourn until 10:00 o'clock tomorrow morning unless a verdict from the jury is received at 4:45 P. M.

(Whereupon at 4:00 o'clock P. M. the jury retired for deliberation.)

The Court: Note all jurors present.

Mr. Di Girolamo: It is so stipulated.

Mr. Gerlack: Yes, it is so stipulated.

The Court: Have each and all of you agreed upon a verdict?

Foreman of the Jury: We have, your Honor.

The Court: You may read the verdict, Mr. Clerk.

The Clerk: "In the United States District Court for [358] the Southern District of California, Central Division, Wilson A. Holland, Plaintiff, against United States of America, Defendant, No. 8415-C, Law Verdict.

> "We, the Jury in the above-entitled cause, find for the Plaintiff and fix the date of his total and permanent disability, as that term is defined in his policy, beginning August 30, 1933.
>
> "Dated: Los Angeles, California, March 1, 1939,
>
> C. M. NEUNER,
>
> Foreman of the Jury."

Is that your verdict, gentlemen, each and all?

The Jury: It is.

The Court: File the verdict.

(Whereupon, at 4:40 o'clock P. M., the hearing in the above-entitled matter was concluded.) [359]

REQUESTED INSTRUCTIONS OF THE DEFENDANT

Instruction No. 1

Even though plaintiff is suffering from a disease which he had while his insurance was still in force, which disease is incurable and will ultimately cause permanent and total disability, the insurance does not mature until the disease has reached that stage;

and if he allows his insurance to lapse before the disease has rendered him permanently and totally disabled he cannot recover.

Wilkes vs. US, 65 F (a) 775 et seq.

Instruction No. 2

If you find from the evidence that the plaintiff worked after his policy lapsed and that that work was done to the detriment of his health and against prescribed treatment, then you must find for the defendant because that leaves the question of whether the plaintiff was permanently and totally disabled in the realm of speculation for plaintiff might have recovered if he had not worked but adhered to medical advice.

Instruction No. 3

You are instructed that the definition of permanent total disability in converted insurance, such as in this case, is that total permanent disability is any impairment of mind or body which continuously renders it impossible for the disabled person to follow any substantially gainful [360] occupation, and which is founded upon conditions which render it reasonably certain that it will continue throughout the life of the person suffering from it.

In other words, before the plaintiff is entitled to recover in this case, you must find that he has been continuously unable to follow some substantially gainful occupation. If the plaintiff has been able to follow some substantially gainful occupation for a short period of time, he then has not been continuously unable to follow a substantially gainful occupation and is not entitled to recover upon this policy of insurance.

Instruction No. 4

You are instructed that an insured who is suffering from a disability while covered by insurance cannot through his own neglect and action and failure to follow proper medical care and treatment permit a disease to progress after the policy has lapsed to a total degree of disability and then assert liability upon his insurance contract on the ground that the disease was permanent and total prior to the lapse of his insurance.

US vs. Ivy, 64 F (2) 653.

Instruction No. 5

There is no liability for permanent and total disability occurring after lapse of war risk insurance policy even though caused by injury suffered during military ser- [361] vice and while the policy is in force, but liability must be founded on total permanent disability while the policy is in force.

Lumbra vs. US, 63 F (2) 797.

Instruction No. 6

You are instructed that if you find that the chief disability the plaintiff was suffering from at the time of the lapse of his insurance is pulmonary tuberculosis, and if you further find that his pulmonary tuberculosis at that time was arrested, then you must find for the defendant. As a matter of law, arrested tuberculosis is not a permanent and total disability.

US vs. Chandler, 77 F (2) 452;
US vs. Murray, 81 F (2) 743.

Instruction No. 7

You are instructed that the insured agreed to pay to the United States certain premiums on his contract of insurance in consideration of which the United States Government agreed to pay to him in the event he became permanently and totally disabled the sum of $57.50 per month during the continuance of said total and permanent disability, provided always that these contingencies happened while the contract was in force and effect. According to the terms of the contract if the premiums were not paid thereon when due or [362] within thirty-one days, the grace period, the contract lapsed and the Government was under no further obligation to the insured on his contract, even though the insured prior to that time was partially disabled and which at some later date, subsequent to lapse, became total.

U.S. vs. Cole, 45 F (2) 339;
Misenhalter vs. U.S., 28 F (2) 771;
U.S. vs. McPhee, 31 F (2) 243.

Instruction No. 8

If you find that the plaintiff after the lapse of his insurance has been engaged at a substantially gainful occupation continuously for a period of approximately three years the effect of this steady profitable employment is an unanswerable refutation to any claim that he was totally disabled during the years of that employment. A finding that a man cannot do what he in fact did cannot stand. To so hold is to strike out the language of the contract and to render a judgment contrary to the physical facts. This Court and other Courts have consistently held that there can be no recovery where the employment was of much shorter duration and much less continuity than the employment here involved.

U.S. vs. John L. Hammons. Decided Aug, 22, 1933, April Term 10th Circuit. [363]

When the physical facts admitted as evidence in the case positively contradict the statement of a witness or witnesses then the physical facts must control and the jury cannot disregard them.

U. S. vs. Kerr, 6616 F. (2) 800;

American Car and Foundry Co. vs. Kinderman, 216 F. 499;

Hansen vs. U. S., 70 F. (2) 230;

Deadrich vs. U. S., 74 F. (2) 619.

Instruction No. 9

I instruct you that the proper treatment of tuberculosis includes complete rest. Not until treatment including complete rest has been tried and found unavailing can it be said that a reasonable certainty of the permanance of the tuberculosis appears. I further instruct you that the insured must pay his premiums until that permanency appears and if the insured fails to do so, he cannot recover.

U. S. vs. Brewer, 97 F. (2) 899; C. C. A. 5;
Hammond vs. U. S., 87 F. (2) 226; C. C. A. 5.

[364]

State of California,
County of Los Angeles—ss.

I, Byron Oyler, hereby certify that on the 1st day of March, 1939, I was the acting court reporter of the United States District Court for the Southern District of California; that as such reporter I took down in shorthand writing all proceedings in the case of: Wilson Alvin Holland, Plaintiff, vs. United States of America, Defendant, No. 9415-RJ, Law, which was heard before the Hon. Jeremiah Neterer, Judge Presiding, on the date hereinabove mentioned.

I further certify that the attached transcript consisting of pages 180 to 317, both inclusive, are a full, true and correct transcription of my said shorthand notes, and that the same is a full, true and complete transcript of said proceedings.

Dated this 1st day of March, 1939.

BYRON OYLER
Reporter

Subscribed and sworn to before me this 25th day of August, 1939.

BYRON OYLER
Notary Public in and for the County of Los Angeles, State of California.

[Endorsed]: Reporter's Transcript. Filed Aug. 25, 1939. [365]

[Endorsed]: No. 9281. United States Circuit Court of Appeals for the Ninth Circuit. United States of America, Appellant, vs. Wilson A. Holland, Appellee. Transcript of Record Upon Appeal from the District Court of the United States for the Southern District of California, Central Division.

Filed August 30, 1939.

PAUL P. O'BRIEN,
Clerk of the United States Circuit Court of Appeals for the Ninth Circuit.

In the United States Circuit Court of Appeals for the Ninth Circuit

No. 9281

UNITED STATES OF AMERICA,

Appellant,

vs.

WILSON A. HOLLAND,

Appellee.

STATEMENT OF THE POINTS UPON WHICH APPELLANT INTENDS TO REPLY ON THE APPEAL HEREIN

(Rule 19, Subdivision 6 of C. C. A., Ninth Circuit.)

The appellant herein and the appellee having by stipulation designated the parts of record necessary for the consideration of the appeal herein, the said appellant hereby designates the points upon which it intends to rely upon the appeal herein as follows:

1. That the Court erred in finding that plaintiff submitted due proof of permanent and total disability to the defendant on March 12, 1937 (R. 252-266).

2. That the Court erred in refusing to instruct the jury as requested by the defendant in its requested instructions Nos. 1 to 9, inclusive, on the ground that the Court's instructions were insufficient to cover defendant's requested instructions as to the law of the case (R. 299-317).

3. That the Court erred in admitting in evidence the X-ray report made at the State Narcotic Hospital at Spadra, California, in August, 1933 (Plaintiff's Exhibit No. 2) on the ground that the proper foundation had not been laid for the introduction for the said exhibit, and on the further ground that said exhibit was not made in the regular course of treatment and was not an official record of the State Narcotic Hospital, Spadra, California (R. 36 to 41, inclusive). [368]

4. That the Court erred in denying the defendant's motion for a directed verdict and submitting the case to the jury for its determination on the ground that the plaintiff had failed to show by substantial evidence that he became permamently and totally disabled while his contract of insurance was in force (R. 252 and 266).

5. That the Court erred in making and entering its Minute Order of March 20, 1939 denying defendant's motion for judgment notwithstanding the verdict.

Dated this 29th day of August, 1939.

BEN HARRISON
United States Attorney for the Southern District of California
ERNEST D. FOOKS
Attorney,
Department of Justice
Attorneys for Appellant [369]

[Title of Circuit Court of Appeals and Cause.]

AFFIDAVIT OF SERVICE BY MAIL

United States of America,
Southern District of California—ss.

Eva P. King, being first duly sworn, deposes and says:

That she is a citizen of the United States and a resident of Los Angeles County, California; that her business address is 677 U. S. P. O. and Court House, Los Angeles, California; that she is over the age of eighteen years, and not a party to the above entitled action;

That on August 29, 1939, pursuant to Rule 19, Subdivision 6 of the Rules of the United States Circuit Court of Appeals for the Ninth Circuit, she deposited in the United States Mails in the Post Office at Temple and Main Streets, Los Angeles, California, in the above entitled action, in an envelope bearing the requisite postage, a copy of Statement of the Points upon which appellant intends to reply on the Appeal herein, addressed to Alvin Gerlack, Attorney-at-Law, Suite 845 Mills Building, Bush and Montgomery Streets, San Francisco, California, at which place there is a delivery service by United States Mail from said post office.

EVA P. KING

Subscribed and sworn to before me this 29th day of August, 1939.

[Seal] MARY M. DONETTE

Notary Public in and for the County of Los Angeles, State of California.

[Endorsed]: Filed Aug. 30, 1939. Paul P. O'Brien, Clerk. [370]

[Title of Circuit Court of Appeals and Cause.]

STIPULATION DESIGNATING THE RECORD NECESSARY FOR THE CONSIDERATION OF THE APPEAL HEREIN.

(Rule 19, Subdivision 6, of Circuit Court of Appeals, Ninth Circuit.)

It is hereby stipulated by and between the parties hereto through their respective counsel pursuant to Rule 19, Subdivision 6, of the Rules of the Circuit Court of Appeals for the Ninth Circuit, that the record as designated in the stipulation filed in the District Court on the 26th day of August, 1939, dated the 25th day of August, 1939, and each and every part thereof, shall be and is hereby designated as the parts of the record necessary for the consideration of the appeal herein.

Dated this 25th day of August, 1939.

BEN HARRISON
United States Attorney for the Southern District of California.

ERNEST D. FOOKS
Attorney,
Department of Justice.
Attorneys for Appellant.

AL. GERLACK
Attorney for Appellee.

[Endorsed]: Filed Aug. 30, 1939. Paul P. O'Brien, Clerk. [372]

[Title of Circuit Court of Appeals and Cause.]

STIPULATION AND ORDER THAT CERTAIN VOLUMINOUS EXHIBITS NEED NOT BE PRINTED IN THE PRINTED RECORD ON APPEAL.

It is hereby stipulated, with the approval of the Court, by counsel for the respective parties herein, that in addition to the printed record on appeal heretofore agreed upon, the hereinafter enumerated original exhibits introduced at the trial of the above-entitled cause, said exhibits not constituting a part of the printed record on appeal, may be incorporated in and made a part of the record on appeal by reference only, said exhibits being specifically enumerated as follows:

Defendant's Exhibits "H", "I", "J", "J-1", "J-2", "J-3", "J-4", "J-5", "J-6", "J-7", "J-8", "J-9", "J-10", "J-11", "J-12", "J-13", "J-14", "J-15", "J-16", "J-17"; Plaintiff's Exhibits "1", "2", "18", "19", "20",, and "29". [374]

Dated: this 7th day of Sept. 1939.

BEN HARRISON
United States Attorney for the Southern District of California.

ERNEST D. FOOKS
Attorney, Department of Justice.
Attorneys for Appellant.

AL. GERLACK
Attorney for Appellee.

It is so ordered, this 7th day of Sept. 1939.

CURTIS D. WILBUR,
Judge, United States Circuit Court of Appeals, for the Ninth Circuit.

[Endorsed]: Filed Sept. 7, 1939. Paul P. O'Brien, Clerk. [375]

[Title of Circuit Court of Appeals and Cause.]

STIPULATION AND ORDER AS TO THE RECORD ON APPEAL.

It Is Hereby Stipulated by and between the parties hereto, through their respective counsel, with the approval of the Court, that the stipulation as to the record on appeal incorporated in Volume I of the Transcript of Record on Appeal may be substituted by this stipulation and that the following hereinafter enumerated parts of the record, proceedings and evidence be included in and shall constitute the record on appeal herein pursuant to Rule 75 (f) of the Rules of Civil Procedure for the District Courts of the United States:

1. Complaint;
2. Notice of filing complaint; [377]
3. Affidavit of service of complaint;
4. Answer;
5. Affidavit of service of Answer;
6. Minute Order directing filing of jury verdict and the verdict;
7. Judgment;
8. Amended Judgment;
9. Second Amended Judgment;
10. Defendant's Notice of Motion for Judgment Notwithstanding the Verdict;
11. Defendant's Motion for Judgment Notwithstanding the Verdict;
12. Minute Order Denying Defendant's Motion for Judgment Notwithstanding the Verdict;
13. Certified Reporter's Transcript of all proceedings, except the pages hereinafter enumerated, which will be omitted or corrected, as follows:

Volume I, pages 2, 3, 4, 5, 6, and lines 1 to 8, inclusive, of page 7, to be omitted;

Volume I, line 20, page 27, to be changed to read: "Q. They told you you had T.B. in 1924, didn't they?", instead of as shown by Reporter's Transcript;

Volume I, page 148, beginning at line 7, and continuing to and including line 14 of page 150, to be omitted;

Volume II, page 180, to be omitted;

Volume II, page 224, beginning at line 7, to be omitted;

Volume II, page 266, beginning at line 26, and continuing to and including line 23 of page 298, to be omitted.

14. Exhibits introduced in evidence at the trial, hereinafter enumerated as follows:

Government's Exhibits "A" to "F", inclusive, and Defendant's Exhibits "G" and "K";

Only pages 21, 22 and first 16 lines of page 23, ending with the word "died", of Plaintiff's Exhibit 20; [378]

Plaintiff's Exhibits 21 to 28, inclusive.

15. Notice of Appeal;

16. Order extending time to August 30, 1939, to file the record on appeal and to docket the cause;

17. Stipulation and Order for transmitting all Exhibits;

18. Stipulation and orders of Trial Judge and the Senior Circuit Judge that the quoted language of the Trial Court appearing in the certified Reporter's Transcript of the proceedings, beginning at line 17, page 264, with the word "Upon" and continuing to and ending with the word "Waived"

at line 24 of page 264, and the quoted language of the Trial Court in the said Transcript, beginning with the word "total" at line 26, page 264, and continuing to and ending with the word "interest" at line 4, page 265, may be substituted by different language;

19. This stipulation designating the contents of the record on appeal;

20. Certificate of Clerk authenticating the record.

21. Stipulation and Order dated September 7, 1939, that certain voluminous exhibits need not be printed in the printed record on appeal.

Dated: This 7th day of September, 1939.

BEN HARRISON,
United States Attorney for the Southern District of California,

ERNEST D. FOOKS,
Attorney, Department of Justice,
Attorneys for Appellant.

AL. GERLACK,
Attorney for Appellee.

It Is So Ordered This 7th Day of September, 1939.

CURTIS D. WILBUR,
Judge, United States Circuit Court of Appeals for the Ninth Circuit.

[Endorsed]: Filed Sept. 7, 1939. Paul P. O'Brien, Clerk. [379]

Jurisdiction......
Statement of the case..
Question presented
Statement of points....
Pertinent statutes and reg...
Summary of the evidence
Argument...
There was no substantial
became totally and pe
1933, or before the la
December 31, 1933
Conclusion.....

Cases:

Bennett v. *United States*

Eggen v. *United States*,
Falbo v. *United States*,
291 U. S. 646..
Franklin v. *United States*,
Hunter v. *United States*,
Lumbra v. *United States*,
McDonald v. *United States*
304 U. S. 594..
Mason v. *United States*,
Nalbantian v. *United States*
Nicolay v. *United States*,
Robinson v. *United States*
United States v. *Alvord*,
291 U. S. 661
United States v. *Andrews*
United States v. *Bishop*,
United States v. *Brewer*,
United States v. *Bryan*
May 2, 1936.......
United States v. *Clemons*
United States v. *Crews*,
United States v. *Diehl*,
United States v. *Huiner*

190009—39——1

INDEX

Page

Jurisdiction ---- 1
Statement of the case ---- 2
Question presented ---- 3
Statement of points ---- 4
Pertinent statutes and regulations ---- 4
Summary of the evidence ---- 5
Argument ---- 13
There was no substantial evidence to establish that plaintiff became totally and permanently disabled on August 30, 1933, or before the lapse of the insurance contract on December 31, 1933 ---- 15
Conclusion ---- 20

CITATIONS

Cases:

Bennett v. *United States*, decided August 7, 1939, unreported ---- 18
Eggen v. *United States*, 58 F. (2d) 616 ---- 17
Falbo v. *United States*, 64 F. (2d) 948, affirmed per curiam. 291 U. S. 646 ---- 17, 19
Franklin v. *United States*, 73 F. (2d) 655 ---- 13
Hunter v. *United States*, 94 F. (2d) 194 ---- 18
Lumbra v. *United States*, 290 U. S. 551 ---- 13
McDonald v. *United States*, 94 F. (2d) 893, certiorari denied, 304 U. S. 564 ---- 18
Mason v. *United States*, 63 F. (2d) 791 ---- 14
Nalbantian v. *United States*, 54 F. (2d) 63 ---- 13
Nicolay v. *United States*, 51 F. (2d) 170 ---- 14, 18
Robinson v. *United States*, 87 F. (2d) 343 ---- 18
United States v. *Alvord*, 66 F. (2d) 455, certiorari denied, 291 U. S. 661 ---- 13, 15
United States v. *Anderson*, 76 F. (2d) 337 ---- 19
United States v. *Bishop*, 90 F. (2d) 65 ---- 14
United States v. *Brewer*, 97 F. (2d) 899 ---- 17, 18
United States v. *Bryan*, 82 F. (2d) 784, rehearing denied May 2, 1936 ---- 18
United States v. *Clements*, 96 F. (2d) 533 ---- 17
United States v. *Crew*, 84 F. (2d) 869 ---- 19
United States v. *Diehl*, 62 F. (2d) 343 ---- 13
United States v. *Hainer*, 61 F. (2d) 581 ---- 13

190502—39——1

Cases—Continued. Page

United States v. *Hammond*, 87 F. (2d) 226 ... 17

United States v. *Hansen*, 70 F. (2d) 230, certiorari denied, 293 U. S. 604 ... 13

United States v. *Harrison*, 49 F. (2d) 227 ... 13

United States v. *Ivey*, 64 F. (2d) 653 ... 19

United States v. *LaFavor*, 96 F. (2d) 425 ... 13

United States v. *Lancaster*, 70 F. (2d) 515 ... 19

United States v. *Linkhart*, 64 F. (2d) 747 ... 13

United States v. *McCreary*, 61 F. (2d) 804 ... 13, 15

United States v. *McRae*, 77 F. (2d) 88, certiorari denied, 295 U. S. 759 ... 18

United States v. *Middleton*, 81 F. (2d) 205 ... 18

United States v. *Spaulding*, 293 U. S. 498, rehearing denied, 294 U. S. 731 ... 13

United States v. *Walker*, 77 F. (2d) 415, certiorari denied, 296 U. S. 612 ... 19

United States v. *Wilfore*, 66 F. (2d) 255 ... 19

Statutes:

War Risk Insurance Act of October 6, 1917 (c. 105, secs. 400, 402, 40 Stat. 409) ... *

Section 5 of the World War Veterans' Act, 1924, as amended July 3, 1930, c. 849, sec. 1, 46 Stat. 991 (U. S. C., Title 38, Sec. 426) ... *

In the United States Circuit Court of Appeals for the Ninth Circuit

No. 9281

UNITED STATES OF AMERICA, APPELLANT

v.

WILSON A. HOLLAND, APPELLEE

UPON APPEAL FROM THE DISTRICT COURT OF THE UNITED STATES FOR THE SOUTHERN DISTRICT OF CALIFORNIA, CENTRAL DIVISION

BRIEF FOR THE APPELLANT

JURISDICTION

This is a suit on a contract of United States Government (converted) insurance. The complaint alleged that application for insurance benefits filed with the Veterans' Administration on or about February 12, 1937, was denied May 14, 1938 (R. 3–4). The answer averred that claim for insurance filed March 16, 1937, was denied May 9, 1938, and notice of denial mailed the same date (R. 10). The jurisdictions of this court and the District Court have been properly invoked under Section 19 of the World War Veterans' Act, 1924, as amended (38 U. S. C. 445).

A judgment was entered in favor of the plaintiff March 2, 1939 (R. 14–17), based on a jury verdict (R. 14). Notice of appeal was filed June 1, 1939 (R. 28).

STATEMENT OF THE CASE

Wilson A. Holland, plaintiff-appellee, brought this suit against the United States, defendant-appellant, seeking a recovery of total permanent disability benefits under a contract of United States Government (converted) insurance.

Facts admitted by the pleadings were that plaintiff served with the military forces from May 6, 1917, to August 3, 1920, and while in service applied for and obtained war risk term insurance in the sum of $10,000, which lapsed for nonpayment of the monthly premium due September 1, 1920. Effective April 1, 1927, he reinstated and converted his insurance to a $10,000 contract of United States Government life insurance, upon which he continued to pay the premiums to include the month of November 1933, extending protection under the terms of the policy to the expiration of the grace period on December 31, 1933. No premium payments were made after that date and the policy lapsed (R. 2, 9–10).

The issue, as raised by the pleadings, was whether the contract matured by total and permanent disability on August 30, 1933, the plaintiff alleging (R. 2–4), and the defendant denying (R. 10–11), that total permanent disability occurred on this date. The disabilities were alleged to be pulmonary tuberculosis, chest trouble, and other disabilities (R. 3).

This issue was tried before the Honorable Jeremiah Neterer, District Judge, and a jury, resulting in a jury verdict for the plaintiff, after a motion for a directed verdict made by the defendant at the close of the evidence, upon the ground that there was no substantial evidence of total permanent disability to take the case to the jury, was overruled (R. 337, 362, 364). The jury fixed the date of total permanent disability as of August 30, 1933 (R. 14).

The question presented on this appeal is whether the trial court erred in overruling the motion for a directed verdict, it being the Government's contention that the trial court did so err, the evidence affirmatively establishing that the plaintiff was gainfully employed at various occupations for a substantial period of time after the date of his alleged total permanent disability. The evidence bearing upon this question is summarized herein under the title "Summary of the Evidence."

QUESTION PRESENTED

Whether there was any substantial evidence to establish that plaintiff became totally and permanently disabled on August 30, 1933, or before the expiration of the grace period on December 31, 1933.

STATEMENT OF POINTS

(R. 385)

4. That the Court erred in denying the defendant's motion for a directed verdict and submitting the case to the jury for its determination on the ground that the plaintiff had failed to show by substantial evidence that he became permanently and totally disabled while his contract of insurance was in force (R. 252 and 266).

5. That the Court erred in making and entering its Minute Order of March 20, 1939, denying defendant's motion for judgment notwithstanding the verdict.

PERTINENT STATUTES AND REGULATIONS

The contract sued upon was issued pursuant to the provisions of the War Risk Insurance Act of October 6, 1917 (c. 105, secs. 400, 402, 40 Stat. 409), and insured against death or total permanent disability occurring during the life of the contract.

Section 5 of the World War Veterans' Act, 1924, as amended July 3, 1930, c. 849, sec. 1, 46 Stat. 991 (U. S. C., Title 38, Sec. 426), is, in part, as follows:

> The director, subject to the general direction of the President, shall administer, execute, and enforce the provisions of this Act, and for that purpose shall have full power and authority to make rules and regulations, not inconsistent with the provisions of this Act, which are necessary or appropriate to carry out its purposes, * * *.

Total permanent disability is defined in the converted policy as follows:

> 9. Total permanent disability as referred to herein is any impairment of mind or body which continuously renders it impossible for the disabled person to follow any substantially gainful occupation and which is founded upon conditions which render it reasonably certain that it will continue throughout the life of the person suffering from it. * * *

SUMMARY OF THE EVIDENCE

Plaintiff worked in a United States Post Office in Iowa from March 1922 to September 1924, when he became ill and went on a leave of absence (R. 50–51).

On December 30, 1924, he was examined by a Veterans' Bureau physician and his condition was diagnosed as pulmonary tuberculosis, chronic, minimal, active; pleuritis, chronic, purulent (R. 48, 70–74).

In the fall of 1924 he received treatment in a private hospital, and in January of 1925 he was admitted to the Veterans' Bureau Hospital at Fort Lyon, Colorado, where he remained until May 1925 (R. 39).

Medical reports made by Government physicians during the period he was hospitalized at Fort Lyon, and thereafter until he returned to work in June of 1927, contained the following diagnoses:

> February 4, 1925: Moderate tuberculosis of the right apex and upper. Far advanced tuberculosis of the left chest with an empyema which is filled with pus (R. 74).
>
> February 24, 1925: Chronic pulmonary tuberculosis, active, far advanced; empyema, left chest (R. 76).
>
> May 5, 1925: Chronic pulmonary tuberculosis, active, far advanced; tuberculous empyema, drainage, left chest (R. 77).
>
> October 1, 1925: Chronic pulmonary tuberculosis, active; empyema, left, healed; chronic pleurisy with fibrosis, left (R. 79).
>
> October 6, 1925: A sputum analysis resulted in a finding of tubercle bacilli (R. 79).
>
> August 19, 1926: Chronic pulmonary tuberculosis, moderately advanced, quiescent, improved (R. 80–81).
>
> March 2, 1927: Chronic pulmonary tuberculosis, moderately advanced, apparently arrested; pleurisy, suppurative, healed, left chest (R. 81).

In April 1927 he reinstated and converted his insurance, and was examined at that time (R. 58).

Upon the advice of Veterans' Bureau physicians that he could do so safely, he returned to work (R. 41), and worked from June or July to December 1927 in a Post Office at Glendale, California (R. 51).

From December 1927 to January 1931 he worked for the Pickwick Corporation, Los Angeles, California, at weekly wages of $25.00 (R. 51, 211, 235)

From January 1931 to March 1933, with the exception of a two-months' period of temporary employment as a deputy assessor at $140.00 per month, he attended Southwestern University (R. 52–53).

After this he was employed as follows:

March 1, 1933, to August 31, 1933—6 months: Bookkeeper at State Hospital, Spadra, California, $120.00 per month plus a monthly allowance of $11.00 for maintenance; total, $786.00 (R. 253–260).

December 13, 1933, to April 30, 1934—4½ months: Bookkeeper for State Relief Administration, San Francisco, California, commencing at monthly wages of $125.00; total, $594.68 (R. 259–261).

May 27, 1934, to June 13, 1934—8 days: Bookkeeper at Preston School of Industry, Ione, California, $120.00 per month; total, $31.35 (R. 261–262).

June 7, 1934, to July 25, 1935—59 weeks: Consulting Accountant and Supervisor for State Relief Administration, $33.30 to $39.25 per week; total, $2,164.32 (R. 53–54, 242, 246–249).

July 26, 1935, to June 19, 1936—11 months: Acting Chief of Administrative Division, State Accounts Office, U. S. Treasury, San Francisco, California, $225.00 per month; total, $2,475.00 (R. 287–288, 293, 298).

His last employment was terminated because of a hemorrhage of the lungs, and he has done nothing since then (R. 44).

190502—39——2

He was hospitalized at the Veterans' Administration Hospital, San Fernando, California, from June 13, 1936, to June 19, 1937 (R. 38, 44). He was readmitted on October 1, 1938, and was a patient there at the time of the trial on February 19, 1939 (R. 38).

Examination reports made by Veterans' Administration physicians subsequent to the reinstatement of plaintiff's insurance on April 1, 1927, contained the following diagnoses:

September 30, 1927: Chronic pulmonary tuberculosis, moderately advanced, arrested; post anterior, left, emphysema, healed; chronic pleurisy, fibrous, left base (R. 82).

October 15, 1927: "After a careful review of all the medical evidence in file, the undersigned members of the T. B. Board conclude that claimant did manifest pulmonary tuberculosis from date of separation from service. Definitely arrested." (Signed by three doctors.) (R. 83.)

March 16, 1931: Chronic pulmonary tuberculosis, moderately advanced, with chronic fibrous pleurisy left base, arrested; postoperative emphysema (R. 83, 84).

February 13, 1932: (a) Chronic pulmonary tuberculosis, moderately advanced, arrested; (b) pleurisy, fibrous, chronic, left, following empyema (R. 84, 85).

June 12–27, 1936: Chronic pulmonary tuberculosis, far advanced, active; chronic pleurisy, fibrous, left base (R. 87).

September 18, 1936: Chronic pulmonary tuberculosis, far advanced, active (R. 87).

Describing his condition on August 30, 1933, plaintiff testified:

> Well, at that time I felt very tired all the time. It just seemed as though I could never get rested. I would go to bed at night and put in a full night's sleep, from eight to ten hours, and when I would wake up the next morning it just seemed as though I had never been to bed, like I had been working all night instead of sleeping. I was rather nervous; in fact, little things seemed to upset me, like noise. I occasionally had some night sweats at that time. I coughed some and raised some sputum; but the main feeling I had was one of fatigue. I was just always tired (R. 39).

He further testified that he had felt more or less the same since he was stricken with tuberculosis in 1924 (R. 39), and that there was very little difference in his feeling at the present time (R. 47).

During the fall and early winter of 1933 he rested in bed about 20 hours per day (R. 42–43), and as a result "felt a great deal better, but * * * was still tired." His nervousness improved (R. 43).

He returned to work in December 1933, as it was financially necessary for him to do so, accepting his position with the State Relief Administration, which had been offered him because of his familiarity with the state accounting system in California (R. 44).

There was testimony that he worked hard (R. 124); that he was an excellent bookkeeper (R. 62); and that his services were satisfactory (R. 108–110, 289, 297–298). There was also testimony that he lost time from work (R. 45–47, 117, 108, 291–292, 299, 306); that he seemed to tire easily (R. 108, 119, 295); that he rested and refrained from social activities, spending all of his week ends in bed (R. 46, 101–102); that he was slight of build, underweight, and undernourished R. 62, 117, 271, 294, 297); and that he suffered from frequent colds (R. 102, 119, 299–300).

From February 12, 1932, to June of 1936, plaintiff was not examined by and did not seek treatment from the Veterans' Administration (R. 50). Asked why he did not return to the Veterans' Hospital for further treatment if he was feeling so badly, he answered: "Because I had had examinations before. They seldom ever tell you anything at the Veterans' Administration when they give you an examination" (R. 55).

Applications which the plaintiff filed with the Los Angeles County Civil Service Commission on November 28, 1931 (R. 182–191), January 20, 1932 (R. 191–199), February 19, 1932 (R. 199–207), November 3, 1932 (R. 230–239), and November 29, 1933 (R. 208–213), in which he represented under oath that his health was good, were introduced.

Dr. Robert E. Wyres, plaintiff's witness, testified that he examined plaintiff's chest on August 30, 1933, and made a diagnosis of chronic pulmonary tuberculosis, active, "on the borderline between moderately advanced and far advanced" (R. 63, 90). An X-ray picture confirmed this diagnosis (R. 63). He was of the opinion that the case was a permanent or chronic one (R. 69). Considering the physical findings recorded on the various examination reports which were introduced, together with plaintiff's testimony, he expressed the opinion that plaintiff had only "a small chance," about one in ten, of "becoming an arrested case of tuberculosis on August 30, 1933, even had he taken the best of medical care, including going to a sanitarium" (R. 89–90).

On cross-examination he testified that he advised plaintiff "that he had to take care of himself, that he needed rest" (R. 97–98). He thought that plaintiff's working until June 1936 "changed the outlook somewhat" as to his chances for recovery in August 1933 (R. 98). He further stated that with a tubercular condition, rest is one of the "most therapeutic measures we have," and that "work would aggravate his condition and make it worse" (R. 98).

Dr. Harry Cohn, a specialist in tuberculosis, testified for the plaintiff (R. 121–123), that he first examined plaintiff in January 1937; that an X-ray picture was taken (R. 123) which revealed active tuberculosis (R. 126). Shown the X-ray made of the plaintiff on August 30, 1933 (R. 127), he testified that it very definitely showed active tuberculosis (R. 128). He was of the opinion, based upon a consideration of the several examination reports which had been introduced, his own report, and the X-ray picture of August 30, 1933, that the probabilities of plaintiff obtaining an arrest or cure of his tuberculosis at the time of his examination in January 1937 were very poor (R. 129). His diagnosis was far-advanced, active tuberculosis, with additional complications (R. 130). Asked to consider the findings on the reports made by Government doctors, and to state what the probabilities were of plaintiff obtaining an arrest of his tuberculosis, with the best of medical care, on August 30, 1933, he stated that the odds were very much against his securing an arrest of his tuberculosis at that time (R. 130). He thought the X-ray picture made on August 30, 1933, showed tuberculosis which was at least moderately advanced (R. 137).

Dr. Mary Jones Mentzer, a chest specialist, testified for the plaintiff by deposition that she examined him on September 19, 1935 (R. 153), and diagnosed his condition as bilateral pulmonary tuberculosis, active, bordering between moderately advanced and far advanced; empyema; and acute pleurisy (R. 154–156). The diagnosis was confirmed by X-ray (R. 156). Predicating her opinion on the examination reports in evidence and her own examination, she expressed the opinion that the probable effect of plaintiff following an occupation or of engaging in physical or mental labor in September 1935 was disastrous (R. 162). She thought that plaintiff had very little chance of getting well "then or now" (R. 166–167).

Dr. Leon Shulman, Government witness, testified that the X-ray picture of August 30, 1933, revealed fibrosis and an arrested condition, and that it did not show active tuberculosis (R. 309, 312–313).

ARGUMENT

There was no substantial evidence to establish that plaintiff became totally and permanently disabled on August 30, 1933, or before the lapse of the insurance contract on December 31, 1933

Relying upon the principle announced by the Supreme Court in *Lumbra* v. *United States,* 290 U. S. 441, and *United States* v. *Spaulding,* 293 U. S. 498, rehearing denied, 294 U. S. 731, and by various United States Circuit Courts of Appeals in numerous decisions,[1] that work performed by an insured

---

[1] *United States* v. *McCreary*, 61 F. (2d) 804 (C. C. A. 9th); *United States* v. *Hansen*, 70 F. (2d) 230 (C. C. A. 9th), certiorari denied, 293 U. S. 604; *United States* v. *Hainer*, 61 F. (2d) 581 (C. C. A. 9th); *United States* v. *LaFavor*, 96 F. (2d) 425 (C. C. A. 9th); *United States* v. *Alvord*, 66 F. (2d) 455 (C. C. A. 1st), certiorari denied, 291 U. S. 661; *United States* v. *Harrison*, 49 F. (2d) 227 (C. C. A. 4th); *Franklin* v. *United States*, 73 F. (2d) 655 (App. D. C.); *United States* v. *Diehl*, 62 F. (2d) 343 (C. C. A. 4th); *Nalbantian* v. *United States*, 54 F. (2d) 63 C. C. A. 7th), certiorari denied, 285 U. S. 536; *United States* v. *Linkhart*,

after the date of alleged total permanent disability may be of such duration and character as to conclusively negative the claim, it is submitted that the work performed by the plaintiff after August 30, 1933, refuted his claim that he became totally and permanently disabled on that date. The evidence established that he had been regularly employed for two and one-half years after the lapse of his contract and received salary in excess of $5,200. As stated by the Supreme Court in *Lumbra* v. *United States, supra:*

> It may be assumed that occasional work for short periods by one generally disabled by impairment of mind or body does not as a matter of law negative total permanent disability. But that is not this case. Petitioner, while claiming to be weak and ill and, contrary to the opinion and diagnoses of examining physicians that he was really unable to work, did in fact do much work. For long periods amounting in the aggregate to more than five years out of the ten following the lapse of the policy he worked for substantial pay. No witness, lay or expert, testified to matters of fact or expressed opinion tending to support petitioner's claim that he had suffered "total permanent disability" before his policy lapsed. Unless by construction these words are given a

---

64 F. (2d) 747 (C. C. A. 7th); *Nicolay* v. *United States*, 51 F. (2d) 170 (C. C. A. 10th); *United States* v. *Bishop*, 90 F. (2d) 65 (C. C. A. 6th); *Mason* v. *United States*, 63 F. (2d) 791 (C. C. A. 2d).

> meaning far different from that they are ordinarily used and understood to convey the evidence must be held not sufficient to support a verdict for petitioner. The trial court should have directed a verdict for the United States. *Gunning* v. *Cooley,* 281 U. S. 90, 93. *Stevens* v. *The White City,* 285 U. S. 195, 204.

Also, as stated by this court in *United States* v. *McCreary,* 61 F. (2d) 804:

> The physical facts positively contradict the statements of conclusion of the witnesses, and must control. The Court may not disregard them. * * * Judgments should not stand upon statements or conclusions that are not predicated upon facts * * *.

This same principle was stated by the United States Circuit Court of Appeals for the First Circuit in *United States* v. *Alvord,* 66 F. (2d) 455, certiorari denied, 291 U. S. 661:

> To say that a person, who could do, and did do, the amount of work which the plaintiff performed following his discharge from the army, was during that period "totally and permanently disabled," is to say something which is obviously not so, if the words be given their usual meaning. They are powerful words carrying a high content of meaning which perhaps has not always been fully recognized in cases of this character * * *.

Although the authorities recognize that employment for relatively short periods, performed at a risk to an insured's health, should not defeat a claim, and plaintiff endeavored, through the testimony of his medical witnesses, to bring his case within this rule, it is submitted that such a case was not made out, for medical evidence was lacking to show that his tuberculosis was active during the period he was working. For aught that appears, the disease was arrested during this period, as it had been earlier, for none of his medical witnesses had examined him between the dates of August 30, 1933, and September 19, 1935, and he did not seek or receive medical treatment from the Veterans' Administration between the dates of February 13, 1932, and June 13, 1936, although aware of his right to do so. Thus there was left in the realm of speculation the question as to whether the work which he performed materially injured his health. The opinions of his medical witnesses, based largely upon the X-ray of August 30, 1933, that work at that time would be harmful, would hardly seem sufficient to sustain the burden of proof resting upon the plaintiff of establishing that he could not with safety to his health follow the gainful occupations which he did in fact pursue. In the *Spaulding* case there was positive medical opinion testimony to the effect that Spaulding's work was injurious to his health, and in holding that such testimony must yield to the facts the Supreme Court stated:

> The opinions of respondent's medical witnesses that work impaired his health and tended to shorten his life had no substantial bearing upon the question whether total disability while the policy was in force continued during the subsequent years. As against the facts directly and conclusively established, this opinion evidence furnishes no basis for opposing inferences.

Cf. *United States* v. *Clements,* 96 F. (2d) 533 (App. D. C.).

Moreover, the fact that he did work for such a substantial period without being under the compulsion of seeking medical attention would strongly suggest that the activity found on Dr. Wyres' examination of August 30, 1933, was not then permanent in the sense that it would not yield to proper treatment as formerly, had such treatment been promptly undertaken. It is, of course, well settled that when the claimed disability is tuberculosis, it is incumbent upon the plaintiff to prove by substantial evidence that the disease has progressed during the life of the insurance contract to the stage where it is beyond the reasonable expectation of arrest before there is proof of permanency,[2]

---

[2] *Falbo* v. *United States*, 64 F. (2d) 948 (C. C. A. 9th), affirmed *per curiam*, 291 U. S. 646; *Eggen* v. *United States*, 58 F. (2d) 616 (C. C. A. 8th); *United States* v. *Hammond*,

and that this must always remain uncertain where treatment which may effect an arrest or cure is not undertaken.[3] An insured's only alternative in such a situation is to keep his policy in force by the payment of premiums until permanency definitely develops. As stated in *United States* v. *Brewer,* 97 F. (2d) 899 (C. C. A. 5th):

> An insured who suspects his presently total disability may prove permanent must pay his premiums until permanency fairly appears. This rule not only accords with the Secretary of the Treasury's definition of permanency, but seems to us the fair basis for such insurance, especially where no claim has been made under the policy when it is suffered to lapse. * * *

Failure to take treatment destroys the probative force that might otherwise attach to the continu-

---

87 F. (2d) 226 (C. C. A. 5th); *Hunter* v. *United States*, 94 F. (2d) 194 (C. C. A. 5th); *McDonald* v. *United States*, 94 F. (2d) 893 (C. C. A. 5th), certiorari denied, 304 U. S. 564; *United States* v. *Bryan*, 82 F. (2d) 784 (C. C. A. 5th), rehearing denied May 2, 1936; *United States* v. *Middleton*, 81 F. (2d) 205 (C. C. A. 6th), *United States* v. *McRae*, 77 F. (2d) 88 (C. C. A. 4th), certiorari denied, 295 U. S. 759; *Robinson* v. *United States*, 87 F. (2d) 343 (C. C. A. 2d); *Bennett* v. *United States* (App. D. C.), decided August 7, 1939, not yet reported; *Nicolay* v. *United States*, 51 F. (2d) 170 (C. C. A. 10th).

[3] *United States* v. *Brewer*, 97 F. (2d) 899 (C. C. A. 5th); *United States* v. *Hammond*, *supra; Robinson* v. *United States*, *supra; McDonald* v. *United States*, *supra.*

ance of the disability.[4] The mere fact that a permanent and total disability may have resulted subsequent to the lapse of the policy from active tuberculosis existing prior thereto, does not afford a basis for a finding that the disease became totally and permanently disabling at the requisite time.[5]

Nor does the plaintiff's testimony that it was financially necessary for him to work change the complexion of the case for, as stated in *Falbo* v. *United States,* 64 F. (2d) 948 (C. C. A. 9th), affirmed per curiam, 291 U. S. 646:

> But we cannot believe that liability upon these contracts of insurance should be determined by the conduct of the insured after the policy has lapsed, nor by economic circumstances which may influence that conduct. * * *

Finally, plaintiff's action in permitting his policy to lapse for nonpayment of premiums in December 1933, without claiming benefits thereunder, and delaying the filing of claim until more than three years later, indicated that he did not

---

[4] *United States* v. *Anderson*, 76 F. (2d) 337 (C. C. A. 4th); *United States* v. *Walker*, 77 F. (2d) 415 (C. C. A. 5th), certiorari denied, 296 U. S. 612; *United States* v. *Lancaster*, 70 F. (2d) 515 (C. C. A. 4th); *United States* v. *Ivey*, 64 F. (2d) 653 (C. C. A. 10th).

[5] *United States* v. *Crew*, 84 F. (2d) 869 (C. C. A. 5th); *Robinson* v. *United States*, *supra.* Cf. *United States* v. *Wilfore*, 66 F. (2d) 255 (C. C. A. 2d).

consider his disability totally and permanently disabling while his insurance was in force.

CONCLUSION

As plaintiff worked for two and one-half years after the lapse of his insurance contract and was not shown to be suffering from active tuberculosis while so employed, it is respectfully submitted that his claim of total permanent disability was refuted and the judgment should be reversed.

BENJAMIN HARRISON,
United States Attorney.

ATTILIO DI GIROLAMO,
Attorney, Department of Justice.

JULIUS C. MARTIN,
Director, Bureau of War Risk Litigation.

WILBUR C. PICKETT,
Special Assistant to the Attorney General.

THOMAS E. WALSH,
Attorney, Department of Justice.

NOVEMBER 1939.

United States
Circuit Court of Appeals
For the Ninth Circuit

United States of America,
Appellant,

vs.

Wilson A. Holland,
Appellee.

Upon Appeal from the District Court of the United States for the Southern District of California, Central Division.

APPELLEE'S REPLY BRIEF.

Alvin Gerlack,
220 Bush Street,
San Francisco, Calif.
Attorney for Appellee.

PARKER PRINTING COMPANY, 545 SANSOME STREET, SAN FRANCISCO

Subject Index

Page

Statement of Facts 1

Dr. Wyres' Testimony 2

Definition of Total Permanent Disability 5

Points Relied upon by Appellant 6

Additional Point Raised by Appellee 8

Question Presented (With Citations Only)

Is there any substantial evidence to sustain the jury's verdict? 11

The Rule 14

Argument 18

There is abundant substantial evidence in the record to sustain the jury's verdict 18

Preliminary Statement 18

Appellee's condition on August 30, 1933, (the date the jury found total permanent disability) 18

History of Appellee's tuberculosis prior to 1933 20

Appellee's testimony 21

Appellee's tubercular condition after August 30, 1933, including his health while employed 21

Appellee's Medical Evidence 26

Dr. Cohn's testimony 26

Active pulmonary tuberculosis—what it is and how it acts 29

Dr. Mentzer's testimony (deposition) 37

Is there any substantial evidence of appellee's total permanent disability on or prior to August 30, 1933? 41

Since what work the Appellee did was at the risk of his health and life, his work record does not bar him from recovery under his insurance contract 42

Appellee's "work record" 52

Policy incontestable 56

Our Answer to Appellant's Contentions 56

Conclusion 58

Table of Authorities Cited

Pages

Aspinwall, United States v. (C. C. A. 9), 96 Fed. (2d) 867 ..... 7, 11, 53

Barksdale v. United States (C. C. A. 10), 46 Fed. (2d) 762 13
Boyett v. United States (C. C. A. 5), 86 Fed. (2d) 66 7

Carlson v. Benton, 66 Neb. 486, 92 N. W. 600, 1 Am. Cas. 159, 51 L. R. A. (N. S.) 558 7
Carter v. United States (C. C. A. 4), 49 Fed. (2d) 221 ..... 13, 17, 49
Clark v. Arizona Mut. Sav. & Loan Ass'n., 217 Fed. 644 9
Corrigan v. United States (C. C. A. 9), 82 Fed. (2d) 106 17
Corsicana National Bank v. Johnson, 251 U. S. 68, 40 S. Ct. Rep. 82, 64 L. Ed. 141 ..... 11, 17

Diller v. No. Cal. Power Co., 162 Cal. 531 7
Drew v. United States, 104 Fed. (2d) 939 13

Farmers & Merchants Bank v. Arizona Mut. Sav. & Loan Ass'n. (C. C. A. 9), 220 Fed. 1 10
Ford v. United States (C. C. A. 1), 44 Fed. (2d) 754 ..... 13, 17

Gilmore v. United States (C. C. A. 5), 93 Fed. (2d) 774 57
Gray v. United States (C. C. A. 8), 76 Fed. (2d) 233 14
Gunning v. Cooley, 281 U. S. 90, 50 S. Ct. 231, 74 L. Ed. 721 ..... 11, 15

Hartford Life and Annuity Ins. Co. v. Unsell, 144 U. S. 439, 12 S. Ct. 671, 36 L. Ed. 496 7
Hayden v. United States (C. C. A. 9), 41 Fed. (2d) 614 ..... 11, 17

Kelley v. United States (C. C. A. 1), 49 Fed. (2d) 897 ..... 13, 18
Kimball v. Northern Electric Co., 159 Cal. 225 7
King v. Chase, 15 N. H. 9 (41 Am. Dec. 675) 9
Knickerbocker Life Ins. Co. v. Pendleton, 112 U. S. 696, 5 S. Ct. 314, 28 L. Ed. 866 7

Pages
La Marche v. United States (C. C. A. 9), 28 Fed. (2d) 828 11
Law v. United States (D. C. Mont.), 290 Fed. 972 42
Lumbra v. United States, 290 U. S. 551, 54 S. Ct. 272, 78 L. Ed. 492 11, 42, 47, 48, 49, 55

Malavski v. United States (C. C. A. 7), 43 Fed. (2d) 974 13, 17
Marsh v. United States, 33 Fed. (2d) 554 11
McNally v. United States (C. C. A. 4), 52 Fed. (2d) 440 57
Mulivrana v. United States (C. C. A. 9), 41 Fed. (2d) 734 12, 17

Nicolay v. United States, 51 Fed. (2d) 170 47

Parsons v. Bedford, 3 Peters 433, 7 L. Ed. 732 11, 14
Putney v. United States (D. C. Colo.), 4 Fed. Supp. 376, 378 57

Reynolds v. Stockton, 140 U. S. 265, 11 S. Ct. 773, 35 L. Ed. 467 9, 10
Royal Ins. Co. v. Martin, 192 U. S. 149, 24 S. Ct. 247, 48 L. Ed. 385 7
Rye, United States v. (C. C. A. 10), 70 Fed. (2d) 150 47

Sorvik v. United States (C. C. A. 9), 52 Fed. (2d) 406 12, 17
Sprow v. United States, 99 Fed. (2d) 38 12
Standard Oil Co. v. Missouri, 224 U. S. 270, 32 Sup. Co. 406, 56 L. Ed. 760, Ann. Cas. 1913D, 936 10

United States v. Adams, 70 Fed. (2d) 486 13
United States v. Albano (C. C. A. 9), 63 Fed. (2d) 677 13, 42
United States v. Anderson, 70 Fed. (2d) 537 13
United States v. Aspinwall (C. C. A. 9), 96 Fed. (2d) 867 7, 11, 53
United States v. Balance (App. D. C.), 59 Fed. (2d) 1040 57
United States v. Barker, 36 Fed. (2d) 556 11, 17
United States v. Brown (C. C. A. 10), 72 Fed. (2d) 608 13, 45
United States v. Burke (C. C. A. 9), 50 Fed. (2d) 653 12, 15
United States v. Burleyson (C. C. A. 9), 44 Fed. (2d) 868 12, 51
United States v. Dudley (C. C. A. 9), 64 Fed. (2d) 743 12, 16
United States v. Flippence (C. C. A. 10), 72 Fed. (2d) 611 13, 44, 55

Pages

United States v. Francis (C. C. A. 9), 64 Fed. (2d) 865...12, 51, 52
United States v. Godfrey (C. C. A. 1), 47 Fed. (2d) 126 ...13, 17, 48
United States v. Harless (C. C. A. 4), 76 Fed. (2d) 317... 14
United States v. Higbee (C. C. A. 10), 72 Fed. (2d) 773 ...14, 46, 57
United States v. Hill (C. C. A. 9), 99 Fed. (2d) 755 ...11,17, 42, 54, 56
United States v. Kane (C. C. A. 9), 70 Fed. (2d) 396... 12
United States v. Klener (C. C. A. 9), 93 Fed. (2d) 15, 16... 11
United States v. Lawson (C. C. A. 9), 50 Fed. (2d) 646 ...12, 17, 49, 50, 51
United States v. Lesher (C. C. A. 9), 59 Fed. (2d) 53...12, 17
United States v. Meserve, 44 Fed. (2d) 549...12, 17
United States v. Nickel (C. C. A. 8), 70 Fed. (2d) 873... 42
United States v. Patryas, 303 U. S. 341, 58 S. Ct. 551... 56
United States v. Phillips (C. C. A. 8), 44 Fed. (2d) 689...13, 48
United States v. Ranes (C. C. A. 9), 48 Fed. (2d) 582... 7
United States v. Rasar (C. C. A. 9), 45 Fed. (2d) 545...12, 17
United States v. Rice (C. C. A. 9), 47 Fed. (2d) 749...12, 17
United States v. Rye (C. C. A. 10), 70 Fed. (2d) 150... 47
United States v. Sligh (C. C. A. 9), 31 Fed. (2d) 737...46, 57
United States v. Sorrow (C. C. A. 5), 67 Fed. (2d) 372...13, 45, 55
United States v. Stamey (C. C. A. 9), 48 Fed. (2d) 150...12, 17
United States v. Stephens (C. C. A. 9), 73 Fed. (2d) 695... 41
United States v. Storey (C. C. A. 10), 60 Fed. (2d) 484... 13
United States v. Suomy (C. C. A. 9), 70 Fed. (2d) 542... 12
United States v. Thompson (C. C. A. 9), 92 Fed. (2d) 137 ...11, 57
United States v. Todd (C. C. A. 9), 70 Fed. (2d) 540... 12
United States v. Tyrakowski (C. C. A. 7), 50 Fed. (2d) 766 ...13, 18
United States v. White (C. C. A. 9), 77 Fed. (2d) 757... 8, 41
United States v. White (C. C. A. 9), 48 Fed. (2d) 584... 7

Vance v. United States (C. C. A. 7), 43 Fed. (2d) 975...13, 17
Vietti v. Hines, 48 Cal. App. 266, 192 Pac. 80... 14
Wallace v. Penn. R. R. Co., 222 Pa. 556... 7

TABLE OF AUTHORITIES CITED

Pages

STATUTES

Section 307 World War Veterans Act of 1924, as amended July 3, 1930 (38 U. S. C. A. 518) 56

MISCELLANEOUS

Cooley's Briefs on Insurance, Vol. 7, p. 6019 et seq. .... [illegible]

Treasury Decision 20 Bureau of War Risk Insurance, dated March 9, 1918 42

No. 9281

United States Circuit Court of Appeals

For the Ninth Circuit

UNITED STATES OF AMERICA, *Appellant*, vs. WILSON A. HOLLAND, *Appellee*.	}

Upon Appeal from the District Court of the United States for the Southern District of California, Central Division.

APPELLEE'S REPLY BRIEF.

STATEMENT OF FACTS.

This is another "fact" case arising out of a suit at law upon a $10,000.00 policy of United States Government (Converted) life insurance which the insured appellee carried with the defendant's Veterans Administration, and upon which policy the premiums were paid until December 31, 1933.

Appellee served overseas in the Philippine Islands and also in Siberia with the American Expeditionary Forces (R. 101).

The jury by their verdict found as a fact that appellee by reason of chronic, active, advanced and incurable tuberculosis of the lungs, became totally and permanently disabled on August 30, 1933.

He was then employed as accountant at the California State Hospital at Spadra, California, and was on this date physically examined (including X-ray) by Dr. Robert E. Wyres, Assistant Superintendent and one of the doctors on duty there, who testified (R. 62):

> "Q. How was his health at that time? [May to August, 1933]
>
> A. Poor, I would say.
>
> Q. Tell the Court and jury what he looked like at that time.
>
> A. He was lean, lank, and cadaverous looking very much as he is now, undernourished. You would see that he didn't have much energy or that he was not very active, but he was a good bookkeeper and seemed to manage to get by with his work very well.
>
> Q. Were his duties as a bookkeeper arduous at that time?
>
> A. No, it is an occupation where there is no physical exertion. It was light work, and especially so at an institution like we are working in.
>
> Q. Doctor, did you ever make an examination of him during the time he was at Spadra?
>
> A. Yes, sir.

Q. Did you take any x-rays?

A. Yes, sir.

Q. Was that a chest examination?

A. Yes.

Q. Tell the jury what examination you made and what your findings were and what your diagnosis was.

A. As a general rule we do not take care of employees, that is, we don't do that now at all, but at that time we didn't make a special effort to treat employees because they were with us for the purpose of working rather than hospitalization. In his case he was complaining to me about some trouble in his shoulder, some pain, and as I recall a stitch in his side.

Well, I thought that we would give him an examination, so I went over his chest and I took some of his history in the meantime. He had told me that he was or had been having trouble with tuberculosis. After a chest examination I decided we would take an x-ray plate, which I did, and from my examination I would say he had tuberculosis without question. The x-ray plate showed it as well as my examination did.

Q. Was his tuberculosis active at that time?

A. I felt so, yes.

Q. What was the degree of advancement?

A. It would be on the borderline between moderately advanced and far advanced."

and (R. 69):

"Q. Now, Doctor Wyres, at the time of your examination of Mr. Holland here, on August 30, 1933, in your opinion was his tuberculosis then of a temporary or of a permanent nature?

A. It was a permanent or chronic case, I would say, of course.

Q. Chronic?

A. Yes."

also (R. 89):

"Q. Now, Doctor, I will ask you to base your opinion not upon the findings (diagnoses)—you know the difference between findings and diagnoses—disregard the diagnoses—base your opinion merely upon the findings and upon your own examination and findings as shown by your testimony here, and assuming the facts or the evidence as given by Mr. Holland under oath on the witness stand to be true, basing your opinion on those facts, will you tell us in your opinion what were the probabilities of Mr. Holland becoming an arrested case of tuberculosis on August 30, 1933 even had he taken the best of medical care including going to a sanitarium?

A. Well, I would say a small chance, perhaps one in ten.

Q. You mean that the strong probabilities were that he would not have gotten well even had he taken the best of medical care?

A. That is right."

and again (R. 98):

"Q. What effect did work have on his condition, Doctor?

A. Well, in a tubercular condition, of course, naturally, rest is one of the most therapeutic measures we have.

Q. What is therapeutic?

A. Well, it includes direct therapeutics, light therapeutics, and treatment.

Q. In other words, work would aggravate his condition and make it worse?
A. Yes."

Total permanent disability, under his policy, (R. 42, Plaintiff's Exhibit No. 1) reads:

"*Total Permanent Disability.* 11. Total permanent disability as referred to herein is any impairment of mind or body which continuously renders it impossible for the disabled person to follow any substantially gainful occupation, and which is founded upon conditions which render it reasonably certain that the total disability will continue throughout the life of the disabled person. The total permanent disability benefits may relate back to a date not exceeding six months prior to receipt of due proof of such total permanent disability, and any premiums paid after receipt of due proof of total permanent disability, and within the six months, shall be refunded without interest. * * *"

"*Recovery from Disability.* 12. Notwithstanding proof of total permanent disability may have been accepted as satisfactory, the Insured shall at any time, on demand, furnish proof satisfactory to the Director of the United States Veterans Bureau of the continuance of such total permanent disability, and if the Insured shall fail to furnish such proof, all payments of monthly installments on account of such total permanent disability hereunder shall cease, and all premiums thereafter falling due shall be payable in conformity with this policy. * * *"

Counsel for appellant in their brief raise the sole question: Whether there is any substantial evidence to support the jury's verdict and the trial court's action in overruling the defendant's motion for a directed verdict, and denying the defendant's motion for judgment notwithstanding the verdict.

It impresses us that counsel for the appellant are "conveniently brief" in their recitation of the facts in their brief, and as a determination of this appeal on its merits depends upon an examination of the Record to determine if there is *any* substantial evidence to support the verdict, it will therefore be necessary to quote from the Record itself in order to determine if it contains evidence sufficient to justify the verdict.

Counsel for the appellant made and presented a motion for a directed verdict and also a motion to enter judgment for the defendant notwithstanding verdict, and the trial court, in the exercise of a sound judicial discretion, having considered such motion and the evidence as introduced at the trial and having denied the motions, is a determination by the trial court, as well as by the jury, that the verdict was just and amply supported by the evidence.

POINTS RELIED UPON BY APPELLANT.

Counsel for appellant specify five points upon which they intend to rely on their appeal (R. 384).

However, in their brief (page 4), counsel abandon the first three points.

However, appellant's point No. 1 is without merit.

See

Boyett v. United States, (C. C. A. 5th) 86 F. (2d) 66;

United States v. Ranes, (C. C. A. 9th) 48 Fed. (2d) 582;

United States v. White, (C. C. A. 9th) 48 Fed. (2d) 584;

Knickerbocker Life Ins. Co. v. Pendleton, 112 U. S. 696, 5 S. Ct. 314, 28 L. Ed. 866;

Hartford Life and Annuity Ins. Co. v. Unsell, 144 U. S. 439, 12 S. Ct. 671, 36 L. Ed. 496;

Royal Ins. Co. v. Martin, 192 U. S. 149, 24 S. Ct. 247, 48 L. Ed. 385;

Cooley's Briefs on Insurance, Vol. 7, p. 6019 et seq.

Appellant's point No. 2 is also without merit.

These requested instructions were either covered by other instructions given by the Court, or are obviously not a correct statement of the law.

See, also

United States v. Aspinwall, (C. C. A. 9th) 96 Fed. (2d) 867.

Appellant's point No. 3 is likewise without merit.

In addition to Dr. Wyres' testimony (R. 63-67), see:

Carlson v. Benton, 66 Nebr. 486, 92 N. W. 600, 1 Ann. Cas. 159, 51 L. R. A. (N. S.) 558;

Kimball v. Northern Electric Co., 159 Cal. 225;

Wallace v. Penn. R. R. Co., 222 Pa. 556;

Diller v. No. Cal. Power Co., 162 Cal. 531.

ADDITIONAL POINT RAISED BY APPELLEE.

That this Court can notice a plain error not assigned or relied upon is, of course, beyond dispute.

See:

> *United States v. White,* (C. C. A. 9th) 77 Fed. (2d) 757.

The plain errors to which appellee directs the Court's attention is the language inserted over appellee's objection, in the original judgment filed March 2, 1939 (R. 16), reading as follows:

> "* * * less a policy lien of $608.30."

and also the language inserted without appellee's knowledge or consent in the Amended Judgment filed March 13, 1939 (R. 22), reading as follows:

> "* * * after deducting any sums due to the United States for any outstanding lien and interest thereon created by plaintiff upon his insurance policy."

And likewise the language inserted, without appellee's knowledge or consent in the Second Amended Judgment filed March 28, 1939 (R. 26), reading as follows:

> "* * * after deducting any sums due to the United States for any outstanding lien and interest thereon created by plaintiff upon his insurance policy."

There is neither allegation nor proof of any lien or policy loan against the policy. In fact nowhere in the record, except in the judgments themselves, is there even the slightest suggestion of any policy loan or lien against the policy.

In *Clark v. Arizona Mut. Sav. & Loan Ass'n.,* 217 Fed. 644, the late Honorable Wm. W. Sawtelle, then District Judge, in deciding that a judgment containing relief provisions not embraced within the pleadings was void, in a very able opinion, quoted the United States Supreme Court as follows:

> "In Reynolds v. Stockton, 140 U. S. 265, 11 S. Ct. 773, 35 L. Ed. 467, the court uses this language:
>
> > '* * * A defect in a judgment, arising from the fact that the matter decided was not embraced within the issue, has not, it would seem, received much judicial consideration; and yet I cannot doubt that, upon general principles, such a defect must avoid a judgment.'
>
> The court then proceeds to discuss the validity of a judgment which is not embraced within the issues, and says:
>
> > 'A judgment upon a matter outside of the issue must, of necessity, be altogether arbitrary and unjust, as it concludes a point upon which the parties have not been heard. * * * "The matter in issue" has been defined in a case of leading authority as "that matter upon which the plaintiff proceeds by his action, and which the defendant controverts by his pleading." King v. Chase, 15 N. H. 9 (41 Am. Dec. 675). But without multiplying authorities, the proposition suggested by those referred to, and which we affirm, is that in order to give a judgment, rendered by even a court of general jurisdiction, the merit and finality of an adjudication between the parties, it must, with the limitations heretofore stated, be responsive to the issues tendered by the pleadings.'

A judgment must accord with and be warranted by the pleadings of the party in whose favor it is rendered; if it is not supported by the pleadings, it is fatally defective. 23 Cyc. 816, and cases cited. There are many cases in the state courts which decide the same questions, but as the decisions of the Supreme Court are decisive of the issue it has not been thought necessary to cite them."

The above case was affirmed by this Court in *Farmers & Merchants Bank v. Arizona M. S. & L. Ass'n.*, 220 Fed. 1, where Honorable Wm. B. Gilbert, the late distinguished Circuit Judge of this Court, after quoting from *Reynolds v. Stockton*, supra, on page 6 says:

"In *Standard Oil Co. v. Missouri*, 224 U. S. 270, 32 Sup. Ct. 406, 56 L. Ed. 760, Ann. Cas. 1913D, 936, the court said:

'The federal question is whether in that court, with such jurisdiction, the defendants were denied due process of law. Under the fourteenth amendment they were entitled to notice an opportunity to be heard. That necessarily required that the notice and the hearing should correspond, and that the relief granted should be appropriate to that which had been heard and determined on such notice, for even if a court has original general jurisdiction, criminal and civil, at law and in equity, it cannot enter a judgment which is beyond the claim asserted, or which, in its essential character, is not responsive to the cause of action on which the proceeding was based.' "

This plain error, we submit, strongly indicates that this Court should modify the judgment by striking out therefrom the language pertaining to such purported lien.

QUESTION PRESENTED.

(With Citations Only)

IS THERE ANY SUBSTANTIAL EVIDENCE TO SUSTAIN THE JURY'S VERDICT?

Parsons v. Bedford, 3 Peters 433, 7 L. Ed. 732;
Corsicana National Bank v. Johnson, 251 U. S. 68, 40 S. Ct. Rep. 82, 64 L. Ed. 141;
Gunning v. Cooley, 281 U. S. 90, 50 S. Ct. 231, 74 L. Ed. 721;
Lumbra v. United States, 290 U. S. 551, 54 S. Ct. 272, 78 L. Ed. 492;
United States v. Aspinwall, 96 Fed. (2d) 867;
United States v. Hill, 99 Fed. (2d) 755;
United States v. Thompson, (C. C. A. 9) 92 Fed. (2d) 135;
United States v. Klener, (C. C. A. 9) 93 Fed. (2d) 15, 16;
La Marche v. United States, (C. C. A. 9) 28 Fed. (2d) 828;
Marsh v. U. S., 33 Fed. (2d) 554;
United States v. Barker, 36 Fed. (2d) 556;
Hayden v. United States, (C. C. A. 9) 41 Fed. (2d) 614;

Mulivrana v. United States, (C. C. A. 9) 41 Fed. (2d) 734;

United States v. Burke, (C. C. A. 9) 50 Fed. (2d) 653;

United States v. Meserve, (C. C. A. 9) 44 Fed. (2d) 549;

United States v. Rasar, (C. C. A. 9) 45 Fed. (2d) 545;

United States v. Rice, (C. C. A. 9) 47 Fed. (2d) 749;

United States v. Stamey, (C. C. A. 9) 48 Fed. (2d) 150;

Sprow v. United States, 99 Fed. (2d) 38;

United States v. Lawson, (C. C. A. 9) 50 Fed. (2d) 646;

Sorvik v. United States, (C. C. A. 9) 52 Fed. (2d) 406;

United States v. Lesher, (C. C. A. 9) 59 Fed. (2d) 53;

United States v. Dudley, (C. C. A. 9) 64 Fed. (2d) 743;

United States v. Francis, (C. C. A. 9) 64 Fed. (2d) 865;

United States v. Burleyson, (C. C. A. 9) 44 Fed. (2d) 868;

United States v. Todd, (C. C. A. 9) 70 Fed. (2d) 540;

United States v. Suomy, (C. C. A. 9) 70 Fed. (2d) 542;

United States v. Kane, (C. C. A. 9) 70 Fed. (2d) 396;

Vance v. United States, (C. C. A. 7) 43 Fed. (2d) 975;

Malavski v. United States, (C. C. A. 7) 43 Fed. (2d) 974;

Ford v. United States, (C. C. A. 1) 44 Fed. (2d) 754;

United States v. Phillips, (C. C. A. 8) 44 Fed. (2d) 689;

Barksdale v. United States, (C. C. A. 10) 46 Fed. (2d) 762;

United States v. Godfrey, (C. C. A. 1) 47 Fed. (2d) 126;

Carter v. United States, (C. C. A. 4) 49 Fed. (2d) 221;

Kelley v. United States, (C. C. A. 1) 49 Fed. (2d) 897;

United States v. Tyrakowski, (C. C. A. 7) 50 Fed. (2d) 766;

United States v. Storey, (C. C. A. 10) 60 Fed. (2d) 484;

United States v. Albano, (C. C. A. 9) 63 Fed. (2d) 677;

Drew v. United States, 104 Fed. (2d) 939;

United States v. Sorrow, (C. C. A. 5) 67 Fed. (2d) 372;

United States v. Adams, (C. C. A. 10) 70 Fed. (2d) 486;

United States v. Anderson, 70 Fed. (2d) 537;

United States v. Flippence, (C. C. A. 10) 72 Fed. (2d) 611;

United States v. Brown, (C. C. A. 10) 72 Fed. (2d) 608;

United States v. Higbee, 72 Fed. (2d) 773;
United States v. Harless, (C. C. A. 4) 76 Fed. (2d) 317;
Gray v. United States, (C. C. A. 8) 76 Fed. (2d) 233;
Vietti v. Hines, 48 Cal. App. 266, 192 Pac. 80.

We submit the jury's verdict is amply supported by substantial evidence as shown by the record.

THE RULE.

Regarding jury trials, almost one hundred years ago Justice Story of the United States Supreme Court, in *Parsons v. Bedford,* 3 Peters 433, 7 L. Ed. 732, said:

> "The trial by jury is justly dear to the American people. It has always been an object of deep interest and solicitude and every encroachment upon it has been watched with great jealousy. The right to such a trial is, it is believed, incorporated in and secured in every state constitution in the Union * * *. One of the strongest objections originally taken against the Constitution of the United States was the want of an express provision securing the right of trial by jury in civil cases. As soon as the Constitution was adopted, this right was secured by the Seventh Amendment of the Constitution proposed by Congress; and which received an assent of the people so general as to establish its importance as a fundamental guarantee of the rights and liberties of the people."

Probably the leading case in the Federal courts on the quantum of evidence necessary to sustain a jury's verdict is *Gunning v. Cooley,* 281 U. S. 90, 50 S. Ct. 231, 74 L. Ed. 721, in which the court, per Mr. Justice Butler, said (50 S. Ct. 233):

> "Issues that depend on the credibility of witnesses, and the effect or weight of evidence, are to be decided by the jury. And in determining a motion of either party for a peremptory instruction, the court assumes that the evidence for the opposing party proves all that it reasonably may be found sufficient to establish, and that from such facts there should be drawn in favor of the latter all the inferences that fairly are deducible from them. (Citing cases.) Where uncertainty as to the existence of negligence arises from a conflict in the testimony or because, the facts being undisputed, fair-minded men will honestly draw different conclusions from them, the question is not one of law but of fact to be settled by the jury. (Citing cases.)"

And the rule regarding the quantum of evidence necessary to sustain a verdict in the Ninth Circuit has been very aptly stated by the late distinguished Circuit Judge Sawtelle, in our opinion one of the ablest judges ever to have sat on the Circuit Court of Appeals for the Ninth Circuit. In *United States v. Burke,* 50 Fed. (2d) 653, at page 656, Judge Sawtelle said:

> "Courts often experience great difficulty in determining whether a given case should be left to the decision of the jury or whether a verdict

should be directed by the court. Fortunately however, the rule in this circuit has been definitely settled and almost universally observed. Judge Gilbert, for many years and until recently, the distinguished senior judge of this court, whose gift for expression was unsurpassed has stated the rule as follows:

'Under the settled doctrine as applied by all the federal appellate courts, when the refusal to direct a verdict is brought under review on writ of error, the question thus presented is whether or not there was any evidence to sustain the verdict, and whether or not the evidence to support a directed verdict as requested, was so conclusive that the trial court in the exercise of a sound judicial discretion should not sustain a verdict for the opposing party.'

And on a motion for a directed verdict the court may not weigh the evidence, and if there is substantial evidence both for the plaintiff and the defendant, it is for the jury to determine what facts are established even if their verdict be against the decided preponderance of the evidence. (Citing cases.)"

And in *United States v. Dudley,* 64 Fed. (2d) 743, this Court said:

"The question before us is whether or not this evidence is so substantial as to justify submission of the case to the jury. We do not weigh the evidence; what our verdict would have been as jurymen is immaterial."

See also the following decisions of this Court:

United States v. Hill, 99 Fed. (2d) 755;
United States v. Lesher, 59 Fed. (2d) 53;
United States v. Barker, 36 Fed. (2d) 556;
United States v. Meserve, 44 Fed. (2d) 549;
United States v. Rice, 47 Fed. (2d) 749;
United States v. Stamey, 48 Fed. (2d) 150;
United States v. Lawson, 50 Fed. (2d) 646;
Corrigan v. United States, 82 Fed. (2d) 106;
Hayden v. United States, (C. C. A. 9) 41 Fed. (2d) 614;
Mulivrana v. United States, (C. C. A. 9) 41 Fed. (2d) 734;
United States v. Rasar, (C. C. A. 9) 45 Fed. (2d) 545;
Sorvik v. United States, 52 Fed. (2d) 406.

See also:

Corsicana National Bank v. Johnson, 251 U. S. 68, 40 S. Ct. Rep. 82, 64 L. Ed. 141;
Vance v. United States, (C. C. A. 7) 43 Fed. (2d) 975;
Malavski v. United States, (C. C. A. 7) 43 Fed. (2d) 974;
United States v. Godfrey, (C. C. A. 1) 47 Fed. (2d) 126;
Ford v. United States, (C. C. A. 1) 44 Fed. (2d) 754;
Carter v. United States, (C. C. A. 4) 49 Fed. (2d) 221;

Kelley v. United States, (C. C. A. 1) 49 Fed. (2d) 897;

United States v. Tyrakowski, (C. C. A. 7) 50 Fed. (2d) 766.

Bearing in mind the rule, we now turn to an examination of the record to see if there is any substantial evidence upon which the verdict can be sustained under this rule.

ARGUMENT.

THERE IS ABUNDANT SUBSTANTIAL EVIDENCE IN THE RECORD TO SUSTAIN THE JURY'S VERDICT.

Preliminary Statement.

The plaintiff and appellee cannot agree that the statement of facts set forth by counsel for the defendant and appellant in their brief is either fair or accurate. We feel that counsel for the appellant, in setting forth their version of the facts, have utterly disregarded the basic rule of appellate procedure that all conflicts in the evidence are to be resolved in favor of appellee and all reasonable inferences to be drawn therefrom must likewise be resolved in favor of the party in whose favor the jury so found. Applying this rule to the facts we believe the facts as found by the jury to be substantially as follows:

Appellee's condition on August 30, 1933, the date the jury found total permanent disability.

Dr. Robert E. Wyres, the Assistant Superintendent of the California State Hospital at Spadra, where appellee was employed as an accountant, gave appellee a thorough physical examination, including taking an X-ray, and found active, advanced, incurable tuberculosis on the very day the jury found by their verdict that appellee became totally and permanently disabled as a fact. Dr. Wyres' testimony quoted ante (pages 2-5) is sufficient in itself to establish appellee's total permanent disability at the time in question.

Appellee (R. 39) testified concerning his condition on August 30, 1933:

> "Q. Now, will you tell us how you felt, so far as your bodily manifestations were concerned, on August 30, 1933?
>
> A. Well, at that time I felt very tired all the time. It just seemed as though I could never get rested. I would go to bed at night and put in a full night's sleep, from eight to ten hours, and when I would wake up the next morning it just seemed as though I had never been to bed, like I had been working all night instead of sleeping. I was rather nervous, in fact, little things seemed to upset me, like noise. I occasionally had some night sweats at that time. I coughed some and raised some sputum; but the main feeling I had was one of fatigue. I was just always tired."

and again (R. 41):

> "Q. Now, why did you quit that employment? [At Spadra on August 30, 1933]
>
> A. Why, I was just so worn out, so tired out that I just had to rest, and upon the advice of a physician that I should rest I did so; but even without his advice I felt that I could not carry on for the time being any further."

At the time of the trial (February 28, 1939), appellee was and still is a patient at the Government's Veterans Tubercular Hospital at San Fernando, California, suffering from chronic, active, far advanced tuberculosis, with complications, and was then and still is a twenty-four hour bed patient. He got up out of bed to attend the trial.

There is an abundance of additional evidence in the Record on this point, with which we will not burden the Court.

History of Appellee's tuberculosis prior to 1933.

Appellee's tuberculosis began in 1924, was pronounced far advanced (which in most cases is equivalent to being incurable) in February, 1925, by Government doctors at the Government Hospital at Fort Lyon, Colorado (R. 74). In 1927, the Government doctors examined him and made a diagnosis of arrested tuberculosis. He was then permitted to convert his insurance into the present policy which now forms the basis of the present suit. He paid all premiums due on this policy until November, 1933. He was told by the Government doctors in 1927 when they examined him and pronounced his tuberculosis arrested, that it was safe for him to go out and follow a job (R. 57).

Appellee testified (R. 40-41):

> "Q. Did you follow an occupation after you got out of the hospital in 1925?
>
> A. Well, not immediately, not for some two years.

Q. You did after that?

A. More than two years later, I did.

Q. Who advised you that you were able to go to work?

A. The Veterans' Bureau doctors told me I was able to go to work.

Q. It was on their advice that you went back to work?

A. Yes, sir."

Appellee's tubercular condition after August 30, 1933, including his health while employed.

Appellee testified (R. 42-47):

"Q. What did you do after that? [Aug. 30, 1933]

A. Well, I rested for a few months until I didn't have any more money with which to eat.

* * * * * * *

Q. Mr. Holland, after you ceased your employment there what did you do next?

Mr. Di Girolamo: What date is that, please?

Mr. Gerlack: Q. When did you quit, August 30 or 31?

A. I think it was the last day of August.

Q. The 31st?

A. I believe so.

Mr. Di Girolamo: What year?

Mr. Gerlack: 1933.

Q. Did you do anything after that, Mr. Holland?

A. Well, for the first few months I rested. I stayed home and rested.

Q. In what manner did you rest?

A. Well, I stayed in bed nearly all the time.

Q. 24 hours a day?

A. No, not 24 hours a day. I got up for my meals, but I daresay I spent 20 hours a day in bed.

Q. How did you feeling during that time?

A. Well, I was resting. I felt a great deal better, but I was still tired. My nervousness improved quite a little bit.

A Juror: What improved, please?

The Witness: My nervousness, my feeling of nervousness had improved, but I couldn't overcome this feeling of fatigue so quickly or easily as that.

Mr. Gerlack: Q. Did you attempt to work again after that?

* * * * * *

A. Yes, I attempted to work after that.

The Court: Just what was said there, Mr. Holland?

The Witness: I went back to work with the State Relief Administration. They wanted me to take a job and come to work there because I was familiar with the California State System of Accounting procedure. It seems that my name had been gotten out of the Civil Service list as one who was experienced in that line of work. Since it was necessary for me to go back to work I accepted this position. I remained on that job up until the Summer of 1935, and then I got this job with the United States Treasury Department in San Francisco where I remained until I finally had a hemorrhage from the lungs and had to enter the hospital at San Fernando, California in the Summer of 1936.

Mr. Gerlack: Q. You have not done anything since then, Mr. Holland?

A. No, sir.

Q. Now, how much wages did you receive on this S. R. A. job?

A. The initial salary was set up at $125.00 a month, and then when the office was transferred to San Francisco they made some adjustments in all of the salaries, and I believe they raised that to $170.00 a month. There had been an intermediate adjustment for all accountants and they were raised to $150.00. They seemed to feel that $125.00 was hardly the sort of salary for men to receive who were doing that type of work. $170.00, I believe, was the final salary we received.

Q. Just tell us how you felt, so far as your health was concerned, while you worked on that job, Mr. Holland?

A. Well, it didn't differ from what I just told you about the way I felt when I was working at Spadra, at the State Hospital, except if anything is worse because I got to coughing more at that time and I got so tired. Sometimes I didn't think I could pull the day through and very frequently I didn't. I just simply had to go home in the afternoon or at other times I just begged for a day off or sometimes a couple of days, and I would just stay in bed 24 hours a day and rest. Then, feeling a little refreshed, I came back. Other times I would feel extremely fatigued. One time, three months after I went to work on this job, I just got so all in I had to take a week off and I went down on the desert with a friend of mine, somewhere on a ranch down there, and I just spent my time out there living in the sunshine and eating good food. I stayed in bed whenever I felt like it which was just about all the time. Then I would come back to work again. That is the way I carried on all the way through this employment.

Q. What were your duties, were they arduous or light?

A. It wasn't what you would call a difficult job. My fellow workers who had more or less similar jobs didn't regard them as difficult.

Q. I know, but was your work supervisory or what?

A. Well, it was a little of each. I had some supervisory work and then a little later on I had less supervisory work. I actually worked on the accounts themselves trying to set them up in the general ledger.

Q. Now, how long did you work for the Treasury Department, the Treasury Accounts Division?

A. I was there approximately ten months. I believe my appointment dated from some time in August, 1935, and it was early in June, 1936, that I had to leave and enter the hospital after this hemorrhage from my lungs.

Q. How did you get on, how did you feel on that job compared to the way you felt previously?

A. Well, there was no change. You might express it as no change.

Q. When you were not at work, for instance, on evenings, and Saturdays and Sundays, did you enjoy dancing and social activities?

A. Oh, no.

Q. What did you do?

A. That has been out for a good many years. Why, I went to bed. I was always so tired when I got home at night that I didn't feel like eating and went to bed.

Q. You spoke of going home early in the afternoon. How much of the time did you do that?

A. Well, it is a little hard to estimate that, but it happened rather frequently.

Q. Rather frequently?

A. Naturally I tried not to go home any oftener than necessary.

Q. Who was your superior on that State job?

A. H. A. R. Carleton, the State Director.

Q. He was your immediate superior?

A. He was in charge of the whole office.

Q. Now, how did you feel today when you came here? How do you feel now as compared to the way you felt when you quit your work at Spadra?

A. Well, there is very little difference, very little difference. Of course, the fact that I am resting all of my time at home in bed, helps somewhat, but I can't overcome this feeling of fatigue. I just want to rest. I can't get away from that, so I shouldn't say there is a great deal of difference in feeling between the way I feel now and the way I felt in 1933.

Q. How do you feel now as compared to the time you worked on the S. R. A. job?

A. I can't say I feel much different.

Q. What would you say comparing the way you feel now, as compared to the way you felt when you worked for the Treasury Department?

A. Just about the same."

Appellee was also corroborated as to his condition by his wife (R. 101), his immediate employer Harold A. R. Carleton (R. 105) and a fellow employee Roy W. Burton (R. 115).

Appellee's Medical Evidence.

The official government Veterans' Administration medical reports show that appellee had active tuberculosis in 1924 (R. 70-74) which was rated by them as active, far advanced in 1925 (R. 74-76) and arrested in 1927 (R. 83), 1931 (R. 84), and 1932 (R. 85).

We have already quoted from Dr. Wyres' testimony (R. 62, 63, 69) showing that on August 30, 1933 (the date of total permanent disability as found by the jury) appellee had active, advanced and incurable tuberculosis, which condition was permanent and which condition would be aggravated by work or activity of any kind.

Dr. Harry Cohn, now head of the Tuberculosis Division of the Los Angeles City Health Department and one of the outstanding tuberculosis experts of the United States as shown by his qualifications, first explained and interpreted certain X-ray films which he took of appellee in January, 1937, and on February 27, 1939, and stated that those films both showed very definitely, active tuberculosis which Dr. Cohn pointed out to the jury.

Dr. Cohn also examined and interpreted Plaintiff's Exhibit No. 2 which was the X-ray film of appellee taken at Spadra on August 30, 1933. Dr. Cohn then testified (R. 127-130):

> "Q. Now, Doctor, I will show you a film that has been introduced here, Plaintiff's Exhibit 2, which has been testified was an x-ray taken of Mr. Holland at the Spadra Colony, under date of Au-

gust 30, 1933, and ask you to examine that and tell us whether that shows any tuberculosis, active tuberculosis?

A. Any time there is an inflammation in the lungs there is a change in the density of the film.

Juror White: You are holding that up against a light background.

Mr. Gerlack: Q. Hold it here, against the light, Doctor.

A. All right.

Now you see what we call either a cotton density or a snowflake deposit in the lung, from here above, from here above (indicating), while here the lung field is clear (indicating). These shadows here are made up of the arteries and veins. We call that a Hilon shadow present in most cases. There is an absolute condition here (indicating), but from here up you have something that is——

Juror White (Interrupting): The ribs on this side do not appear in their entirety. What causes that?

The Witness: That is caused by the density of the white shadow. The white shadow comes down here on the left side, being more on the left than on the right, and you will find that picture more indefinite there, while above it is more definite; but the ribs here come over from the spine, as you see (indicating).

Mr. Gerlack: Q. That definitely shows he had active tuberculosis?

A. Very definitely.

Q. At the time that film was taken, August 30, 1933?

A. Yes, sir.

Q. Now, Doctor, were you in court this morning when these medical examinations were read?

A. Yes, sir.

Q. You examined those documents personally outside of having heard them?

A. Yes, sir.

Q. You sat at the table and read them, did you not?

A. Yes, sir.

Q. Now, Doctor, assuming the facts to be true as shown by those Government records, and basing your opinion not upon the diagnoses, but merely the findings as shown by those medical reports, and basing your opinion upon this x-ray finding, or this x-ray that you have just interpreted which has been introduced in evidence here, and as the testimony shows was taken at Spadra of Mr. Holland on August 30, 1933, and bearing in mind your own examination of him, in your opinion, I will ask you, first, what were the probabilities of his tuberculosis being cured or even arrested, or apparently arrested, even with the best of medical treatment of the time you first examined him in January, 1937?

A. They were poor.

Q. You mean by that, that the probabilities were against him?

A. Very strongly against him recovering from the existing tuberculosis.

Q. By the way, what is your present diagnosis of his condition?

A. He is classified as far advanced, a far advanced active case of tuberculosis with additional complications.

Q. Now, assuming that, and assuming the findings of these Government reports by Government doctors, in your opinion, what were the probabilities of his tuberculosis becoming arrested even with the best of medical care on August 30, 1933?

A. The odds were very much against his securing an arrest of his tuberculosis in 1933.

Q. At the time the film was taken, do you mean?

A. At the time the film was taken, yes.

Q. Doctor, in your opinion, what is the effect of following an occupation or engaging in any physical or mental labor by persons suffering from active tuberculosis?

A. Generally speaking, it tends to aggravate the existing tuberculosis. There are exceptions, of course, but the rule is what governs."

Active pulmonary tuberculosis—What it is and how it acts.

In describing the disease of tuberculosis, Dr. Cohn testified:

"Q. Doctor, will you give us, for the record, and for the information of the jury here—will you explain this disease of tuberculosis, what it is, how it progresses and what effect the disease has upon its victim?

A. Well, briefly, the disease of tuberculosis, like any other infectious disease, is due to a specific organism, in this case the tubercle bacillus. Fortunately, infection in tuberculosis does not very often mean disease. We know by tuberculosis tests that 30 to 45 or perhaps 50 per cent of the population have taken into their bodies at some time or other a few tubercle bacilli, but a very small percentage ever develop the disease of tuberculosis itself.

The disease of tuberculosis develops owing to certain factors peculiar to the individual. In the first place, you have to take within your body the germ. In addition to that, the host has to be in such a condition that he is unable to resist the infection of the germ. In other words, those in good health need not fear the tubercle bacillus; but if the vital forces are depleted from overwork or overstudy or by burning the midnight oil, in riotous living, or by infectious diseases from existing illnesses, we may become candidates for tuberculosis should we at that time take within our bodies some tubercle bacilli. They are usually deposited in the lungs by being inhaled. They drop down like pieces of dust.

Q. Is tuberculosis ever hereditary, Doctor?

A. No, it is not hereditary because it has not been proven, except in rare instances of what we call hereditary tuberculosis in a family, but the opportunities for inhaling these bacilli are so great that if the grandfather or the father or mother had tuberculosis they are very likely to hand it on down. They are very likely to hand it down to the offspring due to the reason that they have intimate contact with one another. Heredity was blamed for direct infection in that way.

Now, after the tubercle is inhaled, immediately the body starts throwing up a barrier, trying to wall these germs so that they don't travel any farther. The white blood cells come to the little capillaries and pile on this area. Pretty soon you have a little microscopic mound built up. You cannot see it with the x-ray until it is about six weeks old. You may spread from that one tubercle by working through the barrier, finding its way into the little lymph channel, or many of them may go together and make one large mass of thousand of tubercles, and then you have pneumonia or a quick type of consumption; or it may spread through the blood and you may get tuberculosis meningitis, or bone tuberculosis, or spine tuberculosis. Or, perhaps, it may break down, form a pus, and discharge through the long nasal chamber, and then you have a hole in the lung. However, it is different in every individual and it has to be studied from an individual standpoint. The statements I have made govern generally the things which may happen as a result of tuberculosis.

Q. How does working or following occupation affect the disease? In what manner does it hasten the progress of tuberculosis?

A. That is explained this way. You are already dealing with a wasting disease. Patients with tuberculosis lose weight. They have a fever. They have a rapid pulse. They have a loss of appetite. They get poison into their system or usually have little spots on the lungs. When the patient exercises he just washes more of that poison out of lungs into the blood stream. He gets more poison into it. He loses weight more rapidly. He may cough more. He may have a higher fever and it may break down faster so that with active tuberculosis we say the symptoms are extenuated and the disease is aggravated by work, whereas rest has the opposite result.

Q. Now, Doctor, where a man has active tuberculosis and he is later examined and found the tuberculosis is not active, does that mean the man has an arrested case?

A. Not at all. In any chronic disease, in practically all chronic disease, you have periods where the disease is quite evident, not only in tuberculosis, but also every chronic disease. Then it quiets down and the unwary patient may assume they are well and do things they shouldn't do and in that way spoil their chances for recovery. That is the delusion and scare particularly in tuberculosis. The patient goes to bed a month or two, possibly, and sometimes it quiets down because he does not absorb so much poison into his system. He gets a false sense of security. He gets up and starts out again and the next thing he knows he has a spread of tuberculosis. He becomes ill again and stays in bed until he gets over his sickness. He may call it a cold or he may call it bronchitis, but it is tuberculosis. Every one of these reactive agents means a spreading of the disease into new territory until you have so much territory infected that a man is sick all the time, and even then he may be sick for a week or two and then it will quiet down.

Q. What symptoms does a man feel in the manifestation of tuberculosis?

A. Unfortunately, he may not feel any symptoms at all. That is the unfortunate thing about tuberculosis. It does not make people sick. They don't have pain with the disease usually. He may have quite extensive tuberculosis and not realize that there is anything seriously wrong with him. A man may tire out more easily than he did and cough, but he blames it on something else. Maybe he is working too hard, smoking too much, or not getting enough rest, so that he becomes tired. Outside of that little coughing, a little loss of weight, and tired feeling, the patient does not show any symptoms unless he should expectorate some blood.

Q. Is there any medicine or specific that will take care of the disease?

A. No, no one has ever found, nor is it probable any will ever be found, due to the peculiar formation of the tubercle. The tubercle is in the blood supply. If you can inject chemicals into the body to destroy the tubercle you could not get to the tubercle because there is no blood supply in the tubercle itself. You would destroy the cells around the tubercle, but not the tubercle itself.

Q. In other words, you would kill the man before you killed the germ?

A. That is correct.

Q. What is your treatment for this disease, Doctor?

A. The orthodox treatment is a so-called sanitorium treatment, a regime of living, using simple principles like rest, freedom from worry, proper food, and so on. After a while, prescribed exercises are given. While the remedies are simple, it requires a very fine judgment on the part of physicians and nurses in their treatment of cases because you are dealing with human beings while they are sick. They are still human and each individual has to be treated differently.

In the last 10 or 15 years the addition of surgery into the treatment of tuberculosis has materially aided people in recovering from that disease so that the outlook in this day and age is very much better than it was a decade or two ago.

Q. Were you in the courtroom this morning, Doctor, when Mr. Whittingham was asking questions about fibrosis of the witness, one of the jurors?

A. Yes.

Q. Can you answer the juror's question?

A. Fibrosis is simply a scar tissue formation. For instance, if you get your hand cut, fibrous tissue forms interlacing it in. The same thing happens in the lungs except it is a different structure, made up of different kinds of cells, and the reaction is different; but the air cells and the disease part are replaced by scar tissue.

Q. Doctor, what are the principal functions of the lungs?

A. The lungs are chiefly an organ for the interchange of gases. In other words, through a rather complicated mechanism you take the red blood cells through the homoglobus portion, which pick up the oxygen which has been breathed in, and deposit the oxygen into the tissues where it is utilized. After it is deposited, they in return pick up carbon dioxide and carry it back to the lungs and deposit it there and out it goes. It is an organ for the interchange of gases.

Q. In other words, the lungs aerate blood?

A. Yes, and they carry off gases.

Q. When a man has tuberculosis, which I understood you to say is a consuming disease, where the disease consumes or eats the lungs away and replaces it with scar tissue, has that scar tissue any ability to aerate blood?

A. It has no function except to seal up the diseased part. It is not able to do anything.

Q. How much of a person's lung can be lost and still be useful?

A. Well, we have about five times as much lung tissue as is necessary to carry on the vital functions at complete rest.

A Juror: Would you repeat that, please?

The Witness: I said we have about five times as much lung tissue to carry on the function of living at rest.

Mr. Gerlack: Q. In other words, at complete rest, a man could lose four-fifths of his lungs and keep the one-fifth?

A. Yes, but he would have to be very quiet.

Q. Does that explain why a person could live for years with tuberculosis even though they had lost considerable portion of their lungs?

A. That is part of the explanation.

Q. How much of the lung capacity has Mr. Holland left at the present time?

A. Well, I would just have to conjecture that because there are tests that will tell you very definitely how much is left. I would say that he has, at the present time, about two-thirds of his lung capacity.

Mr. Di Girolamo: He still has?

The Witness: He still has, because the air cells at the bottom of the lung have enlarged. He has what we call empyema (emphysema) at the bottom of both lungs. The cells there have to do extra work because of the cells which have been destroyed by the disease of the upper portions.

Mr. Gerlack: Q. Are you able to say from reading the x-ray taken at Spadra on August 30, 1933, as to the degree of advancement of his tuberculosis, as to whether or not it was moderately advanced or far advanced?

A. That Spadra films shows tuberculosis which is at least moderately advanced. There are two or three spots in that film—I think it is in the left upper—where they may be a beginning cavity formation; if they were proven he would be up in the far advanced stage, but it is not a probability.

Q. Would you say at that time there was no hope of his coming to complete health?

A. No, I will explain that tuberculosis has to start somewhere. This man's tuberculosis is shown by the age of his lesions. It started at the extreme top of the lungs, probably the right lung. It spread to the top of the left lung, and from both of those spots it spread down into both lung field. In other words, he has had a spread of tuberculosis from one lung to another, and it has traveled downward. Had it remained in one lung his chances of realizing a recovery would have been good, but where you have two lungs diseased, the disease spreads downward and the chances for securing an arrest is not good.

Q. Is he using both lungs uniformly, Doctor?

A. There has been an effort made in the last x-ray, through the use of starch, to arrest it as much as possible. In other words, they put air into the abdomen by the use of a needle and pushed the diaphragm up and collapsed the lungs a little.

Mr. Gerlack: I think that is all.

Juror Whittingham: May I ask a question?

The Court: What is it?

Juror Whittingham: The doctor this morning said something about calcium salt in the Spadra picture. What has that to do with the Plaintiff's condition?

The Witness: I often refer to calcium salt as lime salt. They are anonymous terms in the healing of these microscopic tubercles. Nature throws that wall of tissue around them, and later lime salt may be carried in impregnating the new tissue. That is the so-called lime or calcium salt deposit which you can see on the top of the Spadra film.

Juror Whittingham: May I ask another question?

The Doctor speaks of passing from one lung to another. Is there any rate or time as to its passing?

The Witness: No, there is no time because the change may take place through the bronchial tubes. He may expectorate through the bronchial tubes and out through the mouth and he might drop something over on the other side and get a seeding, and it would start to grow there. On the other hand, some may pass through the blood stream. That is why I say I don't know how long it takes. Here there is not much difference in age, although there may be a year or two difference."

The Diagnostic Standards of the National Tuberculosis Association (Plaintiff's Exhibit No. 20) (R. 332), which diagnostic standards are universally recognized and accepted among all tuberculosis experts as authentic (R. 319) were offered in evidence.

While working for the Treasury Department in San Francisco, appellee was examined by Dr. Mary Jones Mentzer, a tuberculosis specialist, who testified by deposition (R. 153-156):

"Q. Did you ever have occasion to examine and treat professionally the plaintiff in this case, Wilson A. Holland?

A. I did, yes.

Q. You have your records?

A. Yes, right here.

Q. Can you tell when he first came under your professional care?

A. On September 19, 1935.

Q. Just tell us, doctor, what examination you made of him at that time and what you found on that examination.

A. He had a disease of the chest—I took his height, weight, time of the examination, time of taking his temperature, which was 2:10. I examined his eyes, lids, teeth, membranes, tongue, tonsils, glands, thyroid, nails, hands, heart, chest.

Q. What diagnosis was made as a result of your examination?

A. Bilateral tuberculosis (both lungs)—pulmonary, more extensive on right. The physical signs were of empyema [emphysema] at the left base. According to the roentgen examination this diagnosis was pleural thickening and adhesions at the left base. He also had acute pleurisy at that time.

Q. Was his tuberculosis active at that time?

A. It was active at that time.

Q. What would you say as to the degree of advancement—whether minimal—moderate degree of advancement—or far advanced?

A. It was right on the border-line. According to our rules, I would say he had an involvement of about the whole of one lung * * * that can either go on the moderately or far-advanced side according to the National Tuberculosis Association standards followed by us. He told me he had had a cold with a cough and expectoration for about ten days and that he felt well enough along through the days unless something untoward happened—if he had a cold, or became excited—then he wasn't so well. And I think this is very important—he said for about a year and a half he had been troubled with heartburn and occasional constipation, and he was exceedingly nervous—this with heartburn and constipation indicated that he was getting second-stage symptoms—that is why I consider this important. There was nervousness and interrupted sleep, and of course loss of weight. I can give you those figures if you want them as they were given to me. High weight in 1918, when he entered the army was 140, with a minimum of 90 at the time of the empyema, and 113 in September, 1924. For several years he had carried a dressed weight of 120 to 125. I got him at 120 that day, dressed. He was a man that would call for a weight of about 165. I have a copy here of the x-ray findings.

Q. Did you order an x-ray taken?

A. Yes.

Q. Did you see it yourself?

A. Surely.

Q. Were you able to say from the x-ray and examination—were you able to say that that was his x-ray?

A. Yes.

Q. What were the findings on the x-ray, Doctor?

A. (Reading from x-ray report); Bony frame work: Right upper chest contracted. Right diaphragm negative. Left diaphragm shows several basilar adhesions over dome and attached to chest wall in axillary region. Heart of the dropped cylindrical type. Aorta negative; trachea distorted to the right; Right lung: Marked old heavy fibrosis scattered about fourth rib and fifth dorsal spine, which contains numerous mottled areas. Pleura thickened over upper chest. Left Lung: Old heavy fibrosis scattered about third rib and fifth dorsal spine, which also contains numerous scattered coarse mottled areas. Pleura thickened over apex and base. Conclusions: Pulmonary tuberculosis, active. Signed by Dr. G. A. Fogerty, Saint Francis Hospital.

Q. That was also your interpretation of the x-rays, Doctor?

A. Also more at the left base than they had.

Q. Were your findings the same, or not, Doctor?

A. My findings were practically the same as those except at the left base he says there were pleural thickenings over the right, and that the thickenings came up into the axillary. I found it a little more extensive than that and there was quite a flat area and no breath sounds over that at all.

Q. Was that x-ray compatible with your opinion on your physical examination as to the degree of advancement of his tuberculosis?

A. Yes, moderately between far and moderately advanced."

And again (R. 162-163):

"Q. Now, Doctor, bearing in mind your own examination taken in September, 1935, at that time, what would have been the effect of following an occupation or engaging in any physical or mental labor, what would the effect have been on this man?

A. Disastrous.

Q. In what respect?

A. Well, in the first place, the first principle of treatment in tuberculosis is rest, and we think it would aggravate the condition if any activity were engaged in such as a person would enter into if he or she were to work.

Q. Do you mean by that, Doctor, that even mental activity would aggravate such a condition and would make it worse, and that if he did not engage in such activity he would make progress more rapidly than otherwise?

A. Yes."

There is, of course, an abundance of other testimony on behalf of plaintiff, most of it lay evidence, but we think the foregoing a sufficient answer to the question:

"IS THERE ANY SUBSTANTIAL EVIDENCE OF APPELLEE'S TOTAL PERMANENT DISABILITY ON OR PRIOR TO AUGUST 30, 1933?"

Having in mind the facts of the case we now turn to the law applicable thereto.

Analytically speaking—and bearing in mind that no longer (since *United States v. Stephens,* supra, and *United States v. White,* supra) is it permissible to ask a doctor whether a person is totally and permanently disabled or whether he is able to follow continuously a gainful occupation—were we to "break down" the definition of total permanent disability, we find:

1. That a work record in and of itself is not conclusive, but merely evidence for the jury's

consideration; likewise vocational training (see particularly *U. S. v. Albano,* (C. C. A. 9) 63 Fed. (2d) 677; *U. S. v. Nickel,* (C. C. A. 8), 70 Fed. (2d) 873; *Law v. U. S.,* (D. C. Mont.) 290 Fed. 972; *United States v. Hill,* 99 Fed.(2d) 755.

2. That if work is intermittent or spasmodic due to poor health, it is not "continuous" under the definition, and

3. If work aggravates the disease or physical condition and makes it worse or shortens life, it is not substantially gainful (*United States v. Hill,* 99 Fed.(2d) 755).

Since what work the appellee did was at the risk of his health and life, his work record does not bar him from recovery under his Insurance Contract.

In the leading case on what constitutes permanent total disability and the interpretation of the definition (Treasurer's Decision 20 W. R. dated March 9, 1918) the Supreme Court in *Lumbra v. United States,* 290 U. S. 551, 561; 54 S. Ct. 272, 78 L. Ed. 492 (at page 275, 54 S. Ct.) said:

"The war risk contract unqualifiedly insures against 'total permanent disability.' The occasion, source, or cause of petitioner's illness is therefore immaterial. His injuries, exposure, and illness before the lapse of the policy and his condition in subsequent years have significance, if any, only to the extent that they tend to show whether he was in fact totally and permanently disabled during the life of the policy. March 9, 1918, in pursuance of the authorization contained in the War

Risk Insurance Act, the director of the Bureau ruled (T. D. 20 W. R.): 'Any impairment of mind or body which renders it impossible for the disabled person to follow continuously any substantially gainful occupation shall be deemed * * * to be total disability. Total disability shall be deemed to be permanent whenever it is founded upon conditions which render it reasonably certain that it will continue throughout the life of the person suffering from it.'

The phrase 'total permanent disability' is to be construed reasonably and having regard to the circumstances of each case. As the insurance authorized does not extend to total temporary or partial permanent disability, the tests appropriate for the determination of either need not be ascertained. The various meanings inhering in the phrase make impossible the ascertainment of any fixed rules of formulae uniformly to govern its construction. That which sometimes results in total disability may cause slight inconvenience under other conditions. Some are able to sustain themselves, without serious loss of productive power, against injury or disease sufficient totally to disable others."

And again, on page 276, the Supreme Court said:

"Total disability does not mean helplessness or complete disability, but it includes more than that which is partial. 'Permanent disability' means that which is continuing as opposed to what is temporary. Separate and distinct periods of temporary disability do not constitute that which is permanent. The mere fact that one has done some work after the lapse of his policy is not of itself sufficient to defeat his claim of total permanent disability. He may have worked when really unable and at the risk of endangering his health or life."

And further, on page 276, the Supreme Court said:

> "It may be assumed that occasional work for short periods by one generally disabled by impairment of mind or body does not as a matter of law negative total permanent disability."

In *United States v. Flippence* (C. C. A. 10), 72 Fed.(2d) 611, at page 613, the Court said:

> "On the other hand, it is settled by high authority, that if one, unable to work in the sense that he is afflicted with a disease where rest is indicated nevertheless works 'when really unable and at the risk of endangering his health or life' such work does not bar recovery if the proof shows the insured to be otherwise entitled to recover. (Citing cases) If, during the life of his policy, an insured is afflicted with a disease which may be cured by a period of rest, but if, instead of following that course, he works until the disease reaches the incurable stage after his policy lapses, he cannot recover; not, however, because barred by his work record, but because at the time his policy lapsed his disease was curable and his disability temporary. *On the other hand, if, as here, the malady is incurable before lapse, and if it is of a nature where complete rest is necessary to prolong life, then work done thereafter endangers his life and does not necessarily bar recovery."* (Italics ours.)

In *United States v. Brown* (C. C. A. 10), 72 Fed. (2d) 608, at page 610, the Court said:

> "Employment may be of such a nature and duration that it conclusively refutes any idea of total and permanent disability. On the other hand, a person who is incapacitated to work, impelled by necessity and aided by a strong will, may engage in work that aggravates his condition and hastens his death. (Citing cases)
>
> *One who has a serious and incurable ailment for which rest is the recognized treatment and which will be aggravated by work of any kind, is nevertheless totally and permanently disabled, although he may for a time engage in gainful employment. One so incapacitated may only work at the risk of injury to his health and danger to his life.*" (Italics ours.)

In *United States v. Sorrow* (C. C. A. 5), 67 Fed. (2d) 372, the Court said:

> "One is totally disabled when he is not, without injury to his health, able to make his living by work."

That active pulmonary tuberculosis is considered totally disabling has long been recognized by this and all other courts. In no case can we recall where any doctor ever contended that it was safe for a person suffering from active pulmonary tuberculosis to work or engage in any physical or mental activity. As far back as March, 1929, this Court, per Mr. Circuit Judge

Dietrich, in *United States v. Sligh,* (C. C. A. 9) 31 Fed. (2d) 735 at page 737, said:

> "The fact that during the major part of the period in question appellee was receiving a substantial salary is material, but not conclusive. Aside from the consideration that the testimony tended to show that the employer was moved by sentiment and sympathy, fairly construed, the policy is to be understood as meaning not present ability in an absolute sense, but a capacity that may be legitimately exercised; that is, without serious peril to the life or health of the insured. That appellee was afflicted with active tuberculosis is admitted, and in the medical profession the view seems to prevail that at that stage hope of curing, or even staying, the progress of the malady, is largely conditioned upon complete rest. Had appellee put aside concern for the immediate necessities of his family, and, yielding to the advice of a conservative physician, wholly refrained from work, it may be doubted whether any question would have been raised of his right to receive the insurance. But manifestily his 'ability' in a legal sense would be the same in one case as in the other."

Other cases of this and other courts on this point are legion.

In the case of *United States v. William J. Higbee* (C. C. A. 10), 72 Fed. (2d) 773, the Court laid down the well recognized rule, which we submit is applicable to this case, as follows:

"He has worked since then but it apparently was done in a commendable effort to earn a living. Total and permanent disability does not require that one be an invalid or confined to his bed. He may work spasmodically with frequent interruptions, caused by his physical condition, and still be totally and permanently disabled. (Nicolay v. United States, 51 Fed. (2d) 170; United States v. Rye, 70 Fed. (2d) 150.) And work done under pressure of necessity, when health requires rest, does not necessarily disprove disability. The jury may well have found that insured was totally and permanently disabled; that his condition required rest and inactivity, but that the inescapable necessity to earn a livelihood for himself and his family spurred him to work with injury and aggravation of his physical condition. If so, he is not barred from recovering upon his contract. (Citing cases.) Neither the fact that he received vocational training nor his long delay in instituting this action is conclusive against his right to recover. Both are circumstances for consideration of the jury under appropriate instructions of the court."

We believe that there can be no question but that there was substántial evidence that appellee worked when really unable and at the risk of endangering his health or life. See *Lumbra v. United States,* 290 U. S. 551, 54 S. Ct. 273, 78 L. Ed. 492.

The Supreme Court in deciding the *Lumbra* case, and in its opinion after making the statement quoted above cites several cases. The first case cited by the

Supreme Court in the note is that of *United States v. Phillips,* in which the Court said:

> "Some persons, who are totally incapacitated for work, by virtue of strong will power may continue to work until they drop dead from exhaustion, while others with lesser will power will sit still and do nothing. Some who have placed upon them the burdens of caring for aged parents or indigent relatives, feeling deeply their responsibility and actuated by affection for those whom they desire to assist, will keep on working when they are totally unfit to do so. The mere fact that insured did work for Smith-McCord-Townsend Dry Goods Company and also for Montgomery Ward & Company does not necessarily prove that he could follow continuously a gainful occupation. The evidence shows that this work was carried on under great difficulty and was a light class of work." See United States v. Phillips (C. C. A. 8), 44 Fed. (2d) 689.

The Supreme Court likewise cites, on page 499, of the *Lumbra* case, the case of *United States v. Godfrey.* In the *Godfrey* case, it appeared that the veteran was constantly on a payroll from October 14, 1919, until February 3, 1927, earning thirty to thirty-five dollars a week, and yet the verdict of the jury was accepted and the judgment affirmed, the Circuit Court for the First Circuit, saying:

> "The evidence is persuasive that Godfrey was a war victim. He was entitled to the most favorable view of the evidence. * * * To hold him remediless because he tried, manfully, to earn a

living for his family and himself, instead of yielding to justifiable invalidism, would not, in our view, accord with the treatment Congress intended to bestow on our war victims."

United States v. Godfrey (C. C. A. 1), 47 Fed. (2d) 126.

The next case cited in the footnote on page 499 of the *Lumbra* case is that of *Carter v. United States,* wherein Judge Parker stated the principle of law that we believe to be applicable in this case, which is:

"To say that the man who works, and dies, is as a matter of law precluded from recovery under the policy, but that one who following the advice of his physician refrains from such work, and lives, is entitled to recovery, presents an untenable theory of law and fact, and emphasizes the necessity for a determination upon the facts in each case whether the man * * * was able to continuously pursue a substantially gainful occupation."

Carter v. United States (C. C. A. 4), 49 Fed. (2d) 221.

The next case cited in the footnote to the *Lumbra* case, on page 499, is the case of *United States v. Lawson* decided by this Court (50 Fed. (2d) 646). In the *Lawson* case the veteran went to work on May 15, 1920, at a salary of $1100 per annum, plus a bonus of $240, and worked for this for one year, and then after doing some other work, on April 1, 1921, he was given a probationary appointment as forest ranger at a salary of $1220 per year, plus an annual bonus of $240, serving in this capacity until August 31, 1923. On September 1, 1923, he was appointed as a forest clerk at a basis salary of $1100 per year, in which capacity he served until April 15, 1924. The latter part of September, 1924, he became Postmaster at Spencer, Idaho, his annual pay being $1100, and he held that job at that salary continuously until the time of the trial in 1930, and this Court per Mr. Circuit Judge Sawtelle, said:

> "It might be argued that the fact that plaintiff managed to hold several positions for the greater part of the time during the years in question, and actually engaged in work, proves that he was able to work and not totally and permanently disabled. But this does not necessarily follow. It is a matter of common knowledge that many men work in the stress of circumstances, when they should not work at all. When they do that they should not be penalized, rather should they be encouraged. A careful examination and consideration of the evidence herein convinces us that the plaintiff worked when he was physically unable to do so, and that, but for the gratuitous assistance of friends and relatives who did much of his heavy work and the assistance of those whom plaintiff employed at his own expense, he would have been unable to retain his several positions. Under such circumstances, he should not be made to suffer for carrying on when others less disabled than he would have surrendered."

United States v. Lawson (C. C. A. 9), 50 Fed. (2d) 646, at 651.

We believe that the case at bar is a much stronger case than the *Lawson* case in favor of the veteran, for the reason that Lawson was still holding his position as postmaster at the time of the trial and at the time the appeal was decided.

In a case decided by this Court, that of *United States v. Burleyson,* 64 Fed. (2d) 868, it appeared that the veteran had worked continuously since service and was alive at the time of the trial, and this Court sustained the verdict, saying:

> "On this diagnosis the experts disagree, nor is it entirely clear from their testimony that it was detrimental to the veteran's health to work as he did in the event that he was suffering from Buerger's disease. However, the weight of this evidence was for the jury. Their verdict is to the effect that for the veteran to work continuously would impair his health. In view of this situation, no matter how unsatisfactory the condition of the record, we must hold that there was substantial evidence to go to the jury upon the question of the total and permanent disability of the veteran before the lapse of his war risk insurance policy."
>
> *United States v. Burleyson,* 64 Fed. (2d) 868 at 872.

In a case which involved a heart disability it appeared that the veteran had earned $15,000. (*United States v. Francis* (C. C. A. 9), 64 Fed. (2d) 865.) The verdict of the jury in behalf of the veteran was sustained upon the theory that it was for the jury to determine whether the work that he had done had been injurious to his life or health.

In summarizing Francis' work record, this Court per Mr. Circuit Judge Wilbur, said:

> "It is claimed by the veteran that notwithstanding his long periods of work and substantial remuneration therefor, aggregating in all about $15,000., he was 'totally and permanently disabled' during that whole period. Within the meaning of that phrase as defined by the Treasury Department regulations and by the decisions of the courts. This view was sustained by the jury under proper instructions from the court and the question is whether or not the court erred in denying the motion of the Government for directed verdict.
>
> The testimony in favor of the veteran on the trial was directed to the proposition that although he did in fact work, and although he did so continuously for long periods of time, he was unable to do so because he thereby imperiled his health and shortened his life by reason of the excessive load put upon his heart, whose functions had been seriously impaired by the wound and resulting pus infection."
>
> *United States v. Francis,* 64 Fed. (2d) 865.

Appellee's "work record".

A large part of the Government's evidence immaterially relates to appellee's work *before* August 30, 1933. The record was further "stuffed" by appellant with excessive and unnecessary corroboration of his work record both before and after the crucial date of August 30, 1933.

Appellee testified on direct examination that after August 30, 1933, he worked (under the conditions and while in the state of health set forth in his testimony already quoted) off and on for almost two and one-half years, at a salary ranging from $120.00 to $225.00 per month, in positions ranging from bookkeeper and accountant to executive, such employment being abruptly terminated by a pulmonary hemorrhage from the lungs, which put him in the hospital where he has been a bed patient ever since.

Appellee contends that this employment aggravated his active tubercular condition, accelerated its progress and shortened his life, and that thus considered, the amount of money which he earned was not "substantially gainful" within the definition of total permanent disability found in the policy.

If he were in *fact* totally and permanently disabled on August 30, 1933 (and we submit the evidence very persuasively shows this to be true), then what he did thereafter is of little importance.

This precise question arose in the recent case of *United States v. Aspinwall,* (C. C. A. 9). 96 Fed. (2d) 867, where this Court approved an instruction to the jury that:

> "* * * if you find he was permanently and totally disabled upon June 30, 1919, it makes absolutely no difference whether he went to a doctor or not. He didn't have to. The Govern-

> ment didn't put that in his policy. If they wanted him to be bound by such a stipulation, they were bound to put it in the policy. He did not have to take any care of himself whatsoever."

There is no evidence whatsoever in the Holland case to show that plaintiff's neglect of his health or his working converted a temporary total disability into a permanent total disability. The evidence here shows, we submit, conclusively, at least to the satisfaction of the jury, that plaintiff became permanently and totally disabled from following continuously any substantially gainful occupation without material injury to his health, before his insurance lapsed. These conditions being present, the policy matured and he was entitled to his money.

This Court in a recent case (*United States v. Hill*, 99 Fed. (2d) 755), decided similarly. In that case Miss Frances Hill served overseas in the Army Nurses Corps and prior to her discharge was found to be suffering from moderately advanced, active tuberculosis and an incurable heart disease. Nevertheless she worked spasmodically and intermittently for twelve years (1919 to 1931), part of the time taking private nursing jobs out of a Nurses Registry, besides working as a nurse for seven months at the Government's Indian Sanitorium, then for five months at a Copper Company's hospital and after that as a nurse for the Government's Indian School for five months. In affirming the judgment for plaintiff this Court, per Mr. Circuit Judge Wilbur, said:

"It is claimed, and it must be conceded, that the appellee's heart condition, and the diagnosis that the tuberculosis was moderately advanced, differentiates her case from those in which it has been held that incipient tuberculosis is a curable disease and that recovery for total and permanent disability cannot be based upon such a diagnosis. The testimony of experts called by the appellee, who had made physical examinations of her, was to the effect that her heart condition was permanent; that rest was the proper treatment for both the tubercular condition and the heart disease; that she could not work without aggravating both heart and lung conditions, and that such work as she did aggravated both, and that she could not carry on the work of a nurse or any other work without further impairing her health. This evidence brings the case squarely within the rule that if an insured cannot work without imperiling his health, the fact that work is done under such circumstances does not negative the claim of total and permanent disability. *Lumbra v. United States,* 290 U. S. 551, 54 S. Ct. 272, 78 L. Ed. 492; *United States v. Flippence,* 10 Cir., 72 F. (2d) 611; *United States v. Sorrow,* 5 Cir., 67 F. (2d) 372.

It appears from the evidence that appellee frequently worked as nurse for compensation. If this evidence stood alone it might justify the conclusion that because appellee did in fact work, there were periods when she was not totally disabled, and, consequently, that her condition was not permanent. But, as we have stated, there was substantial evidence from which the jury could have determined that she was not able to work without impairing her health at the time she worked."

Policy incontestable.

That the policy is incontestable from its issuance is, of course, beyond question.

See:

United States v. Patryas, 303 U. S. 341, 58 S. Ct. 551;

Sec. 307, World War Veterans Act of 1924, as amended July 3, 1930 (38 U. S. Code Ann. 518);

Paragraph No. 9 of Plaintiff's Policy (Plaintiff's Exhibit No. 1).

OUR ANSWER TO APPELLANT'S CONTENTIONS.

We have no quarrel with any of the cases cited by counsel for the appellant in his brief. Attention is invited, however, to the fact that in none of those cases are the facts similar to the facts in the Holland case. Besides counsel cited and this Court fully considered practically all of those cases in *United States v. Hill,* supra.

Counsel suggests that a wait of three years to make a claim under the policy indicates appellee did not consider himself totally and permanently disabled. We disagree violently with this contention. It impresses us that a three-year wait under a six-year statute of limitation is not unreasonable. But, be that as it may, if the jury found that his three-year wait was not unreasonable, that finding in view of the evidence in the record, is now conclusive here.

See:

Gilmore v. United States, (C. C. A. 5) 93 Fed. (2d) 774;

United States v. Higbee, (C. C. A. 10) 72 Fed. (2d) 773.

The cases cited by counsel in their brief, we submit, are not in point, on the question of total permanent disability, for as this Court has recently held, each war risk insurance case must stand on its own peculiar facts.

See

United States v. Thompson, (C. C. A. 9) 92 Fed.(2d) 137, 139.

Furthermore, "All legitimate doubts as to whether appellee was totally permanently disabled must be resolved in appellee's favor."

See:

United States v. Sligh, (C. C. A. 9) 31 Fed. (2d) 737;

United States v. Balance, (D. C. App.) 59 Fed. (2d) 1040;

McNally v. United States, (C. C. A. 4) 52 Fed. (2d) 440;

Putney v. United States, (D. C. Colo.) 4 Fed. Supp. 376.

CONCLUSION.

We realize this brief is somewhat protracted, but we felt the matter is of such importance to the appellee that it was incumbent upon us to urge every important point in his favor on this appeal.

Then again, in order to do justice to his cause and to answer the inquiry, "Is there *any* substantial evidence in the record to justify the jury's verdict?" we felt it necessary to point out in the record that evidence—tested in the light of the leading cases on the subject—which in our humble opinion fully meet the legal requirements concerning what evidence is necessary to constitute total permanent disability.

Trying to stand far enough away from this case to get the proper perspective, it appears to us, that here is a veteran whose tuberculosis was probably in the incipient or beginning stage during his arduous service in Siberia during the World War; which disease actually manifested itself clinically in 1924; was rated far advanced in 1925; in 1927 thought to be arrested on an insufficient examination or basis (see R. 220 and Plaintiff's Exhibit 20—R. 332-335); his policy converted in 1927, at which time the Government doctors told him it was safe for him to go back to work; that he took their advice and worked as a bookkeeper and accountant; that he broke down again and his tuberculosis pronounced active, advanced and incurable by competent medical authority, including x-ray, on August 30, 1933, the very day the jury found total permanent disability; his return to work again on account of dire financial necessity (R. 42); his four different jobs during this two and one-half year period; the last job terminating in a pulmonary hemorrhage from the lungs; and his twenty-four hour per day bed hospitalization ever since certainly spell total permanent disability as defined by the policy and the decisions of the courts and thoroughly entitle him to the benefits payable under this contract of insurance.

In conclusion we submit there is ample evidence in the record to justify the jury's verdict and that this Court should modify the judgment by striking out the so-called "lien clauses" therein and as so modified the judgment should be affirmed.

December 5, 1939.

Respectfully submitted,

ALVIN GERLACK,
Attorney for Appellee.

No. 9287

United States
Circuit Court of Appeals
For the Ninth Circuit.

G. M. FOSTER, individually, G. M. FOSTER, Assistant Secretary, Standard Oil Company of California, a Delaware corporation, and STANDARD OIL COMPANY OF CALIFORNIA, a Delaware corporation,

Appellants,

vs.

UNITED STATES OF AMERICA,

Appellee.

Transcript of Record

Upon Appeal from the District Court of the United States for the Southern District of California, Central Division.

No. 9287

United States
Circuit Court of Appeals
For the Ninth Circuit.

G. M. FOSTER, individually, G. M. FOSTER, Assistant Secretary, Standard Oil Company of California, a Delaware corporation, and STANDARD OIL COMPANY OF CALIFORNIA, a Delaware corporation,

Appellants,

vs.

UNITED STATES OF AMERICA,

Appellee.

Transcript of Record

Upon Appeal from the District Court of the United States for the Southern District of California, Central Division.

INDEX

[Clerk's Note: When deemed likely to be of an important nature, errors or doubtful matters appearing in the original certified record are printed literally in italic; and, likewise, cancelled matter appearing in the original certified record is printed and cancelled herein accordingly. When possible, an omission from the text is indicated by printing in italic the two words between which the omission seems to occur.]

Page

Appeal:

Designation of Contents of Record on.......... 105

Designation of Additional Contents of Record on 107

Notice of 92

Statement of Points on.......... 102

Attorneys, Names and Addresses of.......... 1

Clerk's Certificate 94

Clerk's Certificate (to Supplemental Transcript) 100

Designation of Contents of Record on Appeal.......... 105

Designation of Additional Contents of Record on Appeal 107

Memorandum in support of motion to quash.......... 58

Points and authorities.......... 63

Memorandum of Ruling on Motions to Quash Subpoena Duces Tecum.......... 82

Minute Orders:

August 21, 1939.......... 77

August 29, 1939.......... 79

August 29, 1939.......... 89

Pages

August 31, 1939 ... 91

September 7, 1939 ... 96

September 8, 1939 ... 99

Notice of Appeal ... 92

Notice of Motion to Quash Subpoena Duces Tecum ... 20

Affidavit of G. M. Foster ... 26

Order deferring appearance of witness until August 29, 1939. (Minutes of August 21, 1939) ... 77

Order deferring appearance of witness until September 6, 1939. (Minutes of August 29, 1939) ... 79, 89

Order deferring appearance of witness until September 8, 1939. (Minutes of August 31, 1939.) ... 91

Order deferring appearance of witness until September 21, 1939. (Minutes of September 8, 1939) ... 99

Order extending term of Grand Jury. (Minutes of September 7, 1939) ... 96

Statement of points upon appeal ... 102

Subpoena Duces Tecum, with Return of Service thereon ... 2

Annex I—To subpoena ... 3

NAMES AND ADDRESSES OF ATTORNEYS

For Appellants, G. M. Foster, individually, G. M. Foster, Assistant Secretary, Standard Oil Company of California, a Delaware corporation, and Standard Oil Company of California, a Delaware corporation,

OSCAR LAWLER, Esq.,
Standard Oil Building,
Los Angeles, California,

FELIX T. SMITH, Esq.,
Standard Oil Building,
San Francisco, California,

PILLSBURY, MADISON & SUTRO,
Standard Oil Building,
San Francisco, California,

LAWLER, FELIX & HALL,
Standard Oil Building,
Los Angeles, California.

For Appellee, United States of America,

BEN HARRISON, Esq.,
United States Attorney,
Los Angeles, California,

JOSEPH E. BRILL, Esq.,

M. S. HUBERMAN, Esq.,

HENRY McCLERNAN, Esq.,

ROBERT H. MARQUIS, Esq.,

L. P. SHERFY, Esq.,
Special Assistants to the
Attorney General,
Los Angeles, California. [1*]

*Page numbering appearing at the foot of page of original certified Transcript of Record.

In the District Court of the United States of America, Southern District of California

The President of the United States of America: To ~~J. H. Tuttle, Secretary,~~ G. M. Foster, Assistant Secretary, Standard Oil Company of California, 225 Bush Street, San Francisco, California. Greeting:

You and Each of You Are Hereby Commanded, That all and singular business and excuses being laid aside, you, and each of you, be and appear in your proper person before the Second Grand Jury empanelled by the District Court of the United States for the Southern District of California, during the February Term of said Court, at the Hearing Room of said Second Grand Jury in the United States Post Office and Court House Building, in the City of Los Angeles, State of California, on the 25th day of August, A. D. 1939, at 11:00 o'clock in the forenoon, then and there to testify and give evidence before said Second Grand Jury, and that you produce at the time and place aforesaid all of those certain books, records, documents and papers which are more particularly described in Annex I, attached to and made a part hereof, and which are in your possession or custody, and not to depart without leave of the Court or the United States Attorney.

And this you are not to omit, under pain of being adjudged guilty of a contempt of said Court.

Witness, the Honorable Paul J. McCormick, Judge of said District Court for the Southern District of California, this 19th day of July, in the year of our Lord one thousand nine hundred and thirty-nine.

[Seal] R. S. ZIMMERMAN,

Clerk

By (Signed) J. M. HORN

Deputy Clerk

M. S. HUBERMAN,

Special Assistant to the Attorney General.

[Endorsed]: MD 46001 Crim. Received Jul 22 1939. U. S. Marshal's Office, San Francisco, Calif.

[2]

ANNEX I—(TO SUBPOENA DUCES TECUM DIRECTED TO J. H. TUTTLE)

The phrase or term "corporation herein named," as used hereinafter, designates and refers to Standard Oil Company of California.

1. Articles of incorporation and the certificate of incorporation or other charter of the corporation herein named, and all amendments thereto.

2. Books and records which show the names of all the officers and directors of the corporation herein named and their residence addresses during the period from January 1, 1935, to date.

3. All minute books and other papers, records, and documents containing the minutes or record of proceedings at meetings of stockholders, directors, any executive committee, or any other committees or boards of the corporation herein named, during the period from January 1, 1935, to date.

4. Copies of the annual, quarterly and other periodic reports made by the corporation herein named to its stockholders, during the period from January 1, 1935, to date.

5. Copies of all of the monthly reports entitled "Petroleum Situation in the Pacific Coast Territory" or "Monthly Petroleum Situation in the Pacific Coast Territory," made by the corporation herein named to the United States Bureau of Mines during the period from January 1, 1938, to date.

6. Such of the books, records, accounts, and memoranda regularly kept by the corporation herein named in the regular course of business as are sufficient to show:

(a) The quantity of crude oil produced in the State of California by the corporation herein named, its subsidiaries and affiliates, each month from January 1, 1935, to date.

(b) The number and daily capacity of refineries located in the states of California, Oregon, Washington, Nevada, and [3] Arizona (hereinafter referred to collectively as "Pacific Coast territory") and owned by the corporation herein named, its subsidiaries and affiliates, on January 1 of each year, from January 1, 1935, to date.

(c) The quantity of gasoline produced within the Pacific Coast territory by the corporation herein named, its subsidiaries and affiliates, each month from January 1, 1935, to date.

(d) The mileage and location of crude oil and gasoline pipelines located in the Pacific Coast territory and owned by the corporation herein named, its subsidiaries and affiliates, on January 1 of each year, from January 1, 1935, to date.

(e) The gasoline stocks owned within the Pacific Coast territory by the corporation herein named, its subsidiaries and affiliates, on the last day of each month from December 31, 1934, to date, including amounts separately shown for "first structure," "second structure," "third structure," and other commercial finished gasolines, and the amounts of each type owned within the Pacific Coast territory on each of said days at refineries and at bulk terminals, respectively.

(f) The monthly quantities of crude oil and of gasoline, and of other petroleum products delivered and received within the Pacific Coast territory from January 1, 1935, to date, by the corporation herein named, its subsidiaries and affiliates, pursuant to exchange account or accounts with any corporation, copartnership or person, including its subsidiaries and affiliates, engaged in the business of producing gasoline within the Pacific Coast territory.

(g) The monthly quantities of crude oil and of gasoline imported from January 1, 1935, to date, by the corporation herein named, its subsidiaries and affiliates, into the Pacific Coast territory. [4]

(h) The monthly quantities of crude oil and of gasoline shipped from January 1, 1935, to date, by the corporation herein named, its subsidiaries and affiliates, from points within the Pacific Coast territory to points outside that territory.

(i) The monthly quantities of gasoline (including the total of all gasolines and separate totals for "first structure," "second structure," and "third structure" gasolines) sold by the corporation herein named, its subsidiaries and affiliates, from January 1, 1935, to date, to consumers and sellers of gasoline located within the Pacific Coast territory (including separate totals for each state in said territory), exclusive of sales to corporations, copartnerships and persons engaged in the business of producing gasoline within the Pacific Coast territory, and including the quantity or the percentage of such monthly quantities sold by the corporation herein named and by its subsidiaries and affiliates to or through retail outlets, and including further the quantity or the percentage sold to or through retail outlets handling exclusively the gasolines of the corporation herein named or exclusively the gasolines of its subsidiaries or affiliates, and the quantity or percentage sold to or through retail outlets not selling exclusively the gasolines of any corporation, copartnership or person.

(j) The quantity of gasoline consumed within the Pacific Coast territory each month, from January 1, 1935, to date, by the corporation herein named, its subsidiaries and affiliates.

(k) The ownership on January 1 of each year, from January 1, 1935, to date, by the corporation herein named of the legal title to or beneficial interest in the stock of any other corporation engaged in the production, transportation or refining of crude oil or in the manufacture, transportation, marketing or sale of gasoline, including all books, records and accounts showing the number of shares of such stock owned [5] legally or beneficially on each of said days.

(l) The dates and amounts and the recipients of each contribution or payment made from January 1, 1935, to date, by the corporation herein named, its subsidiaries and affiliates, to any association of retail dealers in gasoline within the Pacific Coast territory and to any association of producers of gasoline within that territory.

7. All original books, records, contracts, and invoices showing purchases during the period from January 1, 1935, to date, of gasoline physically located at time of delivery within the Pacific Coast territory, by the corporation herein named or by any of its subsidiaries or affiliates engaged in producing or marketing gasoline within that territory,

excluding, however, purchases of gasoline by said subsidiaries or affiliates from the corporation herein named, and excluding purchasers of gasoline by the corporation herein named from its subsidiaries or affiliates, and including books, records, contracts, and invoices disclosing specifically the following information with reference to each such purchase:

(a) Name of vendor.

(b) Date purchased.

(c) Date shipped.

(d) Quantity purchased and shipped.

(e) Octane rating and other specifications of gasoline so purchased.

(f) Whether "first structure," "second structure," "third structure," or other type of gasoline.

(g) Name and address of broker, agent, agency or person through whom purchased.

(h) Point from which shipped.

(i) Point or points to which shipment was moved at the direction of the corporation herein named, or of its subsidiary or affiliate. [6]

(j) Price paid to the vendor for each such purchase.

(k) Whether purchased by contract and the description and date of such contract.

(l) Whether such gasoline was moved by the corporation herein named or by its subsidiary or affiliate to refineries or bulk terminals or bulk stations or service stations operated by the corporation herein named or by its subsidiary or affiliate.

(m) Whether, if such gasoline was not moved to any of the facilities mentioned in paragraph 7 (l) hereof, such gasoline was resold, and in the case of each such resale, the date thereof, the date of delivery, whether sold or delivered on contract, and the description and date of such contract, the name and address of the vendee, the price at which sold, and the place at which delivery was made.

8. All original books, records, contracts, and invoices showing sales during the period from January 1, 1938, to date, of gasoline physically within the Pacific Coast territory at or prior to time of delivery by the corporation herein named or by its subsidiaries or affiliates to Shell Oil Company, Incorporated, Shell Oil Company, Tide Water Associated Oil Company, Associated Oil Company, Union Oil Company of California, The Texas Company (California), Richfield Oil Corporation, William C. McDuffie, as Receiver or as Trustee of Richfield Oil Company of California, General Petroleum Corporation of California, Socony-Vacuum Oil Co., Inc., Seaside Oil Company, Sunset Oil Company, Gilmore Oil Company, Rio Grande Oil Inc., Rio Grande Oil Company, and Rio Grande Oil Corporation, excluding sales in which the quantity of the individual sale is less than three thousand gallons, including books, records, contracts, and invoices disclosing specifically the following information with reference to each such sale.

(a) Date of sale.

(b) Date of delivery. [7]

(c) Whether sold or delivered on contract and the description and date of such contract.

(d) Name and address of vendee.

(e) Price at which sold.

(f) Quantity of each sale.

(g) The octane rating and other specifications of the product so sold.

(h) Place at which delivery was made.

9. All original books, records, contracts, and invoices showing sales made by the corporation herein named, its subsidiaries or affiliates, to any corporation, copartnership or person during the period from April 1, 1936, to date, of gasoline physically within the Pacific Coast territory at or prior to the time of delivery, at or below the following prices, exclusive of taxes:

(a) In the case of sales from April 1, 1936, to March 22, 1937, 8-1/4 cents per gallon plus, in the event delivery is made at points outside the City of Los Angeles, the price differential prevailing at the time of sale between said city and the point of delivery;

(b) In the case of sales from March 23, 1937, to March 24, 1938, 8-1/2 cents per gallon plus, in the event delivery is made at points outside the City of Los Angeles, the price differential prevailing at the time of sale between said city and the point of delivery;

(c) In the case of sales from March 25, 1938, to date, 7-¾ cents per gallon plus, in the event delivery is made at points outside the City of Los Angeles, the price differential prevailing at the time of sale between said city and the point of delivery;

including books, records, contracts, and invoices disclosing specifically with reference to each such sale the date of sale, date of delivery, place of delivery, whether sold or delivered on contract and the [8] description and date of such contract, name and address of vendee, price at which sold, quantity of each sale, and the octane rating and other specifications of products sold.

10. All original letters, telegrams, teletype messages, contracts, reports, interoffice or other memoranda and other documents, or copies thereof where the originals cannot be produced, made, written, sent or received during the period from January 1, 1935, to date, by or between or among any of the following named corporations, copartnerships, associations, and persons:

Ajax Oil & Refining Co.,
Aromalene, Inc.,
Associated Oil Company,
Bachmann Petroleum Corp.,
Bell View Oil Syndicate,
R. R. Bush Oil Company,
California Oil & Refining Co.,
California Refining Co.,

Caminol Co., Ltd.,
Century Oil Company,
Eagle Oil and Refining Co., Inc.,
East West Refining Company,
El Camino Oil Co., Ltd.,
Edington Oil & Refining Co., Ltd.,
Elm Oil Co.,
El Tejon Oil and Refining Corporation,
Envoy Petroleum Company,
Estado Petroleum Corp., Ltd.,
Exeter Refining Company,
Fletcher Oil Company, Inc.,
General Petroleum Corporation of California,
Gilmore Oil Company,
Hancock Oil Company of California, [9]
Harbor Refining Company,
Krieger Oil Company of California,
Lake View Oil & Refining Co.,
Los Alamitos Refining Co.,
Los Nietos Producing & Refining Company, Ltd.,
M. M. McCallen Refining Company,
M. M. McCallen Refining and Producing Co.,
Macmillan Petroleum Corporation,
Mercury Petroleum Corporation,
Mohawk Petroleum Company,
Monarch Refiners, Ltd.,
The Norwalk Company,
Olympic Refining Company,
Operators Oil & Refining Co.,
The Petrol Corporation,
Richfield Oil Corporation,

Rio Grande Oil Company,
Rio Grande Oil, Inc.,
Rocket Oil Company,
Rothschild Oil Company,
St. Helens Petroleum Company, Ltd.,
San Fernando Refining Company,
Seaside Oil Company,
Shell Oil Company,
Shell Oil Company, Incorporated,
Signal Oil Company,
Socal Oil & Refining Company,
Standard Oil Company of California,
Walter Steiner Refining Co.,
Sunset Oil Company,
The Texas Company (California),
Tide Water Associated Oil Company, [10]
Triangle Oil & Refining Co.,
Union Oil Company of California,
White Star Refining Company,
Wilshire Oil Company,
Committee of Independent Refiners,
Fair Practices Association (Petroleum Products),
Independent Refiners' Association of California, Inc.,
O. F. Collinge, Inc.,
F. R. Long, Inc.,
Regional Code Compliance Committee,
Retail Petroleum Dealers Association,
M. M. McCallen,
Henry Brown, doing business as Operators Oil & Refining,

and the officers, directors, agents and employees of said corporations, copartnerships, associations and persons, and all other corporations, copartnerships, associations and persons, relating to the following subjects:

(a) Dealings in or negotiations regarding the purchase and sale of gasoline between corporations, copartnerships or persons engaged in the business of producing gasoline within the Pacific Coast territory or between any such corporation, copartnership or person, and any association or associations (whether incorporated or not) composed in whole or in part of such corporations, copartnerships, or persons.

(b) Refinery, wholesale, tank wagon, tank truck, industrial consumer, commercial consumer, agricultural consumer, tank car, spot market, contract, or tanker prices or quotations of prices of gasoline in the Pacific Coast territory.

(c) Terms of sale of gasoline to or forms of contracts for the sale of gasoline with brokers, jobbers, [11] wholesalers, bulk plant operators, service station operators, retailers or consumers of gasoline in the Pacific Coast territory, or the gross or net margins or allowances received or to be received by them.

(d) Decreases or increases in the prices of gasoline in the Pacific Coast territory or the maintenance or establishment of such prices at or above or below any level or levels.

(e) Agreements or arrangements or understandings between or among corporations, copartnerships or persons engaged in the business of producing gasoline within the Pacific Coast territory regarding the restriction, limitation or regulation of the quantity of gasoline produced or to be produced by any corporation, copartnership or person engaged in the business of producing gasoline within the Pacific Coast territory.

(f) The non-solicitation or non-acceptance by any corporation, copartnership or person engaged in the business of marketing or selling gasoline within the Pacific Coast territory of the accounts of gasoline customers of a competitor or competitors of such corporation, copartnership or person.

(g) Agreements or arrangements or understandings between or among corporations, copartnerships or persons engaged in the business of producing or selling gasoline within the Pacific Coast territory regarding the price or prices of gasoline or the terms or conditions of sale thereof between any such corporation, copartnership or person and purchasers of gasoline, or any policy or practice relating to the marketing of gasoline.

(h) The policy or practice of any corporation, copartnership or person engaged in the business of marketing [12] or selling gasoline within the Pacific Coast territory of requiring purchasers of gasoline within that territory to maintain specified or particular prices in the resale of gasoline.

(i) The refusal by any corporation, copartnership or person engaged in the business of marketing or selling gasoline within the Pacific Coast territory to supply gasoline to purchasers within that territory failing or refusing to resell gasoline at any specified or particular price or prices.

(j) The activities of price checkers or other persons engaged in ascertaining the prices for gasoline posted or charged within the Pacific Coast territory by sellers of gasoline.

(k) The policy or practice of any corporation, copartnership or person engaged in the business of marketing or selling gasoline within the Pacific Coast territory, of selling gasoline only to purchasers of gasoline within that territory who, at the places of business where such purchasers sell the gasolines of such corporation, copartnership or person, do not sell any other gasolines.

(l) The refusal by or failure of any corporation, copartnership or person owning or operating within the Pacific Coast territory a pipeline or pipelines for the transportation of crude oil or petroleum products, to make such pipeline or pipelines available for use by, or the transportation of commodities of, other corporations, copartnerships or persons engaged in the business of producing, refining, purchasing, selling or transporting crude oil or petroleum products.

(m) Negotiations by any corporation, copartnership or person engaged in the business of producing, selling or marketing gasoline in the Pacific Coast territory regarding purchase or attempted purchase of tetraethyl lead, or obtaining [13] or attempting to obtain a right, license or permit to use the same in the manufacture or blending of gasoline in the Pacific Coast territory, or to sell or market in that territory gasoline so manufactured or blended or regarding acquisition or attempted acquisition of any license or permit for the use of any "cracking" process in the manufacture of gasoline in the Pacific Coast territory.

11. All original price lists, records and other documents showing the prices posted from January 1, 1935, to date, by the corporation named herein at each of the cities of Los Angeles, San Francisco, and Fresno, California; Portland, Oregon; Seattle and Spokane, Washington; Phoenix, Arizona; and Reno, Nevada, for the sale of gasolines and fuel oil to resellers or consumers, including price lists, records and other documents showing the price, differential or allowance established by the corporation herein named with respect to each type or class of such resellers or consumers.

12. All original letters, memoranda, reports, surveys, compilations, summaries, analyses and

estimates, or copies thereof where the originals cannot be produced, passing between the corporation herein named, its officers, directors, and employees, and Independent Refiners' Association of California, Inc., its officers, directors, and employees, during the period from January 1, 1936, to date, and relating to production, prices, sales, purchases or consumption of gasoline within the Pacific Coast territory.

13. Such of the books, records, accounts and memoranda regularly kept by the corporation herein named in the regular course of business as are sufficient to show the names and addresses of all persons who, during the period from January 1, 1936, to date, have been employed by the corporation herein named as salesmen, within the Pacific Coast territory, of gasoline, and of all employees of the corporation herein named who, during said period, have had supervision, either direct or indirect, over all or any of said salesmen. [14]

14. (a) All contracts or agreements, including all amendments and supplements thereto, in effect at any time during the period from January 1, 1935, to date, and all correspondence and memoranda relating thereto, or copies thereof where the originals cannot be produced, made, written, sent or received by the corporation herein named with reference to the sale or consignment in the Pacific Coast territory of gasoline by the corporation herein named to Signal Oil Company, or with reference to

the marketing or sale of gasoline by the last named corporation in the Pacific Coast territory.

(b) Such of the books, records, accounts and memoranda regularly kept by the corporation herein named in the regular course of business as are sufficient to show the monthly quantities of gasoline (including the total of all gasolines and separate totals for "first structure," "second structure," and "third structure" gasoline) sold or delivered by the corporation herein named or by its subsidiaries or affiliates from January 1, 1935, to date, within the Pacific Coast territory, to Signal Oil Company.

[Endorsed]:

RETURN ON SERVICE OF WRIT

United States of America
Northern District of California—ss:

I hereby certify and return that I served the annexed Subpoena ad testificandum and duces tecum on the therein-named G. M. Foster, Assistant Secretary Standard Oil Company of California by handing to and leaving a true and correct copy thereof with G. M. Foster, *Assitant* Secretary Standard Oil Company of California personally at San Francisco in said District on the 26th day of July, A. D. 1939. George Vice U. S. Marshal. By Emile J. Canepa, Deputy.

[Endorsed]: Filed Aug. 4, 1939. [15]

In the District Court of the United States for the Southern District of California Central Division

In the Matter of the Subpoena returnable before the Second Grand Jury impanelled by Honorable Paul J. McCormick, Judge of the above entitled Court, during the February Term thereof, which Subpoena was issued out of and over the Seal of said Court, Honorable Paul J. McCormick, Judge thereof, on July 19, 1939, directed to "G. M. Foster, Assistant Secretary, Standard Oil Company of California, 225 Bush Street, San Francisco, California."

NOTICE OF MOTION TO QUASH SUBPOENA DUCES TECUM [16]

To the United States of America, and to M. S. Huberman, Esq., Special Assistant to the Attorney General, Its Attorney:

Please take notice that on Monday, August 21, 1939 at the hour of ten o'clock A. M., or as soon thereafter as counsel can be heard, the undersigned, G. M. Foster, both as an individual and as Assistant Secretary of Standard Oil Company of California, a Delaware corporation, and said Standard Oil Company of California, a Delaware corporation, will move the Honorable, the above entitled court, in the courtroom of the Honorable Paul J. McCormick, judge thereof, in the Federal Building,

Los Angeles, California, for an order with reference to the above described subpoena (a copy of which was handed to said G. M. Foster on or about July 24, 1939, and a copy of which is hereto attached), as follows:

1. Quashing and vacating said subpoena.
2. Quashing and vacating each numbered paragraph or item of Annex I to said subpoena and each lettered subdivision of each such paragraph or item.
3. For such other relief as may be meet in the premises.

Said motion will be made by the moving parties jointly, and by each of them severally, and by said G. M. Foster, both in his personal capacity and in his capacity as Assistant Secretary of said Standard Oil Company of California. Said motion will be made on the grounds stated in the affidavit hereto attached and on the following grounds, severally and collectively:

1. Said subpoena is unreasonable and oppressive, and the enforcement thereof would be an abuse of the process of this court.
2. The enforcement of said subpoena would constitute an unreasonable search and seizure, contrary to and in violation [17] of the rights, privileges, and immunities of the moving parties, and of each of them, under the Fourth Amendment to the Constitution of the United States.
3. The enforcement of said subpoena would result in the taking of property of said Standard Oil Company of California, namely, its books and rec-

ords necessary to the conduct of its business, including, without limitation of the foregoing, books and records containing trade secrets and current contracts and records, without compensation and without due process of law, in violation of and contrary to its rights, privileges, and immunities under the Fifth Amendment to the Constitution of the United States.

4. Said subpoena purports to cast on the witness G. M. Foster the burden of going through a mass of papers and selecting those which, in his judgment, relate to the subject of said subpoena and to cast upon said witness the burden of saying what papers are and what papers are not relevant to or sufficient to show the matters therein mentioned and legally competent and material in that behalf.

5. Said subpoena purports to call for the production of documents and papers relating to business done wholly within particular states and which are, therefore, not pertinent to any investigation within the jurisdiction of said Grand Jury.

6. The enforcement of said subpoena with respect to documents and papers relating solely to the intrastate business of Standard Oil Company of California would be in excess of the authority and jurisdiction of said Grand Jury and of this court, as said authority and jurisdiction are defined and limited by subdivision 3 of section 8 of Article I of the Constitution of the United States.

7. Said subpoena purports to call for the production of documents and papers without any

showing that they, or any of them, [18] contain evidence relevant to any issue under investigation by said Grand Jury, or are legally competent and material in that behalf.

8. Said subpoena does not purport to call for the production of particular documents and papers, specifically described and identified, but calls for the production of a mass of material described only in the broadest and most general terms.

9. Said Standard Oil Company of California has, over a period of about three years, at the request of the United States, accorded to the United States and said Huberman information necessary to enable them to identify, specify, and describe with reasonable particularity any and all documents and any other things in said books and records which may be required for presentation to said Grand Jury, and such information is now, and was at and before the issuance of said subpoena, in the possession of the United States and Huberman.

10. There is no authority in statute or in the rulings or practice of the courts of the United States for the issuance of said subpoena.

11. Without waiving any objection to the generality, indefiniteness, and illegality of said subpoena, or any part thereof, and without admitting that it would be possible to comply therewith, the moving parties specify that it would be a physical impossibility to comply with said subpoena within the time thereby allowed, and compliance would in-

volve the work of many persons over a period of months and years.

12. That said subpoena calls for matters of public record and other information as accessible to the United States as to these moving parties, and for matters not in the possession of these moving parties.

13. Copies of most of the reports of which copies are required by paragraph 4 and by paragraph 5 of said Annex I have been supplied to and are in the possession of the United States and said Huberman, as set forth in the attached affidavit. [19]

14. Other material has been supplied to and is in the possession of the United States and said Huberman, as set forth in the attached affidavit.

The moving parties, severally and collectively, as aforesaid specify the foregoing grounds severally and collectively with regard to said subpoena as a whole and with regard to each individual numbered paragraph and each lettered subdivision of Annex I thereto.

Said motion will be based on all records and files of this court relating to said Grand Jury and to said subpoena and on this notice of motion and on the attached copy of said subpoena and on the attached affidavit of G. M. Foster and upon such oral testimony and other evidence as the court may permit to be offered at the hearing hereon, and on the memorandum of authorities hereto attached.

Dated: Los Angeles, California, August 11, 1939.

OSCAR LAWLER
Standard Oil Building,
Los Angeles, California
Telephone: TRinity 5111.

FELIX T. SMITH
Standard Oil Building,
San Francisco, California,
Telephone: GArfield 6133.

Attorneys for G. M. Foster, individually, G. M. Foster, Assistant Secretary of Standard Oil Company of California, and Standard Oil Company of California.

G. M. FOSTER
G. M. Foster, individually, and as Assistant Secretary of Standard Oil Company of California.

[Seal] STANDARD OIL COMPANY OF CALIFORNIA

By A. K. STEVENSON
Assistant Secretary

PILLSBURY, MADISON & SUTRO,
Standard Oil Building,
San Francisco, California

LAWLER, FELIX & HALL,
Standard Oil Building,
Los Angeles, California
Of Counsel. [20]

[Title of District Court and Cause.]

AFFIDAVIT OF G. M. FOSTER [21]

State of California
City and County of San Francisco—ss.

G. M. Foster, being first duly sworn, deposes and says: He is and has been for about eight years an assistant secretary of Standard Oil Company of California, and is the person named in the subpoena duces tecum issued out of this court July 19, 1939, a copy of which is filed herewith. A copy of said subpoena was handed to affiant on July 26, 1939, in San Francisco. Immediately on receipt thereof affiant consulted about said subpoena with counsel for Standard Oil Company of California and officials and employees of said company, who, with affiant, have ever since that time been making diligent inquiry to ascertain in what respects, if at all, the duces tecum feature of said subpoena can be complied with.

Said subpoena relates for the most part to matters of which affiant has no personal knowledge and which are foreign to affiant's duties with said corporation, and the statements in this affidavit are based for the most part not on affiant's personal knowledge, but on information obtained from those persons connected with said corporation whom affiant believes to have knowledge of the matters herein stated.

The minutes of meetings of stockholders of said corporation contain nothing, so far as affiant knows or can ascertain, which is pertinent to anything involved in this Grand Jury investigation mentioned in said subpoena.

The minutes of meetings of directors of said corporation cover a variety of subjects relating to the business of said corporation, and so far as affiant knows or can ascertain, there is nothing therein relating or pertaining to anything involved in said Grand Jury investigation. There is but one copy of said [22] minutes which is in current use in the business of said corporation.

There are more than twenty committees of said corporation at San Francisco, California, and there are many more (the exact number being unknown to affiant) at other places where said corporation conducts its business. These committees deal with various matters, including such things as social security, advertising, annuities, interpretation of overtime rules, technical employment, loan plan, manufacturing personnel, etc., etc. The minutes of such of said committees as keep minutes, as affiant believes, relate to a variety of subjects, none of which so far as affiant knows, is pertinent to said Grand Jury investigation. As to many of these minutes production thereof is impossible without long delay.

Affiant is informed that since early in 1936 the United States, and particularly the Federal Trade Commission and Department of Justice, have conducted an extensive examination, which included examination by the Department of Justice, at the office of said corporation, of a large part of its records. During such investigation said corporation and its employees and counsel have assisted agents and employees of said Commission and said Department of Justice.

Through said inquiry and investigation, and through material supplied to them by said corporation, M. S. Huberman and government agents acting under him have become sufficiently acquainted (as hereafter will be more fully shown) with the records of said corporation, to know what parts of its voluminous records are pertinent to said Grand Jury inquiry, and to be able to describe them with reasonable certainty. Huberman is in possession not only of the material supplied to him and his subordinates, but also of that supplied to the Federal Trade Commission, as shown by the press release of the Department of Justice, dated May 1, 1939, [23] reading in part as follows:

> "Pacific Coast Oil Monopoly
>
> Investigation of alleged monopolistic practices by oil companies in the Pacific Coast Area in the distribution of petroleum products. Department of Justice Release of May 1, 1939.
>
> The Department of Justice will begin in the near future an inquiry before a Federal grand jury in the Southern District of California with reference to alleged monopolistic practices by oil companies in the Pacific Coast Area in the distribution of petroleum products. This

> statement is issued in accordance with the established policy of the Department to make public its reasons for instituting such an inquiry.
>
> * * * * * * *
>
> In 1936 the Federal Trade Commission at the request of the Attorney General investigated complaints charging that monopolistic practices similar to those which led to the 1930 decree were being resorted to. As a result of the facts reported by the Commission, the Department in November, 1937, undertook a comprehensive field investigation.
>
> The purpose of the inquiry before the grand jury is to present the facts obtained in the course of the investigations conducted by the Department and the Federal Trade Commission as well as such other facts as may appear to be pertinent, in order to ascertain whether prosecutions for violation of the antitrust laws should be had."

Affiant has made inquiry concerning said investigation by said Federal Trade Commission and Department of Justice above referred to and therefrom states that he is informed and believes as follows:

By letter dated October 14, 1936, James A. Horton, chief examiner of said Federal Trade Commission, submitted to said corporation a schedule of inquiries to which reply by said corporation was requested, and to this letter the corporation on or about October 29, 1936, replied:

> "* * * the Company is willing and desirous of fully cooperating with the Commission in its Petroleum Decree investigation. As a matter of fact, prior to the receipt of your letter of October 14, 1936, the Company had already delivered to Mr. Herbert L. Propst, [24] one of your representatives, replies to a number of questions set forth in the schedule * * *. The Company is now engaged in the preparation of replies to the remainder of the queries * * *."

Said inquiry continued thence forward over a long period. Responsive thereto said corporation supplied a vast amount of data and information from its records, including expensive summaries and abstracts of accounts and photostatic and other copies of papers. Said inquiry by the Federal Trade Commission was later merged into an inquiry by the Department of Justice, under the direction of M. S. Huberman, who informed said corporation that the material supplied to the Federal Trade Commission had been turned over to him and, at the request of Huberman, said corporation amplified and made current the latter material.

One of the series of inquiries submitted by said Commission on or about October 14, 1936, was entitled, "Schedule for Preparation from the Records of Standard Oil Company of California." Responsive thereto said corporation supplied particulars of its organization, including date of incorporation, amount of capital stock, number of shares outstanding, absence of bonded indebtedness, nature of the corporation's business, names and addresses of its then officers and directors, copies of all annual and other periodical reports to its stockholders from 1930, to December, 1936. This material was delivered to the Federal Trade Commission at Los Angeles, California, and a copy thereof delivered to Richard C. Heaton as Special Assistant to the Attorney General of the United States, 910 Stock Exchange Building, Los Angeles, California, and, as affiant is informed and believes is included in the material directed to be presented to said Grand Jury as aforesaid. [25]

The articles of incorporation of said corporation are on file in the office of the Secretary of State of the State of Delaware, and a certified copy is the only means by which the same can be produced before said Grand Jury. Such a certified copy is on file with the Secretary of State of the State of California, and a like copy is filed with the county clerk of many of the counties of California, including Los Angeles County, and the copies so filed are a part of the public records available to anyone desiring the same. Said corporation is willing to procure and furnish such certified copy, but affiant is advised and believes that the subpoena duces tecum requiring the production by it of a public record is unreasonable.

There are about twenty persons who are, or during the period since January 1, 1935, have been officers and directors of said corporation. The residence address of each such officer and director appears in a great many places in the books and records of said corporation, and to find them it will be necessary to make exhaustive examination of such books and records, such as stock records, income tax data, reports and social security records.

On or about May 1, 1938, at the request of said Huberman, a list of names and *address* of said officers and directors of said corporation was brought down to May 1, 1938. On the same day copies of all of said corporation's reports to stockholders during the period intervening between delivery of said information to the Federal Trade Commission and May 1, 1938, were furnished to said Huberman.

On February 18, 1938, at the request of said Huberman, said corporation delivered to him photostatic copies of each monthly report made by it to the United States Bureau of Mines [26] from January, 1935, to December, 1937, both inclusive.

The records of said corporation relating to the production by it of crude oil, gasoline and other petroleum products, and to stocks, deliveries and receipts, exchange accounts, imports, shipments, sales, purchases, and consumption of gasoline, search of which will be required in order to comply with said subpoena, are kept at many places where said corporation carries on its operations and are extremely voluminous. For example, said subpoena calls for or requires examination of invoices of various kinds. One type of invoice, namely, service station slips showing sales of gasoline through five states, would probably exceed 40,000,000 in number (affiant being unable to state the exact number) over the period therein mentioned.

The volume and extent of said records mentioned in said subpoena is such as to require many months to inspect the same and render it physically impossible to examine even a substantial part thereof in the time intervening between July 26 and August 25, 1939.

In the latter part of January, 1938, Huberman, after numerous conferences with said corporation, presented to said corporation a series of blank so-called "schedules" calling for information from the records of said corporation relating to various subjects and requested said corporation to fill them out and show on each schedule the company representative who prepared it and the company source of the information supplied. Said schedules were filled in and delivered to said Huberman, and each schedule showed the representative who prepared it and the source of the matter appearing thereon.

The title and subject matter of each such schedule is [27] as follows:

> Quantity of gasoline produced by it in the Pacific Coast territory each month from January, 1935, to December, 1937, inclusive.
>
> Gasoline stocks owned by it in said Pacific Coast territory on the last day of each month from December, 1934, to December, 1937, inclusive, including gasoline stocks at refineries and

at bulk terminals and amounts of gasoline owed to or by said corporation on exchange at the close of each month;

Gasoline exchange receipts by it from January, 1935, to December, 1937, inclusive;

Gasoline deliveries by it pursuant to exchange accounts from January, 1935, to December, 1937, inclusive;

Gasoline shipments by it from Pacific Coast territory by months from January, 1935, to December, 1937, inclusive;

Total sales of gasoline separately in each of the States of California, Oregon, Washington, Nevada and Arizona by months from January, 1935, to December, 1937, inclusive, showing separately first, second and third structures, and other gasolines;

Total sales of gasoline made by it or its subsidiaries from January, 1935, to December, 1937, inclusive;

Consumption of gasoline by it within said Pacific Coast territory from January, 1935, to December, 1937, inclusive;

Gasoline purchased by it from January, 1935, to December, 1937, inclusive, separately indicating as to each purchase, classification of gasoline by structure, [28] amount, price, place of disposition and date of commitment to purchase;

Gasoline sales made by it to refiners, showing name of each vendee, the classification of gasoline, quantity, price, place of delivery, date of commitment to purchaser as to each sale from January, 1935, to December, 1937, inclusive;

Total deliveries of gasoline by structure and otherwise to Signal Oil Company in Pacific Coast territory, from January, 1935, to December, 1937, both inclusive;

Taxable sales of motor fuel in Pacific Coast territory through Signal Oil Company;

Taxable sales of motor fuel in Pacific Coast territory;

Gasoline sales to Continental Oil Company.

On or about December 10, 1936, said corporation delivered to the Federal Trade Commission statements showing the mileage and location of crude oil and gasoline pipe lines located in the Pacific Coast territory and owned by said corporation and by its subsidiaries, with the capacity of each line, points connected thereby, length, capacity and location of all gathering lines and the extent to which said lines were made available to major companies, independent refiners or producers desiring to sell to independent refiners. About December 10, 1936, said corporation also delivered to said Commission a statement showing the following:

Quantity of crude oil produced by said corporation in California, each month, from June 1, 1935, to July 1, 1936; quantities by months of (1) crude oil (2) casinghead gasoline and (3) gasoline imported by said corporation into said Pacific Coast territory showing sources of supply from June,

1935, to [29] October, 1936, inclusive; quantities by months of crude oil shipped by said corporation from points within the United States to points in the United States outside of the Pacific Coast territory and the State of Utah.

In December, 1937, Huberman presented at the office of said corporation one Whitson, stating that he, Huberman, desired to have a survey made by Whitson of the Company's records relating to gasoline purchases, gasoline sales to other refiners (domestic), casinghead purchases and casinghead sales to other refiners (domestic), exchanges of gasoline and exchanges of casinghead—receipts and deliveries, sale price of gasoline and sales policies involved in the marketing of gasoline, including any correspondence between other companies in relation to prices or marketing policies for gasoline, any correspondence, memoranda, or telephone calls, etc., either with the Independent Refiner's Association or with other companies concerning the formation or activities of the Independent Refiner's Association. In so far as there were any such records, said Whitson was thereupon made acquainted with them.

In January, 1938, Huberman presented one Johnson at the office of said corporation, stating that he, Huberman, desired Johnson to examine the records of said corporation relating to the subjects enumerated in the foregoing paragraph. Said corporation then provided Johnson with an office and office accommodations and he proceeded, over a period of several months, to make such examination, during which, and pursuant to his request, copies of a large number of records, forms of contracts and other papers relating to prices and price postings were supplied to him.

Johnson also requested said corporation to furnish "Schedules showing posted prices from January 1, 1935, to date [30] for each of the three major brands of gasoline * * * at San Francisco, Los Angeles, Fresno, Portland, Seattle, Spokane, Phoenix and Reno," together with all postings at each of said points, including all classes of trade and types of deliveries for which prices were posted and said request was complied with.

Johnson also made to said corporation request that "all information reported by the Company in response to the (Federal Trade Commission) questionnaire should be brought down to date," as to a large number of specified items, which request was complied with.

Thereafter Huberman, through one Patterson, requested said corporation to provide copies of a large number of telegrams, letters and other documents from the files of said corporation which had been theretofore examined by said Johnson. In said request the various papers, copies of which were desired as aforesaid, were described not only by reference to the Company's file in which they were found, but by particular description; said request was complied with.

Patterson also requested information with reference to specifications, including octane ratings of the Company's gasolines, and indicated particular original specification sheets which he desired to inspect. Responsive thereto he was provided with all the papers referred to.

Early in 1938, Huberman presented at the offices of said corporation one Fierstone, an accountant acting under Huberman, with statement that he desired Fierstone to examine various records of the corporation relating to sales of gasoline and showing prices at which gasoline was sold by it. Fierstone thereupon examined the records so indicated, during which examination he was provided with particulars regarding contracts of [31] large purchasers of gasoline from said corporation.

On June 28, 1938, Patterson requested certain additional papers, and upon being supplied therewith stated that he knew of nothing further which was needed.

Standard Oil Company of California is a Delaware corporation, having its principal office in San Francisco, California; it is, and for many years past has been, engaged in all branches of the petroleum business, including the producing and marketing of crude oil and the manufacturing and marketing of petroleum products in the so-called Pacific Coast territory and elsewhere. In addition to its principal office, it has more than 650 branch and suboffices at various places throughout said Pacific Coast territory, at most if at not all of which there are records whereof examination is required by said subpoena duces tecum. Said corporation is, and for many years past has been, engaged in conducting both an intrastate and interstate business.

Affiant is further informed and believes and states the fact to be that, in its efforts to comply with the request of the United States and its officers and agents in the making of said investigation, as aforesaid, said corporation has been required to expend a great many thousands of dollars and from time to time to divert from their regular duties a large number of its employees. Affiant is informed and believes that to make the searches and investigation required to comply with said annex to said subpoena duces tecum will necessitate constant service and diversion from their regular duties of a large number of employees of said corporation for several months and require examination of practically all of the records of its sales and other departments, and will require the expenditure of many thousands of dollars. Affiant respectfully states that such indiscriminate search and expenditure [32] of time and money can be avoided by a subpoena duces tecum which specifies with reasonable particularity the papers whose production is desired, and which relates the same to a reasonable scope.

Affiant respectfully states that production of the records of said corporation referred to in said subpoena will withdraw from the custody and possession of said corporation material essential to the conduct of its current business.

Affiant is ready and willing to appear personally and to testify before said Grand Jury, and he and said corporation are, and each of them is, ready and willing not only to comply with requirements of a reasonable and lawful subpoena, but also to assist in the expeditious production of such material as may be reasonably required for said Grand Jury investigation.

Wherefore, affiant, both individually and as an officer on behalf of said Standard Oil Company of California, respectfully prays that said subpoena duces tecum be quashed.

G. M. FOSTER

Subscribed and sworn to before me this 10th day of August, 1939.

[Seal] FRANK L. OWEN

Notary Public in and for the City and County of San Francisco, State of California. [33]

In the District Court of the United States of America, Southern District of California

The President of the United States of America: To ~~J. H. Tuttle, Secretary,~~ G. M. Foster, Assistant Secretary, Standard Oil Company of California, 225 Bush Street, San Francisco, California. Greeting:

You and Each of You Are Hereby Commanded, That all and singular business and excuses being laid aside, you, and each of you, be and appear in your proper person before the Second Grand Jury empanelled by the District Court of the United States for the Southern District of California, during the February Term of said Court, at the Hearing Room of said Second Grand Jury in the United States Post Office and Court House Building, in the City of Los Angeles, State of California, on the 25th day of August, A. D. 1939, at 11:00 o'clock in the forenoon, then and there to testify and give evidence before said Second Grand Jury, and that you produce at the time and place aforesaid all of those certain books, records, documents and papers which are more particularly described in Annex I, attached to and made a part hereof, and which are in your possession or custody, and not to depart without leave of the Court or the United States Attorney.

And this you are not to omit, under pain of being adjudged guilty of a contempt of said Court.

Witness, the Honorable Paul J. McCormick, Judge of said District Court for the Southern District of California, this 19th day of July, in the year of our Lord one thousand nine hundred and thirty-nine.

[Seal] R. S. ZIMMERMAN,
Clerk

By J. M. HORN
Deputy Clerk

M. S. HUBERMAN,
Special Assistant to the Attorney General. [34]

M.

ANNEX I—(TO SUBPOENA DUCES TECUM DIRECTED TO J. H. TUTTLE

The phrase or term "corporation herein named," as used hereinafter, designates and refers to Standard Oil Company of California.

1. Articles of incorporation and the certificate of incorporation or other charter of the corporation herein named, and all amendments thereto.

2. Books and records which show the names of all the officers and directors of the corporation herein named and their residence addresses during the period from January 1, 1935, to date.

3. All minute books and other papers, records, and documents containing the minutes or record of proceedings at meetings of stockholders, directors, any executive committee, or any other committees or boards of the corporation herein named, during the period from January 1, 1938, January 1, 1935, to date.

4. Copies of the annual, quarterly and other periodic reports made by the corporation herein named to its stockholders, during the period from January 1, 1935, to date.

5. Copies of all of the monthly reports entitled "Petroleum Situation in the Pacific Coast Territory" or "Monthly Petroleum Situation in the Pacific Coast Territory," made by the corporation herein named to the United States Bureau of Mines during the period from.. to date.

6. Such of the books, records, accounts, and memoranda regularly kept by the corporation herein named in the regular course of business as are sufficient to show:

(a) The quantity of crude oil produced in the State of California by the corporation herein named, its subsidiaries and affiliates, each month from January 1, 1935, to date.

(b) The number and daily capacity of refineries located in the states of California, Oregon, Washintgon, Nevada, and [35] Arizona (hereinafter referred to collectively as "Pacific Coast territory") and owned by the corporation herein named, its subsidiaries and affiliates, on January 1 of each year, from January 1, 1935, to date.

(c) The quantity of gasoline produced within the Pacific Coast territory by the corporation herein named, its subsidiaries and affiliates, each month from January 1, 1935, to date.

(d) The mileage and location of crude oil and gasoline pipelines located in the Pacific Coast territory and owned by the corporation herein named, its subsidiaries and affiliates, on January 1 of each year, from January 1, 1935, to date.

(e) The gasoline stocks owned within the Pacific Coast territory by the corporation herein named, its subsidiaries and affiliates, on the last day of each month from December 31, 1934, to date, including amounts separately shown for "first structure," "second structure," "third structure," and other commercial finished gasolines, and the amounts of each type owned within the Pacific Coast territory on each of said days at refineries and at bulk terminals, respectively.

(f) The monthly quantities of crude oil and of gasoline, and of other petroleum products delivered and received within the Pacific Coast territory from January 1, 1935, to date, by the corporation herein named, its subsidiaries and affiliates, pursuant to exchange account or accounts with any corporation, copartnership or person, including its subsidiaries and affiliates, engaged in the business of producing gasoline within the Pacific Coast territory.

(g) The monthly quantities of crude oil and of gasoline imported from January 1, 1935, to date, by the corporation herein named, its subsidiaries and affiliates, into the Pacific Coast territory. [36]

(h) The monthly quantities of crude oil and of gasoline shipped from January 1, 1935, to date, by the corporation herein named, its subsidiaries and affiliates, from points within the Pacific Coast territory to points outside that territory.

(i) The monthly quantities of gasoline (including the total of all gasolines and separate totals for "first structure," "second structure," and "third structure" gasolines) sold by the corporation herein named, its subsidiaries and affiliates, from January 1, 1935, to date, to consumers and sellers of gasoline located within the Pacific Coast territory (including separate totals for each state in said territory), exclusive of sales to corporations, copartnerships and persons engaged in the business of producing gasoline within the Pacific Coast territory, and including the quantity or the percentage of such monthly quantities sold by the corporation herein named and by its subsidiaries and affiliates to or through retail outlets, and including further the quantity or the percentage sold to or through retail outlets handling exclusively the gasolines of the corporation herein named or exclusively the gasolines of its subsidiaries or affiliates, and the quantity or percentage sold to or through retail outlets not selling exclusively the gasolines of any corporation, copartnership or person.

(j) The quantity of gasoline consumed within the Pacific Coast territory each month, from January 1, 1935, to date, by the corporation herein named, its subsidiaries and affiliates.

(k) The ownership on January 1 of each year, from January 1, 1935, to date, by the corporation herein named of the legal title to or beneficial interest in the stock of any other corporation engaged in the production, transportation or refining of crude oil or in the manufacture, transportation, marketing or sale of gasoline, including all books, records and accounts showing the number of shares of such stock owned [37] legally or beneficially on each of said days.

(l) The dates and amounts and the recipients of each contribution or payment made from January 1, 1935, to date, by the corporation herein named, its subsidiaries and affiliates, to any association of retail dealers in gasoline within the Pacific Coast territory and to any association of producers of gasoline within that territory.

7. All original books, records, contracts, and invoices showing purchases during the period from January 1, 1935, to date, of gasoline physically located at time of delivery within the Pacific Coast territory, by the corporation herein named or by any of its subsidiaries or affiliates engaged in producing or marketing gasoline within that territory, excluding, however, purchases of gasoline by said subsidiaries or affiliates from the corporation herein named, and excluding purchases of gasoline by the corporation herein named from its subsidiaries or affiliates, and including books, records, contracts,

and invoices disclosing specifically the following information with reference to each such purchase:

(a) Name of vendor.

(b) Date purchased.

(c) Date shipped.

(d) Quantity purchased and shipped.

(e) Octane rating and other specifications of gasoline so purchased.

(f) Whether "first structure," "second structure," "third structure," or other type of gasoline.

(g) Name and address of broker, agent, agency or person through whom purchased.

(h) Point from which shipped.

(i) Point or points to which shipment was moved at the direction of the corporation herein named, or of its subsidiary or affiliate. [38]

(j) Price paid to the vendor for each such purchase.

(k) Whether purchased by contract and the description and date of such contract.

(l) Whether such gasoline was moved by the corporation herein named or by its subsidiary or affiliate to refineries or bulk terminals or bulk stations or service stations operated by the corporation herein named or by its subsidiary or affiliate.

(m) Whether, if such gasoline was not moved to any of the facilities mentioned in paragraph 7 (l) hereof, such gasoline was resold, and in the case of each such resale, the date thereof, the date of delivery, whether sold or delivered on contract, and the description and date of such contract, the name and address of the vendee, the price at which sold, and the place at which delivery was made.

8. All original books, records, contracts, and invoices showing sales during the period from January 1, 1938, to date, of gasoline physically within the Pacific Coast territory at or prior to time of delivery by the corporation herein named or by its subsidiaries or affiliates to Shell Oil Company, Incorporated, Shell Oil Company, Tide Water Associated Oil Company, Associated Oil Company, Union Oil Company of California, The Texas Company (California), Richfield Oil Corporation, William C. McDuffie, as Receiver or as Trustee of Richfield Oil Company of California, General Petroleum Corporation of California, Socony-Vacuum Oil Co., Inc., Seaside Oil Company, Sunset Oil Company, Gilmore Oil Company, Rio Grande Oil Inc., Rio Grande Oil Company, and Rio Grande Oil Corporation, excluding sales in which the quantity of the individual sale is less than three thousand gallons, including books, records, contracts, and invoices disclosing specifically the following information with reference to each such sale:

(a) Date of sale.

(b) Date of delivery. [39]

(c) Whether sold or delivered on contract and the description and date of such contract.

(d) Name and address of vendee.

(e) Price at which sold.

(f) Quantity of each sale.

(g) The octane rating and other specifications of the product so sold.

(h) Place at which delivery was made.

9. All original books, records, contracts, and invoices showing sales made by the corporation herein named, its subsidiaries or affiliates, to ANY corporation, copartnership or person during the period from APRIL 1, 1936, to date, of gasoline physically within the Pacific Coast territory at or prior to the time of delivery, at or below the following prices, exclusive of taxes:

(a) In the case of sales from April 1, 1936, to March 22, 1937, 8¼ cents per gallon plus, in the event delivery is made at points outside the City of Los Angeles, the price differential prevailing at the time of sale between said city and the point of delivery;

(b) In the case of sales from March 23, 1937, to March 24, 1938, 8½ cents per gallon plus, in the event delivery is made at points outside the City of Los Angeles, the price differential prevailing at the time of sale between said city and the point of delivery;

(c) In the case of sales from March 25, 1938, to date, 7¾ cents per gallon plus, in the event delivery is made at points outside the City of Los Angeles, the price differential prevailing at the time of sale between said city and the point of delivery;

including books, records, contracts, and invoices disclosing specifically with reference to each such sale the date of sale, date of delivery, place of delivery, whether sold or delivered on contract and the [40] description and date of such contract, name and address of vendee, price at which sold, quantity of each sale, and the octane rating and other specifications of products sold.

10. All original letters, telegrams, teletype messages, contracts, reports, interoffice or other memoranda and other documents, or copies thereof where the originals cannot be produced, made, written, sent or received during the period from January 1, 1935, to date, by or between or among any of the following named corporations, copartnerships, associations, and persons:

Ajax Oil & Refining Co.,
Aromalene, Inc.,
Associated Oil Company,
Bachmann Petroleum Corp.,
Bell View Oil Syndicate,
R. R. Bush Oil Company,
California Oil & Refining Co.,
California Refining Co.,
Caminol Co., Ltd.,

Century Oil Company,
Eagle Oil and Refining Co., Inc.,
East West Refining Company,
El Camino Oil Co., Ltd.,
Edington Oil & Refining Co., Ltd.,
Elm Oil Co.,
El Tejon Oil and Refining Corporation,
Envoy Petroleum Company,
Estado Petroleum Corp., Ltd.,
Exeter Refining Company,
Fletcher Oil Company, Inc.,
General Petroleum Corporation of California,
Gilmore Oil Company,
Hancock Oil Company of California, [41]
Harbor Refining Company,
Krieger Oil Company of California,
Lake View Oil & Refining Co.,
Los Alamitos Refining Co.,
Los Nietos Producing & Refining Company, Ltd.,
M. M. McCallen Refining Company,
M. M. McCallen Refining and Producing Co.,
Macmillan Petroleum Corporation,
Mercury Petroleum Corporation,
Mohawk Petroleum Company,
Monarch Refiners, Ltd.,
The Norwalk Company,
Olympic Refining Company,
Operators Oil & Refining Co.,
The Petrol Corporation,

Richfield Oil Corporation,
Rio Grande Oil Company,
Rio Grande Oil, Inc.,
Rocket Oil Company,
Rothschild Oil Company,
St. Helens Petroleum Company, Ltd.,
San Fernando Refining Company,
Seaside Oil Company,
Shell Oil Company,
Shell Oil Company, Incorporated,
Signal Oil Company,
Socal Oil & Refining Company,
Standard Oil Company of California,
Walter Steiner Refining Co.,
Sunset Oil Company,
The Texas Company (California),
Tide Water Associated Oil Company, [42]
Triangle Oil & Refining Co.,
Union Oil Company of California,
White Star Refining Company,
Wilshire Oil Company,
Committee of Independent Refiners,
Fair Practices Association (Petroleum Products),
Independent Refiners' Association of California, Inc.
O. F. Collinge, Inc.,
F. R. Long, Inc.,
Regional Code Compliance Committee,
Retail Petroleum Dealers Association,
M. M. McCallen,

Henry Brown, doing business as Operators Oil & Refining, and the officers, directors, agents and employees of said corporations, copartnerships, associations and persons, and all other corporations, copartnerships, associations and persons, relating to the following subjects:

(a) Dealings in or negotiations regarding the purchase and sale of gasoline between corporations, copartnerships or persons engaged in the business of producing gasoline within the Pacific Coast territory or between any such corporation, copartnership or person, and any association or associations (whether incorporated or not) composed in whole or in part of such corporations, copartnerships, or persons.

(b) Refinery, wholesale, tank wagon, tank truck, industrial consumer, commercial consumer, agricultural consumer, tank car, spot market, contract, or tanker prices or quotations of prices of gasoline in the Pacific Coast territory.

(c) Terms of sale of gasoline to or forms of contracts for the sale of gasoline with brokers, jobbers, [43] wholesalers, bulk plant operators, service station operators, retailers or consumers of gasoline in the Pacific Coast territory, or the gross or net margins or allowances received or to be received by them.

(d) Decreases or increases in the prices of gasoline in the Pacific Coast territory or the maintenance or establishment of such prices at or above or below any level or levels.

(e) Agreements or arrangements or understandings between or among corporations, copartnerships or persons engaged in the business of producing gasoline within the Pacific Coast territory regarding the restriction, limitation or regulation of the quantity of gasoline produced or to be produced by any corporation, copartnership or person engaged in the business of producing gasoline within the Pacific Coast territory.

(f) The non-solicitation or non-acceptance by any corporation, copartnership or person engaged in the business of marketing or selling gasoline within the Pacific Coast territory of the accounts of gasoline customers of a competitor or competitors of such corporation, copartnership or person.

(g) Agreements or arrangements or understandings between or among corporations, copartnerships or persons engaged in the business of producing or selling gasoline within the Pacific Coast territory regarding the price or prices of gasoline or the terms or conditions of sale thereof between any such corporation, copartnership or person and purchasers of gasoline, or any policy or practice relating to the marketing of gasoline.

(h) The policy or practice of any corporation, copartnership or person engaged in the business of marketing [44] or selling gasoline within the Pacific Coast territory of requiring purchasers or gasoline within that territory to maintain specified or particular prices in the resale of gasoline.

(i) The refusal by any corporation, copartnership or person engaged in the business of marketing or selling gasoline within the Pacific Coast territory to supply gasoline to purchasers within that territory failing or refusing to resell gasoline at any specified or particular price or prices.

(j) The activities of price checkers or other persons engaged in ascertaining the prices for gasoline posted or charged within the Pacific Coast territory by sellers of gasoline.

(k) The policy or practice of any corporation, copartnership or person engaged in the business of marketing or selling gasoline within the Pacific Coast territory, of selling gasoline only to purchasers of gasoline within that territory, who at the places of business where such purchasers sell the gasolines of such corporation, copartnership or person, do not sell any other gasolines.

(l) The refusal by or failure of any corporation, copartnership or person owning or operating within the Pacific Coast territory a pipeline or pipelines for the transportation of crude oil or petroleum products, to make such pipeline or pipelines available for use by, or the transportation of commodities of, other corporations, copartnerships or persons engaged in the business of producing, refining, purchasing, selling or transporting crude oil or petroleum products.

(m) Negotiations by any corporation, copartnership or person engaged in the business of producing, selling or marketing gasoline in the Pacific Coast territory regarding purchase or attempted purchase of tetraethyl lead, or obtaining [45] or attempting to obtain a right, license or permit to use the same in the manufacture or blending of gasoline in the Pacific Coast territory, or to sell or market in that territory gasoline so manufactured or blended or regarding acquisition or attempted acquisition of any license or permit for the use of any "cracking" process in the manufacture of gasoline in the Pacific Coast territory.

11. All original price lists, records and other documents showing the prices posted from January 1, 1935, to date, by the corporation named herein at each of the cities of Los Angeles, San Francisco, and Fresno, California; Portland, Oregon; Seattle and Spokane, Washington; Phoenix, Arizona; and Reno, Nevada, for the sale of gasolines and fuel oil to resellers or consumers, including price lists, records and other documents showing the price, differential or allowance established by the corporation herein named with respect to each type or class of such resellers or consumers.

12. All original letters, memoranda, reports, surveys, compilations, summaries, analyses and estimates, or copies thereof where the originals cannot be produced, passing between the corporation herein named, its officers, directors, and employees, and Independent Refiners' Association of California, Inc., its officers, directors, and employees, during the period from January 1, 1936, to date, and relating to production, prices, sales, purchases or consumption of gasoline within the Pacific Coast territory.

13. Such of the books, records, accounts and memoranda regularly kept by the corporation herein named in the regular course of business as are sufficient to show the names and addresses of all persons who, during the period from January 1, 1936, to date, have been employed by the corporation herein named as salesmen, within the Pacific Coast territory, of gasoline, and of all employees of the corporation herein named who, during said period, have had supervision, either direct or indirect, over all or any of said salesmen. [46]

14. (a) All contracts or agreements, including all amendments and supplements thereto, in effect at any time during the period from January 1, 1935, to date, and all correspondence and memoranda relating thereto, or copies thereof where the originals cannot be produced, made, written, sent or received by the corporation herein named with reference to the sale or consignment in the Pacific Coast terri-

tory of gasoline by the corporation herein named to Signal Oil Company, or with reference to the marketing or sale of gasoline by the last named corporation in the Pacific Coast territory.

(b) Such of the books, records, accounts and memoranda regularly kept by the corporation herein named in the regular course of business as are sufficient to show the monthly quantities of gasoline (including the total of all gasolines and separate totals for "first structure," "second structure," and "third structure" gasoline) sold or delivered by the corporation herein named or by its subsidiaries or affiliates from January 1, 1935, to date, withing the Pacific Coast territory, to Signal Oil Company. [47]

[Title of District Court and Cause.]

MEMORANDUM IN SUPPORT OF MOTION TO QUASH [48]

The subpoena attacked by this motion is, in our judgment, unparalleled. We have found nothing to match its sweeping, indefinite, and unreasonable character, though we have read the pertinent federal cases, as well as many state decisions.

The subpoena was issued in aid of a Federal Grand Jury investigation. For some three years prior to the convening of the Grand Jury, first the Federal Trade Commission and then the Department of Justice carried on an investigation of the oil industry on the Pacific Coast, the Department of Justice acting through M. S. Huberman, Special Assistant to the Attorney General, whose name is signed to this subpoena. Standard Oil Company of California extended every assistance to the making of this investigation. Employees of the Company were withdrawn from their duties for months at a time and diverted to compiling and supplying information requested by the government.

On May 1, 1939, the Department of Justice made a press release, stating that it was starting a grand jury investigation of alleged monopolistic practices by oil companies in the Pacific Coast area in the distribution of petroleum products. This release, in part, said:

> "The purpose of the inquiry before the grand jury is to present the facts obtained in the course of the investigations conducted by the Department and the Federal Trade Commission as well as such other facts as may appear to be pertinent, in order to ascertain whether prosecutions for violation of the antitrust laws should be had."

This shows that the Department of Justice has all of the information given to the Federal Trade Commission, as well as that given to the Department itself. [49]

Now the Grand Jury has been convened and a subpoena has been served asking a witness to produce in thirty days a mass of documents and information which could not be produced in that time, if it could be produced at all. There is no showing of the materiality or competency of any of these papers, and much of them are obviously immaterial and incompetent on any theory.

The sweeping character of this subpoena cannot be exaggerated. In ONE paragraph (Annex I, para. 10), it calls for "All original letters, telegrams, teletype messages, contracts, reports, interoffice or other memoranda and other documents * * * from January 1, 1935, to date, by or between or among any of" SIXTY-EIGHT named concerns, THEIR "OFFICERS, DIRECTORS, AGENTS AND EMPLOYEES" (How many hundreds or thousands fall in this category?), and "all other corporations, co-partnerships, associations and persons." This blanket demand is for documents on fourteen so-called subjects. ONE part of ONE of these subjects is dealings or negotiations regarding the purchase and sale of gasoline from any and all producers within the Pacific Coast territory. Another subdivision of the same paragraph calls for all documents bearing on all "Agreements or arrangements or understandings * * * regarding * * * ANY POLICY OR PRACTICE RELATING TO THE MARKETING OF GASOLINE" (on the Pacific Coast) (Annex I, para. 10, subd. (g)).

Another paragraph of the subpoena (Annex I, para. 6—with twelve subdivisions of sweeping generality) calls on the witness to produce books and records "sufficient to show" a list of things which would fill volumes of statistics. ONE of these subdivisions (subd. (i)) would require the witness to examine all the service station slips which have been issued to patrons of the Company's Pacific Coast service stations during a period of nearly five years—the number of which probably exceeds 40,000,000. [50] Other paragraphs of the subpoena call for ALL PURCHASE AND SALE CONTRACTS—documents which are in use every day, and without which the corporation could not do business. There is no possible justification for depriving it of these records without any showing as to why such action is necessary or proper.

In other paragraphs (Annex I, paras. 4, 5), the subpoena calls for documents which have already been supplied to the government attorney. Nowhere has the information supplied to him and in his possession been used to prepare a reasonable description of what is wanted or to eliminate immaterial documents.

We have given a few samples of the character of the subpoena; we now pass to the legal principles under which the motion to quash it should be granted. These are simple and well settled:

1. A subpoena is the court's process; the court, while allowing a liberal use of the subpoena in furtherance of the ends of justice, should also control it

to the end of avoiding unnecessary and unreasonable annoyance and expense. An arbitrary and oppressive subpoena is an abuse of the process of the court.

2. An unreasonable subpoena duces tecum is an unreasonable search and seizure contrary to the Fourth Amendment. Corporations as well as individuals are entitled to the protection of this Amendment against unreasonable searches and seizures.

3. A Grand Jury has no right to subpoena all the papers of a corporation to see whether they contain some evidence of violation of the law. A dragnet, general warrant, or omnibus demand is invalid.

4. The Grand Jury cannot, by subpoena duces tecum, compel the witness to go through an unspecified mass of papers and select [51] those which in his judgment are "sufficient to show" the matters stated in the subpoena, nor can it use a subpoena duces tecum for a testimonial purpose, i.e., to produce information as distinguished from documents.

5. Most particularly are the above principles applicable in this case where the government, acting through the very man whose name is signed to the subpoena, has been voluntarily given such information as should enable it to specify with at least some particularity what is wanted, and to make some showing of its legal materiality and competence.

6. While a corporation has no privilege against self-incrimination under the Fifth Amendment, it is entitled to the protection of the due process clause of that Amendment. To withdraw current records and contracts necessary for the operation of a business is, if the subpoena is unreasonable and not fairly warranted by the necessities of the case, a taking of property without due process of law contrary to the Fifth Amendment.

7. Not only does the subpoena fail to afford any evidence whatever of the materiality of the papers demanded, but it purports to apply indiscriminately, and without any showing of reason therefor, to intrastate transactions as well as to interstate transactions.

8. The court is not obliged to go through a dragnet subpoena item by item to see whether perhaps some of the material embraced in its sweeping specifications might properly be called for. The subpoena should be quashed, allowing the party desiring it to prepare a proper subpoena covering such material as he is entitled to have. [52]

POINTS AND AUTHORITIES

1. The court has inherent power to control its process to prevent abuse thereof.

In Gumbel v. Pitkin (1888) 124 U. S. 131, the court said (pp. 143-144):

" 'The grounds of this procedure are the duty of the court to prevent its process from being abused to the injury of third persons * * *. So the equitable powers of courts of law over their own process, to prevent abuses, oppression, and injustice, are inherent and equally extensive and efficient * * *.' "

See also authorities cited infra and 15 C. J. 813.*

2. Corporations as well as individuals are entitled to the protection of Fourth Amendment and to protection thereunder against unreasonable subpoenas duces tecum.

In Hale v. Henkel (1906) 201 U. S. 43, involving a grand jury subpoena in an antitrust investigation, the court said (pp. 75-76):

> "Although, for the reasons above stated, we are of the opinion that an officer of a corporation which [53] is charged with a violation of a statute of the State of its creation, or of an act of Congress passed in the exercise of its constitutional powers, cannot refuse to produce the books and papers of such corporation, we do not wish to be understood as holding that a corporation is not entitled to immunity under the Fourth Amendment, against *unreasonable* searches and seizures. A corporation is, after

---

*"Every court has inherent power to control execution of its orders or processes to the end of preventing an abuse of them" (15 C. J. 813).

all, but an association of individuals under an assumed name and with a distinct legal entity. In organizing itself as a collective body it waives no constitutional immunities appropriate to such body. Its property cannot be taken without compensation. It can only be proceeded against by due process of law, and is protected, under the Fourteenth Amendment, against unlawful discrimination. Gulf &c. Railroad Company v. Ellis, 165 U. S. 150, 154, and cases cited. Corporations are a necessary feature of modern business activity, and their aggregated capital has become the source of nearly all great enterprises.

We are also of opinion that an order for the production of books and papers may constitute an unreasonable search and seizure within the Fourth Amendment" (court's italics).

See also:

Federal Trade Commission v. American Tobacco Co. (1924) 264 U. S. 298, 305-307;

Essgee Co. v. United States (1923) 262 U. S. 151, 156 ("* * * the search thus made was an unreasonable one against which the corporation was protected by the Fourth Amendment * * *");

Federal Trade Commission v. Smith (S.D. N.Y., 1929) 34 F. (2d) 323, 324. [54]

3. A blanket subpoena is an unreasonable search and seizure; it cannot serve as a roving commission to hunt through corporate papers.

In Hale v. Henkel (1906) 201 U. S. 43, supra, involving, as already stated, a grand jury subpoena in an antitrust investigation, the court said (pp. 76-77):

> "Applying the test of reasonableness to the present case, we think the subpoena duces tecum is far too sweeping in its terms to be regarded as reasonable. It does not require the production of a single contract, or of contracts with a particular corporation, or a limited number of documents, but all understandings, contracts or correspondence between the MacAndrews & Forbes Company, and no less than six different companies, as well as all reports made, and accounts rendered by such companies from the date of the organization of the MacAndrews & Forbes Company, as well as all letters received by that company since its organization from more than a dozen different companies, situated in seven different States in the Union.
>
> If the writ had required the production of all the books, papers and documents found in the office of the MacAndrews & Forbes Company, it would scarcely be more universal in its operation, or more completely put a stop to the business of that company. Indeed, it is difficult

to say how its business could be carried on after it had been denuded of this mass of material, which is not shown to be necessary in the prosecution of this case, and is [55] clearly in violation of the general principle of law with regard the the particularity required in the description of documents necessary to a search warrant or subpoena. Doubtless many, if not all, of these documents may ultimately be required, but some necessity should be shown, either from an examination of the witnesses orally, or from the known transactions of these companies with the other companies implicated, or some evidence of their materiality produced, to justify an order for the production of such a mass of papers. A general subpoena of this description is equally indefensible as a search warrant would be if couched in similar terms."

In Federal Trade Commission v. American Tobacco Co. (1924) 264 U. S. 298, where the court denied mandamus to compel disclosure of records to the Federal Trade Commission under a blanket demand, the court said (pp. 305-306, 307):

(Holmes, J.) "The mere facts of carrying on a commerce not confined within state lines and of being organized as a corporation do not make men's affairs public, as those of a railroad company now may be. Smith v. Interstate Commerce Commission, 245 U. S. 33, 43. Anyone who respects the spirit as well as the letter of the Fourth Amendment would be loath to believe that Congress intended to authorize one of its subordinate agencies to sweep all our traditions into the fire (Interstate Commerce Commission v. Brimson, 154 U. S. 447, 479), and to direct fishing expeditions into private papers on the possibility that they may disclose evidence of crime. We do not discuss the question whether it could do so if it [56] tried, as nothing short of the most explicit language would induce us to attribute to Congress that intent. The inerruption of business, the possible revelation of trade secrets, and the expense that compliance with the Commission's wholesale demand would cause are the least considerations. It is contrary to the first principles of justice to allow a search through all the respondents' records, relevant or irrelevant, in the hope that something will turn up. The unwillingness of this Court to sustain such a claim is shown in Harriman v. Interstate Commerce Commission, 211 U. S. 407, and as to correspondence, even in the case of a common carrier, in United States v. Louisville & Nashville R. R. Co., 236 U. S. 318, 335. The question is a different one where the State granting the charter gives its Commission power to inspect.

The right of access given by the statute is to documentary evidence—not to all documents, but to such documents as are evidence. The analogies of the law do not allow the party wanting evidence to call for all documents in order to see if they do not contain it. Some ground must be shown for supposing that the documents called for do contain it. Formerly in equity the ground must be found in admissions in the answer. Wigram, Discovery, 2d ed., § 293. We assume that the rule to be applied here is more liberal but still a ground must be laid and the ground and the demand must be reasonable. Essgee Co. v. United States, 262 U. S. 151, 156, 157. A general subpoena in the form of these petitions would be bad. Some evidence of the materiality of the papers demanded must be produced. Hale v. Henkel, 201 U. S. 43, 77. [57]

* * *

The argument for the Government attaches some force to the investigations and proceedings upon which the Commission had entered. The investigations and complaints seem to have been only on hearsay or suspicion—but, even if they were induced by substantial evidence under oath, the rudimentary principles of justice that we have laid down would apply. We cannot attribute to Congress an intent to defy the Fourth Amendment or even to come so near to doing so as to raise a serious question of constitutional law."

See also, involving grand jury subpoena:

In re American Sugar Refining Co. (C. C. N. Y., 1910) 178 Fed. 109;

United States v. Medical Society of the District of Columbia (D. C., 1938) 26 F. Supp. 55, 56-57;

Ex parte Brown (1880) 72 Mo. 83, 93-96 (approved in Hale v. Henkel, supra, 201 U. S. 77);

And see:

United States v. Union Trust Co. of Pittsburgh (W.D.Pa., 1936) 13 F. Supp. 286, 287 ("* * * blanket demand for the production of the minutes * * * for the years 1931 and 1932 * * * is violative of * * * the Fourth Amendment * * *."—See present subpoena, Annex I, para. 3).

And generally:

Boyd v. United States (1886) 116 U. S. 616, 622, et seq.;

Carpenter v. Winn (1911) 221 U. S. 533;

Rawlins v. Hall-Epps Clothing Co. (5th C.C.A., 1914) 217 Fed. 884, 887-888 (Bankruptcy subpoena);

Federal Trade Commission v. Smith (S. D. N. Y., 1929) 34 F. (2d) 323, 324 (Federal Trade Commission order);

Elting v. United States (1892) 27 Ct. Cl. 158 (quoted infra);
Ex parte Clarke (1899) 126 Cal. 235, 238.

In no one of these cases was the process condemned by the court even remotely comparable for sweeping generality and general oppressiveness with the subpoena here involved. [58]

4. A subpoena duces tecum cannot compel the witness to go through a mass of papers to ascertain which ones are "sufficient to show" matters stated in the subpoena.

In Elting, Adm'r. v. United States (1892) 27 Ct. Cl. 158, the court said, referring to R. S. 877 (U.S.C. 28:655), which is the statutory authority for issuance of subpoenas by the federal courts (p. 164):

> "The duty of a witness under the writ, as regulated by the statute, is simply to bring a specified paper to a designated place. Under a writ ad testificandum a party can not make a man his lawyer, or physician, or scientific instructor by subpoenaing him as a witness and examining him as an expert. Under neither writ is he entitled to the judgment, discretion, opinion, or professional service of the witness. *He cannot compel him to go through a mass of papers and select those which in his (the witness's) judgment relate to the subject of litiga-*

tion; neither can he cast on the witness the responsibility of saying what papers do, and what papers do not, bear upon the issue to be tried" (italics ours).

See also Rawlins v. Hall-Epps Clothing Co. (5th C.C.A., 1914) 217 Fed. 884, 887.

These cases rest on the obvious principle that a subpoena duces tecum cannot serve a testimonial purpose; it cannot require the giving of information as distinguished from the production of documents (Murray v. Louisiana (1896) 163 U. S. 101, 107). [59]

5. The above principles are peculiarly applicable where the government has full information to enable it to specify material matters with fair particularity.

In Schuricht v. McNutt (D. Conn., 1928) 26 F. (2d) 388, the court said on a motion to quash a subpoena duces tecum (p. 390):

"Furthermore, even if the operativeness of the Swiss ammunition was material, the subpoena should be recalled under the rule that a subpoena should not issue where the facts to be proved by the papers wanted can be otherwise established, as where a party has in his possession or under his control the means for acquiring the information he seeks to obtain, In re Romaine (D. C.) 138 F. 837, at page 843, and cases there cited * * *."

In Mobile Gas Co. v. Patterson (M.D. Ala., 1923) 288 Fed. 884, in denying a motion by a public utility commission for production of records, the court said (pp. 888-889):

> "It also appears that the commission subsequently sent its auditor to Chicago to make such examination of the books and records of the Mobile Gas Company as the commission directed. And it further appears that these engineers and these accountants were given access to all that they sought to examine. Such examinations necessarily constitute great burdens to any utility that must submit thereto, and they ought not to be subjected to repetition thereof at the instance of the commission upon the theory that the commission and its representatives did not do their duty in making such examination thorough. To require a public utility to submit to an examination of its properties and [60] of its records by engineers and accountants representing the commission and to pay them large sums of money for the expenses thereof in addition to the interruption of its business, which is incident thereto, and then again to require them to go through this same expensive proceeding, without any better reason than the allegation of the commission that its examinations were not sufficient to justify its own action, and that the proceedings

which it has taken cannot be upheld without further fishing expedition through the same property and same writings savors of the oppression, and is within the spirit of the prohibition of the Fourth Amendment of the Constitution of the United States * * *." [61]

6. Corporation entitled to protection under due process clause of Fifth Amendment against unnecessary deprivation of records necessary to its business, disclosure of trade secrets, etc.

See authorities supra, namely:

Hale v. Henkel (1906) 201 U. S. 43, 76;

Federal Trade Commission v. American Tobacco Co. (1924) 264 U. S. 298, 306;

Rawlins v. Hall-Epps Clothing Co. (5th C. C. A., 1914) 217 Fed. 884, 887.

7. A subpoena duces tecum cannot validly apply to intrastate and interstate transactions indiscriminately.

See Federal Trade Commission v. American Tobacco Co. (1924) 264 U. S. 298, 307, supra.

See also Federal Trade Commission v. Smith (S.D.N.Y., 1929) 34 F. (2d) 323, where the court said (p. 324):

"So far as is shown by the present papers, the books and vouchers that are sought by petitioners relate not alone to interstate business of the Electric Bond & Share Company, but to its intrastate business as well. And even as to interstate business, petitioner, in the absence of a well-founded basis, canot say to a suspected corporation, 'Stand and deliver the possible evidences of the crime of which you are suspected.' " [62]

8. The court should quash the subpoena.

In Miller v. Mutual Reserve Fund Life Ass'n. (C.C.N.Y., 1905) 139 Fed. 864, the court said (p. 864):

> "This court did, as counsel for complainant suggests, heretofore lay down the rule that a subpoena duces tecum should be first obeyed by bringing the documents into court, and that thereupon the court would inspect them to see if they were relevant or material, and such as might be offered in evidence. Edison Electric Light Co. v. U. S. Electric Lighting Co. (C. C.) 44 Fed. 294, 45 Fed. 55. That decision had reference, of course, to the concrete case then before the court. It was not expected that any such grotesque subpoena duces tecum as we have here would ever be taken out, calling for apparently a cart load of books and papers, nearly all of which, so far as their description indicates, have nothing whatever to do with the issues raised by the pleadings. The motion to punish for failure to obey this omnibus subpoena is denied. If in this long enumeration there are a few items which possibly might

have some bearing on the controversy, complainant may take out new and separate subpoenas for them. The court will then look into the merits of each separate application to produce. To undertake a recitation of this mass of irrelevant material would be a useless waste of time."

See also Hoppe v. W. R. Ostrander & Co. (C. C. N. Y., 1910) 183 Fed. 786, and authorities supra, particularly Hale v. Henkel [63] (1906) 201 U. S. 43, 76-77, and Federal Trade Commission v. American Tobacco Co (1924) 264 U. S. 298, 307.

We respectfully submit that the motion should be granted.

Dated: Los Angeles, California, August 11, 1939.

OSCAR LAWLER
Standard Oil Building,
Los Angeles, California,
Telephone: TRinity 5111.

FELIX T. SMITH
Standard Oil Building,
San Francisco, California,
Telephone: GArfield 6133.

Attorneys for G. M. Foster, individually, G. M. Foster, Assistant Secretary of Standard Oil Company of California, and Standard Oil Company of California.

PILLSBURY, MADISON & SUTRO
Standard Oil Building,
San Francisco, California,
LAWLER, FELIX & HALL
Standard Oil Building,
Los Angeles, California,
Of Counsel.

[Endorsed]: Received copy of the within Notice of Motion to Quash Subpoena Duces Tecum, this 11 day of August, 1939. M. S. Huberman & Joseph E. Brill, Special Assistants to the Attorney General.

[Endorsed]: Filed Aug. 11, 1939. [64]

At a stated term, to wit: The February Term, A. D. 1939, of the District Court of the United States of America, within and for the Central Division of the Southern District of California, held at the Court Room thereof, in the City of Los Angeles, California, on Monday, the 21st day of August, in the year of our Lord one thousand nine hundred and thirty-nine.

Present: The Honorable Paul J. McCormick, District Judge.

[Title of Cause.]

This matter coming before the Court at this time, M. S. Huberman, Esq., Special Assistant to the

Attorney General, appearing for the Government; Oscar Lawler, Esq., appearing for the Standard Oil Company of California, and G. M. Foster, who is present in court; Hubert T. Morrow, Esq., appearing for the Texas Company and E. B. Liles, who is present in court; R. M. Searles, Esq., appearing for Tide Water Associated Oil Company and J. P. Edwards, who is present; L. R. Martineau, Jr., Esq., appearing for Richfield Oil Corporation, Rio Grande Oil Inc., a corporation, and Cleve B. Bonner, who is present; Martin J. Weil, Esq., appearing for General Petroleum Corporation of California, and D. W. Woods, who is present; V. E. Robinson, Esq., appearing for Gilmore Oil Company and S. M. Salisbury, who is present; Harrison Ryon, Esq., appearing for Seaside Oil Company and G. C. Howell, who is present; Wm. E. Wright, Esq., appearing for Shell Oil Company, Incorporated, and A. R. Bradley, who is present; L. A. Gibbons, Esq., appearing for Union Oil Company of California and W. R. Edwards, who is present; and Harold Judson, Esq., appearing for Signal Oil Company, and H. J. March, who is present; R. T. Doidge, appearing as court reporter and reporting the proceedings;

Oscar Lawler, Esq., now makes a statement relative to the further appearance of respondent, G. M. Foster, under the Subpoena Duces Tecum, and counsel for all other respondents appearing as [65] aforesaid having made similar statements, now, pursuant to consent and stipulation, it is ordered that said respondents today appearing under the subpoenas, may be now excused to again appear on Tuesday, August 29, 1939, at the hour of ten o'clock a. m., the Subpoenas Duces Tecum as to aforesaid respondents to continue in force without any waiver of any rights under the pending Motions to Quash interposed herein, hearing on which is now set for August 23, 1939, at 10 o'clock a. m., and subject to the further order of the Court pursuant to any ruling and decision that may be rendered on said motions. [66]

At a stated term, to wit: The February Term, A. D. 1939, of the District Court of the United States of America, within and for the Central Division of the Southern District of California, held at the Court Room thereof, in the City of Los Angeles on Tuesday the 29th day of August in the years of our Lord one thousand nine hundred and thirty-nine.

Present: The Honorable Paul J. Mccormick, District Judge.

[Title of Cause.]

At the hour of 10:07 o'clock a. m., this matter coming before the court for further proceedings; Joseph E. Brill, Esq., M. S. Huberman, Esq., Henry McClernan, Esq., Robert H. Marquis, Esq., L. P. Sherfy, Esq., Special Assistants to the Attorney General, appearing on behalf of the Government; Oscar Lawler, Esq., appearing for G. M.

Foster, individually, and as Assistant Secretary of, and the Standard Oil Company of California, a Corp.; Hubert T. Morrow, Esq., appearing for E. B. Liles, individually, and as Assistant Secretary of, and The Texas Company, a Corp.; Harold A. Black, Esq.; appearing for A. R. Bradley, and Shell Oil Company Incorporated; L. R. Martineau, Jr., Esq. appearing for Cleve B. Bonner, individually, and as Secretary of, and Richfield Oil Corporation, and Cleve B. Bonner, individually, and as Secretary of, and Rio Grande Oil Inc., a Corp.; Harold Judson, Esq. appearing for H. J. March, individually, and as Secretary of, and Signal Oil Company, a Corp.; Harrison Ryon, Esq. appearing for G. C. Howell, Secretary of, and the Seaside Oil Company, a Corp.; Verne E. Robinson, Esq. appearing for Stuart M. Salisbury, individually, and as Secretary of, and Gilmore Oil Company, a Corp.; Wm. I. Robinson, Esq. appearing for J. P. Edwards, Executive Secretary of, and the Tide Water Associated Oil Company; M. E. Harrison, Esq., of the firm of Brobeck, Phleger & Harrison, and L. A. Gibbons, Esq., appearing for W. R. Edwards, Secretary of, and the Union Oil Company of California, and Martin J. Weil, Esq., appearing for D. W. Woods, [67] individually, and as Secretary of, and General Petroleum Corporation of California; H. A. Dewing, appearing as court reporter and reporting the proceedings; the Court now reads and hands down "Memorandum of Ruling on Motions to Quash Subpoenas Duces

Tecum", and orders same filed and entered herein, same being as follows, to-wit:

[For aforesaid Memorandum of Ruling—see page 82.]

now, accordingly, it is ordered that each separate Motion to Quash Subpoena Duces Tecum of each of the movants herein be denied. Exceptions to the ruling are noted by counsel appearing for the respective aforesaid movants.

Joseph E. Brill, Esq., now makes a statement relative to the further appearance of witnesses under Subpoena Duces Tecum, who have previously been excused by the Court until this time, and now moves that all witnesses who have been so excused, be directed and ordered to appear, under the said Subpoenas, before the Second Grand Jury, on Wednesday, September 6th, 1939, at ten o'clock a. m., and it is so ordered.

Harrison Ryon, Esq., on behalf of the respondents whom he represents, now moves for a stay and supersedeas, and said motion is ordered denied. [68]

In the District Court of the United States,
Southern District of California,
Central Division

No. Miscellaneous

In the Matter of Various Motions to Quash Subpoena Duces Tecum Returnable Before Second Grand Jury, February, 1939, Term.

MEMORANDUM OF RULING ON MOTIONS TO QUASH SUBPOENAS DUCES TECUM

McCormick, District Judge:

As I view the motions before the court, in the light of applicable decisions of the United States Supreme Court and of other appellate federal courts, the sole litigable issue at this time is whether or not, under the movants' chargeable knowledge of the scope of investigations by the Second Grand Jury, the documents called for are indicated to the corporate officers served with reasonable specification as to subjects and subject matter and are reasonably limited as to dates.

Hale v. Herkel, 201 U. S. 43; Nelson v. U. S., 201 U. S. 92; Consolidated Rendering Co. v. Vermont, 207 U. S. 541; Wilson v. U. S., 221 U. S. 362; Blair v. U. S., 250 U. S. 273; Essgee Co. v. U. S., 262 U. S. 151; Norcross v. U. S. (C. C. A. 9) 209 Fed. 13; Consolidated Mines v. Securities & Exchange Comm'r. (C. C. A. 9) 97 F.(2d) 704; In re Black (C. C. A. 2) 47 F.(2d) 542.

The policy of the government in the investigation of alleged violation of anti-trust laws of the

United States has been disclosed in an article by the present Attorney General, who has charge of such matters in the Department of Justice, in 47 Yale Law Journal (1303), where he stated:

> "I conceive of the duty of the Department of Justice both to the courts and to Congress. To the courts they owe the duty of fair and able presentation of the particular cases which they prosecute. To Congress they owe the duty of marking out an intelligible line of policy of law enforcement. No other department can possibly outline that duty for them in a field where rules of thumb are not possible. Therefore, acting under the advice of the Attorney General, I propose to announce in connection with par- [69] ticular cases or investigations which are instituted in the future enough information so that the exercise of the discretion in selecting the cases may be as consistent as public announcement and public criticism can make it."

This governmental policy relating to restraint of trade was followed prior to the impanelment of the Second Grand Jury in this division of the court, when, in a press release by the Department of Justice on May 1, 1939, it was stated:

> "The Department of Justice will begin in the near future an inquiry before a Federal Grand Jury in the Southern District of California with reference to alleged monopolistic practices by oil companies in the Pacific Coast

Area in the distribution of petroleum products. This statement is issued in accordance with the established policy of the Department to make public its reasons for instituting such an inquiry.

"The major oil companies produce 84% of the gasoline refined and distribute 85% of the gasoline marketed in the Pacific Coast Area. In 1936 the price of gasoline rose sharply throughout the Pacific Coast Area, and it has since exhibited a stability without precedent in the area. By reason of two price advances in April, 1936, the majors' retail price for third structure gasoline in Los Angeles went from 7½¢ to 12¢ per gallon, exclusive of taxes; on first and second structure gasoline the advance was 4¢ a gallon. At the same time prices on all three grades were raised 4½¢ throughout the balance of the area. In March, 1937 the majors made an additional advance of ½¢ a gallon on all grades throughout the area. There have been no general reductions since April, 1936, in the majors' posted prices for gasoline.

"These price advances have made the practices in the Pacific Coast Area the subject of complaints and government investigations extending over a considerable period of time. The complaints have charged that by resort to various practices all substantial competition in the marketing of petroleum products is being eliminated. A comparatively small number of companies occupy such a predominant position in the Pacific Coast oil industry, that concerted action to restrict competition may easily place in the hands of a few companies the power to fix monopolistic prices. Under such circumstances and in view of the well known importance of petroleum products, it is the duty of the Department to exercise extreme vigilance and to take vigorous action whenever it appears that current practices definitely restricting competition may be the product of concerted action.

"An earlier investigation by the Department, following complaints of monopolistic practices, resulted in the entry of a consent decree on September 15, 1930 against a number of the Pacific Coast oil companies. In 1936 the Federal Trade Commission at the request of the Attorney General investigated complaints charging that monopolistic [70] practices similar to those which led to the 1930 decree were being resorted to. As a result of the facts reported by the Commission, the Department in November, 1937 undertook a comprehensive field investigation.

"The purpose of the inquiry before the grand jury is to present the facts obtained in the course of the investigations conducted by the Department and the Federal Trade Commission as well as such other facts as may appear to be pertinent, in order to ascertain whether prosecutions for violation of the anti-trust laws should be had."

It is not claimed that movants as responsible officers of the oil companies affected by the subpoenas duces tecum have not had knowledge of the activities of the government as published relating to the corporate business of their principals prior to and during the proceedings of the Second Grand Jury and of the problems of the petroleum industry with which the inquisitorial body is concerned, and the designation in the subpoenas of the documentary evidence required is, we think, adequate to enable the respective officers to respond to the process. The materiality of the evidence sought by the process is apparent from a consideration of the public announcement by the Department of Justice, the empanelment of the Second Grand Jury by the court, and the contents of the subpoenas. All such matters are so closely related to the business of movants that the parties served cannot fail to understand what evidence is desired.

It is undeniably true that the subpoena requires the production of a great mass of material. It imposes an unusual and severe burden. This is unavoidable, by reason of the magnitude of the enterprises that are the subject of the investigation and the ramifications and complexities of detail that normally occur in the operation of great industrial concerns. The reasonableness of the requirements of a subpoena duces tecum in a valid grand jury investigation under the laws of the United States is a concrete matter. Essgee Co. v. U. S., supra. It depends upon the specific situation that is the subject of inquiry, having in mind at all times that in every bona fide investigation by a federal grand jury no unnecessary initiatory action should be judicially taken that is likely to impede investigation and obstruct the impartial administration of justice. [71]

It was stated by the Special Assistant Attorney General in the argument of these motions that the record in this court shows "that some forty subpoenas, substantially similar in form and in content" to those here under attack "had issued out of this court, and that they met with compliance" by other operating oil companies and their officers, doing business within the Pacific Coast Territory. These statements were not challenged by counsel for the objecting companies and have not been refuted by any of the movant oil companies. We think that if other operating oil concerns have undertood like process and have been able to identify and supply documentary material in their files and records similar to that required by the subpoenas under attack, there is good reason to feel that the movants can do likewise.

Affidavits that are uncontradicted have been filed by movants in support of objections to the subpoenas which show that different agencies of the government and one of the Special Assistant Attorneys General who is appearing before the present grand jury in the investigation of the petroleum industry in the Pacific Coast Area have been during the last two years examining into the affairs of the movant oil companies, and that much material and many documents have been voluntarily supplied and are now presumably available to the grand jury. It is claimed by the movants that material called for in the subpoenas has been already obtained in these previous contacts. Undoubtedly the grand jury is not required to accept such earlier furnished matter and is entitled to have produced before it competent fresh evidence. Application of Texas Co., 27 F. Supp. 847. Unless the grand jury deems such course necessary or pertinent to an adequate investigation or inquiry, duplication of work or production can be avoided and economy of time and resources, both public and private, preserved. The paramount and indispensable requirement is the production and consideration of evidence that is competent, credible, sufficient and satisfactory to the grand jury. We assume that the Department of Justice will conform to the method stated in the May 1, 1939, announcement for the presentation of facts to the grand jury. [72]

The time specified in the subpoenas or in the order of the court made this day may not be considered by the grand jury as sufficient to enable the person served to comply with the terms of the subpoena. In that event the time may be enlarged to meet unavoidable exigencies and the material ordered to be produced may be presented periodically and in such installments as not to unnecessarily impede the normal business of the oil companies or to inordinately congest the archives of the grand jury. Documents should not be unnecessarily retained, and should be guardedly and securely kept from outside contact with unauthorized sources, so that they may be reasonably returned intact to owners, unless otherwise ordered by the court. Such precautions, with the sanctity of the oath of grand jurors, and the attitudes of confidence and ethical suasion by government officers and agents, adequately safeguard all property rights of the movants.

Each motion to quash the subpoena duces tecum is denied, and the clerk will enter separate orders accordingly.

Dated this August 29, 1939. [73]

At a stated term, to wit: The February Term, A. D. 1939, of the District Court of the United States of America, within and for the Central Division of the Southern District of California, held at the Court Room thereof, in the City of Los Angeles on Tuesday the 29th day of August in the year of our Lord one thousand nine hundred and thirty-nine.

Present: The Honorable Paul J. McCormick, District Judge.

Misc.

In the Matter of the Motion of G. M. Foster, individually, and as Assistant Secretary of Standard Oil Company of California, a Corp., and Standard Oil Company of California, a Corp., to Quash Subpoena Duces Tecum, etc.

At the hour of 10:07 o'clock a. m., this matter coming before the court for further proceedings; Joseph E. Brill, Esq., M. S. Huberman, Esq., Henry McClernan, Esq., Robert H. Marquis, Esq., L. P. Sherfy, Esq., Special Assistants to the Attorney General, appearing on behalf of the Government; Oscar Lawler, Esq., appearing for G. M. Foster, individually, and as Assistant Secretary of, and the Standard Oil Company of California, a Corp.; H. A. Dewing, appearing as court reporter and reporting the proceedings; the Court now reads and hands down "Memorandum of Ruling on Motions to Quash Subpoenas Duces Tecum", and orders same filed and entered herein; now, accordingly.

It is ordered that the Motion of G. M. Foster, individually, and as Assistant Secretary of, and the Standard Oil Company of California, a Corp. to Quash Subpoena Duces Tecum be denied. Exception to said ruling is noted by Oscar Lawler, Esq.

Joseph E. Brill, Esq., now makes a statement relative to the further appearance of witnesses under Subpoenas Duces Tecum, who have previously been excused by the Court until this time, and now moves that all witnesses who have been so excused, be directed and ordered to appear, under said Subpoenas, before the Second Grand Jury, on Wednesday, September 6th, 1939, at ten o'clock a. m., and it is so ordered. [74]

At a stated term, to wit: The February Term, A. D. 1939, of the District Court of the United States of America, within and for the Central Division of the Southern District of California, held at the Court Room thereof, in the City of Los Angeles on Thursday the 31st day of August in the year of our Lord one thousand nine hundred and thirty-nine.

Present: The Honorable Paul J. McCormick, District Judge.

[Title of Cause.]

At the hour of 3:10 o'clock P. M., this matter coming on for hearing on the Motion of G. M. Foster, individually, and as Assistant Secretary of Standard Oil Company of California, a Corporation, and Standard Oil Company of California, for stay of proceedings herein; Oscar Lawler, Esq., appearing for said movant; Joseph E. Brill, Esq., and M. S. Huberman, Esq., Special Assistants to the Attorney General, appearing on behalf of the Government; W. A. Weigel, appearing as court reporter and reporting the proceedings; the Court orders that hearing proceed; whereupon,

Oscar Lawler, Esq., argues in support of the Motion, and thereafter, Joseph E. Brill, Esq., makes a statement in opposition thereto, and the matter being submitted to the Court, whereupon,

It is ordered that the motion for a stay and supersedeas be denied.

Thereafter, pursuant to stipulation of counsel, and consent of Oscar Lawler, Esq., on behalf of G. M. Foster, individually, it is further ordered that the time for Mr. Foster to appear before the Second Grand Jury, under the subpoena duces tecum herein, be enlarged, and that said witness appear before said Second Grand Jury on Friday, September 8th, 1939, at the hour of ten o'clock A. M. [79]

[Title of District Court and Cause.]

NOTICE OF APPEAL [81]

Notice is hereby given that G. M. Foster, individually, G. M. Foster, Assistant Secretary, Standard Oil Company of California, a Delaware corporation, and Standard Oil Company of California, a Delaware corporation, hereby appeal to the United States Circuit Court of Appeals for the Ninth Circuit from the order of the District Court of the United States for the Southern District of California, Central Division, made August 29, 1939, entitled "In the Matter of various Motions to Quash Subpoenas Duces Tecum Returnable before Second Grand Jury, February, 1939, Term," denying the motion of G. M. Foster, individually, and as Assistant Secretary of Standard Oil Company of California, a Delaware corporation, and of said Standard Oil Company of California, a Delaware corporation, to quash and vacate each numbered paragraph and each lettered subdivision of each such numbered paragraph of that certain subpoena duces tecum directed to the said G. M. Foster, Assistant Secretary, Standard Oil Company of California, issued out of and under the seal of the said District Court of the United States under date of July 19, 1939, which said order was entered August 29th, 1939.

Dated: Los Angeles, California, August 31st, 1939.

OSCAR LAWLER
Standard Oil Building,
Los Angeles, California,
Telephone: TRinity 5111.
FELIX T. SMITH
Standard Oil Building,
San Francisco, California,
Telephone: GArfield 6133.

Attorneys for G. M. Foster, individually, G. M. Foster, Assistant Secretary of Standard Oil Company of California, and Standard Oil Company of California. [82]

PILLSBURY, MADISON & SUTRO,
Standard Oil Building,
San Francisco, California.

LAWLER, FELIX & HALL,
Standard Oil Building,
Los Angeles, California.
Of Counsel.

Copy of the above Notice mailed to Joseph E. Brill, Esq., Special Assistant to the Attorney General, U. S. Postoffice & Courthouse Bldg., Los Angeles, Calif., on August 31, 1939.

R. S. ZIMMERMAN,
Clerk
By L. B. FIGG,
Deputy.

[Endorsed]: Filed Aug. 31, 1939. [83]

[Title of District Court and Cause.]

CLERK'S CERTIFICATE

I, R. S. Zimmerman, Clerk of the District Court of the United States for the Southern District of California, do hereby certify the foregoing pages, numbered from 1 to 91, inclusive, contain full, true and correct copies of original Subpoena Duces Tecum, with Return of Service thereon; Notice of Motion to

Quash Subpoena Duces Tecum; Minute Order, entered on August 21, 1939; Minute Order, entered on August 29, 1939; Memorandum of Ruling on Motions to Quash Subpoena Duces Tecum; Minute Order, entered on August 29, 1939; Motion for Stay of Proceedings; Minute Order entered on August 31, 1939; Stipulation filed September 6, 1939; Stipulation filed September 1, 1939; Notice of Appeal; Designation of Contents of Record on Appeal; Bond on Appeal; which constitute the record on appeal to the United States Circuit Court of Appeals for the Ninth Circuit.

I do further certify that the fees of the Clerk for comparing, correcting and certifying the foregoing record amount to $35.05, and that said amount has been paid me by the Appellants herein.

Witness my hand and the Seal of the District Court of the United States for the Southern District of California, this 6th day of September, A. D. 1939.

[Seal] R. S. ZIMMERMAN,
Clerk

[Endorsed]: No. 9287. United States Circuit Court of Appeals for the Ninth Circuit. G. M. Foster, individually, G. M. Foster, Assistant Secretary, Standard Oil Company of California, a Delaware corporation, and Standard Oil Company of California, a Delaware corporation, Appellants, vs.

United States of America, Appellee. Transcript of Record. Upon Appeal from the District Court of the United States for the Southern District of California, Central Division.

Filed, September 7, 1939.

PAUL P. O'BRIEN,

Clerk of the United States Circuit Court of Appeals for the Ninth Circuit.

At a stated term, to wit: The February Term, A. D. 1939, of the District Court of the United States of America, within and for the Central Division of the Southern District of California, held at the Court Room thereof, in the City of Los Angeles on Thursday the 7th day of September in the year of our Lord one thousand nine hundred and thirty-nine.

Present: The Honorable Paul J. McCormick, District Judge.

In the Matter of Extending the Term of Office of the Second Grand Jury Impaneled in and for the February, 1939 Term, of this Court.

At 10:05 o'clock A. M. Court convenes. The roll of the Second Grand Jury is called, twenty-one Grand Jurors being present; and Joseph E. Brill, M. S. Huberman, Henry McClernan, Robert H. Marquis, and L. P. Sherfy, Special Assistants to the Attorney General, being present; and A. M.

Randol, being present as Court Reporter and reporting the proceedings;

The Court now advises the Grand Jurors present that upon the certificate of the United States Attorney for the Southern District of California, which is now ordered filed and entered herein, which Certificate is as follows, to-wit:

"[Title of District Court and Cause.]

CERTIFICATE OF THE UNITED STATES ATTORNEY

To the Honorable Paul J. McCormick, District Judge:

Now comes the United States Attorney for the Southern District of California and respectfully certifies as follows:

Whereas, Section 421 of Title 28, United States Code, provides that a district judge may, upon request of the district attorney, by order authorize any grand jury to continue to sit during the term succeeding the term at which such request is made, to finish investigations begun but not finished by such grand jury, and

Whereas, the Second Grand Jury, impaneled in and for the February, 1939, Term of this court has begun investigations during said February, 1939, Term which have not been completed and cannot be completed before the end of said February, 1939, Term,

Now, therefore, Ben Harrison, United States Attorney for the Southern District of California, requests that an order be entered authorizing the Second Grand Jury, impaneled in and for the February, 1939, Term of this Court, to continue to sit during the September, 1939, Term of said Court to finish investigations begun but not finished by such Second Grand Jury.

Dated at Los Angeles, California, this 5 day of September, 1939.

BEN HARRISON

United States Attorney for the Southern District of California"

[Endorsed]: Filed Sep. 7, 1939.

And, pursuant thereto it is ordered that the Second Grand Jury be authorized to continue to sit during the September, 1939, Term of this Court in order that it may complete investigations begun, but not finished, during said February, 1939, Term. Order thereon is now signed by the Court and ordered filed and entered herein, same being as follows, to-wit:

"[Title of District Court and Cause.]

ORDER TO CONTINUE THE FEBRUARY 1939 SECOND GRAND JURY

The United States Attorney for the Southern District of California, having certified to a district judge of said district that the Second Grand Jury, impaneled in and for the February 1939 Term of this Court, has begun investigations which have not as yet been completed and which cannot be completed during said February, 1939, Term of this Court, and the facts set forth in such certificate having been duly considered, it is, on this 7th day of September, 1939, by the said District Judge,

Ordered that the Second Grand Jury, impaneled in and for the February 1939 Term of this Court, be and it is hereby authorized to continue to sit during the September 1939 Term of this Court in order that it may complete investigations begun but not finished during said February 1939 Term of this Court.

PAUL J. McCORMICK

District Judge.

Dated: September 7, 1939."

[Endorsed]: Filed Sep. 7, 1939.

And said grand jurors now are excused to resume their deliberations.

At a stated term, to wit: The February Term, A. D. 1939, of the District Court of the United States of America, within and for the Central Division of the Southern District of California, held at the Court Room thereof, in the City of Los Angeles on Friday the 8th day of September in the year of our Lord one thousand nine hundred and thirty-nine.

Present: The Honorable Paul J. McCormick, District Judge.

Misc.

In the Matter of the Subpoena Duces Tecum issued out of the above-entitled Court, returnable before the Second Grand Jury, directed to G. M. Foster, individually, and as Assistant Secretary of Standard Oil Company of California, a Corporation, and Standard Oil Company, a Corporation, etc.

At the hour of 10:20 o'clock A. M., this matter coming on for further proceedings; Joseph E. Brill, Esq., Special Assistant to the Attorney General, appearing on behalf of the Government; Oscar Lawler, Esq., appearing for G. M. Foster, individually, and as Secretary of, and Standard Oil Company of California, a Corporation, said G. M. Foster being present, now, pursuant to stipulation of counsel, and by consent,

It is ordered that the time of said G. M. Foster to appear under the Subpoena Duces Tecum herein, be enlarged and continued to September 21, 1939, at 10 o'clock A. M., and the Court now directs said G. M. Foster to appear at the said time.

[Title of District Court and Cause.]

I, R. S. Zimmerman, Clerk of the District Court of the United States for the Southern District of California, do hereby certify that the foregoing pages, numbered from 1 to 6, inclusive, contain a full, true and correct copy of Minute Order, made and entered on September 7th, 1939; Minute Order, made and entered on September 8th, 1939; and Praecipe, filed September 13th, 1939, which constitute the supplementary record on appeal to the United States Circuit Court of Appeals for the Ninth Circuit.

Witness my hand and the Seal of the District Court of the United States for the Southern District of California, this 13th day of September, A. D. 1939.

[Seal]: R. S. ZIMMERMAN,
Clerk
By B. B. HANSEN,
Deputy Clerk.

[Endorsed]: No. 9287. United States Circuit Court of Appeals for the Ninth Circuit. G. M. Foster, individually, and as Assistant Secretary of Standard Oil Company of California, and Standard Oil Company, etc., Appellants, vs. United States of America, Appellee. Supplementary Record on Appeal from the District Court of the United States for the Southern District of California, Central Division. Filed Sep. 14, 1939. Paul P. O'Brien, Clerk.

In the United States Circuit Court of Appeals for the Ninth Circuit.

No. 9287

In the Matter of the Subpoena returnable before the Second Grand Jury impaneled by Honorable Paul J. McCormick, Judge of the United States District Court for the Southern District of California, Central Division, during the February Term thereof, which Subpoena was issued out of and over the Seal of said Court, Honorable Paul J. McCormick, Judge thereof, on July 19, 1939, directed to "G. M. Foster, Assistant Secretary, Standard Oil Company of California, 225 Bush Street, San Francisco, California."

CONCISE STATEMENT OF POINTS ON WHICH APPELLANTS INTEND TO RELY, AND DESIGNATION OF PARTS OF THE RECORD WHICH THEY THINK NECESSARY FOR THE CONSIDERATION THEREOF

To the Clerk of the above entitled Court, and to Messrs. J. E. Brill, Esq., and M. S. Huberman, Esq., Special Assistants to the Attorney General of the United States, attorneys for the United States:

You are, and each is, hereby advised that the following is a concise statement of the points on which the appellants, G. M. Foster, individually, and as

Assistant Secretary of Standard Oil Company of California, a corporation, and said Standard Oil Company of California, intend to rely, on said appeal, and designation by said appellants of parts of the record which they think necessary for the consideration thereof, to-wit:

CONCISE STATEMENT OF POINTS ON WHICH APPELLANTS INTEND TO RELY

That the order denying motion to quash Annex I attached to said subpoena duces tecum and directing obedience to said subpoena duces tecum, is erroneous, for the following reasons:

1. Clauses 2, 3, 6, 7, 8, 9, 10, 13 and 14b of said Annex I to said subpoena duces tecum do not, nor does either of said clauses, specify, identify or describe any document required to be produced by said subpoena duces tecum;

2. Clauses 6, 13 and 14b of said Annex I to said subpoena duces tecum, and each of said clauses, calls for information, and neither thereof calls for any document which is either specified, identified or described therein;

3. Clauses 2, 6, 7, 8, 9, and 10 of said Annex I do not, nor does either of said clauses, specify, identify or describe any document, but require, and each of said clauses requires, an indiscriminate search through a mass of material to ascertain whether there is therein any document relating to either or

all of the several subjects mentioned in said several clauses;

4. Clauses 6, 13 and 14 of said Annex I to said subpoena duces tecum do not, nor does either thereof, specify, identify or describe any document, but each of said clauses requires an indiscriminate search through a great mass of material to ascertain whether in any thereof there is matter which, in the opinion of the witness, is sufficient to show either of many stated facts, and a selection of such papers as in the opinion of the witness are sufficient to show either or any of such facts;

5. Clauses 2, 3, 6, 7, 8, 9, and 10 of said Annex I to said subpoena duces tecum do not, nor does either thereof, specify, identify or describe any document, but each of said clauses requires the production of a mass of material, without regard to the evidential character of any thereof, and without any indication or showing that the production of all or any thereof is proper or necessary;

6. That Clauses 2, 3, 6, 7, 8, 9, 10, 13 and 14b of said Annex I to said subpoena duces tecum require, and each of said clauses requires, and compliance therewith or either thereof as required by said order will constitute, an unreasonable search of the Standard Oil Company of California, in violation of the Fourth Amendment to the Constitution of the United States;

7. That Clauses 2, 3, 6, 7, 8, 9, 10, 13 and 14b of said Annex I to said subpoena duces tecum require,

and each of said clauses requires, and compliance therewith or either thereof as required by said order will constitute, the taking of property of said Standard Oil Company of California, in violation of the Fifth Amendment to the Constitution of the United States;

8. That the requirements of Clauses 2, 3, 6, 7, 8, 9, 10, 13 and 14b of said Annex I to said subpoena duces tecum are, and each of said clauses is, unreasonable and oppressive, and compliance therewith as required by said order will be unreasonable and oppressive and an abuse of the process of said Court.

DESIGNATION OF PARTS OF THE RECORD NECESSARY FOR THE CONSIDERATION OF THE FOREGOING POINTS

(The page of the record transmitted by the Clerk of the District Court at which the part of the record referred to appears, is indicated in parentheses.)

1. Notice of appeal (61);
2. Subpoena duces tecum, with return of service (2);
3. Notice of motion to quash subpoena duces tecum, with affidavit of G. M. Foster [copy of subpoena duces tecum], and memorandum of points and authorities, thereto attached (16);
4. Minute order entered August 21, 1939, deferring appearance of witness until August 29, 1939 (65);

5. Minute order entered August 29, 1939, denying motion of G. M. Foster, individually and as Assistant Secretary of Standard Oil Company of California, a corporation, and said Standard Oil Company of California to quash said subpoena duces tecum, and deferring appearance of witness until September 6, 1939 (74);

6. Minute order entered August 31, 1939, denying motion for stay, and deferring appearance of witness until September 8, 1939 (79);

7. Any and all minute orders made after August 31, 1939, with reference to the appearance of the witness and obedience to said subpoena duces tecum, transmitted by the Clerk of the District Court to the Clerk of the Circuit Court of Appeals after the transmission of the original record herein.

Dated: September 8th, 1939.

FELIX T. SMITH
OSCAR LAWLER
Attorneys for G. M. Foster, individually and as Assistant Secretary of Standard Oil Company of California, a corporation, and said Standard Oil Company of California.

Received copy of the within Concise Statement of Points on Which Appellants Intend to Rely, and Designation of Parts of the Record Which They

Think Necessary for the Consideration Thereof, this 8th day of September, 1939.

JOSEPH E. BRILL
M. S. HUBERMAN
Attorneys for the United States

[Endorsed]: Filed Sept. 11, 1939. Paul P. O'Brien, Clerk.

[Title of Circuit Court of Appeals and Cause.]

DESIGNATION BY APPELLEE OF PARTS OF RECORD CONSIDERED NECESSARY FOR CONSIDERATION OF APPEAL IN ADDITION TO THOSE PARTS HERETOFORE DESIGNATED BY APPELLANTS

To the Clerk of the above entitled Court and to attorneys for appellants:

You are, and each is, hereby advised that appellee designates the following parts of the record as necessary for consideration of the appeal herein, in addition to those parts heretofore designated by appellants;

(The page of the record transmitted by the Clerk of the District Court at which appears the part of the record referred to in (1) and (2) below, is indicated in parenthesis):

(1) Memorandum of ruling on motions to quash subpoena duces tecum [69];

(2) Minute Order, entered on August 29, 1939 (67).

(The following are parts of the supplemental record on appeal transmitted by the Clerk of the District Court);

(3) Minute Order, entered on September 7, 1939, continuing the February 1939 Second Grand Jury;

(4) Minute Order, entered on September 8, 1939, extending the time of appearance before the Second Grand Jury of G. M. Foster to September 21, 1939, at 10:00 o'clock a. m.

Dated: September 13, A. D. 1939.

JOSEPH E. BRILL
M. S. HUBERMAN
HENRY McCLERNAN
ROBERT H. MARQUIS
LAWRENCE P. SHERFY
CHARLES S. BURDELL
A. ANDREW HAUK

Special Assistants to the Attorney General Attorneys for the United States of America, 254 U. S. Post Office and Court House, Los Angeles, California.

Received copy of the foregoing Designation by Appellee of Parts of Record Considered Necessary for Consideration of Appeal in Addition to Those Parts Heretofore Designated by Appellants, and inclusion of parts of record so designated by appellee is hereby agreed to.

OSCAR LAWLER
FELIX T. SMITH
PILLSBURY, MADISON & SUTRO; and
LAWLER, FELIX & HALL

Attorneys for G. M. Foster, individually, G. M. Foster, Assistant Secretary, Standard Oil Company of California, a Delaware Corporation, and Standard Oil Company of California, a Delaware Corporation.

By OSCAR LAWLER

By C. E.

[Endorsed]: Filed Sept. 13, 1939. Paul P. O'Brien, Clerk.

TOPICAL INDEX.

PAGE

Jurisdictional statement 1

Statement of the case 3

Questions involved on appeal 6

Manner in which questions are raised, and errors relied on 8

Summary of argument 8

1. Nature of subpoena duces tecum, and judicial control over it 10

2. The subpoena is oppressive, unreasonable and invalid, because

   (a) It does not identify documents desired 13

   (b) It does not call for documents but for information.... 22

   (c) It requires indiscriminate search for, and opinion of witness as to nature of, documents to be produced 24

   (d) It requires indiscriminate search to ascertain whether there is any document relating to suggested subjects 27

   (e) It requires production of mass of material, without regard to its evidential character or any showing that production proper or necessary 32

   (f) It requires unreasonable search, in violation of Fourth Amendment 34

   (g) It requires taking of property without compensation, in violation of Fifth Amendment 38

3. Comments on opinion of District Court 39

4. Conclusion 41

TABLE OF AUTHORITIES CITED.

CASES. PAGE

American Car and Foundry Co. v. Alexandria Water Co. (Pa.), 70 Atl. 867 .... 16, 28

Bank of America v. Douglas, 105 Fed. (2d) 100 .... 10, 15, 33, 36, 37

Brewster v. Hartog, 111 N. Y. S. 1026 17

Brown, Ex parte, 72 Mo. 83 .... 11, 16, 36

Carpenter v. Winn, 221 U. S. 533 31

Carson v. Hawley (Minn.), 84 N. W. 746 .... 13, 29

Compton v. Jesup, 68 Fed. 263 11

Cudahy Packing Co. v. United States, 15 Fed. (2d) 133 13

Dickey v. Turner, 49 Fed. (2d) 998 11

Elting v. United States, 27 Court of Claims 158 .... 22, 25

Essgee v. United States, 262 U. S. 151 34

Federal Trade Commission v. American Tobacco Co., 264 U. S. 298 .... 17, 27, 31, 33, 36

Foster, In re, 124 N. Y. S. 667 11

Go-Bart v. United States, 282 U. S. 344 .... 12, 13, 35

Gould, Ex parte (Tex.), 132 S. W. 364 16

Gumbel v. Pitkin, 124 U. S. 131 11

Hale v. Henkel, 201 U. S. 43 .... 10, 13, 16, 30, 33, 35

Hale, In re, 139 Fed. 496 14

Hoyt v. Jackson, 3 Dem. (N. Y.) 390 10

Johnson Co. v. North Branch Co., 48 Fed. 191 10

Jones v. Securities Exchange Comm., 298 U. S. 1 37

Keiffe v. La Salle Realty Co. (La.), 112 So. 799 11

Krippendorf v. Hyde, 110 U. S. 276 11

McMann v. Securities Exchange Commission, 87 Fed. (2d) 377 .... 10, 37, 39

Mobile Gas Co. v. Patterson, 288 Fed. 884 .... 25, 28

PAGE

Murray v. Louisiana, 163 U. S. 101 23
National Window Glass Workers, In re, 287 Fed. 219 11
New Hampshire Gas Co. v. Morse, 42 Fed. (2d) 490 18
People v. Reynolds (Ill.), 182 N. E. 754 16
Rawlins v. Hall-Epps Clothing Co., 217 Fed. 884 .... 25, 28
Silverthorne v. United States, 251 U. S. 385 .... 10, 39
United States v. Medical Society, 26 Fed. Supp. 55 13
United States v. Union Trust Co., 13 Fed. Supp. 286 33
Wilson v. United States, 221 U. S. 361 34
Zimmermann v. Wilson, 81 Fed. (2d) 847 .... 38, 41

Court Rules.

Rules of Civil Procedure, Rule 45 .... 2, 12, 15
District Court, Southern District of California, Rule 33 .... 2, 12

Statutes.

United States Code, Annotated, Title 28, Sec. 225a 2
United States Code, Annotated, Title 28, Sec. 647 15

Text Books.

70 Corpus Juris, p. 50 31
70 Corpus Juris, p. 51 23
Hughes on Federal Practice, Sec. 4030 15
Thompson on Trials, 2nd Ed., p. 660 10
Wigmore on Evidence, Sec. 2200 15

United States Constitution.

Fourth Amendment 3, 15
Fifth Amendment 3

No. 9287

In the United States
Circuit Court of Appeals
For the Ninth Circuit.

G. M. Foster, individually, G. M. Foster, Assistant Secretary, Standard Oil Company of California, a Delaware corporation, and Standard Oil Company of California, a Delaware corporation,

Appellants,

vs.

United States of America,

Appellee.

APPELLANTS' OPENING BRIEF.

Statement of Facts Upon Which It Is Contended That the District Court Had Jurisdiction and That This Court Has Jurisdiction Upon Appeal.

Appellant Foster was served with subpoena *duces tecum* issued pursuant to praecipe of M. S. Huberman, Esq., as Special Assistant to the Attorney General, commanding him to appear before a Grand Jury at Los Angeles "then and there to give evidence * * * and * * * produce * * * all of those certain books, records, documents and papers" of said Standard Oil Company of California "which are more particularly described in Annex I attached to and made a part" of said subpoena [R. 2].[1]

Standard Oil Company of California intervened and, jointly with Foster, as well as severally, moved to quash and vacate "each numbered paragraph and item of Annex I to said subpoena, and each lettered subdivision of each such paragraph or item", upon the grounds stated, including the ground that the several clauses of the subpoena are unreasonable and oppressive [R. 20].[2]

The District Court, after hearing, denied the motions severally and directed Foster to obey the subpoena *duces tecum* [R. 90-91]. Standard Oil Company of California, and Foster, individually and as Assistant Secretary of the corporation, jointly and severally appeal from the order.

Jurisdiction of the District Court exists by virtue of its inherent power to prevent oppression and injustice by means of its process, also by virtue of Rule 45 of the Rules of Civil Procedure, which requires the court, upon motion promptly made for that purpose, to quash a subpoena *duces tecum* which is unreasonable or oppressive, and by virtue of Rule 33 of said District Court, which provides that the Rules of Civil Procedure shall govern criminal proceedings "in so far as they are applicable directly or by analogy."

The jurisdiction of this Court exists by virtue of Section 225A, Title 28, of the United States Code Annotated.

---

[1]The subpoena was issued July 19, 1939 [R. 2-3], served July 24 [R. 19] and returnable August 25, 1939 [R. 2].

[2]Hearing of the motion was set for August 21, 1939 [R. 21]; on that date response by the witness to the subpoena *duces tecum* was deferred until August 29, and the hearing continued until August 23, 1939 [R. 79]; August 29, the motions were denied and response of the witness deferred until September 6 [R. 90-91]; August 31, notice of appeal was filed, and, while application for stay pending appeal was denied, the District Court further deferred response of the witness until September 8 [R. 92]; on the latter date, response was further deferred until September 21 [R. 100]; this court has granted further stay until October 9, 1939, at which time the appeal will be heard.

Statement of the Case.

Annex I to the subpoena contains fourteen numbered paragraphs and fifty-one lettered subdivisions [R. 2-19]. Pertinent particulars thereof will be hereinafter specifically referred to.[3]

Briefly, the grounds of the motion are that the subpoena is unreasonable and oppressive, that its enforcement would constitute an unreasonable search in violation of the Fourth Amendment, and the taking of property of the corporation in violation of the Fifth Amendment to the Constitution [R. 21-22]; that it requires search through a mass of papers and selection of those which, in the judgment of the searcher, relate to the subjects mentioned in said subpoena, and requires determination as to what papers are relevant to or sufficient to show the matters mentioned in the subpoena [R. 22]; that it calls for the production of papers relating solely to intrastate business [R. 22]; that it does not call for documents described and identified, but for a mass of material described in general terms [R. 23]; that prior to the subpoena, said Special Assistant to the Attorney General and his subordinates had extensively examined the corporation's records and been provided with information sufficient to enable them to identify, specify and describe with reasonable particularity any documents which might be required [R. 23];

---

[3]Due to error in the served copy of the subpoena, it was assumed that paragraphs 4 and 5 called for the reports therein mentioned from January 1, *1935* (as stated in the copy) to the date of the subpoena, instead of from January 1, 1938 (as indicated on the original). In their notice movants objected that the call was unreasonable except as to reports after 1937, because reports to and including that year had been previously furnished to the Government [R. 32]. The error was not discovered until the hearing on August 24, whereupon movants stated they waived the right to move to quash the defective service and had no objection to furnishing the copies called for by the original subpoena and that no point would be made because of the mistake in the served copy.

that compliance would involve the work of many persons over a period of months and years [R. 23-24]; that matters of public record as accessible to the United States as to the moving parties, and not in the possession of the latter, are called for [R. 24]; that copies of most of the reports required by paragraphs 4 and 5 have been previously supplied and are in the possession of said Huberman [R. 24];[4] that other material has been supplied to and is in the possession of the United States and said Huberman as set forth in the affidavit, and that Huberman had been directed by the Attorney General to submit all the facts so obtained to said Grand Jury [R. 29].

The supporting affidavit is not controverted. It shows: That Standard Oil Company of California, a Delaware corporation, with principal office at San Francisco, is and has been for many years engaged in all branches of the petroleum business; that it has 650 branch and sub-offices scattered throughout the Pacific Coast territory; that examination of records at most of these offices will be required in order to supply information called for by the subpoena; that the corporate records, search of which would be necessary to qualify anyone to give the information called for by the subpoena, are located at many different places where the corporation carries on business, are extremely voluminous, and will require many months for their examination;[5] that since early in 1936 Government agents, including Assistant Attorney General Huberman and his subordinates (some of the latter being accountants), with the cooperation of the corporation,

[4]This objection was predicated on the mistake in the served copy heretofore indicated.

[5]For example, more than 40,000,000 invoices of *one type* must be examined pursuant to one of the clauses of said subpoena [R. 31-32].

have carried on an extensive survey of the latter's records and accounts relating to the subjects referred to in the subpoena [R. 27-38];[6] that in connection with such examinations and surveys there were furnished to said Huberman a schedule showing posted prices for all classes of gasoline and trade and types of deliveries at San Francisco, Los Angeles, Fresno, Portland, Seattle, Spokane, Phoenix, and Reno,[7] and extensive summaries and abstracts of the corporate accounts [R. 33-36] each certified to by a corporate representative and showing the corporate source of all data therein set forth, which summaries and abstracts covered the various parts of the company's business referred to in said subpoena;[8] that there were also delivered to Mr. Huberman statements showing location of the company's oil and gas pipe lines [R. 35; 6d], copies of contracts with purchasers of gasoline, and many other papers [R. 36-37].

The affidavit further shows that the company spent thousands of dollars and diverted many of its employees from their regular duties, in assisting the Government in its examination, and that to make the search necessary to

---

[6]The subjects covered by such examinations (with record references to the affidavit and the clauses of the subpoena referring to the same subject shown in brackets) are as follows: gasoline purchases [R. 34; 7], sales to refiners [R. 34; 8], exchanges [R. 34; 6f], sales prices [R. 37; 11] and marketing policies and correspondence relating thereto; corporate files and correspondence relating to Independent Refiners Association [R. 36; 12], and to contracts and other matters relating to Signal Oil Company [R. 35, 36-37, 38; 14a], correspondence relating to prices [R. 36, 38; 7j, 10b], sales [R. 36, 38; 6i, 8 and 9], purchases [R. 36; 7k], and consumption [R. 34; 6j] of gasoline by the corporation.

[7]See subpoena clause 11.

[8]The subjects covered by said respective summaries and abstracts (with record references to the affidavit and the clauses of the subpoena referring to the same subject shown in brackets) are as follows: gasoline production [R. 33; 6c], stocks [R. 33; 6e], exchange accounts [R. 34; 6f], sales [R. 34; 6i], consumed by the corporation [R. 34; 6j], crude oil production [R. 35; 7], gasoline imports [R. 35; 6g], shipments of crude oil [R. 36; 6h], posted prices from January 1, 1935, for all classes of trade and types of delivery [R. 37; 11].

comply with Annex I will necessitate the constant services of a large number of employees for several months, examination of practically all of the records of the company's sales and other departments, and the expenditure of additional thousands of dollars [R. 39]; that the papers referred to are essential to the conduct of its business [R. 39]; and that the corporation is ready and willing to comply with a reasonable subpoena and to assist in the production of material which may be reasonably required [R. 40].

Other features of the affidavit will be referred to in the discussion of subjects to which they are pertinent.

Questions Involved in This Appeal.

1. Should the motion to quash each numbered clause and each lettered subdivision of each numbered clause of Annex I to said subpoena *duces tecum* have been granted?

2. Do the respective clauses 2, 3, 6, 7, 8, 9, 10, 13 and 14b of Annex I to said subpoena *duces tecum* and the respective lettered subdivisions of each of said numbered paragraphs specify, identify or describe any document required to be produced?

3. Do clauses 6, 13 and 14b of said Annex I to said subpoena *duces tecum* and does each of said clauses call for information rather than for any specified, identified or described document?

4. Do clauses 2, 6, 7, 8, 9 and 10 of said Annex I to said subpoena *duces tecum,* and does each of said clauses, require an indiscriminate search through a mass of material to ascertain whether there is in such mass of material any document relating to either or all of the several subjects mentioned in said respective clauses?

5. Do clauses 6, 13 and 14 of said Annex I to said subpoena *duces tecum,* and does each thereof, require an indiscriminate search through a mass of material to ascertain whether in such mass of material there is matter which, in the opinion of the witness, is sufficient to show either of many facts stated in said subpoena, and a selection of such papers as may be found as a result of said search as, in the opinion of the witness, are sufficient to show either or any of the facts stated?

6. Do clauses 2, 3, 6, 7, 8, 9 and 10 of said Annex I to said subpoena *duces tecum,* and does each thereof, require the production of a mass of material without regard to the evidential character of any thereof and without identification of any thereof or any showing that the production of all or any thereof is proper or necessary?

7. Do clauses 2, 3, 6, 7, 8, 9, 10, 13 and 14b of said Annex I to said subpoena *duces tecum* require and does each of said clauses require, and will compliance therewith or with either thereof as required by the order appealed from constitute, an unreasonable search of the Standard Oil Company of California in violation of the Fourth Amendment to the Constitution of the United States?

8. Do clauses 2, 3, 6, 7, 8, 9, 10, 13 and 14b of said Annex I to said subpoena *duces tecum* require and does each of said clauses require, and will compliance therewith or with either thereof as required by the order appealed from constitute, the taking of property of said Standard Oil Company of California in violation of the Fifth Amendment to the Constitution of the United States?

9. Are the requirements of clauses 2, 3, 6, 7, 8, 9, 10, 13 and 14b of said Annex I to said subpoena *duces tecum,*

or are the requirements of either of said clauses, unreasonable and oppressive, and will compliance therewith as required by the order appealed from be unreasonable and oppressive and an abuse of the process of the District Court?

Manner in Which the Foregoing Questions Are Raised.

The respective questions aforesaid were raised in the District Court by motion to quash each numbered paragraph and item of Annex I to said subpoena *duces tecum* and each lettered subdivision of each such paragraph or item.

The errors relied upon are:

> The Court erred in denying motion to quash each numbered clause and each lettered subdivision of each such clause of Annex I to said subpoena *duces tecum.*
>
> The Court erred in ordering appellant Foster to comply with said subpoena *duces tecum.*

Summary of the Argument.

1. A SUBPOENA DUCES TECUM IS A JUDICIAL PROCESS OVER WHICH THE COURTS HAVE INHERENT POWER OF CONTROL TO PREVENT OPPRESSION OR INJUSTICE.

2. THE SUBPOENA DUCES TECUM IS OPPRESSIVE, UNREASONABLE AND INVALID BECAUSE.

(a) It does not specify, describe or otherwise identify the documentary evidence production of which is desired.

(b) It does not call for documents, but for information.

(c) It requires, and its enforcement will involve, an indiscriminate search through a mass of material to ascertain whether there is anything therein evidential or otherwise, which is, in the opinion of the witness, sufficient to show either or any suggested facts, and, if so, to select and produce such matter.

(d) It requires, and its enforcement will involve, an indiscriminate search through a mass of material to ascertain whether there is anything therein, evidential or otherwise, relating to suggested subjects.

(e) It requires, and its enforcement will involve, production of a mass of material without regard to the evidential character thereof, and without any indication or showing that the production of all or any thereof is proper or necessary.

(f) It requires, and its enforcement will involve, an unreasonable search of Standard Oil Company of California, in violation of the Fourth Amendment to the Constitution of the United States.

(g) It requires, and its enforcement will involve, a taking of the property of Standard Oil Company of California without compensation in violation of the Fifth Amendment to the Constitution of the United States.

3. Comments on opinion of the judge of the District Court.

4. Conclusion.

1. A Subpoena Duces Tecum Is a Judicial Process Over Which the Courts Have Inherent Power of Control to Prevent Oppression or Injustice.

In advance of a discussion of particular provisions of the subpoena *duces tecum,* some preliminary observations concerning the nature, purpose, and limitations of such a writ and the powers and duty of the court with reference thereto are deemed appropriate:

A subpoena *duces tecum* is a compulsory judicial process, in the nature of a search warrant, to compel the production of *evidential* documents.

> *Hale v. Henkel,* 201 U. S. 43, 77;
> *Johnson Co. v. North Branch Co.,* 48 Fed. 191, 193;
> *Hoyt v. Jackson,* 3 Dem. (N. Y.) 390;
> *Thompson on Trials,* 2nd Ed., p. 660.

Because "an order for the production of books and papers may constitute an unreasonable search and seizure within the Fourth Amendment" (*Hale v. Henkel,* 201 U. S. 43, 76), and because the compulsory taking of private records under illegal process deprives the owner of property in violation of the Fifth Amendment (*Silverthorne v. U. S.,* 251 U. S. 385, 391-2), and because a subpoena *duces tecum* whose "requirements are out of proportion to the end sought" will constitute an unreasonable search in violation of the Fourth Amendment and an abuse of judicial process (*McMann v. Securities Exchange Commission* (C. C. A. 2), 87 Fed. (2d) 377, 379; *Bank of America v. Douglas* (D. C. App.), 105 F. (2d) 100, 106-7), the question as to whether such a subpoena is, or the enforcement thereof will be, unreasonable or oppressive, is always a matter of grave concern, not only to the person served and to the party whose papers are sought, but to the courts and to the public.

As said by the District Court for the Eastern District of Ohio, following analysis of a number of decisions by the Supreme Court of the United States and of several of the Circuit Courts of Appeal:

> "The process by which witnesses are compelled to attend the grand jury investigation *is the court's process.* * * * It can therefore never become an immaterial matter to the court what may be done with its process. * * * A supervisory duty not only exists but is imposed upon the court to see that its grand jury and its process are not abused or used for purposes of oppression and injustice."[9]

In re National Window Glass Workers (1922), 287 Fed. 219, 225.

Chief Justice Taft, while a member of the Circuit Court of Appeals for the Sixth Circuit, said:

> "* * * Every court has inherent equitable power to prevent its own process from working injustice to anyone,"

and held that such power might be invoked by *simple motion by the party aggrieved,* by *intervention,* or by ancillary bill.

Compton v. Jesup (C. C. A. 6), 68 Fed. 263, 279.

See, also,

Krippendorf v. Hyde, 110 U. S. 276, 283;

Gumbel v. Pitkin, 124 U. S. 131, 145;

Dickey v. Turner (C. C. A. 7), 49 Fed. (2d) 998, 1000;

Ex parte Brown, 72 Mo. 83;

In re Foster, 124 N. Y. S. 667;

Keiffe v. LaSalle Realty Co. (La.), 112 So. 799.

---

[9]Italics supplied unless otherwise herein indicated.

This judicial obligation to prevent oppressive and unreasonable use of the subpoena *duces tecum* is crystallized in Rule 45 of the new Rules of Civil Procedure; it provides that the clerk may issue subpoena

> "commanding the person to whom it is directed to produce the books, papers or documents designated therein, *but the court,* upon motion made promptly * * *, *may quash the subpoena if it is unreasonable or oppressive.*"

Rule 33 of the District Court declares that the Rules of Civil Procedure shall govern in criminal proceedings "in so far as they are applicable directly or by analogy."

Under Rule 45 the party concerned may not wait until the witness responds to the subpoena *duces tecum,* but must seek relief "*promptly* and in any event at or before the time specified * * * for compliance therewith", by motion to quash. Upon such motion, it is the duty of the court to determine whether the requirements of the writ are, or their enforcement will be oppressive or unreasonable, and, therefore, an abuse of judicial process.

Whether the requirements of a subpoena *duces tecum* are, or their enforcement will be, unreasonable or oppressive, is to be ascertained not alone from the writ, but from circumstances *de hors* the writ.

> "There is no formula for the determination of unreasonableness. Each case is to be decided on its own facts and circumstances."
>
> *Go-Bart v. United States,* 282 U. S. 344, 357.
>
> "The decision (*Brown v. U. S.,* 276 U. S. 134) and others of the court, establish the rule that a subpoena *duces tecum* must be limited to a reasonable period of time and specify with reasonable par-

ticularity the subjects to which the desired writings relate. *Each case must be judged according to the peculiar facts arising from the subpoena itself and other proper sources.*"

U. S. v. Medical Soc., 26 Fed. Supp. 55, 57.

2a. The Subpoena Duces Tecum Is Oppressive, Unreasonable and Invalid Because It Does Not Specify, Describe or Otherwise Identify the Documentary Evidence Production of Which Is Desired.

A subpoena *duces tecum,* from its very nature, must specify or describe with reasonable precision the documentary evidence whose production is directed.

"While it is within the power of the court to require the production of any instrument, paper, or book containing evidence material to the issue involved in a legal controversy, *the probable existence of such evidence should be known to the party demanding it, and a description of the same sufficient to apprise the witness of what is demanded,* so as to intelligibly identify it, *is an essential prerequisite* to require such production. Thomp. Trials, Sec. 590."

Carson v. Hawley (Minn. 1901), 84 N. W. 746, 750.

No uncertainty or confusion is permissible in connection with either laws or orders concerning the production of documentary evidence.

Cudahy Packing Co. v. United States (C. C. A. 7), 15 F. (2d) 133, 136;

Go-Bart v. United States, 282 U. S. 344, 357.

In this respect, the rules are similar to those applicable to search warrants, and are analogous to, but stricter than, those governing notices to produce and discovery.

The Supreme Court of the United States, in *Hale v. Henkel* (201 U. S. 43, 76, 77), holds that:

> "An order for the production of books and papers may constitute an unreasonable search and seizure within the Fourth Amendment. * * * The substance of the offense is the compulsory production of private papers, whether under a search warrant or a subpoena *duces tecum,* against which the person, be he individual or corporation, is entitled to protection."

and, referring to the subpoena there in question, said that it was

> "clearly in violation of the general principle of law with regard to the *particularity required in the description of documents necessary to a search warrant or subpoena.*"

Circuit Judge Wallace, condemning the same subpoena denounced by the Supreme Court in *Hale v. Henkel,* said:

> "The legality of *search warrants* has been sanctioned on the ground of public necessity * * *. Because of the obnoxious character of the process, *very great particularity is required in designating the articles to be searched for* before the officers of the law are permitted to invade the premises where the articles sought are supposed to be. * * *
>
> *"Any process which is issued to perform the office of a search warrant* should conform in some remote degree, at least, in certainty and specific description, to the requirements of a valid search warrant."

In re Hale (C. C. N. Y., 1905), 139 Fed. 496, 503-4.

See, also,

Bank of America v. Douglas (D. C. App. 1939), 105 F. (2d) 100, 106-7.

The Fourth Amendment forbids issuance of search warrant except upon affidavit *particularly describing* "the place to be searched and * * * *things to be seized* * * *."

Section 647, Title 28, United States Code Annotated (formerly Sec. 869, R. S.), requires that the judge ordering issuance of a subpoena *duces tecum* in a civil case *must be satisfied* by affidavit or otherwise *that the document sought is in the possession or control of the party named, and that it must be described.*

Rule 45 of the Rules of Civil Procedure requires that the "books, papers or documents" required to be produced by the subpoena must *"be designated therein"*.

See, also, *Hughes on Federal Practice,* sections 4030 and 4031.

> "A peculiarity of the subpoena *duces tecum* is that, in the nature of things, it must specify with as much precision as is fair and feasible the particular documents desired, because the witness ought not to be required to bring what is not needed, and he cannot know what is needed unless he is informed beforehand."

4 *Wigmore on Evidence* (2d ed.), Sec. 2200.

> "The same reasonable certainty in describing what is required should be observed in a subpoena *duces*

tecum as is held necessary in the case of applications for orders to produce books and papers."

American Car and Foundry Co. v. Alexandria Water Co. (Pa.), 70 Atl. 867, 869.

See, also,

People v. Reynolds (Ill.), 182 N. E. 754, 756-7;

Ex parte Brown, 72 Mo. 83, 94;

Ex parte Gould (Tex. 1910), 132 S. W. 364, 365.

It is admitted that the Assistant to the Attorney General who signed the praecipe for this subpoena and his subordinates extensively examined the company's records, correspondence and accounts, and was provided with abstracts and summaries with source material indicated on each, covering practically every subject mentioned in the subpoena [R. 33-38], and that he was directed by the Attorney General to present the facts thus obtained to the Grand Jury [R. 29].

It is thus apparent that the Government's representative, in procuring the issuance of this suboena *duces tecum,* failed to either avail himself of the complete knowledge admittedly in his possession, or take the testimony of witnesses of whose identity and familiarity with the facts he was fully apprised, in order to adequately describe the documents desired or "to justify an order for the production of such a mass of papers."

Hale v. Henkel, 201 U. S. 43, 77.

"It would be much better practice for the plaintiffs to examine the officers of the corporation, and thus ascertain what books or accounts were kept which might tend to prove an agreement * * * and then obtain an order for the inspection of such books as are shown to be material."

Brewster v. Hartog, 111 N. Y. S. 1026, 1027.

See, also:

Federal Trade Commission v. American Tobacco Co., 264 U. S. 298, 306.

In few, if any, of the clauses of this subpoena is there any attempt to specify, describe or identify any document.

In *Clause 2* there is complete absence of definition [R. 3]; it calls for no particular book or record, either by reference to subject-matter or otherwise; it is a blanket call for *every* corporate book and record (regardless of nature, subject-matter, number or pertinency) in which the name or residence address of any officer or director, throughout a period of about five years, appears [R. 3]; thus, pension records, payrolls, social security records, insurance, correspondence, stock books, contracts, etc., etc., without limit or restriction, must be searched in order to locate each place where each such name and address appears, and to produce *all* of the records there found, without reference to whether any particular book or record so produced is of any evidential value for any purpose whatever!

The suggestion that all that is wanted is the name and residence address of each officer and director aggravates the objection. The answer is three-fold: first, the suggestion does not accord with the writ, which must be "literally interpreted" (*N. H. Gas Co. v. Morse,* 42 Fed. (2d) 490, 494), and no such assumption is permissible; second, the information suggested had been previously furnished [R. 32], and even if assumption were permissible it is unreasonable to suppose that duplication of material already furnished was desired; and, third, it is not (as will be hereafter shown, *infra,* p. 22) the function of a subpoena *duces tecum* to obtain *information.*

Clause 3 contains no identification or description of any document, either by date, subject-matter, or otherwise [R. 3]; it is a blanket call for *all* minutes since January 1, 1935, not only of stockholders and directors, but of *any executive or other committee or board of the corporation.* Obviously, minutes of stockholders and directors cover a multitude of subjects; Foster deposes that there is nothing therein pertaining to said investigation [R. 27]; that there is but one copy, which is in constant use in the conduct of the corporation's business.

The call for minutes of all committees and boards of the corporation is wholly lacking in specification or description, by subject-matter or otherwise. *There are more than twenty such committees at San Francisco, and many more at other places* [R. 26-27]. They respectively deal with such subjects as social security, advertising, annuities, interpretation of overtime rules, technical employment, loan plan, manufacturing personnel, etc.; that none thereof, so far as known, is pertinent to said investigation, and that the production of much thereof is impossible without long delay [R. 27].

Clause 6 and its several subdivisions are devoid of description [R. 4-7]. Subdivision 6i alone, as shown by the Foster affidavit [R. 32-33], would require examination of more than 40,000,000 service station slips at stations scattered throughout the five western states in order to obtain information necessary to the general classification of records from which the required selection must be made. Aside from other infirmities, which are hereafter discussed (*infra,* p. 24), this clause, so far from describing any document, does not even assume the existence of any document, but requires inquiry and search to ascertain whether there is or ever was such a document.

Clause 7 neither describes nor identifies any document [R. 7]. It requires an examination of company records in order to ascertain what, if any, purchases were made by the corporation and its "subsidiaries and affiliates engaged in producing or marketing gasoline", of gasoline physically located in the Pacific Coast territory at or before the time of delivery; also, whether any record so found discloses whether any purchase was by contract and, if so, the description and date of the contract.

Clause 8 [R. 9] is likewise devoid of description or means of identification. It requires examination of all records and invoices showing sales to refiners in order to ascertain what, if any, of the gasoline sold was physically within the Pacific Coast territory *at or prior to* the time of delivery and, if there was any such sale, to produce the papers.

Obviously, there *can* be no identification or description of a document which has not even hypothetical existence, and where the witness is required, as a preliminary to the search therefor, to ascertain whether a corporation, partnership or person is a subsidiary or affiliate of Standard Oil Company of California, and then to ascertain whether such a subsidiary or affiliate was concerned with a purchase referred to therein and is "engaged in producing or marketing gasoline", also whether any of a very large number of gasoline purchases were pursuant to contracts, and whether the gasoline sold was, *at any time* prior to sale, in the Pacific Coast area. Each of these is an undertaking of serious proportions, requiring excursions entirely collateral to the writ itself, to ascertain, first, whether there was any transaction such as that described; second, whether any document exists relating thereto, and (if the witness is able to affirmatively answer in these two respects) to then make the selection required by the subpoena. This is the antithesis of that specification, description and identification of particular papers required in process directing the production of evidence.

Clause 9 contains no identification or description of any document [R. 10]. It requires examination of all the company records and invoices showing sales to anyone, anywhere, of gasoline, in order to select therefrom such, if any, sale or sales as were *below* specified prices (such prices supposedly being subject to geographical price differentials at the time of each sale) during the time specified. This clause requires ascertainment of facts (and corresponding selection of papers, if any there are), including whether the gasoline subject-matter of any sale was physically within the Pacific Coast territory *at any time* prior to the time of delivery, the ascertainment and calculation of price differentials, if any, at the time and place of each sale, and whether there are any records bearing on such subjects. Here, again, in addition to absence of description, the scope of collateral inquiry necessary in order to determine whether any document exists such as that called for, and the duty of selection, are almost without limit.

Clause 10 contains no description [R. 11]. It requires exhaustive search throughout all of the company's records and files to find out whether there is therein any paper including "inter-office or other memoranda and other documents" made by or passing between any persons anywhere, regardless of whether the company had anything to do with it, or whether it is mere gossip, newspaper comment or other non-evidential matter, relating to thirteen subjects. Production cannot be based upon any description in this clause, but must be predicated upon the witness' interpretation of the documents examined.

It is submitted that each clause of the subpoena *duces tecum* utterly disregards the fundamental requirement that such a writ must specify and describe with reasonable accuracy each document required to be produced.

2b. The Subpoena Duces Tecum Is Oppressive, Unreasonable and Invalid Because It Does Not Call for Documents, But for Information.

A subpoena *duces tecum* is mechanical—not testimonial—in operation; it commands production of described documentary evidence; the witness has no choice, he can exercise no discretion or judgment; the writ must be literally interpreted and literally complied with; the witness' duty is to examine the subpoena and produce the very paper therein described.

> "The duty of a witness under the writ as regulated by statute is simply to bring a specified paper to a designated place. Under a writ *ad testificandum* a party cannot make a man his lawyer, or physician, or scientific instructor by subpoenaing him as an * * * expert. Under neither writ is he entitled to the judgment, discretion, opinion or professional service of the witness. * * * *The writ required the administrator to assort all the papers* of an insurance office *and select those which in his judgment 'shall in anywise bear'* upon either of the claims of the seventeen underwriters who procured the writ. *This would involve not only judgment and discretion, but a study of the pleadings* in the seventeen cases. * * * *It is manifest that the witnesses were commanded to do that which was unreasonable, if not impossible.*"

Elting v. United States, 27 Court of Claims 158, 165.

No document is described or assumed to exist in either Clause 2, 6, 7, 8, 9, 10, 13 or 14b; these clauses seek information as to whether the facts, conditions, transactions, or contracts therein referred to exist and whether there is any paper relating thereto—in other words, seeks information.

> "* * * the subpoena *duces tecum* is not proper to be used for the purpose of obtaining facts or information * * * or general inquisitorial examination of books * * * with a view to ascertaining whether something of value may not show up * * *."

70 *Corpus Juris,* p. 51, Sec. 37.

The Supreme Court of the United States, affirming refusal of a trial court to issue a subpoena *duces tecum* requiring the registrar of voters to furnish the number of white voters, of colored voters, and total number of voters who could sign their names, who had voted at the preceding congressional election, said:

> "The court was of opinion that either the defendant should have specified the books or documents required, or, *if he wished information* from the registrar, he should have subpoenaed him to attend and testify. We perceive no error in this action."

Murray v. Louisiana, 163 U. S. 101.

See, also:

70 *Corp. Jur.,* Sec. 37, p. 51, and note 70.

2c. The Subpoena Duces Tecum Is Oppressive, Unreasonable and Invalid Because It Requires, and Its Enforcement Will Involve, an Indiscriminate Search Through a Mass of Material to Ascertain Whether There Is Anything Therein, Evidential or Otherwise, Which Is, in the Opinion of the Witness, Sufficient to Show Either or Any Suggested Facts, and, If So, to Select and Produce Such Matter.

Clause 6 of this subpoena is unique [R. 4]. It not only requires a search of the entire corporate files to ascertain whether there is any document relating to either or all of a dozen suggested subjects, but directs that if any such document is found, then, from examination thereof or by inquiry, determination as to whether there is anything therein which, *in the opinion of the witness,* is sufficient to show the respective facts suggested, and, if so, to produce any such paper or papers.

Clauses 13 [R. 18] and 14b [R. 19] contain similar requirements.

It is respectfully submitted that such a requirement transcends the legitimate functions of a subpoena *duces tecum.*

Not only is an indiscriminate search through a mass of papers required, but the exercise of choice, discretion, opinion and judgment on the part of the searcher.

The language of Mr. Justice Noll, of the Court of Claims, referring to a subpoena requiring production of "all the books, papers, documents and records * * * which shall in anywise bear upon" certain French Spoliation Claims, heretofore quoted (*ante*, p. 22), is especially pertinent.

Elting v. United States, 27 Ct. of Cl. 158, 165.

The Circuit Court of Appeals for the Fifth Circuit, reversing as unreasonable an order requiring production of all books of account from which might be ascertained any of the matters covered by a proposed examination, said that the order should have apprised the parties of *what specific documents were required,* that it was unreasonable in that it required production of documents "without proper description to enable the bankrupts to know with sufficient certainty what specific books and documents they were expected to produce" and that it was therefore, equivalent to a requirement to produce *all* the books and papers belonging to their business.

Rawlins v. Hall-Epps Clothing Co. (C. C. A. 5), 217 Fed. 884, 887-8;

Mobile Gas Co. v. Patterson, 288 Fed. 884, 885-6.

To be effective, a writ issued by a judicial tribunal must not leave obedience to the opinion, choice or judgment of the party served; it must, when taken by its four corners, specify the duty of the addressee with such precision as to render disobedience subject to prosecution with the same certainty as violation of a criminal statute.

If the coercive remedy, without which a subpoena *duces tecum* (or any judicial process, for that matter) is ineffective, be borne in mind, the futility of a requirement such as that of clauses 6, 13 and 14b of this subpoena is at once obvious. When, as a basis for production, it is left to the witness to determine whether the contents of a document or other circumstances are sufficient to show a given fact, no standard or description is fixed by which the court can determine whether its process is being flaunted or evaded. What answer could be made to a witness' response that he had examined the corporate records and that, while papers had been found containing matter bearing on one or more of the many subjects suggested, there was nothing therein sufficient, in his opinion, to show any or all of the long list of facts? The only alternative would be production of *all* of his papers in order that the court might determine whether the witness' opinion was correct. Such a consequence would render judicial process ridiculous.

2d. The Subpoena Duces Tecum Is Oppressive, Unreasonable and Invalid Because It Requires, and Its Enforcement Will Involve, an Indiscriminate Search Through a Mass of Material to Ascertain Whether There Is Anything Therein, Evidential or Otherwise, Relating to Suggested Subjects.

As pointed out in previous discussion (*ante*, pp. 17 *et seq.*) clauses 2, 6, 7, 8, 9 and 10 describe no document; on the contrary, each requires an exhaustive search to find out whether a document exists relating to either of the many subjects suggested and, if it does, whether it contains the matter referred to. The attempt to use judicial process designed to produce *specific* documentary evidence known to exist for any such exploratory purpose has been condemned by the highest authority:

> "* * * *It is contrary to the first principles of justice to allow a search through all the respondents' records, relevant or irrelevant, in the hope that something will turn up.* * * * The right of access given by the statute is to documentary *evidence*—not to all documents, but to such documents as are evidence. The analogies of the law do not allow the party wanting evidence to call for all documents in order to see if they do not contain it. * * * A general subpoena in the form of these petitions would be bad."
>
> *Federal Trade Commission v. American Tobacco Co.*, 264 U. S. 298, 305-6.

> "An order to produce all papers concerning the matter in dispute is not sufficiently specific * * *. It is unreasonable to ask for a blanket list of persons and firms with whom contracts had been made during the year. In the absence of all particularity in

specifying what was wanted, and without any showing of materiality, the court was right in sustaining the objection to the demand for a general list of contracts with other persons."

American Car and Foundry Co. v. Alexandria Water Co. (Pa.), 70 Atl. 867, 869.

Referring to a motion requiring production which specified documents "such as might contain material evidence", the District Court for Alabama said:

"The rule is well established that every motion for the production of documents * * * must describe the documents which it seeks to have produced * * *. The defendants in this cause seek to escape the necessity of describing the books and documents which they desire to examine * * * *by referring to them as such as may contain the material evidence* in the cause, *so as to cast the burden upon the plaintiffs of determining at their peril what ought to be produced and what withheld.*"

Citing and quoting from *Rawlins v. Hall-Epps Clothing Co.* (C. C. A. 5) 217 Fed. 884, the court held that no such requirement could be cast upon the recipient of the order.

Mobile Gas Co. v. Patterson (D. C. Ala. 1923) 288 Fed. 884.

Clause 10, although heretofore adverted to (*supra* p. 21) requires additional consideration in this connection. It approaches the grotesque—it must be read to be fully appreciated [R. 11]. Its very terms clearly indicate absence of any thought or suggestion by its drafter of the existence of any particular paper; on the contrary, it is purely inquisitorial. It calls for no particular paper, but for any and every conceivable memorandum, paper, or even newspaper article, written at any time "by, between or among" any and every corporation, partnership or person on earth, and any and all agents and officers thereof, which contains *anything* relating to thirteen subjects (many of which, such as marketing and other policies, have long been controversial and the subject of general public and private discussion).

> "To require the production of all the books and papers of any person, of his business, for a period of three months, does not indicate any knowledge on the part of the person demanding a particular piece of evidence, or of any book or paper, desired, and permits the allowance of an improper inquisition into the affairs of the witness, outside of the scope of the judicial inquiry then under investigation. No party can be allowed to fish for evidence in this way. To permit such a course would deny the privilege of the citizen to protection from improper search and seizure of his papers, in violation of his plain constitutional right in that respect."
>
> *Carson v. Hawley* (Minn. 1901), 84 N. W. 746, at 750.

This call is without reference to whether either the witness or Standard Oil Company of California had anything to do with either or any paper referred to, and is without regard to the evidential character of anything called for. The entire files of the corporation must be searched, not for a described document or documentary evidence, but to find out whether there is *anything* relating to either of the thirteen subjects.

Pertinent to a consideration of this clause is the language of the Supreme Court condemning the subpoena involved in *Hale v. Henkel:*

> "* * * the subpoena *duces tecum* is far too sweeping in its terms to be regarded as reasonable. It does not require the production of a single contract, or of contracts with a particular corporation, or a limited number of documents, but all understandings, contracts or correspondence between the MacAndrews & Forbes Company, and no less than six different companies, * * * all reports made and accounts rendered by such companies from the date of the organization of the MacAndrews & Forbes Company, * * * all letters received by that company since its organization from more than a dozen different companies situated in seven different states in the Union. * * * Doubtless many, if not all, of these documents may ultimately be required, *but some necessity should be shown* either from an examination of the witnesses orally, or from the known transactions of these companies with the other companies implicated, or some evidence of their materiality produced, *to justify an order for the production of such a mass of papers.* A general subpoena of this description is equally indefensible as a search warrant would be if couched in similar terms."
>
> *Hale v. Henkel,* 201 U. S. 43, 76, 77.

The subpoena in that case characterized generally the papers called for, and its scope, though unconscionably broad, was not without limit. This clause, however, does not suggest even the *nature* of the papers required, and its scope has no horizon. It would be difficult to imagine a more sweeping and, we respectfully submit, a more unreasonable and oppressive requirement.

In this connection, it is to be further remembered that the purpose of a subpoena *duces tecum* is to produce *evidential* documents, not any and every paper, whether evidential or not.

> "Generally speaking, a subpoena *duces tecum* may be used to compel the production of any proper documentary *evidence* * * * but not for the production of property of any other kind * * *."
>
> 70 *Corpus Juris* 50.

> "The right of access given by the statute is to documentary *evidence*—not to all documents, but to such documents as are *evidence*. The analogies of the law do not allow the party wanting evidence to call for all documents in order to see if they do not contain it."
>
> *Federal Trade Commission v. American Tobacco Co.*, 264 U. S. 298, 306-7.

In *Carpenter v. Winn* (1911), 221 U. S. 533, the Supreme Court said that bills of discovery (p. 540)

> "cannot be used merely for the purpose of enabling the plaintiff * * * to pry into the case of his adversary to learn its strength or weakness. * * * Such a bill *must seek only evidence* which is material to the support of the complainant's own case, and prying into the nature of his adversary's case will not be tolerated."

2e. The Subpoena Duces Tecum Is Oppressive, Unreasonable and Invalid Because It Requires, and Its Enforcement Will Involve, Production of a Mass of Material Without Regard to the Evidential Character Thereof, and Without Any Indication or Showing That the Production of All or Any Thereof Is Proper or Necessary.

As heretofore pointed out (*ante,* pp. 17-18), Clause 2 requires production of every record and paper of the corporation in which the name or address of any officer or director of the corporation during the past five years appears, without regard to whether any such record or paper has the slightest pertinency or is of evidential character.

Clause 3 is a *blanket requirement* for "all minute books and other papers, records and documents" containing minutes of stockholders, directors, "any executive committee or any other committees or boards * * * from January 1, 1938, January 1, 1935, to date," [R. 3] without regard to any subject to which such minutes relate. It is not questioned and is obvious that the minutes of directors and stockholders cover a multitude of subjects; it is equally obvious that few, if any, of the host of company committees whose minutes are asked for can have any possible relation to the subject of this investigation [R. 27]. Yet, *all* must be produced!

In a case in which the Revenue Department sought to compel a trust company to obey subpoena *duces tecum* issued by the Board of Tax Appeals requiring, among other things, the corporate minutes, the company responded that to require such production would constitute an unreasonable search. The court said (p. 287):

> "This paragraph is a blanket demand for the production of the *minutes of the Union Trust Company for the years 1931 and 1932. Lacking specification as it does, the paragraph is violative of the rights of the Union Trust Company under the Fourth Amendment, and the production of the records demanded by it will not be ordered.*"

United States v. Union Trust Co. (D. C. Pa., 1936), 13 Fed. Supp. 286.

That the other clauses of the subpoena *duces tecum* violate the fundamental requirement that such a writ must be reasonable in scope is obvious from a mere reading thereof, and, as to many thereof, has been previously pointed out (*ante*, pp. 18-21; 24-28). The clear and explicit language of the Supreme Court heretofore quoted from *Hale v. Henkel* (201 U. S. 43, 77) (*ante*, p. 29) and *Federal Trade Commission v. American Tobacco Co.* (264 U. S. 298, 305-6) (*ante* p. 27) branding illegal such process, renders further discussion superfluous.

See:

Bank of America v. Douglas (D. C. App. 1939), 105 F. (2d) 100, 106-7.

2f. The Subpoena Duces Tecum Is Oppressive, Unreasonable and Invalid Because It Requires, and Its Enforcement Will Involve, an Unreasonable Search of Standard Oil Company of California, in Violation of the Fourth Amendment to the Constitution of the United States.

A corporation may, of course, be compelled by *due and lawful process* to produce its books and papers; if the requirements, however, of a subpoena *duces tecum* requiring such production are not confined *"within limits which reason imposes in the circumstances of the case"*, it is not "due and lawful" in that the Constitutional guaranty against unreasonable search is thereby violated.

> *Essgee Company v. United States,* 262 U. S. 151, 155;
>
> *Wilson v. United States,* 221 U. S. 361, 382.

> "The first clause of the Fourth Amendment declares: 'The right of the people to be secure in their persons, houses, papers, and effects, against unreasonable searches and seizures shall not be violated.' It is general and forbids every search that is unreasonable; it protects all, those suspected or known to be offenders as well as the innocent, and unquestionably extends to the premises where the search was made and the papers taken. *Gouled v. United States,* 255 U. S. 298, 307. The second clause declares: 'and no Warrants shall issue, but upon probable cause, supported by Oath or affirmation, and particularly describing the place to be searched, and the persons or things to be seized.' This prevents the issue of warrants on loose, vague or doubtful bases of fact. It emphasizes the purpose to protect against all general searches. Since before the creation of our government, such searches have been deemed

obnoxious to fundamental principles of liberty. They are denounced in the constitutions or statutes of every State in the Union. *Agnello v. United States,* 269 U. S. 20, 33. The need of protection against them is attested alike by history and present conditions. The Amendment is to be liberally construed and all owe the duty of vigilance for its effective enforcement lest there shall be impairment of the rights for the protection of which it was adopted. *Boyd v. United States,* 116 U. S. 616, 623. *Weeks v. United States, supra,* 389-92."

Go-Bart Co. v. United States, 282 U. S. 344, 356-57.

The unlimited and unreasonable requirements of the process here involved have been heretofore pointed out (*ante,* pp. 17-21; 24-31). It specifies no particular paper but requires an indiscriminate search through all the corporation's records, "relevant or irrelevant, in the hope that something will turn up".

In a case cited with approval in *Hale v. Henkel,* 201 U. S. 43, the Supreme Court of Missouri said:

"*To permit an indiscriminate search* among all the papers in one's possession *for no particular paper, but some paper which may throw some light on some issue involved* in the trial of some cause pending, *would lead to consequences that can be contemplated only with horror, and such a process is not to be tolerated among a free people.* A grand jury has a general inquisitorial power. They may ask a witness * * * without reference to any particular offense which is the subject of inquiry, what he knows touching the violation of any section of the criminal code. Give such a body, in addition, the power to search any man's papers for evidence of some crime committed, and you convert it into a tribunal which would soon become as odious to American citizens as the Star Chamber was to Englishmen or the Spanish Inquisition to the civilized world."

Ex parte Brown, 72 Mo. 83, 94.

See, also,

Federal Trade Comm. v. American Tobacco Co., 264 U. S. 298, 306;

Bank of America v. Douglas (D. C. App.), 105 F. (2d) 100, 106-7.

The wholesale and sweeping requirements of this subpoena are not, as erroneously assumed by the District Court, accounted for, explained, or justified by the magnitude of the business operations of Standard Oil Company of California. Requirements such as those in clauses 2, 6, and 10 would be equally indefensible and unreasonable if imposed on any institution, large or small. A grand jury proceeding is inquisitorial, but a subpoena *duces tecum* is not an inquisition. If it is, the reforms due to reactions from the ill-famed Star Chamber and the vagaries of Justice Jeffreys were lost in the framing of our Constitution. Appropriate is the language of the Supreme Court in a recent case:

"No one can read those two great opinions (Entick v. Carrington, 19 Howell's St. Trials, 1030, 1074, followed by this court in Boyd v. United States, 116 U. S. 616, 629-30) and the opinions in the Pacific Railway Commission case * * * without perceiving how closely allied in principle are the three protective rights of the individual—that against compulsory self-accusation, that against unlawful searches and seizures, and that against unlawful inquisitorial investigations. They are among those intolerable abuses of the Star Chamber * * *. Even the shortest step in the direction of curtailing one of these rights must be halted *in limine,* lest it serve as a precedent for further advances in the same direction, or for wrongful invasion of the others."

> *Jones v. Securities Exchange Comm.,* 298 U. S. 1, 28.

This subpoena is inherently *bad* for the reasons pointed out. Even if its sanction were unobjectionable, it is, under the facts here admitted, void because it imposes an unreasonable search and constitutes an abuse of judicial process.

"* * * though the information was not itself protected, it does not follow that all means of extracting it were lawful. Some certainly were not; among them, an unreasonable search. * * * No doubt a subpoena may be so onerous as to constitute an unreasonable search (Hale v. Henkel, 201 U. S. 43; Federal Trade Commission v. American Tobacco Co., 264 U. S. 298). Even then, the sanction is unobjectionable, unlike a descent upon one's dwelling or the seizure of one's papers; the search is unreasonable only because it is out of proportion to the end sought, as when the person served is required to fetch all his books at once to an exploratory investigation whose purposes and limits can be determined only as it proceeds."

> *McMann v. Securities Exchange Commission* (C. C. A. 2, 1937), 87 Fed. (2d) 377, 379;
>
> *Bank of America v. Douglas* (D. C. App.), 105 F. (2d) 100, 106-7.

2g. The Subpoena Duces Tecum Is Oppressive, Unreasonable, and Invalid Because It Requires, and Its Enforcement Will Involve, a Taking of the Property of Standard Oil Company of California Without Compensation in Violation of the Fifth Amendment to the Constitution of the United States.

It is sought by this subpoena *duces tecum* addressed to Foster to obtain books and records of his employer, Standard Oil Company of California. It is not, of course, questioned that production of documents from the records of that company can be obtained by such a writ, properly drawn and reasonable in scope, and the company has repeatedly avowed and here repeats that it is, and at all times has been, ready and willing to comply promptly with any such writ.

The objections to unnecessary and wholesale excursions into private business and records are practical and obvious and have received emphatic recognition by the Supreme Court in the *Boyd* case and numerous other decisions. It is for this and other reasons that specification and reasonable limits in such a subpoena are imperative. The Circuit Court of Appeals for the Third Circuit, referring to books in the hands of third persons containing accounts of taxpayers, said:

> "* * * It is the information the bankers' books contain, and not the books in which that information is recorded, that is the property right of these taxpayers, a property right this court protects by injunctive relief."

Zimmermann v. Wilson (C. C. A. 3), 81 Fed. (2d) 847, 849.

As said by Mr. Justice Holmes,

> "the rights of a corporation against unlawful search and seizure are to be protected even *if the same result might have been achieved in some other way.*"
>
> *Silverthorne v. United States,* 251 U. S. 285, 392.

It is respectfully submitted that the facts here admitted demonstrate lack of warrant or justification for either the absence of specification or description, or for the vague and limitless scope of the requirements of this subpoena, and that it violates the Constitutional guarantees against unreasonable searches and seizures.

3. Comments on Opinion of the Judge of the District Court.

The District Court did not in its opinion [R. 82-89] consider the provisions of either of the several clauses or subdivisions of the subpoena. It conceded that the writ "requires the production of a great mass of material. It imposes a severe burden." It apparently believed that objection to a subpoena *duces tecum* should be deferred pending operation of the process. This, however, overlooks the obvious purpose of Rule 45 of the Rules of Civil Procedure and the principle that "a subpoena may be so onerous as to constitute an unreasonable search" because of the disproportion of its requirements to the purpose sought. (*McMann v. Securities Exchange Commission* (C. C. A. 2), 87 Fed. (2d) 377, 379.)

The court below also said that because of a magazine article attributed to an Assistant Attorney General of the United States (which does not refer to any form of process and of which there is no suggestion that either Foster or the corporation had the slightest knowledge) and because "it is not claimed that movants * * * have not had knowledge of the activities of the Government as published relating to the corporate business * * * prior to and during the proceedings of the Second Grand Jury and of the problems of the petroleum industry, with which the inquisitorial body is concerned, * * * the designation in the subpoenas of the documentary evidence required is * * * adequate to enable the respective officers to respond to the process." This presents a most unusual basis upon which to predicate denial of the motion to quash the subpoena. It must be remembered that we are here concerned with the subpoena *duces tecum* itself and whether it adequately describes the documents desired. Neither statements in a magazine article nor activities of public officials, *even if in the record,* can be resorted to for the purpose of supplying requisite description and specification in the writ.

The court below also said that a statement made by Government counsel at the argument that many other subpoenas substantially similar in form had been complied with was not challenged. This observation overlooks the impossibility of challenging statements made during arguments of counsel which are outside the record. Besides, the unreasonableness of a subpoena *duces tecum* is to be determined in the light of its own terms and the proven or admitted circumstances; there is nothing in this record showing either the forms of the subpoenas referred to or the situation or circumstances of the parties to whom they were addressed or to which they apply, or the extent, if any, of the asserted "compliance".

4. Conclusion.

The nature and requirements of this subpoena, and its disregard for those ordinary restraints essential to the maintenance of respect for judicial process render appropriate the language of the Circuit Court of Appeals for the Third Circuit, in condemning a subpoena which, in both substance and effect, was, compared to the present one, modesty itself:

> "A hundred fifty years ago the far-seeing men who framed the Constitution, mindful of the fact that they had been wrongfully subjected to unreasonable search, placed the rugged barrier, 'the right of the people to be secure in their * * * papers, * * * against unreasonable searches' in the pathway of the government then to be established, and made the courts the stern guardians of that barrier if government was tempted to violate it."
>
> *Zimmermann v. Wilson* (C. C. A. 3), 81 Fed. (2d) 847, 849.

It is respectfully submitted that the order denying the motion to quash the subpoena *duces tecum* and directing the witness to obey the same should be reversed.

FELIX T. SMITH,
Standard Oil Building,
San Francisco, California,
Telephone: GArfield 6133.

OSCAR LAWLER,
Standard Oil Building,
Los Angeles, California,
Telephone: TRinity 5111.

Attorneys for Appellants.

PILLSBURY, MADISON & SUTRO,
Standard Oil Building,
San Francisco, California,

LAWLER, FELIX & HALL,
Standard Oil Building,
Los Angeles, California,

Of Counsel.

No. 9287

In the United States Circuit Court of Appeals

For the Ninth Circuit.

G. M. Foster, individually, G. M. Foster, Assistant Secretary, Standard Oil Company of California, a Delaware corporation, and Standard Oil Company of California, a Delaware corporation,

Appellants,

vs.

United States of America,

Appellee.

BRIEF FOR THE UNITED STATES OF AMERICA.

Joseph E. Brill,
M. S. Huberman,
Henry McClernan,
Robert H. Marquis,
Laurence P. Sherfy,
Charles S. Burdell,
A. Andrew Hauk,
Special Assistants to the Attorney General,

U. S. Postoffice and Court House Bldg.,
Los Angeles, California,

Attorneys for Appellee.

Parker & Baird Company, Law Printers, Los Angeles.

No. 9287

In the United States
Circuit Court of Appeals
For the Ninth Circuit.

C. M. Foster, individually, C. M. Foster, Assistant Secretary, Standard Oil Company of California, a Delaware corporation, and Standard Oil Company of California, a Delaware corporation,

Appellants,

vs.

United States of America,

Appellee.

BRIEF FOR THE UNITED STATES OF AMERICA

[illegible] E. Smith,
[illegible] Hubbman,
[illegible] McClellan,
[illegible] H. Marquis,
Lawrence P. Stewart,
[illegible] S. P[illegible],
A. Andrew Hauk,
Special Assistants to the Attorney General,

U. S. Postoffice and Court House Bldg.,
Los Angeles, California,

Attorneys for Appellee.

Parker & Baird Company, Law Printers, Los Angeles.

INDEX.

PAGE

Introductory Statement 1

Jurisdictional Considerations: Renewal of Motion to Dismiss the Appeal 3

Summary of Issues Presented 5

Summary of Argument 6

Argument 8

I. Where a subpoena duces tecum is issued to compel the production of documentary evidence before a grand jury, no showing as to the relevancy, materiality, competency and propriety of such evidence is required prior to the issuance of such subpoena or apart from the duces tecum clauses therein contained 8

II. Where a corporate officer is subpoenaed duces tecum to produce corporate documents before a grand jury investigating alleged violations of the Sherman Anti-trust Act, such officer has no standing to challenge, by an allegation that certain of the called for documents relate solely to intrastate transactions, the authority and jurisdiction of the grand jury to investigate matters to which such documents relate 15

III. Where a subpoena duces tecum requiring the production by a corporate officer of corporate documents before a grand jury is not an unreasonable search and seizure within the meaning of the Fourth Amendment to the Federal Constitution, production of such documents cannot be refused upon the ground that expense, inconvenience or disclosure of "trade secrets" attendant thereon would deprive the corporation of property without due process of law in violation of the Fifth Amendment 17

PAGE

IV. A subpoena duces tecum issued in connection with a grand jury proceeding may properly, and without violating any of the prohibitions of the Fourth Amendment, require the production of documents "relating to," "showing," "sufficient to show," or "disclosing specifically" certain facts "with respect to" stated subjects and subject matters, provided that such subjects and subject matters are specifically enumerated and described, and provided also that there is proper limitation as to the period of time which the documents called for are to cover 24

V. The previous informal investigations conducted by the Government do not in any way limit the extent of and means used to make effective a subsequent investigation by a grand jury of possible violations of Federal statutes 35

VI. Tested in the light of the foregoing legal principles the subpoena here in question is reasonable and valid........ 41

Reply to Appellants' Comments on the Opinion of the District Court 52

Conclusion 54

CITATIONS.

CASES: PAGE

American Medical Ass'n., Chicago, Ill., In re, 26 F. Supp. 58 (D.C.D.C., 1938) 16

Bank of America Nat. Trust & Sav. Ass'n v. Douglas, 105 F. (2d) 100 (App. D.C., 1939) 26

Black, In re, 47 F. (2d) 542 (C.C.A. 2nd, 1931) 13

Blair v. United States, 250 U.S. 273 (1919) 13, 16

Bolster, In re, 59 Wash. 655, 110 Pac. 547 (1910) 19

Boyd v. United States, 116 U.S. 616 (1886) 17

Brown v. United States, 276 U.S. 134 (1928) 12, 29, 36, 39, 49, 54

Consolidated Mines v. Securities and Exchange Com'n, 97 F. (2d) 704 (C.C.A. 9th, 1938) 16, 31

Consolidated Rendering Co. v. Vermont, 207 U.S. 541 (1908) 21, 28, 45, 48

Elting v. United States, 27 Ct. Cl. 158 (1892) 25

Essgee Co. v. United States, 262 U.S. 151 (1923) 18

Federal Trade Commission v. American Tobacco Co., 264 U.S. 298 (1924) 25

Greenbaum v. United States, 98 F. (2d) 574 (C.C.A. 9th, 1938.. 46

Hale v. Henkel, 201 U.S. 43 (1906) 12, 22, 23, 25

Johnson Steel Street-Rail Co. v. North Branch Steel Co., 48 Fed. 191 (C.C.W.D. Pa., 1891) 19

Mobile Gas Co. v. Patterson, 288 Fed. 884 (D.C.M.D. Ala., N.D., 1923) 25

Nelson v. United States, 201 U.S. 92 (1906) 26, 45, 48

Newfield v. Ryan, 91 F. (2d) 700 (C.C.A. 5th, 1937) 32

Norcross v. United States, 209 Fed. 13 (C.C.A. 9th, 1913) 9, 11, 12, 30, 44, 45, 48

PAGE

Rawlins v. Hall-Epps Clothing Co., 217 Fed. 884 (C.C.A. 5th, 1914) 25, 26

Silverthorne Lumber Co. v. United States, 251 U.S. 385 (1920) 17, 18

State v. Superior Court, 109 Wash., 634, 187 Pac. 358 (1920) 19, 20

Subpoenas Duces Tecum, In re, 248 Fed. 137 (D.C.E.D. Tenn., S.D., 1916) 9

Wertheim v. Continental Ry. & Trust Co., 15 Fed. 716 (C.C.S.D. N.Y., 1883) 19, 20

Wheeler v. United States, 226 U.S. 478 (1913) 12

Wilson v. United States, 221 U.S. 361 (1911) 9, 19

Zimmerman v. Wilson, 81 F. (2d) 847 (C.C.A. 3d, 1936) 17, 18

Statutes:

49 Stat. 1561 46

United States Code Annotated, Title 28, Sec. 225(a) 4

United States Code Annotated, Title 28, Sec. 695 46

No. 9287

In the United States Circuit Court of Appeals

For the Ninth Circuit.

G. M. FOSTER, individually, G. M. FOSTER, Assistant Secretary, Standard Oil Company of California, a Delaware corporation, and STANDARD OIL COMPANY OF CALIFORNIA, a Delaware corporation,

Appellants,

vs.

UNITED STATES OF AMERICA,

Appellee.

BRIEF FOR THE UNITED STATES OF AMERICA.

Introductory Statement.

The appeal taken herein is from an order of the District Court of the United States for the Southern District of California denying a motion to quash a subpoena *duces tecum* issued out of said Court and directed to G. M. Foster, Assistant Secretary of the Standard Oil Company of California, a Delaware corporation. The subpoena required said Foster to appear and testify before the Second Grand Jury, impaneled in and for the February 1939 Term of said District Court, and there to produce certain books and papers of said Standard Oil

Company of California specified in Annex I of the subpoena [R. 2-19].

The Second Grand Jury was duly impaneled in and for the February 1939 Term of said District Court to investigate possible violations of the Sherman Antitrust Act by oil companies and others engaged in or connected with the petroleum industry [R. 83-86, 96-99]. On May 1, 1939, and prior to such impanelment, the United States Department of Justice, in accordance with its usual practice in such cases, issued a press release in which were set out the reasons underlying the institution of the Grand Jury investigation [R. 84-86].[1]

During the course of the Grand Jury's inquiries, subpoenas *duces tecum* similar to that involved on this appeal were directed to and complied with by officers of some forty corporations and firms engaged in the petroleum industry, without resort on their part to any legal action challenging the validity of the process [R. 87]. In the case of eleven other subpoenas *duces tecum* directed to officers of as many different corporations, all of which were substantially identical in form and in content, motions to quash were filed in the District Court by the corporate officers who had been served with process, as well as by the corporations themselves [R. 77-91].

After hearing, the District Court entered its order denying *in toto* the several motions to quash and directing that the subpoenas be complied with by the corporate officers on whom they had been served [R. 77-91]. No re-

---

[1]The press release is set out in full in the opinion of the District Court [R. 84-86].

view of the District Court's ruling has been sought in respect to ten of the eleven subpoenas, compliance with which was directed by the District Court. From so much of the District Court's order, however, as denies the motion to quash filed by G. M. Foster, individually and as Assistant Secretary of the Standard Oil Company of California, and by said Standard Oil Company of California, the present appeal has been taken.

Subsequent to the date on which notice of appeal was given by appellants herein, the Second Grand Jury was duly authorized by order of the United States District Court for the Southern District of California, made and entered on September 7, 1939, to continue during the September 1939 Term of said Court investigations which it had begun but not completed during the February 1939 Term [R. 96-99].

Jurisdictional Considerations:

Renewal of Motion to Dismiss the Appeal.

The subpoena *duces tecum* involved on this appeal was the process of the District Court. It is of course not open to question that a court possesses control over its own process. The District Court, therefore, undoubtedly possessed jurisdiction to entertain motions to quash this and other subpoenas which had been issued under its authority.

Appellants state at page 2 of their brief that jurisdiction on the part of this Court to hear and determine the present appeal exists by virtue of Section 225(a), Title 28, of the United States Code Annotated. Such title and section confer upon Circuit Courts of Appeals, however, jurisdiction to hear and determine only appeals from final orders, as well as appeals from interlocutory orders in certain limited classes of cases.

The order entered by the District Court in this instance does not fall within that class of interlocutory orders which are appealable. Hence this appeal will lie only if the order of the District Court is held to be final.

It is the Government's position that the order in question is not final, and that the present appeal therefore does not lie. The question of the non-appealability of the order has heretofore been raised by appellee in a motion to dismiss the present appeal. Such motion has heretofore been argued before the Court.[2] No decision having been reached by the Court on such motion, and leave having been granted to renew the same at the time of argument on the merits, the motion is accordingly renewed at the present time.[3]

---

[2]Argument on appellee's motion to dismiss the appeal was heard by the Court at Portland, Oregon, on September 18, 1939. After argument, the motion was submitted. Thereafter, the Court entered an order vacating such submission, and granting leave to appellee to renew the motion at the time when the appeal should be argued on the merits.

[3]Legal argument in connection with the motion to dismiss is not included in the present brief, since appellee has previously stated what it believes to be the applicable principles of law in a Memorandum of Points and Authorities, filed in support of the motion, to which Memorandum the Court is respectfully referred.

Summary of Issues Presented.

In their brief, appellants set out separately the grounds of their motion to quash (at p. 3); the questions which they state are involved in the appeal (at pp. 6-8); and a summary of their argument (at pp. 8-9). Since different questions of law and of fact are differently stated under each of these three sections of appellants' brief, appellee here summarizes what it believes to be (apart from jurisdictional considerations) the issues presented on this appeal:

1. Where a subpoena *duces tecum* is issued to compel the production of documentary evidence before a grand jury, is any showing required as to the relevancy, materiality, competency and propriety of such evidence prior to the issuance of such subpoena or apart from the *duces tecum* clauses therein contained?

2. Where a corporate officer is subpoenaed *duces tecum* to produce corporate documents before a grand jury investigating alleged violations of the Sherman Antitrust Act, may such officer, by an allegation that certain of the called for documents relate solely to intrastate transactions, challenge the authority and jurisdiction of the grand jury to compel production of such documents and to investigate matters to which they relate?

3. Where a subpoena *duces tecum* requiring the production by a corporate officer of corporate documents before a grand jury is not an unreasonable search and seizure within the meaning of the Fourth Amendment to the Federal Constitution, can production of such documents be refused on the ground that expense, inconvenience or disclosure of "trade secrets" attendant thereon would deprive the corporation of property without due process of law in violation of the Fifth Amendment?

4. May a subpoena *duces tecum* issued in connection with a grand jury proceeding properly, and without violating the prohibitions of the Fourth Amendment, require production of documents "relating to," "showing," "sufficient to show," or "disclosing specifically" certain facts "with respect to" stated subjects and subject matters, provided that such subjects and subject matters are specifically enumerated and described, and provided further that there is proper limitation as to the period of time which the documents called for are to cover?

5. Do the previous informal investigations conducted by the Government in any way limit the extent of and means used to make effective a subsequent investigation of possible violations of Federal criminal statutes by a grand jury?

6. Tested in the light of established legal principles, is the subpoena here in question reasonable and valid?

Summary of Argument.

1. Where a subpoena *duces tecum* is issued to compel the production of documentary evidence before a grand jury, no showing as to the relevancy, materiality, competency and propriety of such evidence is required prior to the issuance of such subpoena or apart from the *duces tecum* clauses therein contained.

2. Where a corporate officer is subpoenaed *duces tecum* to produce corporate documents before a grand jury investigating alleged violations of the Sherman Antitrust Act, such officer has no standing to challenge, by an al-

legation that certain of the called for documents relate solely to intrastate transactions, the authority and jurisdiction of the grand jury to investigate matters to which such documents relate.

3. Where a subpoena *duces tecum* requiring the production by a corporate officer of corporate documents before a grand jury is not an unreasonable search and seizure within the meaning of the Fourth Amendment to the Federal Constitution, production of such documents cannot be refused upon the ground that expense, inconvenience or disclosure of "trade secrets" attendant thereon would deprive the corporation of property without due process of law in violation of the Fifth Amendment.

4. A subpoena *duces tecum* issued in connection with a grand jury proceeding may properly, and without violating any of the prohibitions of the Fourth Amendment, require the production of documents "relating to," "showing," "sufficient to show," or "disclosing specifically" certain facts "with respect to" stated subjects and subject matters, provided that such subjects and subject matters are specifically enumerated and described, and provided also that there is proper limitation as to the period of time which the documents called for are to cover.

5. The previous informal investigations conducted by the Government do not in any way limit the extent of and means used to make effective a subsequent investigation by a grand jury of possible violations of Federal statutes.

6. Tested in the light of the foregoing legal principles, the subpoena here in question is reasonable and valid.

ARGUMENT.

I.

Where a Subpoena Duces Tecum Is Issued to Compel the Production of Documentary Evidence Before a Grand Jury, No Showing as to the Relevancy, Materiality, Competency and Propriety of Such Evidence Is Required Prior to the Issuance of Such Subpoena or Apart From the Duces Tecum Clauses Therein Contained.

Appellants apparently contend that prior to the issuance of a subpoena *duces tecum* in connection with a grand jury proceeding, and apart from the *duces tecum* clauses thereof, there must be some showing that the documents called for are relevant, material, competent, proper and necessary to be produced [R. 22-23; Appellants' Brief pp. 32-33]. This contention is advanced in the face of decisions of the Supreme Court of the United States and other Federal appellate courts which hold that a subpoena *duces tecum* in grand jury proceedings may be issued by the clerk, as of course, without prior showing to the Court; that the relevancy, competency and propriety of matter called for under such subpoena may be gathered merely from a reading of the *duces tecum* clauses therein contained; and that the relevancy, materiality, competency and propriety of evidence desired by a grand jury is no concern of the witness.

It is well settled that a subpoena *duces tecum* to compel the production of evidence before a grand jury may be issued by the clerk, as of course, without the necessity of any prior showing to the Court of the materiality, competency or propriety of the evidence sought. *Wilson v. United States,* 221 U. S. 361 (1911); *Norcross v. United States,* 209 Fed. 13 (C. C. A. 9th, 1913); *In re Subpoenas Duces Tecum,* 248 Fed. 137 (D. C. E. D. Tenn., S. D., 1916).

The rule of law is well stated in *In re Subpoenas Duces Tecum, supra.* In that case, the clerk of the court requested instructions as to whether he was authorized to issue subpoenas *duces tecum* in criminal proceedings. Answering in the affirmative the question thus propounded, Judge Sanford (later Mr. Justice Sanford of the Supreme Court of the United States) stated (at pp. 137-138):

> "Under R. S. Secs. 868 and 869 (Comp. St. 1916, Secs. 1479, 1480), a subpoena **duces tecum,** commanding a witness to produce documents before a commissioner authorized to take testimony under a **dedimus potestatem,** is only issued upon application to a judge and order to the clerk. And this requirement as to a preliminary order of the court seems to have been frequently followed in equity practice in the Federal courts, where the document is to be produced before an examiner or other officer taking a deposition **de bene esse** under R. S. Sec. 863 (Comp. St. 1916, Sec. 1472), or under the equity rules. Simk. Fed. Eq. Suit (2d Ed.) 552, 553, and cases cited. This rule, in so far as not dependent upon statute, is apparently based upon the practical inconvenience, if not impossibility, of otherwise adequately protecting a witness appearing before such

officer from producing and making public privileged matters. Obviously, however, it has no application where the witness is merely required to produce the document before the grand jury or the court itself, since in either case he may claim his privilege when called upon to produce the document before the grand jury or the court, and upon application to the court will be protected in any privilege he may have before being required to make the disclosure sought.

"Direct authority is furthermore found, by necessary implication, in *Wilson v. United States,* 221 U. S. 361, 370, 376, 31 Sup. Ct. 538, 540, 542 (55 L. Ed. 771, Ann. Cas. 1912D, 558). In this case a subpoena *duces tecum* had been issued, apparently as of course, requiring a corporation to produce certain documents before the grand jury. The president of the company having appeared with the documents, declined to permit them to be inspected by the grand jury, and upon application to the court was committed for contempt. Among other objections relied on by him to the sufficiency of the subpoena, as stated in the opinion, was the fact that the subpoena **duces tecum** 'was not issued pursuant to an order of court.' The court, after reviewing the several other objections thus interposed, but without referring again to this specific objection, said that 'no ground appears upon which the corporation could have resisted the writ'; and again, that it concluded 'that the subpoena was valid and that its service imposed upon the corporation the duty of obedience.' It must hence be taken as conclusively determined

> that no preliminary order of the court is essential to the validity of a subpoena **duces tecum** for a witness required to appear before a grand jury in a criminal proceeding; but that the same may be issued by the clerk, as of course, upon due application."

In *Norcross v. United States, supra,* one of the grounds taken in a motion to quash a subpoena *duces tecum* addressed to the secretary of a corporation was that the subpoena had issued irregularly and without authority in that no order of court had first been secured directing it to issue. The conclusion of the trial court on this point (set out at 209 Fed. 14) was that:

> "No order of court is required, either by statute or by the practice in this district as a prerequisite to the valid issuance by the Clerk of a subpoena **duces tecum** to compel the attendance of a witness before the grand jury."

The judgment below was affirmed by this Court.

Similarly, the rule is established that, as no showing of materiality, relevancy, competency and propriety need be made prior to the issuance of a subpoena *duces tecum* in connection with grand jury proceedings, no such showing need be made in the subpoena itself apart from that which may be gathered from the description of the documents therein called for. The only case cited by appellants which casts any doubt upon the validity of this principle is *Hale v. Henkel,* 201 U. S. 43 (1906). There, it is true, the Court said (p. 77):

> "Doubtless many, if not all, of these documents may ultimately be required, but some necessity should be shown, either from an examination of the witnesses orally, or from the known transactions of these companies with the other companies implicated, or some evidence of their materiality produced, to justify an order for the production of such a mass of papers."

The decision in *Hale v. Henkel, supra,* is discussed at greater length *infra.* It is sufficient to note, as to the point here raised, that the language of the Court was obiter and it cannot now be accepted in view of the decision in *Brown v. United States,* 276 U. S. 134 (1928), where the Supreme Court said (p. 143):

> "The probable materiality of the documents is sufficiently indicated by the descriptions of their subject matter contained in the subpoena."

Moreover, subpoenas *duces tecum* have been upheld in many cases where the subpoenas contained no statement as to relevancy or materiality apart from the description of the papers called for in the subpoenas. See for example, in addition to *Brown v. United States, supra, Wheeler v. United States,* 226 U. S. 478, 482-483 (1913); *Norcross v. United States,* 209 Fed. 13, 15-17 (C. C. A. 9th, 1913).

Further, the relevancy, materiality, competency and propriety of evidence sought to be obtained by a grand jury through a subpoena *duces tecum* is not for the determination of the person who is served with the subpoena. This is not a suit in equity, an action at law, or a proceeding before the Federal Trade Commission, where the relevancy or materiality of evidence sought can readily be determined from an examination of the pleadings. The Government is not obliged to disclose to one subpoenaed as a witness before the grand jury the precise nature or extent of the matters under investigation. As was said in *In re Black,* 47 F. (2d) 542, 543 (C. C. A. 2nd, 1931):

> "Every bona fide investigation by a grand jury seeks to ferret out crime and criminals. To detect crime and to present charges against the guilty required the most ample power of investigation. *Frequently neither the nature of the crime itself, nor the identity of criminals can be forecast. To be compelled to state either in advance we think is likely unnecessarily to impede investigation and obstruct the administration of justice."* (Italics supplied.)

The position of a witness before the grand jury—and such is the position of the corporate officer subpoenaed here—is succinctly stated in *Blair v. United States,* 250 U. S. 273, 281-282 (1919):

> "But, aside from exceptions and qualifications—and none such is asserted in the present case—the witness is bound not only to attend but to tell what he knows in answer to questions framed for the pur-

pose of bringing out the truth of the matter under inquiry.

"*He is not entitled to urge objections of incompetency or irrelevancy, such as a party might raise, for this is no concern of his. Nelson v. United States,* 201 U. S. 92, 115.

"On familiar principles, he is not entitled to challenge the authority of the court or of the grand jury, provided they have a *de facto* existence and organization.

"He is not entitled to set limits to the investigation that the grand jury may conduct. The Fifth Amendment and the statutes relative to the organization of grand juries recognize such a jury as being possessed of the same powers that pertained to its British prototype, and in our system examination of witnesses by a grand jury need not be preceded by a formal charge against a particular individual. *Hale v. Henkel,* 201 U. S. 43, 65. *It is a grand inquest, a body with powers of investigation and inquisition, the scope of whose inquiries is not to be limited narrowly by questions of propriety or forecasts of the probable result of the investigation, or by doubts whether any particular individual will be found properly subject to an accusation of crime.* As has been said before, the identity of the offender, and the precise nature of the offense, if there be one, normally are developed at the conclusion of the grand jury's labors, not at the beginning. *Hendricks v. United States,* 223 U. S. 178, 184." (Italics supplied.)

II.

Where a Corporate Officer Is Subpoenaed Duces Tecum to Produce Corporate Documents Before a Grand Jury Investigating Alleged Violations of the Sherman Antitrust Act, Such Officer Has No Standing to Challenge, by an Allegation That Certain of the Called for Documents Relate Solely to Intrastate Transactions, the Authority and Jurisdiction of the Grand Jury to Investigate Matters to Which Such Documents Relate.

One of the grounds upon which appellants object to the subpoena is that "it calls for the production of papers relating solely to intrastate business" (Appellants Brief p. 3), or as stated in appellants' notice of motion to quash the subpoena:

> "The enforcement of said subpoena with respect to documents and papers relating solely to the intrastate business of Standard Oil Company of California would be in excess of the authority and jurisdiction of said Grand Jury and of this court, as said authority and jurisdiction are defined and limited by subdivision 3 of section 8 of Article I of the Constitution of the United States." [R. 22.]

Lengthy discussion of this contention seems unnecessary, inasmuch as appellants, since they do not argue the point in their brief, have apparently abandoned it. It is sufficient to note that the contention represents an effort to attack the jurisdiction of the Grand Jury. That appellants have no standing to attack the Grand Jury's jurisdiction has been explicitly ruled by the United States Supreme Court in *Blair v. United States*, 250 U. S. 273, 282-283 (1919), in which the Court said:

> "And, for the same reasons, witnesses are not entitled to take exception to the jurisdiction of the grand jury or the court over the particular subject-matter that is under investigation. In truth it is in the ordinary case no concern of one summoned as a witness whether the offense is within the jurisdiction of the court or not. At least, the court and grand jury have authority and jurisdiction to investigate the facts in order to determine the question whether the facts show a case within their jurisdiction."

And see also *Consolidated Mines v. Securities and Exchange Com'n*, 97 F. (2d) 704 (C. C. A. 9th, 1938); *In re American Medical Ass'n, Chicago, Ill.*, 26 F. Supp. 58 (D. C. D. C., 1938).

III.

Where a Subpoena Duces Tecum Requiring the Production by a Corporate Officer of Corporate Documents Before a Grand Jury Is Not an Unreasonable Search and Seizure Within the Meaning of the Fourth Amendment to the Federal Constitution, Production of Such Documents Cannot Be Refused Upon the Ground That Expense, Inconvenience or Disclosure of "Trade Secrets" Attendant Thereon Would Deprive the Corporation of Property Without Due Process of Law in Violation of the Fifth Amendment.

Another of the grounds upon which appellants attack the subpoena is that it would allegedly deprive the Standard Oil Company of California of property without due process of law, in violation of the Fifth Amendment. Such deprivation, it is intimated, would consist in the disclosure of "trade secrets" [R. 22], and in the inconvenience and expense which would follow from enforcement of the subpoena [R. 39].

The three cases cited by appellants in support of their position (at pp. 38-39 of their Brief) are *Boyd v. United States,* 116 U. S. 616 (1886); *Silverthorne Lumber Co. v. United States,* 251 U. S. 385 (1920); and *Zimmermann v. Wilson,* 81 F. (2d) 847 (C. C. A. 3rd, 1936).

No one of these cases remotely concerns any right possessed by corporations under the Fifth Amendment. The issue under the Fifth Amendment in the *Boyd* case had to do with the rights of individuals against self-incrimination, rights which corporations do not possess. As was said by the Supreme Court in *Essgee Co. v. United States,* 262 U. S. 151 (1923), in holding that a motion for the return of corporate documents and papers secured by subpoenas had been properly denied (p. 158):

> "Appellants cite the cases of *Boyd v. United States,* 116 U. S. 616; *Weeks v. United States,* 232 U. S. 383, and *Gouled v. United States,* 255 U. S. 298, to support their contention that the proceedings complained of herein violate their rights under the Fourth and Fifth Amendments. Those cases were all unreasonable searches of documents and records belonging to individuals. The distinction between the cases before us and those cases lies in the more limited application of the Amendments to the compulsory producton of corporate documents and papers as shown in the *Henkel, Wilson* and *Wheeler* cases."

The *Silverthorne* and *Zimmermann* cases had to do with the application of the Fourth Amendment rather than the Fifth.

In respect to the argument advanced that enforcement of the subpoena would result in the disclosure of trade secrets, it must be apparent from a reading of the subpoena that nothing is required to be produced which has to do with any secret process constituting a "trade secret," as that term is ordinarily employed in a legal sense. It may be true that enforcement of the subpoena would necessitate disclosure of information concerning the operations of a private business, but such information is not a technical "trade secret." It is well settled law that a corporation cannot object to the production of books and papers merely because they contain information that is confidential or which relates to the conduct of the corporation's private affairs. *Johnson Steel Street-Rail Co. v. North Branch Steel Co.,* 48 Fed. 191 (C. C. W. D. Pa., 1891); *Wertheim v. Continental Ry. & Trust Co.,* 15 Fed. 716 (C. C. S. D. N. Y., 1883); *In re Bolster,* 59 Wash. 655, 110 Pac. 547 (1910); *State v. Superior Court,* 109 Wash. 634, 187 Pac. 358 (1920). As was stated in *In re Bolster,* 110 Pac. 547, 548:

> "But a corporation or other person keeping books is not relieved from producing them, when they contain matters material to an issue, merely because they are private. A witness can be compelled to testify orally to private affairs connected with his business when material, and his books and documents stand at no higher plane."

The argument that the inconvenience and expense to which the Standard Oil Company of Californa would be put in complying with the subpoena would result in a deprivation of property without due process of law is clearly without merit. A corporation possesses no immunity in respect to the production of documents "when a writ, suitably specific and properly limited in its scope, calls for the production of documents which, as against their lawful owner to whom the writ is directed, the party procuring its issuance is entitled to have produced." (*Wilson v. United States,* 221 U. S. 361, 376 (1911).) The writ in such case is itself due process, and no denial thereof follows from any inconvenience or expense which may result from its enforcement.

The general rule applicable in this regard is undoubtedly that which was stated in *Wertheim v. Continental Ry. & Trust Co.*, 15 Fed. 716, 717 (C. C. S. D. N. Y., 1883), where the Court said:

> "It may be inconvenient, and sometimes embarrassing, to the managers of a corporation to require its books and papers to be taken from its office and exhibited to third persons, but it is also inconvenient and often onerous to individuals to require them to do the same thing. Considerations of inconvenience must give way to the paramount right of litigants to resort to evidence which it may be in the power of witnesses to produce, and without which grave interests might be jeoparded, and the administration of justice thwarted."

In *State v. Superior Court,* 109 Wash. 634, 187 Pac. 358 (1920), the Spokane & Eastern Trust Company objected to the production of books and records under a subpoena directed to it in connection with a civil suit to which it was not a party on the grounds, among others, that the records sought were not competent evidence and did not show anything of value to the party at whose instance the subpoena was issued; that the books and records in question "would weigh half a ton" and were "constantly used in the bank's business"; and that their production would result in great inconvenience and expense to the bank. Answering these contentions, the Court said (187 Pac. 358, 361):

> "The Spokane & Eastern Trust Company further asserts that Daniel did not make the entries contained in the books, and that those entries would not even tend to indicate the sources from which deposits were derived, and that therefore the entries could

not affect the rights of Daniel in the accounting. Although it may be that they are not the books of the accounts of the defendant, and not books of original entries, still they are proper evidence and will throw some light upon the accuracy of the account submitted by the defendant Daniel, and it is not for the Spokane & Eastern Trust Company to say the amount of weight they will carry nor the conclusiveness of their showing upon the referee. The witness subpoenaed in a case and the witness subpoenaed **duces tecum** are not in any different position before the court. It is not for either to comply or to refuse to comply with the subpoena by determining for themselves the admissibility of the evidence sought nor the weight thereof.

"This observation also applies to the further objection of the Spokane & Eastern Trust Company that it would be a great inconvenience to it to respond to the subpoena. If it were the rule that witnesses might respond or not to the subpoena according to the inconvenience they might suffer by responding, lawsuits would be conducted according to private rather than public convenience. The further objection of the Spokane & Eastern Trust Company that to comply with the subpoena would entail great expense is answered in the same way."

In *Consolidated Rendering Co. v. Vermont,* 207 U. S. 541 (1908), one ground of objection to a subpoena *duces tecum* was the inconvenience and expense which would result from its enforcement, and it was urged that the order enforcing the subpoena be at least conditioned upon the tender of an amount sufficient to defray the expense of producing the documents called for. The Supreme Court upheld the decision of the courts of Vermont that the statutory fee payable to witnesses was all that could legally be required.

In *Hale v. Henkel,* 201 U. S. 43 (1906), it is true, the Court spoke of the possible effect upon the corporation concerned should it be denuded of its books and records in accordance with the subpoena there under consideration. That part of the opinion which dealt with the validity of the subpoena was obiter dictum since the actual decision of the Court was that Hale, the corporate officer who had been subpoenaed, was properly adjudged in contempt for failure to produce any of the books and records required. The opinion was rendered by a divided court. Two of the Justices dissented. Two other Justices concurred in the holding, but stated in their opinion that the Fourth Amendment has no application to corporations whatsoever, and that the power of visitatorial search possessed by grand jurors in connection with corporate affairs is in effect unlimited. It is clear that the language in the majority opinion respecting the validity of the subpoena was based on the belief that the terms of the subpoena were so broad as to violate the prohibitions of the Fourth Amendment against unreasonable searches and seizures. While the Court spoke of the possible effect on the business of a corporation, it clearly envisioned the possibility that possession of all of the books and records called for might nevertheless have been gained under a proper subpoena, saying (p. 77):

> "Doubtless many, if not all, of these documents may ultimately be required, * * *."

The dictum in the case as to the unreasonableness of the subpoena has since often been cited in connection with the general principle therein stated, but in actual application it has been more often distinguished than followed. In any event, however, the dictum in question rested upon the application of the Fourth Amendment rather than the Fifth, and it is impossible to believe by a reading of the case that the Court had in mind any possible deprivation of property without due process apart from the unreasonableness of the subpoena under the Fourth Amendment.

The subpoena which the Court had under consideration in *Hale v. Henkel* did not relate to specific subject matters, and the Court stated (p. 77) that it might as well have required "the production of all the books, papers, and documents found in the office of the MacAndrews & Forbes Company, * * *."

It is thus clearly established that the inconvenience or expense incident to compliance with this subpoena affords no basis for relieving appellants from the obligation of responding thereto. The fact stressed by appellants that, because the Standard Oil Company of California is of great size, possessing some 650 branch offices and sub-offices in the Pacific Coast territory [R. 38], and because its transactions and the records thereof are numerous, a large volume of records and papers would have to be examined and produced under the subpoena, can obviously constitute no justification for the claim that enforcement of the subpoena would in any way violate the provisions of the Fifth Amendment.

IV.

A Subpoena Duces Tecum Issued in Connection With a Grand Jury Proceeding May Properly, and Without Violating Any of the Prohibitions of the Fourth Amendment, Require the Production of Documents "Relating to," "Showing," "Sufficient to Show," or "Disclosing Specifically" Certain Facts "With Respect To" Stated Subjects and Subject Matters, Provided That Such Subjects and Subject Matters Are Specifically Enumerated and Described, and Provided Also That There Is Proper Limitation as to the Period of Time Which the Documents Called for Are to Cover.

The argument most strongly relied upon by appellants is that the subpoena casts upon Foster, the corporate officer served with process, the duty of exercising judgment in the selection of material to be produced pursuant to the subpoena. This argument is directed to those paragraphs of the subpoena which require the production of documents "relating to," "with reference to," "showing," "sufficient to show," or "disclosing specifically the following information with reference to" certain specifically enumerated and described subjects and subject matters, in each case with limitation as to dates. The position of appellants seems to be that it is necessarily improper to require the production of books and papers relating to or showing certain transactions and subject matters, even though the transactions and subject matters are specifically enumerated and described. Instead, appellants take the position that each book, record, document or paper desired must be individually and separately described by name, date, or otherwise (Appellants' Brief p. 21).

In support of their position, appellants cite a number of cases, most of which have nothing to do with subpoenas issued in grand jury proceedings, and all of which, in so far as they relate to the validity of particular subpoenas, are readily distinguishable on their facts. Such cases, for example, as *Hale v. Henkel,* 201 U. S. 43 (1906), *Federal Trade Commission v. American Tobacco Co.,* 264 U. S. 298 (1924), *Rawlins v. Hall-Epps Clothing Co.,* 217 Fed. 884 (C. C. A. 5th, 1914), *Mobile Gas Co. v. Patterson,* 288 Fed. 884 (D. C. M. D. Ala., N. D., 1923), and *Elting v. United States,* 27 Ct. Cl. 158 (1892), are not authority, as apparently claimed by appellants, for the proposition that a subpoena may not validly require the production of books and papers relating to specifically described subject matters. Such cases merely follow the well established rule that the production of books and papers may not be required unless the subpoena specifically describes the subject matters to which such books and papers relate and unless there is proper limitation as to dates. This was precisely the test adopted by the District Court in considering the subpoena here involved, when it said that the sole litigable issue was whether "the documents called for are indicated to the corporate officers served with reasonable specification as to subjects and subject matter and are reasonably limited as to dates" [R. 82].

The subpoenas in *Hale v. Henkel* and *Federal Trade Commission v. American Tobacco Co., supra,* did not even purport to relate the books or records called for to any subject matter whatsoever. The references to subject matters in *Rawlins v. Hall-Epps Clothing Co., Mobile Gas Co. v. Patterson,* and *Elting v. United States, supra,* were in such general terms that there was in effect no description of particular subject matters. Thus, *Rawlins v. Hall-Epps Clothing Co.* involved an order requiring the production before a referee by a partnership named in an involuntary bankruptcy petition of "all of the books of account of said Rawlins Mercantile Company, and other writings and memoranda from which may be ascertained any of the matters and things, hereinbefore mentioned, and to be covered in said examination" (217 Fed. 884, 887).

Certain other cases cited by appellants in this connection have nothing whatsoever to do with the problem involved. An example is *Bank of America Nat. Trust & Sav. Ass'n v. Douglas,* 105 F. (2d) 100 (App. D. C. 1939), where the Court held that a subpoena *duces tecum* issued by the Securities and Exchange Commission was unreasonable and invalid, not because the subpoena was too broad in scope but because it required that the Bank of America, having its principal place of business in San Francisco, California, produce the documents called for by the subpoena in an investigation to be conducted in Washington, D. C., which proceeding could as well have been held in San Francisco, California.

That a subpoena may validly call for books and papers relating to or showing particular subject matters rather than specifying individually each book or paper that is required, is clearly established by the following cases:

Nelson v. United States, 201 U. S. 92, 99-100 (1906), where the Court upheld the validity of subpoenas described by it as follows:

> "The subpoenas required plaintiffs in error to produce the account books, including the journals, ledgers and other books kept by or under the control of the companies respectively, of which plaintiffs in

error were respectively officers, (a) showing the amounts, kinds and grades of paper manufactured by the respective companies and sold by or through the General Paper Company, and were shipped since the fifth of July, 1900; (b) the prices, amounts or credits received for such paper from the paper company between the fifth of July and the present time, including entries, showing the manner in which the prices and amounts received by the respective companies for any and all of its products so sold have been equalized with the prices and amounts received or realized of any and all of the other defendant companies for which the paper company is or has been the exclusive agent; (c) the amounts and proportions of earnings or profits of the paper company received by the respective companies from and through the paper company, either in the form of rebates, credits or otherwise.

"Second. All contracts, agreements, writings and account books, including journals, ledgers and other books, kept by or under the control of the respective companies, showing the agreement, arrangement or understanding under and pursuant to each, and the manner in which the prices and amounts realized by the respective companies upon the various kinds and grades of paper manufactured by it and sold by and through the paper company, are and have been, since July 5, 1900, equalized, or the profits arising from the sale of such paper distributed or apportioned, as between the respective companies and other defendants manufacturing and selling through the paper company similar kinds or grades of paper, or among all of the defendants manufacturing similar kinds or grades of paper, and then and there to testify and the truth to say, in a certain matter in controversy in said court, between the United States as complainant against the General Paper Company *et al.*, defendants, on the part of the complainant."

Consolidated Rendering Co. v. Vermont, 207 U. S. 541, 554 (1908), where the Supreme Court upheld the validity of a subpoena requiring the production of "such books or papers *as related to, or concerned,* any dealings or business between January 1, 1904, and the date of the notice, October, 1906, with the parties named therein, who were cattle commissioners of the State of Vermont, and which papers were to be used relative to the matter of complaint pending, and then and there to be investigated by the grand jury, in which the persons named in the notice were charged with having unlawfully sold diseased meat for food purposes at Burlington." (Italics supplied.) As the Court said in that case (at page 554):

> "* * * But unless it can be said that the court or grand jury never has any right to call for all the books and papers, or correspondence, between certain dates and certain persons named, in regard to a complaint which is pending before such court or grand jury, we think the objection here made is not well founded. We see no reason why all such books, papers and correspondence which related to the subject of inquiry, and were described with reasonable detail, should not be called for and the company directed to produce them. Otherwise the State would be compelled to designate each particular paper which it desired, which presupposes an accurate knowledge of such papers, which the tribunal desiring the papers would probably rarely, if ever, have. The notice is not nearly so sweeping in its reach as in the case of *Hale v. Henkel, supra.*"

Brown v. United States, 276 U. S. 134, 138-139 (1928), where the Court upheld a subpoena *duces tecum* directed to the National Alliance of Furniture Manufacturers and commanding it to produce before a grand jury:

> " 'All letters or copies of letters, telegrams or copies of telegrams, incoming and outgoing, passing between the National Alliance of Furniture Manufacturers and its predecessor, the National Alliance of Case Goods Associations, their officers and agents, and the several members of said National Alliance of Furniture Manufacturers and its predecessor, the National Alliance of Case Goods Associations (including corporations, partnerships, and individuals, and their respective officers and agents) during the period from January 1, 1922, to June 15, 1925, relating to the manufacture and sale of case goods, and particularly with reference to—
>
> " '(a) general meetings of Alliance
>
> " '(b) Zone meetings of Alliance members
>
> " '(c) costs of manufacture
>
> " '(d) grading of various types of case goods
>
> " '(e) issuing new price lists
>
> " '(f) discounts allowed on price lists
>
> " '(g) exchanging price lists
>
> " '(h) maintaining prices
>
> " '(i) advancing prices

"'(j) reducing prices

"'(k) rumors of charges of price cutting

"'(l) discounts, terms and conditions of sale, etc.

"'(m) curtailment of production

"'(n) the pricing of certain articles or suits of furniture by W. H. Coye

"'(o) cost bulletins

"'(p) intention of W. H. Coye and A. C. Brown to attend furniture markets or expositions at Jamestown, N. Y., Grand Rapids, Mich., Chicago, Ill., and New York City, N. Y., and meetings of members held prior to and during said furniture markets or expositions

"'(q) conditions obtaining at various furniture markets or expositions at Jamestown, N. Y., Grand Rapids, Mich., Chicago, Ill., and New York City, N. Y.

"'(r) manufacturers maintaining a fair margin of profit between cost prices and selling prices.'"

Norcross v. United States, 209 Fed. 13, 15-17 (C. C. A. 9th, 1913), where this Court upheld a subpoena requiring the production of all books, papers, records and vouchers of the Western Fuel Company, "showing," among other things, the amount and weight of all coal in the company's bunkers on January 1, 1904, in the state of California; "showing" the total amount and weight of coal delivered from all bunkers between January 1, 1904, and August 14, 1913; "showing" the weight of each load of coal taken from all bunkers of the Western Fuel Company between January 1, 1904, and August 14, 1913; and "also showing the name of the person or persons to whom each of said loads of coal was sold or delivered, the date or dates upon which each of said loads of coal was so sold or delivered, and the amount charged to the person or persons to whom each of said loads of coal was so sold or delivered, and the amount paid for each of said loads of coal so sold or delivered."

Consolidated Mines v. Securities and Exchange Com'n, 97 F. (2d) 704 (C. C. A. 9th, 1938), where this Court upheld the validity of a subpoena issued in connection with an investigation conducted by the Securities and Exchange Commission, which directed the production of (p. 707):

> " '1. All the engineers' reports, together with covering letters, exhibits, supporting data and supplements in the possession of the company, *concerning* the McKisson, Grand Prize and/or Mineral Lode Properties in Calaveras County, California.
>
> " '2. All mining records and assay records in the possession of Consolidated Mines of California, *pertaining* to the McKisson, Grand Prize and/or Mineral Lode Properties in Calaveras County, California, for the period from January 1, 1934, to October 1, 1937,

including all sampler's books, assay certificates, assay records, sample maps, the assay and routine records of the McKisson mill, with the head assays, tail assays, concentrate assays, records of tonnage handled, plus the daily records of mill operation, smelter settlement sheets and mint returns, all reports from officers or employees at the properties, all ore reserve estimates including tonnage and grade calculations and maps relative thereto, all records of receipts and disbursements *pertaining* to any of said properties, including payroll records, material and equipment purchases, maintenance accounts and segregation records showing segregation of receipts and disbursements against development, mining, milling, selling or other costs; the general journal and general ledger of the company *concerning* said properties, all said records being for the period from January 1, 1934, to October 31, 1937.'" (Italics supplied.)

Newfield v. Ryan, 91 F. (2d) 700 (C. C. A. 5th, 1937), sustaining two subpoenas *duces tecum* issued in connection with an investigation by the Securities and Exchange Commission. One of said subpoenas required the production of (p. 701):

"'Any and all telegrams or copies thereof in your custody or control, sent or received between the dates of January 1, 1937, and March 12, 1937, by Florida Tex Oil Co., Lewis Sacker, Edmund A. Aldridge and Income Royalties, Inc., *which mention or refer or relate* to the Class A common stock of Florida Tex Oil Company or to interests in oil royalties, or oil leases in the Walker farm or tract of the Crescent pool, Oklahoma, the Fitts pool, Oklahoma, or the Jacob pool, Texas, or to any transactions or proposed transaction in any such securities, and particularly any and all telegrams or copies thereof, sent to or received from George C. Creager, Oklahoma City, or M. A. Childers, San Antonio, Texas.'" (Italics supplied.)

The second of said subpoenas required the production of (p. 701):

"'Any and all telegrams or copies thereof in your custody or control, sent or received between the dates of May 1, 1936, and March 30, 1937, by Ryan-Florida Corporation, Frank J. Ryan, Thomas J. McReynolds, Jr. and J. E. Stillman, *which mention or refer to or relate to* investment contracts or certificates of participation in profit sharing agreements, pertaining to oil royalties or interests in oil rights or leases, or to any transaction or proposed transaction in any of said securities, and pertaining particularly to oil royalties or interests in oil rights or leases in the Wilmauna Section of Hillsborough County, Florida.'" (Italics supplied.)

Appellants state in their brief (at pp. 25-26), that a subpoena "must not leave obedience to the opinion, choice or judgment of the party served * * *." Where the party served, they say, is required to produce documents "sufficient to show" a given fact, the court will be unable to determine whether its process is being flaunted or evaded. What answer could be made, they ask, to a witness' response that he examined the corporate records and found nothing which was sufficient to show a particular fact or facts.

An obvious response to the query put by appellants is that the same problem may conceivably arise in connection with the enforcement of any subpoena *duces tecum,* however limited its demands and however specific the description therein contained of the document or documents required to be produced. Judicial process requiring production of a single document, described by name, date and other identifying characteristics, might conceivably be met by a statement of the party served, impossible or impracticable in the nature of things to refute, that such document does not exist. It is normally expected that the court's process will be complied with rather than evaded.

Further, the cases cited above uniformly hold that a subpoena may properly call for documents "showing" a particular fact or facts. A witness called upon to determine whether documents "show" specified facts must necessarily determine that such documents are "sufficient to show" such facts.

Appellants' argument is therefore advanced in the face of decisions of the Supreme Court of the United States, as well as of this and other Federal appellate courts, which are directly opposed to their position.

V.

The Previous Informal Investigations Conducted by the Government Do Not in Any Way Limit the Extent of and Means Used to Make Effective a Subsequent Investigation by a Grand Jury of Possible Violations of Federal Statutes.

Apart from the general question as to whether a subpoena *duces tecum* may properly call for books and papers relating to or showing specified subject matters, appellants contend that the Government is under more than an ordinary duty to specify particularly—apparently by individual description—the books and papers which it desires to secure because of the opportunity that it previously had for examination of such books and papers in the course of prior investigations conducted by it. Appellants also contend that, because the Standard Oil Company of California furnished certain material to the Government during the course of such previous informal investigations, it should not now be required to furnish books and papers called for under the present subpoena.

In respect to appellants' contention that previous governmental investigations create a duty to describe individually each document called for in this subpoena, such contention is unworthy of any consideration unless appellants are in a position to assert that they cannot determine from the subpoena what books and papers they are required to produce. An examination of the subpoena clearly shows that there is ample specification of material called for to enable appellants to comply therewith. Indeed, this contention of appellants necessarily assumes that they have been able to ascertain from an examination of the subpoena that they have heretofore furnished or made available for inspection all or some of the documents now required to be produced before the Grand Jury. If this assumption be accepted, and appellants are hardly in a position to contend otherwise in view of the allegations made in the sworn affidavit of G. M. Foster submitted in support of the motion, the so-called burden of selecting the books and records called for by the subpoena is shown to be a mere sham and pretext. To the extent that appellants have not heretofore made available to the Government material specified in this subpoena, the Government is obviously in no position to itemize the particular documents included in such material. To the extent that appellants have heretofore made available material called for in this subpoena, there is and can be no burden cast upon them in producing such material before the Grand Jury. In the last analysis, the only consideration before the Court is whether the subpoena *duces tecum* apprises Foster with reasonable certainty of the records and documents which he is called upon to produce. That it does so is apparent from the face of the subpoena and by the assertions here advanced by appellants.

The situation in this respect is similar to that in *Brown v. United States, supra.* There a subpoena directed to an unincorporated association was attacked as unreasonable, although it appeared that the president of the association had, on a prior occasion, produced the same books and records under a subpoena directed to him as an officer rather than to the association itself. In this connection the Court said (p. 143):

> "But the form of the subpoena aside, it appears from Brown's own statement that, prior to the issue of the subpoena in question, a subpoena *duces tecum* had been directed to and served upon him personally, commanding him to produce the same documents, and

> that in answer thereto he had appeared before the grand jury with them. This is equivalent to a demonstration that the description contained in the subpoena was sufficient to enable Brown to know what particular documents were required and to select them accordingly. Having produced them once without difficulty and without undue interference with the affairs of the association, so far as appears, there is no reason why he should not produce them again in response to another subpoena identical in terms. See *Lee v. Angas,* L. R. 2 Eq. 59, 64; *Starr v. Mayer & Co.,* 60 Ga. 546, 549."

In connection with the second phase of their argument, appellants apparently contend that the production before the Grand Jury of the material called for in the subpoena is unnecessary and improper because material containing similar information has previously been furnished to Government investigators.

It is true that various types of information and documentary material have previously been submitted in connection with investigations conducted by the Federal Trade Commission and the Department of Justice over a period of approximately three years. The only allegations of fact submitted in support of the motion to quash are those contained in the affidavit of G. M. Foster [R. 26-40]. A reading of this affidavit demonstrates that there is manifest exaggeration in the statement contained at page 16 of appellants' brief that: "It is admitted that the Assistant to the Attorney General who signed the praecipe for this subpoena and his subordinates extensively examined the company's records, correspondence and accounts, and was provided with abstracts and summaries with source material indicated on each, covering practically every subject mentioned in the subpoena [R. 33-38], and that he was directed by the Attorney General to present the facts thus obtained to the Grand Jury [R. 29]."

As is indicated by Foster's affidavit [R. 29-38] two types of material were submitted during the prior investigations. The first consisted of written answers by the Standard Oil Company of California to questions propounded at various times during the conduct of such investigations; and of compilations and schedules based on, but not inclusive of, its original records. The second consisted of copies of various types of correspondence and other material in its files.

An examination of the subpoena and of Foster's affidavit readily discloses that the answers to questions and the compilations furnished in the course of the prior informal investigations relate to only some of the subjects referred to in the subpoena and even in those instances cover only a portion of the period embraced in the subpoena. Further, such answers and compilations were not made in response to any compulsory process but as a result of voluntary acquiescence by the Standard Oil Company of California in connection with such of the questions as it was willing to answer and such of the compilations as it was willing to make. Obviously, the Grand Jury is not compelled to rely upon the accuracy or completeness of information given without compulsion of legal process; and, further, it is entitled to examine the relevant original records and other documents which will furnish accurately the information desired. It matters not that the Standard Oil Company of California has in the past submitted certain documents, at its offices, for inspection by Government investigators; the Grand Jury itself is entitled to a full examination of such documents, and of all other documents which may be pertinent to its investigation. See *Brown v. United States,* 276 U. S. 134, 143 (1928). As was said by the District Court in its opinion [R. 88]: "It is claimed by the movants that material called for in the subpoenas has been already obtained in these previous contacts. Undoubtedly the grand jury is not required to accept such earlier matter and is entitled to have produced before it competent fresh evidence. Application of Texas Co., 27 F. Supp. 847."

There is nothing in Foster's affidavit to establish that it is unnecessary for the Grand Jury to examine all of the books, papers and records called for by the subpoena. Certainly, at least in the absence of any showing that the Grand Jury investigation is being conducted in bad faith, and there is not one shred of fact alleged in the affidavit to support such a showing, the Court should not assume the burden of making a detailed examination of the facts disclosed and the precise character of the evidence obtained in the course of the prior informal investigations; nor should the Government be required to reveal its reasons for selecting particular methods of presenting the evidence in preference to other methods.

Under the contention of appellants, it would be necessary in all cases of this character for the courts to examine in detail into every item of information obtained in a prior informal investigation, to review in detail the Government's plan of presentation of the evidence to the Grand Jury, and to explore in advance all of the issues which may be presented in an indictment which may be returned.

For example, Foster's affidavit shows that the great bulk of the information furnished in the prior informal investigations was in the form of statistical schedules and answers to questionnaires filled out by the Standard Oil Company of California. Apart from the question already referred to, as to whether the Grand Jury should be compelled to rely on the accuracy of information not given under legal compulsion, we need only suggest here the familiar rule that the admissions of a conspirator are not binding upon his or its co-conspirators unless shown to be declarations in furtherance of the conspiracy. This is the type of question into which the Court would have to go if it entertained the suggestion that the Grand Jury is calling for records unnecessary to its investigation.

Clearly, in the absence of any showing of bad faith, such a suggestion should not be entertained. Unless bad faith be shown, it must be assumed that the demand for the books and papers specified in the subpoena is based upon *bona fide* necessities, and that the Grand Jury and the Government are performing their functions in a lawful and proper manner.

VI.

Tested in the Light of the Foregoing Legal Principles, the Subpoena Here in Question Is Reasonable and Valid.

While the legal principles applicable in determining the validity of a subpoena *duces tecum* are clear, the application of those principles necessitates consideration of the individual facts of each case and of the clauses contained in the particular subpoena involved.

An examination of the requirements contained in each paragraph of the subpoena here in question is of particular importance in view of the fact that Foster's affidavit attacks the subpoena only in the broadest and most general terms. The affidavit states that enforcement of the subpoena will require an "indiscriminate search" [R. 39]; that much of the material required to be produced is—in the opinion of affiant— irrelevant and immaterial to the Grand Jury's inquiry [R. 26-27]; and that the "volume and extent of said records mentioned in said subpoena" is very great [R. 33].

With negligible exceptions, the affidavit fails to specify, however, the particular portion or portions of the subpoena which it is claimed would require production of voluminous quantities of documents. Apparently the notion is that a mass attack upon several paragraphs collectively enables affiant to escape the duty of specifying any unreasonable burden claimed to be imposed by any particular paragraph or subdivision thereof considered individually. No information is furnished with respect to the types of books, records and other documents of the Standard Oil Company of California which would satisfy those portions of the subpoena calling for books, records and documents showing, sufficient to show or relating to the specific subjects and subject matters enumerated.

The Government submits that a corporate officer or corporation seeking to quash a subpoena *duces tecum* issued in connection with a grand jury investigation on the ground that such subpoena would cast upon him or it an unreasonable burden, is under an obligation to show with definiteness and certainty the nature and extent of the unreasonable burden alleged. Generalizations and sweeping statements offer no adequate substitute for such a showing. For these reasons, the affidavit can be of little or no assistance in determining the reasonableness of the subpoena under consideration. Such determination must therefore be predicated principally, if not exclusively, upon the terms of the subpoena itself, in addition to facts concerning the petroleum industry of which the Court may take judicial notice.

Paragraph One of the subpoena [R. 3] requires production of the articles of incorporation and the certificate of incorporation, with amendments thereto, of the Standard Oil Company of California. Appellants apparently concede that this paragraph is neither indefinite, uncertain, nor otherwise open to objection, since it is not attacked in their brief. In appellants' motion papers it was suggested only that the Government should obtain copies of the articles and certificate of incorporation, presumably by a subpoena *duces tecum,* from the Secretary of State of California or from some county office of the State where such copies might be on file [R. 24, 31], rather than from the corporation itself or an officer thereof. The Government is unaware of any principle of law which requires it, in a grand jury proceeding, to select a particular one of several possible sources from which desired documents may be obtained by subpoena.

Paragraph Two [R. 3] requires the production of "books and records which show the names of all the officers and directors of the corporation" and their residence addresses from January 1, 1935 to date. The names and addresses of those who have been responsible for corporate acts under investigation are unquestionably pertinent to the Grand Jury's inquiry. Appellants contend, however, that this paragraph will require the production of *every* book and record which contains any mention by name of any one of the officers or directors during the period mentioned. Such construction of the paragraph, it is submitted, is strained and unnatural. In other portions of the subpoena, where *all* books and records showing or relating to certain subject matters were considered necessary, the subpoena expressly calls for *all* books and records [R. 3, 4, 7, 9, 10, 11, 17, 18]. In Paragraph Two, the word "all" is omitted. A reading of the paragraph is sufficient to indicate that what the Grand Jury desires are the names and residence addresses of the officers and directors during the period stated, and that any book, record or other document containing the desired information will suffice to comply with the terms of the paragraph.

Paragraph Three [R. 3] requires the production of books containing the minutes of meetings of stockholders, directors, and committees, also from January 1, 1935 to date. Appellants do not contend that this paragraph is uncertain in its requirements. They attack it solely on the ground that the minutes of meetings of a large number of committees will be required. The number of committees of a particular corporation presumably varies more or less in direct proportion to its size. The size of a given corporation or the volume of records in which that size has resulted can play no part in determining the reasonableness of a requirement that certain of its records be produced. That to require production of a corporation's minute books is not unreasonable was specifically held in *Norcross v. United States,* 209 Fed. 13 (C. C. A. 9th, 1913).

Paragraph Four [R. 4] requires the production of the annual, quarterly and other periodic reports made by the corporation to its stockholders from January 1, 1935 to date. Such reports are obviously relevant to the inquiry. Among other things they bear on the size of the corporation and the degree of economic control which it is in a position to exercise, questions of vital import in any investigation under the Sherman Antitrust Act. As this paragraph is not attacked in appellants' brief, nor specified in any of the questions listed by them as involved in the appeal, they presumably concede its reasonableness and validity.

Paragraph Five [R. 4] requires the production of copies of monthly reports made by the Standard Oil Company of California to the United States Bureau of Mines. This paragraph, also, has not been attacked by appellants in their brief, nor specified in connection with the questions stated by them to be involved on the appeal. It may be noted that production is required only in connection with reports which have been made by the Standard Oil Company of California to the Bureau of Mines since January 1, 1938, copies for the period January 1, 1935 to January 1, 1938 having previously been furnished [R.

32]. This fact clearly shows that in drawing the present subpoena, every effort was made to avoid duplicating material already furnished where it was possible to do so.

Paragraph Six [R. 4-7] requires the production of such of the books, records, accounts and memoranda regularly kept by the corporation in the regular course of its business as are sufficient to show specified matters concerning, among other things, the production, sales, and assets of the corporation in the Pacific Coast territory from January 1, 1935 to date; and also the interests of the corporation in other corporations or firms which are a part of the petroleum industry, and its contributions and payments to associations of retailers or refiners of gasoline. In view of the importance in Sherman Antitrust Act investigations of economic facts concerning the industry involved and its members, particularly with reference to the economic position in the industry of each such member, the relevancy to the inquiry of the matters specified is apparent. This paragraph is attacked by appellants on the ground that a subpoena cannot validly require the person on whom it is served to select books, records and documents which are "sufficient to show" specifically enumerated subject matters. As previously shown, appellants' contention in respect to this paragraph is directly contrary to the decisions in such cases as *Consolidated Rendering Co. v. Vermont,* 207 U. S. 541 (1908), *Nelson v. United States,* 201 U. S. 92, 99-100 (1908), *Norcross v. United States,* 209 Fed. 13, 15-17 (C. C. A. 9th, 1913), and other cases hereinbefore cited.

In addition, appellee desires to point out that the language used in this and other paragraphs of the subpoena was chosen for the very purpose of requiring production of as few records as possible. Formerly it would have been necessary, in order to obtain legally competent and admissible evidence concerning the various subject matters involved, to call for books of original entry or books containing first permanent entries in respect to the matters specified. See *Greenbaum v. United States,* 98 F. (2d) 574 (C. C. A. 9th, 1938). By the terms of 28 U. S. C. A., section 695 (49 Stat. 1561), it is provided, however:

> "In any court of the United States and in any court established by Act of Congress, any writing or record, whether in the form of an entry in a book or otherwise, made as a memorandum or record of any act, transaction, occurrence, or event, shall be admissible as evidence of said act, transaction, occurrence, or event, if it shall appear that it was made in the regular course of any business, and that it was the regular course of such business to make such memorandum or record at the time of such act, transaction, occurrence, or event or within a reasonable time thereafter. All other circumstances of the making of such writing or record, including lack of personal knowledge by the entrant or maker, may be shown to affect its weight, but they shall not affect its admissibility. The term 'business' shall include business, profession, occupation, and calling of every kind."

Paragraph Six and other paragraphs [R. 18, 19] of the subpoena were drafted in the light of the foregoing statute for the express purpose of dispensing with the production of the books of original entry or books containing first permanent entries wherever possible. For example, subsection (a) of Paragraph Six requires the production of such of the books, records, accounts, and memoranda as are sufficient to show the quantity of crude oil produced in California by the corporation, its subsidiaries and affiliates, monthly from January 1, 1935 to date. If the corporation regularly keeps in the course of its business a monthly record showing the quantity of crude oil produced, production of such records suffices in compliance with this subsection of the subpoena, without the necessity of producing the books, papers and memoranda from which such records were compiled. Wherever possible the subpoena calls only for such books and records as show or are sufficient to show the facts and matters in respect to which evidence is necessary. Where this has not been possible, the subpoena requires production of all books, records, and papers which show the necessary information. Appellants, with no apparent consistency, attack the first type of requirement on the ground that the Government's effort to limit that which is to be produced results in indefiniteness, while attacking the second type of requirement as being too broad.

Paragraph Seven [R. 7-9] requires the production of books, records, contracts, and invoices showing purchases from January 1, 1935 to date of gasoline physically located within the Pacific Coast territory at the time of delivery, by the corporation, its subsidiaries and affiliates. Here again, relevancy to the inquiry of the matter sought is hardly open to dispute. It is necessary only to suggest the effect of purchases in aid of any possible monopoly or conspiracy in restraint of trade which is the subject matter of this investigation. The basis of appellants' attack on this paragraph is, again, that a subpoena may not validly call for books and papers "showing" or "disclosing specifically information with respect to" enumerated and described subjects and subject matters. That appellants' position is fundamentally unsound is demonstrated by a reading of the *Nelson, Consolidated Rendering Co., Norcross* and other cases cited *supra.*

Paragraph Eight [R. 9-10] requires the production of books, records, contracts and invoices showing sales of gasoline by the corporation, its subsidiaries and affiliates, to several named corporations. What has been said regarding Paragraph Seven is equally applicable here. This paragraph, moreover, furnishes another illustration of the effort made to limit the amount of material called for wherever possible, in that: (1) No material is called for under this paragraph prior to January 1, 1938; and (2) individual sales of less than three thousand gallons are excluded.

Paragraph Nine [R. 10-11] requires the production of books, records, contracts and invoices showing sales made by the corporation, its subsidiaries and affiliates, from April 1, 1936 to date, of gasoline physically within the Pacific Coast territory at or prior to delivery, at or below certain specified prices. The relevancy of this material is not and cannot be seriously disputed. The description of the material called for is specific, and there can be no reasonable ground for doubt as to that which is required to be produced. Appellants attack the validity of this paragraph on grounds similar to those already stated and discussed in connection with Paragraphs Seven and Eight.

Paragraph Ten [R. 11-17] requires the production of original letters, telegrams, teletype messages, contracts, reports, memoranda or copies thereof, made, written, sent, or received from January 1, 1935 to date, relating to certain specified subject matters which are patently relevant and material to the Grand Jury's investigation. This paragraph is attacked on the ground that production "cannot be based upon any description in this clause, but must be predicated upon the witness' interpretation of the documents examined" (Appellants' Brief p. 21). The objection goes to the validity of a call for documents which "relate to" specifically enumerated subject matters. That such a call is reasonable and valid was expressly held by the Supreme Court of the United States in *Brown v. United States,* 276 U. S. 134, 138-139 (1928). It is of course true that, since the Standard Oil Company of California presumably is larger than was the association involved in *Brown v. United States,* the volume of correspondence required to be produced may be greater. However, the size of the corporation concerned can play no part in determining whether the call contained in the subpoena is reasonable and valid.

Paragraph Eleven [R. 17] requires the production of original price lists, records, and other documents showing the prices posted from January 1, 1935 to date by the corporation in various cities located in the Pacific Coast area. This paragraph is not open to attack on the ground either of irrelevancy or indefiniteness. Appellants apparently concede its validity, since it is not mentioned in their brief in connection with any of the questions stated to be involved in this appeal.

Paragraph Twelve [R. 17-18] of the subpoena requires the production of letters, memoranda, reports, surveys, compilations, summaries, analyses, and estimates passing between the Standard Oil Company of California and the Independent Refiners' Association of California, Inc., their officers, directors and employees, from January 1, 1936 to date, relating to production, prices, sales, purchases or consumption of gasoline in the Pacific Coast territory. What has been said in discussing Paragraph Ten of the subpoena, with respect to the validity of a call for documents "relating to" specifically enumerated subject matters, is equally applicable in connection with Paragraph Twelve. Curiously enough, although appellants attack the validity of Paragraph Ten they apparently concede the validity of Paragraph Twelve since it, too, is not mentioned in their brief as having any relation to the questions involved in this appeal.

Paragraph Thirteen [R. 18] of the subpoena requires production of such books, records, accounts and memoranda regularly kept by the corporation in the regular course of its business as are sufficient to show the names and addresses of persons employed by it as salesmen or as supervisors of sales forces in the Pacific Coast territory from January 1, 1936 to date. As previously stated, the Grand Jury's investigation is concerned with possible restraints of trade in connection with the marketing of gasoline and other petroleum products. The requirement in this paragraph of the subpoena is obviously for the purpose of enabling the Grand Jury to identify the personnel of the Standard Oil Company of California who have actually carried out the marketing practices under investigation. Appellants do not and cannot seriously dispute the right of the Grand Jury to obtain such material, nor can they, in view of the narrowly defined subject matter of this paragraph, claim either that they do not know what the Grand Jury wants or that this requirement is unreasonable. The only ground upon which appellants attack this paragraph is in connection with the use of the words "sufficient to show," a question which has already been fully discussed.

Paragraph Fourteen [R. 18-19] requires production of all contracts or agreements, in effect at any time from January 1, 1935 to date, together with correspondence and memoranda relating thereto, made, written, sent or received by the Standard Oil Company of California, with reference to the sale or consignment of gasoline by the Standard Oil Company of California to the Signal Oil Company, or to the marketing or sale of gasoline in the Pacific Coast territory by the Signal Oil Company; and such of the books, records, accounts and memoranda regularly kept by the Standard Oil Company in the course of its business as are sufficient to show the monthly quantities of gasoline sold or delivered by it, or by its subsidiaries and affiliates, to the Signal Oil Company from January 1, 1935 to date. It is not contended by appellants that this paragraph of the subpoena calls for material which is irrelevant to the Grand Jury's investigation. Their objection goes, again, solely to the use of the words "sufficient to show" in subsection (b) of this paragraph.

Reply to Appellants' Comments on the Opinion of the District Court.

Appellants state in their brief, at page 39, that the District Court "conceded" that the subpoena "requires the production of a great mass of material. It imposes a severe burden." It may not be amiss, however, to add the following sentence of the Court's opinion: "This is unavoidable, by reason of the magnitude of the enterprises that are the subject of the investigation and the ramifications and complexities of detail that normally occur in the operation of great industrial concerns" [R. 86].

The statement of appellants, in their brief at page 39, that the District Court "apparently believed that objection to a subpoena *duces tecum* should be deferred pending operation of the process" finds no basis or support in any part of the Court's opinion. On the contrary, the Court considered the objections to the subpoena interposed by appellants and, overruling them, sustained the subpoena *in toto*.

Appellants also take exception to the mention made in the District Court's opinion of a statement by counsel for the Government during the argument that some forty additional subpoenas substantially similar in form were not challenged, but instead had been complied with by those to whom they were addressed. It is, of course, hardly necessary to point out that the subpoenas in question were on file with the clerk of the District Court and, as the Court's own process, could be judicially noticed by the Court.

There is a suggestion in appellants' brief that the District Court assumed in its opinion knowledge on the part of appellants concerning a magazine article written by an Assistant Attorney General of the United States, which magazine article, appellants say, formed a partial basis for the District Court's conclusion (Appellants' Brief, pp. 39-40). A reading of the District Court's opinion indicates clearly that the Court cited the article in question only as indicative of the policy of the Government in its enforcement of the Sherman Antitrust Act to make public announcement of contemplated cases or investigations; it neither imputed knowledge of such article to appellants nor based its decision upon anything which the article contained. It did, in discussing the materiality of the documents called for by the subpoena, consider that the contents of a press release issued by the Department of Justice as a preliminary to the present investigation were known to appellants. That the District Court's assumption of appellants' familiarity with the contents of the press release was not without basis is sufficiently indicated by the fact that such release was quoted in Foster's affidavit [R. 28, 29], and in appellants' memorandum of points and authorities [R. 59].

Conclusion.

An investigation under the Sherman Antitrust Act of an industry as large as the petroleum industry necessarily requires analysis of a voluminous amount of statistical and other information. Of necessity, subpoenas cannot possibly specify individually every document that is required, and it is this fact which undoubtedly led to the decision in *Brown v. United States, supra,* and like cases. Undue limitation on the rights of the Government in this respect, and in respect also to the quantity of documents and records which may be required to be produced, would necessarily result in making difficult, if not impossible, the proper enforcement of the antitrust laws in the public interest.

The judgment of the District Court should be affirmed.

Respectfully submitted,

Joseph E. Brill,
M. S. Huberman,
Henry McClernan,
Robert H. Marquis,
Laurence P. Sherfy,
Charles S. Burdell,
A. Andrew Hauk,
Special Assistants to the Attorney General,

Attorneys for Appellee.

No. 9289

United States

Circuit Court of Appeals

For the Ninth Circuit.

CARROLL HENDERSON, as Receiver of the Reno National Bank, Reno, Nevada, a national banking association, organized and existing under the laws of the United States of America,

Appellant,

vs.

CARROLL HENDERSON, as Receiver of the First National Bank of Winnemucca, Nevada, a national banking association, organized and existing under the laws of the United States of America,

Appellee.

Transcript of Record

Upon Appeal from the District Court of the United States for the District of Nevada.

No. 9289

United States

Circuit Court of Appeals

For the Ninth Circuit.

CARROLL HENDERSON, as Receiver of the Reno National Bank, Reno, Nevada, a national banking association, organized and existing under the laws of the United States of America,

Appellant,

vs.

CARROLL HENDERSON, as Receiver of the First National Bank of Winnemucca, Nevada, a national banking association, organized and existing under the laws of the United States of America,

Appellee.

Transcript of Record

Upon Appeal from the District Court of the United States for the District of Nevada.

INDEX

[Clerk's Note: When deemed likely to be of an important nature. errors or doubtful matters appearing in the original certified record are printed literally in italic; and, likewise, cancelled matter appearing in the original certified record is printed and cancelled herein accordingly. When possible, an omission from the text is indicated by printing in italic the two words between which the omission seems to occur.]

Pages

Accounting by receiver of the Reno National Bank 81

Amended judgment 93

Answer 16

Exhibit to answer:

A—Subordination agreement 32

Appeal:

Designation of contents of record on (District Court) 96

Notice of 94

Statement of points on 221

Telegram authorizing 95

Certificate of clerk, United States District Court 99

Conclusions of law 58

Conclusions of law, defendant's proposed 74

Decree 59

Decision, memorandum and orders 44

Findings of fact and conclusions of law 49

Index **Page**

Findings of fact and conclusions of law, defendant's proposed 68

Exhibit to findings of fact and conclusions of law:

A—Subordination agreement 76

Findings of fact and conclusions of law, defendant's objections to plaintiff's 63

Judgment 83

Judgment, amended 93

Judgment, defendant's proposed 80

Names and addresses of attorneys of record 1

Notice of appeal 94

Reply 36

Statement of points on appeal 221

Stipulation for corrected judgment 85

Telegram for general council, bureau of comptroller of the currency to receiver of Reno National Bank authorizing appeal 95

Testimony 101

Exhibits for defendant:

A—Statement of total loss 206

B—Subordination agreement 32

Exhibits for plaintiff:

1—Statement of pro rata distribution 160

2—Letter from Receiver of First National Bank of Winnemucca to comptroller of the currency 172

Index Page

Exhibits for defendant: (cont.)
3—Letter from deputy comptroller to board of directors, First National Bank of Winnemucca 174
4—Deposition of J. G. Moore 176
Exhibit A—Letter dated October 11, 1932 to J. G. Moore from J. Sheehan 198

Witnesses for defendant:
Butler, Walter E.
—direct 200
—cross 207
Tobin, W. J.
—direct 207
—cross 213

Witnesses for plaintiff:
Henderson, Carroll
—direct 153
Moore, J. G. (Deposition)
—direct 178
—cross 195
Nelson, P. L.
—direct 139
—cross 145
Sheehan, John
—direct 101
—cross 125
—redirect 135
—recross 136

NAMES AND ADDRESSES OF ATTORNEYS OF RECORD:

N. J. BARRY, ESQ.,
Reno, Nevada,
For the Defendant and Appellant.

THOS. J. SALTER, ESQ.,
Winnemucca, Nevada,
For the Plaintiff and Appellee. [1*]

In the District Court of the United States of America, in and for the District of Nevada

No. H-207

CARROLL HENDERSON, as Receiver of the First National Bank of Winnemucca, Nevada, a national banking association, organized and existing under the laws of the United States of America,

Plaintiff,

vs.

W. J. TOBIN, as Receiver of the Reno National Bank, Reno, Nevada, a national banking association, organized and existing under the laws of the United States of America,

Defendant.

COMPLAINT

Plaintiff complains of the defendant, and for cause of action alleges:

*Page numbering appearing at the foot of page of original certified Transcript of Record.

I.

That on or about the 9th day of December, 1932, The First National Bank of Winnemucca, Nevada, being then and there a banking corporation duly organized and existing under the banking laws of the United States of America, and having its office and principal place of business at Winnemucca, Nevada, suspended by resolution of its Board of Directors, and the Comptroller of the Currency of the United States of America, being satisfied of the insolvency of said bank, appointed a receiver thereof; that on or about the 2nd day of March, 1937, Carroll Henderson was duly appointed as receiver thereof, thereupon qualified as such Receiver, and ever since has been and now is the duly appointed, qualified and acting Receiver of said Bank. [2]

II.

That on or about the 9th day of December, 1932, The Reno National Bank, Reno, Nevada, being then and there a banking corporation duly organized and existing under the banking laws of the United States of America, and having its office and principal place of business at Reno, Nevada, suspended by resolution of its Board of Directors, and the Comptroller of the Currency of the United States of America, being satisfied of the insolvency of said bank, appointed a receiver thereof; that on or about the 9th day of December, 1932, W. J. Tobin was duly appointed as Receiver thereof, thereupon qualified as such Receiver, and ever since has been and now is the duly appointed, qualified and acting Receiver of said bank.

III.

That for many years prior to June 30, 1932, Geo. Wingfield, was the President, and J. Sheehan the Vice President of The First National Bank of Winnemucca, Nevada, plaintiff herein, and were respectively President and Vice President of The Reno National Bank, Reno, Nevada, defendant herein, and that both of said banks were subject to their control as such President and Vice President.

IV.

That prior to said June 30, 1932, The First National Bank of Winnemucca, Nevada, was the owner and holder of certain notes, which said notes were secured by mortgages, and which mortgages are described as follows:

Chattel Mortgage dated May 12, 1930, between Saturnino Alcorta and Justa Alcorta, of town of McDermitt, County of Humboldt, State of Nevada, as Mortgagors, and The First National Bank of Winnemucca, Nevada, Mortgagee, said mortgage securing an indebtedness of $7,250, plus interest; Recorded in Book I, page 30 of Chattel Mortgages, records of Humboldt County, Nevada.

Chattel Mortgage dated October 24, 1929, between Alex Dufurrena, Manuel Begino, Frank Laurnaga, Pierre Ahuntcain and Fortunato Arbeloa, co-partners, doing business under the firm name and style of Alex Dufurrena & Co., all of Humboldt County,

Nevada, as Mortgagors; and The First National Bank of Winnemucca, Nevada, as Mort- [3] gagee; said mortgage securing an indebtedness of $47,-500.00, plus interest; recorded in Book H of Chattel Mortgages, Page 585, Records of Humboldt County, Nevada.

Chattel Mortgage dated August 23, 1928, executed by W. A. Johnstone and Minnie A. Johnstone, his wife, both of Humboldt County, Nevada, as Mortgagors, to The First National Bank of Winnemucca, Nevada, as Mortgagee, drawn to secure an indebtedness of $32,500.00; recorded in Book H of Chattel Mortgages, Page 531, records of Humboldt County, Nevada.

Chattel Mortgage dated October 15, 1930, executed by Joe Larribeau, Gregorio Ocamica and Frank Amuchastegui, co-partners, all of the town of McDermitt, County of Humboldt, State of Nevada, as Mortgagors; to The First National Bank of Winnemucca, Nevada, as Mortgagee; said mortgage drawn to secure an indebtedness of $60,000.00, plus interest; recorded in Book I, page 53, Chattel Mortgages, records of Humboldt County, Nevada.

Chattel Mortgage dated March 5, 1932, between Joe Yragui, of Twin Falls, County of Twin Falls, State of Idaho, as Mortgagor, and The First National Bank of Winnemucca, Nevada, Mortgagee, securing an indebtedness of $52,500.00, plus interest, recorded in County of Twin Falls, State of Idaho, on March 5, 1932.

Real and Chattel Mortgage dated September 4, 1929, executed by Daniel Gabica, Constantina Gabica, his wife, Frank Gabica and Marsellina Gabica, his wife, and Gabica Brothers, a co-partnership, of Humboldt County, Nevada, as Mortgagors, to The First National Bank of Winnemucca, Nevada, as Mortgagee; said mortgage drawn to secure an indebtedness of $85,000.00; plus interest; recorded in Book I of Real and Chattel Mortgages, page 325, Records of Humboldt County, Nevada.

Real Mortgage dated September 12, 1930, executed by Juan Jaca, Ramona Jaca, his wife, Silbestre Jaca and Florentina Jaca, his wife, of Humboldt County, State of Nevada, as Mortgagors, to The First National Bank of Winnemucca, Nevada, as Mortgagee; said mortgage drawn to secure an indebtedness of $151,000.00, plus interest; recorded in Book N of Real Mortgages, page 307, records of Humboldt County, Nevada.

Also, Chattel Mortgage dated September 12, 1930, executed by Juan Jaca, Ramona Jaca, his wife, Silbestre Jaca and Florentina Jaca, his wife, of Humboldt County, State of Nevada, as Mortgagors, to The First National Bank of Winnemucca, Nevada, as Mortgagee; said mortgage drawn to secure an indebtedness of $151,000.00, plus interest; recorded in Book I of Chattel Mortgages, page 45, records of Humboldt County, Nevada.

Chattel Mortgage dated August 13, 1928, executed by Juan Belaustgui & Co., John Belaustgui, Antonio Beabe and Martina Belaustgui, of Lander County,

Nevada, as Mortgagors, to The First National Bank of Winnemucca, Nevada, as Mortgagee, said Mortgage drawn to secure an indebtedness of $31,000.83, plus interest, recorded in office of County Recorder, Lander County, Nevada. [4]

Migratory Chattel Mortgage dated April 29, 1936, executed by Alex Dufurrena, Manuel Begino, Frank Laurnaga, Pete Bidaurreta, and Fortunato Arbeloa, doing business under the firm name and style of Alex Dufurrena and Company; Alex Dufurrena as a co-partner of said firm and individually; and Julia Dufurrena, his wife; Manuel Begino, as a co-partner of said firm and individually, and Clarice Begino, his wife; Frank Laurnaga, as a co-partner of said firm and individually; Pete Bidaurreta as a co-partner and individually, and Fortunato Arbeloa, as a co-partner and individually, all as Mortgagors, and The Reno National Bank, in liquidation, Reno, Nevada, and The First National Bank of Winnemucca, Nevada, as Mortgagees; said Mortgage recorded in the office of the County Recorder of Humboldt County, Nevada, on May 1, 1936; said mortgage securing an indebtedness of $45,369.32, plus interest.

V.

That on or about June 30, 1932, at the direction of J. Sheehan, Vice President aforesaid, The First National Bank of Winnemucca, Nevada, sold, assigned, and delivered to The Reno National Bank, Reno, Nevada, all of the notes and mortgages above described.

VI.

That at the time the said notes and mortgages were so sold, assigned and delivered to the said Reno National Bank, and for many years prior thereto it was, and had been, the custom, usage, agreement and understanding between The First National Bank of Winnemucca, Nevada, and The Reno National Bank, and the officials thereof, that for the purpose of protecting the assets covered by the security so sold, that from time to time The First National Bank of Winnemucca, Nevada, would advance to the debtors named in said notes and mortgages, certain sums of money, and take from said debtors a note or notes for such advances, or in lieu of said notes, charge the same against the account of said debtors in the nature of an overdraft or overdrafts.

That such advances or overdrafts were to be secured by the mortgages hereinabove mentioned in pursuance to the provisions contained in each of said mortgages that any future loans or advances to the debtors would be covered by the said mortgages;

That from time to time within six years last past and prior [5] to suspension of said banks pursuant to said custom, usage, agreement and understanding between The First National Bank of Winnemucca, Nevada, and The Reno National Bank, Reno, Nevada, The First National Bank of Winnemucca, Nevada, did make certain advances to the debtors herein mentioned and took notes for the same or charged the same against the said debtors' accounts as overdrafts, in the amounts as follows, to-wit:

Note dated July 14, 1932, Saturnino Alcorta and Justo Alcorta, Balance Due	1,273.14	
Overdraft dated October 14, 1932 to November 25, 1932, Balance Due	507.09	
Total		1,7
Note dated January 18, 1932, Alex Duferrena Co. Sheep Account, Balance Due	3,500.00	
Note dated July 14, 1932, Alex Dufurrena Co. Sheep Account, Manuel Begino, Balance Due	500.00	
Overdraft dated August 22, 1932, to November 25, 1932, Balance Due	1,576.42	
Total		5,5
Note dated July 13, 1932, Gabica Brothers, Daniel Gabica, Balance Due	2,198.84	2,1
Note dated July 27, 1932, Juan Jaca, Ramona Jaca, Silbestre Jaca, & Florentina Jaca, Balance Due	2,967.29	
Overdraft dated September 25, 1932, to November 25, 1932, Balance Due	2,538.34	
Total		5,5
Note dated July 27, 1932, W. A. Johnstone and Minnie A. Johnstone, Balance Due	999.33	
Overdraft dated September 9, 1932, to November 25, 1932, Balance Due	494.95	
Total		1,4
Note dated September 6, 1932, Joe Larribeau Company, Gregorio Ocamica	1,000.00	
Overdraft dated October 20, 1932, to November 25, 1932, Balance Due	1,536.89	
Total		2,5
Note dated July 27, 1932, Joe Yragui, Balance Due	1,914.08	1,9
Overdraft dated October 12, 1932, to November 25, 1932, Juan Belaustegui Co., Balance Due	58.10	5

VII.

That as each advance was made by The First National Bank of Winnemucca, Nevada, to the said debtors, as hereinabove listed, The Reno National Bank, Reno, Nevada, was duly notified by The First National Bank of Winnemucca, Nevada, of the date and amount of such advances.

VIII.

That the defendant herein as Receiver of The Reno National Bank, Reno, Nevada, has from time to time liquidated the indebtedness of the debtors herein listed, either in whole or in part, and has collected such assets and appropriated the same to the use of his trust;

That although demand has been made for an accounting of such assets and collections, and that the defendant herein pay over to plaintiff his pro rata of such assets and collections, the defendant has failed and refused to make such accounting or to pay over to the plaintiff herein the sums representing the plaintiff's pro rata so due from defendant to plaintiff.

IX.

That there is now due, owing and unpaid from defendant to plaintiff the sums as hereinabove mentioned, representing said amounts due on said balances, or the pro rata thereof based on the total amount of the indebtedness represented by the said notes and mortgages as the said advances bear to the total thereof.

For a Second Cause of Action the Plaintiff realleges the matters and things set forth in Paragraphs I, II and III, of his [7] Complaint herein, and asks that the same be treated as though realleged herein in haec verba.

X.

That on or about March 12, 1932, John G. Taylor, Inc., a corporation organized under the laws of the State of Wyoming, executed a note in favor of The Reno National Bank, Reno, Nevada, in the sum of $700,000.00 with interest, and to secure said note executed a chattel mortgage to The Reno National Bank, Reno, Nevada, which said mortgage was recorded in Book I of Chattel Mortgages, page 214, Records of Humboldt County, Nevada.

XI.

That the time the said note and mortgage were so executed and for many years prior thereof it was, and had been the custom, usage, agreement and understanding between The First National Bank of Winnemucca, Nevada, and The Reno National Bank, Reno, Nevada, and its officials, that for the purpose of protecting the assets covered by the security held by said Reno National Bank that from time to time The First National Bank of Winnemucca, Nevada, would advance to the debtor named in said note and mortgage certain sums of money and take from said debtor a note or notes for such advances, or in lieu of said notes charge the same against the account of said debtor in the nature of an overdraft or overdrafts;

That such advances or overdrafts were to be secured by the mortgage hereinabove mentioned in pursuance to the provision contained therein, that any future loans or advances would be covered by the said mortgage.

That from time to time within six years last past, and prior to the suspension of said banks pursuant to said custom, usage, agreement and understanding, between The First National Bank of Winnemucca, Nevada, and The Reno National Bank, Reno, Nevada, The First [8] National Bank of Winnemucca, Nevada, did make certain advances to the debtor, took notes for the same or charged the same against the said debtor's accounts as overdrafts, in the amounts as follows, to-wit:

Note dated September 16, 1932, John G. Taylor Inc., Balance Due	25,000.00	
Note dated September 29, 1932, John G. Taylor Inc., Balance Due	5,000.00	
Overdraft dated October 5, 1932, to November 25, 1932, Balance Due	15,142.18	
Total		45,142.18

XII.

That as each advance was made by The First National Bank of Winnemucca, Nevada, to the said debtor, as hereinabove listed, The Reno National Bank, Reno, Nevada, was duly notified by The First National Bank of Winnemucca, Nevada, of the date and amount of such advances.

XIII.

That the defendant herein, as Receiver of The Reno National Bank, Reno, Nevada, has from time to time liquidated the said indebtedness, either in whole or in part, and has collected such assets and appropriated the same to the use of his trust;

That although demand has been made for an accounting of such assets and collections, and that the defendant herein pay over to plaintiff his pro rata of such assets and collections, the defendant has failed and refused to make such accounting or to pay over to the plaintiff herein the sums representing the plaintiff's pro rata so due from the defendant to plaintiff.

XIV.

That there is now due, owing and unpaid from defendant to plaintiff the sums as hereinabove mentioned, representing amounts due on said balances, or the pro rata thereof based on the total amount of the indebtedness represented by the said note and mortgage as the said advances bear to the total thereof. [9]

For a Third Cause of Action the Plaintiff realleges the matters and things set forth in paragraph I, II, and II of his Complaint herein, and asks that the same be treated as though realleged herein in haec verba.

XV.

That on or about March 24, 1931, St. John Laborde and Michel Cadet, co-partners, doing business under the firm name and style of Laborde Brothers & Company, County of Lander, State of Nevada, executed notes, one in the sum of $42,000.00, and one in the sum of $28,000.00, and to secure said notes executed a real and chattel mortgage to The Reno National Bank, Reno, Nevada, which said mortgage was recorded in Book I of Real and Chattel Mortgages, page 234, records of Lander County, Nevada.

XVI.

That thereafter the Reno National Bank, Reno, Nevada, sold, assigned and delivered to The First National Bank of Winnemucca, Nevada, the note in the sum of $28,000.00, executed by the above named parties, and secured by the said mortgage, for which the said First National Bank of Winnemucca, Nevada, paid to The Reno National Bank, Reno, Nevada, the sum of $28,000.00.

XVII.

That at the time the said note of $28,000.00 was so purchased by The First National Bank of Winnemucca, Nevada, and for many years prior thereto it was and had been the custom, usage, agreement and understanding between The First National Bank of Winnemucca, Nevada, and The Reno National Bank, Reno, Nevada, and its officials, that for the purpose of protecting the assets covered by the security so sold that any notes sold by The Reno National Bank to The First National Bank of Winnemucca, Nevada, were to be secured by any mortgages given as security for the said notes. [10]

XVIII.

That The Reno National Bank, through the defendant herein, as such Receiver, has liquidated the indebtedness covered by the said mortgage of the said debtors, and has collected the assets therefrom and appropriated the same to the use of his trust;

That although demand has been made for an accounting of such assets and collections, and that the defendant herein pay over to plaintiff his pro rata of such assets and collections, the defendant has failed and refused to make such accounting or to pay over to the plaintiff herein the sum representing the plaintiff's pro rata so due from defendant to plaintiff on account of said indebtedness.

XIX.

That there is now due, owing and unpaid from defendant to plaintiff the sum of $27,102.98, together with overdraft in the sum of $3,612.49, with interest, representing balance due on said balances, or the pro rata thereof based on the total amount of the indebtedness represented by the said notes and mortgage as the said sum of $30,715.47 bears to the total thereof.

XX.

That all of the assets in this Complaint mentioned came into the possession of plaintiff, as such Receiver, as assets of The First National Bank of Winnemucca, Nevada, and that plaintiff is now the legal owner and holder thereof.

Wherefore Plaintiff Prays:

1. That the defendant herein be ordered to render unto plaintiff a full, true and correct accounting of all sums collected and assets reduced on account of each of the mortgages and notes set forth in Paragraph IV of this Complaint. [11]

2. That defendant herein be ordered to render unto plaintiff a full, true and correct accounting of all sums collected and assets reduced on account of the note and mortgage mentioned in paragraph X of this complaint.

3. That defendant herein be ordered to render unto plaintiff a full, true and correct accounting of all sums collected and assets reduced on account of the note and mortgage mentioned in paragraph XV of this complaint.

4. That plaintiff have Judgment against the defendant for his pro rata of the sums collected by plaintiff and the interest thereon, on account of the several causes of action herein set forth as such sums so found to be due bear to the total indebtedness of the various debtors herein set forth.

5. For costs of suit and for such other and further relief as to the Court may seem equitable.

THOS. J. SALTER,

Attorney for Plaintiff.

State of Nevada,
County of Humboldt—ss.

Carroll Henderson, being first duly sworn, deposes and says:

That he is the plaintiff in the above entitled action; that he has read the above and foregoing Complaint and knows the contents thereof, that the same is true of his own knowledge, except as to those matters which are therein stated on his information and belief, and as to those matters he believes it to be true.

CARROLL HENDERSON.

Subscribed and sworn to before me this 22nd day of June, 1938.

[Seal] THOS. J. SALTER,
Notary Public.

[Endorsed]: Filed June 24, 1938. [12]

[Title of District Court and Cause.]

ANSWER

Now comes the defendant above named, and answering plaintiff's complaint on file herein, admits, alleges and denies as follows:

I.

Answering Paragraph VI of the first count of said complaint defendant alleges that he has not sufficient knowledge or information upon which to base a belief, and basing his denial upon that ground, denies generally and specifically each and every allegation of said paragraph. [13]

II.

Answering Paragraph VII of the first count of said complaint, defendant alleges that he has not sufficient knowledge or information upon which to base a belief, and basing his denial upon that ground, denies generally and specifically each and every allegation contained in said Paragraph.

III.

Answering Paragraph VIII of the first count of said complaint, defendant denies that as Receiver of The Reno National Bank, Reno, Nevada, or otherwise, he has from time to time or at all liquidated the said indebtedness either in whole or in part and has, or has, collected such assets and appropriated, or appropriated the same to the use of his trust.

Further answering said paragraph, defendant denies that plaintiff has any pro rata of such assets and collections, or assets, or collections, or that defendant has failed and refused, or failed or refused, to make accounting or pay over to plaintiff any sums of money due from defendant to plaintiff.

IV.

Answering Paragraph IX of the first count of said complaint, defendant denies that there is now due, owing and unpaid, or due, or owing, or unpaid from defendant to plaintiff the sums as theretofore in said count mentioned, or any sums representing said amounts due on said balances or otherwise, or the pro rata thereof based on the total amount of the indebtedness represented by said notes and mortgages as the said advances bear to the total thereof or otherwise.

V.

Answering Paragraph XI of the second count of said complaint, defendant alleges that he has not sufficient knowledge or infor- [14] mation upon which to base a belief, and basing his denial upon such ground, denies generally and specifically each and every allegation in said paragraph XI contained.

VI.

Answering Paragraph XII of the second count of said complaint, defendant alleges that he has not sufficient knowledge or information upon which to base a belief, and basing his denial upon such ground, denies generally and specifically each and every allegation in said paragraph XII contained.

VII.

Answering Paragraph XIII of the second count of said complaint, defendant denies that as Receiver of The Reno National Bank, Reno, Nevada, or otherwise, he has from time to time or at all liquidated the said indebtedness either in whole or in part and has, or has, collected such assets and appropriated, or appropriated the same to the use of his trust.

Further answering said Paragraph, defendant denies that plaintiff has any pro rata of such assets and collections, or assets, or collections, or that defendant has failed and refused, or failed, or refused, to make accounting or pay over to plaintiff any sums of money due from defendant to plaintiff.

VIII.

Answering Paragraph XIV of the second count of said complaint, the defendant denies that there is now due, owing and unpaid, or due, or owing, or unpaid, from defendant to plaintiff the sums thereinabove mentioned, or any sums representing amounts due on said balances or otherwise, or the pro rata thereof based on the total amount of the indebtedness represented by said note and mortgages as the said advances bear to the total thereof, or otherwise. [15]

IX.

Answering Paragraph XVI of the third count of said complaint, defendant denies that thereafter, or at all, The Reno National Bank, Reno, Nevada, sold, assigned and delivered, or sold, or assigned, or delivered to The First National Bank of Winnemucca, Nevada, the note in the sum of $28,000 executed by the above named parties and secured, or secured, by said mortgage, and denies that The First National Bank of Winnemucca, Nevada, paid to The Reno National Bank, Reno. Nevada, the sum of $28,000, or any sum whatsoever.

X.

Answering Paragraph XVII of the third count of said complaint, defendant alleges that he has not sufficient knowledge or information upon which to base a belief, and basing his denial upon that ground, denies generally and specifically each and every allegation contained in said paragraph.

XI.

Answering Paragraph XVIII of said third count of said complaint, defendant denies that The Reno National Bank, through the defendant herein as such Receiver, or otherwise, has liquidated the indebtedness covered by said mortgage of said debtors and has collected, or has collected, the assets therefrom and appropriated, or appropriated, the same to the use of his said trust.

Further answering said paragraph, defendant denies that plaintiff has any pro rata of such assets and collections, or assets, or collections, or that defendant has failed and refused, or failed, or refused, to make accounting or pay over to plaintiff any sums of money due from defendant to plaintiff.

XII.

Answering Paragraph XIX of said third count of said complaint, [16] defendant denies that there is now due, owing and unpaid, or due, or owing, or unpaid, from the defendant to plaintiff the sum of $27,102.98, or any sum, together with overdraft in the sum of $3,612.49, or any sum, with interest, or otherwise, representing balance due on said balances or the pro rata thereof based on the total amount of the indebtedness represented by the said notes and mortgages as the said sum of $30,715.47 bears to the total thereof, or otherwise.

XIII.

Answering Paragraph XX of said third count of said complaint, defendant alleges that he has not sufficient knowledge or information upon which to base a belief, and basing his denial upon that ground, denies generally and specifically each and every allegation contained in said paragraph.

Further answering the first count of said complaint, and as a defense to said cause of action, defendant alleges:

I.

That the notes and mortgages securing the same alleged and set forth in paragraph IV of the plaintiff's complaint were assigned to The Reno National Bank on or about the 30th day of June, 1932, and said notes and mortgages were thereupon delivered to The Reno National Bank, and that The Reno National Bank paid to The First National Bank of Winnemucca the full face value thereof; that all of said notes and mortgages were by The Reno National Bank hypothecated to the Reconstruction Finance Corporation, a corporation organized and existing under the laws of the United States, as security for a loan from said Reconstruction Finance Corporation to The Reno National Bank, and that by reason of said loan secured from said Reconstruction Finance Corporation, said The Reno National Bank was [17] able to pay and did pay to The First National Bank of Winnemucca the full face value of said notes and mortgages, and The First National Bank of Winnemucca was thereby enabled to continue in business and avoid the closing of its doors through inability to meet its obligations; that if said The Reno National Bank had not secured said loan and paid said The First National Bank of Winnemucca the full face value of said notes and mortgages, said The First National Bank of Winnemucca would have been compelled to close its doors and cease to conduct its banking business;

II.

That prior to the securing of said loan from said Reconstruction Finance Corporation, and made a condition thereof, said The First National Bank of Winnemucca made and entered into a subordination agreement with the Reconstruction Finance Corporation, a copy of which said agreement is attached hereto, marked "Exhibit A" and made a part hereof, and that by the terms of said agreement, said The First National Bank of Winnemucca waived all right and recourse to participation in the proceeds arising from the liquidation of the said notes and mortgages assigned to The Reno National Bank, as aforesaid, and so pledged to the Reconstruction Finance Corporation, as aforesaid, until and unless said securities were paid in full, dollar for dollar;

III.

That said notes and mortgages described in plaintiff's complaint as being assigned to The Reno National Bank and herein referred to as being hypothecated to the Reconstruction Finance Corporation were liquidated, not by the defendant, but by the Reconstruction Finance Corporation while held by said Reconstruction Finance Corporation, and the proceeds realized applied on the idebtedness of The Reno National Bank to Reconstruction Finance Corporation; [18]

That said Alcorta notes and mortgage was paid in full.

That the Dufurrena mortgaged indebtedness was liquidated at a loss of $29,823.39.

That the Johnstone mortgaged indebtedness was liquidated at a loss of $49,378.27.

That the Larribeau mortgaged indebtedness was liquidated at a loss of $28,231.76.

That the Yragui mortgaged indebtedness was liquidated at a loss of $25,135.78.

That the Gabica mortgaged indebtedness was liquidated at a loss of $87,949.08.

That the Jaca mortgaged indebtedness was liquidated at a loss of $107,880.90.

That the Belaustgui mortgaged indebtedness was liquidated at a loss of $2,769.11.

IV.

That the entire indebtedness of The Reno National Bank to said Reconstruction Finance Corporation was subsequently fully paid, satisfied and discharged; that defendant was compelled to make up said deficiencies or losses out of other assets of The Reno National Bank pledged to the Reconstruction Finance Corporation, and said The Reno National Bank thereby suffered a loss on the above described mortgaged indebtedness in the sum of $331,170.51.

As a further defense to plaintiff's first cause of action, defendant alleges:

I.

That defendant is informed and believes, and upon such information and belief alleges the fact to be that whatever custom, usage, agreement and understanding was used or had between The First Na- [19] tional Bank of Winnemucca and The Reno National Bank as to The First National Bank of Winnemucca making loans and advancements for the protection of the assets so assigned by The First National Bank of Winnemucca to The Reno National Bank were not in writing, and that any such custom, usage, agreement and understanding, if any were in fact ever made, were promises on the part of The Reno National Bank to answer for the debt, default or miscarriage of another.

As a second further defense to plaintiff's first cause of action, defendant alleges:

I.

That the note of Alex Duferrena Company of date January 18, 1932, is barred by the provisions of Section 8524, Nevada Compiled Laws of 1929.

Further answering the second count of said complaint, and as a defense to said cause of action, defendant alleges:

I.

That the entire indebtedness of John G. Taylor, Inc., which was originally unsecured, originated in The First National Bank of Winnemucca, and was represented by miscellaneous notes totalling the sum of $700,000 which were sold and transferred to The Reno National Bank and for which The First National Bank of Winnemucca received from said The Reno National Bank the full face value thereof; that The Reno National Bank was attempting to borrow money from the Reconstruction Finance Corporation, and that said Reconstruction Finance Corporation required collateral security for such loan; that in order to meet the requirements of the Reconstruction Finance Corporation, it was necessary to secure the said indebted- [20] ness of John G. Taylor, Inc., with a real and chattel mortgage which was then taken as a matter of convenience in favor of said The Reno National Bank, and that the entire then existing bank indebtedness of said John G. Taylor, Inc:, was incorporated in one note in the sum of $700,000 and secured by a mortgage on the real and personal property of said John G. Taylor, Inc., and that the said note and mortgage were by said The Reno National Bank hypothecated to the Reconstruction Finance Corporation as collateral security for a loan by the Reconstruction Finance Corporation to said The Reno National Bank, and said The Reno National Bank was thereby able to pay and did pay from the money secured by said loan the full face value of said note and mortgage to The First National Bank of Winnemucca, and said The First National Bank of Winnemucca was thereby enabled to continue in business and avoid the closing of its doors through inability to meet its obligations; that if said The Reno National Bank had not secured said loan and paid said The First National Bank of Winnemucca the full face value of said note and mortgage, said The First National Bank of Winnemucca would have been compelled to close its doors and cease to conduct its banking business.

II.

That prior to the securing of said loan from said Reconstruction Finance Corporation, and made a condition thereof, said The First National Bank of Winnemucca made and entered into a subordination agreement with the Reconstruction Finance Corporation, a copy of which said agreement is attached hereto, marked "Exhibit A" and made a part hereof, and that by the terms of said agreement, said The First National Bank of Winnemucca waived all right and recourse to participation in the proceeds arising from the liquidation of the said notes and mortgages assigned to The Reno National Bank, as [21] aforesaid, and so pledged to the Reconstruction Finance Corporation, as aforesaid, until and unless said securities were paid in full, dollar for dollar.

III.

That said note and mortgage described in plaintiff's second count of said complaint and referred to as being hypothecated to the Reconstruction Finance Corporation were liquidated, not by defendant, but by the Reconstruction Finance Corporation while held by the Reconstruction Finance Corporation, and the proceeds realized applied on the indebtedness of The Reno National Bank to the Reconstruction Finance Corporation; that said John G. Taylor, Inc., indebtedness was liquidated at a loss of $295,-700.39.

IV.

That the entire indebtedness of The Reno National Bank to the Reconstruction Finance Corporation was subsequently fully paid, satisfied and discharged, and defendant was compelled to make up the loss of said John G. Taylor, Inc., mortgaged indebtedness out of other assets of The Reno National Bank pledged to the Reconstruction Finance Corporation, and said The Reno National Bank thereby suffered a loss on the John G. Taylor, Inc., indebtedness in the sum of $295,700.39.

As a further defense to plaintiff's second cause of action, defendant alleges:

I.

That defendant is informed and believes, and upon such information and belief alleges the fact to be that whatever custom, usage, agreement and understanding was used or had between The First

National Bank of Winnemucca and The Reno National Bank as to The First National Bank of Winnemucca making loans and advancements [22] for the protection of the assets so assigned by The First National Bank of Winnemucca to The Reno National Bank were not in writing, and that any such custom, usage, agreement and understanding, if any were in fact ever made, were promises on the part of The Reno National Bank to answer for the debt, default or miscarriage of another.

Further answering the third count of said complaint and as a defense to said cause of action, defendant alleges:

I.

That the entire indebtedness of Laborde Brothers & Company, totalling $70,000, originated in The First National Bank of Winnemucca and was unsecured; that $42,000 of this indebtedness was sold by said The First National Bank of Winnemucca to The Reno National Bank for which said The First National Bank of Winnemucca received full face value; that $28,000 of said indebtedness was retained by said The First National Bank of Winnemucca;

That to improve the position of said The First National Bank of Winnemucca, it was decided to obtain a real and chattel mortgage securing the entire indebtedness of $70,000; that two notes were taken, one for $42,000 representing that portion of the indebtedness of said Laborde Brothers & Company held by said The Reno National Bank, and one note for $28,000 representing that portion of the indebtedness held by said The First National Bank of Winnemucca, which said latter note was delivered to The First National Bank of Winnemucca to replace the previous existing indebtedness of Laborde Brothers & Company to said The First National Bank of Winnemucca in like amount;

That the Laborde Brothers & Company note and mortgage executed to The Reno National Bank were hypothecated to the Reconstruction [23] Finance Corporation as collateral security for a loan by said Reconstruction Finance Corporation to said The Reno National Bank, and that by reason of said loan secured from said Reconstruction Finance Corporation, said The Reno National Bank was able to pay and did pay to The First National Bank of Winnemucca the full face value of said note of $42,000, and said The First National Bank of Winnemucca was thereby enabled to continue in business and avoid the closing of its doors through inability to meet its obligations; that if said The Reno National Bank had not secured said loan and paid said The First National Bank of Winnemucca the full face value of said note of $42,000, said The First National Bank of Winnemucca would have been compelled to close its doors and cease to conduct its banking business.

II.

That prior to the securing of said loan from said Reconstruction Finance Corporation, and made a condition thereof, said The First National Bank of Winnemucca made and entered into a subordination agreement with the Reconstruction Finance Corporation, a copy of which said agreement is attached hereto, marked "Exhibit A" and made a part hereof, and that by the terms of said agreement, said The First National Bank of Winnemucca waived all right and recourse to participation in the proceeds arising from the liquidation of said notes and mortgages assigned to The Reno National Bank, as aforesaid, and so pledged to the Reconstruction Finance Corporation, as aforesaid, and waived all rights to participation in the proceeds arising from the liquidation of the collateral security held by the Reconstruction Finance Corporation as to any notes or obligations of the same maker held by The First National Bank of Winnemucca, until and unless said securities were paid in full, dollar for dollar. [24]

III.

That said note and mortgage described in plaintiff's third count of said complaint and referred to as being hypothecated to the Reconstruction Finance Corporation were liquidated, not by defendant, but by the Reconstruction Finance Corporation while held by the Reconstruction Finance Corporation, and the proceeds realized applied on the indebtedness of The Reno National Bank to the Reconstruction Finance Corporation; that said Laborde Brothers & Company mortgaged indebtedness was liquidated at a loss of $5,977.77.

IV.

That the entire indebtedness of The Reno National Bank to the Reconstruction Finance Corporation was subsequently fully paid, satisfied and discharged, and defendant was compelled to make up the loss of said Laborde Brothers & Company mortgaged indebtedness out of other assets of The Reno National Bank pledged to the Reconstruction Finance Corporation, and said The Reno National Bank thereby suffered a loss on the Laborde Brothers & Company indebtedness in the sum of $5,977.77.

As a further defense to plaintiff's third cause of action, defendant alleges:

I.

That defendant is informed and believes, and upon such information and belief alleges the fact to be that whatever custom, usage, agreement and understanding was used or had between The First National Bank of Winnemucca and The Reno National Bank as to The First National Bank of Winnemucca making loans and advancements for the protection of the assets so assigned by The First National Bank of Winnemucca to The Reno National Bank were not in writing, and that any such custom, usage, agreement and understanding, if any were in fact ever made, were promises on the part of The Reno National Bank [25] to answer for the debt, default or miscarriage of another.

Wherefore, defendant prays that plaintiff take nothing by his action, and that defendant have his costs herein expended and such other and further relief as to the Court may seem meet and proper in the premises and conformable to equity.

N. J. BARRY,
Attorney for Defendant. [26]

State of Nevada,
County of Washoe—ss.

W. J. Tobin, being first duly sworn, deposes and says:

That he, as Receiver of The Reno National Bank, is the defendant in the above entitled action; that he has read the within and foregoing Answer and knows the contents thereof, and that the same is true of his own knowledge, except as to those matters which are therein stated on information and belief, and as to those matters, he believes it to be true.

W. J. TOBIN.

Subscribed and sworn to before me this 28th day of July, 1938.

[Notarial Seal] MARY THOMPSON,
Notary Public in and for the County of Washoe, State of Nevada. [27]

"EXHIBIT A"

SUBORDINATION AGREEMENT

Whereas, Reno National Bank, Reno, Nevada, hereinafter called "the bank", has applied to Reconstruction Finance Corporation, hereinafter called "the corporation", for a loan to be made to it upon its note and/or notes secured by certain collateral notes, which collateral notes are in turn secured by mortgages and/or deeds of trust upon real and personal property and other miscellaneous collateral; and

Whereas, the undersigned will derive a real and valuable consideration from any loans made by the corporation to the bank, and such loans and the assistance thereby rendered to the bank will be of direct and material benefit to the undersigned; and

Whereas, it appears that some of the collateral notes pledged by said bank with said corporation as security for the indebtedness of said bank to said corporation are made by the same persons, firms and corporations as notes held by the undersigned; and

Whereas, the corporation requires as a condition precedent to the making of further loans and advances to said bank that the undersigned agree that in all cases where the undersigned holds or may hold and/or acquire any notes or other obligations which the undersigned claims or may claim are secured by mortgages, deeds of trust, or other security assigned to or in the possession of the corporation, the right of recourse of the undersigned against the real or personal property or other security securing such notes shall be subordinated and made secondary to the right of the corporation to receive from such property payment in full of any indebtedness due the corporation and secured by such property;

Now, Therefore, in consideration of the premises and of the making of any loan by the corporation to the bank, the undersigned does hereby undertake and agree to and with the corporation that all loans and/or advances secured by mortgages and/or deeds of trust upon real or personal property and/or any other collateral which may at any time be pledged by the bank to the corporation as collateral security for loans made or to be made to the bank by the corporation, shall have priority in right and remedy over any claims however evidenced for other loans heretofore and/or hereafter made by the undersigned and/or heretofore and/or hereafter acquired by the undersigned in so far as recourse against the property securing the notes held by the corporation is concerned. In all cases where it appears that the corporation and the undersigned hold notes or other obligations of the same maker, the undersigned waives any and all right of recourse, right of foreclosure and/or right of participation in the proceeds arising from foreclosure and/or sale in any and all collateral security of whatever kind or character held or which may be held to secure notes in the possession of the corporation and/or held by it as collateral security for any advances or loans made by it to said bank. It is the intent hereof that any note or other obligation secured by mortgage, deed of trust and/or other collateral security [28] pledged by the bank to the corporation shall as between the undersigned, its successors and assigns, and the corporation be deemed the sole obligation so secured and that until full payment thereof shall have been made to the corporation the mortgaged property and/or the property covered by the deed of trust and/or other collateral security and all proceeds from the sale or disposition thereof shall be held solely as security for the repayment of indebtedness due the corporation and for the sole benefit of the corporation.

The foregoing shall apply to all obligations of makers whose notes the corporation may hold as collateral security for any debt of said bank to said corporation and shall apply to any and all notes and/or other obligations of the same makers whether acquired by the undersigned through purchase thereof from said bank or otherwise or through original loans made by the undersigned to the makers of said notes.

In Witness Whereof, the undersigned has caused these presents to be executed in its name by its president and secretary thereunto duly authorized, and its corporate seal to be hereunto affixed, this 25th day of July, 1932.

[Corporate Seal] FIRST NATIONAL BANK OF WINNEMUCCA, NEVADA.

By GEO. WINGFIELD,
President.

By J. G. MOORE,
Secretary.

[Endorsed]: Filed August 1, 1938. [29]

[Title of District Court and Cause.]

REPLY

Now comes the plaintiff herein and replying to the Answer and defense of the defendant, admits, alleges and denies:

I.

Replying to subdivision I, on page 6 of defendant's defense, plaintiff denies that because of the payment to The First National Bank of Winnemucca of the face value of the notes it was enabled to continue in business and avoid the closing of its doors through inability to meet its obligations; and

Denies that said bank would have been compelled to close its doors and cease to conduct its banking business if they had not sold said notes and mortgages to The Reno National Bank; and

Alleges that the allegations contained in said subdivision I do not constitute a defense to plaintiff's complaint.

II.

Replying to subdivision II, page 6, of defendant's defense, plaintiff denies that by the execution of the Subordination Agreement, defendant's Exhibit "A" to the Reconstruction Finance Cor- [30] poration, that the First National Bank of Winnemucca waived all or any right and recourse to participation in the proceeds arising from the liquidation of said notes and mortgages as against The Reno National Bank; and, alleges the fact to be that the said First National Bank of Winnemucca received no benefit whatever by virtue of the execution of the said Subordination Agreement; and,

Alleges that the allegations contained in said subdivision II do not constitute a defense to the plaintiff's Complaint.

III.

Replying to subdivision III, pages 6 & 7, defendant's defense, the plaintiff alleges that the allegations contained in said subdivision III do not constitute a defense to the plaintiff's complaint.

Plaintiff denies that any part of the sum of $1,780.23 due on the Alcorta note and mortgage to The First National Bank of Winnemucca has been paid to said First National Bank of Winnemucca.

On information and belief, plaintiff denies that the Dufurrena mortgaged indebtedness was liquidated at a loss of $29,823.39, or in any sum whatever; and,

On information and belief alleges that some money was received by said defendant on account of the liquidation of the said mortgage, and that none of said receipts have been paid to the plaintiff herein;

On information and belief plaintiff denies that the Johnstone mortgaged indebtedness was liquidated at a loss of $49,378.27, or in any sum whatever; and,

On information and belief alleges that some money was received by said defendant on account of the liquidation of the said mortgage, and that none of said receipts have been paid to the plaintiff herein; [31]

On information and belief plaintiff denies that the Larribeau mortgaged indebtedness was liquidated at a loss of $28,231.76, or in any sum whatever; and,

On information and belief alleges that some money was received by said defendant on account of the liquidation of the said mortgage, and that none of said receipts have been paid to the plaintiff herein;

On information and belief plaintiff denies that the Yragui mortgaged indebtedness was liquidated at a loss of $25,135.78, or in any sum whatever; and,

On information and belief alleges that some money was received by said defendant on account of the liquidation of the said mortgage, and that none of said receipts have been paid to the plaintiff herein;

On information and belief plaintiff denies that the Gabica mortgaged indebtedness was liquidated at a loss of $87,949.08, or in any sum whatever; and,

On information and belief alleges that some money was received by said defendant on account of the liquidation of the said mortgage, and that none of said receipts have been paid to the plaintiff herein.

On information and belief plaintiff denies that the Jaca mortgaged indebtedness was liquidated at a loss of $107,880.90, or in any sum whatever; and,

On information and belief alleges that some money was received by said defendant on account of the liquidation of the said mortgage, and that none of said receipts have been paid to the plaintiff herein.

On information and belief plaintiff denies that the Belaustgui mortgaged indebtedness was liquidated at a loss of $2,769.11, or in any sum whatever; and, [32]

On information and belief alleges that some money was received by said defendant on account of the liquidation of the said mortgage, and that none of said receipts have been paid to the plaintiff herein.

IV.

Replying to subdivision IV, page 7, of defendant's defense, plaintiff alleges that said allegations do not constitute a defense to the plaintiff's complaint.

V.

Replying to subdivision I on pages 7 and 8 of defendant's further defense, the plaintiff denies each and every allegation therein contained and the whole thereof; and,

In this connection alleges that the allegations therein contained do not constitute a defense to the plaintiff's complaint.

VI.

Replying to subdivision I on page 8 of defendant's second further defense, the plaintiff denies each and every allegation therein contained and the whole thereof.

VII.

Replying to subdivision I, pages 8 and 9, of the answer to the second count, the plaintiff denies that because of the payment to the First National Bank of Winnemucca of the face value of the notes, it was enabled to continue in business and avoid the closing of its doors through inability to meet its obligations; and,

Denies that The First National Bank of Winnemucca would have been compelled to close its doors and cease to conduct its banking business if they had not sold the said mortgage to The Reno National Bank.

The plaintiff further alleges that the allegations therein contained do not constitute a defense to the plaintiff's complaint. [33]

VIII.

Replying to subdivision II, pages 9 and 10 of the answer to the second count, the plaintiff denies that by the execution of the Subordination Agreement, defendant's Exhibit "A", that The First National Bank of Winnemucca waived all or any right and recourse to participation in the proceeds arising from the liquidation of said notes and mortgages as against The Reno National Bank, and alleges the fact to be that the said First National Bank of Winnemucca received no benefit whatever by virtue of the execution of the said Subordination Agreement; and,

Further alleges that the allegations contained in said subdivision II aforesaid do not constitute a defense to the plaintiff's complaint.

IX.

Replying to subdivision III on page 10 of the answer of defendant's to the second count, on information and belief plaintiff denies that The Reno National Bank suffered a loss of $295,700.39, or any sum whatever, on the John G. Taylor indebtedness; and,

On information and belief alleges that some money was received by said defendant on account of the liquidation of the said mortgage; and that none of said receipts has been paid to the plaintiff herein;

And further alleges that the allegations therein contained do not constitute a defense to the plaintiff's complaint.

X.

Replying to subdivision IV on page 10 of the answer of defendant's to the second count, plaintiff alleges that the allegations therein contained do not constitute a defense to the plaintiff's complaint. [34]

XI.

Replying to subdivision I on pages 10 and 11 of defendant's further defense to plaintiff's second cause of action, plaintiff denies each and every allegation therein contained and the whole thereof.

XII.

Replying to subdivision I, on pages 11 and 12 of the defendant's answer to the third count, the plaintiff denies that because of the purchase by The Reno National Bank of the Laborde Brothers note in the sum of $42,000.00 that The First National Bank of Winnemucca was thereby enabled to continue in business and avoid the closing of its doors through inability to meet its obligations; and,

Denies that if the said sum had not been paid to The First National Bank of Winnemucca that it would have been compelled to close its doors and cease to conduct its banking business; and,

Alleges that the allegations therein contained do not constitute a defense to the plaintiff's complaint.

XIII.

Replying to subdivision II on page 12 of the defendant's answer to the third count, the plaintiff denies that by the execution of the Subordination Agreement, defendant's Exhibit "A", that The First National Bank of Winnemucca waived any or all right and recourse to participation in the proceeds arising from the liquidation of said notes and mortgages as against The Reno National Bank; and,

Alleges the fact to be that the said First National Bank of Winnemucca received no benefit whatever by virtue of the execution of the said Subordination Agreement; and, further alleges that the allegations contained in said subdivision II do not constitute a defense to the plaintiff's complaint. [35]

XIV.

Replying to subdivision III on page 13 of the defendant's answer to the third count, on information and belief, plaintiff denies that the Laborde Brothers & Company mortgaged indebtedness was liquidated at a loss of $5,977.77, or in any sum whatever; and on information and belief alleges that some money was received by said defendant on account of the liquidation of the said mortgage, none of which has been paid to the plaintiff herein; and,

Further alleges that the allegations therein contained do not constitute a defense to the plaintiff's complaint.

XV.

Replying to subdivision IV, on page 13 of defendant's answer, on information and belief, plaintiff denies that The Reno National Bank suffered a loss on Laborde Brothers & Company indebtedness in the sum of $5,977.77, or in any sum whatever; and,

On information and belief alleges that some money was received by said defendant on account of the liquidation of the said mortgage, none of which has been paid to the plaintiff herein; and,

Alleges that the allegations therein contained do not constitute a defense to the plaintiff's Complaint.

XVI.

Replying to subdivision I on pages 13 and 14 of defendant's further defense to plaintiff's third cause of action, the plaintiff denies each and every allegation therein contained and the whole thereof; and,

Alleges that the allegations therein contained do not constitute a defense to the plaintiff's complaint.

Wherefore, Plaintiff Prays that he have Judgment as in his Complaint prayed for.

THOS. J. SALTER,
Attorney for Plaintiff. [36]

State of Nevada,
County of Humboldt—ss.

Carroll Henderson, being first duly sworn, deposes and says:

That he, as Receiver of The First National Bank of Winnemucca, is the plaintiff in the above entitled action; that he has read the above and foregoing Reply and knows the contents thereof, and that the same is true of his own knowledge, except as to those matters which are therein stated on information and belief, and as to those matters, he believes it to be true.

CARROLL HENDERSON.

Subscribed and sworn to before me this 5th day of August, A. D. 1938.

[Seal] THOS. J. SALTER,
Notary Public.

[Endorsed]: Filed Aug. 8, 1938. [37]

[Title of District Court and Cause.]

MEMORANDUM DECISION AND ORDERS

This is a suit by plaintiff to require an accounting by defendant to plaintiff of the proceeds received by or on account of defendant in the matter of the liquidation of certain securities held by The Reno National Bank prior to a transfer of the same to the Reconstruction Finance Corporation as security for a loan made to said bank, and later liquidated by or on account of said Finance Corporation and accounted for to defendant.

The securities in question were in the form of notes secured by mortgages, real and chattel, the latter, in the main, covering livestock. The mortgages not only secured the original notes given by the several debtors but secured and were intended to secure any [75] loans or advances subsequently made to enable said debtors to carry on their livestock business.

The two banks in question now represented by plaintiff and defendant receivers, were, in the main, for many years, preceding the depression, controlled by the same personnel. The Winnemucca Bank while located more nearly in the center of the livestock industry of the state, because of its limited capital, was restricted in the making of loans in amounts not exceeding $30,000.00 to any individual, partnership, or corporation. This restriction was in the main complied with. Whether the loan was originally made in the name of the Winnemucca Bank or the Reno Bank it was the practice for each bank to carry a portion of the loan when the amount exceeded $30,000.00. This was effected by the assignment of notes and credit given therefor in the accounts of the respective banks. Because of this custom the same mortgages secured accounts in both banks.

At the time the Reno Bank was negotiating for a loan in the total sum of $3,000,000.00 from the Reconstruction Finance Company, designed not only to aid in the maintenance of the credit of the Reno Bank but also that of the Winnemucca Bank and a number of state banks dominated by the same personnel, it called upon the Winnemucca Bank to make a number of additional assignments of notes held by it and take credit therefor upon the books of the Reno Bank. At or about the same time, July, 25, 1932, the Winnemucca Bank executed with the Reconstruction Finance Corporation an agreement subrogating any rights it had in the securities to be so pledged by the Reno National Bank to the Finance Corporation. On December 9, 1932, both the said Reno and Winnemucca Banks were taken over by the Comptroller of the Currency and receivers appointed respectively therefor; [76] since which time said books have been and now are in course of liquidation. Following the said Receiverships, the loan made by the Finance Corporation to the Reno Bank was paid; payment being accomplished in part by a liquidation of the debts here in question. An accounting for all the debts pledged for security was made as between the Finance Corporation and the Receiver of the Reno National Bank.

Plaintiff alleges failure upon the part of defendant Receiver to account to him for the proportion of the amounts received from the pledged securities which would be represented by the relative interests of the two banks in such securities. Plaintiff's complaint lists ten debtors whose pledged securities represented in part debts owing to the Winnemucca Bank. It is the contention of plaintiff that of the total amounts received by plaintiff or applied on account of the settlement of the Finance Corporation loan to the Reno Bank, defendant should account for and pay to plaintiff the total of several amounts derived from the securities so pledged by said debtors as the total of the several amounts owed by said respective debtors to the Winnemucca Bank bears to the total of the several amounts owed by said debtors to the Reno Bank. The total amount so claimed to be accounted for and paid by Defendant and Plaintiff is the sum of $78,502.53.

Defendant denies any liability to plaintiff based on an accounting as prayed for and alleges a loss in the liquidation of the assets of the several debtors named in the aggregate sum of $632,848.67. From an exhibit filed upon the part of plaintiff the aggregate amount of the loss which should be taken into consideration is approximately $115,000.00.

In any accounting between Plaintiff and Defendant, notes originally made by debtors to the Winnemucca Bank and by the bank later [77] transferred to the Reno Bank at times prior to negotiations for a loan from the Reconstruction Finance Corporation would not be within the purview of the accounting here involved as such transfers would be deemed to have been made in the ordinary course of business between the respective banks. The situation thus presented would involve simply the relation of debtor and creditor.

The matters which plaintiff is entitled to an accounting on the basis of proceeds received by or on account of the Reno Bank from a sale of pledged securities given by the Reno Bank to the Finance Corporation for its loan, is notes or securities transferred by the Winnemucca Bank to the Reno Bank at the latter's request to aid in securing said loan, and further loans or advances thereafter made by the Winnemucca Bank to a debtor or debtors at the request of the Reno Bank, as in the case of loans and advances by the Winnemucca Bank to the debtor Taylor or Taylor, Inc.

Subject to the limitation above stated, Plaintiff is entitled to a decree requiring an accounting by Defendant and payment of the amount found to be due thereon.

It is so Ordered.

It is further Ordered that Plaintiff submit proposed Findings of fact, conclusions of Law and form of decree and serve copies thereof upon counsel for Defendant.

Dated this 13th day of February, 1939.

(Signed) FRANK H. NORCROSS,
District Judge.

[Endorsed]: Filed Feb. 13, 1939. [78]

In the District Court of the United States of America, in and for the District of Nevada.

No. H-207

CARROLL HENDERSON, AS RECEIVER OF THE FIRST NATIONAL BANK OF WINNEMUCCA, NEVADA, A NATIONAL BANKING ASSOCIATION, ORGANIZED AND EXISTING UNDER THE LAWS OF THE UNITED STATES OF AMERICA,

Plaintiff,

vs.

CARROLL HENDERSON, AS RECEIVER OF THE RENO NATIONAL BANK, RENO, NEVADA, A NATIONAL BANKING ASSOCIATION, ORGANIZED AND EXISTING UNDER THE LAWS OF THE UNITED STATES OF AMERICA,

Defendant.

FINDINGS OF FACT AND CONCLUSIONS OF LAW

This cause came on regularly for trial before the Court without a jury on the 9th day of December, 1938; plaintiff, Carroll Henderson, as Receiver of The First National Bank of Minnemucca, Nevada, appearing by and through his attorney, Thos. J. Salter, and the then defendant, W. J. Tobin, as Receiver of The Reno National Bank, Reno, Nevada, appearing by and through his attorney, N. J. Barry.

Whereupon, evidence both oral and documentary

was introduced on the part of plaintiff and on the part of defendant; and the cause being submitted, the Court files its Findings of Fact and Conclusions of Law herein:

I.

That plaintiff is the duly appointed, qualified and acting Receiver of The First National Bank of Winnemucca, Nevada, a banking corporation, organized and existing under the banking laws of [79] the United States of America.

II.

That defendant is the duly appointed, qualified and acting Receiver of The Reno National Bank, Reno, Nevada, a banking corporation, organized and existing under the banking laws of the United States of America.

III.

That for many years prior to June 30, 1932, George Wingfield was the President, and J. Sheehan the Vice President, of The First National Bank of Winnemucca, Nevada, plaintiff herein, and were respectively President and Vice President of The Reno National Bank, Reno, Nevada, defendant herein, and that both of said banks were subject to their control as such President and Vice President;

IV.

That prior to June 30, 1932, The First National Bank of Winnemucca, Nevada, was the owner and holder of certain notes, which said notes were secured by mortgages, to-wit:

Notes of Saturnino Alcorta and Justa Alcorta in the sum of $13,000.00.

Notes of Alex Dufurrena, Manuel Begino, Frank Laurnaga, Pierre Ahuntcain and Fortunato Arbeloa, co-partners doing business under the firm name and style of Alex Dufurrena & Company, in the sum of $65,500.00.

Notes of W. A. Johnstone and Minnie A. Johnstone, his wife, in the sum of $45,500.00.

Notes of Joe Larribeau, Gregorio Ocamica and Frank Amuchastegui, co-partners, in the sum of $69,500.00.

Notes of Joe Yragui in the sum of $58,000.00.

Notes of Daniel Gabica, Constantina Gabica, his wife, Frank Gabica and Marsellina Gabica, his wife, and Gabica Brothers, a co-partnership, in the sum of $110,668.48.

Notes of Juan Jaca, Ramona Jaca, his wife, Silbestre Jaca and Florentina Jaca, his wife, in the sum of $141,000.00.

Notes of Juan Belaustgui & Co., John Belaustgui, Antonio Meabe and Martina Belaustgui, in the sum of $34,500.83. [80]

V.

That on or about the 30th day of June, 1932, The Reno National Bank was negotiating for a loan in the total sum of $3,000,000.00 from the Reconstruction Finance Corporation, which loan was designed to aid in the maintenance of the credit of The Reno National Bank, that of The First National Bank and a number of state banks dominated by the same director personnel;

Whereupon, at about the said date, at the direction of J. Sheehan, Vice President of both banks, plaintiff and defendant herein, The First National Bank sold, assigned and delivered to The Reno National Bank, without recourse, all of the notes and mortgages described in paragraph IV of these Findings, for the purpose of Consolidating the split loans held by these banks and providing additional security to the R. F. C. for such loan;

That thereafter The Reno National Bank did pledge to the R. F. C. the securities herein listed, together with other securities held by it, by means of which the loan was procured.

VI.

That The First National Bank of Winnemucca received credit on the books of The Reno National Bank in a sum covering the principal amounts of the notes; to-wit, $537,669.31;

That on December 9, 1932, the date of the suspension of the two banks here involved, The Reno National Bank owed to The First National Bank the sum of $147,746.66 representing a credit of The First National Bank on the books of The Reno National Bank, and the sum of $22,540.35 representing the interest on the notes of the above listed debtors, for which sums The First National Bank has filed claims against The Reno National Bank, as in the case of other creditors.

VII.

That on or about March 12, 1932, John G. Taylor, Inc., a [81] corporation organized under the laws of the State of Wyoming, executed a note in favor of The Reno National Bank, Reno, Nevada, in the sum of $638,145.59 with interest, and to secure said note executed a chattel mortgage to said bank.

VIII.

That on or about March 24, 1931, St. John Laborde and Michel Cadet, co-partners, doing business under the firm name and style of Laborde Brothers & Company, executed notes, all in the sum of $70,500.00, and one in the sum of $28,000.00, and to secure said notes executed a real and chattel mortgage to The Reno National Bank, Reno, Nevada.

That The Reno National Bank, Reno, Nevada, was the owner of the notes so executed in the sum of $70,500.00, and The First National Bank of Winnemucca, Nevada, was the owner of the note in the sum of $28,000.00 executed by said debtor, all of which said notes were secured by the mortgage so executed by the said debtor.

IX.

That The First National Bank of Winnemucca, Nevada, because of its limited capital, was restricted in the making of loans in amounts not exceeding $30,000.00 to any individual, partnership, or corporation, and whether the loan was originally made in the name of The First National Bank or The Reno National Bank it was the practice for each bank to carry a portion of the loan when the amount exceeded $30,000.00; that this was effected by the assignment of notes and credit given therefor in the accounts of the respective banks; that because of this custom the same mortgages secured accounts in both banks.

X.

That for the purpose of protecting the assets covered by the securities listed in paragraph IV of these Findings, and those of John G. Taylor, Inc., and Laborde Brothers & Company, and to enable [82] the debtors to carry on their livestock business, and pursuant to the practice and custom of the banks herein involved, The First National Bank advanced to the debtors therein named certain sums of money and took from such debtors notes for such advances, or in lieu of said notes, charged the same against the account of the debtors in the nature of overdrafts, to-wit:

Name of Debtor	Date	Amount
Saturnino Alcorta and Justa Alcorta	Note dated July 14, 1932 and Overdraft dated October 14, 1932, to October 29, 1932	2,007.14
Alex Dufurrena, et al	Note dated January 18, 1932 Note dated July 14, 1932 and Overdraft dated August 22, 1932, to October 29, 1932	5,576.42
W. A. Johnstone and Minnie A. Johnstone	Note dated July 27, 1932 and Overdraft dated September 9, 1932, to October 29, 1932	1,495.28

Name of Debtor	Date	Amount
Joe Larribeau, et al	Note dated September 6, 1932, and Overdraft dated October 20, 1932, to October 29, 1932	2,536.89
Joe Yragui	Note dated July 27, 1932	2,000.00
Daniel Gabica, et al	Note dated July 13, 1932	2,500.00
Juan Jaca, et al	Note dated July 27, 1932 and Overdraft dated September 25, 1932, to October 29, 1932	5,538.34
Juan Belaustegui & Co. et al	Overdraft dated October 12, 1932, to October 29, 1932	58.10
John G. Taylor, Inc.	Note dated September 16, 1932, $25,000.00. Note dated September 29, 1932, $5,000.00. and Overdraft dated October 5, 1932, to October 29, 1932, $15,142.18. Total	45,142.18
Laborde Brothers & Company	Note dated March 24, 1931, $28,000.00. and Overdraft dated September 9, 1932, to October 29, 1932, $3,612.49. Total	31,612.49

[83]

XI.

That the said mortgages of the debtors listed as aforesaid in these Findings secured the original notes given by the several debtors therein named and secured and were intended to secure the loans or advances so made by The First National Bank as hereinabove set forth, pursuant to the provisions contained in said mortgages.

XII.

That as each advance was made by The First National Bank of Winnemucca, Nevada, to the debtors above listed, The Reno National Bank, Reno, Nevada, was duly notified by The First National Bank of Winnemucca, Nevada, of the date and amount of such advances.

XIII.

That on or about July 25, 1932, The First National Bank executed with the R. F. C. an agreement subrogating any rights it had in the securities to be so pledged by The Reno National Bank to the R. F. C.;

That such subordination agreement between the The First National Bank and the R. F. C. did not constitute a waiver from The First National Bank in favor of The Reno National Bank of the provision contained in the mortgages of the debtors herein listed that such mortgages secured and were intended to secure the loans or advances made subsequent to the execution of such mortgages, and did not affect the right of the plaintiff to an accounting and payment from the defendant of the pro rata of proceeds collected through liquidation of the securities of the debtors herein listed.

That on or about December 9, 1932, both The Reno National Bank and The First National Bank were taken over by the Comptroller of the Currency and receivers appointed respectively therefor, since which time said banks have been and now are in the course of liquidation; [84]

That following the said receiverships, the loan made by the R. F. C. to The Reno National Bank was paid, payment being accomplished in part by a liquidation of the debts herein question, and an accounting for all the debts pledged for security was made as between the R. F. C. and the receiver of The Reno National Bank.

XIV.

That during the course of liquidation of the securities of the debtors herein listed certain losses were sustained by reason of the insufficiency of the assets of the debtors to cover their total indebtedness, which losses should be borne pro rata by the trusts herein involved as their interests appear.

XV.

That no accounting was ever made by The Reno National Bank to The Frst National Bank of the proceeds from such liquidation of these securities herein listed representing the pro rata of the advances made and indebtedness held by The First National Bank and secured by said mortgages.

That the accounting from the defendant to the plaintiff should be based upon the pro rata of such proceeds collected by the liquidation of the securities listed herein as the total amount of the indebtedness held by The Reno National Bank bears to the total advances made and indebtedness held by The First National Bank to the same debtors.

XVI.

That as to the defense of defendant set up in the "second further defense to plaintiff's first cause of action" the Court finds:

That the statute of limitations does not apply in respect to the note of Alex Dufurrena et al, for the reason that this note, with the original notes executed by these debtors, was secured by [85] the mortgage executed by these parties, and which mortgage has been liquidated. Section 9048, N. C. L., 1929, relating to one form of action for the recovery of a debt secured by mortgage, applies to the question involved.

As

CONCLUSIONS OF LAW

from the foregoing facts, the Court finds:

That the plaintiff is entitled to judgment for an accounting from the defendant for plaintiff's pro rata of such proceeds realized from the liquidation of the securities of the debtors listed in paragraph IV of these Findings, and those of John G. Taylor, Inc., and Laborde Brothers & Company.

That the plaintiff's pro rata of such proceeds be based on the total amount of indebtedness held by

The Reno National Bank and the total advances made and indebtedness held by The First National Bank of the debtors hereinabove mentioned, and that the said amount so ascertained be paid by the defendant to the plaintiff herein.

That each of the parties, plaintiff and defendant, should bear pro rata as their interests appear the losses sustained during the course of liquidation of the securities of the debtors herein listed.

That the right of plaintiff to recover from the defendant its pro rata of the amount of the proceeds collected on the Alex Duffurrena, et al security, is not barred by the statute of limitations.

That the plaintiff is entitled to his costs of suit herein expended.

Let Judgment be entered herein accordingly.

Dated: May 25th, 1939.

FRANK H. NORCROSS,
Judge of said Court.

[Endorsed]: Lodged March 3, 1939. Filed May 25, 1939. [86]

[Title of District Court and Cause.]

DECREE.

This cause came on regularly for trial before the Court without a jury on the 9th day of December, 1938; the plaintiff, Carroll Henderson, as Receiver of The First National Bank of Winnemucca,

Nevada, appearing by and through his attorney, Thos. J. Salter, and the then defendant, W. J. Tobin, as Receiver of The Reno National Bank, Reno, Nevada, appearing by and through his attorney, N. J. Barry.

Whereupon evidence both oral and documentary was introduced on the part of plaintiff and on the part of defendant; and the cause having been submitted and the Court having filed herein its Findings of Fact and Conclusions of Law——

It Is Hereby Ordered, Adjudged and Decreed:

That the plaintiff do have and recover from the defendant a money judgment for the pro rata of the proceeds collected through the liquidation of the mortgages given by those certain debtors hereinafter listed, based upon the total amount of the indebted- [87] ness held by the Reno National Bank covered by original notes, and of the total amount of the indebtedness held by The First National Bank of Winnemucca, Nevada, covered by advances made and evidenced by notes and overdrafts of the following debtors, to-wit:

Notes held by The Reno National Bank:

Saturnino Alcorta and Justa Alcorta	$ 13,000.00
Alex Dufurrena, Manual Begino, Frank Laurnaga, Pierre Ahuntcain and Fortunato Arbeloa, co-partners doing business under the firm name and style of Alex Dufurrena & Company	65,500.00
W. A. Johnstone and Minnie A. Johnstone, his wife	45,500.00

Joe Larribeau, Gregorio Ocamica and Frank Amuchastegui, co-partners	69,500.00
Joe Yragui	58,000.00
Daniel Gabica, Constantina Gabica, his wife, Frank Gabica and Marsellina Gabica, his wife, and Gabica Brothers, a co-partnership	110,668.48
Juan Jaca, Ramona Jaca, his wife, Silbestre Jaca and Florentina Jaca, his wife	141,000.00
Juan Belaustgui & Co., John Belaustgui, Antonio Meabe and Martina Belaustgui	34,500.83
John G. Taylor, Inc.	638,145.59
Laborde Brothers & Company	70,500.00

Notes and Overdrafts held by The First National Bank of Winnemucca, Nevada:

Saturnino Alcorta and Justa Alcorta		2,007.14
Alex Dufurrena, Manuel Begino, Frank Laurnaga, Pierre Ahuntcain and Fortunato Arbeloa, co-partners doing business under the firm name and style of Alex Dufurrena & Company		5,576.42
W. A. Johnstone and Minnie A. Johnstone, his wife		1,495.28
Joe Larribeau, Gregoiro Ocamica and Frank Amuchastegui, co-partners		2,536.89
		[88]
Joe Yragui		2,000.00
Daniel Gabica, Constantina Gabica, his wife, Frank Gabica and Marsellina Gabica, his wife, and Gabica Brothers, a co-partnership		2,500.00
Juan Jaca, Ramona Jaca, his wife, Silbestre Jaca and Florentina Jaca, his wife		5,538.34
Juan Belaustgui & Co., John Belastgui, Antonio Meabe and Martina Belaustgui		58.10
John G. Taylor, Inc.		45,142.18
Laborde Brothers & Company	28,000.00	
	3,612.49	
		31,612.49

It is further ordered that a full, true and correct accounting be made forthwith by the defendant to the plaintiff showing in detail the amount of the indebtedness held by The Reno National Bank against the said debtors; the amount of the proceeds realized through the liquidation of the said mortgages; the amount of the indebtedness held by The First National Bank of Winnemucca, Nevada, against the said debtors, and the amount due The First National Bank of Winnemucca, Nevada out of the proceeds so collected.

It is further ordered that the statement of such accounting be filed in this cause subject to the approval of the Court, and that plaintiff have judgment against the defendant for the amount, based upon such statement, so found by the Court to be due from the defendant to the plaintiff.

It is further ordered that the plaintiff do have and recover from the defendant his costs expended in this action.

Dated, May 25, 1939.

FRANK H. NORCROSS,
Judge of said Court. [89]

Service, by copy, of the within and foregoing Decree is hereby admitted this 20th day of February, 1939.

N. J. BARRY,
Attorney for Defendant.

[Endorsed]: Lodged Feb. 21, 1939. Filed May 25, 1939. [90]

[Title of District Court and Cause.]

DEFENDANT'S OBJECTIONS TO PLAINTIFF'S PROPOSED FINDINGS AND JUDGMENT.

Comes now the defendant, W. J. Tobin, as Receiver of The Reno National Bank, and objects and excepts to plaintiff's proposed Findings of Fact and Conclusions of Law, and to plaintiff's proposed form of Judgment heretofore served and filed herein, for the reasons and upon the grounds following, to-wit:

I.

Objects to Paragraph V of said proposed Findings upon the ground and for the reason that the same is not warranted by the evidence and is contrary to the evidence. [91]

II.

(a) Objects to that portion of Paragraph VI of said proposed Findings commencing with the word "That", line 14 and ending with the word "overdrafts", line 25, page 3 upon the ground and for the reason that the same is not warranted by the evidence and is contrary to the evidence;

(b) Objects to that portion of Paragraph VI of said proposed Findings, being line 2, page 4, upon the ground and for the reason that the same is not warranted by the evidence and is contrary to the evidence.

(c) Objects to that portion of Paragraph VI of said proposed Findings, being lines 8, 9, 10, 11, 12, 13 and 14, page 4 upon the ground and for the reason that the dates of such advances are not given, and asks that the dates of such advances be inserted.

III.

Objects to Paragraph VII of said proposed Findings upon the ground and for the reason that the same is not warranted by the evidence.

IV.

Objects to all that portion of Paragraph VIII of said proposed Findings, as follows: "or by The Reno National Bank", upon the ground and for the reason that the same is not warranted by the evidence and is contrary to the evidence.

V.

Objects to the proposed Conclusions of Law contained in Paragraph IX of said proposed Findings upon the ground and for the reason that said conclusions are not based upon any valid findings of fact and are not based upon fact or law.

VI.

Objects to Paragraph XII of said proposed Findings upon the [92] ground and for the reason that there is no evidence to warrant such finding.

VII.

Objects to Paragraph XIII of said proposed Findings upon the ground and for the reason that there is no evidence to warrant such finding.

VIII.

Objects to the conclusions of law of the Court found in Paragraph XIV of said proposed Findings for the reason that said conclusions are not based upon a valid finding and that the same are against the facts and the law.

IX.

(a) Objects to that portion of Paragraph XVII of said proposed Findings beginning on line 12 and ending on line 20, page 7 upon the ground and for the reason that the same is not warranted by the evidence and is contrary to the evidence.

(b) Objects to that portion of said Paragraph XVII of said proposed Findings beginning with the word "and" after the word "debtor", line 26 and ending with the word "banks", line 27, page 7 upon the ground and for the reason that the same is not warranted bý the evidence and is contrary to the evidence.

X.

Objects to that portion of Paragraph XVIII of said proposed Findings beginning with the word "That", line 2, and ending with the word "therefrom", line 4, page 8, upon the ground and for the reason that the same is not warranted by the evidence and is contrary to the evidence.

XI.

Objects to the conclusions of the Court found in Paragraph XIX of said proposed Findings upon the ground and for the reason [93] that the same are not based upon any valid finding of fact and are not based on fact or law.

XII.

Objects to all the conclusions of the Court beginning on line 17, page 8 and ending on line 4, page 10 of said proposed Findings upon the ground and for the reason that the same are not based upon any valid findings of fact and are not based upon fact or law.

XIII.

Objects to the proposed form of Judgment upon the ground that said proposed Judgment is not based upon any valid findings of fact or conclusions of law, and that it is against the facts and against the law.

XIV.

Objects to said proposed Findings of Fact and Conclusions of Law for the reason that defendant, in his answer, plead the statute of limitations that as to the note of Alex Dufurrena & Company, of date January 18, 1932, the same was barred by the provisions of Section 8524, Nevada Compiled Laws of 1929, and that there is no finding as to said allegation.

XV.

Objects to said proposed Findings of Fact and Conclusions of Law for the reason that the defendant alleged in his answer that plaintiff waived all his right to an accounting or to participate in the proceeds from the liquidation of the notes and mortgages assigned to The Reno National Bank by a subordination agreement, a copy of which was attached to the answer, and that the Court made no finding in relation thereto. [94]

Defendant herewith files the annexed Defendant's Proposed Findings of Fact and Conclusions of Law and Defendant's Proposed Judgment, and requests the Court to approve, adopt, sign, file and cause to be entered and filed after hearing, and that these matters may be heard and determined by the Court after notice to the plaintiff, and requests that after hearing, the Court may reject the Plaintiff's Findings of Fact and Conclusions of Law and Judgment objected to, and may adopt, sign and enter the Defendant's Proposed Findings of Fact and Conclusions of Law and Judgment in lieu thereof.

Dated: February 21, 1939.

N. J. BARRY,

Attorney for Defendant.

[Endorsed]: Filed Feb. 23, 1939. [95]

[Title of District Court and Cause.]

DEFENDANT'S PROPOSED FINDINGS OF FACT AND CONCLUSIONS OF LAW.

This cause came on regularly for trial before the Court without a jury on the 9th day of December, 1938; plaintiff Carroll Henderson, as Receiver of The First National Bank of Winnemucca, appearing by and through his attorney, Thos. J. Salter, and W. J. Tobin, as Receiver of The Reno National Bank, appearing by and through his attorney, N. J. Barry.

Whereupon, evidence both oral and documentary was introduced on the part of plaintiff and on the part of defendant, and the [96] cause being submitted, the Court files its Findings of Fact and Conclusions of Law herein, as follows:

I.

That plaintiff is the duly appointed, qualified and acting Receiver of The First National Bank of Winnemucca, a banking corporation organized and existing under the banking laws of the United States of America.

II.

That defendant is the duly appointed, qualified and acting Receiver of The Reno National Bank, a banking corporation organized and existing under the banking laws of the United States of America.

III.

That for many years prior to June 30, 1932, George Wingfield was the President, and J. Sheehan the Vice President of The First National Bank of Winnemucca, and were respectively, President and Vice President of The Reno National Bank, and that both of said banks were subject to their control as such President and Vice President.

IV.

That prior to June 30, 1932, The First National Bank of Winnemucca was the owner and holder of certain notes, which said notes were secured by mortgages, to-wit:

Notes of Saturnino Alcorta and Justa Alcorta in the sum of $13,000 secured by chattel mortgage dated May 12, 1930.

Notes of Alex Dufurrena, Manuel Begino, Frank Laurnaga, Pierre Ahuntcain and Fortunato Arbeloa, co-partners doing business under the firm name and style of Alex Dufurrena & Company, in the sum of $65,500, secured by chattel mortgage dated October 24, 1929.

Notes of W. A. Johnstone and Minnie Johnstone, his wife, in the sum of $45,500, secured by chattel mortgage dated August 23, 1928. [97]

Notes of Joe Larribeau, Gregorio Ocamica and Frank Amuchastegui, co-partners, in the sum of $69,500, secured by chattel mortgage dated October 15, 1930.

Notes of Joe Yragui in the sum of $58,000 secured by chattel mortgage dated March 5, 1932.

Notes of Daniel Gabica, Constantina Gabica, his wife, Frank Gabica and Marsellina Gabica, his wife, and Gabica Brothers, a co-partnership, in the sum of $110,668.48, secured by real and chattel mortgage dated September 4, 1929.

Notes of Juan Jaca, Ramona Jaca, his wife, Silbestre Jaca and Florentina Jaca, his wife, in the sum of $141,000 secured by real and chattel mortgage dated September 12, 1930.

Notes of Juan Belaustegui & Co., John Belaustegui, Antonio Beabe and Martina Belaustegui, in the sum of $34,500.83, secured by chattel mortgage dated August 13, 1928.

V.

That on or about the 30th day of June, 1932, the notes and mortgages described in Paragraph IV of these Findings were sold, assigned and delivered to The Reno National Bank, and that The Reno National Bank paid to The First National Bank of Winnemucca the full face value thereof, and that on the same day, all of said notes and mortgages were by The Reno National Bank hypothecated to the Reconstruction Finance Corporation, a corporation organized and existing under the laws of the United States of America, as security for a loan from said Reconstruction Finance Corporation to The Reno National Bank, and that such assignment, sale and delivery was then and there known to The First National Bank of Winnemucca.

VI.

That thereafter, The First National Bank of Winnemucca made certain advancements to the debtors mentioned in the mortgages, as follows: [98]

Name of Debtor	Date	Advances
S. & J. Alcorta	July 14, 1932	$2,007.14
Gabica Bros.	July 13, 1932	2,500.00
Juan Jaca et al	July 27, 1932	5,538.34
W. A. and Minnie Johnstone	July 27, 1932	1,495.28
Joe Larribeau Company	Sept. 6, 1932	2,536.89
Joe Yragui	July 27, 1932	2,000.00
Juan Belaustegui	Nov. 25, 1932	58.10

VII.

That all the advancements above described were made after the assignment of the notes mentioned in Paragraph IV of these Findings to the Reconstruction Finance Corporation, and with full knowledge of said assignment by The First National Bank of Winnemucca.

VIII.

That plaintiff, on the 18th day of January, 1932, advanced to Alex Dufurrena Company the sum of $5,576.42; that the plaintiff permitted said claim to become barred by the Statute of Limitations.

IX.

That on the 25th day of July, 1932, The Frst National Bank of Winnemucca made, executed and delivered to the Reconstruction Finance Corporation a subordination agreement, a copy of which is attached hereto, marked "Exhibit A" and made a part hereof.

X.

That after the notes and mortgages mentioned in Paragraph IV of these Findings were assigned to the Reconstruction Finance Corporation by The Reno National Bank, The Reno National Bank had no further connection with the same, and that the same were liquidated entirely by the Reconstruction Finance Corporation and applied on the entire indebtedness of The Reno National Bank to the Reconstruction Finance Corporation. [99]

XI.

As to plaintiff's second cause of action, the Court finds that the $700,000 indebtedness of John G. Taylor, Inc. was represented by a note of John G. Taylor, Inc. to The Reno National Bank, and that a mortgage was given by John G. Taylor, Inc. to The Reno National Bank to secure the payment of said note, and that The First National Bank of Winnemucca was not a party to the note or the mortgage.

XII.

That immediately on the execution of said note and mortgage, the same were assigned by The Reno National Bank to the Reconstruction Finance Corporation to secure the payment of money borrowed by The Reno National Bank from the Reconstruction Finance Corporation; that all the advancements made by The First National Bank of Winnemucca to John G. Taylor, Inc. were made after the making and execution of said mortgage and the assignment of the same to the Reconstruction Finance Corporation by The Reno National Bank and were made by The First National Bank of Winnemucca with full and complete knowledge of such assignment by The Reno National Bank to the Reconstruction Finance Corporation.

XIII.

That on the 25th day of July, 1932, The First National Bank of Winnemucca made, executed and delivered to the Reconstruction Finance Corporation a subordination agreement, a copy of which is attached hereto, marked "Exhibit A" and made a part hereof.

XIV.

As to plaintiff's third cause of action, the Court finds that all the Laborde Brothers & Company indebtedness originated in the First National Bank of Winnemucca and was evidenced by several notes; that to consolidate the indebtedness, a note was [100] given to The Reno National Bank in the sum of $42,000, and The First National Bank of Winnemucca received credit in the sum of $42,000! that a note for $28,000 was executed by Laborde Brothers & Company to The First National Bank of Winnemucca, and was included in the mortgage; that said note and mortgage were assigned to the Reconstruction Finance Corporation by The Reno National

Bank as security for money borrowed by The Reno National Bank from the Reconstruction Finance Corporation; that said The First National Bank of Winnemucca had full knowledge and notice of such assignment.

XV.

That on the 25th day of July, 1932, The First National Bank of Winnemucca made, executed and delivered to the Reconstruction Finance Corporation a subordination agreement, a copy of which is attached hereto, marked "Exhibit A" and made a part hereof.

As

CONCLUSIONS OF LAW

from the foregoing facts, the Court finds:

I.

That as to plaintiff's first cause of action, plaintiff is not entitled to an accounting from or to pro rate with the defendant in the proceeds of the liquidation of said notes and mortgages for the reason that the advancements made by The First National Bank of Winnemucca were made after said notes and mortgages had passed into the hands of third persons.

II.

That as to the indebtedness of Alex Dufurrena Company, plaintiff is not entitled to an accounting from or to pro rate with the defendant in the proceeds of the liquidation of said indebt- [101] edness for the reason that The First National Bank of Winnemucca permitted said indebtedness to become barred by the Statute of Limitations.

III.

That plaintiff is not entitled to an accounting from or to pro rate with the defendant in the proceeds of the liquidation of said notes and mortgages for the reason that The First National Bank of Winnemucca, by said subordination agreement of date July 25, 1932, waived all its right to participate in the proceeds of the liquidation of said notes and mortgages.

IV.

That as to plaintiff's second cause of action, plaintiff is not entitled to an accounting from or to pro rate with the defendant in the proceeds of the liquidation of said John G. Taylor, Inc. indebtedness for the reason that The First National Bank of Winnemucca was not a party to the John G. Taylor, Inc. mortgage and was without authority in fact or in law to make advancements after the making of said note and mortgage and the assignment of the same to the Reconstruction Finance Corporation by The Reno National Bank.

V.

That plaintiff is not entitled to an accounting from or to pro rate with the defendant in the proceeds of the liquidation of said John G. Taylor, Inc. indebtedness for the reason that The First National Bank of Winnemucca, by said subordination agreement of date July 25, 1932, waived all its right to participate in the proceeds of the liquidation of said note and mortgage.

VI.

That as to plaintiff's third cause of action, plaintiff is not entitled to an accounting from or to pro rate with the defendant in the proceeds of the liquidation of said Laborde & Company [102] indebtedness for the reason that The First National Bank, by said subordination agreement of date July 25, 1932, waived all its right to participate in the proceeds of the liquidation of said indebtedness.

VII.

That the defendant is entitled to his costs of suit herein expended.

It Is Ordered that judgment be entered herein in accordance herewith.

Dated: February ...., 1939.

....

District Judge. [103]

EXHIBIT A

SUBORDINATION AGREEMENT

Whereas, Reno National Bank, Reno, Nevada, hereinafter called "the bank", has applied to Reconstruction Finance Corporation, hereinafter called "the corporation", for a loan to be made to it upon its note and/or notes secured by certain collateral notes, which collateral notes are in turn secured by mortgages and/or deeds of trust upon real and personal property and other miscellaneous collateral; and

Whereas, the undersigned will derive a real and valuable consideration from any loans made by the corporation to the bank, and such loans and the assistance thereby rendered to the bank will be of direct and material benefit to the undersigned; and

Whereas, it appears that some of the collateral notes pledged by said bank with said corporation as security for the indebtedness of said bank to said corporation are made by the same persons, firms and corporations as notes held by the undersigned; and

Whereas, the corporation requires as a condition precedent to the making of further loans and advances to said bank that the undersigned agree that in all cases where the undersigned holds or may hold and/or acquire any notes or other obligations which the undersigned claims or may claim are secured by mortgages, deeds of trust, or other security assigned to or in the possession of the corporation, the right of recourse of the undersigned against the real or personal property or other security securing such notes shall be subordinated and made secondary to the right of the corporation to receive from such property payment in full of any indebtedness due the corporation and secured by such property;

Now, Therefore, in consideration of the premises and of the making of any loan by the corporation to the bank, the undersigned does hereby undertake and agree to and with the corporation that all loans and/or advances secured by mortgages and/or deeds of trust upon real or personal property and/or any other collateral which may at any time be pledged by the bank to the corporation as collateral security for loans made or to be made to the bank by the corporation, shall have priority in right and remedy over any claims however evidenced for other loans heretofore and/or hereafter made by the undersigned and/or heretofore and/or hereafter acquired by the undersigned in so far as recourse against the property securing the notes held by the corporation is concerned. In all cases where it appears that the corporation and the undersigned hold notes or other obligations of the same maker, the undersigned waives any and all right of recourse, right of foreclosure and/or right of participation in the proceeds arising from foreclosure and/or sale in any and all collateral security of whatever kind or character held or which may be held to secure notes in the possession of the corporation and/or held by it as collateral security for any advances or loans made by it to said bank. It is the intent hereof that any note or other obligation secured by mortgage, deed of trust and/or other collateral security [104] pledged by the bank to the corporation shall as between the undersigned, its successors and assigns, and the corporation be deemed the sole obligation so secured and that until full payment thereof shall have been made to the corporation the mortgaged property and/or the property covered by the deed of trust and/or other collateral security and all proceeds from the sale or disposition thereof shall be held solely as security for the repayment of indebtedness due the corporation and for the sole benefit of the corporation.

The foregoing shall apply to all obligations of makers whose notes the corporation may hold as collateral security for any debt of said bank to said corporation and shall apply to any and all notes and/or other obligations of the same makers, whether acquired by the undersigned through purchase thereof from said bank or otherwise or through original loans made by the undersigned to the makers of said notes.

In Witness Whereof, the undersigned has caused these presents to be executed in its name by its president and secretary thereunto duly authorized, and its corporate seal to be hereunto affixed, this 25th day of July, 1932.

FIRST NATIONAL BANK OF WINNEMUCCA, NEVADA.

By GEO. WINGFIELD,
President.

[Corporate Seal]

By J. G. MOORE,
Secretary.

[Endorsed]: Lodged Feb. 23, 1939. [105]

[Title of District Court and Cause.]

DEFENDANT'S PROPOSED JUDGMENT

This cause came on regularly for trial before the Court without a jury on the 9th day of December, 1938; plaintiff Carroll Henderson, as Receiver of The First National Bank of Winnemucca, appearing by and through his attorney, Thos. J. Salter; and defendant W. J. Tobin, as Receiver of The Reno National Bank, appearing by and through his attorney, N. J. Barry.

Whereupon, evidence both oral and documentary was introduced on the part of plaintiff and on the part of defendant; and the cause having been submitted and the Court having filed herein its [106] Findings of Fact and Conclusions of Law:

It Is Hereby Ordered, Adjudged and Decreed:

That the plaintiff, Carroll Henderson, as Receiver of The First National Bank of Minnemucca, is not entitled to an accounting from or to pro rate with the defendant, W. J. Tobin, as Receiver of The Reno National Bank, in the proceeds of the liquidation of the notes and mortgages in the Complaint and the Findings particularly set forth; that plaintiff take nothing by this action and that defendant have his costs herein expended.

Dated: February ...., 1939.

....

District Judge

[Endorsed]: Lodged Feb. 23, 1939. [107]

[Title of District Court and Cause.]

ACCOUNTING BY RECEIVER OF THE RENO NATIONAL BANK.

To the Honorable, the Above Entitled Court:

Pursuant to Decree rendered and filed by the Court in the above entitled cause May 25, 1939, I, the undersigned, Carroll Henderson, Receiver of The Reno National Bank, render to the Court a full, true and correct accounting showing in detail the amount of the indebtedness held by The Reno National Bank against the debtors named in this case; the amount of the proceeds realized through the liquidation of the mortgages executed by the said debtors; and the amount of the indebtedness held by The First National Bank of Winnemucca, Nevada, against the said debtors; and the amount due The First National Bank of Winnemucca, Nevada, out of the proceeds collected by the Receiver of The Reno National Bank, as follows, to-wit: [108]

Account	Amount of Original Debt Held by the Reno National Bank	Amount of Original Debt Held by the First National Bank
1. S. & J. Alcorta	13,000.00	$ 2,007.14
2. Alex Dufurrena	65,500.00	5,576.42
3. W. A. & Minnie A. Johnstone	45,500.00	1,495.28
4. Joe Larribeau Co.	69,500.00	2,536.89
5. Joe Yragui	58,000.00	2,000.00
6. Gabica Bros.	110,668.48	2,500.00
7. Juan Jaca, et al.	141,000.00	5,538.34
8. Juan Belaustegui	34,500.83	58.10
9. John G. Taylor, Inc.	638,145.59	45,142.18
10. Laborde Bros. Co.	72,500.00	31,612.49
Total	$1,248,314.90	$98,466.84

Account No.	Net Proceeds Collected	Per Cent Due Reno National Bank	Per Cent Due First National Bank	Amount Due First National Bank
1.	$15,884.09	86.63%	13.37%	$2,123.70
2.	58,572.78	92.15%	7.85%	4,597.96
3.	15,240.42	96.818%	3.182%	484.95
4.	57,185.19	96.48%	3.52%	2,012.92
5.	35,091.23	96.67%	3.33%	1,168.54
6.	66,796.06	97.791%	2.209%	1,475.52
7.	88,046.52	96.22%	3.78%	3,328.16
8.	42,311.25	99.83%	.17%	71.93
9.	594,964.47	93.393%	6.607%	39,309.30
10.	93,844.47	69.636%	30.364%	28,494.93
Total	$1,067,936.48			$83,067.91

[109]

Forward Amount due First National Bank.........................$83,067.91

Account No.	Amount Collected by First National Bank for which Reno National Bank Should Have Credit	
1.	$ 229.45	
3.	1.00	
5.	85.92	
6.	305.24	
7.	3,582.92	
8	.29	
10.	901.39	
Total	$5,106.21	–$ 5,106.21

Net Amount Due First National Bank..............................$ 77,961.70
Amount Retained by Reno National Bank.......................... 989,974.78

Total...$1,067,936.48

Respectfully submitted,

CARROLL HENDERSON

Receiver of The Reno National Bank, Reno, Nevada.

[Endorsed]: Filed June 2, 1939. [110]

In the District Court of the United States of America, in and for the District of Nevada.

No. H-207

CARROLL HENDERSON, AS RECEIVER OF THE FIRST NATIONAL BANK OF WINNEMUCCA, NEVADA, A NATIONAL BANKING ASSOCIATION, ORGANIZED AND EXISTING UNDER THE LAWS OF THE UNITED STATES OF AMERICA,

Plaintiff,

vs.

CARROLL HENDERSON, AS RECEIVER OF THE RENO NATIONAL BANK, RENO, NEVADA, A NATIONAL BANKING ASSOCIATION, ORGANIZED AND EXISTING UNDER THE LAWS OF THE UNITED STATES OF AMERICA,

Defendant.

JUDGMENT

This cause having come on regularly for trial before the Court without a jury on the 9th day of December, 1938, the plaintiff, Carroll Henderson, as Receiver of The First National Bank of Winnemucca, Nevada, appearing by and through his attorney, Thos. J. Salter, and the then defendant, W. J. Tobin, as Receiver of The Reno National Bank, Reno, Nevada, appearing by and through his attorney, N. J. Barry, and the Decree of the Court having been filed herein May 25, 1939, and the same having been entered as of that date, wherein it was ordered that a full, true and correct accounting be made by the defendant to the plaintiff, showing in detail the amount of the indebtedness held by The Reno National Bank against the debtors in said Decree named; the amount of the proceeds realized through the liquidation of the mortgages of the debtors; and the amount of indebtedness held by The First National Bank of Winnemucca, Nevada, against the said debtors, and the amount due The First National Bank of Winnemucca, Nevada, out of the proceeds so collected; and it was further ordered that the [111] statement of such accounting be filed in this cause, subject to the approval of the Court; and such account and statement having been made and filed herein, and the Court having given due consideration thereof, and finding the accounting and statement to be full, true and correct—

It Is Hereby Ordered, Adjudged and Decreed:

That the plaintiff do have and recover from the defendant a money Judgment for the sum of $77,961.70.

It is further ordered that the Plaintiff do have and recover from the defendant his costs expended in this action in the sum of $.................................

Dated: June 8, A. D. 1939.

FRANK H. NORCROSS,
Judge of said Court

[Endorsed]: Filed June 8, 1939. [112]

[Title of District Court and Cause.]

STIPULATION

It is stipulated by and between plaintiff herein and the defendant herein that the corrected statement of pro rata distribution of net liquidation of split lines due by The Reno National Bank, Reno, Nevada, to The First National Bank of Winnemucca, Nevada, be, and the same is accepted by both parties herein as showing the correct amount for which judgment should have been entered in this case, to-wit, $75,276.76.

It is further stipulated that each of the parties are to pay their own costs in this action.

Dated: June 20, 1939.

THOS. J. SALTER
Attorney for Plaintiff
CARROLL HENDERSON
Receiver of The First National Bank of Winnemucca, Nevada,
Plaintiff
N. J. BARRY
Attorney for Defendant
CARROLL HENDERSON
Receiver of The Reno National Bank, Reno, Nevada,
Defendant. [113]

STATEMENT OF PRORATA 'DISTRIBUTION OF NET LIQUIDATION OF SPLIT LINES DUE BY THE RENO NATIONAL BANK, RENO, NEVADA, TO FIRST NATIONAL BANK OF WINNEMUCCA, NEVADA

RECAPITULATION

Debtor	Amount
Alcorta, S. & J.	$ 1,985.05
Belaustegui, Juan	70.81
Dufurrena Co. Alex	4,595.03
Gabica Bros.	1,107.28
Jaca, Juan et al	255.65 (Red)
Johnstone, W. A. & Minnie A.	483.95
Laborde Bros. Co	27,593.55
Larribeau Co. Joe	2,014.06
Taylor, Inc. John G.—Taylor, John G	36,626.01
Yragui, Joe	1,083.67
	$75,276.76

[114]

btedness eld by	Name of Debtor	Original Amount	Payments to Reno Prin.	Int.	Net Liquidation
o Nat'l Bank					
	S. & J. Alcorta	$13,000.00	$13,000.00	$2,654.64	
N/B Wncca					
	S. & J. Alcorta	2,007.14			
		$15,007.14	$13,000.00	$2,654.64	$15,654.64

*$229.45 receuved frin W. J. Tobin, Receiver Reno National Bank to apply

	Total Indebtedness	Percent	Reno Net Liquidation	Prop D
Reno Nat'l Bank	$13,000.00	86.625	$15,654.64	
1st N/B Wncca	2,007.14	13.375	15,654.64	
	$15,007.14	100.		$15,

Payments to				
1st N/B Wncca	$229.45	86.625% due Reno	$198.76	
		13.375% due Wncca	30.69	
			$229.45	

[

Indebtedness Held by	Name of Debtor	Original Amount	Payments to Reno Prin.	Payments to Reno Int.	Liq
Reno Nat'l Bank	Juan Belaustegui	$34,500.83	$34,500.83	$7,810.13	
1st N/B Wncca	Juan Belaustegui	58.10			
		$34,558.93	$34,500.83	$7,810.13	$42,3

	Total Indebtedness	Percent	Reno Net Liquidation	Propo Du
Reno Nat'l Bank	$34,500.83	99.832	$42,310.96	
1st N/B Wncca	58.10	.168	42,310.96	
	$34,558.93	100.		$42,3

Payments to				
1st N/B Wncca	.29	99.832% due Reno	.28	
		.168% due Wncca	.01	
			.29	

[1

Indebtedness Held by	Name of Debtor	Original Amount	Payments to Reno Prin.	Int.	Li
Reno Nat'l Bank	Alex Dufurrena Co. (Sheep Acc't)	$65,500.00	$58,326.67	$246.11	
1st N/B Wncca	Alex Dufurrena Co. (Sheep Acc't)	5,576.42			
		$71,076.42	$58,326.67	$246.11	$58,

	Total Indebtedness	Percent	Reno Net Liquidation	Pr
Reno National Bank	$65,500.00	92.155	$58,572.78	
1st Nat'l Bank, Wncca	5,576.42	7.845	58,572.78	
	$71,076.42	100.		$58,5

Proportion due 1st Nat'l Bank, Wncca $4,595.03

[

Indebtedness Held by	Name of Debtor	Original Amount	Payments to Reno Prin.	Int.	N Liquic
Reno Nat'l Bank	Gabica Bros.	$110,668.48	$66,208.34	$282.48	
1st N/B Wncca	Gabica Bros.	2,500.00			
		$113,168.48	$66,208.34	$282.48	$66,4

	Total Indebtedness	Percent	Reno Net Liquidation	Propor Du
Reno Nat'l Bank	$110,668.48	97.791	$66,490.82	
1st N/B Wncca	2,500.00	2.209	66,490.82	
	$113,168.48	100.		$66,4

Payments to 1st N/B Wncca	$305.24	97.791% due Reno	$298.50
		2.209% due Wncca	6.74
			$305.24

[1

Indebtedness Held by	Name of Debtor	Original Amount	Payments to Reno Prin.	Payments to Reno Int.	N Liqui
Reno Nat'l Bank	Juan Jaca et al...	$141,000.00	*$79,325.20*	$5,138.40	
1st N/B Wncca	Juan Jaca et al...	5,538.34			
		$146,538.34	*$79,235.20*	$5,138.40	$84,4

	Total Indebtedness	Percent	Reno Net Liquidation	Prop
Reno Nat'l Bank...........	$141,000.00	96.221	$84,463.60	
1st N/B Wncca...............	5,538.34	3.779	84,463.60	
	$146,538.34	100.		$84,4

Payments to 1st N/B Wncca			
$3,582.92	96.221%	due Reno	$3,447.52
	3.779%	due Wncca	135.40
			$3,582.92

Indebtedness Held by	Name of Debtor	Original Amount	Payments to Reno Prin.	Payments to Reno Int.	N Liqui
Reno Nat'l Bank	W. A. Johnstone............... Minnie A. Johnstone	$45,500.00	$14,986.26	$253.16	
1st N/B Wncca	W. A. Johnstone............... Minnie A. Johnstone	1,495.28			
		$46,995.28	$14,986.26	$253.16	$15,2

	Total Indebtedness	Percent	Reno Net Liquidation	Prop
Reno Nat'l Bank.............	$45,500.00	96.818	$15,239.42	
1st N/B Wncca................	1,495.28	3.182	15,239.42	
	$46,995.28	100.		$15,2

Payments to
1st N/B Wncca.....................$1.00 96.818% due Reno .97
3.182% due Wncca .03

$1.00

[

Indebtedness Held by	Name of Debtor	Original Amount	Payments to Reno Prin.	Int.	Ne Liquid
Reno Nat'l Bank					
	Laborde Bros. Co....	$72,500.00	$72,499.00	$20,444.08	
1st N/B Wncca					
	Laborde Bros. Co....	31,612.49			
		$104,112.49	$72,499.00	$20,444.08	$92,9

	Total Indebtedness	Percent	Reno Net Liquidation	Prop
Reno National Bank.....	$72,500.00	69.636	$92,943.08	
1st N/B Wncca..................	31,612.49	30.364	92,943.08	
	104,112.49	100.		$92,9

Payments to
1st N/B Wncca...............$901.39 69.636% due Reno $627.69
30.364% due Wncca 273.70

$901.39

[

Indebtedness Held by	Name of Debtor	Original Amount	Payments to Reno Prin.	Payments to Reno Int.	N Liqui
Reno Nat'l Bank					
	Joe Larribeau Co.	$69,500.00	$52,052.10	$5,133.09	
1st N/B Wncca					
	Joe Larribeau Co.	2,536.89			
		$72,036.89	$52,052.10	$5,133.09	$57,1

	Total Indebtedness	Percent	Reno Net Liquidation	Propc D
Reno Nat'l Bank	$69,500.00	96.478	$57,185.19	
1st Nat'l Bank Wncca	2,536.89	3.522	57,185.19	
	$72,036.89	100.		$57,1

Proportion due 1st Nat'l Bank, Wncca $2,014.06

[

Indebtedness Held by	Name of Debtor	Original Amount	Payments to Reno Prin.	Payments to Reno Int.	N Liqui
Reno Nat'l Bank					
	John G. Taylor, Inc.				
	John G. Taylor, End	$688,145.59	$594,964.47	—	
1st N/B Wncca					
	John G. Taylor, Inc	45,142.18			
	John G. Taylor, End				
		$733,287.77	$594,964.47	0	$594,9

	Total Indebtedness	Percent	Reno Net Liquidation	Prop D
Reno National Bank	688,145.59	93.844	594,964.47	
1st Nat'l Bank Wncca	45,142.18	6.156	594,964.47	
	733,287.77	100.		594,9

Proportion due 1st Nat'l Bank, Wncca $36,626.01

[

Indebtedness Held by	Name of Debtor	Original Amount	Payments to Reno Prin.	Int.	N Liqui
Reno Nat'l Bank........................					
	Joe Yragui.....	$58,000.00	$28,489.90	$6,515.41	
1st N/B Wncca..........................					
	Joe Yragui....	2,000.00			
		$60,000.00	$28,489.90	$6,515.41	$35,0

	Total Indebtedness	Percent	Reno Net Liquidation	Pro
Reno Nat'l Bank............	$58,000.00	96.667	$35,005.31	
1st N/B Wncca................	2,000.00	3.333	35,005.31	
	$60,000.00	100.		$35,0

Payments to			
1st N/B Wncca.................$85.92	96.667%	due Reno	$83.06
	3.333%	due Wncca	2.86
			$85.92

[Endorsed]: Filed June 23, 1939. [124]

In the District Court of the United States of America, In and for the District of Nevada.

No. H-207

CARROLL HENDERSON, AS RECEIVER OF THE FIRST NATIONAL BANK OF WINNEMUCCA, NEVADA, A NATIONAL BANKING ASSOCIATION, ORGANIZED AND EXISTING UNDER THE LAWS OF THE UNITED STATES OF AMERICA,

Plaintiff,

vs.

CARROLL HENDERSON, AS RECEIVER OF THE RENO NATIONAL BANK, RENO, NEVADA, A NATIONAL BANKING ASSOCIATION, ORGANIZED AND EXISTING UNDER THE LAWS OF THE UNITED STATES OF AMERICA,

Defendant.

AMENDED JUDGMENT.

The original judgment in the above entitled Court and cause having been filed herein on the 8th day of June, 1939, awarding the plaintiff judgment in the sum of $77,961.70, and the defendant herein, as Receiver of The Reno National Bank, having filed herein a corrected statement of the amount due from the defendant to the plaintiff, covering the pro rata share of the liquidation of assets upon which this action was based, showing that the true amount due from the defendant to the plaintiff is the sum of $75,276.76, and the parties herein having filed a stipulation to that effect; and the Court finding that the said sum of $75,276.76 is the correct amount for which judgment should have been entered in this action——

It Is Hereby Ordered, Adjudged and Decreed that the plaintiff do have and recover from the defendant a money judgment of $75,276.76, in lieu of the amount of $77,961.70 as shown in the original judgment herein.

Dated: July 7th, 1939.

FRANK H. NORCROSS,
Judge of said Court.

[Endorsed]: Filed July 7, 1939. [125]

[Title of District Court and Cause.]

NOTICE OF APPEAL.

To Carroll Henderson, as Receiver of The First National Bank of Winnemucca, and to Thos. J. Salter, His Attorney:

You, and Each of You, Will Please Take Notice that the defendant, Carroll Henderson, as Receiver of The Reno National Bank, hereby appeals to the United States Circuit Court of Appeals for the Ninth *District* from that certain Judgment entered in the United States District Court for the District of Nevada in the above entitled action on the 8th day of June, 1939, and from the Amended Judgment made and entered in said action on the 7th day [126] of July, 1939, in favor of the plaintiff in said action and against said defendant, and from the whole thereof.

Dated: July 31, 1939.

N. J. BARRY,
Attorney for defendant Carroll Henderson, as Receiver of The Reno National Bank.

[Endorsed]: Filed Aug. 1, 1939. [127]

Postal Telegraph

F69 58 DL Collect 5 EX-PXX Washington DC 19 212P

1939 Jul 19 PM 12 48

Carroll Henderson
Receiver Reno National Bank Reno Nev.

In view of the statements in attorney Barrys letter to you June first and his letter to us July fourteenth you are directed to perfect an appeal from the decision of your United States District Court in the case of the Receiver of the First National Bank of Winnemucca versus your Reno Receivership.

GEORGE P. BARSE
General Counsel Bureau of the Comptroller of the Currency.

[Endorsed]: Filed Aug. 1st, 1939. [128]

[Title of District Court and Cause.]

DESIGNATION OF CONTENTS OF RECORD ON APPEAL.

To the Clerk of the Above Entitled Court:

You will please prepare a transcript of the record in the above entitled cause to be filed with the United States Circuit Court of Appeals for the Ninth Circuit, incorporating therein the following portions of the record, to-wit:

1. Complaint.
2. Answer to Complaint.
3. Reply to Answer.
4. Decision of the Court.
5. Transcript of Testimony, including all Exhibits described therein. (Two copies of the Transcript of Testimony are filed herewith.) [129]
6. Findings of Fact and Conclusions of Law.
7. Defendant's Objections to Findings of Fact and Conclusions of Law.
8. Defendant's Proposed Findings of Fact and Conclusions of Law.
9. Defendant's Proposed Judgment.
10. Judgment in favor of Plaintiff.
11. Amended Judgment in favor of Plaintiff.
12. Notice of Appeal.
13. Telegram of Comptroller of the Currency of the United States authorizing appeal.

Dated: August 5, 1939.

N. J. BARRY

Attorney for Defendant.

[Endorsed]: Filed Aug. 5, 1939. [130]

[Title of District Court and Cause.]

AFFIDAVIT OF SERVICE.

State of Nevada,
County of Washoe—ss.

Mary McKinnon, being first duly sworn, deposes and says:

That she is a citizen of the United States over the age of twenty-one years, and that she is Secretary in the office of N. J. Barry, an attorney and counselor at law of the City of Reno, County of Washoe, State of Nevada; that said N. J. Barry is the attorney of record for Defendant in the above entitled action, and that Thos. J. Salter is the attorney of record for Plaintiff in said action. [131]

That said N. J. Barry resides at and has his office in the City of Reno, County of Washoe, State of Nevada, and that said Thos. J. Salter resides at and has his office in the City of Winnemucca, County of Humboldt, State of Nevada.

Affiant further says that there is a United States Post Office in said City of Reno, and a United States Post Office in said City of Winnemucca, and between said Cities of Reno and Winnemucca, there is a daily communication by United States Mail.

Affiant further says that she served the within and foregoing Designation Of Contents Of Record On Appeal on Thos. J. Salter, attorney for the Plaintiff, on the 4th day of August, 1939, by depositing a true copy of said Designation of Contents of Record on Appeal in the United States Post Office in the City of Reno, County of Washoe, State of Nevada, enclosed in an envelope properly addressed to said Thos. J. Salter, Winnemucca, Nevada, the place wherein said Thos. J. Salter resides and has his office;

Affiant further says that she prepaid the postage thereon.

MARY McKINNON.

Subscribed and sworn to before me this 4th day of August, 1939.

[Notarial Seal]

N. J. BARRY,

Notary Public in and for the County of Washoe, State of Nevada.

[Endorsed]: Filed Aug. 5, 1939. [132]

[Title of District Court and Cause.]

CERTIFICATE OF CLERK, U. S. DISTRICT COURT.

United States of America,
District of Nevada—ss.

I, O. E. Benham, Clerk of the District Court of the United States for the District of Nevada, do hereby certify that I am custodian of the records, papers and files of the said United States District Court for the District of Nevada, including the records, papers and files in the case of Carroll Henderson, as Receiver of The First National Bank of Winnemucca, Nevada, a national banking association, organized and existing under the laws of the United States of America, Plaintiff, vs. Carroll Henderson, As Receiver of The Reno National Bank, Reno, Nevada, a national banking association, organized and existing under the laws of the United States of America, Defendant, said case being No. H-207 on the equity docket of said court.

I further certify that this transcript, consisting of 214 typewritten pages and numbered from 1 to 214, inclusive, contains a full, true and correct transcript of the proceedings in said [133] matter and of all papers filed therein, as set forth in the Designation of Contents of Record on Appeal filed in said case and made a part of the transcript attached hereto, as the same appear from the originals of record and on file in my office as such Clerk in Carson City, State and District aforesaid.

I further certify that accompanying this record, not attached hereto but made a part hereof, is a full, true and correct copy of Transcript of Testimony, filed December 12, 1938, being pages Nos. 135 to 214, inclusive.

And I further certify that the cost of preparing and certifying to said record, amounting to $42.25, has been paid to me by Carroll Henderson, as Receiver of The Reno National Bank, the appellant herein.

Witness my hand and the seal of said United States District Court this 7th day of September, A. D. 1939.

[Seal] O. E. BENHAM,

Clerk, U. S. District Court.

[134]

[Title of District Court and Cause.]

TRANSCRIPT OF TESTIMONY

Reno, Nevada,
December 9, 1938

MARIE D. McINTYRE,

Reporter. [135]

Be It Remembered, That the above-entitled matter came on regularly for trial before the Court at Reno, Nevada, on Friday, the 9th day of December, 1938, at 10:00 o'clock A. M. Hon. F. H. Norcross, Judge, presiding.

Appearances: Thos. J. Salter, Esq.,
Attorney for Plaintiff,
N. J. Barry, Esq.,
Attorney for Defendant.

Statement of pleadings was made by respective counsel, whereupon the following testimony was had:

MR. SHEEHAN

was called as a witness on behalf of plaintiff, sworn and testified as follows: [137]

Direct Examination

By Mr. Salter:

Q. Will you state your name please sir.

A. J. Sheehan.

Q. Where do you live, Mr. Sheehan?

A. Reno.

(Testimony of John Sheehan.)

Q. How long have you lived in the State of Nevada? A. About all my life.

Q. Have you, in the past, been connected with The First National Bank of Winnemucca?

A. I have.

Q. Do you remember when you first became connected with that bank? A. About 1905.

Q. And in what capacity?

A. First as clerk, assistant cashier, cashier and vice-president.

Q. And were you also connected with The Reno National Bank? A. I was.

Q. And in what capacity? A. Vice-president.

Q. And what duties did you perform there with reference to supervision over other banks in the State?

A. Well, the usual duties that attach to an executive officer.

Q. Well, were you an executive officer of the Wingfield chain of banks? A. Not all of them.

Q. What banks were you the executive officer of, Mr. Sheehan?

A. The Reno National Bank, Bank of Nevada, The First National Bank of Winnemucca, Churchill County Bank, Bank of Sparks, Virginia City Bank, Tonopah Banking Corporation, John S. Cook. [138]

Q. Now, then, as executive officer, did you supervise the business and the running of all of the banks that you have testified to?

(Testimony of John Sheehan.)

A. Each bank had a separate board of directors and I attended each meeting that I could.

Q. With reference to The First National Bank and The Reno National Bank, were part of the directors of The Reno National Bank also directors of The First National Bank?

A. There were two of them.

Q. And which two?

A. Mr. Wingfield and myself.

Q. And that was true of all the rest of the Wingfield chain? A. It was.

Q. Mr. Sheehan, do you remember a transaction whereby, about June 30, 1932, certain notes and mortgages were sold by The First National Bank to the Reno National Bank?

A. I know that such a thing happened but I can't recall the date. Each bank was doing the same thing.

Q. Do you remember the note and mortgage of S. & J. Alcorta?

A. I knew we had that account, but didn't know there was an application.

Q. You know that about that time there were certain notes and mortgages sold by The First National Bank to The Reno National Bank?

A. I do.

Q. Could you state why that transaction took place?

A. Well, we were arranging for a loan from the R. F. C. and many of the loans were brought to

(Testimony of John Sheehan.)

Reno to bring the different [139] notes together into one application and often it is done for the purpose of avoiding an excess loan in the bank at Winnemucca or any other bank, sometimes to build up the reserve in one bank, sometimes to give earnings to the bank if they needed it. I don't recall why that was made, but I think it was to obtain money from the R. F. C.

Q. You obtained about that time from the R.F.C. quite a lot of money and placed with them certain notes and mortgages that you held in The Reno National Bank? A. Yes sir.

Q. How did you dispose of the money that you got from the R. F. C.?

A. It was credited out to the various banks entitled to the credit to the amount of the securities that they contributed.

Q. But all the money was handled by The Reno National Bank? A. It was, yes sir.

Q. Do you know if any of this money that you received from the R. F. C. was ever sent to The First National Bank of Winnemucca?

A. Well, The First National Bank of Winnemucca, or any other bank, received credit when they sent in their notes.

Q. Now, with reference to the notes and mortgages that were sold by The First National Bank to The Reno National Bank, were those notes and mortgages so sold without recourse, or how?

A. The endorsement on the notes was without recourse.

(Testimony of John Sheehan.)

Q. Then you would say that that was an absolute sale to The Reno National Bank?

A. Well, it was, yes, as far as the banks were concerned.

Q. Now were these notes and mortgages that were sold by The [140] First National Bank to the Reno National Bank—what was the custom, usage and understanding between the two banks with reference to the proceeds that might be derived from the liquidation or collection?

A. Well, that is the first time we had occasion to borrow money on the notes, but prior to that, in the distribution of notes, it was understood that all banks were to be protected.

Q. Do you know if each one of these mortgages carried a provision that any advances made were to be secured by the mortgages?

A. It was, I think; both the trust deeds and the mortgages contained that provision.

Q. Up until the time of this transaction, up to that time, in case you bought mortgages and notes from another bank and you had liquidation of them or collected them, what was your understanding and practice as to the distribution of those notes?

A. We distributed upon prorata, according to the holdings of each bank, as near as we could.

Q. In other words, if you foreclosed on a mortgage and there were certain advances made on those mortgages held by The Reno National Bank that had been sold to you, you would calculate the pro-

(Testimony of John Sheehan.)

rata and then you would remit to those banks that had made the advances, according to the prorata?

A. The practice was to take up the last note first from the proceeds of sale of cattle, or whatever it was. For instance, we sent an excess loan here, and then followed by expense note, the expense note should be taken up first. We tried to do that.

Q. You mean by that that where The Reno National Bank held a note and mortgage that they bought from The First National Bank, [141] and certain advances had been made to those borrowers by The First National Bank, that from the first proceeds of the collection of this mortgage, or mortgages, that you would remit to The First National Bank the amount of their overdrafts or notes, is that right?

A. I think I have your point; it was, yes.

Q. In other words, you would get those proceeds from the sale of sheep or wool during the year and it was your custom to pay these advances which were carried in the nature of notes or overdrafts first before you started liquidating the notes?

A. That is the idea. The First National Bank of Winnemucca had a limit of $30,000. If the excess note was $10,000, it was sent to The Reno National Bank; then followed by another note of $5,000, The Reno National Bank probably sent the $5,000 to the Tonopah Banking Corporation; then when the proceeds came in, we would ask The Reno National

(Testimony of John Sheehan.)

Bank to take up the $5,000; The Reno National Bank would take up the $5,000 and send it to Tonopah; that was the last note issued. Sometimes we couldn't do that.

Q. That was your intention and custom to do that? A. That was the intention, yes sir.

Q. In other words, if I understand your testimony, it was your custom and practice for many years, in the handling of these accounts, that advances made by the bank selling the notes and mortgages to The Reno National Bank would have the same protection as to those advances as The Reno National Bank would holding the notes and mortgages? A. That was the intention, yes sir.

Q. Mr. Sheehan, with reference to the advances made on these [142] notes and mortgages sold to you by The First National Bank and covered in this complaint, will you state whether or not those advances were made by the officers of The First National Bank under your direction?

A. Well, yes. I will state that when they start to make up these applications they are nearly all done at the same time. I couldn't supervise all of them, so the authority was delegated to a man like Mr. Moore, the vice-president of the Winnemucca bank, and sent down here and then the R. F. C. sent their own man to assist in the work. After that time I was part of the time on the R. F. C. in San Francisco and part of the time in Washington.

Q. Then that authority then would apply to the Alcorta advances, the Dufurrena advances, the Ga-

(Testimony of John Sheehan.)

bica advances, the Juan Jaca advances, the Johnstone advances, the Larribeau advances, the Yragui advances and the Belaustegui advances?

A. It would.

Q. Will you state whether or not as each of these advances were made to The First National Bank, if it was the custom for you to be notified of those advances? A. Yes sir.

Q. Do you know how often that statement came down?

A. Sometimes by telephone every day.

Q. So that you were kept informed at all times as to what advances had been made by The First National Bank?

A. I was, and then had weekly statement, a summary of everything.

Q. Mr. Sheehan, do you remember the transaction where the John G. Taylor, Inc. executed a note secured by chattel mortgage in [143] the sum of $700,000? A. I do.

Q. Who took that note and mortgage, The Reno National Bank or The First National Bank?

A. Well, it was given, as I recall, to The Reno National Bank for the purpose of consolidating into one mortgage all of the indebtedness held by the various banks.

Q. After the execution of that note and mortgage by John G. Taylor, Inc., did you instruct J. G. Moore, vice-president of The First National Bank of Winnemucca, to make certain loans and honor

(Testimony of John Sheehan.)

checks of the John G. Taylor, Inc., and to carry the same on his books as overdrafts and notes?

A. I did.

Q. How did you instruct him, Mr. Sheehan, by letter or wire or both?

A. By phone. Mr. Moore called up and said Mr. Taylor was there and needed, I think, $15,000. He said he would have a check from his land within three or four days and I said if he knew that check was coming, we would carry it as an overdraft. The check came after they closed and was turned over to the R. F. C.

Q. Now then, if the records show that John G. Taylor borrowed $25,000 on September 16, 1932, and $5,000 on September 29, 1932, and $15,142.18 on November 25, 1932, from The First National Bank, was that thru your authority?

A. Most of it was. There might be some there that I wasn't here, but most of it was by my authority.

Q. That is direct authority? [144]

A. Yes sir.

Q. Was it the understanding that these advances were to be made by John G. Moore? A. Yes sir.

Q. Did you also write him a letter stating——

A. I probably did. I probably confirmed the telephone message.

Q. Would you state what your understanding was with reference to that account, as to how it would be prorated, if at all?

(Testimony of John Sheehan.)

A. Well, that wasn't to be prorated. That was an overdraft and I always felt that the R. A. C. C. should have returned that check from the lands directly over to The First National Bank of Winnemucca.

Q. In other words, as they made collections they would take up these overdrafts and loans first?

A. Yes sir.

Q. Suppose you had liquidated that $700,000, how would you have prorated the proceeds?

A. Well, the same as it was prorated. After getting the money it was distributed to all banks entitled to it.

Q. And that was the custom with reference to this particular loan as it was to all others?

A. It was, yes sir.

Q. And you were notified, of course, of these loans at the same time? A. I was.

Q. Now, Senator, do you remember a loan made to Lobarde Bros. & Company for $70,000 about March 24, 1931? A. I do. [145]

Q. Do you remember that transaction, is that in your mind clearly?

A. Well, yes, I think it comes back to me.

Q. Would you state what those circumstances were?

A. The amount was practically the amount due The First National Bank at Winnemucca and The Reno National Bank and I think the mortgage was taken in favor of The Reno National Bank and the

(Testimony of John Sheehan.)

entire loan brought down here, leaving Winnemucca with the $30,000 that it could handle.

Q. Do you remember when this loan of $70,000 was made that a mortgage was given covering that amount to The Reno National Bank, $70,000, mortgage and two notes were given, one for $42,000 and one for $28,000? A. Yes sir.

Q. Do you remember that The Reno National Bank kept $42,000? A. Yes sir.

Q. And that the $28,000 was sent to The First National Bank? A. It was.

Q. And then under this mortgage the $42,000 was secured as well as the $28,000? A. It was.

Q. What was your understanding and custom and usage with reference to the proceeds which might be derived from foreclosure or collection of those notes and mortgages?

A. Well, the collateral pledge was for the benefit of both banks.

Q. And it was the understanding, then, that they should prorate according to the amount that each held? [146]

A. There was no understanding had at that time, but that was the way we handled that.

Q. That was always your custom, was it?

A. Yes sir.

Q. Do you remember if afterwards an advance was made of $3,612.49 by The First National Bank to these debtors, under your authority?

A. It was.

(Testimony of John Sheehan.)

Q. And you were so notified?

A. Just the same as the Taylors, at the same time.

Q. Mr. Sheehan, with reference to the notes and mortgages that were sold to The Reno National Bank by the First National Bank about the 30th of June, 1932, do you remember if you gave The First National Bank credit on your books immediately after receiving those securities?

A. I don't remember, but that's the way we should handle it; should have credit immediately upon sending the notes down here. They would receive credit for the face value of the amount.

Q. In other words, you wouldn't carry it there in your bank and make those entries later?

A. No sir.

Q. So if those notes and mortgages were sent down to you on the 30th of June, 1932, you would immediately credit The First National Bank with the amount of those mortgages and notes?

A. We would.

Q. Now do you remember the execution of a subordination agreement between The First National Bank of Winnemucca and the Reconstruction Finance Corporation, dated the 25th of July, 1932?

[147]

A. I can't recall as I do, but we had one about that time. I don't know who signed it.

Q. I will show you a paper, which is defendant's Exhibit A in this suit, purporting to have been

(Testimony of John Sheehan.)

signed by The First National Bank of Winnemucca, Nevada, by George Wingfield, President, and J. G. Moore, Secretary, corporate seal. Would that refresh your memory as to the signing of that Exhibit A or the transaction?

A. Well, it was signed by Mr. Wingfield, you say, and J. G. Moore, not by me.

Q. Do you remember, or do you know, by whose authority that paper was executed?

A. That would indicate that I wasn't here at that time.

Q. What was Mr. Wingfield's position with reference to The Reno National Bank and The First National Bank? A. President of both banks.

Mr. Barry: We admit that that subordination agreement was made on that date.

Mr. Salter: Will you also stipulate it was made by direction and authority of George Wingfield, President of both banks?

Mr. Barry: It was made by authority of the Wingfield bank.

Mr. Salter: No, we want to show it was made by authority of George Wingfield, President of both banks.

Mr. Barry: And no one else?

Mr. Salter: Well, may it be stipulated that George Wingfield, President of The Reno National Bank, and also President of The First National Bank, a member of the Board of Directors of both banks, by authority of the directors of The First

(Testimony of John Sheehan.)

National Bank of Winnemucca, executed this paper? [148]

Mr. Barry: I think we will admit that that subordination agreement was made with the authority of the directors of The First National Bank of Winnemucca and that George Wingfield at that time was a director of The First National Bank of Winnemucca and also a director of The Reno National Bank.

Mr. Salter: That is all right.

Q. What authority, if you know, Mr. Sheehan, did George Wingfield exercise over the Wingfield chain of banks?

A. He was the president, in complete authority; he was the majority stockholder in all of the banks.

Q. And he exercised authority then with you over the entire Wingfield banks, as far as business transactions and loans were concerned?

A. He did, yes sir.

Q. Now, Mr. Sheehan, bearing in mind that these securities that we base this suit on were sold to The Reno National Bank without recourse by The First National Bank on June 30, 1932, and credited to The First National Bank of Winnemucca, and this subordination agreement was executed on July 25, 1932, would you say that any part of that money that you received from the R. F. C. was sent to The First National Bank in Winnemucca?

A. I don't think that was anything to do with that money. I think The Reno National Bank

(Testimony of John Sheehan.)

credited The First National Bank with the full amount of the application and the First National Bank would check out as she needed it.

The Court: I don't understand what is meant by that answer. I would like to have it explained a little more fully. [149]

A. For instance, if the amount of the application was $400,000 and was sent from Winnemucca to Reno, Reno would credit The First National Bank immediately with that amount, then The Reno National Bank would include those notes in the application to the R. F. C. and when the amount came back, it was credited to The Reno National Bank, so that The Reno National Bank perhaps didn't receive the full amount that she credited Winnemucca with. The whole application, as I understand, was about a million two hundred thousand dollars and in that was included the notes from all of the banks and the one million two hundred thousand would be credited to the Crocker National Bank and the Crocker National Bank would be charged that amount and we would credit the other banks up here in proportion to the amount they had in the application.

The Court: Then there would be a portion of that amount carried on the books of The Reno National Bank as on open account or something for The First National Bank of Winnemucca?

A. Yes sir.

Q. (Mr. Salter): Let me see if I can straighten this out a little bit, Mr. Sheehan——

(Testimony of John Sheehan.)

A. Now, when you speak of July 25th, I was in Washington. I am a little hazy on how they handled that while I was gone, but that would be my thought of it.

Q. Now, about June 30, 1932, and for some little time prior to that, say from the 9th of June, 1932, to the 30th of June, 1932, The First National Bank sold to The Reno National Bank about $575,000 worth of paper, which is covered in our complaint. Immediately after receiving those securities from The First [150] National Bank, you would credit The First National Bank of Winnemucca with that entire amount?

A. That is my understanding.

Q. That is all about the 9th to 30th of June, 1932. That paper was sold to The Reno National Bank without recourse? A. It was.

Q. And you had instructions from the Comptroller of the Currency to handle that paper in that manner, is that true?

A. It was. I do not know as there were any direct instructions from the Comptroller.

Q. Well, I will show you a resolution, if you don't remember, Mr. Sheehan, that was passed by The First National Bank directors on that point.

A. That is what the bank examiners required, but I do not know as it came from the Comptroller.

Q. I show you a copy of a letter which is pasted in the minutes of The First National Bank of Winnemucca, Nevada, on page 141, Book No. 3, dated

(Testimony of John Sheehan.)

June 13, 1925, addressed to the Comptroller of the Currency, Washington, D. C., purported to have been signed by J. Sheehan, George E. Stall, Wm. F. Stock, John G. Taylor, J. G. Moore, J. O. Walther and George Wingfield, and ask you if you remember writing that letter to the Comptroller of the Currency of the United States?

A. Well, I don't know as I remember it.

Q. Well, do you know the signatures?

A. My signature and the signatures of all the others.

Q. Just read this if you will, Mr. Sheehan.

A. First National Bank, Winnemucca, Nevada. June 13, 1925. [151] Comptroller of the Currency, Washington, D. C. Dear Sir: In connection with the examination of our bank completed May 23rd, our attention has been called by your examiner, C. S. Coffin, to the following matters: Sold Paper. You are advised that this bank is in no way liable, either directly or indirectly, on any paper sold. You are further advised that efforts will be made to have customers who require seasonal lines of credit in excess of our legal limit make arrangements direct with the Reno National Bank. Respectfully, (signed) J. Sheehan, Geo. E. Stall, Wm. F. Stock, John G. Taylor, J. G. Moore, J. O. Walther, Geo. Wingfield, Directors.

Mr. Barry: Just a minute. I don't see the materiality of this.

(Testimony of John Sheehan.)

Mr. Salter: I am merely trying to show, if the Court please, that when these notes and mortgages were sold to The Reno National Bank they were sold without recourse.

Mr. Barry: They are so endorsed, aren't they?

Mr. Salter: Yes. Mr. Sheehan didn't remember whether that was true or not and I am trying to refresh his memory of it. I think you admit, Judge Barry, that all this paper was sold to The Reno National Bank without recourse?

Mr. Barry: If that is the fact.

Q. That is a fact, is it, Mr. Sheehan?

A. It was. We had authority to make some changes sometimes. I can explain the reason for this.

Q. If you will, please.

A. There was one loan aggregating, I think, $30,000 in excess of the amount that Winnemucca held, but some way or other, when the [152] property was sold off the proceeds were distributed on the banks outside and Winnemucca took all the loss. In other words, Winnemucca took several thousand dollars more than she could loan and the bank examiner discovered it and insisted that some letter of that kind be written.

Q. Now, when The Reno National Bank bought these mortgages and securities from The First National Bank, did they become the owners of that paper without recourse on The First National Bank? A. Yes sir.

(Testimony of John Sheehan.)

Q. Now then, do you know when you borrowed this money from the R. F. C., The Reno National Bank borrowed from the R. F. C.?

A. It was pending a long while. It seems to me we started in February, 1932, and didn't get the money until along about the last of May, I think.

Q. Then in this subordination agreement executed by The First National Bank, dated the 25th of July, 1932, you had already credited The First National Bank on this paper bought for a month, is that right?

A. I would take that as probably the second application. There was probably one application made on this, one in July.

Q. You mean by The Reno National Bank?

A. Yes; and I don't remember whether Winnemucca was included in it or not.

Q. Did The First National Bank ever make an application for loan from the R. F. C. direct about this time? A. Yes, I think they did.

Q. That was a separate transaction from the loan that you made from The Reno National Bank? [153]

A. Yes, for which The Reno National Bank couldn't be held at all.

Q. And that loan that The First National Bank of Winnemucca made from the R. F. C. was repaid and wiped out, was it?

A. I couldn't say as to that. That happened after the bank closed.

(Testimony of John Sheehan.)

Q. But any way the application that you made on behalf of The Reno National Bank had nothing to do with any application made by The First National Bank with the R. F. C.?

A. Not the first one, no sir.

The Court: Let me see if I understand that situation. I had the impression heretofore that the only application for the R. F. C. loan was made with The Reno National Bank, but was it also included in the application by The First National Bank and other banks?

A. I think, your Honor, there was an application made independent of The Reno National Bank direct from The First National Bank, but I wouldn't be sure.

Q. (Mr. Barry): You mean the Winnemucca bank when you say The First National Bank?

A. Winnemucca, yes sir. I am a little hazy for the reason that the State banks had only limited borrowing power, on account of their capital, and those banks naturally then were turned over to The Reno National Bank and I don't know whether The First National Bank at Winnemucca was included in that or not.

The Court: If it is important that can be looked up and found out later.

Q. (Mr. Salter): Mr. Sheehan, do you remember whether there was [154] a joint application made by The First National Bank and The Reno National Bank for loan from the R. F. C.?

(Testimony of John Sheehan.)

A. No, I can't say.

Q. Was it your custom to gather up a lot of paper from the various banks in the State and bring that into The Reno National Bank and then make a loan with that paper which you had brought to The Reno National Bank with the R. F. C.?

A. Yes sir.

Q. And then The Reno National Bank took credit for that entire loan, isn't that right?

A. They did.

Q. And then there wasn't any distribution then to the other banks of that particular loan?

A. Well, they were given credit for the amount of their securities that were included in that loan.

Q. But isn't it true that you had already given these various banks credit? A. Yes.

Q. Before you made the loan on that paper from the R. F. C.? A. Yes, that is true.

The Court: I think at this point we will take our usual recess for about 10 minutes.

(Recess taken at 11:00 o'clock)

11:10 A. M.

MR. SHEEHAN

resumes the stand on further direct examination.

Q. (Mr. Salter): Now, Mr. Sheehan, referring to the latter part of June, 1932, and the date that these mortgages and notes were [155] sold to The Reno National Bank by The First National Bank, do you know the condition of The First National

(Testimony of John Sheehan.)

Bank at that time, whether it was solvent or insolvent? A. Well, I maintain it was solvent.

Mr. Barry: I move to strike that out. That isn't the answer; that is conclusion.

The Court: That may stand subject to the objection.

Q. From your knowledge of the financial condition of The First National Bank of Winnemucca, was it necessary for that paper to have been transferred from The First National Bank to The Reno National Bank for The First National Bank's protection?

A. I don't know as it was. I think The First National Bank of Winnemucca was going along pretty well by itself.

The Court: Let me ask a question right here. It has been brought out in the testimony that there was a limit on the amounts which The First National Bank could loan. How was that limitation arrived at?

A. The capital surplus of the bank is $300,000. Under the National Bank Law it could loan ten per cent of that amount.

The Court: That is to one individual?

A. Yes sir.

The Court: That is, the limit to any single loan?

A. Yes, sir.

Q. (Mr. Salter): Now, from your knowledge of the financial condition of The First National Bank, notwithstanding the loan on October 29, 1932, when

(Testimony of John Sheehan.)

it closed its doors, what was the condition of The First National Bank, solvent or insolvent? [156]

Mr. Barry: I object; it calls for conclusion. This witness hasn't shown he has qualifications to testify. That would require quite an investigation to determine whether it was solvent or not. I understand it paid 60 per cent, so it isn't very solvent.

The Court: I will permit the question to be answered, subject to the objection. The Court had occasion to consider this matter subject to The Reno National Bank, that where the bank had been closed under the Governor's proclamation and then later taken over by the Comptroller of the Currency, there was a presumption that the insolvency would relate back to the time of closing of the bank. I have forgotten just what that ruling was; it may not apply here.

Mr. Barry: That was the ruling in the case of Cantor against The Reno National Bank, and the Court took judicial knowledge that the bank was insolvent at the closing of its doors.

The Court: We will consider those matters later. This answer may be given subject to the objection. I think that the ruling was substantially to this effect, that in the absence of any showing to the contrary, the presumption related back to the date of foreclosure.

Q. (Mr. Salter): Now, Mr. Sheehan, as vice-president and executive officer of all these banks, were you familiar with the financial condition of each one? A. I was. [157]

(Testimony of John Sheehan.)

Q. Did you receive, from time to time, reports from each of these banks? A. I did.

Q. Did you receive, from time to time, report as to the financial condition of The First National Bank? A. I did.

Q. And did you familiarize yourself with those reports? A. I did.

Q. You are familiar, then, with all the transactions and all the paper, all the loans and the assets of The First National Bank of Winnemucca?

A. Yes sir.

Mr. Barry: This goes in over our objection, of course.

The Court: Yes.

Q. Now, in having The Reno National Bank buy this paper from The First National Bank, was that for the purpose of strengthening the financial condition of The First National Bank or otherwise?

A. Well, I don't know just how to answer that.

Q. Well, was The First National Bank in such a condition financially that you thought it was necessary to buy this paper to protect the interests of The First National Bank, or was The First National Bank in good condition financially if they had kept the $575,000 worth of paper?

A. Well, I think if they had kept it they would have been about as well off. This money was all borrowed for the general good of the State and each bank was expected to stand in and help out in se-

(Testimony of John Sheehan.)

curing of the money to bring it in here, putting up that [158] collateral and securing it.

Mr. Salter: I think that is all.

Cross Examination

By Mr. Barry:

Q. As I understand this borrow from the R. F. C. was for the purpose of assisting all of the State banks in the Wingfield chain?

A. Yes sir, wherever needed.

Q. Wherever they needed it? A. Yes sir.

Q. Would you say at the time these notes were transferred by the Winnemucca bank that they needed it?

A. I don't think they did at that time.

Q. Had they made an application before that to borrow money from the R. F. C.?

A. I think they had.

Q. And had received some money?

A. I think so.

Q. Then what was the purpose of that transfer of the notes down here?

A. To go into the general application to get the money.

Q. So as to get money from the R. F. C. to assist all of the banks?

A. Yes sir. I think that was the suggestion of the R. F. C.

Q. These notes, none of them, were in excess of the loan, were they? Yes, some of the notes were in excess of the amount they could loan?

(Testimony of John Sheehan.)

A. Yes sir. [159]

Q. Now as to those notes, the idea was to help The First National Bank of Winnemucca make a loan for the amount allowed and you take up the surplus?

A. In order to reduce the excess, that is true.

Q. In that sense it was an accommodation to The First National Bank? A. It was.

Q. The directors of The First National Bank of Winnemucca passed a resolution declaring that they were insolvent and asking to be taken over, did they? A. We did.

Q. And that was because the bank at that time was insolvent?

A. Yes sir; that was in the fall, I think.

Q. In the fall of 1932?

A. About October, I think.

Q. Then later, if not on that date, The First National Bank was insolvent, so that wouldn't have made them insolvent? A. It was.

Q. Now when those notes came down here, totalling some $578,000, The Reno National Bank gave The First National Bank credit for them?

A. The face amount.

Q. That was the same as cash in banking, wasn't it? A. It was; they were using it.

Q. You don't send out cash in these deals; it was all done by check and *credit?*

Q. You give them credit so that they can draw on that bank to the amount of those notes? [160]

(Testimony of John Sheehan.)

A. That is right.

Q. And when they did so, you took care of overdrafts and checks? A. We did.

Q. Then immediately hypothecated those securities to the R. F. C., did you not? A. We did.

Q. And I think you stated in your direct examination that you didn't get as much credit from the R. F. C. as you had given credit to the Winnemucca bank?

A. I don't mean to specify any particular bank. For instance, our application may have been for two million dollars and we got credit for a million and a quarter.

Q. But you would have to send in a whole lot more security than that? A. Yes sir.

Q. You didn't get the full face value of your security? A. No sir.

Q. So on these notes that you took over out there from the Winnemucca bank, you didn't get the face value in a loan from the R. F. C.?

A. Well, I would have to check that over. There were some loans the R. F. C. allowed in full in the application and others they cut down to probably 50 per cent.

Q. But so far as the Winnemucca bank was concerned, the transaction was closed? A. Yes sir.

Q. And whatever you got from the R. F. C. you retained in The Reno National Bank? [161]

A. We did.

Q. Because these notes were yours and you had paid for them. Now did the Winnemucca bank know,

(Testimony of John Sheehan.)

at the time you took these notes, that you were going to hypothecate them?

A. That was the purpose, they understood.

Q. One of the purposes? A. Yes sir.

Q. That and the excess loan limit?

A. Yes sir.

Q. Now when this subordination agreement was made by the Winnemucca bank, previous to that you had taken over these notes on the 25th of July, 1932?

A. Yes, I think we had.

Q. And that transaction was just the same as if you had paid cash for them. You bought the notes from the Winnemucca bank? A. Yes.

Q. Then in consideration of that, the Winnemucca bank made a subordination agreement to the R. F. C.? A. Yes.

Q. Now on this endorsing of the notes without recourse, if you hadn't endorsed without recourse, you couldn't have avoided the excess limit—if they could come back with it, it wouldn't be avoiding the excess limit, isn't that what it was done for?

A. That is what it was done for, yes sir.

Q. And wasn't there an understanding, in a measure, if they could that the Winnemucca bank would take those notes back?

A. Well, it wasn't absolutely necessary.

Q. But they could take them back and pay you for them? [162] A. Yes sir.

Q. Now they have set up in their complaint here that it was the agreement, custom, usage and prac-

(Testimony of John Sheehan.)

tice that the bank selling its securities to another bank might make advances and those advances should be pro rated. Now between The Reno National Bank and the Winnemucca bank was there anything said at all in the agreement, or did you just rely upon the usage?

A. There was no agreement entered into but the matter had been talked over among perhaps Mr. Wingfield and myself.

Q. That advances should be taken care of?

A. Yes sir.

Q. You testified on your direct examination that, for instance, if a $35,000 indebtedness occurred in the Winnemucca bank, that the Winnemucca bank, in taking the note and mortgage, would hold $30,000 of that indebtedness, more or less, and say five thousand would be sent to The Reno National Bank, the excess? A. That is correct.

Q. And then The Reno National Bank would send that $5,000 to the Tonopah Banking Corporation? A. Yes sir.

Q. And the first money you realized from the mortgaged property you would pay the Tonopah bank? A. If we could, yes sir.

Q. Wasn't that the custom all of the time, that the party who took up this excess should be paid out of the first monies? A. That is correct.

Q. Now on this John G. Taylor matter—John G. Taylor gave a mortgage of $700,000 and then you advanced him certain advance- [163] ments on over-

(Testimony of John Sheehan.)

drafts and notes; that is, the Winnemucca bank did that. I believe you testified that you authorized the officers of The First National Bank to do that?

A. I did.

Q. Did you do that as an officer of The Reno National Bank or as an officer of The First National Bank?

A. First National Bank. In that transaction The Reno National Bank was hardly known.

Q. And you did that as an officer of The First National Bank?

A. The First National Bank. That was between The First National Bank of Winnemucca and the R. A. C. C.

Q. You mean the R. F. C.?

A. No sir, the R. A. C. C.

The Court: What is the full name?

A. Regional Agricultural Credit Corporation.

Q. They take care of expenses on personal property and make loans?

A. They had just come in here about that time, a man by the name of Westgate was in charge; and as I explained, check for this amount was turned over to him and he kept it for future expenses for Mr. Taylor's outfit, when I had pledged it to take up the overdraft at Winnemucca, and he kept it, so I am informed, and that is the reason for the overdraft at Winnemucca.

Q. In this deal with the Winnemucca bank, in taking over those securities in June, 1932, at the

(Testimony of John Sheehan.)

time you gave them credit for some $578,000, could you have done that unless you got a loan from the R. F. C.?

A. No, we wouldn't have done it. [164]

Q. You wouldn't have done it?

A. No sir. We asked all banks, I think, to come in with their applications.

Q. You wouldn't have done it if you hadn't known that you were going to get the money from the R. F. C.? A. No.

Q. Well, that did assist the Winnemucca bank in keeping its doors open, didn't it?

A. Yes sir.

Q. And was a benefit?

A. It was. I think they had quite a balance on hand with us at the time but nevertheless, it didn't do them any harm.

Q. Well, they needed it, didn't they? A. Yes.

Q. When you took over these notes from the Winnemucca bank, the first notes that were taken in June, 1932, did you have any idea as to their value? A. Well, I did at that time, yes.

Q. Did you think they were worth the money that you were giving them credit for? A. I did.

Q. Take this Laborde indebtedness; as I understand the situation, Laborde had got into the Winnemucca Bank in the sum of about $70,000?

A. That is correct.

Q. And that had originated in the Winnemucca bank; The Reno National Bank had nothing to do with it.

(Testimony of John Sheehan.)

A. Well, it would never amounted to that amount unless we knew [165] we had an outlet for the surplus.

Q. But the money went to Laborde from the Winnemucca bank, the $70,000?

A. Well, I would have to go back and explain that a little bit.

Q. Go ahead.

A. At the time Laborde bought out his outfit he paid $60,000, as I remember it, and he had some money besides. We couldn't loan him that amount of money. We loaned him up to our limit and sent the surplus down here. Then as time went along, the same as with other stockmen, the loan increased instead of decreasing, and the excess above the $30,000 was always taken here.

Q. But he did get the credit from the Winnemucca bank? A. He did.

Q. And you sent $43,000 of that down to this bank? A. Yes sir.

Q. And you did this so you could carry Laborde, make the loan to him of $30,000?

A. That is right.

Q. Then that was an accommodation to the Winnemucca bank to have The Reno National Bank take them over, wasn't it? A. It was.

Q. Then The Reno National Bank took over that $30,000 to save the Winnemucca bank from violating the excess limit?

A. Well, that is the way it appears now, but nothing was said about that at that time. It was

(Testimony of John Sheehan.)

considered a very fine loan. About that time a lot of these little banks could hardly exist unless they could get some 8% paper from some source and we were trying to get them going. [166]

Q. That was the Wingfield banks?

A. Yes sir. The Winnemucca bank never knew where their notes went to after they left. They were sent to The Reno National Bank, might have been held in Tonopah, Carson or somewhere else.

Q. Do you remember the date of the subordination agreement between The Reno National Bank and the R. F. C.? A. I do not.

Q. Is that your signature? A. It is.

Q. Is that the signature of P. L. Nelson?

A. It is.

Mr. Barry: That is the original subordination agreement. The only purpose, if the Court please, is to show the date of it. I do not want to put it in because it is necessary for Mr. Tobin to keep it. I want it understood that this is the date.

Mr. Salter: All right.

Mr. Barry: This is dated the 19th of March, 1932. Let the record so show. That is the subordination agreement between The Reno National Bank and the Reconstruction Finance Corporation.

Q. You have testified to the practice, usage and custom here that when, say the Winnemucca bank, would make an excess of loan and they would send the excess to The Reno National Bank, it was the usage and practice and custom that the Winnemucca

(Testimony of John Sheehan.)

bank might go on and take care of overdrafts and future advances and be secured under the mortgage. Was that the custom? A. Yes sir.

Q. Didn't you have some such dealings with the Crocker Bank, The Reno National Bank, wherein you turned over excess and things [167] like that to the Crocker Bank?

A. Only once that I can recall. That was loaned direct to Taylor.

Q. The Crocker Bank took a direct loan of $700,-000?

A. That was direct loan, it seems to me, about $500,000, with the understanding that we would take care of any expenses.

Q. You eventually got that back, didn't you?

A. We got that back.

Q. Wasn't it the understanding at that time out of any proceeds the Crocker Bank was to be paid first and you were to take care of any advances?

A. Oh well, we were borrowing temporary amounts from Crocker while the blanks were being made up and then when we got the loan from the R. F. C., the Crocker advance was first on the application.

Q. But they wouldn't stand for advances or future notes? A. Notes?

Q. Wasn't that the custom, where a correspondent bank takes care of papers, isn't it the usage, custom and practice that out of the first moneys the correspondent bank is taken care of?

(Testimony of John Sheehan.)

A. That is our custom, but lots of times we are taking this excess paper for the benefit of these little banks, so as to make this 8 per cent money.

Q. You were doing that as an accommodation to the little banks? A. Yes sir.

Q. But the usage and custom is, where you borrow from these correspondent banks, that their loan is to be taken care of first? [168]

A. First, yes sir.

Mr. Barry: I think that is all.

Redirect Examination

By Mr. Salter:

Q. Now, Mr. Sheehan, with reference to the Laborde matter, the final result was that The Reno National Bank took two notes, one for $42,000 and one for $28,000, secured by one mortgage, is that correct? A. That is right.

Q. The Reno National Bank kept $42,000 note and the $28,000 note was sent to the Winnemucca bank, is that right? A. That is right.

Q. So that it was the understanding that when this mortgage was foreclosed that The Reno National Bank would get $42,000 and the Winnemucca Bank would get $28,000, if it was collected in full?

A. That is the way we expected it to work out.

Q. And if it didn't collect the mortgage in full, that the amounts so collected were to be pro-rated?

A. That is our way of doing things.

(Testimony of John Sheehan.)

Q. Now isn't it a fact when you took these mortgage and these two notes from Laborde for The Reno National Bank, in the sum of $70,000, The Reno National Bank sold to The First National Bank the note for $28,000, isn't that the way that transaction was?

A. Well, that is the intimation, but the fact of the matter was there was a participating loan, in which the two banks agreed to join and take it and we could only take at Winnemucca $30,000. I think when the loan was first arranged, before coming to Reno, if I remember right, Winnemucca was to participate in that loan [169] for $30,000, and The Reno National Bank for the balance of the $42,000 note.

Q. And you can't remember whether or not The Reno National Bank sold The First National Bank the $28,000 note and received credit on the books of The First National Bank at Winnemucca?

A. I don't remember, but I think that they did.

Mr. Salter: That is all.

Recross Examination

By Mr. Barry:

Q. Let us get that straight. We seem to be much at sea on that. As I understand the transaction, the indebtedness occurred at Winnemucca——

A. Naturally they kept their account there and that was his headquarters and when he came in—I don't remember who was the officer or how we

(Testimony of John Sheehan.)

handled it, by letter or telephone—but he had to have some money, so much money, and it was understood and agreed that he could have it and it amounted to $30,000 for Winnemucca and the balance for Reno.

Q. To avoid an excess loan?

A. It was an excess loan but both banks agreed to participate. Had The Reno National Bank refused, the Winnemucca Bank would only loaned $30,000.

Q. They would have been entitled to loan only $30,000? A. Yes.

Q. But they took $28,000 and The Reno National Bank took $42,000?

A. The reason for the amounts, taking a little less than the $30,000, was to leave a little leeway for expenses.

Q. I see, but as a matter of fact, The Reno National Bank didn't sell that $28,000 note to the Winnemucca bank? [170] A. Oh no.

Q. And The Reno National Bank got credit for it?

A. I thought counsel here was referring to the application from the R. F. C.

Mr. Salter: No, what I was referring to is this. If the Court please, my contention is this—and I think I can prove it by the facts—that The Reno National Bank took a mortgage from Laborde for $70,000. They had Laborde make out two notes, one for $42,000, which was retained by The Reno Na-

(Testimony of John Sheehan.)

tional Bank, and one for $28,000, which was sent to The First National Bank at Winnemucca, and The First National Bank at Winnemucca gave The Reno National Bank credit on their books for $28,000. That is the transaction that Jim Moore testified to in his deposition, which I expect to introduce.

Mr. Barry: But that isn't the fact. The transaction was just as you related. Laborde wanted $70,000 worth of credit. The Winnemucca Bank took $28,000 and this bank in here took $42,000. They were both secured by the mortgage, but The Reno National Bank never took credit for $28,000, that was sent out to Winnemucca.

A. Laborde kept the $28,000 and the $42,000. It would seem to me the way it should have been handled when the loan was completed between us; the $70,000 took up the notes that were then outstanding and left enough credit for him to buy the property he intended to buy at that time and that account was so handled at Winnemucca.

Q. And Laborde would have $42,000 to The Reno National Bank and $28,000 to the Winnemucca bank? [171]

A. That is right.

The Court: As I understand it, on the records of The Reno National Bank it would show a loan to Laborde of $70,000? A. Yes sir.

The Court: And two notes were given therefor?

A. Yes sir.

(Testimony of John Sheehan.)

The Court: The original mortgage was made to The Reno National Bank? A. Yes sir.

The Court: And $28,000 was transferred to The First National Bank at Winnemucca and appears on the books as a credit from The Reno National Bank?

A. That is right. The mortgage would naturally run to The Reno National Bank, for the reason it was $70,000, whereas the bank at Winnemucca had only a loaning capacity of $30,000. The mortgage would try to be in line with the amount of our loan.

Mr. Barry: That is all.

The Court: Court will be in recess until 1:30.

(Recess taken at 11:50 A. M.)

Afternoon Session

1:35 P. M.

The Court: You may proceed.

MR. NELSON

was called as a witness on behalf of plaintiff, sworn and testified as follows:

Direct Examination

By Mr. Salter:

Q. Will you state your name please.

A. P. L. Nelson. [172]

Q. Where do you live, Mr. Nelson?

(Testimony of P. L. Nelson.)

A. Reno.

Q. Were you ever connected officially with The Reno National Bank? A. Yes.

Q. In what capacity?

A. Assistant cashier and later cashier.

Q. And do you know how long you were so connected with that up to October 29, 1932?

A. As assistant cashier from 1917 until 1931 and during 1931 I was appointed cashier.

Q. And did you remain cashier then until the bank went into liquidation? A. Yes.

Q. Do you know the policy, practice, custom and usage between the various Wingfield chain of banks with reference to how credits would be transferred from one bank to the other, also called straight loans? A. Yes sir.

Q. What was your practice between all the banks, policy, custom and usage with reference to pro rating collections from mortgages, where a mortgage is held by one bank and advances are made by another to some debtors?

A. Well, it had been the practice among all the banks to pro rate equally on collections that were made on all applications that were secured under the same mortgage or deed of trust, except that seasonal advances that were made after the deed of trust or mortgages were in effect were repaid first out of the [173] proceeds of sales of livestock or wool.

(Testimony of P. L. Nelson.)

Q. Can you elaborate on your system of handling those split loans?

A. Well, the practice of handling split loans originated mostly during the administration of W. H. Doyle, who was vice-president of the Wingfield banks from 1917 to 1920. Prior to that time there were a few participations and the Winnemucca loan was carried by The Reno National Bank. Mr. Doyle conceived the idea of taking the split loans into more general use, as I recall, for two principal reasons—one was to provide the various Wingfield banks with loans in such cases where they wouldn't or couldn't make loans otherwise, in order to find an outlet for their money, and the other reason was to provide to the borrowers, who were mostly up in Humboldt County and Elko County, with funds to carry on their business. You see, none of the banks could carry a very big loan at any time, so it wasn't possible for a borrower up in that section to borrow a loan from, we will say The First National Bank at Winnemucca, due to their small limit. Those borrowers who required, say up to $100,000, couldn't get the loan probably anywhere at all outside of the Wingfield banks. At first I think the practice was to take a combined real and chattel mortgage for the real estate and the livestock and I believe that at first that all ran to The First National Bank at Winnemucca, but such mortgage would cover a series of notes in such amounts that they could be parcelled out to the va-

(Testimony of P. L. Nelson.)

rious banks. Later, I believe the practice became more general and that was especially true in taking ranches, to use wither a deed of trust or the combined real and chattel mortgage [174] for the larger amounts to run directly to The Reno National Bank and also in this case in several loans that could be parcelled out to the various banks and I recall in a number of ranches the deed of trust or mortgage would run to all of the banks jointly to cover, for instance, a $20,000 loan that might previously have been carried by John S. Cook & Company, and we will say $30,000 to The First National Bank of Winnemucca and whatever amounts the borrower owed at that time.

Q. Where The Reno National Bank would buy a mortgage, say from the Winnemucca bank, was it the practice and custom for The First National Bank at Winnemucca to make certain advances to those borrowers and that such advances represented by notes or overdrafts would be secured under the mortgage that had been sold to The Reno National Bank? A. That was the custom.

Q. And in case of foreclosure, what would happen to that mortgage, how would the proceeds be handled?

A. Well, I guess theoretically the later advances would be paid first, but I don't recall any instance of a foreclosure as to how the distribution was made; that is, whether the advances taken subsequent to the deed of trust were repaid in full first

(Testimony of P. L. Nelson.)

or whether they participated on the total amount collected.

Q. Do you remember if The First National Bank of Winnemucca was able to put out a great deal of paper where they didn't have the money to advance and that that paper was valuable to the other banks; that is, in the matter of interest or that the interest would run 8 per cent, the other banks, the Wingfield chain, would get a considerable advantage by giving this 8 per [175] cent paper, is that one of the reasons why the transfer was made?

A. That was one reason. The advantages were mutual. Those banks that needed 8 per cent paper, or any other per cent paper, found an outlet for their funds, but it also provided The First National Bank at Winnemucca with funds of the same nature. I mean to say that The First National Bank at Winnemucca probably wouldn't *had such* a loan at all if it couldn't have taken a part of the loans up.

Q. Are you familiar with negotiations had with the R. F. C., under subordination agreement executed by The Reno National Bank to the R. F. C.?

A. Yes sir.

Q. Will you state what that transaction was and how it was and what paper you used to procure this loan?

A. You mean just with reference to the subordination or just the borrowings in general that the bank made? I didn't quite understand the question.

(Testimony of P. L. Nelson.)

Q. You might cover both, if you will. I want to know what the nature of the transaction was between The Reno National Bank and the R. F. C.

A. Beginning early in the year 1932 The Reno National Bank, as well as the other Wingfield banks, found it necessary to take advantage of the R. F. C. provision for loaning on securities. At first I believe the several banks made individual borrowings from the R. F. C., but due to the fact that State Banks could only borrow up to the extent of their capital and the only other national bank was The First National Bank of Winnemucca, [176] it was found advisable for The Reno National Bank to make all of the remaining borrowings, as I recall, direct to themselves. In order to pledge a certain line, we will say John G. Taylor, to the R. F. C., it was necessary to gather in all of the parts of that loan into one bank, such as The Reno National Bank. If I make myself clear, to put in the other way, the R. F. C. wouldn't make a loan on part of the John G. Taylor paper, for instance, they insisted on having all notes pledged that were secured under the deed of trust or mortgage, so that, as Mr. Sheehan has testified, at various times, in order to make such borrowings, The Reno National Bank called in various notes of the borrowers in order to include them in an application to the R. F. C. for a loan.

Q. Now then, when you gathered all this paper into The Reno National Bank from the various

(Testimony of P. L. Nelson.)

banks over the State, did you give the various banks credit on your books for the notes and mortgages procured from them by The Reno National Bank?

A. Yes, they received immediate credit for such notes.

Q. And then you made up your application for the loan to the R. F. C. and put in all of the paper from the various banks all over the State as a whole, is that right? A. That is right.

Q. Instead of separating The First National Bank paper, the Tonopah paper and paper from other banks, you put it into the R. F. C. as a whole?

A. It all had to be merged into one application.

Q. And one loan then was made to cover all the paper sent to the R. F. C. [177]

A. Well, there were several loans made from the R. F. C., but all paper of one line would be included in a single application.

Cross Examination

By Mr. Barry:

Q. Now, as I understand it, you take these notes that were assigned by the Winnemucca bank, those first notes, outside of Taylor, aggregated some $578,000, when you took those you gave the Winnemucca bank credit for the amount of all those notes? A. Yes.

Q. And that was paid in full then?

A. That was paid in full.

Q. Just the same as if they had cash?

(Testimony of P. L. Nelson.)

A. The First National Bank of Winnemucca was paid in full because that represented what we will call set exchange; it was available the same as cash.

Q. When you got those all in from the various banks you pledged them all to the R. F. C. for loan from the R. F. C. to The Reno National Bank?

A. Yes.

Q. Then if those securities were not realized on at the proper time, it wouldn't affect the Winnemucca bank, because the Winnemucca bank had been paid in full; the different banks were given credit in full? A. That is right.

Q. But The Reno National Bank would have to take the loss, if there was any?

A. That is right.

Q. There was no attempt at any adjustment if you didn't get as [178] much on the loan as the different notes aggregated, that was just too bad for The Reno National Bank—the Winnemucca Bank or the outside banks didn't have to stand any of that loss?

A. There was no attempt of any adjustment whether or not there was a——

Q. Because of the fact they closed—there was no adjustment? A. No adjustment.

Q. Now if you took some notes from the Winnemucca bank and they afterwards made advances on the mortgage, then it would be the custom those advances would be paid first?

(Testimony of P. L. Nelson.)

A. It was the custom.

Q. The outside chain banks making advances wouldn't be protected in the mortgage unless they had some notes covered by the mortgage—just any bank wouldn't make advances?

A. The other banks wouldn't make advances. If these loans originated in Winnemucca, invariably The First National Bank at Winnemucca would make advances. If some note might be farmed out to other banks, like the Tonopah Banking Corporation, in that event it was the understanding that they would be repaid first out of the proceeds of sale.

Q. Would you have taken up those Winnemucca securities, amounting to about $578,000, unless you knew you were going to get a loan from the R. F. C.? You couldn't have have done it, could you?

A. They did do it, but I presume with the understanding that they were going to get some sort of loan on them. That $578,000, if that is the amount, represented, of course, lines in which Winnemucca might have held a great deal of the paper and other banks some, The Reno National Bank some, but they had to merge [179] in order to get the entire line into this application with the R. F. C. Of course, Winnemucca received credit immediately for that $578,000 because the loan was naturally subsequent to that date.

(Testimony of P. L. Nelson.)

Q. And then one loan was made in May, wasn't there? A. Loan was made in May as I recall.

Q. Would that have anything to do with taking care of this credit to the Winnemucca bank?

A. I don't recall whether any items in the May application to the R. F. C. had any Winnemucca lines in that.

Q. But you did finally get a loan that assisted you, didn't it, in taking care of the Winnemucca credit? A. Oh yes.

Q. And Mr. Sheehan testified that they wouldn't have made the loan unless they expected to get that loan from the R. F. C. A. Probably true.

Q. Now the R. F. C. insisted, before the loan was made, that all these subordinate banks must subordinate their claims?

A. That is right. I recall the testimony regarding July, 1932. I don't recall the dates of subordination.

Q. But that was the condition of getting the R. F. C. loan? A. I would say it was.

Q. If the Winnemucca bank received a credit of $578,000, they were benefited by this loan from the R. F. C.?

A. I don't know as I understand your question exactly.

Q. If you hadn't got the loan from the R. F. C., could you have taken care of that $578,000 that you had of Winnemucca paper?

(Testimony of P. L. Nelson.)

A. That is, could The Reno National Bank have paid for the [180] $578,000 drawn on by the First National Bank of Winnemucca?

Q. Yes.

A. Well, that is a matter that I couldn't say. I imagine the receiver's records would show what cash was available there at that time.

Q. Well, this transaction with the Winnemucca bank was of benefit to them, wasn't it?

A. This particular one of $578,000?

Q. Yes. A. I think it was.

Q. Do you remember anything about the Laborde transaction?

A. I remember the Laborde loan, but don't remember any of the particulars.

Q. Where did it originate, do you know?

A. It was what we called a Winnemucca loan.

Q. And there had been several notes out to the different banks, the chain of banks? A. Yes.

Q. And those were all gathered in and a new mortgage was made covering two notes, one for $42,000 and one for $28,000?

A. I don't remember the details of the new mortgage.

Q. Well, we have the mortgage here. The mortgage is made to The Reno National Bank; that covers two notes, one for $42,000, payable to The Reno National Bank, and one for $28,000, payable to The Reno National Bank. Do you know whether or not this $28,000 note was sold by The Reno Na-

(Testimony of P. L. Nelson.)

tional Bank to The First National Bank at Winnemucca?

A. No, I don't. I don't remember the details of this particu- [181] lar transaction. I can see that it might have happened in two ways and the records will show which is correct.

Q. Now there is another mortgage here and trust deed, dated back in 1924, and in that it set up $55,000 of that indebtedness to the Winnemucca bank, $30,000 to the Carson City Bank, $7500, to the Virginia City Bank and $7500 to John S. Cooke & Company. That would show that back in '24 Laborde owed the Winnemucca bank $55,000——

Mr. Tobin: The Reno National Bank is $55,000; the First National Bank of Winnemucca $30,000.

Mr. Barry: That is right. So that loan, at least $30,000, must have originated in the Winnemucca bank, wouldn't you say? A. Yes.

The Court: Who is the borrower in this?

Mr. Barry: Laborde. Now, Mr. Salter, I don't want to put these in evidence. When we come to make up the record, unless these exhibits are set out in full we have to go to Carson City to the custody of the Clerk to find out what they were and those things are pages and pages of discussion. I would like to just have it show first what they were for, without putting in the mortgage, and I will read them off.

To the Reno National Bank, $55,000.

To the Winnemucca bank, $30,000.

(Testimony of P. L. Nelson.)

To the Carson Valley Bank, $20,000.

To the Virginia City Bank, $7500.

To John S. Cooke, $7500.

Now when the second mortgage was given, was made by Laborde, a co-partnership and Laborde Bros. and Laborde individually, to [182] The Reno National Bank, it covered two notes, one for $42,000 and one for $28,000, and the $28,000 note was sent out to Winnemucca because that covered their loan.

Mr. Salter: Very well.

Q. You don't remember the details of that Laborde transaction? A. No, I do not.

Q. Do you recall any split loan liquidations at a loss and if so, how the proceeds were distributed?

A. There were liquidations that were made at a loss, but I do not recall any particular ones at this time, so I can't recall how the apportionments were made.

Q. Were there some liquidated at a loss?

A. Over a period of years?

Q. Yes. A. Yes.

Q. What ones, if you recall?

A. I don't recall. I recall there were profit and loss statements I helped to prepare from year to year. I know I ran into losses of various amounts, so I know there were losses.

Q. But you don't know how the proceeds were distributed? A. No.

Q. Then there wasn't any custom because you never had any transaction of that kind?

(Testimony of P. L. Nelson.)

A. Yes, there was a custom.

Q. Why do you say there was a custom if you never did it?

A. I didn't say we didn't do it. That was the custom, to pro rate them, pay each one equally. The only exception to that is, as I stated, we would probably take up later advances out of the [183] sale for livestock and wool. What I intended to say here was that I don't recall any particular liquidation made at a loss and don't recall, therefore, particulars regarding what pro rata of distribution was made in any particular case. That was the custom, to pro rate it.

Q. Not to pay the advances in full, but to pro rate?

A. Yes, to pay any later advances in full. Whether, in liquidation, I don't recall, whether they pro rated entirely or whether they paid later advances in full. I would say that the practice probably was in case of liquidation where there were loans, probably pro rated the entire loan.

Q. If a mortgage covered two or three notes, owned by different banks, of course when liquidated those banks will all come in equally, all covered by one mortgage, but you wouldn't say as to advances whether they were pro rated or paid in full?

A. I don't know in any particular liquidation just how they were pro rated.

Mr. Barry: That is all.

Mr. Salter: That is all.

(Testimony of P. L. Nelson.)

The Court: I want to ask a question to clear my mind, that would apply to all these mortgages. Did they all carry—and I assume they do—provisions for covering subsequent advances, like taking care of the feed, or something of that kind?

A. It is my impression that they all provided for advances to be secured on the mortgage or deed of trust.

Mr. Salter: Rather than bring in all these mortgages, may [184] it be stipulated that each of these mortgages carries such a provision?

Mr. Barry: This first one does and the last one refers to covenants. That refers to covenant, 1, 2, 3, 4, 5, 6, 7, 8, 9, 10, 11, 12, 13, 14 and 15. That will save putting the mortgages in.

Mr. Salter: That is all, Mr. Nelson, thank you.

MR. HENDERSON

was called as a witness on behalf of the plaintiff, sworn and testified as follows:

Direct Examination

By Mr. Salter:

Q. Your name is Carroll Henderson?

A. Yes sir.

Q. What official position do you hold, Mr. Henderson, in Winnemucca?

A. Receiver of The First National Bank of Winnemucca.

(Testimony of Carroll Henderson.)

Mr. Salter: In order to save a lot of time, may I ask that if we could admit a lot of these allegations without having to prove them, I will submit each one, so we can save a lot of time.

Mr. Barry: We can talk it over. All right.

Mr. Salter: Admit paragraph I.

Mr. Barry: Yes.

Mr. Salter: That is that Carroll Henderson is the duly appointed and qualified receiver of The First National Bank of Winnemucca.

Mr. Barry: Yes.

Mr. Salter: Admit paragraph II, that W. J. Tobin is the duly appointed, acting receiver of The Reno National Bank. [185]

Mr. Barry: Yes.

Mr. Salter: Admit paragraph III, with reference to the official positions of George Wingfield as president and J. Sheehan as vice-president of The First National Bank of Winnemucca and also of the Wingfield chain of banks.

Mr. Barry: Yes.

Mr. Salter: Admit paragraph IV that about the latter part of June, 1932, The First National Bank of Winnemucca was the owner and holder of certain notes.

Mr. Barry: We have admitted that in the answer by failing to deny.

Mr. Salter: I want to establish the amounts. All the amounts in this complaint are at variance with the figures submitted to Mr. Henderson by W. J.

(Testimony of Carroll Henderson.)

Tobin, Receiver, and I would like to establish those amounts.

Mr. Barry: All right. What is the first one?

Mr. Salter: Alcorta; the sum should be $13,000. In explanation of this, if the Court please, would say that we took our figures from the records in the Recorder's office at Winnemucca and afterwards took this matter up with W. J. Tobin, receiver, and he submitted us figures which we have accepted as being correct.

Mr. Barry: All right.

Mr. Salter: Now the mortgage of Alex Dufurrena, the principal should have been $65,500.

Mr. Barry: $65,500, is that correct, Mr. Tobin?

Mr. Tobin: Yes.

Mr. Salter: The mortgage of W. A. and Minnie A. Johnstone [186] should be $45,500.

Mr. Barry: Yes.

Mr. Salter: The mortgage of Joe Larribeau and others should be $69,500.

Mr. Barry: $69,500.

Mr. Salter: The mortgage of Joe Yragui should be $59,000.

Mr. Tobin: I have $58,000.

Mr. Salter: We will make that $58,000. The mortgage of Daniel Gabica and others should be $110,668.48.

Mr. Barry: $110,668.48.

Mr. Salter: The real mortgage and chattel mortgage of Juan Jaca and others, $141,000.

Mr. Barry: $141,000.

(Testimony of Carroll Henderson.)

Mr. Salter: Mortgage executed by Juan Belaustgui and others, $34,500.83.

Mr. Barry: $34,500.83, all right.

Mr. Salter: Admit paragraph V "That on or about June 30, 1932, at the direction of J. Sheehan, Vice President aforesaid, The First National Bank of Winnemucca, Nevada, sold, assigned, and delivered to The Reno National Bank, Reno, Nevada, all of the notes and mortgages above described."

Mr. Barry: Yes, that is all right, we admit that. Six we deny.

Mr. Salter: Admit paragraph VI.

Mr. Barry: No.

Mr. Salter: To this extent, that the following advances were made to these debtors by The First National Bank and that they were represented by notes or overdrafts. If you don't ad- [187] mit that I will have to have Carroll testify to all of that.

Mr. Barry: Well, we will admit that, but I want the dates of the advances. I want to stipulate that the dates set forth in he complaint are correct.

Mr. Salter: Yes, that is right.

Mr. Barry: We will admit that those advances were made as advances and overdrafts and that the dates are correct as set up in the complaint.

Mr. Salter: Yes, and that these advances are shown on pages 5 and 6, paragraph VI, of the complaint.

Mr. Barry: Yes, that is all right.

(Testimony of Carroll Henderson.)

Mr. Salter: Admit that in the Alcorta account the pro rata of the principal amount of the mortgage to that of the advances made by The First National Bank of Winnemucca would be to The Reno National Bank 86.63; to The First Bank of Winnemucca 13.37.

Mr. Barry: That isn't the pleadings.

Mr. Salter: Well, if I don't get that admission I will have to introduce evidence by Mr. Henderson what the pro rata would be if it is worked out mathematically.

Mr. Barry: You are going outside——

Mr. Salter: I will introduce this then.

Mr. Barry: If it is going to go in, you might as well let it in, but my objection is that it is immaterial and it is outside of any issue in the case, what the pro rata would be.

Mr. Salter: It is merely a matter of mathematics, if the Court please. In other words, if we are entitled to anything or entitled to recover anything, then these would be the figures. That is all I want to get in. [188]

The Court: I will permit it under those circumstances. Has Mr. Tobin had a chance to check over that pro rata?

Mr. Salter: Yes, we sent him a copy of this.

Mr. Tobin: I received a copy of it but I never audited it or tried to verify it.

Mr. Barry: If we admitted it and it wasn't correct mathematically, we could correct it. They pro

(Testimony of Carroll Henderson.)

rated, if they pro rated, in proportion to their indebtedness to what?

The Court: Let this witness testify as to what that is and let it be admitted subject to any correction.

Mr. Salter: We agree to that.

Mr. Barry: What is this based on?

Mr. Salter: The figures that were made up is based on this, if the Court please. Mr. Tobin sent to Carroll Henderson, receiver, a statement of the principal amounts of these notes and mortgages. Mr. Henderson showed on this sheet of paper what those principal amounts were, then he added to those principal amounts the advances made by The First National Bank of Winnemucca, then he broke down that and showed what the proportion of the total of the mortgage and of the advance would be to The Reno National Bank and to the First National Bank.

Mr. Barry: In other words, it would be in proportion to the sum of the advancements to the sum of the notes?

Mr. Salter: Right, and worked out in percentages.

Mr. Barry: We can figure that out if there is any pro rata. We don't need any testimony as to that any more than testimony [189] that 12 x 12 are 144.

Mr. Salter: But I want to show what each would be so it will be before the Court so we can use it in

(Testimony of Carroll Henderson.)

our brief, if we are to make a brief, that these are the figures if they are correct.

The Court: You use the expression "advances", what do you mean by advances?

Mr. Salter: I mean, if the Court please, the monies that were loaned to these debtors and carried on the books of The First National Bank either as overdrafts or as notes.

The Court: I understand.

Mr. Barry: If that is the pro rata there can be no objection to putting that in, but if it isn't correct mathematically, we ask to have it changed.

Mr. Salter: We understand that.

The Court: We will be in recess while you are checking.

(Recess for five minutes)

Mr. Salter: If the Court please, I offer in evidence statement of pro rata distribution of net liquidation of split lines due by Reno National Bank, Reno, Nevada to The First National Bank of Winnemucca, Nevada, each one set out separately as stated in our complaint, and ask it be marked plaintiff's Exhibit 1.

Mr. Barry: With the understanding that if those are not mathematically correct they may be changed.

Mr. Salter: Yes.

The Court: That may be admitted.

(Testimony of Carroll Henderson.)

PLAINTIFF'S EXHIBIT No. 1.

STATEMENT OF PRORATA DISTRIBUTION OF NET LIQUIDATION OF SPLIT LINES DUE BY RENO NATIONAL BANK, RENO, NEVADA TO FIRST NATIONAL BANK OF WINNEMUCCA, NEVADA

RECAPITULATION

Debtor	Amount	
Alcorta, S. & J.	$ 1,894.25	
Belaustegui, Juan	71.64	
Dufurrena Co. Alex (Sheep Account)	4,597.96	
Gabica Bros.	1,170.28	
Jaca, Juan et al	254.76	(Red)
Johnstone, W. A. & Minnie A.	483.95	
Laborde Bros. Co.	28,151.92	
Larribeau Co. Joe	2,012.92	
Taylor, Inc. John G.	39,309.30	
Yragui, Joe	1,065.07	
	$78,502.53	

[38]

btedness eld by	Name of Debtor	Original Amount	Payments Prin.	Payments Int.	Net Liquidation
o Nat'l Bank					
	S. & J. Alcorta	$13,000.00	$13,000.	$2,654.64	
N/B Wnncca					
	S. & J. Alcorta	2,007.14	* 229.45	—	
		15,007.14	$13,229.45	$2,654.64	$15,884.09

*$227.86 received from W. J. Tobin, Receiver Reno National Bank to apply

(Testimony of Carroll Henderson.)

	Total Indebtedness	Percent	Net Liquidation	Prop D
Reno National Bank	$13,000.00	86.63	$15,884.09	
1st Nat'l Bank, Wncca.	2,007.14	13.37	15,884.09	
	$15,007.14	100.		$15,8

Proportion due 1st. N/B. Wncca	$2,123.70
Amount received	229.45
Proportion due	$1,894.25

Indebtedness Held by	Name of Debtor	Original Amount	Payments Prin.	Int.	Liqu
Reno Nat'l Bank	Alex Dufurrena Co. (Sheep Account)	$65,500.	$58,326.67	$246.11	
1st N/B Wncca.	Alex Dufurrena Co. (Sheep Account)	5,576.42	—	—	
		$71,076.42	$58,326.67	$246.11	$58,5

	Total Indebtedness	Percent	Net Liquidation	Prop D
Reno National Bank	$65,500.00	92.15	$58,572.78	
1st Nat'l Bank, Wncca	5,576.42	7.85	58,572.78	
	$71,076.42	100.		$58,5

Proportion due 1st Nat'l Bank, Wncca $4,597.96

(Testimony of Carroll Henderson.)

Indebtedness Held by	Name of Debtor	Original Amount	Payments Prin.	Int.	N Liqui
Reno Nat'l Bank	Gabica Bros	$110,668.48	$66,208.34	$282.48	
1st N/B Wncca.	Gabica Bros	2,500.00	305.24	—	
		113,168.48	66,513.58	282.48	$66,7

	Total Indebtedness	Percent	Net Liquidation	Propo Du
Reno Nat'l Bank	$110,668.48	97.791	$66,796.06	
1st Nat'l Bank, Wncca	2,500.00	2.209	66,796.06	
	$113,168.48	100.		$66,7

Proportion due 1st N/B Wnnca	$1,475.52
Amount received	305.24
Balance due 1st N/B Wnnca	$1,170.28

Indebtedness Held by	Name of Debtor	Original Amount	Payments Prin.	Int.	Ne Liquid
Reno Nat'l Bank	Juan Jaca et al	$141,000.00	$79,325.20	$5,138.40	
1st N/B Wncca.	Juan Jaca et al	5,538.34	32.71	—	
		$146,538.34	$79,357.91	$5,138.40	$84,4

	Total Indebtedness	Percent	Net Liquidation	Propo Du
Reno National Bank	$141,000.00	96.22	$84,496.31	
1st Nat'l Bank, Wncca	5,538.34	3.78	84,496.31	
	$146,538.34	100.		$84,4

(Testimony of Carroll Henderson.)

	Total Indebtedness	Percent	Ins. Funds rec'd by 1st N/B Wncca Held in Tr. for O	Prop
Reno National Bank	$141,000.00	96.22	$3,550.21	
1st N/b Wncca	5,538.34	3.78	3,550.21	
	$146,538.34	100.		$3,5

Proportion due 1st Nat'l Bank, Wncca	$3,193.96	
	134.20	$3,328.16
Received by 1st Nat'l Bank, Wncca	$ 32.71	
Ins. Funds held in Tr. for Owners by 1st Nat'l Bank, Wncca	3,550.21	3,582.92
Due Reno Nat'l Bank by 1st N/b Wncca		254.76 (

Indebtedness Held by	Name of Debtor	Original Amount	Payments Prin.	Int.	N Liqui
Reno Nat'l Bank	W. A. Johnstone Minnie A. Johnstone	$45,500.00	$14,986.26	$253.16	
1st N/B. Wncca	W. A. Johnstone Minnie A. Johnstone	1,495.28	1.00	—	
		$46,995.28	14,987.26	253.16	$15,2

	Total Indebtedness	Percent	Net Liquidation	Propor Du
Reno Nat'l Bank	$45,500.00	96.818	$15,240.42	
1st N/B Wncca	1,495.28	3.182	15,240.42	
	$46,995.28	100.		$15,2

Proportion due 1st N/B Wncca	$484.95
Amount received	1.00
	$483.95

(Testimony of Carroll Henderson.)

Indebtedness Held by	Name of Debtor	Original Amount	Payments Prin.	Int.	N Liqui
Reno Nat'l Bank					
	Joe Larribeau Co........	$69,500.00	$52,052.10	$5,133.09	
1st N/B Wncca					
	Joe Larribeau Co........	2,536.89	—	—	
		$72,036.89	$52,052.10	$5,133.09	$57,1

	Total Indebtedness	Percent	Net Liquidation	Propc D
Reno National Bank...........	$69,500.00	96.48	$57,185.19	$55,1
1st Nat'l Bank Wncca......	2,536.89	3.52	57,185.19	2,0
	72,036.89	100.		$57,1

Proportion due 1st Nat'l Bank, Wncca........................ $2,012.92

Indebtedness Held by	Name of Debtor	Original Amount	Payments Prin.	Int.	N Liqui
Reno Nat'l Bank					
	Joe Yragui....	$59,000.00	$28,489.90	$6,515.41	
1st N/B Wncca					
	Joe Yragui....	2,000.00	85.92	—	
		$61,000.00	$28,575.82	$6,515.41	$35,0

	Total Indebtedness	Percent	Net Liquidation	Prop D
Reno National Bank.......	$59,000.00	96.72	$35,091.23	
1st Nat'l Bank, Wncca.	2,000.00	3.28	35,091.23	
	$61,000.00	100.		$35,0

Proportion due 1st Nat'l Bank, Wncca........................ $1,150.99
Amount received.. 85.92

Balance due 1st Nat'l Bank, Wncca........................ $1,065.07

(Testimony of Carroll Henderson.)

Indebtedness Held by	Name of Debtor	Original Amount	Payments Prin.	Int.	N Liqui
Reno Nat'l Bank	Juan Belaustegui	$34,500.83	$34,500.83	$7,810.13	
1st N/B Wncca	Juan Belaustegui	58.10	.29	—	
		34,558.93	34,501.12	7,810.13	$42,3

	Total Indebtedness	Percent	Net Liquidation	Propo Du
Reno Nat'l Bank	$34,500.83	99.83	$42,311.25	
1st Nat'l Bank, Wncca	58.10	.17	42,311.25	
	$34,558.93	100.		$42,3

Proportion due 1st N/B Wncca	$71.93
Amount received	.29
Balance due 1st N/B Wncca	$71.64

Indebtedness Held by	Name of Debtor	Original Amount	Payments Prin.	Int.	Liqu
Reno Nat'l Bank	John G. Taylor, Inc.	$638,145.59	$594,964.47	—	
1st N/B Wncca	John G. Taylor, Inc. John G. Taylor	45,142.18	—	—	
		$683,287.77	$594,964.47	0	$595,9

	Total Indebtedness	Percent	Net Liquidation	Prop D
Reno National Bank	$638,145.59	93.393	$594,964.47	
1st Nat'l Bank, Wncca	45,142.18	6.607	594,964.47	
	$683,287.77	100.		$594,9

Proportion due 1st Nat'l Bank, Wncca $39,309.30

(Testimony of Carroll Henderson.)

debtedness Held by	Name of Debtor	Original Amount	Payments Prin.	Int.	Net Liquidation
no Nat'l Bank	Laborde Bros. Co.	$70,500.00	$72,499.00	20,444.08	
t N/B Wncca	Laborde Bros. Co...	31,612.49	901.39	—	
		$102,112.49	$73,400.39	$20,444.08	$93,844.47

	Total Indebtedness	Percent	Net Liquidation	Proportion Due
no Nat'l Bank	$70,500.00	69.041	$93,844.47	$64,791.16
t Nat'l Bank Wncca.	31,612.49	30.959	93,844.47	29,053.31
	$102,112.49	100.		$93,844.47

oportion due 1st N/B Wncca	$29,053.31
ount received	901.39
lance due 1st N/B Wncca	$28,151.92

[Endorsed]: Plaintiff's Exhibit No. 1. Filed Dec. 9, 1938. [48]

Mr. Salter: Admit paragraph VIII to this extent, that W. [190] J. Tobin, as receiver of The Reno National Bank, has from time to time liquidated the indebtedness of the debtors herein.

Mr. Barry: We don't admit that.

Mr. Salter: What do you admit?

Mr. Barry: We never liquidated.

Mr. Salter: Who did?

Mr. Barry: The R. F. C.

Mr. Salter: In behalf of The Reno National Bank?

Mr. Barry: In their own behalf.

(Testimony of Carroll Henderson.)

Mr. Salter: Well, would you admit they were liquidated and leave out who liquidated them?

Mr. Barry: No, we want to prove that they were liquidated by the R. F. C.

Mr. Salter: All right, leave that out then, if you expect to prove that. Will you admit, under that paragraph, that W. J. Tobin, as receiver, has made no accounting of any of these claims to The First National Bank of Winnemucca?

Mr. Tobin: I made no accounting because there was nothing to account for.

Mr. Salter: I merely want to know if you made an accounting.

Mr. Barry: Our contention is there is nothing to account for.

The Court: The only question now is upon the fact that he has made no accounting.

Mr. Barry: Admitted.

Mr. Salter: Further admit that he has not paid over to The First National Bank any of the amounts claimed in our com- [191] plaint?

Mr. Barry: That is right.

Mr. Salter: With reference to the second cause of action on page 6, admit paragraph X, having reference to the execution by John G. Taylor, Inc. of a note in favor of The Reno National Bank, secured by mortgage in the sum of $700,000?

Mr. Barry: Well, that arose at Winnemucca; that was a Winnemucca transaction.

(Testimony of Carroll Henderson.)

Mr. Salter: No, this merely states that such a mortgage was executed to The Reno National Bank.

Mr. Barry: Yes, if we are going to admit to save time, that was an indebtedness that arose at Winnemucca.

Mr. Salter: I don't believe that is true. You will have to prove that. All I want here is admission on paragraph X.

Mr. Barry: They gave a mortgage, yes.

Mr. Salter: Then it is admitted that John G. Taylor, Inc., on March 12, 1932, did execute a note to The Reno National Bank, secured by mortgage, in the sum of $700,000?

Mr. Barry: Yes.

Mr. Salter: Admit a portion of paragraph XI that the following advances were made to John G. Taylor, Inc. by The First National Bank of Winnemucca and were represented by notes or overdrafts?

Mr. Barry: All right.

Mr. Salter: That there is a note dated September 16, 1932, of $25,000, note dated September 29, 1932 of $5,000, overdraft dated October 5, 1932 of $15,142.18, a total of $45,142.18?

Mr. Barry: Yes. [192]

Mr. Salter: That overdraft of $15,142.18 was between October 5, 1932 and November 25, 1932, between those dates?

Mr. Barry: Yes, that is right.

(Testimony of Carroll Henderson.)

Mr. Salter: Admit part of paragraph XIII, that no accounting has been made by The Reno National Bank to The First National Bank of that amount?

Mr. Barry: Yes.

Mr. Salter: And that no part of that has been paid by The Reno National Bank to The First National Bank?

Mr. Barry: That is all right.

Mr. Salter: Referring to the third cause of action, admit paragraph XV. Admit "that on March 24, 1931, St. John Laborde and Michel Cadet, copartners, doing business under the firm name and style of Laborde Brothers & Company, County of Lander, State of Nevada, executed notes, one in the sum of $42,000.00, and one in the sum of $28,000.00, and to secure said notes executed a real and chattel mortgage to The Reno National Bank, Reno, Nevada, which said mortgage was recorded in Book I of Real and Chattel Mortgages, page 234, records of Lander County, Nevada."

Mr. Barry: That is right.

Mr. Salter: Admitted, under paragraph XVI, that The Reno National Bank at Reno, Nevada held the $42,000 note and that The First National Bank of Winnemucca held the $28,000 note?

Mr. Barry: Yes.

Mr. Salter: Both of which were secured by said mortgage.

(Testimony of Carroll Henderson.)

Mr. Barry: Yes. That cuts out that The First National Bank at Winnemucca paid The Reno National Bank $28,000. [193]

Mr. Salter: Well, I don't know. We better take a little testimony on that.

Q. Do you know from your records and files what that transaction was?

A. Yes. The Reno National Bank made a loan of $70,000 to the Laborde Brothers & Company, secured by a mortgage. In making the loan they made two notes, one for $42,000 and one for $28,000, and afterwards The First National Bank of Winnemucca bought the $28,000 note from The Reno National Bank, bought it, I would think, by charge against the account of The First National Bank of Winnemucca.

Q. Is that what your records and files show?

A. Yes, sir.

Mr. Salter: Do you want to cross-examine on that?

Mr. Barry: No.

Mr. Salter: Admit under paragraph XVIII that no accounting has been made of the Laborde account by The Reno National Bank to The First National Bank.

Mr. Barry: Yes.

Mr. Salter: And that no part of that sum has been paid by The Reno National Bank to The First National Bank.

(Testimony of Carroll Henderson.)

Mr. Barry: Yes.

Mr. Salter: I believe that is all.

Q. (Mr. Salter) Now, Mr. Henderson, you, as receiver of The First National Bank of Winnemucca, have in your possession the Minute Book of The First National Bank of Winnemucca?

A. I have.

Q. I will show you a paper which has been certified to by you [194] and ask if this is an exact copy of a letter addressed to the Comptroller of the Currency, Washington, D. C., and signed by the directors of The First National Bank of Winnemucca, taken from the Minute Book of the Board of Directors of The First National Bank of Winnemucca?

A. Yes sir. This copy was made from the Minute Book of the First National Bank of Winnemucca.

Mr. Salter: I ask that that certified copy be admitted in evidence in lieu of the Minute Book itself.

Mr. Barry: That is all right, under our objection that it is immaterial.

The Court: It may be admitted subject to the objection.

Clerk: Plaintiff's 2.

(Testimony of Carroll Henderson.)

PLAINTIFF'S EXHIBIT No. 2

First National Bank, Winnemucca, Nevada.

June 13, 1925.

Comptroller of the Currency,
Washington, D. C.

Dear Sir:

In connection with the examination of our bank completed May 23rd, our attention has been called by your examiner, C. S. Coffin, to the following matters:

Sold Paper. You are advised that this bank is in no way liable, either directly or indirectly, on any paper sold. You are further advised that efforts will be made to have customers who require seasonal lines of credit in excess of our legal limit make arrangements direct with the Reno National Bank.

Respectfully,
(Signed) J. SHEEHAN
GEO. E. STALL
WM. F. STOCK
JOHN G. TAYLOR
J. G. MOORE
J. O. WALTHER
GEO. WINGFIELD
Directors.

I hereby certify that the above and foregoing is a true and correct copy of an extract of a letter

(Testimony of Carroll Henderson.)

from the Board of Directors of the First National Bank of Winnemucca, Nevada, to the Comptroller of the Currency as of June 13, 1925.

CARROLL HENDERSON
Receiver, First National Bank of Winnemucca, Winnemucca, Nevada.

[Endorsed]: Plff's Exhibit No. 2. Filed Dec. 9, 1938. [49]

Q. I show you letter addressed to the Board of Directors of The First National Bank of Winnemucca, signed by I. W. J. Weller, Deputy Comptroller, and dated August 11, 1925, purporting to be certified by you, and ask you if that is an exact copy of the letter that you have in your files from the Comptroller of the Currency?

A. Yes, this is the exact copy of the letter from I. W. J. Weller, Deputy Comptroller of the Currency, the original of which I have in my files.

Mr. Salter: I ask that that be admitted in evidence, if the Court please, in lieu of the original letter.

Mr. Barry: Same objection.

The Court: It may be admitted subject to the objection.

Clerk: Plaintiff's No. 3.

(Testimony of Carroll Henderson.)

PLAINTIFF'S EXHIBIT No. 3

TR-12 S-3575

Office of
Comptroller of the Currency
Treasury Department
Washington

Address Reply to
Comptroller of the Currency

August 11, 1925.

Board of Directors,
First National Bank,
Winnemucca, Nevada.

Dear Sirs:

The report of an examination of your bank, completed May 23, is at hand, together with your letter of June 13.

It is observed by the report that paper amounting to $1,410,750.38 has been placed with other banks. The practice of placing paper with other banks is objectionable to this office because of the possible liability that, in case of default, may be incurred by the sending bank. The objections to the practice are, however, largely overcome if the paper is placed in such a manner as to relieve the sending bank of any such liability. The report shows that in your case the paper has been placed without liability. In the absence of any information to controvert this statement it will be accepted as correct. You are advised, however, that whether liability exists or not may depend upon the facts sur-

(Testimony of Carroll Henderson.)

rounding the transaction of placing the paper. It is suggested, therefore, that the safest course to pursue would be to accept from the bank taking the paper a statement that it was taken without any liability whatever upon your part.

Respectfully

(Signed) I. W. J. WELLER

Deputy Comptroller.

I hereby certify that the above and foregoing is a true and correct copy of an extract of a letter from the Comptroller of the Currency addressed to the Board of Directors of The First National Bank of Winnemucca, Nevada, as of August 11, 1925.

CARROLL HENDERSON

Receiver, First National Bank of Winnemucca, Winnemucca, Nevada.

Date: October 17, 1938.

[Endorsed]: Plff's Exhibit No. 3. Filed Dec. 9, 1938. [50]

Mr. Salter: That is all, Mr. Henderson. [195]

Cross Examination

By Mr. Barry:

Q. Mr. Henderson, have you the record showing that Laborde transaction?

A. No sir, I have not. You mean the letters?

Q. No, the bank record.
A. No, I haven't the bank record.

Mr. Salter: Now, if the Court please, the Clerk has deposition from J. G. Moore. Does your Honor desire me to read this deposition or shall I just offer it in evidence?

The Court: You may offer it and might state the substance of it. It is quite long.

Mr. Barry: It is along the same line of Mr. Sheehan's testimony. I suggest it be admitted in evidence and we can refer to it in our briefs and the Court can verify it.

Mr. Salter: We offer this deposition, together with the exhibit attached thereto, of J. G. Moore in evidence.

The Court: It may be admitted.

Clerk: Plaintiff's No. 4.

Mr. Salter: That is all.

PLAINTIFF'S EXHIBIT NO. 4

[Title of District Court and Cause.]

COMMISSION

State of Nevada,
To Geo. S. Hoskins:—

Whereas, it appears to the Judge of the above entitled Court that James G. Moore, residing at Winnemucca, Nevada, is a material witness in a certain action now pending in our said Court, between

(Plaintiff's Exhibit No. 4 Continued)

Carroll Henderson, as Receiver, Plaintiff, and W. J. Tobin, as Receiver, Defendant, we, in confidence of your prudence and fidelity, have appointed you, and by these presents do appoint you as commissioner to take the deposition of said witness, and therefore we authorize and empower you, at certain days and places, to be by you for that purpore appointed, diligently to examine said witness in answer to all interrogatories propounded to him, and upon his corporal oath, first taken before you, which oath you are hereby authorized to administer, and cause the said examination of the said witness to be reduced to writing and subscribed by the same witness and then certify and return the same annexed to this commission, unto the Clerk of our District Court aforesaid; with all convenient speed, enclosed in a sealed envelope directed to said [51] Clerk and forwarded to him by United States mail or other usual channel of conveyance.

Witness: Hon. Frank H. Norcross, Judge of the above entitled Court, this 25th day of November, A. D. 1938.

[Seal] O. E. BENHAM,
Clerk.

[Endorsed]: Filed Nov. 30, 1938. [52]

[Title of District Court and Cause.]

Be It Remembered: That pursuant to Stipulation of the parties hereto, Order that Commission issue, on file herein, and the Commission annexed here-

(Deposition of James G. Moore.)

(Plaintiff's Exhibit No. 4 Continued)

unto, on the 28th day of November, 1938, at Winnemucca, Humboldt County, Nevada, before me, J. A. Langwith, a Notary Public in and for the State of Nevada, duly appeared James G. Moore, a witness produced on behalf of plaintiff in the above entitled action now pending in the above entitled Court, who, being by me duly sworn, was then and there examined and interrogated by Thos. J. Salter, Esq., Counsel for said plaintiff, and by N. J. Barry, Esq., counsel for said defendant, and testified as follows:

JAMES G. MOORE,

after being duly sworn by J. A. Langwith, Notary Public, testified as follows: [53]

Mr. Salter: Will you state your name, please?

A. J. G. Moore.

Q. Where do you live, Mr. Moore?

A. Winnemucca, Nevada.

Q. How long have you lived in Winnemucca, Nevada?

A. Since January the first, 1911.

Q. Do you know of The First National Bank of Winnemucca, Nevada? A. I do.

Q. Were you ever employed by that bank?

A. I was.

Q. When did you first enter into the employment of that bank? A. January 1st, 1911.

Q. And how long did you continue in its employment? A. Until December 9, 1932.

(Deposition of James G. Moore.)

(Plaintiff's Exhibit No. 4 Continued)

Q. Did you ever hold an official position in that bank? A. I did.

Q. Were you ever a member of the Board of Directors? A. I was.

Q. On what day were you made a member of the Board of Directors?

A. On the 17th day of January, 1922.

Q. And how long did you continue as a member of the Board of Directors?

A. Until the bank closed, December 9, 1932.

Q. Were you ever made Cashier of the bank?

A. I was.

Q. On what date? A. January 10, 1924.

Q. How long were you employed as Cashier of the bank?

A. Until the bank closed, December 9, 1932.

Q. Now did you hold any other official position?

A. Vice President. [54]

Q. When were you made Vice President of the bank? A. 14th day of January, 1926.

Q. How long did you continue as Vice President? A. Until December 9, 1932.

Q. Now, Mr. Moore, during the time that you held your official position in that bank as Cashier and Vice President, from whom did you receive your orders as to the conduct of the business of the bank?

A. From George Wingfield and J. Sheehan.

Q. What official position did they hold in that bank?

(Deposition of James G. Moore.)

(Plaintiff's Exhibit No. 4 Continued)

A. Mr. Wingfield was President of the bank and Chairman of the Board of Directors; and Mr. Sheehan was Vice President of the bank.

Q. Are you acquainted with the so-called Wingfield Chain of Banks? A. I am.

Q. Was The Reno National Bank one of that chain? A. It was.

Q. What official position did Mr. Wingfield and Mr. Sheehan hold in The Reno National Bank?

A. President and Vice President, respectively.

Q. Their residence was at Reno, Nevada?

A. Reno, Nevada.

Q. And all instructions with reference to the conduct of the bank you received from George Wingfield, President, and J. Sheehan, Vice President? A. I did.

Q. Could you state what other banks in the State of Nevada, were members of that Wingfield Chain of banks?

A. Bank of Nevada Savings and Trust. United Nevada Bank. [55] Riverside Bank, Bank of Sparks, Sparks, Nevada., Virginia City Bank, Churchill County Bank, at Fallon, Nevada, Tonopah Banking Corporation, Tonopah, Henderson Banking Company, Elko, Nevada, and the Bank of Wells, Wells, Nevada.

Q. Will you state whether or not George Wingfield and J. Sheehan occupied the same position with reference to the banks you have just named as they

(Deposition of James G. Moore.)

(Plaintiff's Exhibit No. 4 Continued)

did to The Reno National and to The First National Bank of Winnemucca?

A. Mr. Wingfield was President of all the banks; Mr. Sheehan was Vice President of all excepting The Riverside Bank and the Henderson Banking Company and the Bank of Wells, and I am not sure about the United Nevada Bank.

Q. Now with reference to all the banks except the ones you have just named, state whether or not George Wingfield and J. Sheehan exercised the management of all those banks. A. They did.

Q. And all orders with reference to the conduct of those banks were taken from George Wingfield and J. Sheehan? A. They were.

Q. Now, Mr. Moore, during the time you were Cashier and Vice President of The First National Bank of Winnemucca, I will ask you if there was executed to The First National Bank of Winnemucca, the following notes, secured by mortgages in the following amounts:

S. & J. Alcorta	$13,000.00	
Juan Belaustegui	34,500.83	
Alex Dufurrena Co.	65,500.00	
Gabica Bros.	110,668.48	[56]
Juan Jaca et al	141,000.00	
W. A. Johnstone and Minnie A. Johnstone	45,500.00	
Joe Larribeau Company	69,500.00	
Joe Yragui	59,000.00	

(Deposition of James G. Moore.)

(Plaintiff's Exhibit No. 4 Continued)

A. Yes.

Q. Did you personally handle those transactions whereby these notes and mortgages were executed by the above named parties to The First National Bank of Winnemucca? A. I did.

Q. Will you state what became of those notes and mortgages?

A. We sold them to The Reno National Bank on June the 30th, 1932.

Q. And by whose direction?

A. Mr. Sheehan's.

Q. Were those notes sold, transferred and assigned over without recourse by The First National Bank of Winnemucca to The Reno National Bank, of Reno? A. They were.

Q. Do you know whether you received any cash or whether you received credit on the books of The Reno National Bank?

A. We received credit on the books of The Reno National Bank.

Mr. Moore: I would like to make a correction. That on the Gabica Bros. note and the Juan Jaca et al, The Reno National Bank already held a portion of this loan, and it is possible that they held a portion of some of the loans of those other borrowers at that time.

Q. Were those loans what is generally known in the Wingfield Chain of Banks as split-loans?

A. Yes.

(Deposition of James G. Moore.)

(Plaintiff's Exhibit No. 4 Continued)

Q. What do you mean by split-loans? [57]

A. Well, under the National Bank Act we were permited to loan on our capital and surplus $30,000.00; but where under the McFadden law, which superseded the National Bank Act in some respects, we were permitted to loan 25% of our capital and surplus under certain conditions. Now that would be on government bonds, we could loan 25%, or on livestock chattel mortgages, where the collateral was 115% of the amount of the loan.

Q. So that other banks of the Wingfield Chain took over part of those loans from the First National Bank?

A. The Reno National Bank. If there was any excess loan we would forward it to The Reno National Bank, and they would do what we called farm it out to some of the other banks—like send some to Tonopah, Virginia or Fallon, or where ever they wanted to send it. We did business direct with The Reno National Bank and no other bank.

Q. Now, will you state whether or not certain advances were made to the above named debtors by The First National Bank after the execution of the notes and mortgages, in the following amounts:

S. & J. Alcorta	$2,007.14
Juan Belaustegui	58.10
Alex Dufurrena Co.	5,576.42
Gabica Bros.	2,500.00
Juan Jaca et al	5,538.34

(Deposition of James G. Moore.)

(Plaintiff's Exhibit No. 4 Continued)

W. A. Johnstone and Minnie A. Johnstone	1,495.28
Joe Larribeau Company	2,536.89
Joe Yragui	2,000.00

A. Yes.

Q. Now, Mr. Moore, why did The First National Bank make these [58] advances after the notes and mortgages had been sold to The Reno National Bank?

A. We were requested to make the advances by Mr. Sheehan, with the understanding that the proceeds from the sale of lambs in the Fall the R. F. C. would permit these proceeds to be used by these borrowers for expenses, and which would eventually come to us and take up overdrafts and take up these advances that were made.

Q. Were those advances so made for the protection of the assets of The First National Bank represented by these notes and mortgages?

A. They would be the notes and mortgages already transferred to The Reno National Bank. It was for the protection of the assets of The Reno National Bank.

Q. What was the policy between The First National Bank of Winnemucca and The Reno National Bank with reference to securing these advances?

A. It was always the policy that any note given by one of the borrowers secured by a mortgage was to protect all the loan, whether part of it was sent

(Deposition of James G. Moore.)

(Plaintiff's Exhibit No. 4 Continued)

to Reno or one of the other banks, and the same way with The Reno National Bank. If they sent us one of their notes secured by a mortgage, the note sent us was supposed to be secured under the mortgage.

Q. What was the practice?

A. That was the same practice in securing all notes under the mortgage.

Q. And what was the custom?

A. The same.

Q. And what was the usage?

A. The same.

Q. And what was the understanding? [59]

A. The same.

Q. Now suppose the mortgages herein referred to and sold to The Reno National Bank, had been foreclosed, what would become of the proceeds according to your understanding?

A. They would be pro rated among the banks holding the paper.

Q. Now under what authority were these advances made to the debtors named herein?

A. At the request of Mr. Sheehan.

Q. And when the loan was made how did you handle it?

A. We either took a note, placed the amount to the credit of the borrower, or handled it in the form of an overdraft.

Q. And were these advances so handled?

A. They were.

(Deposition of James G. Moore.)

(Plaintiff's Exhibit No. 4 Continued)

Q. And in case of collection of these mortgages by The Reno National Bank or the foreclosure thereof, what would become of the proceeds?

A. Should be pro rated amongst the banks that held the paper.

Q. Would you say as their interest appeared?

A. As their interests appeared.

Q. Now as The First National Bank made these advances that you have just testified to, will you state whether or not the Reno National Bank was notified of such advances?

A. They were. That is, the officers, Mr. Wingfield and Mr. Sheehan.

Q. What notification would that be?

A. We made a weekly report of all new loans and overdrafts.

Q. State whether or not you gave the date of the loan or the advance and the amount?

A. We did.

Q. Was that your regular custom?

A. It was. [60]

Q. Now calling your attention to a note and mortgage executed by John G. Taylor, Inc., on March 12, 1932, in favor of The Reno National Bank, in the sum of $700,000.00, do you remember that transaction? A. Yes.

Q. Do you know that it took place?

A. Well I wasn't there because it was handled in Reno.

(Deposition of James G. Moore.)

(Plaintiff's Exhibit No. 4 Continued)

Q. Were you informed of the transaction by anyone? A. Yes, Mr. Sheehan.

Q. Did you have any instructions from anyone to make any loans to John G. Taylor, Inc., and to take notes and to honor checks? A. I did.

Q. Who did you get those instructions from?

A. Mr. Sheehan.

Q. And how were those instructions communicated to you?

A. Sometimes over the 'phone and I believe he wrote me a letter on the John G. Taylor loan.

Q. Mr. Moore, I hand you a letter purporting to be the original letter from J. Sheehan, Vice President, to J. G. Moore, Cashier, dated October 11, 1932, with reference to the Taylor loan. Will you state whether or not you received that letter?

A. Yes, I did.

Q. And is that the letter that you received from J. Sheehan? A. It is.

Q. About what date would you have received it?

A. That's dated October 11th. I would get it about the 12th.

Mr. Salter: I now ask that this letter be attached to this deposition and marked Plaintiff's Exhibit "A".

Q. I will ask you if after receiving instructions from Mr. [61] Sheehan, if you loaned to John G. Taylor, Inc., $25,000.00 and took a note dated September 16, 1932, as evidence of that indebtedness?

(Deposition of James G. Moore.)

(Plaintiff's Exhibit No. 4 Continued)

A. We made him a loan of $25,000.00; that was prior to receiving the letter, but I was instructed by Mr. Sheehan to make the loan.

Q. And was that loan made?

A. It was made.

Q. Now, Mr. Moore, did you also make a loan to John G. Taylor, Inc., of $5,000.00, September 29, 1932, and take a note evidencing that indebtedness?

A. I did.

Q. Did you on November 25, 1932, make a loan to John G. Taylor, Inc., of the sum of $15,142.18, and carry the same as an overdraft?

A. I did. That was an overdraft caused over a period of time, of course.

Q. Then from September 16, 1932, to November 25, 1932, you made total advances to John G. Taylor, Inc., of $45,142.18? A. I did.

Q. Now under what authority did you make those advances?

A. Under the authority of J. Sheehan.

Q. Did you have any understanding with Mr. Sheehan at that time with reference to these notes and overdrafts?

A. Yes. That the proceeds from the sale of wool and lambs, etc., would be—they had an agreement I believe with the R. F. C. that the proceeds from the sale of the lambs would be turned back to this borrower for expenses. When turned back they would be turned over, of course, to us.

(Deposition of James G. Moore.)

(Plaintiff's Exhibit No. 4 Continued)

Q. What understanding did you have with reference to the security for these advances? [62]

A. That the security would take care of these loans the same as in all other cases.

Q. Do I understand you to say that it was your understanding at that time that if any wool or livestock were sold, that that money would be applied on these advances?

A. To be applied on these advances. It is doubtful, as Mr. Sheehan says there, if it would be applied on the notes, but these were advances for expenses.

Q. What was your understanding in case of foreclosure of this mortgage as to the proceeds?

A. That the proceeds would be pro rated the same as in all other loans.

Q. And what was the practice?

A. That was the practice, usage and custom.

Q. And in case of the collection of the indebtedness, what would happen?

A. That it would be pro rated and the notes taken up, and the money pro rated if it was not enough to take up all the notes.

Q. Do you mean that the proceeds of the notes would be pro rated as the interest of the two banks appeared? A. Yes.

Q. Will you state whether or not as these advances were made to John G. Taylor, Inc., if The

(Deposition of James G. Moore.)

(Plaintiff's Exhibit No. 4 Continued)

Reno National Bank was notified of the dates and amounts of the loans? A. They were.

Q. Now with reference to the indebtedness of the Laborde Bros. & Company. Do you remember that transaction? A. I do.

Q. What was that transaction, Mr. Moore?

A. The Laborde Bros. & Company executed unsecured notes to The First National Bank of Winnemucca in the sum of $70,000.00, and [63] part of which, I believe $42,000.00, was after that time sold and transferred to The Reno National Bank by us, leaving us with $28,000.00. Then to secure the loan The Reno National Bank took a mortgage, taking one note for $42,000.00 and one note for $28,000.00, on their own paper. They sent us the $28,000.00 note to take up the unsecured $28,000.00 note that we were carrying.

Q. With reference to the $42,000.00 note that you *sayd* was sold to the Reno National Bank: how were you credited with that amount on the books of The Reno National Bank?

A. Credited us with the amounts. It didn't all go down at one time, it was probably different notes of different amounts, and they would credit our account.

Q. In any of these transactions did The Reno National Bank ever send to The First National Bank of Winnemucca any cash? A. No.

(Deposition of James G. Moore.)

(Plaintiff's Exhibit No. 4 Continued)

Q. Will you state if after the transaction you have just testified to, whether you made any advances to the Laborde Bros. & Company?

A. Yes. We advanced $3,612.49.

Q. And how did you handle that?

A. This was in the form of an overdraft.

Q. Under what authority?

A. Under the authority of Mr. Sheehan.

Q. Was that also your custom and understanding? A. It was.

Q. Were the proceeds to be pro rated between the two banks? A. They were.

Q. And how were these advances to be secured?

A. Under the mortgage.

Q. As these advances were made, will you state whether The Reno [64] National Bank was notified? A. They were.

Q. You say that it was your understanding, and usage, that these advances were to be secured by the mortgage held by The Reno National Bank?

A. Yes.

Q. And also the note held by you in the sum of $28,000.00?

A. That note was on The Reno National Bank paper, and specifically mentioned in the mortgage.

Q. Now what would happen in case of the sale of any increase of the livestock of the Laborde Bros. & Company?

(Deposition of James G. Moore.)

(Plaintiff's Exhibit No. 4 Continued)

A. The proceeds would be pro rated among the banks holding the paper.

Q. What was your understanding in case of foreclosure or collection?

A. That the proceeds would be pro rated amongst the two banks holding the paper; that is, The Reno National Bank and The First National Bank of Winnemucca.

Q. Now, Mr. Moore, do you remember the execution of a Subordination Agreement between The First National Bank of Winnemucca, and the Reconstruction Finance Corporation? A. I do.

Q. When was the Subordination Agreement executed? A. July the 25th, 1932.

Q. Do you remember executing that Subordination Agreement as Secretary of the corporation?

A. I do.

Q. With George Wingfield, President?

A. I do.

Q. I am now referring to defendant's Exhibit "A" in this case. Do you understand that? [65]

A. I do.

Q. Did you have any authority to execute that Subordination Agreement?

A. Yes. It was sent to me by Mr. Sheehan with instructions to sign it and return to him.

Q. Now up until the time the First National Bank of Winnemucca closed, which was on Decem-

(Deposition of James G. Moore.)

(Plaintiff's Exhibit No. 4 Continued)

ber 9, 1932, did The First National Bank ever receive any money from The Reno National Bank on account of this Subordination Agreement?

A. No.

Q. Did The First National Bank after July 25, 1932, ever borrow any money from the Reconstruction Finance Corporation? A. No.

Q. Did The Reno National Bank give The First National Bank any credit for any money on account of the Subordination Agreement, or monies received from the R. F. C.? A. No.

Q. Mr. Moore, do you know the amount that the First National Bank was credited with on the books of The Reno National Bank on December 9, 1932? A. The sum of $170,287.01.

Q. What did that sum represent?

A. That represented the cash that we had on deposit with them; part of which I believe was interest due on the loans sold; That's about all. I think it was the credit with The Reno National Bank that was $150,000.00, plus interest due on the loans sold them on June 30th.

Q. Were you familiar with the securities held by The First National Bank on notes and mortgages? A. I was.

Q. Would you know the approximate value thereof? Could you [66] estimate the value of the securities held in each case?

(Deposition of James G. Moore.)

(Plaintiff's Exhibit No. 4 Continued)

A. You mean when we closed?

Q. Yes.

A. Say, securities and property that we held I always considered was more than ample to pay off 100% in the bank.

Q. Would you say from your knowledge of the assets and liabilities of The First National Bank that it was solvent on December 9, 1932?

A. I would, and it was solvent at all times.

Q. Now with reference to the sale of these notes and mortgages which you have testified to. Do you know why those notes and mortgages were sold to The Reno National Bank?

A. They were sold to The Reno National Bank at the request of Mr. Sheehan. The Reno National Bank needed money badly. They needed these mortgages and notes in order to get a loan from the R. F. C.

Q. Was The First National Bank in need of money at that time to meet its obligations?

A. No.

Q. Well for whose benefit were these notes and mortgages sold?

A. For the benefit of The Reno National Bank.

Mr. Salter: That is all.

(Deposition of James G. Moore.)

(Plaintiff's Exhibit No. 4 Continued)

Cross Examination

by N. J. Barry.

Mr. Barry: You set up here first in your Complaint that there was a note from the Alcortas in the sum of $7,250.00. The next one was Dufurrena in the sum of $47,500.00; W. A. and Minnie A. Johnstone, $32,500.00; Joe Larribeau, $60,000.00; Yragui, $52,500.00; Gabica Bros., $85,000.00; Jaca, $151,000.00; and Belaustgui, $31,000.83. Now those notes were all assigned or [67] sold, were they not, to The Reno National Bank?

A. Some prior to the sale of other notes. They were all sold. You see, Judge, as I said we couldn't loan $110,000 or we couldn't loan $141,000. to one person, and with these other notes it is possible that some of those notes were already sold and assigned to The Reno National Bank.

Q. Well, ultimately these notes were all assigned to The Reno National Bank?

A. Ultimately, yes.

Q. Well, you got credit with The Reno National Bank for the face value of the notes?

A. Yes, that is those we sent down.

Q. And from that time on those notes and mortgages were the property of The Reno National Bank? A. They were.

Q. Now you have testified that it was the agreement and custom and usage that you would protect

(Deposition of James G. Moore.)

(Plaintiff's Exhibit No. 4 Continued)

those individual notes by making further advances and overdrafts?

A. You see, Judge, all these parties did business with this bank. Now if we had foreseen what was going to happen this bank would have told them to go to the R. F. C. or go to The Reno National and get their expense money.

Q. Yes, well now where I am hung up a little here—you have testified, with the help of Mr. Henderson, that when The Reno National Bank closed you had a credit of some $170,000.00? A. Yes.

Q. Did the credit come out of these notes you sent down and the interest? A. Yes.

Q. Well now, if you sold the notes down there, now why did you have the interest? [68]

A. It was back interest that was due, and the interest was compromised through the receivership. I believe there was due on those notes we sent down $20,000.00 or $30,000.00 back interest.

Q. Now when you made these advances afterward in the way of notes and overdrafts, you knew that all these mortgages securing the loans that you had transferred to The Reno National Bank had been assigned to the R. F. C.? A. I did.

Q. That was the purpose in taking them down there, was to assign them to the R. F. C.?

A. It was.

Q. You testified that you never got any cash from The Reno National Bank?

(Deposition of James G. Moore.)

(Plaintiff's Exhibit No. 4 Continued)

A. That is cash as cash.

Q. But you got credit, which was the same thing? You got credit on the books? You were satisfied? A. Yes.

Q. You say the Winnemucca bank was solvent when the banks closed?

A. That is what I have always believed.

Q. What dividends has it paid? Have they paid in full, dollar for dollar?

A. They have paid 60% up to this time, and a possible 15% more.

Q. It won't pay out dollar for dollar?

A. Did you ever see a receivership that did? I believe I could have liquidated this bank and got dollar for dollar.

Mr. Barry: That is all.

/s/ J. G. MOORE. [69]

(Plaintiff's Exhibit No. 4 Continued)

PLAINTIFF'S EXHIBIT "A"

The Reno National Bank
Capital $700,000.00
Geo Wingfield, President
J. Sheehan, Vice President
H. H. Kennedy, Vice President
P. L. Nelson, Cashier
A. R. McRae, Asst. Cashier
T. L. Wilcox, Asst. Cashier
Reno, Nevada

October 11, 1932.

Mr. J. G. Moore, Cashier
First National Bank,
Winnemucca, Nevada.

Dear Jim:

Mr. Taylor and his bookkeeper were here this afternoon and we completed their application for the return of the proceeds from the sale of wool and lambs totaling about $53,000.00. This money no doubt will be released back to us and will be sent to you for credit to their account. We suggest for the time being that you honor checks against the account of John G. Taylor, Inc., and carry the same as an overdraft.

Do not take a note, for the reason that when the money is released back to us, we can place it to Taylor's credit, which will eliminate the overdraft but we have our doubts as to whether or not any part of it could be used to apply on the note. It is

(Plaintiff's Exhibit No. 4 Continued)

possible that Taylor will contract to sell his cattle within the next few days. I took the matter up with Dodge Bros., today at Fallon and they are to meet with Taylor tomorrow and believe that a sale will be made.

Yours very truly,

/s/ J. SHEEHAN

Vice President.

JS:W [70]

State of Nevada
County of Humboldt—ss.

I, J. A. Langwith, a Notary Public in and for the County of Humboldt, State of Nevada, and commissioner appointed to take the deposition of James G. Moore, a witness in the above entitled cause, do hereby certify that I am a disinterested person therein; that said deposition of James G. Moore was taken before me at Winnemucca, Humboldt County, State of Nevada on the 28th day of November, 1938, commencing at the hour of 10 o'clock A. M. of said day;

That the said witness, James G. Moore, was by me duly sworn to testify to the truth, the whole truth, and nothing but the truth; that thereupon and while said witness was under oath, and in pursuance to said Commission, Thos. J. Salter, Esq., attorney for the plaintiff, and N. J. Barry, Esq., attorney for the defendant, in this cause, examined said witness; which examination was reduced to writing; that

(Plaintiff's Exhibit No. 4 Continued)

when completed said deposition was carefully read to said witness and corrected by him in every particular he desired, and was thereupon subscribed by him in my presence.

That the foregoing is a correct and true transcript of the evidence and words of said witness in answer to examination by the attorneys, and other proceedings, at the taking of said deposition.

That there is attached hereto a letter dated October 11, 1932, addressed to J. G. Moore, Cashier, and signed by J. Sheehan, Vice President, and marked Plaintiff's Exhibit "A".

In Witness Whereof, I have hereunto subscribed my hand and affixed my seal of office this 29th day of November, A. D. 1938.

[Seal] J. A. LANGWITH

Notary Public in and for the County of Humboldt, State of Nevada, and Commissioner appointed to take the deposition of James G. Moore. [71]

[Endorsed]: Plff's Exhibit No. 4. Filed Dec. 9, 1938. [72]

MR. BUTLER

was called as a witness on behalf of the defendant, sworn and testified as follows:

Direct Examination

By Mr. Barry:

Q. What is your name?

A. Walter E. Butler.

(Testimony of Walter E. Butler.)

Q. What is your business or occupation?

A. At present I am unemployed. [196]

Q. But you have some occupation—are you an accountant? A. Yes, I am.

Q. Have you been an assistant to Mr. Tobin in the liquidation of The Reno National Bank?

A. I have.

Q. And the bookkeeper? A. Yes sir.

Q. And you had access to the books of The Reno National Bank? A. I have.

Q. I will ask you to refer to the Laborde indebtedness, what does that show?

A. In what particular respect?

Q. Well, what does the transaction show? How was the $70,000 distributed, the notes for the $70,000?

A. Well, the Laborde indebtedness, at the time the banks closed, comprised $72,500 held by The Reno National Bank and $28,000 by The First National Bank of Winnemucca and an overdraft of $3612.49.

Q. Do those records show that that note of $28,000 was purchased by the Winnemucca bank from The Reno National Bank?

A. This record wouldn't give that information.

Q. It just shows how it was cut up?

A. Just shows distribution between The Reno National Bank and The First National Bank of Winnemucca.

Q. Winnemucca took over how much?

(Testimony of Walter E. Butler.)

A. There was $28,000 and a note of $3612.49 in an overdraft.

Q. Have you kept the books for Mr. Tobin ever since he was appointed Receiver? [197]

A. No, since the summer of 1934.

Q. You took charge of the books in 1934?

A. During the summer of 1934.

Q. Are you familiar with the liquidation of these notes that were transferred by the Winnemucca bank to The Reno National Bank and by The Reno National Bank hypothecated to the R. F. C.?

A. Since that time I have been.

Q. Do you know whether or not The Reno National Bank, in liquidation by the R. F. C., took a loss on these different notes?

Mr. Salter: If the Court please, for the purpose of the record I desire to object to that question and to all questions along this line, on the ground the same is immaterial and does not constitute a defense to this action brought by Carroll Henderson, receiver. Our theory on that is that it is evidently the theory of the defense that The Reno National Bank acted as trustee for the First National Bank in the handling of these papers and that The First National Bank should suffer in a loss that might occur thru the liquidation of this particular paper held in the hands of the R. F. C., whereas it is our theory that there was an absolute sale from The First National Bank to The Reno National Bank and that The Reno National Bank was the owner and holder

(Testimony of Walter E. Butler.)

of all of this paper and that it is immaterial in this case whether The Reno National Bank afterward suffered a loss on account of this paper that they purchased from The First National Bank, and I would like to have my objection go to this entire line of questions and to this entire line of defense.

The Court: Let me ask a question in connection therewith, [198] if it wouldn't at this time avoid going into any of those questions, if instead of whether the bank suffered a loss, a showing would not be made of the amounts subsequently received from the R. F. C.

Mr. Barry: My idea is the same. I get it in a different way. If I take the loss from my total amount, that would show what was subsequently received. If they are going to pro rate with this, they are going to pro rate on what we received.

The Court: I mean put those questions over until later. This evidence can go in now on which there wouldn't be any legal question raised. The thought I had, if you had figures, they would show the amount subsequently received on each of those accounts.

Mr. Barry: I am just offering the losses. I am getting at it in a different way. Take the losses away from the total amount of the notes and that is the amount received.

The Court: I will permit you to put it in evidence, subject to the objection.

(Testimony of Walter E. Butler.)

Mr. Salter: May I have one suggestion, if the Court please. For instance, in this Exhibit 1 which I offered, it shows here the amount of the principal indebtedness of a mortgage held by The Reno National Bank and by The First National Bank; that is, the combined sums. It might be that The First National Bank sent the Reno National Bank notes and The Reno National Bank subsequently loaned some money or already had a note of that same debtor, this Exhibit 1 shows the original [199] amount is $13,000 with Alcorta and the same with reference to all the rest. It shows the amount collected and net liquidation right on thru, so that it seems to me that these questions here are answered by this exhibit, which is admitted to be correct by Judge Barry and Mr. Tobin. This is the total amount and total collected; that would show the amount of loss.

Mr. Barry: I understood you offered this sheet. I didn't see the rest of this at all. As I understand it you just offered that sheet.

Mr. Salter: No, that was merely a summary. I offered the detailed statement of each of those notes and I got those figures from Mr. Tobin.

Mr. Barry: That is all right. I want to put in this statement showing losses.

The Court: If you have a statement to that effect, we will permit it.

Q. Mr. Butler, you went over with me yesterday the different losses. Will you see if that is correct—

(Testimony of Walter E. Butler.)

I will read them off to you. Tobin suffered a loss in the Duffurena account of $29,823.39.

A. That is correct.

Q. W. A. and Minnie Johnstone, $49,378.27?

A. Correct.

Q. Larribeau, $28,231.76? A. Correct.

Q. Yragui, $25,135.78? A. Correct.

Q. Gabica, $87,949.08? [200]

A. That is correct.

Q. Juan Jaca, $107,883.12? A. Correct.

Q. Belastegui, $2,769.11?

A. That is correct.

Q. John G. Taylor, $295,700.39?

A. That is correct.

Q. Laborde, $5,977.77?

A. That is correct.

Q. Now that totals $632,848.67?

A. That is correct.

Mr. Barry: I would like to offer that in evidence.

Mr. Salter: We would like to have our objection go on the ground it is immaterial, on the grounds heretofore that it does not constitute a defense to this action.

The Court: It may be admitted subject to the objection.

Clerk: Defendant's "A".

(Testimony of Walter E. Butler.)

DEFENDANT'S EXHIBIT "A"

TOTAL LOSS

Duffurena	$29,823.39
Johnstone	49,378.27
Larribeau	28,231.76
Yragui	25,231.76
Gabica	87,949.08
Jaca	107,883.12
Belastegui	2,769.11
Taylor	295,700.39
Labordi	5,977.77
Total	632,848.67

[Endorsed]: Deft's Exhibit No. "A". Filed Dec. 9, 1938. [73]

The Court: Let me inquire, so that it is clear in my mind. Do those figures represent the losses including the total of money recovered by the R. F. C.?

Mr. Barry: Yes. The amount recovered by the R. F. C. is that amount short of the original indebtedness, for which we paid dollar for dollar.

Mr. Salter: On this particular paper that you got from The First National Bank?

Mr. Barry: Yes. That is all. [201]

(Testimony of Walter E. Butler.)

Cross Examination

By Mr. Salter

Q. You say there was a loss of how much?

A. $632,848.67.

Q. Well, if the paper that was sold by The First National Bank to The Reno National Bank is only $578,000, how could you lose $632,000?

Mr. Barry: That is Taylor and Laborde.

Mr. Salter: That includes Taylor and Laborde?

Mr. Barry: Yes, something over a million dollars.

Mr. Salter: That is all.

Mr. Barry: That is all.

MR. TOBIN

was called as a witness on behalf of defendant, sworn and testified as follows:

Direct Examination

By Mr. Barry

Q. Your name is W. J. Tobin? A. Yes sir.

Q. You are the receiver of The Reno National Bank? A. Yes sir.

Q. And have been such since about the 9th of December, 1932? A. Yes sir.

Q. I hand you paper, is that the subordination agreement between the Winnemucca bank and the R. F. C.? A. Yes sir.

Mr. Barry: We offer that in evidence.

Clerk: Defendant's "B".

[Defendant's Exhibit No. B, filed December 9,

(Testimony of W. J. Tobin.)

1938, is the same as Exhibit A attached to the Answer of the defendant, filed August 1, 1938. Set out at page 32 of this printed record.] [74]

Q. Mr. Tobin, did you liquidate these securities that are described in the complaint? [202]

A. No sir.

Q. Who liquidated them?

A. The Reconstruction Finance Corporation.

Q. And out of the proceeds of the liquidation do you know what they did with the proceeds?

A. They applied it against the debt of The Reno National Bank to their corporation.

Q. Was the indebtedness of The Reno National Bank to the R. F. C. eventually paid in full?

A. Yes sir.

Q. Mr. Butler has testified there were certain losses here, how were those losses made up to the R. F. C.?

Mr. Salter: May it be understood that my same objection goes to this entire line of testimony?

The Court: I may be so understood.

A. The losses were made up out of the collections realized from other assets pledged.

Q. And you, as Receiver of The Reno National Bank, took a loss of the amounts stated in Mr. Butler's statement? A. Yes sir.

Q. What is your business, outside of being receiver?

A. Well, I have been in the banking business.

(Testimony of W. J. Tobin.)

Q. How many years were you in the banking business? A. About fifteen years.

Q. You were never in the banking business in this locality? A. No sir.

Q. Do you know what the usage and custom of banks is with regard to split loans, where the amount loaned represents an ex- [203] cess in the amount of loan and the excess is taken up by a correspondent bank, as to payment?

Mr. Salter: I object on the ground Mr. Tobin has not qualified himself. He states he is not familiar with the practice in Nevada.

The Court: I will permit it subject to the objection.

A. Yes sir.

Q. What is the custom?

A. The custom is that the correspondent bank taking over from a local institution the excess of any loan, that excess must be repaid out of the first proceeds derived from any liquidation.

Q. Do you know about the Laborde loan?

A. Yes sir.

Q. What do you know about it?

A. Well, I think I know about all there is to know about it.

Q. All right, tell us what it was.

A. The St. John Laborde indebtedness, or Laborde Bros. & Company indebtedness, all originated in The First National Bank of Winnemucca and I

(Testimony of W. J. Tobin.)

can prove by my records here that that is what happened.

Q. How was it ultimately taken care of?

A. Originally the Laborde Bros. gave a deed of trust securing an indebtedness which was subsequently paid and thereafter, for a period of years, the line was carried unsecured. The notes were all given to The First National Bank of Winnemucca and part of them were sold by The First National Bank of Winnemucca to The Reno National Bank. During one of the examinations, the bank examiner criticized the fact that the Laborde indebtedness was [204] unsecured and thereupon the banks made arrangements to secure a real and chattel mortgage. At that time The Reno National Bank held approximately $42,000 in miscellaneous notes, which it had acquired from The First National Bank of Winnemucca, which my records will show the Winnemucca bank had received credit for, and The First National Bank of Winnemucca had in its note pouch approximately $28,000 in Laborde Bros. notes, and correspondence will indicate that it was decided to secure the line and as a matter of convenience the mortgage was drawn in favor of The Reno National Bank. Two notes were taken, one representing the $42,000 in miscellaneous notes which The Reno National Bank acquired from The First National Bank of Winnemucca, the other representing the $28,000 in miscellaneous notes

(Testimony of W. J. Tobin.)

which The First National Bank of Winnemucca already held. The notes were drawn on The Reno National Bank forms and the $28,000 note was exchanged with The First National Bank of Winnemucca for the $28,000 in miscellaneous notes which it had at that time and The Reno National Bank retained the $42,000 note, representing miscellaneous notes aggregating $42,000, which it held.

Q. Would you say that was a sale by The Reno National Bank of the $28,000 note to the Winnemucca bank?

A. No sir. There was no sale there at all. As a matter of fact, the records will show, and I can give you the proof there, that the $42,000 which The Reno National Bank held represented notes that the First National Bank of Winnemucca had sold to The Reno National Bank.

Q. And received credit for? [205]

A. Yes sir.

Q. So, instead of The Reno National Bank selling the Winnemucca bank a note of $28,000, the Winnemucca bank had sold The Reno National Bank a note of $42,000, for which they got credit?

A. Yes sir.

The Court: Let me understand one thing the witness said. I understood you to say that the $28,000 indebtedness held by the Winnemucca bank, that those smaller notes making that up, were transferred to The Reno National Bank at the time The

(Testimony of W. J. Tobin.)

Reno National Bank transferred the $28,000 new note to the Winnemucca bank.

A. Maybe I could explain it in this way, your Honor. The First National Bank at Winnemucca had miscellaneous notes aggregating $28,000, and The Reno National Bank had miscellaneous notes of Laborde Bros. which they had acquired over a period of time from The First National Bank of Winnemucca, aggregating $42,000, and the entire line was unsecured and the examiner criticized that and it was decided to take security and rather than describing all these miscellaneous notes in this mortgage at that time, they consolidated all these miscellaneous notes into one note for $28,000, representing what the Winnemucca bank had, and one note for $42,000, representing the notes which the Winnemucca bank had previously sold to The Reno National Bank.

The Court: These miscellaneous notes then were merged?

A. Yes, your Honor.

Q. What did The Reno National Bank owe the Winnemucca bank at the time of closing? [206]

A. $147,700 odd dollars.

Q. Have you paid them a dividend on that?

A. Yes sir, I paid them a 50 per cent dividend on that.

Q. Did you figure up the total amount of all of the notes that were transferred to The Reno National Bank? A. Yes sir.

(Testimony of W. J. Tobin.)

Q. What does that sum aggregate.

A. Well, the sum as I have set it up, is $1,298,-000. I might explain that that includes the John G. Taylor indebtedness, which amounted to $688,145.59. John G. Taylor carried his account with The First National Bank of Winnemucca. All of the loans that he received were made out originally on the Winnemucca First National Bank notes and they were sold to The Reno National Bank and other banks in the Wingfield group. The Reno National Bank, however, carried the John G. Taylor indebtedness in excess of what Winnemucca could loan legally, but the loan actually originated in The First National Bank of Winnemucca.

Q. Then The Reno National Bank had taken over from the Winnemucca bank a million and some odd dollars, for which they got credit?

A. Yes sir.

Q. Then the difference between that and $147,000 that The Reno National Bank owed the Winnemucca bank would show what they had to meet the demands on the bank in the mean time?

A. Except this part of the John G. Taylor indebtedness that had been sold to other banks in the Wingfield group, which is comparatively small.

Mr. Barry: That is all. [207]

Cross Examination

By Mr. Salter

Q. Mr. Tobin, was all of the paper of The First National Bank sold to The Reno National Bank,

(Testimony of W. J. Tobin.)

including John G. Taylor and Laborde, pledged with the R. F. C.? A. No sir.

Q. What part of the paper was not pledged with the R. F. C.?

A. There was a certain amount of the Gabica Bros. indebtedness, a certain amount of the John G. Taylor indebtedness and a certain amount of the Yragui indebtedness that The Reno National Bank retained in its files.

Q. It was never pledged to the R. F. C.?

A. No sir.

Q. Who liquidated that?

A. I didn't get any liquidation on it because there wasn't enough realized from the Laborde liquidation, the John G. Taylor or Yragui liquidation to pay the amount of the notes that the R. F. C. held.

Q. I don't understand that. Didn't you get any money from the John G. Taylor liquidation at all?

A. No sir.

Q. Was any money realized from the notes and mortgages? A. Yes sir.

Q. Who got it?

A. The Reconstruction Finance Corporation.

Q. But it was liquidated—somebody liquidated it?

A. The Reconstruction Finance Corporation liquidated it.

Q. I thought you said the John G. Taylor was not pledged to the R. F. C. [208]

(Testimony of W. J. Tobin.)

A. I said it wasn't all pledged. I had a note of $50,000 of John G. Taylor in my files on which I didn't get a dime on.

Q. What did you owe the R. F. C. at the time you became receiver, the bank owe?

A. In excess of three million dollars.

Q. What paper was pledged to them, paper from practically every bank in the State?

A. Well, I couldn't answer it that way. I could answer it in this way—that the paper involved in this case was all pledged to the R. F. C. and miscellaneous loans that The Reno National Bank held in its own note pouch, as well as securities, bonds, etc.

Q. Well, there was paper from practically all the banks of the Wingfield chain grouped together and set down to the R. F. C., upon which The Reno National Bank received a loan of over three million dollars, is that right?

A. Well, I couldn't say whether The Reno National Bank had paper from all the banks or not.

Q. Well, there were some outside notes?

A. Yes, from The First National Bank of Winnemucca.

Q. You only had $578,000 of that, wasn't it?

A. Yes.

Q. Plus Taylor and plus Laborde?

A. Yes.

Q. There was other paper besides The First National Bank paper pledged, wasn't there?

(Testimony of W. J. Tobin.)

A. Yes, but not of considerable amount of consequence. The balance of the pledged paper represented assets of The Reno National [209] Bank. It pledged practically all of its assets.

Q. That is what I am getting at. You pledged the assets of The Reno National Bank, together with other assets, to borrow three million dollars for The Reno National Bank. In other words, The Reno National Bank got three million dollars from the R. F. C., is that right?

A. That is correct.

Q. Now then, the R. F. C. liquidated all of these securities themselves and credited your receivership?

A. Liquidated all of them until they were paid out in full, yes sir.

Q. And that meant the liquidation of some of The Reno National Bank assets, as well as assets from the other banks? A. Yes sir.

Q. Now with reference to this custom that you testified to, had it been your custom with the receiver of The First National Bank to carry the split lines, since you have been receiver, where there was so much money coming to The First National Bank and so much money coming to The Reno National Bank?

A. It has been our custom, where the assets were not pledged, to do that.

Q. That is, the assets that were not pledged to the R. F. C.?

(Testimony of W. J. Tobin.)

A. Well, the R. F. C. or Federal Reserve or anybody else. We had a loan from the Federal Reserve at one time.

Q. Outside of assets not pledged to the R. F. C. or R. A. C. C., you have pro rated with The First National Bank of Winnemucca?

A. That is correct, yes sir.

Q. So that it is your contention that it was a custom to pro rate [210] all paper that you and The First National Bank held jointly, except that you have pledged with the R. F. C. or the R. A. C. C.? A. Yes sir, that is correct.

Q. Mr. Tobin, you said that at the closing of The Reno National Bank that you owed $147,500 to The First National Bank, is that right?

A. Yes sir.

Q. I will show you a proof of claim showing $170,287.01, will you explain your discrepancy in that statement and in your testimony?

A. Yes sir.

Q. I wish you would.

A. After suspension of The Reno National Bank, Mr. Streeter, who was the first receiver, made a demand for interest on the notes which The First National Bank of Winnemucca had sold to The Reno National Bank. In other words, he contended that his trust was entitled to interest on those notes for the period of time that they had been carried in The First National Bank of Winnemucca and

(Testimony of W. J. Tobin.)

up to date of sale by The Reno National Bank, and he made a demand for a claim for that interest. It amounted to some $44,000. I refused to honor that demand and we both then referred the matter to the Comptroller and I, in my correspondence, explained to the Comptroller that The Reno National Bank had purchased, prior to suspension, from time to time notes from The First National Bank of Winnemucca, aggregating approximately a million dollars and upon which it was going to take a loss of some five or six hundred thousand dollars and that at the time [211] that these notes had come into The Reno National Bank, or purchased by The Reno National Bank, a lot of them were inadequately secured. In other words, they were known losses on these assets which they purchased from The First National Bank at Winnemucca at the time they came into The Reno National Bank, and in view of that I felt that the depositors of The Reno National Bank had suffered a greater loss by far than would be represented by any interest that The First National Bank of Winnemucca would be entitled to, and I thought that, from the standpoint of equity, The First National Bank of Winnemucca had already received credit for more than it was entitled to on these notes, but rather than have any controversy about it, the Comptroller suggested the matter be compromised and that I allow a claim for 50 per cent of the interest, so that after suspension

(Testimony of W. J. Tobin.)

I set up, as an additional liability of my trust, $22,540, representing 50 per cent of the interest due on the notes that had come in, and that accounts for the difference in this statement.

Q. In other words, when this paper that we are suing on was sent down from The First National Bank to The Reno National Bank, they gave them credit for the principal amount? A. Yes sir.

Q. But did not give The First National Bank credit for interest on that paper?

A. That is correct.

Q. Then after the banks failed there was a claim made and The Reno National Bank also allowed them interest?

A. Under protest, yes sir.

Q. And you allowed them that interest under instruction of the [212] Comptroller?

A. Yes sir.

Mr. Salter: That is all from Mr. Tobin.

Mr. Barry: That is all.

(Recess for 10 minutes)

The Court: I would like to have a complete transcript of this proceeding and then we might informally discuss the submission. I would say, unless there is some reason to the contrary, the cost of the reporting and transcript of the proceedings be divided equally between the two receiverships, subject to change later.

Mr. Barry: That is all right.

Mr. Salter: I want a copy and copy for Judge Norcross and copy for you.

Stipulation by respective counsel that after testimony is furnished plaintiff have 10 days to file brief, defendant 10 days thereafter to file answering brief and plaintiff 10 days to file reply brief.

Court adjourned at 3:15 P. M. [213]

State of Nevada,
County of Ormsby—ss.

I, Marie D. McIntyre, the duly appointed official court reporter, do hereby certify that I took verbatim shorthand notes of the proceedings had and the testimony taken in the case of Carroll Henderson, as Receiver of The First National Bank of Winnemucca, Nevada, Plaintiff, vs. W. J. Tobin, as Receiver of The Reno National Bank, Defendant, No. H-207, at Reno, Nevada, on Friday, the 9th day of December, 1938, and that the foregoing pages, numbered 1 to 77 inclusive, comprise a full, true and correct transcript of said proceedings and testimony, to the best of my knowledge and ability.

Dated at Carson City, Nevada, December 12, 1938.

MARIE D. McINTYRE
Official Reporter.

[Endorsed]: Filed Dec. 12, 1938. [214]

[Endorsed]: No. 9289. United States Circuit Court of Appeals for the Ninth Circuit. Carroll Henderson, as Receiver of the Reno National Bank, Reno, Nevada, a national banking association, organized and existing under the laws of the United States of America, Appellant, vs. Carroll Henderson, as Receiver of the First National Bank of Winnemucca, Nevada, a national banking association, organized and existing under the laws of the United States of America, Appellee. Transcript of Record. Upon Appeal from the District Court of the United States for the District of Nevada.

Filed September 8, 1939.

PAUL P. O'BRIEN,

Clerk of the United States Circuit Court of Appeals for the Ninth Circuit.

[Title of District Court and Cause.]

STATEMENT OF POINTS ON WHICH APPELLANT INTENDS TO RELY ON APPEAL

On the 30th day of June, 1932, The First National Bank of Winnemucca assigned to The Reno National Bank ten real and chattel mortgages securing notes in the sum of $578,000.

Appellant designates Paragraphs IV and V of the first count of plaintiff's complaint, as supporting the above statement of facts, which allegations of the complaint are undenied by the defendant.

That The First National Bank of Winnemucca received payment in the full face value of said notes, to-wit: the sum of $578,000.

Appellant designates Paragraph I of defendant's further answer to the first count of plaintiff's complaint and the admission of plaintiff by his failure to deny; also the testimony of J. Sheehan, Lines 14, 15 and 16, Page 26 of the Transcript of Testimony; also the testimony of P. L. Nelson, Lines 5 to 16, Page 42 of the Transcript of the Testimony; also statement of counsel for plaintiff, lines 20 and 21, Page 62 of the Transcript of Testimony, as supporting the above statement of facts.

That on the same day, to-wit: the 30th day of June, 1932, said notes and mortgages were assigned by The Reno National Bank to the Reconstruction Finance Corporation.

Appellant designates Paragraph I of defendant's further answer to the first count of plaintiff's complaint and the admission of the same by plaintiff by his failure to deny; also the testimony of J. Sheehan, Lines 4, 5 and 6, Page 25 of the Transcript of Testimony, as supporting the above statement of facts.

That the assignment by The First National Bank of Winnemucca to The Reno National Bank was made with full knowledge and understanding by The

First National Bank of Winnemucca that the notes and mortgages would immediately be assigned to the Reconstruction Finance Corporation by The Reno National Bank.

Appellant designates the testimony of J. Sheehan, Lines 2, 3, 4 and 5, Page 26 of the Transcript of Testimony, as supporting the above statement of facts.

That after the assignment of the notes and mortgages above mentioned to The Reno National Bank by The First National Bank of Winnemucca, The First National Bank of Winnemucca, by way of notes and overdrafts, advanced to the debtors described in the notes and mortgages hereinabove mentioned the sum of $21,164.47.

Appellant designates Paragraph VI of the first count of plaintiff's complaint as supporting the above statement of facts.

That there is no evidence showing any agreement between The First National Bank of Winnemucca and The Reno National Bank to the effect that The First National Bank of Winnemucca was to participate in the proceeds of the liquidation of the original notes and mortgages for the advancements and overdrafts made after the assignment of the original notes and mortgages by The First National Bank of Winnemucca to The Reno National Bank.

Appellant designates the testimony of J. Sheehan at Page 27 of the Transcript of the Testimony as supporting the above statement of facts.

That on the 25th day of July, 1932, The First National Bank of Winnemucca signed a subordination agreement to the Reconstruction Finance Corporation of all its claims, both past and future, and waived all right to participate in any of the proceeds from the assets assigned to the Reconstruction Finance Corporation by The Reno National Bank.

Appellant designates Defendant's Exhibit B (the subordination agreement) included in the Transcript of Testimony as supporting the above statement of facts.

That the original notes assigned by The First National Bank of Winnemucca to The Reno National Bank were liquidated by the Reconstruction Finance Corporation, and The Reno National Bank was given credit for the amount of the proceeds derived from the liquidation on the indebtedness of The Reno National Bank to the Reconstruction Finance Corporation.

Appellant designates the testimony of W. J. Tobin, Lines 27 and 28, Page 66, and Lines 1 to 7 inclusive, Page 67 of the Transcript of Testimony as supporting the above statement of facts.

Legal Points Raised on This Appeal as to the First Count of Plaintiff's Complaint:

Defendant's contention is:

(a) That after the assignment of the original notes and mortgages by The First National Bank of Winnemucca to The Reno National Bank, The First National Bank of Winnemucca could not legally make any further advancements by way of notes or overdrafts for the reason that The First National Bank of Winnemucca had parted with all interest in the notes and mortgages and was not a party to and had no interest in the original notes and had no legal right to make any further advancements by way of notes or overdrafts or otherwise.

(b) That when the notes were assigned by The Reno National Bank to the Reconstruction Finance Corporation, The Reno National Bank parted with all interest in the notes and mortgages and had no right thereafter to make, direct, or authorize any further advancements by way of notes or overdrafts or otherwise. That The Reno National Bank thereby passed out of the entire transaction.

(c) That there was no agreement between The Reno National Bank and The First National Bank of Winnemucca for the pro rating of advancements and overdrafts thereafter made by The First National Bank of Winnemucca.

(d) That all the advancements made before or after the assignment of the original notes by The First National Bank of Winnemucca to The Reno National Bank were waived by the subordination agreement.

(e) That the liquidation of said notes and mortgages was made by the Reconstruction Finance Corporation and that if The First National Bank of Winnemucca had any right to participate in the proceeds of the liquidation of the said notes and mortgages, its claim was against the Reconstruction Finance Corporation and not against The Reno National Bank, as The Reno National Bank had passed out of the entire transaction.

Statement of Facts as to Second Count of Plaintiff's Complaint:

On the 12th day of March, 1932, John G. Taylor, Inc. made, executed and delivered to The Reno National Bank its note in the sum of $700,000 and to secure said note, executed a chattel mortgage to The Reno National Bank. Said note and mortgage were by John G. Taylor, Inc. made to The Reno National Bank and no one else was named in the note or mortgage, and The First National Bank of Winnemucca was not named in either the note or the mortgage.

Appellant designates Paragraph X of the second count of plaintiff's complaint; also Paragraph I of Defendant's further answer to the second count of said complaint and the admission by plaintiff by failure to deny in his reply; also admission of counsel for plaintiff and defendant, Lines 17 to 20 inclusive, Page 56 of the Transcript of Testimony, as supporting the above statement of facts.

Said note and mortgage were assigned by The Reno National Bank to the Reconstruction Finance Corporation.

Appellant designates Paragraph I of defendant's further answer to the second count of plaintiff's complaint; also the admission of plaintiff by his failure to deny the same in his reply, as supporting the above statement of facts.

After the execution of the above note and mortgage, The First National Bank of Winnėmucca advanced by way of notes and overdrafts to John G. Taylor, Inc. the sum of $45,142.18.

Appellant designates Paragraph XI of the second count of plaintiff's complaint as supporting the above statement of facts.

That there is no evidence showing any agreement between The First National Bank of Winnemucca and the Reno National Bank to the effect that The First National Bank of Winnemucca was to participate in the proceeds of the liquidation of said note and mortgage for the advancements and overdrafts made after the assignment of said note and mortgage.

Appellant designates the testimony of J. Sheehan at Pages 27 and 28 of the Transcript of the Testimony as supporting the above statement of facts.

The advancements made by The First National Bank of Winnemucca to John G. Taylor, Inc. were not to be prorated with The Reno National Bank as to the sum of $15,000.

Appellant designates the testimony of J. Sheehan, Page 9, Lines 6 to 12, Transcript of Testimony, as supporting the above statement of facts.

Where a bank was not a party to the mortgage, it could not make advances.

Appellant designates the testimony of P. L. Nelson, Lines 13 to 21, inclusive, Page 43 of the Transcript of Testimony, as supporting the above statement of facts.

That on the 25th day of July, 1932, The First National Bank of Winnemucca signed a subordination agreement to the Reconstruction Finance Corporation of all its claims, both past and future, and waived all right to participate in any of the proceeds from the liquidation of the assets assigned to the Reconstruction Finance Corporation by The Reno National Bank.

Appellant designates Defendant's Exhibit B (subordination agreement) included in the Transcript of Testimony as supporting the above statement of facts.

That said John G. Taylor, Inc. note and mortgage were liquidated by the Reconstruction Finance Corporation, and The Reno National Bank was given credit for the amount of the proceeds derived from the liquidation on the indebtedness of The Reno National Bank to the Reconstruction Finance Corporation.

Appellant designates the testimony of W. J. Tobin, Lines 27 to 28, Page 66, and Lines 1 to 7 inclusive, Page 67 of the Transcript of Testimony as supporting the above statement of facts.

That the entire indebtedness of John G. Taylor, Inc., which was originally unsecured, originated in The First National Bank of Winnemucca, was represented by miscellaneous notes totaling the sum of $700,000 which were sold and transferred to The Reno National Bank and for which The First National Bank of Winnemucca received from said The Reno National Bank the full face value thereof.

Appellant designates Paragraph I of defendant's further answer to the second count of plaintiff's complaint, and plaintiff's admission of the same by his failure to deny in his reply as supporting the above statement of facts.

Legal Points Raised on This Appeal as to the Second Count of Plaintiff's Complaint:

Defendant's contention is:

(a) That The First National Bank of Winnemucca had no right to make advancements for the reason that it was not a party to the John G. Taylor, Inc. note and mortgage and was a stranger thereto.

(b) That The Reno National Bank had no legal right to make, direct or authorize any advancements by The First National Bank of Winnemucca for the reason that The First National Bank of Winnemucca was not a party to the note or mortgage.

(c) That after the assignment of the note and mortgage to the Reconstruction Finance Corporation, The Reno National Bank had no right to make, direct or authorize any advancements for the reason that it has assigned all its interest in the note and mortgage to the Reconstruction Finance Corporation and thereby passed out of the entire transaction.

(d) That there was no agreement between The Reno National Bank and The First National Bank of Winnemucca for the pro rating of advancements and overdrafts thereafter made by The First National Bank of Winnemucca.

(*d*) That The First National Bank of Winnemucca waived all its right to participate in the proceeds of the liquidation of the John G. Taylor, Inc. note and mortgage by the subordination agreement made and executed on the 25th day of July, 1932.

(e) That the liquidation of said note and mortgage was made by the Reconstruction Finance Corporation, and that if The First National Bank of Winnemucca had any right to participate in the proceeds of the liquidation of the Taylor note and mortgage, its claim was against the Reconstruction Finance Corporation and not against The Reno National Bank, as The Reno National Bank had passed out of the entire transaction.

Statement of Facts as to the Third Count of Plaintiff's Complaint:

On March 24, 1931, Laborde Brothers & Company were indebted to The First National Bank of Winnemucca in the sum of $70,000. Two notes were given by said Laborde Brothers & Company as evidence of said indebtedness; one for the sum of $42,000, and one for the sum of $28,000, and a mortgage was given by the Laborde Brothers & Company to secure the two notes. $42,000 of this indebtedness was sold by The First National Bank of Winnemucca to The Reno National Bank, for which The First National Bank of Winnemucca received full face value in credit. $28,000 of said indebtedness was retained by The First National Bank of Winnemucca. Thereafter, said $42,000 note and the mortgage were assigned to the Reconstruction Finance Corporation by The Reno National Bank.

Appellant designates Paragraph I of defendant's further answer to the third count of plaintiff's complaint; the admission of plaintiff by his failure to deny the same in his reply, and the testimony of W. J. Tobin, found at Pages 68 and 69 of the Transcript of Testimony, as supporting the above statement of facts.

That after the assignment of the note and mortgage above mentioned to the Reconstruction Finance Corporation by The Reno National Bank, The First National Bank of Winnemucca, by way of notes and overdrafts, advanced to the said Laborde Brothers & Company the sum of $3,612.49.

Appellant designates Paragraph XIX of the third count of plaintiff's complaint as supporting the above statement of facts.

That on the 25th day of July, 1932, The First National Bank of Winnemucca signed a subordination agreement to the Reconstruction Finance Corporation of all its claims, both past and future, and waived all right to participate in any of the proceeds from the assets assigned to the Reconstruction Finance Corporation by The Reno National Bank.

Appellant designates Defendant's Exhibit B (the subordination agreement) included in the Transcript of Testimony as supporting the above statement of facts.

That said note and mortgage above mentioned were liquidated by the Reconstruction Finance Corporation, and The Reno National Bank was given credit for the amount of the proceeds derived from the liquidation on the indebtedness of The Reno National Bank to the Reconstruction Finance Corporation.

Appellant designates the testimony of W. J. Tobin, Lines 27 and 28, Page 66, and Lines 1 to 7 inclusive, Page 67 of the Transcript of Testimony as supporting the above statement of facts.

Legal Points Raised On This Appeal As To The Third Count Of Plaintiff's Complaint:

Defendant's contention is:

(a) That The First National Bank of Winnemucca waived all its right to participate in the proceeds of the liquidation of the Laborde Bros. & Company mortgage by the subordination agreement made and executed on the 25th day of July, 1932.

(b) That the liquidation of said note and mortgage was made by the Reconstruction Finance Corporation, and that if The First National Bank of Winnemucca had any right to particpate in the proceeds of the liquidation of said mortgage, its claim was against the Reconstruction Finance Corporation and not against The Reno National Bank, as The Reno National Bank had passed out of the entire transaction.

Dated: August 4, 1939.

N. J. BARRY,

Attorney for Defendant and Appellant.

[Title of District Court and Cause.]

AFFIDAVIT OF SERVICE.

State of Nevada,
County of Washoe—ss.

Mary McKinnon, being first duly sworn, deposes and says:

That she is a citizen of the United States over the age of twenty-one years, and that she is Secretary in the office of N. J. Barry, an attorney and counselor at law of the City of Reno, County of Washoe, State of Nevada; that said N. J. Barry is the attorney of record for Defendant in the above entitled action; and that Thos. J. Salter is the attorney of record for Plaintiff in said action.

That said N. J. Barry resides at and has his office in the City of Reno, County of Washoe, State of Nevada, and that said Thos. J. Salter resides at and has his office in the City of Winnemucca, County of Humboldt, State of Nevada.

Affiant further says that there is a United States Post Office in said City of Reno, and a United States Post Office in said City of Winnemucca, and between said Cities of Reno and Winnemucca, there is a daily communication by United States Mail.

Affiant further says that she served the within and foregoing Statement of Points on Which Appellant Intends to Rely on Appeal on Thos. J. Salter, attorney for the Plaintiff, on the 4th day of August, 1939, by depositing a true copy of said

Statement of Points on Which Appellant Intends to Rely on Appeal in the United States Post Office in the City of Reno, County of Washoe, State of Nevada, enclosed in an envelope properly addressed to said Thos. J. Salter, Winnemucca, Nevada, the place wherein said Thos. J. Salter resides and has his office.

Affiant further says that she prepaid the postage thereon.

MARY McKINNON.

Subscribed and sworn to before me this 4th day of August, 1939.

[Seal] N. J. BARRY,

Notary Public in and for the County of Washoe, State of Nevada.

[Endorsed]: Filed Aug. 5, 1939. O. E. Benham, Clerk. By O. F. Pratt, Deputy.

[Endorsed]: Filed Sept. 8, 1939. Paul P. O'Brien, Clerk.

8

No. 9289

IN THE

United States Circuit Court of Appeals

For the Ninth Circuit

Carroll Henderson, as Receiver of The Reno National Bank, Reno, Nevada (a national banking association, organized and existing under the laws of the United States of America),

Appellant,

vs.

Carroll Henderson, as Receiver of The First National Bank of Winnemucca, Nevada (a national banking association, organized and existing under the laws of the United States of America),

Appellee.

On Appeal from the District Court of the United States, for the District of Nevada.

BRIEF FOR APPELLANT.

N. J. Barry,
Reno, Nevada,
Attorney for Appellant.

Pernau-Walsh Printing Co., San Francisco

Subject Index

Page

Statement of Facts 3

Statement of Facts as to First Count of Plaintiff's Complaint 7

Statement of Facts as to Second Count of Plaintiff's Complaint 9

Statement of Facts as to Third Count of Complaint........ 12

Legal Points Raised on This Appeal as to the First Count of Plaintiff's Complaint 14

Legal Points Raised on This Appeal as to the Second Count of Plaintiff's Complaint 15

Legal Points Raised on This Appeal as to the Third Count of Plaintiff's Complaint 16

Argument 17

Recapitulation 25

Table of Authorities Cited

Cases

Pages

Atkinson v. Foote, 44 C. A. 149, 186 P. 831............... 20

International Trust Company v. Weeks, 203 U. S. 364..... 2

Larabee Flour Mills v. First National Bank (C. C. A. 8), 13 Fed. (2d) 330.................................... 2

Lehman v. Spurway, 58 Fed. (2d) 227.................. 2

Savings etc. Ass'n v. Burnett, 106 Cal. 514, 39 P. 922..... 21

Schmitt v. Tobin, 15 Fed. Sup. 35...........19, 22, 23, 24, 27, 29

Studebaker Corp. v. First National Bank, 10 Fed. (2d) 590 2

Walker v. Whitmore, et als., 262 S. W. 678............... 19

Codes and Statutes

Federal Rules of Civil Procedure, Rule 73, subds. a, b, c... 3

Title 28, U. S. C. A., Section 870....................... 3

28 U. S. C. 41, subds. 1, 16.............................. 2

Texts

41 C. J. 527, Section 468................................ 21

No. 9289

IN THE

United States Circuit Court of Appeals

For the Ninth Circuit

CARROLL HENDERSON, as Receiver of The Reno National Bank, Reno, Nevada (a national banking association, organized and existing under the laws of the United States of America),

Appellant,

vs.

CARROLL HENDERSON, as Receiver of The First National Bank of Winnemucca, Nevada (a national banking association, organized and existing under the laws of the United States of America),

Appellee.

On Appeal from the District Court of the United States, for the District of Nevada.

BRIEF FOR APPELLANT.

This is an action filed in the District Court of the United States for the District of Nevada on the 24th day of June, 1938, No. H-207, by Carroll Henderson, as Receiver of The First National Bank of Winnemucca, Nevada, a national banking association organized and existing under the laws of the United States of America, Plaintiff, v. W. J. Tobin, as Receiver of The Reno National Bank, a national banking association, organized and existing under the laws of the United States of America, Defendant. (Carroll Henderson substituted as defendant in the place of W. J. Tobin.)

The complaint sets up that certain notes and real and chattel mortgages, the property of The First National Bank of Winnemucca, were assigned to The Reno National Bank; that all the notes and mortgages provided for future advancements; that thereafter, The First National Bank of Winnemucca made certain advances to the mortgagors, as represented by promissory notes, and that The First National Bank of Winnemucca was entitled to prorate in the proceeds of the liquidation of the securities covered by the mortgages.

The suit is one for winding up the affairs of a national banking association cognizable in the United States District Court independent of the amount involved under the provisions of 28 U. S. C. 41, Subdivisions 1 and 16. *International Trust Company v. Weeks,* 203 U. S. 364, 366; *Larabee Flour Mills v. First National Bank* (C. C. A. 8), 13 Fed. (2d) 330; *Studebaker Corp. v. First National Bank,* 10 Fed. (2d) 590, 591, 592; *Lehman v. Spurway,* 58 Fed. (2d) 227.

The trial before the judge presiding without a jury on the pleadings and testimony resulted in a judgment and decree for the plaintiff for the recovery of the sum of $75,276.76 and the costs of the suit, filed July 7, 1939.

Appellant's Notice of Appeal was seasonably filed under Rule 73, Federal Rules of Civil Procedure under Subdivisions a, b and c. Instead of a bond, a telegram from the Deputy Comptroller of the Currency of the United States was filed under the provisions of Section 1001, U. S. Revised Statutes, Title 28, Section 870, U. S. C. A.

The jurisdictional averment of complainant's complaint is found on Pages 1 to 15, Folios 1 to 11 of the Transcript of Record, and in Defendant's Answer, Pages 16 to 32, Folios 12 to 27, and the admissions contained therein; and in the Notice of Appeal found on Pages 94 and 95 and the telegram authorizing the appeal on Page 95.

STATEMENT OF FACTS.

On the 30th day of June, 1932, The First National Bank of Winnemucca assigned to The Reno National Bank promissory notes in the aggregate sum of $578,000, and also assigned the real and chattel mortgages securing said notes.

The First National Bank of Winnemucca received payment from The Reno National Bank in the full face value of said notes.

On the 30th day of June, 1932, the same notes and mortgages were assigned by The Reno National Bank to the Reconstruction Finance Corporation.

The assignment by The First National Bank of Winnemucca to The Reno National Bank was made with full knowledge and understanding on the part of The First National Bank of Winnemucca that the notes and mortgages would immediately be assigned to the Reconstruction Finance Corporation by The Reno National Bank.

After the assignment of the notes and mortgages above mentioned to The Reno National Bank by The First National Bank of Winnemucca, and after the assignment of the notes and mortgages by The Reno National Bank to the Reconstruction Finance Corporation, The First National Bank of Winnemucca, by way of notes and overdrafts, advanced to the mortgagors described in the notes and mortgages the total sum of $21,164.47.

On the 12th day of March, 1932, John G. Taylor, Inc. made, executed and delivered to The Reno National Bank its note in the sum of $700,000, and to secure the note, executed a chattel mortgage to The Reno National Bank. The note and mortgage were by John G. Taylor, Inc. made to The Reno National Bank, and no one else was named in the note or the mortgage, and The First National Bank of Winnemucca was not named in either the note or the mortgage.

The above named note and mortgage were assigned by The Reno National Bank to the Reconstruction Finance Corporation.

After the assignment of the Taylor note and mortgage to the Reconstruction Finance Corporation by The Reno National Bank, The First National Bank of Winnemucca advanced, by way of notes and overdrafts, to John G. Taylor, Inc. the sum of $45,142.18.

On March 24, 1931, Laborde Bros. & Co. were indebted to The First National Bank of Winnemucca in the sum of $70,000. Two notes were given by Laborde Bros. & Co. as evidence of said indebtedness; one for the sum of $42,000 and one for the sum of $28,000; and a mortgage was given by Laborde Bros. & Co. to The Reno National Bank to secure the two notes.

$42,000 of this indebtedness was sold by The First National Bank of Winnemucca to The Reno National Bank, for which The First National Bank received from The Reno National Bank full face value in credit.

After the assignment of all the notes and mortgages by The First National Bank of Winnemucca to The Reno National Bank, and after the assignment of the notes and mortgages by The Reno National Bank to the Reconstruction Finance Corporation, The First National Bank of Winnemucca advanced by way of notes and overdrafts to Laborde Bros. & Co. the sum of $30,715.47.

After the assignment of all the notes and mortgages by The First National Bank of Winnemucca to The Reno National Bank, and after the assignment of the notes and mortgages by The Reno National Bank to the Reconstruction Finance Corporation, and on the 25th day of July, 1932, The First National Bank of Winnemucca signed a subordination agreement to the Reconstruction Finance Corporation waiving all its claims, both past and future, and waiving all right to participate in any of the proceeds from the liquidation of the assets assigned to the Reconstruction Finance Corporation by The Reno National Bank.

All the assigned notes and mortgages mentioned above were liquidated by the Reconstruction Finance Corporation, and The Reno National Bank was given credit for the amount of the proceeds derived from the liquidation of the indebtedness of The Reno National Bank to the Reconstruction Finance Corporation, but the liquidation proceeds were $632,848.69 less than the face value of the notes and the sum for which The First National Bank of Winnemucca was given credit by The Reno National Bank. In other words, The Reno National Bank took a loss in the sum of $632,848.69.

This action was commenced by the Receiver of The First National Bank of Winnemucca against the Receiver of The Reno National Bank to recover a judgment allowing The First National Bank of Winnemucca to prorate in the credit received from the proceeds of the liquidation of the above notes and mortgages by the Reconstruction Finance Corporation and applied on the indebtedness of The Reno National Bank to the Reconstruction Finance Corporation. The pro rata prayed for was the proportion which the advancements made by The First National Bank of Winnemucca would bear to the amount credited to The Reno National Bank by the Reconstruction Finance Corporation on the indebtedness of The Reno National Bank to the Reconstruction Finance Corporation.

In other words, The First National Bank of Winnemucca sought to recover a money judgment from The Reno National Bank in an amount that the total advancements made by it bore to the total credit allowed by the Reconstruction Finance Corporation to The Reno National Bank.

On July 7, 1939, the U. S. District Court for the District of Nevada rendered a judgment in favor of plaintiff, The First National Bank of Winnemucca, as prayed for, in the sum of $75,276.76.

This is an appeal from that judgment.

STATEMENT OF FACTS AS TO FIRST COUNT OF PLAINTIFF'S COMPLAINT.

On the 30th day of June, 1932, The First National Bank of Winnemucca assigned to The Reno National Bank ten real and chattel mortgages securing notes in the sum of $578,000. (Paragraphs IV and V of plaintiff's complaint, Pages 3, 4, 5 and 6 of Tr.)

That The First National Bank of Winnemucca received payment in the full face value of said notes, to-wit: the sum of $578,000. (Paragraph I of defendant's further answer to first count of plaintiff's complaint, Pages 21 and 22 of Tr.; admission of plaintiff by failure to deny; testimony of J. Sheehan, Page 128 of Tr.; testimony of P. L. Nelson, Page 145 of Tr.; statement of counsel for plaintiff, Pages 202 and 203 of Tr.)

That on the same day, to-wit: the 30th day of June, 1932, said notes and mortgages were assigned by The Reno National Bank to the Reconstruction Finance Corporation. (Paragrah I of defendant's further answer to the first count of plaintiff's complaint, Pages

21 and 22 of Tr.; admission of same by plaintiff by his failure to deny; testimony of J. Sheehan, Page 127 of Tr.)

That the assignment by The First National Bank of Winnemucca to The Reno National Bank was made with full knowledge and understanding by The First National Bank of Winnemucca that the notes and mortgages would immediately be assigned to the Reconstruction Finance Corporation by The Reno National Bank. (Testimony of J. Sheehan, Pages 127 and 128 of Tr.)

That after the assignment of the notes and mortgages above mentioned to The Reno National Bank by The First National Bank of Winnemucca, The First National Bank of Winnemucca, by way of notes and overdrafts, advanced to the debtors described in the notes and mortgages hereinabove mentioned the sum of $21,164.47. (Paragraph VI of first count of plaintiff's complaint, Pages 7 and 8 of Tr.)

That there is no evidence showing any agreement between The First National Bank of Winnemucca and The Reno National Bank to the effect that The First National Bank of Winnemucca was to participate in the proceeds of the liquidation of the original notes and mortgages for the advancements and overdrafts made after the assignment of the original notes and mortgages by The First National Bank of Winnemucca to The Reno National Bank. (Testimony of J. Sheehan, Page 129 of Tr.)

That on the 25th day of July, 1932, The First National Bank of Winnemucca signed a subordination agreement to the Reconstruction Finance Corporation of all its claims, both past and future, and waived all right to participate in any of the proceeds from the liquidation of the assets assigned to the Reconstruction Finance Corporation by The Reno National Bank. (Defendant's Exhibit B, the subordination agreement, Pages 32, 33, 34 and 35 of Tr.)

That the original notes assigned by The First National Bank of Winnemucca to The Reno National Bank were liquidated by the Reconstruction Finance Corporation, and The Reno National Bank was given credit for the amount of the proceeds derived from the liquidation on the indebtedness of The Reno National Bank to the Reconstruction Finance Corporation. (Testimony of W. J. Tobin, Page 208 of Tr.)

STATEMENT OF FACTS AS TO SECOND COUNT OF PLAINTIFF'S COMPLAINT.

On the 12th day of March, 1932, John G. Taylor, Inc. made, executed and delivered to The Reno National Bank its note in the sum of $700,000 and to secure said note, executed a chattel mortgage to The Reno National Bank. Said note and mortgage were by John G. Taylor, Inc. made to The Reno National Bank and no one else was named in the note or mortgage, and The First National Bank of Winnemucca was not named in either the note or the mortgage. (Paragraph X of the second count of plaintiff's complaint, Page 10 of Tr.; Paragraph I of Defendant's further answer to the second count of said complaint, Page 27 of Tr.;

admission by plaintiff by failure to deny in his reply; admission of counsel for plaintiff and defendant, Page 168 of Tr.)

Said note and mortgage were assigned by The Reno National Bank to the Reconstruction Finance Corporation. (Paragraph I of defendant's further answer to the second count of plaintiff's complaint, Page 27 of Tr.; admission of plaintiff by failure to deny in his reply.)

After the execution of the above note and mortgage, The First National Bank of Winnemucca advanced by way of notes and overdrafts to John G. Taylor, Inc. the sum of $45,142.18. (Paragraph XI of the second count of plaintiff's complaint, Page 10 of Tr.)

That there is no evidence showing any agreement between The First National Bank of Winnemucca and The Reno National Bank to the effect that The First National Bank of Winnemucca was to participate in the proceeds of the liquidation of said note and mortgage for the advancements and overdrafts made after the assignment of said note and mortgage. (Testimony of J. Sheehan, Pages 129, 130 and 131 of Tr.)

The advancements made by The First National Bank of Winnemucca to John G. Taylor, Inc. were not to be prorated with The Reno National Bank as to the sum of $15,000. (Testimony of J. Sheehan, Pages 109 and 110 of Tr.)

Where a bank was not a party to the mortgage, it could not make advances. (Testimony of P. L. Nelson, Page 147 of Tr.)

That on the 25th day of July, 1932, The First National Bank of Winnemucca signed a subordination agreement to the Reconstruction Finance Corporation of all its claims, both past and future, and waived all right to participate in any of the proceeds from the liquidation of the assets assigned to the Reconstruction Finance Corporation by The Reno National Bank. (Defendant's Exhibit B, subordination agreement, Pages 32 to 35 of Tr.)

That said John G. Taylor, Inc. note and mortgage were liquidated by the Reconstruction Finance Corporation, and The Reno National Bank was given credit for the amount of the proceeds derived from the liquidation on the indebtedness of The Reno National Bank to the Reconstruction Finance Corporation. (Testimony of W. J. Tobin, Page 208 of Tr.)

That the entire indebtedness of John G. Taylor, Inc., which was originally unsecured, originated in The First National Bank of Winnemucca, was represented by miscellaneous notes totalling the sum of $700,000 which were sold and transferred to The Reno National Bank and for which The First National Bank of Winnemucca received from said The Reno National Bank the full face value thereof. (Paragraph I of defendant's further answer to the second count of plaintiff's complaint, Page 27 of Tr.; admission of plaintiff by failure to deny.)

STATEMENT OF FACTS AS TO THIRD COUNT OF COMPLAINT.

On March 24, 1931, Laborde Bros. & Company were indebted to The First National Bank of Winnemucca in the sum of $70,000. Two notes were given by Laborde Bros. & Co. as evidence of said indebtedness; one for the sum of $42,000, and one for the sum of $28,000, and a mortgage was given by the Laborde Bros. & Co. to The Reno National Bank to secure the two notes. $42,000 of this indebtedness was sold by The First National Bank of Winnemucca to The Reno National Bank, for which The First National Bank of Winnemucca received full face value in credit. $28,000 of said indebtedness was retained by The First National Bank of Winnemucca. Thereafter, said $42,000 note and the mortgage were assigned to the Reconstruction Finance Corporation by The Reno National Bank. (Paragraph I of defendant's further answer to the third count of plaintiff's complaint, Page 28 of Tr.; admission of plaintiff by failure to deny in his reply; testimony of W. J. Tobin, Pages 209 to 211 of Tr.)

That after the assignment of the note and mortgage above mentioned to the Reconstruction Finance Corportion by The Reno National Bank, The First National Bank of Winnemucca, by way of notes and overdrafts, advanced to the said Laborde Brothers & Company the sum of $30,715.47. (Paragraph XIX of the third count of plaintiff's complaint, Page 14 of Tr.)

That on the 25th day of July, 1932, The First National Bank of Winnemucca signed a subordination agreement to the Reconstruction Finance Corporation of all its claims, both past and future and waived all right to participate in any of the proceeds from the liquidation of the assets assigned to the Reconstruction Finance Corporation by The Reno National Bank. (Defendant's Exhibit B, the subordination agreement, Pages 32 to 35 of Tr.)

That said note and mortgage above mentioned were liquidated by the Reconstruction Finance Corporation, and The Reno National Bank was given credit for the amount of the proceeds derived from the liquidation on the indebtedness of The Reno National Bank to the Reconstruction Finance Corporation. (Testimony of W. J. Tobin, Page 208 of Tr.)

There are just three questions in this case, the answers to which will solve the suit:

FIRST: Can the owner of a mortgage providing for advancements, after the assignment of the mortgage and the notes for which the mortgage is given as security, make such advancements and be secured under the mortgage?

SECOND: Can anyone who is not a party to a mortgage make advancements to a mortgagor and be secured by the mortgage for such advancements?

THIRD: Can a person who is the owner of claims secured by mortgage, or otherwise, subordinate all his right to the claims to the rights of another for a consideration?

LEGAL POINTS RAISED ON THIS APPEAL AS TO THE FIRST COUNT OF PLAINTIFF'S COMPLAINT.

Defendant's contention is:

(a) That after the assignment of the original notes and mortgages by The First National Bank of Winnemucca to The Reno National Bank, The First National Bank of Winnemucca could not legally make any further advancements by way of notes or overdrafts for the reason that The First National Bank of Winnemucca had parted with all interest in the notes and mortgages and was not a party to and had no interest in the original notes and had no legal right to make any further advancements by way of notes or overdrafts or otherwise.

(b) That when the notes were assigned by The Reno National Bank to the Reconstruction Finance Corporation, The Reno National Bank parted with all interest in the notes and mortgages and had no right thereafter to make, direct, or authorize any further advancements by way of notes or overdrafts or otherwise. That The Reno National Bank thereby passed out of the entire transaction.

(c) That there was no agreement between The Reno National Bank and The First National Bank of Winnemucca for the pro rating of advancements and overdrafts thereafter made by The First National Bank of Winnemucca.

(d) That all the advancements made before or after the assignment of the original notes by The First National Bank of Winnemucca to The Reno National Bank were waived by the subordination agreement.

(e) That the liquidation of said notes and mortgages was made by the Reconstruction Finance Corporation and that if The First National Bank of Winnemucca had any right to participate in the proceeds of the liquidation of the said notes and mortgages, its claim was against the Reconstruction Finance Corporation and not against The Reno National Bank, as The Reno National Bank had passed out of the entire transaction.

LEGAL POINTS RAISED ON THIS APPEAL AS TO THE SECOND COUNT OF PLAINTIFF'S COMPLAINT.

Defendant's contention is:

(a) That The First National Bank of Winnemucca had no right to make advancements for the reason that it was not a party to the John G. Taylor, Inc. note and mortgage and was a stranger thereto.

(b) That The Reno National Bank had no legal right to make, direct or authorize any advancements by The First National Bank of Winnemucca for the reason that The First National Bank of Winnemucca was not a party to the note or mortgage.

(c) That after the assignment of the note and mortgage to the Reconstruction Finance Corporation, The Reno National Bank had no right to make, direct or authorize any advancements for the reason that it had assigned all its interest in the note and mortgage to the Reconstruction Finance Corporation and thereby passed out of the entire transaction.

(d) That there was no agreement between The Reno National Bank and The First National Bank of Winnemucca for the pro rating of advancements and overdrafts thereafter made by The First National Bank of Winnemucca.

(e) That The First National Bank of Winnemucca waived all its right to participate in the proceeds of the liquidation of the John G. Taylor, Inc. note and mortgage by the subordination agreement made and executed on the 25th day of July, 1932.

(f) That the liquidation of said note and mortgage was made by the Reconstruction Finance Corporation, and that if The First National Bank of Winnemucca had any right to participate in the proceeds of the liquidation of the Taylor note and mortgage, its claim was against the Reconstruction Finance Corporation and not against The Reno National Bank, as The Reno National Bank had passed out of the entire transaction.

LEGAL POINTS RAISED ON THIS APPEAL AS TO THE THIRD COUNT OF PLAINTIFF'S COMPLAINT.

Defendant's contention is:

(a) That The First National Bank of Winnemucca waived all its right to participate in the proceeds of the liquidation of the Laborde Bros. & Company mortgage by the subordination agreement made and executed on the 25th day of July, 1932.

(b) That the liquidation of said note and mortgage was made by the Reconstruction Finance Corporation, and that if The First National Bank of Winnemucca had any right to participate in the proceeds of the liquidation of said mortgage, its claim was against the Reconstruction Finance Corporation and not against The Reno National Bank, as The Reno National Bank had passed out of the entire transaction.

ARGUMENT.

As to the first count of the complaint, our contention is that on the same day that the notes were assigned to The Reno National Bank, to-wit: the 30th day of June, 1932, the same notes were immediately assigned by The Reno National Bank to the Reconstruction Finance Corporation. The First National Bank of Winnemucca knew that the notes were going to be assigned to the Reconstruction Finance Corporation and that they had been assigned to the Reconstruction Finance Corporation.

Thereafter, The First National Bank of Winnemucca made the advancements set forth in the first count of the complaint to the mortgagors named in the mortgages alleged to be assigned in that count. Our contention and position is that the plaintiff is not entitled to prorate as to such advancements and overdrafts for the reasons:

(1) The original notes and mortgages were immediately assigned to the Reconstruction Finance Corporation, and while it is true that they were assigned as a pledge for money borrowed from the Reconstruction Finance Corporation, the legal effect is precisely

the same as if the securities had been sold outright to the Reconstruction Finance Corporation, as the securities never came back to The Reno National Bank. While it is true that the mortgages securing the notes assigned by The First National Bank of Winnemucca to The Reno National Bank provided for advancements, it would be absurd to say that after the original notes and mortgages had passed from The First National Bank of Winnemucca to The Reno National Bank and thence to the Reconstruction Finance Corporation, The First National Bank of Winnemucca could go on making advancements in the way of notes and overdrafts, and thus dilute and depreciate the security of the notes held by the Reconstruction Finance Corporation.

(2) All the advancements, except one (that of Alex Duffurena Company), were made after the right of the Reconstruction Finance Corporation to the securities had attached.

(3) On the 25th day of July, 1932, The First National Bank of Winnemucca signed a subordination agreement waiving all its claims, both past and future, and waiving all right to participate in any of the proceeds derived from the liquidation of the assets assigned to the Reconstruction Finance Corporation by The Reno National Bank.

As to our first contention, it may be conceded that it is proper to provide for advancements in mortgages, and it may be further conceded that when a mortgage covers several notes, the holders of the notes are entitled to prorate in the proceeds of the liquidation of the mortgaged property. As to the making of advancements, the advancements must be made by someone who has an interest in the mortgage; that is to say, someone who holds one or more of the notes. An outsider could not make advances; neither could a person who had parted with all interest in the notes and mortgages.

I have searched diligently for an authority to the effect that the holder of a note providing for future advances could not be protected as to such future advances made after the assignment of the note, and I find no authority directly in point. I have read the briefs of the attorneys for the Reconstruction Finance Corporation in the case of *Schmitt v. Tobin,* 15 Fed. Sup. 35-38, an action for a pro rata in a suit similar to the present case, and they dismiss the subject by saying it would be absurd to say that a mortgagee who had parted with title to the mortgage could make future advancements under the terms of the mortgage and be protected in so doing as against the assignee of the mortgages.

The nearest that I can find on the subject is the case of

Walker v. Whitmore, et als., 262 S. W. 678.

I quote from that case as follows:

> "Counsel for appellants concede that the sole question is whether the deed of trust from H. A. Mashburn to J. F. Walker, as trustee, includes advancements made by the mortgagee to Y. E. Whitmore, who was the grantee of H. A. Mashburn, the original mortgagor. The clause which is claimed to have that effect is copied in our state-

ment of facts, and need not be repeated here. It recites that the deed of trust shall be security for any other indebtedness that may be owing by the grantor to said American Trust Company up to the time of the foreclosure of the deed of trust.

"Counsel for appellants claim that this language is sufficiently comprehensive to include subsequent advancements made by the mortgagee to Y. E. Whitmore. We do not think so. The word, 'grantor', as used in the clause in question both in its legal meaning and in its common acceptation, refers to the person executing the deed of trust, of which the clause in question is a part. It would be a stretch of the meaning of the word 'grantor', far beyond this to make it refer to Y. E. Whitmore, who was not a party to the original deed of trust, and who simply acquired the property by mesne conveyances from H. A. Mashburn. If the bank had made any other advancements prior to the time of the foreclosure of the mortgage, the clause in question could cover them because Mashburn is the granter named and referred to in the instrument. Whitmore could in no sense be said to come within the meaning of the word 'grantor', as used in the original deed of trust. Therefore, the chancellor properly held that the original deed of trust from Mashburn to the bank could not be foreclosed for subsequent advances made by the bank to Whitmore."

Also the case of

Atkinson v. Foote, 44 C. A. 149, 186 P. 831,

as follows:

"The mortgage lien of a superior or prior mortgagee will not operate to secure optional advances made under such mortgage after such mortgagee has acquired actual notice of an encumbrance subsequent in point of time to his mortgage so as to defeat or impair the rights of the second encumbrancer."

Savings etc. Ass'n. v. Burnett, 106 Cal. 514, 39 P. 922.

"After notice of the attaching of a junior lien the senior mortgagee will not be protected in making further advances under his mortgage, at least where there is no binding engagement to make such advancements."

41 *C. J.* 527, Sec. 468.

It would seem that if a mortgagee cannot make advances to the grantee of the mortgagor, by parity of reasoning the mortgagee who had parted with his mortgage could not make advances to the mortgagor and be protected, and again, if a mortgagee may not make advances after notice of a junior lien, for a stronger reason, a mortgagee could not make advances after he had parted with all interest in the mortgage.

I have in mind that perhaps the reason there are no direct authorities on this point is because no one has heretofore ever raised so absurd a question as that a party who had parted with his interest in a mortgage or a party who was never a party to the mortgage could make future advancements and be protected as against the assignee of the mortgage.

These notes and mortgages were immediately assigned to the Reconstruction Finance Corporation and the Reconstruction Finance Corporation demanded that The First National Bank of Winnemucca sign a waiver of all its right to participate in the liquidation of the assigned securities and this The First National Bank of Winnemucca did through the subordination agreement.

Counsel contends that the subordination agreement is of no effect as there was no consideration, and bases his contention on the case of *Schmitt v. Tobin,* supra.

In the case cited, The Reno National Bank, through the same board of directors, had assigned to different state banks certain notes and mortgages, and the Court held that under such circumstances, it must be shown that the contending party received some benefit. In that case, the different state banks had paid for the mortgages instead of being paid for them, as in this case, and the Court held that as the state banks had taken the assigned notes and mortgages prior to the assignment of The Reno National Bank of certain assets to the Reconstruction Finance Corporation, the state banks received no benefit thereby. In the present case, The First National Bank of Winnemucca assigned to The Reno National Bank and had received its consideration.

In the case of *Schmitt v. Tobin,* the state banks had paid a consideration instead of receiving a consideration. In the *Schmitt* case, the Court made an exception of all assignments made to the state banks by The Reno National Bank after the assignment by The Reno National Bank to the Reconstruction Finance Corporation, and held that such claims were not entitled to prorate.

As to the second cause of action, the John G. Taylor, Inc. indebtedness of $700,000 was incurred in The First National Bank of Winnemucca. Thereafter, a note was given to The Reno National Bank in that amount to facilitate securing a loan from the Reconstruction Finance Corporation, and The First National Bank of Winnemucca was given credit for the $700,000. After the assignment of the $700,000 note and mortgage to the Reconstruction Finance Corporation by The Reno National Bank, The First National Bank of Winnemucca advanced $45,142.18 and The First National Bank of Winnemucca now asks that as to that amount it be entitled to prorate from the proceeds of the liquidation of the John G. Taylor, Inc. mortgage.

Our contention is that The First National Bank of Winnemucca is not entitled to prorate for the reason that it was not a party to the mortgage, and as to the making of advancements, it was in the position of a stranger.

This situation is similar to the case of *Schmitt v. Tobin,* supra. In that case, The Reno National Bank had a mortgage on the Jenkins property for $400,000. Thereafter, The Reno National Bank advanced $9000 to the Jenkins Company under the advancement clause, and took notes therefor and assigned the notes to the state banks, and the Court held that as these advancements were made after the assignment to the Reconstruction Finance Corporation, they would not be entitled to prorate, and the same holding was made as to this same John G. Taylor, Inc. claim set up in that case.

The reason the Court held that the state banks were not entitled to prorate for advancements assigned to them by The Reno National Bank was because The Reno National Bank had no right to make such advancements after it had made an assignment to the Reconstruction Finance Corporation.

The present case is stronger than the *Schmitt* case for the reason that The Reno National Bank was a party to the mortgage and could have made advancements under the terms of the mortgage prior to the assignment to the Reconstruction Finance Corporation. In the present situation, The Winnemucca Bank was not a party to the mortgage and was a perfect stranger without a shadow of a right to make advancements.

As to this count of the complaint, the subordination agreement applies the same as in the first count.

As to the third count of the complaint, on the 24th day of March, 1931, Laborde Bros. & Co. were indebted to The First National Bank of Winnemucca in the sum of $70,000. Two notes were given by the Laborde Bros. & Co. as evidence of the indebtedness; one for the sum of $42,000 and one for the sum of $28,000; and a mortgage was given by Laborde Bros. & Co. to The Reno National Bank to secure the notes.

$42,000 of this indebtedness had been sold by The First National Bank of Winnemucca to The Reno National Bank, for which The First National Bank of Winnemucca received full face value in credit. $28,000 of this indebtedness was retained by The First National Bank of Winnemucca.

Thereafter, the $42,000 note and the mortgage were assigned to the Reconstruction Finance Corporation by The Reno National Bank. After the assignment of the note and mortgage to the Reconstruction Finance Corporation by The Reno National Bank, The First National Bank of Winnemucca, by way of notes and overdrafts, advanced to Laborde Bros. & Co. the sum of $30,715.47 and The First National Bank of Winnemucca now contends that it is entitled to prorate as to the $30,715.47.

This might be true except for the subordination agreement.

It would seem to be unnecessary to cite authorities to the effect that a lien may be waived by agreement. As far as this case has gone, no question has been raised as to the right of the different banks to sign a subordination agreement. The only question that has been raised is that the subordination agreements were void for the want of consideration. This cannot apply to the present case for the reason that The First National Bank of Winnemucca received credit, which the Vice-President testified was the same as cash, in the sum of $1,298,314.90, and which enabled The First National Bank of Winnemucca to continue in business.

RECAPITULATION.

The plaintiff is not entitled to prorate on its first cause of action for the reason:

The notes were assigned for a valuable consideration, to-wit: the face value thereof, to The Reno

National Bank, and The Reno National Bank, on the same day, assigned the same to the Reconstruction Finance Corporation. The First National Bank of Winnemucca thereby disabled itself from making any further advancements under the mortgages, as it had parted with all title thereto and would not be allowed to dilute or diminish the security held by the Reconstruction Finance Corporation. Any advancements made thereafter by The First National Bank of Winnemucca were the same as though a stranger had made them.

Further, The First National Bank of Winnemucca is estopped by its subordination agreement, the consideration of which and the benefit accruing to The First National Bank of Winnemucca is the credit which it received for the full face value of all the notes.

The plaintiff is not entitled to prorate on its second cause of action for the reason:

First: If the John G. Taylor, Inc. claim was a direct loan from The Reno National Bank to John G. Taylor, Inc. of $700,000, and the note was given to The Reno National Bank, and the mortgage securing the same was given to The Reno National Bank without The First National Bank of Winnemucca being a party to the mortgage, then any advancements made to John G. Taylor, Inc. by The First National Bank of Winnemucca were without authority and were illegal because the advancements were made by a stranger to the mortgage.

Again, if the above situation were true, we would be in the same position as that of the Jenkins Company and John G. Taylor, Inc. in the suit of *Schmitt v. Tobin,* 15 Fed. Sup. 35-38. (See Appendix.) The advancements were made after the right of the Reconstruction Finance Corporation had attached, as was held in that case. The only difference in the two cases is that in the suit of *Schmitt v. Tobin,* the advancements were made by The Reno National Bank and evidenced by notes, and the notes assigned to the state banks, a much stronger situation than the present. In the *Schmitt* case, the notes were regularly made out to The Reno National Bank and assigned to the state banks. Here the advancements were made without authority and would be in a worse position than the assets in the *Schmitt* case.

As to the Laborde claim, the third count of plaintiff's complaint, a large amount of the indebtedness of the Laborde Bros. & Co. had originated in The First National Bank of Winnemucca and was evidenced by many notes. The indebtedness was consolidated. One note for $42,000 was made to The Reno National Bank, and a note for $28,000 was made to The First National Bank of Winnemucca, and was secured by a mortgage running to The Reno National Bank.

Up to this point, it may be conceded that The First National Bank of Winnemucca was entitled to prorate in any of the assets through liquidation of the mortgage security, but The First National Bank of

Winnemucca thereafter made advancements in the sum of $30,715.47 to Laborde Bros. & Co., and the note was taken by The First National Bank of Winnemucca to evidence these advances.

Therefore, it is clear that The First National Bank of Winnemucca had received credit for $42,000 of the Laborde indebtedness.

On the 25th of July, 1932, The First National Bank of Winnemucca subordinated all its claims to the Reconstruction Finance Corporation, both past and future. The consideration for the subordination agreement was the credit of $42,000, which The First National Bank of Winnemucca had received from The Reno National Bank. Not only this, but it had received credit for all the other notes transferred and assigned on the 30th day of June, 1932, a benefit that permitted The First National Bank of Winnemucca to continue in business, to avoid excess loans, and to avoid complications with the Comptroller's Office for the making of excess loans, and to avoid liability of its directors for making such loans, and to receive interest on the excess loans, and to take care of its creditors.

To restate the entire case, the evidence shows that The Reno National Bank has taken over notes from The First National Bank of Winnemucca in order to permit it to exceed the excess loan limit and to continue in business in the sum of $1,298,314.90, and upon these notes assigned to The Reno National Bank, The

Reno National Bank has taken a loss in the liquidation thereof in the sum of $632,848.69.

In the case of *Schmitt v. Tobin,* supra, the state banks took over worthless paper from The Reno National Bank and paid face value therefor and gave The Reno National Bank credit for the full face value of the notes assigned to them, and they received nothing for this credit, which was the same as cash, except a lot of worthless securities, and the Court held in that case for that reason there was no benefit accruing to them and no consideration for the subordination.

In this case, the shoe is on the other foot. We are out, in credit at least, the sum of $1,298,314.90, and we have taken a loss thereon in the sum of $632,848.69. Of course, I do not contend that The Reno National Bank is entitled to the recoupment of its loss. I make the above statement simply to show the difference between this case and the *Schmitt* case which counsel contends is decisive of this case.

There are just three questions in this case, the answers to which will solve the suit:

First: Can the owner of a mortgage providing for advancements, after the assignment of the mortgage and the notes for which the mortgage is given as security, make such advancements and be secured under the mortgage?

Second: Can anyone who is not a party to a mortgage make advancements to a mortgagor and be secured by the mortgage for such advancements?

Third: Can a person who is the owner of claims secured by mortgage, or otherwise, subordinate all his right to the claims to the rights of another for a consideration?

The mere statement of the above should be a sufficient answer.

We respectfully submit that the plaintiff is not entitled to prorate with the defendant in any sum whatsoever.

Dated, Reno, Nevada,
November 1, 1939.

Respectfully submitted,
N. J. Barry,
Attorney for Appellant.

(Appendix Follows.)

[illegible] a party to a mortgage to a mortgagor and be se[illegible] advancements?

[illegible] person who is the owner of claims [illegible] or otherwise, subordinate all [illegible] to the rights of another for a

[illegible] of the above should be a suffi-

[illegible] that the plaintiff is not [illegible] defendant in any sum

[illegible] submitted.

[illegible] J. BARRY,

Attorney for Appellant.

(Appendix Follows.)

Schmitt v. Tobin, 15 Fed. Sup. 35-38.

"Norcross, District Judge:

"A number of questions are involved in this case mainly growing out of the validity of certain subordination agreements entered into by the various State banks of which plaintiff Schmitt is Receiver. At the time of the trial it appeared that the subordination agreements as alleged in the complaint, in só far as they applied to the Bank of Nevada Savings & Trust Company and the Virginia City Bank, were not produced. The question was then for the first time raised as to whether such subordination agreements were ever executed and delivered to the defendant corporation. Without at this time reviewing all of the evidence thereon, it is the opinion of the Court that the evidence is sufficient to establish the execution and delivery of such subordination agreements, both as to the Bank of Nevada Savings & Trust Company and the Virginia City Bank. I will say that the proof in respect to the Bank of Nevada Savings & Trust Company is stronger than the proof in respect to the Virginia City Bank, for in the case of the former bank Mr. Sheehan, Vice-President, testified that he had seen the executed agreement upon his desk, and later on it was taken by one of the clerks in the office assumedly for mailing. It is also in testimony that officers or representatives of defendant had checked over the files in their possession on one or two occasions, and found all subordination agreements therein.

"Two serious questions have been raised with respect to the validity of such agreements; one deals with the question as to whether they were ever lawfully executed by the respective banks. It appears from the evidence that there was no meeting of the Board of Directors of any of the banks authorizing such issuance. The question is then presented respecting the power of the officers who did execute the same. In the view the Court takes with respect to the other question which has been the main contention in the case, it will be unnecessary to pass upon this question of official power.

"It appears from the evidence that all of the several banks involved are a part of what is referred to in the briefs as the Wingfield chain of banks. It appears from the record that the president and vice-president of the Reno National Bank were respectively president and vice-president of all of the other banks of the said chain, including all of the banks referred to in the complaint. It also appears from the evidence that the Board of Directors of all of the banks mentioned in the complaint were the same, or at least a majority thereof were members of the Board of Directors of the Reno National Bank. The rule is well settled that where two or more corporations are controlled by the same or substantially the same board of directors, in transactions between such corporations so dominated, in order for the same to be enforceable against a corporation a party to any such agreement, it must appear that the agreement is advantageous to the corporation against whom such agreement or obligation is sought to be enforced.

In the case of *Geddes v. Anaconda Mining Co.,* 254 U. S. 590, 599, the Supreme Court said:

> " 'The relation of directors to corporations is of such a fiduciary nature that transactions between boards having common members are regarded as jealously by the law as are personal dealings between a director and his corporation, and where the fairness of such transactions is challenged the burden is upon those who would maintain them to show their entire fairness and where a sale is involved the full adequacy of the consideration. Especially is this true where a common director is dominating in influence or in character. This court has been consistently emphatic in the application of this rule, which, it has declared, is founded in soundest morality, and we now add in the soundest business policy. Twin-Lick Oil Co. v. Marbury, 91 U. S. 587, 588; Thomas v. Brownville, Ft. Kearney & Pacific R. R. Co., 109 U. S. 522; Wardell v. Railroad Co., 103 U. S. 651, 658; Corsicana National Bank v. Johnson, 251 U. S. 68, 90.'

"The Geddes case, supra, was on appeal from the Ninth Circuit Court of Appeals, and while the decision of the latter court (245 Fed. 225) was reversed, there was no substantial disagreement respecting the rule applicable in cases of interlocking directors. (See page 235.) See also opinions in same case by Hunt, Circuit Judge, sitting as trial judge, 197 Fed. 860, 864, and Bourquin, District Judge, 222

Fed. 133. See also Idaho-Oregon Light & P. Co. v. State Bank of Chicago, 224 Fed. 39; 14A C. J. 125.

"The principal question to be determined in the case is the question last mentioned. The Court has reached the conclusion that the State banks, assuming they entered into what otherwise would be valid subordination agreements, that such agreements are not binding upon the State banks for the reason it appears from the evidence that the banks were not benefited thereby. It is apparent that the loan in question made by the Reconstruction Finance Corporation was one designed to aid the Reno National Bank in particular to continue business as a banking concern. It is also apparent from the evidence that the other banks would in all probability be benefited by such continuance. However, as subsequently developed, the loan was insufficient, or for other reasons the bank eventually had to suspend, was adjudged insolvent, and taken over by the Controller of the Currency as an insolvent bank. There was nothing to support a consideration or advantage upon the part of the State banks entering into such subordination agreements except the hope or belief that the aid to be extended by the defendant would be sufficient to carry on the Reno National Bank, and which, as the main bank in the said chain would have enabled the other banks also to carry on. However, in so far as the facts appear in this case no advantage whatsoever was derived by the several State banks entering into the subordination agreements. The mere hope of a different situation would not be sufficient to support a consideration for such an agreement. It is therefore the conclusion of the Court that this case in the main comes within the rule heretofore announced that where two or more corporations are controlled by interlocking boards of directors any agreement or obligation between such corporations to be binding and enforceable, must show a supporting advantage, otherwise the agreement is void.

"It is the conclusions of the Court that the subordination agreements referred to in the complaint are not binding upon the several State banks, and hence not binding upon the Receiver thereof. This question becomes of importance because of the allegations in the complaint that certain loans aggregating very substantial amounts of money, made particularly to various corporations and individuals engaged in the live stock industry of the State, had been split and assigned in part to various of the State banks. When the Reno National Bank negotiated its loan or loans from the Reconstruction Finance Corporation it assigned as security the mortgages securing these several notes, together with such notes as were then retained by the Reno National Bank. The question here involved is whether the Receiver now holding certain of the notes so secured has a right to have the defendant Reconstruction Finance Corporation account for such portion of the proceeds of sales of property covered by the various mortgages or other securities as is represented by the notes held by the Receiver. It is the conclusion of the Court that the Receiver has a right to have such an accounting. That is, that where property has been sold by the defendant corporation, the proceeds of any such sale of mortgaged or otherwise incumbered property are subject to apportionment to the Receiver of the several State banks as the amount of notes held by him as such Receiver bear to the total secured by the mortgage.

"While this view covers the main question presented, there remains a question applicable alike to the Seventh and Eighth causes of action. In the Seventh cause of action it appears that the Jenkins Land & Live Stock Company, which had executed notes and mortgages covering a very substantial amount of money, made prior to March 19, 1932, the date of a subordination agreement entered into by the Reno National Bank in favor of the Reconstruction Finance Corporation, and hence prior to April 13, 1932, the date the Jenkins Land & Livestock Company mortgage was assigned to the Reconstruction Finance Corporation as security for its main loan, and that on May 24, 1932, an additional loan in the sum of $9000.00 was made to the Jenkins Land & Livestock Company by the Reno National Bank, and that the note therefor was by it assigned to the Virginia City Bank. On July 12, 1932, the same company, Jenkins Land & Live Stock Company, executed another note for $9000.00 to the Reno National Bank, which in turn was assigned to the Tonopah Banking Corporation. It appears that these two notes were made and assigned subsequent to the assignment of the main mortgage to the Reconstruction Finance Corporation, and subsequent to the subordination agreement executed by the Reno National Bank to the Reconstruction Finance Corporation. It is manifest that the State banks taking these assignments subsequent to the main assignment to the Reconstruction Finance Corporation, took subject to the rights of the Reno National Bank, and could obtain no greater right than that of the Reno National Bank. It is therefore the conclusions of the Court that plaintiff is not entitled to recover upon the Seventh cause of action.

"The Eighth cause of action presents precisely the same question of law referred to respecting the Seventh cause of action. It also deals with subsequent loans made by the Reno National Bank to the John G. Taylor Company, one dated June 21, 1932, for $9000.00, assigned to the Virginia City Bank, another dated July 9, 1932, for $7500.00, assigned to the Tonopah Bank, and another note of August 6, 1932, for $7500.00, assigned to the Carson Valley Bank. As before stated, these several notes are all subsequent to the main assignment by the Reno National Bank to the Reconstruction Finance Corporation, and hence the assignee banks acquire no rights superior to those of the Reno National Bank, and are governed by the subordination agreement of the Reno National Bank of date March 19, 1932. Plaintiff is not entitled to recover upon the Eighth cause of action. The First and Ninth causes of action have heretofore been dismissed by consent of the respective parties.

"In the other causes of action remaining there are a few instances of assignments of notes to the various banks which come within the rule as announced with respect to the Seventh and Eighth causes of action. Where there are such assignments following the so-called main assignment by the Reno National Bank to the Reconstruction Finance Corporation, plaintiff will not be entitled to an accounting thereon, but upon all other notes mentioned, from the Second to the Sixth causes of action, inclusive, plaintiff is entitled to a decree for an accounting of such proportion of the receipts by the defendant corporation from foreclosure or other proceedings in respect to the mortgages and securities therein referred to as may appear. Let decree be entered accordingly. It is so ordered."

No. 9289

IN THE

United States Circuit Court of Appeals

For the Ninth Circuit

CARROLL HENDERSON, as Receiver of The Reno National Bank, Reno, Nevada (a national banking association, organized and existing under the laws of the United States of America), *Appellant,* vs. CARROLL HENDERSON, as Receiver of The First National Bank of Winnemucca, Nevada (a national banking association, organized and existing under the laws of the United States of America), *Appellee.*	

On Appeal from the District Court of the United States, for the District of Nevada.

BRIEF FOR APPELLEE.

THOS. J. SALTER,
Winnemucca, Nevada,
Attorney for Appellee.

PERNAU-WALSH PRINTING CO., SAN FRANCISCO, CALIFORNIA

Subject Index

Page

Statement of the Case.................................... 1

Argument 11

Table of Authorities Cited

Cases

Pages

Schmitt v. Reconstruction Finance Corporation, 20 Fed. Supp. 813 ....14, 25, 29

Statutes

Statutes of Nevada, 1926-1927, p. 190, numbers one to fifteen 3

No. 9289

IN THE

United States Circuit Court of Appeals

For the Ninth Circuit

CARROLL HENDERSON, as Receiver of The Reno National Bank, Reno, Nevada (a national banking association, organized and existing under the laws of the United States of America),

Appellant,

vs.

CARROLL HENDERSON, as Receiver of The First National Bank of Winnemucca, Nevada (a national banking association, organized and existing under the laws of the United States of America),

Appellee.

On Appeal from the District Court of the United States, for the District of Nevada.

BRIEF FOR APPELLEE.

STATEMENT OF THE CASE.

For many years prior to December 9, 1932, the Wingfield chain of banks was operated in the State of Nevada, under the management and control of George Wingfield, President, and J. Sheehan, Vice President and Executive Officer of the entire chain of banks. George Wingfield was a majority stockholder in all the banks, and he and J. Sheehan were members of the Board of Directors of each, thus creating an interlocking directorate.

Executive offices were located in The Reno National Bank, Reno, Nevada, and business of all the banks was transacted through that bank.

Although these banks were separate corporations, George Wingfield and J. Sheehan as members of the Board of Directors of each, and as such common directors, were the dominating influence over the chain of banks to the extent of managing and controlling the business policy of each bank, and the authority for all loans made; distribution of split loans as between the various members of the chain; transfer of securities from one bank to another; handling the cash funds of each bank through The Reno National Bank, and the initiation of customs, usages and understandings between the various banks covering all their business dealings.

The First National Bank of Winnemucca was incorporated under the laws of the United States and pursuant to such laws could only make a loan to any one person in an amount not exceeding ten per cent of its capital and surplus; however, in certain cases covered by the McFadden act, such loan to any one person could be increased to twenty-five per cent.

The First National Bank was situated in the midst of a community of large cattle and sheep operators, and had the opportunity of making loans far in excess of the amounts allowed it by law, whereas other banks in the chain were located in communities where large deposits of cash were available, but no outlet for loans.

Because of this situation, Mr. Wingfield and Mr. Sheehan inaugurated and put into effect the practice of The First National Bank accepting loans covering the needs of the borrower which exceeded the amount The First National Bank could carry and then transferring to The Reno National Bank such excess paper, The First National Bank receiving credit on the books of The Reno National Bank for the amount of the loan so transferred.

The Reno National Bank then transferred to various banks of the chain certain portions of this paper, thereby creating what is known in the organization as split loans.

The technical accomplishment of these transactions was effected by The First National Bank taking the note or notes of the borrower, which notes were secured by chattel mortgage on livestock. In each and every of these mortgages there was contained a provision referred to as statutory covenants (Statutes of Nevada, 1926-1927, page 190, numbers one to fifteen). Covenant No. 5 reads as follows:

> "This mortgage shall be security for any and all renewals of the mortgage debt or of the promissory note or notes evidencing the same, which may be executed and delivered by the mortgagor to the mortgagee, and any and all additional or future advances or loans which may be made by the mortgagee to the mortgagor."

After the execution of the notes and mortgage the borrower invariably required additional funds to be used each year for cutting and stacking hay; for payment of wages to labor; for supplies and general expenses in running his livestock business. For the convenience of the borrower living in the vicinity of Winnemucca, The First National Bank made these advances and took additional notes of the borrower, or carried such advances in the form of overdrafts, all secured by the original mortgage.

These advances were made by authority of Mr. Wingfield and Mr. Sheehan and were justified upon the theory that it was necessary to protect the security covered by the mortgages until liquidation.

During all the years of the operation of the Wingfield chain of banks it was the custom, usage, practice and understanding that these advances should be secured by the mortgage to the same extent as the original notes. And, that upon liquidation of the loan the advances made by The First National Bank should be taken into consideration with the original note and receive its pro rata of the collection made.

It was also understood that where expedient these advances were to be repaid out of the first proceeds realized from the sales of the debtor's wool, lambs, or livestock increase during the year.

Under this procedure, as each advance was made by The First National Bank, The Reno National Bank was notified and the advance added to the account of the debtor upon the records of The Reno National Bank, where the debtors' account was kept.

In pursuance to the usual practice and custom herein referred to, and upon direct instructions of J. Sheehan, executive officer of the banks, from about June 9 to June 30, 1932, The First National Bank transferred to The Reno National Bank notes and mortgages, the subject of this action, of eight debtors, to-wit:

Alcorta, Dufurrena, Johnstone, Larribeau, Yragui, Gabica, Jaca, and Belaustegui,

which amount The Reno National Bank credited to the account of The First National Bank.

The specific purpose of this particular transfer of securities was to enable The Reno National Bank to add them to other securities then held by The Reno National Bank and pledge the whole to the Reconstruction Finance Corporation for a cash loan to The Reno National Bank.

After the transfer of these accounts to The Reno National Bank, The First National Bank made advances to these debtors as shown in the Complaint. These advances were made by authority of Mr. Sheehan and pursuant to the usual understanding covering pro rata distribution of collections.

The accounting made by the Receiver of The Reno National Bank reveals that in addition to the original notes covered by these mortgages The Reno National Bank either held notes or had made advances to these same eight debtors.

Thus The First National Bank and The Reno National Bank were placed upon the same footing in that both banks held notes or had made advances to these debtors, all paper of these debtors outstanding being secured by the same mortgages.

Plaintiff's second cause of action covering the John G. Taylor transaction presents a slight difference in procedure in the handling of this account between the two banks.

On March 12, 1932, John G. Taylor, Inc. made, executed and delivered to The Reno National Bank its note in the sum of $700,000.00, secured by chattel mortgage. After the execution of the note and mortgage The First National Bank advanced to John G. Taylor, Inc. the sum of $45,142.18, which indebtedness was evidenced by notes and overdrafts.

These advances were made not only pursuant to the usual custom and understanding that they would be secured by the mortgage given to The Reno National Bank, but through specific instructions from Mr. Sheehan, the executive officer of these two banks. These facts are testified to by J. Sheehan, Transcript pages 108, 109, 110 and 130. Testimony of P. L. Nelson, Transcript pages 140, 141 and 142. Deposition of James G. Moore, Transcript pages 186, 187, 188 and 189. Letter of authority by J. Sheehan to J. G. Moore, Transcript pages 198 and 199.

The purpose of these advances was to protect the assets covered by the mortgage and for the use of the borrower in paying wages and for supplies and general expenses in running his livestock and ranching business.

Mr. Sheehan further testified that the Taylor mortgage was given to The Reno National Bank for the purpose of consolidating into one mortgage all of its indebtedness held by the various banks. Transcript page 108.

The First National Bank made these advances to Taylor as a matter of convenience to him so that he could transact his business with the bank closest to his headquarters.

Plaintiff's third cause of action covering the Laborde Bros. transaction presents a further slight difference in procedure in the handling of this account between the two banks.

Laborde Bros. and Company owed The First National Bank $28,000.00 and at the same time owed The Reno National Bank $42,000.00, all evidenced by notes. Whereupon, on March 24, 1931, Laborde Bros. executed a mortgage to The Reno National Bank, to secure the total of $70,000.00. The Reno National Bank retained one note amounting to $42,000.00 and sent one note in the sum of $28,000.00 to The First National Bank.

Testimony of J. Sheehan, Transcript pages 110 and 111; Carroll Henderson, Transcript pages 169 and 170; Admission of counsel, Transcript pages 169 and 170; J. G. Moore, Transcript pages 190, 191 and 192.

Thereafter The First National Bank made advances to Laborde Bros. in the sum of $3612.49 and carried the same on its books in the form of an overdraft.

This advance was made pursuant to the usual custom and also by specific authority of J. Sheehan, and with the understanding that upon liquidation The First National Bank would pro rate the proceeds with The Reno National Bank. Testimony J. G. Moore, Transcript pages 191 and 192; J. Sheehan, Transcript page 111.

From the statement furnished by the Receiver of The Reno National Bank it appears that The Reno National Bank also made advances to Laborde Bros. amounting to $30,500.00, which sum was represented by notes or overdrafts, all secured by the mortgage.

In this instance, as in the case of the debtors in our first cause of action, The Reno National Bank also made advances to Laborde Bros., thus placing itself on the same footing with The First National Bank in that both banks held notes or had made advances to the same debtor and all paper of this debtor outstanding being secured by the same mortgage.

After all the securities available from the various banks of the chain had been gathered into The Reno National Bank for the purpose of pledging the same to the Reconstruction Finance Corporation, to secure a loan to The Reno National Bank, Mr. Sheehan put together these securities with other securities held by The Reno National Bank, and sent the same to the Reconstruction Finance Corporation, thereby securing the loan required. Testimony of J. Sheehan, Transcript page 121.

About a month after the consummation of the loan from the Reconstruction Finance Corporation, and on

July 25, 1932, George Wingfield, President of the bank chain, caused The First National Bank to execute to the Reconstruction Finance Corporation a subordinate agreement. Transcript page 32.

This transaction only affected the relations between the Reconstruction Finance Corporation and The First National Bank. It did not modify, change or limit the relations existing between The First National Bank and The Reno National Bank in respect to the interest The First National Bank had in the mortgages, the subject of this action. When the Reconstruction Finance Corporation was repaid the loan made to The Reno National Bank, all interest in these securities that it had, or ever had, was cancelled, so that no issue in this case is presented as between The First National Bank and the Reconstruction Finance Corporation.

The securities herein mentioned were pledged to the Reconstruction Finance Corporation, and not sold to it by The Reno National Bank. When the Wingfield chain of banks was officially closed on December 9, 1932, the loan made by the Reconstruction Finance Corporation to The Reno National Bank remained unpaid, and thereafter the Reconstruction Finance Corporation in cooperation with the Receiver of The Reno National Bank proceeded to liquidate the securities pledged and in so doing liquidated such paper as seemed most expedient at the time, irrespective of whether the paper had originated in any particular bank. The Reconstruction Finance Corporation in this manner eventually received full payment of its loan.

Consequently, the equities in any of the pledged securities remained in The Reno National Bank, and in the banks of the chain to which the borrower was also indebted.

The liquidation of the securities in which The First National Bank had an interest resulted in loss in some instances and a gain in others.

By adding together the amounts due to The Reno National Bank and the advances due to The First National Bank, all secured by the same mortgages, a pro rata distribution of proceeds was arrived at. In this manner, where there was a loss, each bank suffered its pro rata thereof. Where there was a gain, each bank likewise enjoyed its pro rata.

In this respect, we ask the Court to consider the fact that it was the policy of these two banks for The First National Bank to transfer without recourse its excess loans, as well as other loans held by it, to The Reno National Bank—not for the benefit of The First National Bank, but to provide an outlet for the money on deposit in The Reno National Bank and other banks of the chain. In effect, when The First National Bank made a loan to a borrower in excess of the amount it could loan, and transferred such excess loan to The Reno National Bank, or when it transferred other loans held by it, The First National Bank was acting as the agent of The Reno National Bank in procuring loans. Testimony of P. L. Nelson, Transcript pages 141 and 142.

Such transactions were not sales in a strict sense such as would govern ordinary transactions between banks having no interlocking directorate or associated interests. The result of the Wingfield method was that to all intents and purposes The Reno National Bank made the loan direct to the borrower, but caused The First National Bank to handle the transaction in its behalf as an accommodation and for the convenience of the borrower.

Under orders of the comptroller of the Currency all these transfers of securities were without recourse upon The First National Bank. Transcript page 117.

It follows then that all paper transferred to The Reno National Bank by The First National Bank became the property of The Reno National Bank, just as though it had made the loan in the first place; and, in the liquidation of the securities The First National Bank could not be held for any loss sustained because of any depreciation in value of the assets from the time of transfer to The Reno National Bank to the date of liquidation.

ARGUMENT.

The theory upon which the plaintiff brings this action is that George Wingfield, as President, and J. Sheehan, as executive officer of the Wingfield chain of banks, formulated and put into effect the policies governing the relations of the various banks.

One policy so inaugurated was that where the requirements of a borrower was in excess of the amount The First National Bank could loan to such borrower that several notes representing the loan should be taken and that all such notes should be secured by a mortgage upon the assets of the borrower.

That the excess loan notes should be transferred without recourse to The Reno National Bank, where the executive office for all the banks was maintained; and that upon receipt of the notes The Reno National Bank should credit The First National Bank with the face value thereof. Such notes were then distributed to other banks of the chain, thus providing an outlet for their money.

In some instances, particularly where there was a lack of cash in The First National Bank and a surplus of cash in the other banks, the entire loan was transferred to The Reno National Bank, The First National Bank retaining no part of it.

It was also the custom that from time to time The First National Bank should make advances covering the requirements of borrowers living in the vicinity of Winnemucca for general running expenses of their ranches and cattle and sheep business, and for the protection of the assets covered by the mortgage.

All such advances were represented by notes or overdrafts and were secured by the mortgage to the same extent as the original notes, each mortgage carrying a provision to that effect.

Upon liquidation of the assets, or payment of the indebtedness, all banks holding paper, including all advances, covered by the mortgage shared pro rata in the proceeds.

This policy, understanding, custom, and usage was invariably followed by the banks during the entire existence of the Wingfield chain.

The transfer to The Reno National Bank of the securities of the eight debtors, the subject of our first cause of action, was in line with the regular policy of the banks, except that J. Sheehan gave as his reason for this specific transfer that he wished to add these securities to others and pledge the whole to the Reconstruction Finance Corporation for a loan running to The Reno National Bank.

The First National Bank received credit upon the books of The Reno National Bank, but no cash.

At the time the transfer was made the policy of pro rating the proceeds from liquidation was in full force and effect.

In executing the subordination agreement The First National Bank only subordinated its interest in these securities to the Reconstruction Finance Corporation and after the Reconstruction Finance Corporation had received repayment by The Reno National Bank of its loan, the subordination agreement was of no further force or effect, and did not in any respect limit the relations existing between these two banks in respect to a pro rata of the proceeds of liquidation.

The original notes covered by the mortgages occupied no greater degree of dignity than that of the subsequent notes and overdrafts, according to the provision of the mortgage that such advances would be likewise secured thereby, and such advances should be added to the original notes and pro rated between the two banks either in loss or gain.

Schmitt v. Reconstruction Finance Corporation, Volume 20, Federal Supplement, 813.

This decision is based upon substantially the same facts as in the instant case, and involves the relations between the Wingfield chain of banks respecting pro rata of proceeds from liquidation.

In the *Schmitt* case the Reconstruction Finance Corporation set up as a defense that any advances made by The Reno National Bank to the borrower after the pledging of his security could not share pro rata in the proceeds of liquidation. This defense could not have been available to The Reno National Bank against another bank of the chain because of the custom and understanding hereinbefore mentioned, and for the additional reason that such advances were made for the protection of the assets covered by the mortgage.

Even so, we believe that if Schmitt had urged the proposition that these advances in his case had been made with the knowledge of the Reconstruction Finance Corporation and to preserve the assets covered by the mortgage, Schmitt would have recovered on that count as well.

With reference to our second cause of action, the John G. Taylor, Inc. account:

As we have stated, Taylor owed the various banks in the Wingfield chain about $700,000.00. For the purpose of consolidating these loans, Taylor executed a note for this amount to The Reno National Bank and secured the same by mortgage. Testimony of J. Sheehan, Transcript page 108. By virtue of direct instructions of Mr. Sheehan The First National Bank advanced running expenses in the sum of $45,-142.18. It was understood, as in all the other instances, that the mortgage secured these advances. In addition to that it was understood that this money was to be repaid to The First National Bank out of the first sales of wool and lambs. Instead of this being done, the Reconstruction Finance Corporation, or the Regional Agricultural Credit Corporation kept the money and paid The First National Bank nothing. This transaction is no different than all the other dealings between these banks. In view of the fact that Wingfield was the principal stockholder in all the banks it is unreasonable to assume that he would prefer one bank over another in the distribution of proceeds from collections, or allow one bank to hold secured paper and another to hold an unsecured account. The very fact that the mortgage carried the provision that subsequent loans and advances should also be secured by the mortgage precludes any such preference.

Referring to our third cause of action, the Laborde Bros. and Company account:

This account is a typical example of a split loan. The Reno National Bank held a note for $42,000.00 and The First National Bank held a note for $28,-

000.00, both secured by the same mortgage. The Reno National Bank made advances to this debtor for his running expenses and so did The First National Bank. The two banks were on an equal footing insofar as their interests appeared. In the liquidation of this account The Reno National Bank collected from Laborde a sum far in excess of that due it, and yet the Receiver refused to account to The First National Bank for any part of the collection. We cannot conceive the justification for this procedure. The Reno National Bank had no right to any sum in excess of the amount due it, so that under any theory of this case, Laborde was entitled to return of the surplus collected, or The First National Bank was entitled to its pro rata.

Henderson's accounting, Transcript page 90.

Answering counsel's brief for appellant:

On page 3 of his brief under statement of facts it is said that The First National Bank received payment from The Reno National Bank in the full face value of the notes.

The evidence is that The First National Bank was credited with the amount on the books of The Reno National Bank and that when the banks closed on December 9, 1932, The Reno National Bank owed The First National Bank the sum of $170,287.01.

On page 4 of the brief it is stated that The First National Bank was not named in the note and mortgage given by Taylor. While that statement is true, it is also true that, according to Mr. Sheehan's testimony, the note and mortgage was given for the purpose of consolidating into one mortgage all of the indebtedness held by the various banks. The fact that no other bank was named in the mortgage was an immaterial matter in view of the split loan system in use by the various banks of the chain.

On page 5 of the brief it is stated that after the assignment of the Laborde account The First National Bank advanced by way of notes and overdrafts to Laborde the sum of $30,715.47. There is no such evidence in this case upon which to base such a statement. In our Complaint it is alleged that The First National Bank held a note of Laborde in the sum of $28,000.00, secured by mortgage, and that The Reno National Bank held a note, secured by the same mortgage in the sum of $42,000.00. It is further alleged that The First National Bank made advances to this borrower in the sum of $3,612.49. Transcript, pages 13 and 14. Henderson's statement, Transcript page 90, shows that The Reno National Bank made advances to this debtor in the sum of $30,500.00. According to our theory of this case, it makes no difference which bank made the advances, but we do feel that a statement of facts should be accurate and conform to the evidence.

On page 6 of the brief it is stated that The Reno National Bank took a loss on the paper mentioned in the complaint in the sum of $632,848.69. These figures are given by Mr. Tobin in his testimony, but there was no basis for them as they were not involved in this action, and the stipulation of the parties, Transcript page 85, destroyed this testimony.

While we contend that it is no defense to this suit that a general loss to the banks occurred in the liquidation of this paper, we again insist that a statement of facts should be accurate.

Henderson's statement, Transcript pages 86 to 92 inclusive, which is stipulated to by both parties as being accurate, and upon which this judgment is based, Transcript page 85, shows that the total amount of the paper, held by The Reno National Bank was the sum of $1,298,314.90 and further shows that The Reno National Bank received from liquidation of these assets the sum of $1,062,830.27, leaving a loss sustained of $235,484.63 including the Taylor account. We arrive at this result by adding the items of the statement under the head of "total indebtedness, Reno National Bank", and deducting the items of the statement "Reno Net liquidation".

There is no tenable theory which could be advanced in this case whereby The First National Bank could be held responsible for any loss sustained by liquidation of this paper, except its pro rata based on the sum held by The Reno National Bank and the sum held by The First National Bank. This is true because upon the order made by the comptroller of the currency all paper transferred to The Reno National Bank was without recourse upon The First National Bank. Transcript page 174. If this contention of loss is injected in the brief as a plea for sympathy, we suggest that the loss on the Taylor account, in which counsel says we had no interest, was the sum of $93,181.12, and the loss on the paper transferred to The Reno

National Bank was only $142,303.51, and that if The First National Bank had been paid the sum of $170,287.01 due it by The Reno National Bank at its closing, The First National Bank could have assumed the loss, if it could have lawfully done so, and still be ahead on the deal.

On page 8 of the brief it is stated that there is no evidence showing any agreement between The First National Bank and The Reno National Bank to the effect that The First National Bank was to participate in the proceeds of liquidation. We say that no such agreement was necessary among the banks composing the Wingfield chain. Mr. Wingfield and Mr. Sheehan initiated the policy of splitting these loans and pro rating the proceeds of liquidation, and as they had complete authority over these banks, the necessity for a specific agreement was obviated.

On page 10 of the brief, the same statement is made in reference to the Taylor loan, and to which we make the same reply as in the preceding paragraph of this brief.

On page 10 of the brief the further statement is made that the advancements of $15,000.00 were not to be pro rated. Mr. Sheehan, Transcript page 110, explains this transaction. He says that this $15,000.00 should have been repaid from the sale of lambs (reporter in error uses the word "lands") so that he intended to testify that this advance was a preferred one and should have been repaid immediately. Mr. Sheehan further testifies on the same page that upon liquidation of the Taylor assets the proceeds should have been pro rated.

It is stated on page 10 of the brief that where a bank is not a party to the mortgage, it could not make advances.

Mr. Nelson, Transcript page 147, clears up this bald statement. He says that if the loans originated at Winnemucca invariably The First National Bank would make the advances. Naturally the testimony should be construed according to its true meaning. If a borrower did business in this vicinity he would as a matter of course do business with The First National Bank and receive his advances from that bank. Counsel insists that the loans originated at Winnemucca. If this is true, then Mr. Nelson's testimony is altogether consistent.

On page 11 of the brief, it is stated that the Taylor indebtedness in the sum of $700,000.00 was sold by The First National Bank to The Reno National Bank, and that The First National Bank received the full face value thereof.

Although according to our theory of this case The First National Bank is not precluded from recovery of its pro rata of the proceeds from liquidation of this paper as its interests appear, whether the loan originated in The First National Bank or in some other bank, the evidence in this case is that the Taylor note and mortgage for $700,000.00 was handled in Reno. Transcript page 186, testimony of J. G. Moore. Transcript page 108, J. Sheehan testifying that the transaction was consummated at Reno. There is no testimony showing that Taylor owed The First National Bank any sum except $45,142.18 advances.

It is stated on page 12 of the brief that The First National Bank advanced to Laborde $30,715.47. There is no testimony in this case upon which to base that statement. The amount advanced was the sum of $3612.49. Transcript page 191, testimony of J. G. Moore; Transcript page 156, stipulation of counsel.

Counsel says there are three questions in this case, the answers to which will solve this suit: Brief page 13.

In answer to this statement we do not concede that the three general questions cover all the issues in this case or fully cover the theory of the plaintiff.

Referring to the first two questions: We believe that as a matter of law the mortgagor is bound by the terms of the mortgage. It may be that in certain cases, where an independent bank, or a stranger, purchases the note and mortgage, and without his knowledge or consent, advances are made after assignment, such assignee would not be bound thereby. However, in the instant case a different set of facts is presented.

All the banks of the chain were under one management. Under such management it was the policy that when a mortgage was taken by The First National Bank and several notes given thereunder, or advancements thereafter made, the mortgage covered all notes and all advancements, and the mortgage was for the benefit of each bank holding a note as its interest appeared.

In the case of split loans and where the loan originated in The First National Bank, the mortgage was invariably retained by The First National Bank and only a portion of the notes transferred to The Reno National Bank for re-transfer to the various members of the chain. Where convenient, as in the Taylor and Laborde cases, the mortgages were executed to The Reno National Bank, even though the loans may have originated at The First National Bank, the mortgages were retained by The Reno National Bank, and the notes distributed to the various banks.

The Reno National Bank acted as a clearing house for all split loans and no preference was given any one bank because a certain bank retained the mortgage and liquidated the assets. This policy was understood by the comptroller of the Currency and approved by him. The comptroller recognized the right of each bank to share pro rata in the collection of assets covered by the mortgage and made it the rule that where several banks held notes covered by the same mortgage, that such banks could only look to the mortgage security for their pro rata share and could not hold the bank where the loan originated to any responsibility whatever. Hence the rule that all notes transferred were to be without recourse. Under this system any bank in the chain could hold the mortgage and still have no greater right to the assets covered by it than any other bank holding a mere note without evidence of security.

Subsequent advancements, whether represented by notes or overdrafts, occupied the same standing in relation to the mortgage. There was nothing to prevent the transfer of these advance notes to the various banks. Illustrative of the system, we find The First

National Bank making advances on mortgages held by The Reno National Bank and we likewise find The Reno National Bank making advances on mortgages held by The First National Bank. It was all a matter of convenience to the borrower in transacting his business.

In the instant case, where the mortgages were transferred to The Reno National Bank for its convenience in negotiating a loan from the Reconstruction Finance Corporation no change was made in the system. In effect, the notes were transferred without recourse according to custom, but The First National Bank still retained its interest in the mortgages and assets covered thereby.

The liquidation of the assets covered by these mortgages by the Reconstruction Finance Corporation, in cooperation with the receiver of The Reno National Bank, was for the benefit of all banks holding notes against these particular securities.

It will be remembered that The Reno National Bank negotiated a loan from the Reconstruction Finance Corporation and pledged securities gathered in from the various banks in the chain. All these securities, collectively and individually, secured the loan, but the interest each bank held therein being only subordinated for the purpose of guaranteeing the repayment to the Reconstruction Finance Corporation of its loan by The Reno National Bank.

In collecting this loan, the Reconstruction Finance Corporation was not interested in liquidating any particular asset, but liquidated such assets as were expedient from time to time. It follows that the loan was eventually repaid out of the general assets of The Reno National Bank. Some of the securities formerly held by The First National Bank aided in this payment. Some of the securities held by The Reno National Bank and other banks likewise aided. All these securities were held together in the pouch of The Reno National Bank.

It is not equity that any one bank, such as The First National Bank, should bear as guarantor, to the extent of its interest in this security, the burden of repaying this loan just because it might have been that securities in which it had an interest were the first to be liquidated.

The relations existing between the banks of this chain remove them from what might be a general rule of law that under certain circumstances the assignee of a mortgage would not be bound by subsequent advances.

Answering the third question on page 13 of the brief:

When the securities, the subject of this action, were transferred to The Reno National Bank through direct instructions of Mr. Sheehan, it was for the purpose of aiding The Reno National Bank to procure a loan from the Reconstruction Finance Corporation. When the subordination agreement was executed upon direction of Mr. Wingfield, The First National

Bank passed certain rights in and to the securities to the Reconstruction Finance Corporation. The First National Bank did not intend by this act to repay the entire loan made to The Reno National Bank. There were other securities pledged to the Reconstruction Finance Corporation to help bear this burden. As collections were made on any or all of these securities the Reconstruction Finance Corporation credited The Reno National Bank on its note. Even the Reconstruction Finance Corporation had no right to select the securities in which The First National Bank had an interest with which to pay the general loan made to The Reno National Bank. *Schmitt v. Reconstruction Finance Corporation,* Volume 20, Federal Supplement, 813.

Naturally when collections were sufficient to repay the Reconstruction Finance Corporation all the securities remaining in the pouch were retained by The Reno National Bank and the Reconstruction Finance Corporation passed out of the transaction. Then the procedure was for The Reno National Bank to cast up accounts with the various banks, ascertain the interest of each bank in each security, including advances, and pro rate the loss or gain as their interest in each security appeared.

The liquidation of these securities whether made by the Reconstruction Finance Corporation or by The Reno National Bank did not change the situation. The liquidation was accomplished for the benefit of the several banks pro rata to the interest each had in each security. The First National Bank never has received any part of the proceeds collected. Whatever rights the Reconstruction Finance Corporation may have had under the subordination agreement did not affect the relations between the various banks of the chain.

No benefit whatever accrued to The First National Bank when they executed the subordination agreement to the Reconstruction Finance Corporation. The bank never received any part of the loan made to The Reno National Bank, so that the agreement stood and still stands without consideration.

Counsel will say that The First National Bank received credit on the books of The Reno National Bank upon transfer of these securities and therefore received some benefit because of the original transfer. J. G. Moore, Transcript page 194, testified that The First National Bank gained nothing by this transfer. Also testimony of J. Sheehan, Transcript page 124.

Answering the legal points raised in counsel's brief page 14:

The attitude of counsel that The First National Bank in this instance of the transfer of these securities, and during all the previous years of like dealings, enriched itself at the expense of The Reno National Bank, is not justified by the facts covering the relations of these banks.

The First National Bank because of its location in a large sheep and cattle community had the opportunity to loan a great deal of money on splendid security. No other bank in the chain stood in such an advantageous position. The other banks had on hand large deposits, but had little opportunity to make good loans, which is the foundation for earnings in the banking business.

With The First National Bank negotiating these loans as a quasi-agent for the other banks and furnishing them with eight per cent paper from year to year, all the members of the chain prospered.

Even when the paper, the subject of this action, was transferred to The Reno National Bank there was no advantage to The First National Bank, as in the windup The Reno National Bank owed The First National Bank $170,287.01 in cash. The First National Bank would have been in no worse position if it had retained the paper and liquidated it. The First National Bank did not need the money and standing alone could have survived the panic.

I, too, have searched diligently for a decision desired upon the facts covered in the instant case, and cannot find one. The cases cited by counsel are of no help whatever as they are not based upon a similar statement of facts.

Counsel takes the anomalous position that The First National Bank was a stranger to the John C. Taylor mortgage and did at the same time originate the loan which was transferred to The Reno National Bank. It seems rather trite for counsel to remark that any one of the Wingfield chain of banks was a stranger to the other. It seems to me that it was more of a brotherhood.

There is no competent evidence in this case that the Taylor loan was sent to The Reno National Bank and The First National Bank given credit for it. Even if it had been, The Reno National Bank wanted the loan for itself and the other banks, and The First National Bank could not handle it under the law. Mr. Sheehan testified that all this paper was considered good loans at the time made. The Taylor mortgage covered the advances made and it would have made no difference what bank in the chain held it.

In Conclusion, We Submit:

Under the direction of George Wingfield and J. Sheehan, The First National Bank was the feeder bank for the chain, and furnished excess loans and other loans as directed by Mr. Sheehan to The Reno National Bank for distribution to the various members of the Wingfield chain, thus providing an outlet for their cash.

These loans were acceptable to The Reno National Bank and after receipt by it had the same standing as though The Reno National Bank had made the loan in the first place. There is no evidence that The First National Bank received any compensation whatever because of these transactions. It merely handed over to The Reno National Bank its customers so that The Reno National Bank and the other banks could make a profit from the loans.

When there was a split loan, whether represented by original notes or advances, the whole was secured by the same mortgage and the proceeds of liquidation were pro rated.

In transferring the paper, the subject of this action, from The First National Bank to The Reno National Bank, Wingfield and Sheehan exercised their authority in taking the securities for whatever purpose they saw fit and for the benefit of The Reno National Bank as well as all the associated banks.

When The Reno National Bank became the recipient of this transfer of paper such paper constituted an asset of that bank and without recourse on The First National Bank who held the original loans, but The First National Bank nevertheless retained its interest in the mortgaged security.

When The Reno National Bank pledged this security to the Reconstruction Finance Corporation together with other securities that it owned, for a loan to itself, the whole of these securities became liable for repayment of the loan.

When, by direction of Wingfield and Sheehan, The First National Bank executed the subordination agreement, only the interest of The First National Bank in this paper was so subordinated as a guarantee for the payment of The Reno National Bank loan and then for such time only as The Reno National Bank could repay the loan. This subordination was of no benefit to The First National Bank even as against the Reconstruction Finance Corporation as was held by Judge Norcross in the *Schmitt* case. The First National

Bank never received any money whatever because of the transaction.

When the Reconstruction Finance Corporation had been repaid out of the general assets of The Reno National Bank or from the liquidation of the pledged security as a whole, the office of the subordination had been accomplished, the various banks retained their former status in relation to each other and were entitled to their share of liquidation of the assets as their interest appeared in any security.

In a manner of speaking, the Wingfield chain of banks was an association of banks, although separate entities, having a common management and interlocking directorate. They freely transferred paper among themselves as seemed expedient. They shared the gain or suffered the loss of an asset in proportion to the interest each held therein.

These interests were not separated in life and are inseparable in death. Each played its part in the financial structure created by George Wingfield in the State of Nevada. No theory on the part of the able counsel for the defendant can make these banks strangers to each other to the extent of voiding the provision contained in the mortgages that it should be security for advances made from time to time.

The subordination agreements executed to the Reconstruction Finance Corporation by all the banks in the chain in effect only operated as a guarantee that The Reno National Bank would repay its loan. The Reno National Bank was at all times primarily liable for the payment of its debt to the Reconstruction Finance Corporation.

Neither the Reconstruction Finance Corporation nor The Reno National Bank had the right to select the paper in which The First National Bank had an interest, liquidate it, repay the whole loan of The Reno National Bank, and forgive the general assets of The Reno National Bank, as well as the paper remaining and owned by The Reno National Bank, and in which the First National Bank had no interest.

It was the duty of the receiver of The Reno National Bank to liquidate the general assets held by it, including the paper the subject of this action, whether pledged, or not, repay the Reconstruction Finance Corporation therefrom out of the cash on hand, and then distribute the amount due The First National Bank pro rata as its interest appeared in the securities.

He had no right to shift to the guarantor the primary obligation of The Reno National Bank; nor was it in his power to cancel the provision of the mortgages that the advances made were to be secured thereby, nor to void the custom, usage and understanding between these banks and each should share pro rata in collections made from liquidation of the security in which they had an interest.

Dated, Winnemucca, Nevada,
November 29, 1939.

Respectfully submitted,
THOS. J. SALTER,
Attorney for Appellee.

No. 9289

IN THE

United States Circuit Court of Appeals

For the Ninth Circuit

CARROLL HENDERSON, as Receiver of The Reno National Bank, Reno, Nevada (a national banking association, organized and existing under the laws of the United States of America), *Appellant,* vs. CARROLL HENDERSON, as Receiver of The First National Bank of Winnemucca, Nevada (a national banking association, organized and existing under the laws of the United States of America), *Appellee.*	

On Appeal from the District Court of the United States, for the District of Nevada.

APPELLANT'S CLOSING BRIEF.

N. J. BARRY,
Reno, Nevada,
Attorney for Appellant.

PERNAU-WALSH PRINTING CO., SAN FRANCISCO, CALIFORNIA

Table of Authorities Cited

Cases

Pages

Calvert v. Schultz, 106 N. W. 1123 5

Geddes v. Anaconda Mining Co., 254 U. S. 590 11

Schmitt v. Tobin, 15 Fed. Supp. 35 .... 7, 10

Statutes

Nevada Compiled Laws of 1929, Section 1533 5

Nevada Compiled Laws of 1929, Section 8524 8

No. 9289

IN THE

United States Circuit Court of Appeals

For the Ninth Circuit

CARROLL HENDERSON, as Receiver of The Reno National Bank, Reno, Nevada (a national banking association, organized and existing under the laws of the United States of America),

Appellant,

vs.

CARROLL HENDERSON, as Receiver of The First National Bank of Winnemucca, Nevada (a national banking association, organized and existing under the laws of the United States of America),

Appellee.

On Appeal from the District Court of the United States, for the District of Nevada.

APPELLANT'S CLOSING BRIEF.

At the outset, I wish to correct a mistake which was called to my attention in counsel's brief. Where it is stated on Page 5 of my Opening Brief that The First National Bank of Winnemucca advanced by way of notes and overdrafts to Laborde Bros. & Company the sum of $30,715.47, the amount should have been $3,612.49, and wherever the figures $30,715.47 appear in my Opening Brief, the sum should be $3,-612.49. In any event, the question is absolutely immaterial, but I do not want to misstate the facts.

In my opening brief, I stated there were just three questions in this case, the answers to which will solve the suit, to-wit:

First: Can the owner of a mortgage providing for advancements, after the assignment of the mortgage and the notes for which the mortgage is given as security, make such advancements and be secured under the mortgage?

Second: Can anyone who is not a party to a mortgage make advancements to a mortgagor and be secured by the mortgage for such advancements?

Third: Can a person who is the owner of claims secured by mortgage, or otherwise, subordinate all his right to the claims to the rights of another for a consideration?

The only attempt on the part of counsel for Appellee to answer these questions may be found on Page 21 of his brief, wherein he says:

"Referring to the first two questions: We believe that as a matter of law the mortgagor is bound by the terms of the mortgage. It may be that in certain cases, where an independent bank, or a stranger, purchases the note and mortgage, and without his knowledge or consent, advances are made after assignment, such assignee would not be bound thereby. However, in the instant case a different set of facts is presented."

Again, on Page 24:

"The relations existing between the banks of this chain remove them from what might be a general rule of law that under certain circumstances the assignee of a mortgage would not be bound by subsequent advances."

The above and foregoing is no answer at all. When The First National Bank of Winnemucca assigned its interest in the notes and mortgages set forth in the first count of the complaint, the right to make further advances absolutely ceased under any sensible interpretation of the law.

It might be conceded that an agreement could be entered into between The Reno National Bank and The First National Bank of Winnemucca to the effect that The Reno National Bank would take care of the advances, but no such agreement was made and counsel does not argue in his brief that any such agreement was made. In fact, J. Sheehan, on Page 130 of the Transcript, testified as follows:

"Q. * * * I believe you testified that you authorized the officers of The First National Bank to do that?

A. I did.

Q. Did you do that as an officer of The Reno National Bank or as an officer of The First National Bank?

A. The First National Bank. In that transaction The Reno National Bank was hardly known."

In the absence of an agreement, counsel must rely upon usage, custom and practice, as alleged in his complaint. There is no testimony in the record to the effect that a person not a party to the mortgage or a person who was a party to the mortgage, after assignment of the mortgage, could go on and make further advances.

The fact remains that the notes and mortgages mentioned in the first count of the complaint were assigned by The First National Bank of Winnemucca to The Reno National Bank and by The Reno National Bank immediately assigned to the Reconstruction Finance Corporation.

Therefore, the only way in which The Reno National Bank could be held would be by an independent agreement that The First National Bank of Winnemucca might make advances and The Reno National Bank would pay them, or that by usage, practice and custom, The Reno National Bank could be held to pro rate for advancements made after the assignment by The First National Bank of Winnemucca.

However, there would be one drawback to all this.

This would be a case where The Reno National Bank agreed to answer for the debt, default or miscarriage of another; whether by agreement or by usage and custom. If there was any such agreement, usage or custom, just exactly what was The Reno National Bank to do? The answer is: It was to pay the advancements in case the mortgagors did not do so. A plain, straight, specific promise to answer for the debt, the default, or the miscarriage of another.

Under the provisions of Section 1533, Nevada Compiled Laws of 1929, which reads as follows:

> "In the following cases every agreement shall be void, unless such agreement, or some note or memorandum thereof, expressing the consideration, be in writing, and subscribed by the party charged therewith: First, every agreement that, by the terms, is not to be performed within one year from the making thereof; second, every special promise to answer for the debt, default, or miscarriage of another; third, every promise or undertaking made upon consideration of marriage, except mutual promises to carry.",

the Reno National Bank could not make such an agreement unless the agreement were in writing. If it was by usage, custom and practice, then such usage, custom and practice cannot avoid the statute.

> *Calvert v. Schultz,* 106 N. W. 1123. (See Appendix.)

As to the second question: "Can anyone who is not a party to a mortgage make advancements to a mortgagor and be secured by the mortgage for such advancements? 'Counsel answer this question as follows, Page 21 of his brief:

"All the banks of the chain were under one management. Under such management, it was the policy that when a mortgage was taken by The First National Bank and several notes given thereunder, or advancements thereafter made, the mortgage covered all notes and all advancements, and the mortgage was for the benefit of each bank holding a note as its interest appeared."

I do not know where counsel got the foregoing. It is not in the record. In fact, it is in direct violation of the record. On Page 47 of the Transcript, P. L. Nelson, Cashier of The Reno National Bank, testified: "Where a bank was not a party to the mortgage, it could not make advancements."

As to the Taylor mortgage, the $700,000 indebtedness was incurred in The First National Bank of Winnemucca. The note and mortgage were given to The Reno National Bank and The First National Bank of Winnemucca was given credit for $700,000.

As a principle of law, it is absurd to say that advances may be made by one who is not a party to the mortgage.

As to the third question (the subordination agreement), counsel contends:

(1) That such agreement was made to the Reconstruction Finance Corporation; and

(2) That there was no consideration for the same.

I fail to see where it makes any difference that it was made to the Reconstruction Finance Corporation. The Reconstruction Finance Corporation liquidated the securities, and if the liquidation was not satisfactory, or if plaintiff was entitled to pro rate, a suit should have been brought against the Reconstruction Finance Corporation.

Again, suppose the Reconstruction Finance Corporation had reassigned the notes and securities to The Reno National Bank, The Reno National Bank would have taken the assignment subject to all the rights of the Reconstruction Finance Corporation, the subdination agreement included.

As to the want of consideration: The First National Bank of Winnemucca received a credit of $1,298,314.90 which enabled it to continue in business and rendered that bank solvent, according to the contention of Appellee.

Counsel cites the case of *Schmitt v. Tobin,* 15 Fed. Supp. 35-38, set forth in full in the Appendix in my opening brief, to the effect that there was no consideration. While that case is not binding upon this Court and was cited in my brief to show that the same Judge had decided this point, the case is against counsel's contention. I set forth in the Appendix to this brief that portion of the case applicable to this case. There, advancements were made after the assignment to the Reconstruction Finance Corporation, just the same as they were in this case, and the Court held that as to such advancements, the state banks were not entitled to pro rate.

Counsel seeks to make much of the fact that when the banks closed, The First National Bank of Winnemucca had a credit in The Reno National Bank of $147,000 which The First National Bank of Winnemucca lost. Nonetheless, The First National Bank of Winnemucca had the credit and could have drawn on it if it had seen fit. It did use up the difference between $1,298,314.90 and $147,000.

Counsel further argues that The First National Bank of Winnemucca was not insolvent. The record shows that it passed a resolution claiming that it was insolvent. If it was not insolvent, the reason was because of the credit which it had received in return for the assignment of notes and mortgages which lacked a substantial sum of being worth their full face value paid for them by The Reno National Bank.

There are two further questions that should be called to the attention of the Court:

First: The only advancement made prior to the assignment of The First National Bank of Winnemucca to The Reno National Bank was made to Alex Duffurena Company on January 18, 1932, and no payments were ever made thereon. The complaint in this case was filed June 24, 1938. Under the provisions of Section 8524, Nevada Compiled Laws of 1929, this claim would be barred by the statute of limitations, which is six years from date, and the notes were all demand notes. In the trial Court counsel contended that the statute did not apply. As this note was secured by mortgage, there certainly was a duty on the part of the party holding the note to have it renewed or commence an action so as to keep it alive. The amount involved is $3,500. (See Page 8 of Transcript.)

Second: The testimony is clear as shown by the testimony of J. Sheehan at Pages 109 and 110 of the Transcript, that $15,000 of the Taylor advancements was not to be pro rated, so in any event, we would be entitled to a deduction of the sum of $18,500.00 on the pro rata.

CONCLUSION.

The notes set forth in the first count of the complaint were assigned by The First National Bank of Winnemucca to The Reno National Bank, and all the advancements, except the Duffurena advancement of $3,500, were made after such assignment. Not only were the notes assigned to The Reno National Bank, but The Reno National Bank assigned them to the Reconstruction Finance Corporation, which, in law, is of the same effect as though they had been sold outright. All such advancements were made after the assignment to The Reno National Bank and after the assignment to the Reconstruction Finance Corporation, and could not have been made under any authorization of law for the reason that the assignors had parted with all interest therein.

As to the second cause of action, the Taylor claim, the note was made to The Reno National Bank, and The First National Bank of Winnemucca was given credit for the full face value thereof, $700,000. Any advancements were void for the reason that they were made by an institution not a party to the original note and mortgage.

As to the third claim, the Laborde claim, The First National Bank of Winnemucca signed a subordination agreement as to all the claims, and waived its right to participate in any of the proceeds from the liquidation.

It must be borne in mind that the only authority cited in this case as to the subordination agreement is that of *Schmitt v. Tobin,* heretofore cited. In that case, the Court held that any advancements made after the assignment of the original notes and mortgages to the Reconstruction Finance Corporation could not participate in the proceeds of the liquidation.

In my opening brief, I propounded three questions, the answers to which I claimed solve the controversy in this case. The questions are as follows:

FIRST: Can the owner of a mortgage providing for advancements, after the assignment of the mortgage and the notes for which the mortgage is given as security, make such advancements and be secured under the mortgage?

SECOND: Can anyone who is not a party to a mortgage make advancements to a mortgagor and be secured by the mortgage for such advancements?

THIRD: Can a person who is the owner of claims secured by mortgage, or otherwise, subordinate all his right to the claims to the rights of another for a consideration?

Counsel has answered none of these questions. The only attempt to answer them is a number of loose statements warranted neither by the record nor by citation of law. He practically admits the soundness of my position in law, but seeks to avoid it by saying that The Reno National Bank and The First National Bank of Winnemucca had interlocking directors, and therefore, that fact cures everything. He overlooks the rights of the depositors and creditors of The Reno

National Bank and overlooks the rule laid down in the case of

Geddes v. Anaconda Mining Co., 254 U. S. 590-599,

as set forth in the Appendix to my opening brief, to the effect that transactions between interlocking directors must be in all respects just and fair and there must be an adequate consideration, and the burden of proof is on the party seeking to enforce such contracts.

Dated, Reno, Nevada,
December 8, 1939.

Respectfully submitted,
N. J. Barry,
Attorney for Appellant.

(Appendix Follows.)

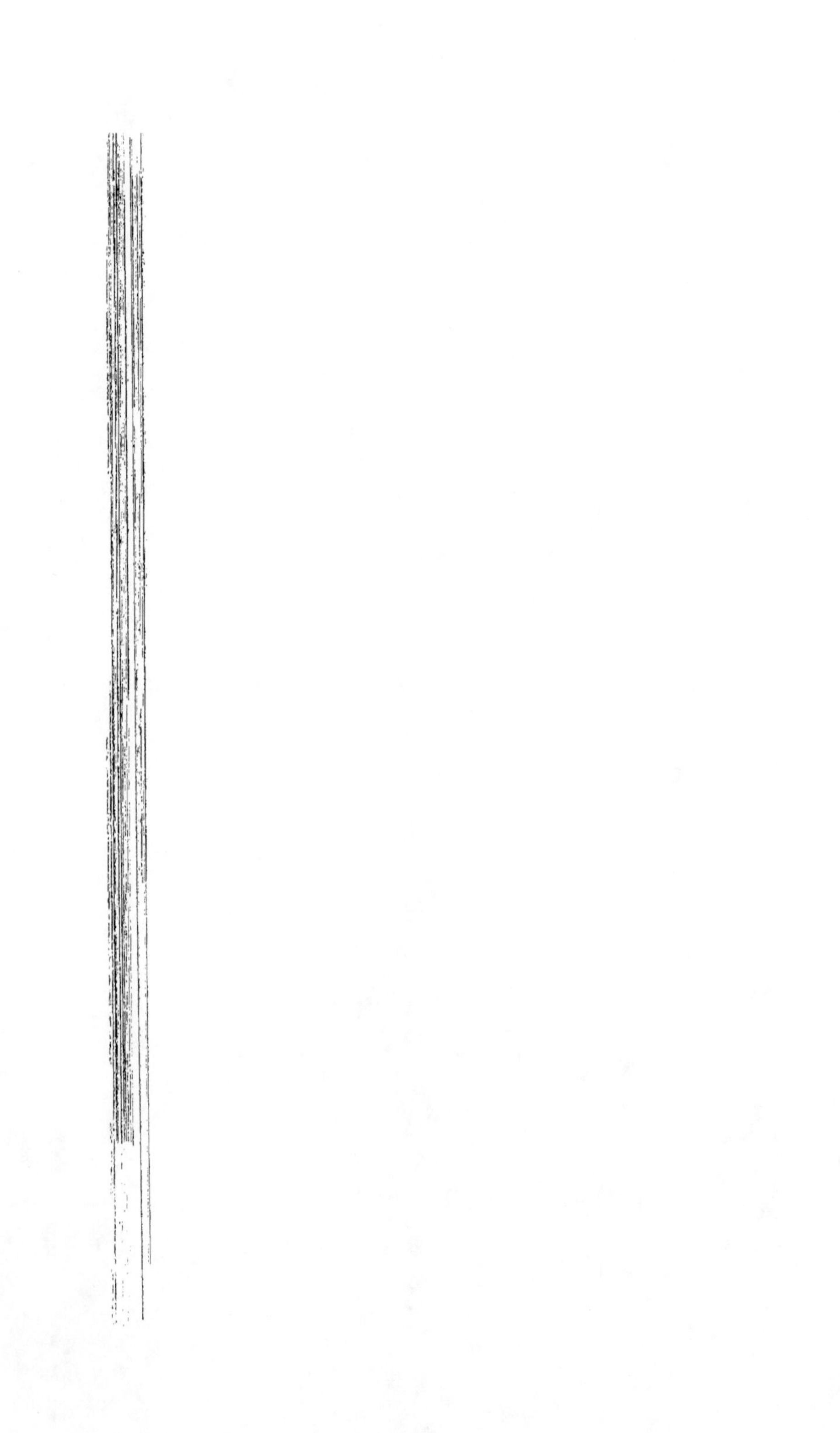

"While this view covers the main question presented, there remains a question applicable alike to the Seventh and Eighth causes of action. In the Seventh cause of action it appears that the Jenkins Land & Livestock Company, which had executed notes and mortgages covering a very substantial amount of money, made prior to March 19, 1932, the date of a subordination agreement entered into by the Reno National Bank in favor of the Reconstruction Finance Corporation, and hence prior to April 13, 1932, the date the Jenkins Land & Livestock Company mortgage was assigned to the Reconstruction Finance Corporation as security for its main loan, and that on May 24, 1932, an additional loan in the sum of $9000.00 was made to the Jenkins Land & Livestock Company by the Reno National Bank, and that the note therefor was by it assigned to the Virginia City Bank. On July 12, 1932 the same company, Jenkins Land & Livestock Company, executed another note for $9000.00 to the Reno National Bank, which in turn was assigned to the Tonopah Banking Corporation. It appears that these two notes were made and assigned subsequent to the assignment of the main mortgage to the Reconstruction Finance Corporation, and subsequent to the subordination agreement executed by the Reno National Bank to the Reconstruction Finance Corporation. It is manifest that the State banks taking these assignments subsequent to the main assignment to the Reconstruction Finance Corporation, took subject to the rights of the Reno National Bank, and could obtain no greater right than that of the Reno National Bank. It is therefore the conclusion of the Court that plaintiff is not entitled to recover upon the Seventh cause of action.

"The Eighth cause of action presents precisely the same question of law referred to respecting the Seventh cause of action. It also deals with subsequent loans made by the Reno National Bank to the John G. Taylor Company, one dated June 21, 1932, for $9000.00, assigned to the Virginia City Bank, another dated July 9, 1932, for $7500.00, assigned to the Tonopah Bank, and another note of August 6, 1932, for $7500.00, assigned to the Carson Valley Bank. As before stated, these several notes are all subsequent to the main assignment by the Reno National Bank to the Reconstruction Finance Corporation, and hence the assignee banks acquire no rights superior to those of the Reno National Bank, and are governed by the subordination agreement of the Reno National Bank of date March 19, 1932. Plaintiff is not entitled to recover upon the Eighth cause of action. The First and Ninth Causes of action have heretofore been dismissed by consent of the respective parties."

Schmitt v. Tobin, 15 Fed. Supp. 35-38.

"March 7, 1903, defendant gave plaintiffs a verbal order for a car of Jackson Hill coal worth $179.03, then in the Michigan Central Railroad yards at Detroit, Mich. Immediately upon receipt of this order, plaintiffs telephoned to the railroad company to turn the car over to defendant, and, on the same day, sent to the railroad company a written order to the same effect. This is the method by which delivery of coal in car load lots is usually made. The same day, an invoice of the coal was sent to the defendant. The car was put on the Twentieth street siding by the railroad company on March 17th. The day before this, March 16th (nine days after the railroad company had been ordered by plaintiffs to turn the car over to defendant), defendant countermanded his order.

"At the trial, defendant claimed the verbal order was within the statute of frauds, and therefore void. Plaintiffs claimed that no written contract was necessary, because of a custom existing among coal dealers, by which the direction to the railroad company to turn the coal over to the purchaser constituted delivery and acceptance. Frequently before this, delivery of other car load lots had been made to defendant himself in accordance with this custom. At the conclusion of plaintiff's testimony, the trial court directed a verdict for defendant because the custom had not been proven. The conclusion reached had not been proven. There was no offer to show an authority conferred by the defendant upon the railroad company to accept this coal for him. In the absence of such authority, delivery to the company was not delivery to the defendant. There was, indeed, no delivery to the carrier; the coal was already in its possession. There was nothing but a direction to the carrier, who held possession for plaintiff, to make delivery to defendant. Defendant was no party to this, except as he became such by virtue of his parol contract wholly void by the statute of frauds. That this was not delivery to or acceptance by defendant is clear. Mechem on Sales, Secs. 356, 358, 365; Smith v. Brennan, 62 Mich. 349, 28 N. W. 892, 4 Am. St. Rep. 867;

Grimes v. Van Vechten, 20 Mich. 410; Gatiss v. Cyr, 134 Mich. 233, 96 N. W. 26. The claimed custom does not change this rule. First, it is apparent that the evidence of acceptance of coal by purchasers under similar circumstances proves no more than that the great majority of purchasers would not insist on the defense of the statute of frauds. In so far as the witnesses undertook to testify that an order to the carrier was a delivery or acceptance by custom, they assumed to testify to legal conclusions. But, however well such custom might have been proved, it could not be permitted to override the express words of the statute. Van Hoesenn v. Cameron, 54 Mich. 609, 20 N. W. 609; 29 Am. & Eng. Enc. L. (2d Ed.) 378, 381.

"The judgment is affirmed."

Calvert v. Schultz, 106 N. W. 1123.

IN THE

UNITED STATES CIRCUIT COURT OF APPEALS

FOR THE NINTH CIRCUIT.

No. 9289.

CARROLL HENDERSON, as Receiver of The Reno National Bank, Reno, Nevada, a national banking association, organized and existing under the laws of the United States of America, *Appellant*,

v.

CARROLL HENDERSON, as Receiver of The First National Bank of Winnemucca, Nevada, a national banking association, organized and existing under the laws of the United States of America, *Appellee*.

MEMORANDUM BRIEF OF THE COMPTROLLER OF THE CURRENCY AS AMICUS CURIAE.

GEORGE P. BARSE,
Washington, D. C.,
Attorney for Preston Delano,
Comptroller of the Currency.

PRESS OF BYRON S. ADAMS, WASHINGTON, D. C.

IN THE

UNITED STATES CIRCUIT COURT OF APPEALS

FOR THE NINTH CIRCUIT.

No. 9289.

Carroll Henderson, as Receiver of The Reno National Bank, Reno, Nevada, a national banking association, organized and existing under the laws of the United States of America, *Appellant*,

v.

Carroll Henderson, as Receiver of The First National Bank of Winnemucca, Nevada, a national banking association, organized and existing under the laws of the United States of America, *Appellee.*

MEMORANDUM BRIEF OF THE COMPTROLLER OF THE CURRENCY AS AMICUS CURIAE.

Comes now, as amicus curiae, Preston Delano, Comptroller of the Currency of the United States, the officer charged by law with the supervision of the liquidation of insolvent national banks, and by leave of Court first had and obtained, respectfully submits his brief in support of the appellant's contention that this honorable court should hear this case on appeal.

The National Banking Act (12 U. S. C. A. 191, 192, 194 and 203) charges the Comptroller of the Currency with the supervision of the liquidation of insolvent national banks. The appellant and appellee, receivers in this case, are the agents of the Comptroller of the Currency, and they act in all respects at his direction. See *Kennedy* v. *Gibson,* 8 Wall. 498, and other cases cited in the annotations following 12 U. S. C. A. 192, note 41.

The National Banking Act contemplates an economical and efficient liquidation of these banks which will result in a maximum recovery for depositors and creditors. Federal taxes are abated where the assets are insufficient to pay depositors;[1] federal courts are given jurisdiction of suits to wind up the affairs of such banks independent of the amount involved;[2] court approval of all sales and compromises is required;[3] advances to protect assets can be made only with the consent of the Secretary of the Treasury;[4] and annual reports of the result of the liquidations are required to be made to Congress.[5] This court will take judicial notice of the annual reports of the Comptroller of the Currency to Congress, *Tempel* v. *United States,* (1918) 248 U. S. 121, 130; *Hardee* v. *Washington Loan & Trust Co.,* (App. D. C. 1937) 91 F. (2d) 314, and these reports will evidence that a total of 2,449 insolvent national banks were liquidated between 1865 and October 31, 1939, and that an average of 92.78 per cent of each dollar collected was paid to the depositors and creditors; the average cost of liquidation, including receivers' salaries, attorneys' fees and all expenses, being 7.22 per cent.

It is the practice of the Comptroller of the Currency to consolidate national bank receiverships when the liquidation has proceeded to the point that consolidation is indi-

---

1 12 U. S. C. 570.

2 28 U. S. C. 41 (16).

3 12 U. S. C. 192.

4 12 U. S. C. 198, 199.

5 12 U. S. C. 14.

cated, and where the rights of the creditors of the separate banks would not be prejudiced by consolidation. This practice is referred to at page 38 of the Seventy-fifth Annual Report of the Comptroller of the Currency to Congress, covering the year ended October 31, 1937, (House Document No. 395, 75th Congress, 2nd Session) as follows:

> "The decrease in percentage cost of liquidation expense during the current year is principally the result of the existing policy of this office in consolidating groups of receiverships under individual receivers, where the remaining asset values in such receiverships plus the additional efficiency and economies to be obtained thereby are found to warrant such consolidations. The effect of these consolidations of receiverships is well evidenced by the fact that a total of 833 receivers in charge of active national bank receiverships as of June 30, 1934, had been reduced to a total of but 367 as of October 31, 1937, with little or no increase in the average salary of individual receivers. This reduction in number of receivers in charge of active receiverships, together with corresponding economical consolidations in the field staff of receivers' clerks and assistants, resulted in the administration of an average of 2.4 receiverships per individual receiver as of October 31, 1937."

The Reno National Bank of Reno, Nevada, was closed by resolution of its board of directors on December 9, 1932. The Comptroller of the Currency appointed Mr. W. J. Tobin receiver for the bank on December 9, 1932, and his service was continuous until his resignation at the close of business February 15, 1939, when he was succeeded by the present receiver, Mr. Carroll Henderson.

Considerations of efficiency and economy indicated as early as 1938 that the receiverships of The Reno National Bank and of The First National Bank of Winnemucca should be consolidated. However, action was postponed until this controversy between the two receiverships, directed by the Comptroller to be presented to the United

States District Court, had been determined by that court. When, on February 13, 1939, the court below filed its "Memorandum Decision and Orders" (R. 44), the Comptroller considered that with the record made and with each bank's creditors represented by separate attorneys, the consolidation could safely be made. Mr. Henderson was then appointed receiver of the Reno bank as of the close of business on February 15, 1939.

When suit was filed in the instant case and when the case was decided by the court below, the banks were represented by separate receivers. The Comptroller of the Currency has a duty to protect the rights of each group of creditors, independent of the duty of the receivers. The instant suit was filed pursuant to the Comptroller's direction. Because of the amount involved and the recommendations to the Comptroller of N. J. Barry, Esq., of Reno, Nevada, the attorney representing the creditors of The Reno National Bank, the Comptroller directed that the controversy be presented to this Court. (R. 95)

We respectfully submit that the interests of each group of creditors have been fully protected, and that this honorable court should decide this case on appeal.

Respectfully submitted,

George P. Barse,
Washington, D. C.,
Attorney for Preston Delano,
Comptroller of the Currency.

CPSIA information can be obtained
at www.ICGtesting.com
Printed in the USA
BVHW031957031118
531990BV00039B/491/P